A VOICE FULL OF CITIES:

THE COLLECTED ESSAYS
OF ROBERT KELLY

A VOICE FULL OF CITIES:

THE COLLECTED ESSAYS
OF ROBERT KELLY

Edited by Pierre Joris & Peter Cockelbergh

Contra Muncum Press   New York · London · Melbourne

The Collected Essays of Robert Kelly

Pierre Joris & Peter Cockelbergh (eds)

Contra Mundum Press

A VOICE FULL OF CITIES

Essays of Robert Kelly

𝒜 Voice Full of Cities © 2014 by Pierre Joris & Peter Cockelbergh; Essays © 2014 by Robert Kelly; Introduction © 2014 Pierre Joris & Peter Cockelbergh.

First Contra Mundum Press edition 2014.

All Rights Reserved under International & Pan-American Copyright Conventions. No part of this book may be reproduced in any form or by any electronic means, including information storage and retrieval systems, without permission in writing from the publisher, except by a reviewer who may quote brief passages in a review.

Library of Congress Cataloguing-in-Publication Data

Kelly, Robert, 1935–

[A Voice Full of Cities: The Collected Essays of Robert Kelly. English.]

A Voice Full of Cities: The Collected Essays of Robert Kelly / Robert Kelly

—1ˢᵗ Contra Mundum Press Edition
806 pp., 6 x 9 in.

ISBN 9781940625065

  I. Kelly, Robert.
  II. Title.
 III. Joris, Pierre.
 IV. Editor.
  V. Cockelbergh, Peter.
 VI. Editor.
 VII. Joris, Pierre.
VIII. Introduction.
 IX. Cockelbergh, Peter.
  X. Introduction.

2014949786

TABLE OF CONTENTS

0   **INTRODUCTION**

     THREADS 1: ROBERT SAYS   2

1. A BOOK OF IMAGES: DEEP & OTHER

8   *Trobar* Editorial
9   Notes on the Poetry of Deep Image
13   Statement for *Nomad*
15   Letter to Ken Irby
18   Song? / After Bread (Notes on Zukofsky's *A 1–12*)
42   The Image of the Body
46   Review of Stan Brakhage's *Metaphors on Vision*
50   On the Art of Vision
52   Letter on "Deep Image"
54   *Duende*, Lorca's Dark Sounds
55   Enstasy
60   Cryptodes
62   Postscript II from *A Controversy of Poets*
68   Intentional Language
73   Poem = Communiqué

     THREADS 2: ROBERT SAYS   76

2. A BOOK CALLED *IN TIME* (1971)

82   (prefix:
83   Letter to the Bear.   Re: Rome
85   Re: The Occult
87   Identity   Preference   Temple Complex

TABLE OF CONTENTS

91	Pokorny on √pel-
96	Beyond the Personal
97	The Frontiers of the Fact
99	The Dream Work
103	re: Snow Jobs / we have got :
105	*Sermo*
106	Given *any* niveau of language:
107	*Tensors*
109	WHAT WHO HOW
111	Program:
112	Hygiene —)
114	*In Historiam*
115	Biotic Diet
117	A spoon of strawberry jam
120	for the Waiblings
121	LABRYS: *Twelve Matters*

THREADS 3: *ROBERT SAYS*   138

3. A BOOK OF THE COMPANY: "Heaven is other people"

144	Statement
	On Paul Blackburn
152	*In on or about the Premises*
153	Introduction to *The Journals*
156	Robert Duncan *&* The Right Time
167	On Olson: Two Reviews and Some Preliminaries
	Five Short Reviews
175	Robert Creeley
176	Philip Lamantia
177	Stephen Jonas

TABLE OF CONTENTS

178	Stan Persky
178	Daphne Marlatt
181	Leroi Jones's *The Dead Lecturer*
184	Edward Dorn's *Gunslinger, Book I*
187	Towards and On Cid Corman
192	Tarn: a Tribute
	On Jonathan Williams
195	*An Ear In Bartram's Tree*
197	*Colonel Generosity*
202	Thirty Passing Remarks on The Black Sparrow Press
206	An Introduction to Thomas Meyer's *Umbrellas of Æsclepius*
211	Preface to Bruce McClelland's *The Dracula Poems*
216	American Direction: On Carolee Schneemann
217	A Note on Nora Jaffe
	Notes & Prefaces for
219	Harvey Bialy
219	George Quasha
220	John Yau
221	Franz Kamin
222	Elizabeth Robinson
223	Towards Enslin's *Forms*
236	On Irby
244	From *Oasis* to *Poasis*: Two Pieces on Pierre Joris
	Three Short Reviews
252	Allen Fisher
252	Thomas Meyer
253	John Taggart
254	For Rothenberg
255	Things I Think About When Eshleman Comes To Mind

TABLE OF CONTENTS

THREADS 4: ROBERT SAYS — 260

4. A BOOK OF DISCOURSE &/ON NARRATIVE

266	On Discourse
290	"On Narrative" from "Injune"
292	From *The Loom*, § 12: "Theory of Narrative"
304	Event: Eleven Propositions, with an Annex
306	Essay on Clarity
307	Some Thoughts on Jung
309	On *The Cruise of the Pnyx*
310	Russian Tales: Experiments in Telling
311	Afterword to *A Transparent Tree*
316	Afterword to the second edition of *The Scorpions*
	Three Book Reviews
320	William Gaddis's *Carpenter's Gothic*
324	I am not a halfback: On Robert Coover's *Whatever Happened to Gloomy Gus of the Chicago Bears?*
328	Poundian Romance: Investigating Thomas McEvilley's Novel *North of Yesterday*
339	Tribute to Thomas McEvilley
341	Notes For An After Dinner Discourse
344	*Come Out*: A Baccalaureate Address
349	Zones of a Non-Linear Discourse…

THREADS 5: ROBERT SAYS — 354

5. A BOOK OF DREAMS

360	Dream Stele
362	An Experimental Program for Dream Research
365	[Position Paper]
368	Seventeen Arcana from the Infinity of Dreams
374	Hypnogeography

Hypnogeography II
376   First Kansas Talk: Introduction
384   Second Kansas Talk: Public Dreaming

THREADS 6: ROBERT SAYS   404

6. A BOOK OF OUTSIDE / INSIDE

410   A Line of Sight
423   A Talking House
427   Buffalo Problem
        Four Short Pieces from *Io*
428   A Note on Dimensionality
429   Maps, Borrowings
430   Why Columbus Discovered America
431   (Œcology)
435   On Human Cloning
438   The World of NULL-E
451   Commentary on Peter Lamborn Wilson's "Atlantis Manifesto"
458   Hudson Valley Sows the Seeds of Tomorrow's Utopia

THREADS 7: ROBERT SAYS   462

7. A BOOK WITH & AGAINST THEORY

468   Lecture on Identity
469   Prynne Picks
470   On Carlos Castaneda
472   A Meditation on Heraclitus
475   From *TEXTS*: 16 [Reading Heidegger]
495   *TEXTS*: 18 [The Bastille]
502   On Michel Foucault
506   On Walter Benjamin

511	Letter to the Editor of $L=A=N=G=U=A=G=E$
513	morning item for bruce andrews
515	Albany Lecture on Theory

THREADS 8: ROBERT SAYS   522

8. A BOOK OF TRANSLATION

528	On Translation
530	Translation All-Pervading
535	All Writing is Collaboration
537	Night Thoughts
544	Reflection for PEN America — On Translation
548	Tensions: A Note on Two Newly Published Translations
551	Introduction to *Œdipus after Colonus and Other Plays*

THREADS 9: ROBERT SAYS   556

9. A BOOK OF THE EYE (MOVING OR NOT)

562	On Kenneth Anger's *Invocation of My Demon Brother*
564	The Mystery of *Kaspar Hauser*
568	Sections on Matt Phillips's Recent Work
571	Notes on Brakhage
576	Brakhage, Spoken in Memory
578	Adamagica: Magic and Iconolatry in Film

THREADS 10: ROBERT SAYS   594

10. A BOOK OF NEARLY EVERYTHING ELSE

600	Biography)
601	Horoscope

TABLE OF CONTENTS

602	"Autobiographical Essay" [excerpts]
627	A New Kind of MFA Program
	Some Letters
629	Letter to Margaret Randall
630	Letters to Lindy Hough & Richard Grossinger
638	Letter to Thomas Bernhard
643	Letter from Joseph Cornell to Dorothea Tanning
646	Note on Kabbalah & Criticism
647	The True Story
650	Faust et Moi
661	"Autobiographical Essay" [Timeline]

THREADS 11: ROBERT SAYS   675

11. A BOOK BETWEEN POEM &/AS STATEMENT

682	"Autobiographical Essay" [excerpts]
	Six Statement-Poems
685	(gloss as preface
687	(prefix: [to *Finding the Measure*]
688	(prefix: [to *The Mill of Particulars*]
689	Purity
690	In Commentary on the Gospel According to Thomas
692	(An Anecdote, as Preface) [to *The Time of Voice*]
693	"Autobiographical Essay" [excerpts]
696	Invited to introduce my work
699	Notes on *Line for Epoch*
703	"To The Reader" From *Not This Island Music*
705	Statements for *Sentence* and *Uncertainties*
706	Poetry is an Art Seeking Infinite Relevance...

	Some Poet-Statements
707	Two Notes on Dante & Shakesper
708	Blake was Best
708	Headnote for *Io* [on Blake]
709	On Keats' "Well-Wrought Urn"
710	Today's the Birthday of Wallace Stevens, so I Plan to Talk as Invited About Pound
712	A Love Affair with Silence: Review of Paul Celan
716	Opening Remarks for Black Mountain Conference
719	Statement on my Poetics for the H.W. Wilson Co.
722	Bard College 40th Anniversary Celebration
726	Statement for the Modern Poetry Conference at CUNY
727	Poetry, Archipelago, Island

THREADS 12: ROBERT SAYS   730

12. A BOOK OF MUSIC

736	Lection) H A R M O N I C S
737	A Plucked Flute
741	Against Music
746	Piano Tuning
750	The Lost Chord

756	**ALSO BY ROBERT KELLY**

INTRODUCTION

*Don't waste their time, say it or be silent. Never apologize, never explain —,
that has always been your rule. Why otherwise now?*
"Autobiographical Essay, #6"

Most of the poets & writers of the second part of the 20C, in emulation of their modernist predecessors — from Pound to Breton, from Rilke to Mandelstam — have produced a more or less abundant flow of meta-writing, in terms of essays & reflections on poetry & poetics. In the U.S. this is true for both the experimental or avant-garde schools of writing & for many poets of the more traditional or "quietist" schools of middle-of-the-road verse: all wrote & published on their poetics at length in forms ranging from highly theoretical & often formally innovative essays to at times pedestrian skill-expounding "how-to" accounts for aspiring creative writers. There exists however a generation of poets who decided to focus primarily on the writing & publishing of poetry — though that in great quantity —, only sporadically composing statements, essays, articles or theoretical writings. This focus on the poem short or long, that often & for essential reasons included a stating of a poetics in poem-rather than in essay-form, led to a very varied, rich, & copious output whose publication in magazine-, chapbook-, & volume-form, demanded much energy & concentrated attention. The other forms of poetological writing — essay, review, statement, manifesto, interview, etc. — while indeed engaged in, seem to have rather been ad hoc productions, written & published on the spur of the moment often goaded by events or the urging of a "little magazine" editor. Maybe rightly considered as the discardable scaffolding for the real work, the poem, these texts became ephemera, their visibility that of the eye-blink life-span of the mimeo magazine, as their creators often did not bother to gather them into books. This was the case with, for instance, Paul Blackburn (who did indeed die too young to have been able to do so), Jerome Rothenberg, Robert Kelly, Clayton Eshleman, Diane Wakoski, or David Antin — all poets who, incidentally, took part in one way or another in the original short-lived mid-1960s Deep Image movement. But over the years even sporadic "writings on" can make for a large & varied collection, & so we have recently (finally!) seen the publication of, for example, David

Antin's *Radical Coherency* (2011), Jerome Rothenberg's *Poetics & Polemics* (2008) & *Eye of Witness* (2013), or Eshleman's *Companion Spider* (2002) & *Grindstone of Rapport* (2008). Unfortunately, no similar collection of Robert Kelly's essays has been available (except for *In Time*, published in 1971 & unavailable for some decades now) even though he too has been writing on his (& others') poetry & poetics since the early '60s.

This is all the more surprising, bearing in mind RK's long, distinguished career. Robert Kelly was born in Brooklyn on 24 September 1935. Barely in his teens, he attended CCNY from which he graduated in 1955, & then he enrolled in the Columbia University Graduate School to pursue work in medieval literature, working with Roger Loomis on material that has kept him fascinated ever since (the Grail narratives) & studying 17C literature with Marjorie Nicholson & Pierre Garay. During those formative years — from the early fifties *Wanderjahre*, as he has called them, of discovering Manhattan & beyond, to the *Studienjahre* of the end of the decade — he meets a range of young poets who were to constitute the *communitas* of mind & work for decades to come: David Antin who introduced him to Jerome & Diane Rothenberg; George Economou (with whom he started the magazines *Chelsea Review* and *Trobar*) & Rochelle Owens; Clayton Eshleman; Diane Wakoski, Ursule Molinaro, Armand Schwerner, Gerrit Lansing & Paul Blackburn, among many others. It is also then that he makes contact with the older poets whose personal occasions & poetics were to remain exemplary for him: Louis & Celia Zukofsky, Robert Duncan &, in 1962, Charles Olson.

In 1958, the call for poetry had come in the form of a sudden, true spiritual awakening. Here is how he describes that moment:

> On an October evening, blue sky and cool, I walked down Lexington Avenue going home from work, tired and absurd, three years in graduate school, three years translating rat tests and liver jaundice. It seemed that the sky opened quietly and an Understanding spoke in me, saying that if I dedicated myself to writing, if I gave myself to that truth I knew as somehow the sky and the voice that speaks inside and the good of the world, if I gave myself over to writing for the good of the world, it would be well, and it would be well with me. [p.663]

As he has commented elsewhere: "That October commitment is the story. To write every day was the method. To attend to what is said. To listen. To prepare myself for writing by learning everything I could, by hanging out in languages & enduring overdetermined desires, by tolerating my own inclinations as if they had the physical accuracy of gravity. To listen, and say what I heard." As the title of his first book (published in 1961 by Jerome Rothenberg's Hawk's Well Press) suggests, this commitment was to be an "Armed Descent" — a title drawn from a reflection by Paul Valéry: "Who would descend into the self must go armed to the teeth." Later glossed by Kelly thus: "To go down into the self, armed with everything I have of flesh or dream or information. Armed, but not armored. To go down into the self, not especially my self but the sense of, steady beating pulsing beautiful soon lost forever physiology of the, self." These are also the times of the elaboration with Jerome Rothenberg & others of "Deep Image," (see Book 1 in this volume) considered but quickly abandoned as a possible communal & public proposition for a new poetics.

Since 1961, RK has been teaching at Bard College, where he is now Asher B. Edelman Professor of Literature & where for a number of years he also codirected the Avery Graduate School of the Arts. Annandale proved a most fertile ground for Kelly's work: in the year he moved up into the mid-Hudson valley he wrote more than he did in the 10 previous years. This immense productivity has continued ever since, so that it is no exaggeration to suggest that he may be America's most prolific poet: to date he has published close to 60 collections of poetry, as well as 12 volumes of prose fictions. The published work however constitutes only a small part of the actual writing. Jed Rasula calculated that by June 1982 (i.e., about thirty years ago), the typescript binders on RK's shelves contained about 30,000 pages of unpublished poetry — excluding prose work, like Kelly's unpublished 1,200-page novel, *Parsifal*.[1] It is important to stress, furthermore, that these binders don't contain notes, outlines, or drafts, but full & first-rate poems that simply happen not (yet) to be published.

---

1. Cf. Jed Rasula, "Ten Different Fruits on One Different Tree: Reading Robert Kelly." In: *Credences*, Vol. 3, № 1 (Spring 1984) 138–139.

Robert Kelly is, however, not only the most productive contemporary American poet, but certainly also one of the very best America has produced in the 2nd part of this just past century. Literally breathtaking is the range of his offerings, from freshly minted *trobar clus* & contemporized sonnet forms, to long epic narratives & non-narratives — we are thinking here of five major achievements in the genre of the 20C American long poem, the long out-of-print *Axon Dendron Tree*, the series gathered as *The Common Shore*, the magical journey known as *The Loom*, & the first two installments, *Fire Exit* & *Uncertainties*, of an ongoing trilogy — via every possible *inventio*, both in length & genre & mode. Just as breathtaking, even if the breath makes for shorter poems, thus follows a different music, are such volumes as *Finding the Measure, Songs I-XXX, Not this Island Music, The Flowers of Unceasing Coincidence & Lapis*, or his writing-through of Shelley's poem *Mont Blanc*. And this is leaving unmentioned RK's other collaborations (with Hölderlin, Schuldt, Brigitte Mahlknecht, Birgit Kempker), the "selected" works, such as *Red Actions, The Time of Voice*, Jed Rasula's *The Alchemist to Mercury*, his prose books, & so much more.

One emblematic early collection, for instance, is the 1971 volume *Flesh Dream Book*, the title of which gives what we think are the major concerns even today: "The flesh of sensory experience, dream & vision, & the holy book of tradition and learning, shared through time." As Kelly says concerning that title: "Perhaps at least it sets the priorities straight." It may be the massiveness of the work & its steadily accumulating variety & size that have scared critics off over the years, for it is extremely surprising that an œuvre of such richness & multi-phasic complexity, that gives such "feeding for the intelletto," has not had its analysts & exegetes. The absence of a substantial volume of essays on his own poetics, by the poet himself will, as signaled, also have contributed to that state.

This is what the present, long over-due project for two books tries to redress. A forthcoming companion volume, *A City Full of Voices*, will gather critical essays on RK's work by a wide range of contributors. *A Voice Full of Cities*, the volume at hand, gathers Kelly's essays, key statements & poem-statements, as well as prefaces, postludes & afterwords, reviews & articles from the various little magazines RK wrote for or edited himself, other discursive writings, talks &, finally, texts & notes from both his personal archives as well as from those at the University at Buffalo (from which we also drew the materials that serve as frontispieces to each of the twelve so-called "books" this volume consists of). Yet, not being Hegelian (i.e., not believing that "das Wahre ist das Ganze") but more — how to put it? — "Kellyan" ("nothing truer than fragment"), & bearing in mind the scattered nature of Kelly's prose writings on poetry & the vastness of the œuvre, the editors would like to qualify or finetune the *collected* scope of this book. Simply put, this is a "Collected" not a "Complete Essays." Beyond our decision to gather as wide & eclectic a range of writings as possible we have of course made sure that all key texts, spanning some sixty years of writing, are included — though this has also entailed making a de facto selection.

Suffice it to briefly sketch the nature of omitted materials. In the mid-eighties, for instance, Kelly started to regularly review (mainly) novels for the *New York Times Book Review*. However, because these texts are by & large standard, even if well-written reviews, & above all because one can readily consult them in the NYT online archive,[2] we have decided to include only a sample in "A Book of Discourse &/on Narrative." Similarly, "A Catena," a chain of statements Kelly made at different occasions between 1960 & 1980, has not been included, because the original essays used in the making of "A Catena" are all present as such.[3] There is a further range of minor materials from the archives that in our judgment did not warrant inclusion, for being too fragmentary, occasional, unfinished, etc., or because they represented early or unsatisfactory sketches or

---

2. Kelly reviewed, amongst others, Toby Olson's *The Woman who Escaped from Shame* (June 1st, 1986), Janet Kauffman's *Obscene Gestures for Women* (September 24th, 1989), *Loving Letters from Ogden Nash* (February 11th, 1990), Donald Hall's *Life Work* (October 3rd, 1993), Reynolds Price's *A Whole New Life* (July 10th, 1994), William Gass's *The Tunnel* (February 25th, 1995), Umberto Eco's *The Island of the Day Before* (October 22nd, 1995), Philip Roth's *I Married a Communist* (October 11th, 1998), Mark Z. Danielewski's *House of Leaves* (March 26th, 2000), Padgett Powell's *Mrs. Hollingsworth's Men* (November 5th, 2000), John Dufresne's *Deep in the Shade of Paradise* (June 9th, 2002)...

3. Namely "Notes on the Poetry of Deep Image," "A Plucked Flute," "On Discourse" & the Postlude to *Not This Island Music*.

drafts of thoughts realized better elsewhere. All noteworthy omissions have, however, been signaled in one way or another. In a few of the included pieces reproduced from archival manuscripts, there are occasional words or sentences missing; these are indicated by [...].

Rather than standardize the styles of the various pieces, the editors have tried to reproduce the original layout & spelling of Kelly's texts as much as possible, especially in the case of typescripts, poem-statements, schemas, Kelly's own magazine pieces, or when typographical idiosyncrasies were at stake. Such idiosyncratic use of the typewriter (& later, if to a lesser degree, the computer) is an integral part of RK's style of composition in the wake of Ezra Pound's much more insistent typographical experiments — & Robert Kelly is certainly in many aspects a direct descendant of Pound. A differential representation over the time of these writings (stretching over half a century) helps, we think, to give a quasi-visual depth-of-time perception to the book. We have of course silently corrected what were clear & unintended mistakes. Except for straightforward prose pieces, we have thus attempted to give the book the visual multiplicity typical of an essay collection properly speaking.

It is also important to note that, although the editors have carefully assembled twelve specific "books," they have respected a *broad* chronological focus only, both throughout the entire volume & within each of its twelve "books." However, we give below each text either the date provided by Kelly at the moment of composition, or, set between parentheses, the date & place of first publication. Square brackets have been used to indicate tentative dates.

Organizing the wealth of materials into smaller (more or less) self-contained "books" has the advantage of offering the reader the choice & ease of reading those thematically organized "books" separately & according to his or her specific interests, though of course the whole of the twelve "books" does form an *ensemble*. Finally, a *broad* chronological focus also puts different texts, genres, & literary contexts into play, & keeps the concept of "writing on" open enough — both in terms of focus & form — as this is furthermore a vital aspect of RK's writing at large. In short, we have not chosen to categorize the texts by either a strict (& often stultifying) chronological line-up, or by subordinating them to the usual labels of "reviews," "interviews," "critical essays" or what have you. What, then, do these twelve "books" offer?

INTRODUCTION

A Book of Images: Deep and Beyond, probably the most chronological section, opens with Kelly's first takes on poetics, gathering texts from the early to mid-sixties. The frontispiece, an early draft of "The Poetry of Image: 20 Points" (which would soon be rewritten into the well-known "Notes on the Poetry of Deep Image"), introduces the thematic focus of this first book: Kelly's involvement with image, Deep & Other. This may also be the occasion to rethink "Deep Image," the intense, visionary even if fore-shortened & self-dismantled "movement" started by Jerome Rothenberg & Robert Kelly in the early sixties (& that has nothing to do with the cheapened version peddled for some time by Wright, Bly & Co.). Such a re-evaluation would, in our judgment, show the ineptitude of the editorial decision Paul Hoover made when preparing the 2013 edition of his *Postmodern American Poetry: A Norton Anthology*, to drop all of his earlier commentary on "deep image" & to eliminate the poems of both Jerome Rothenberg & Robert Kelly. To his credit, Hoover did leave Clayton Eshleman in, the one "deep image" poet who has persisted throughout his career with an image-based poetics, where image transformations impel the poem forward, expanding Kelly's early insight that "the rhythm of the images constitut[es]… the deep structure of the poem."

Most of the texts in this opening "book" were first published in crucial little magazines of the period: *Trobar* & *Matter*, edited by RK himself, but also *Nomad*, *Kulchur*, *Sum* or *El Corno Emplumado*. It is interesting to note that, chronologically speaking, other pieces could have been placed in this book — notably some of the reviews (of Leroi Jones/Amiri Baraka's *The Dead Lecturer*, or the *Caterpillar* reviews —. all from **A Book of the Company**), as well as the *Sullen Art* interview with David Ossman (which can be found in **A Book of Interrogations**).[4] Here, too, Stan Brakhage makes a first, important appearance in no less than three essays — two of which were published in *Film Culture*.

---

4. **A Book of Interrogations**, which can be found in the companion volume *A City Full of Voices*, features three complete interviews: the early conversation with David Ossman (1963), the mid-seventies five-way talk with George Quasha & Charles Stein (1973), & Clayton Eshleman's recent "20 Questions for Robert Kelly" (2007).

Brakhage, an artist of major importance for Kelly, will reappear in the **Book of the Eye (Moving or not)**, in two more recent pieces.

A Book Called *In Time* (1971) constitutes a second beginning: published in book form in 1971 by Harvey Brown's Frontier Press, *In Time* is Kelly's sole book of essays properly speaking. At the time of its appearance this book constituted for one of us the singular most stimulating collection of post-Olson essays on poetics, especially via the concept of the poet as last "scientist of the Whole" in an age of overspecialization. Both of us have kept coming back to this most useful figure even & especially today, a decade & a half into a 21C where the overarching problematics are the knot made by various religio-ideological strands interwoven with an encroaching ecological disaster against a background of globalized late-capitalist economic exploitation.

In Time mainly gathers texts from the mid- to late sixties, some of which were previously published in little magazines, like "Letter to the Bear. Re: Rome" (*Floating Bear* #11, 1961), "Re: The Occult" (*Aion* #1, 1964), "Identity Preference Temple Complex" (*Matter* #4, 1968), "The Frontiers of the Fact" (*Sum* #2, 1964) & consecutive sections of "The Dream Work" in *Matter* #1–4 (with, remarkably, a fifth section that was added later & published in *Io* #8, 1971, & which opens **A Book of Dreams**). Although *In Time* coincides chronologically at least partly with **A Book of Images**, we have kept RK's organization of his collection entirely intact, thus also setting it up in this volume as a sort of counterpart to the first book.

With its subtitle, "Heaven is other people," suggested by Kelly himself, **A Book of the Company** features a wide range of essays, reviews, statements, introductions, prefaces & in certain cases even blurbs on & for poets, writers, & artists, many of them friends, whose work is often core or kin to Kelly's own preoccupations. Like the schema that figures as this book's frontispiece, the line-up is obviously incomplete: these writings are indicative of, but in no way an exhaustive take on Kelly's always expanding "Company" itself.

Again, it is interesting to note that this book, in many ways, inevitably cuts across the two previous books, as many of these pieces, too, were published in the 1960s (notably in *Caterpillar*) or 1970s (*Truck, Oasis, Credences*...). In this book, we also come across the first two installments of RK's proposed & sketched out "critical organon" (never realized as an actual book) — on Ted Enslin & Pierre Joris —, while a third installment, on Matt Phillips, can be found in **A Book of the Eye (Moving or not)**. Although all three are part of this never completed critical project of the mid- to late seventies, they are, along with the Irby piece, a turning point in Kelly's approach to "writing on" or essayistic poetics. In the headnote to the Enslin piece, he announces a turn away from traditional "literary criticism" toward what he calls the "deictic," which he defines as follows: an "act of criticism [that] means to represent a new possibility, not a Criticism but a Deicticism, deictic (Greek *deiknumi*, I demonstrate, rather than *krino*, I judge). This new or deictic possibility means to gesture towards, walk along beside, assert ontologies, abstain from evaluations, prestiges."

Also indicative of this turn is the relative absence of texts directly on the Company during the 1980s & the better part of the 1990s. From the late 1990s, the Company reemerges in the writing, as can be seen from the many double entries of early & later pieces (which we have mostly kept together). Thus, after three books of beginnings that each in their own way started somewhere in the 1960s, we head into the next books with the "critical organon" — Kelly obviously didn't stop producing new essays; they simply cover different grounds.

The next three books thus not only open onto the 70s & after, they also interlace, &, incidentally, feature key contributions to *Io* magazine,[5] conceived by Richard Grossinger to some extent according to Kelly's own idea of what a magazine should be. I.E., a place to gather the various heterogeneous multi-disciplinary matters (RK's own magazine of the sixties was called *Matter* after all) & materials that would be necessary for the information-hungry "poet as world scholar," poets that, as he said in *In Time*, "do not have hobbies" but "eat everything." **A Book of**

---

5. After much consideration, the editors have decided not to include Kelly's "An Alchemical Journal," first published in *Io* #4 (summer 1967), & reprinted in Jed Rasula's *The Alchemist to Mercury* (1981). Although a seminal text in RK's œuvre, we feel it falls beyond the scope of this "Collected Essays" — hoping, however, that it will be made available again elsewhere beyond this recent serialization on Nomadics blog (pierrejoris.com/blog).

Discourse &/on Narrative starts off with a crucial sequence called "On Discourse," consisting in a substantial set of musings, statements, & poems published in *Io #20* "Biopoesis" (1974). This opening sequence also links back to **A Book Called *In Time***: as Kelly states in his introductory remark, "On Discourse" resumes & carries forward *In Time*. Although in a very Kellyan manner these are touche-à-tout texts, it may be useful to think of them as speaking to the differentials he perceives between poetry & prose when reminding us "that poetry begins in speech as prose never does, prose, that late form, that abstraction" — & that to think beyond (or below or around or through) those staid categories, would mean to focus on "writing" ("*writing* is the plane of event"). Apart from other early (poem-)statements, this book also offers three "generic" clusters: prefaces & afterwords to Kelly's own novels & short stories, a sample selection of book reviews, &, finally, "discourses" with a slightly different ring to the word.

A Book of Dreams & **A Book of Outside / Inside** might, each in their way, be said to pick up on *In Time* too — thinking of the already mentioned "Dream Work" on the one hand, & of "Hygiene —)" or "Biotic diet" carried forward in an "oecological" focus on the other. Both of these books are furthermore closely related — the texts & talks on "hypnogeography" squarely in-between, thus literally linking dream & place. The latter book nonetheless branches out, from the early Black Sparrow pamphlet *A Line of Sight* (& the more recent "A Talking House" for & on John Ashbery) still directly tied in with dream & place, to talk of cloning, "entertainment" & the Hudson Valley, as well as Peter Lamborn Wilson's *Atlantis Manifesto* on which RK recently wrote a long commentary.

With the *TEXTS* series at its core, **A Book with & against Theory** is a further twist in the poetics road. The installments of this sequence were mainly published in *Wch Way* (with *TEXTS* : 16 in *Sixpack* & an additional version of *TEXTS* : 18 in *Curtains*). Given that the 24 sections of *TEXTS* are largely comprised of poems, the editors have selected those fragments relevant for this book's purposes only. What interested us here specifically is the way Kelly's thinking about philosophical & theoretical matters takes shape in a realm of "writing" one can formally situate *between* poetry & prose (thus an in-between realm, a *barzakh*, to use Ibn Arabi's sufi terminology) that allows it to escape the double bind of straightjacketed footnote-beholden academic theorizing & the metaphor-strangled image-grounded (or ungrounded / Ungrund-ed) realm of the lyric. Of further notice are the responses to Frederic Grab's (Bard College) faculty seminars on Foucault & Benjamin, & the statement regarding theory given as a keynote address at the University at Albany. **A Book of Translation** then functions as a supplement to its predecessor, moving from more theoretical considerations on translation to concrete authors & texts (Edward Young, *Gilgamesh* & *Beowulf*, or five of RK's "adaptions" of Greek tragedies) — considerations that, in turn, already point to the "Poet-Statements" subsection of **A Book between Poem &/as Statement**.

The paradoxically short **Book of Nearly Everything Else** & **A Book of the Eye (Moving or not)** are organized thematically, as is the final **Book of Music**. The middle book hinges on art & especially film (Anger, Herzog, & Brakhage), thus picking up "images" from a different viewpoint, *and* going back to "the Company" (Schneemann, Jaffe, a "critical organon" et cetera). The latter book talks of, to, & through music — so essential in Kelly's poetry & poetics that it seemed to the editors a perfect "outro." And the first mentioned **Book of nearly Everything else**, finally, deals indeed with "nearly everything else," gathering a small selection of published letters,[6] notes, & extracts from the "Autobiographical Essay" for *Gale Research*.

The remaining extracts from that fascinating text can be found at the opening of **A Book between Poem &/as Statement** — thereby literally linking poetry & poetics to everything else. In-between those additional Gale extracts, the editors placed a set of six crucial "poem-statements," with a seventh coming at the very end of the book. Along with a set of "poet-statements" (on Dante, Blake, Keats, Pound/Stevens, & Celan), these two subsections serve as hinges for the many statements on poetry this book consists of (discourse, essay, talk, reply to questionnaires,

---

6. Although there's a considerable amount of published letters available, the editors have opted to make a small selection only — even within series of letters published in the same magazine, such as, e.g., the sole letter we retained from *El Corno Emplumado*.

et cetera). And so these statements move between poetry & poetics, between poem-statement & statement on poems, &, along with **A Book of Music**, appropriately direct the reader back to Kelly's daily work as a poet, i.e., to his books of poetry.

Picking up our cue from the tantric weavings of *The Loom*, as well as from one of Kelly's syntactically experimental books of poems, *Threads*, we have woven twelve *THREADS* across this volume of RK's collected essays, continued, in turn, in the companion volume of critical essays on his work. These twelve sections of *THREADS* — in which "Robert says" — consist of various interview excerpts that directly, or indirectly, speak to the "books" they precede & to the other *THREADS* they are woven into. In the present volume, the editors have used Kelly's words only, whereas in the companion volume the voices of both Kelly & his interviewers resound.[7] In this way, both volumes together offer the reader not only a "collected" & "critical" essays, but also a *"SELECTED INTERVIEWS."* The *THREADS* furthermore signal one way in which *A Voice Full of Cities* & *A City Full of Voices* speak to each other, indeed, overlap & fold into one another — as indicated by their titles & internal structural organization as an assemblage of "books." A key topos in his poetry & poetics, Kelly's voice thus literally opens up on a myriad of cities the reader is invited to visit & explore.

---

7. For the *THREADS* of this volume, the editors made use of the following interviews: Joshua Stolle, "An Interview with Robert Kelly" (ca. 1970s); James Stalker, "Interview" (ca. 1980); Dennis Barone, "Nothing but Doors: an Interview with Robert Kelly" (early 1980s); Larry McCaffery, "A Rose to Look at: an Interview with Robert Kelly" (1988); Bradford Morrow, "Robert Kelly: *Conjunctions* Interview" (spring 1989); Bonnie Langston, "Interview with Robert Kelly for the Kingston *Freeman*" (July 13th, 1994); Simone dos Anjos & Pietro Aman, "*The Modern Review* Interview" (2006); Mark Thwaite, "Robert Kelly *ReadySteadyBooks* Interview" (2006); Sam Lohmann, "*Peaches & Bats* Interview with Robert Kelly" (April 2007, published Winter 2008); Leonard Schwartz's *CrossCultural Poetics*, "#93 Listening hard" (2005), "#99 Red Actions" (2006) & "#202 Path & Counterpath" (2009).

INTRODUCTION

Finally, the editors & the author of these essays wish to thank deeply & loudly a number of friends the writer Cassandra Seltman, who flawlessly typed hundreds of pages of often scarce-legible originals to produce files that were used in this book; the novelist Ashley Mayne, who at the last moment typed in the autobiographical essay; & the poet Tamas Panitz who helped proofread the whole typescript with alertness, precision, & understanding, & who further helped dig up some of the final missing materials. The editors also wish to thank the staff of the New York Public Library for their kind help with retrieving many sought-after little magazines. Special thanks go to James Maynard, associate curator of poetry for the wonderful Special Collections of the University at Buffalo, who enthusiastically provided us with always new archival treasure boxes of RK's writings; to Christina Milletti & Dimitri Anastasopoulos for their warm hospitality; to Jed Rasula, whose precise RK bibliography (*Credences* Vol. 3, № 1, spring 1984) has proven an invaluable aid; to Nicole Peyrafitte for the gorgeous cover illustration; to Alessandro Segalini for his typesetting efforts; to Rainer J. Hanshe for his generous support & precise understanding throughout, & for backing a project of this magnitude; &, finally, the editors' thanks go to Robert Kelly himself, for kindly, patiently, & gracefully responding to endless queries, practical & other, via mail or over a cup of coffee. This book could not exist without them.

Pierre Joris & Peter Cockelbergh
Brooklyn, Paris, Lille

A VOICE FULL OF CITIES:

THE COLLECTED ESSAYS
OF ROBERT KELLY

THREADS 1: ROBERT SAYS

(Certainly [...] I don't like to use that word [i.e., image] anymore. It became like a slogan. At that time, I didn't have enough sense... I did have enough sense, but I realized there would be some value in a slogan, too. It doesn't have that value for me now. But certainly the sense of an image that penetrates the mind and [...] the interesting thing about an image — and I said that even back then in that essay, and I hardly knew what I meant —, is that an image is not just a shield as I was saying now, it's a door, and of course a door is a notable shield, isn't it? The enemy is coming, we close the door in his face. That's the shield aspect. But an image is something we open and go through. This long poem that has just been published in Boston, Fire Exit, which is a poem not as long as The Loom, but it's the next longest thing I've ever done and it's a poem that has been the preoccupation over the last three years or so. A long, continuous and very dense poem, as an attempt — the name is Fire Exit, and exit is what it's about, it's the image, as opening the image to flee from the fire, through the image. [...] I'm glad you brought up the Deep Image thing as, in a way, tired as I am of hearing about it, nonetheless I, in that sense, stand by it, or rather I open it up and run through it, escaping... The image as a doorway is the main thing to think about, I think.

in conversation with Leonard Schwartz (2009)

Thinking about it almost fifty years later, only now do I realize that I was in the position say Alban Berg was — my first and favorite modernist composer — caught between the intense emotional tonality of late romanticism, but seeing a starkly radical beauty possible, a cutting through, a suddenness. Back then, I was looking for suddenness. That sudden upwelling my friends and I found best articulated in Lorca's marvelous, seductive essay on the duende, still I think the best expression we have to hand of the sudden presence of deity in our struggling song and dance. And we called that thing, our blue flower, the Deep Image. Deep not out of appeal to depth psychology so-called, more with reference to the "deep structure" of linguistics — the rule beneath the apparent feature, deep too because the image we meant did not have to be (as in the miraculous rejuvenation of the early 1900s, Pound's Imagisme), the image did not have to be a visualizable, namable thing. But thingliness had always been our best guide. When I explain this to students nowadays, I say: I am trying to teach you to write Thinglish. Deep image was Thinglish Grammar forgotten into dream and awakened by music.

in conversation with Simone dos Anjos & Pietro Aman (2006)

Chelsea was distributed by that Spanish-Dutchman named B. DeBoer, an irascible man, but very useful. He used to come around in his station wagon to pick up copies. George Economou and I left Chelsea in 1960. Chelsea took on two new editors who were lover and lover or something. David Ignatow came on when it became clear that the others did not have a handle on American Poetry. Ignatow came on to save them. […] Trobar was interesting because at that point there were lots of paperback bookshops. So, we sold them by mail and in bookstores. There weren't many printed. We'd print maybe 500–1,000 copies. It sold very quickly. Matter, as you say, was sent to a mailing list of people. Not quite to whoever asked for it. More like who I thought should get it. People whose work interested me or people who indicated to me that it might be of some use to them. The idea of Matter was matter; to provide the material for poems, rather than just a magazine of poems. Of course, it didn't entirely do that. Every so often I'm tempted to do another since I can do it so much better than anyone else and blah, blah, blah. And yet, I couldn't.

in conversation with Dennis Barone [early 1980s]

Several weeks ago I read that deep image essay for the first time in many years, & I found myself still able to stand by it. There's hardly anything that I disown except that rather shrill tone (today I'd probably make it shriller). My manifesto writing, which I've done a lot of over the years, always seems to return to this issue of permission: don't say I can't do this, don't take away this possibility, don't let decorum replace possibility. I don't think my writing has ever taken advantage of all the possibilities I have had, let alone those that someone has presented. As a poet, I was after something that was not exhausted by describing the outer reality or by the kind of decorum I had been facing, as we all were, of the Wilbur's and all the other tired '40-ish writing that came to life briefly again in the '50s when Dylan Thomas's comet-like blaze came through us and then died down into mere imitations because Thomas was doing something you can't imitate. But after years of facing that decorum, to turn & face the decorum of the Williamsites, who were going to tell me that I couldn't use language, that I could only mention the names of objects (as if the names of objects were somehow more concrete than the names of feelings were; whereas in fact they are both just names, the names of "hate" and "lust" and "envy" being just as concrete as "wheelbarrow" because these are all just words, imputations, and "wheelbarrow" is just as abstract as "anger" or "embarrassment"). So there was one more decorum to deal with — this one based on a naïve literalism of "the real" which not even Williams himself believed. And of course as we all know, the duration of every generation is brief indeed — you get only an 18-month period between the language school and Raymond Carver. But the keynote is decorum, which one cannot rail against without being excluded from the poetic mainstream.

in conversation with Larry McCaffery (1988)

1.

A BOOK OF IMAGES: DEEP & OTHER

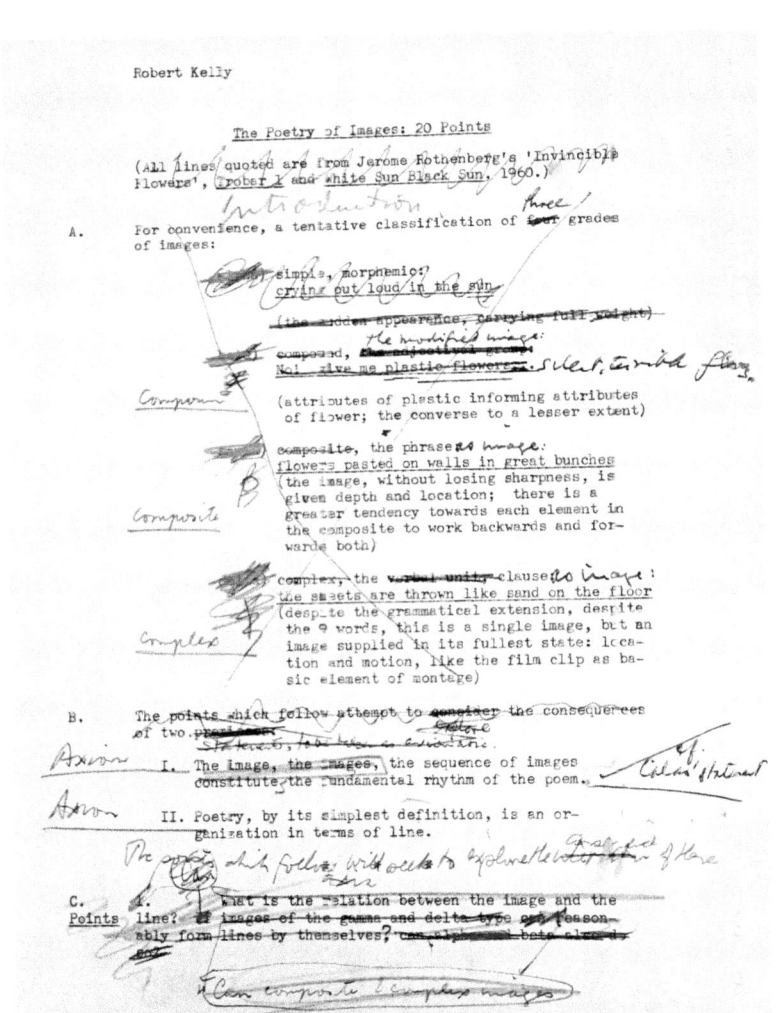

TROBAR EDITORIAL

The primal gestures of language: ox foraging on the grassland, the archer pulling his bow with all his powers. And we had planned a rough target as our present emblem. And there is a hunter, the organon of movements and powers, the deliberate mind but the fingers curved. And at a certain point there is only rummaging around for rocks and roots to throw and feed on, the hunter scouring the ground. But deeper: not till the rock is pulled from the ground is its size or nature known, can it be used.

It is the capture of the primal vigor of poetry, the visible substance of the mystery. A poet's passion roots itself to things, and it is, after all vision and all craft, his business to discover the substance and bearings of those roots which are the inescapable content of dream and discipline, which are deep images.

Poetry is itself a power of life. The editors of TROBAR believe that American poetry today must re-establish contact with the perennial strength of the deep image as a mode of working within the poem, as statement and as vision.

But TROBAR will not be confined to the poetry of any single approach. The purpose of TROBAR is to publish American poetry of intensity & immediacy, apparitions of the native duende, articulate in power of word, dynamic in the space of music, made with all the powers of poetry, moving alive and passionate.

(*Trobar* #2, 1961)

NOTES ON THE POETRY OF DEEP IMAGE

> ... *the movement of images is rhythm.*
> — Nicolas Calas

These notes represent my attempt to understand and use this statement. The climate of the notes is the atmosphere of excitement and confrontation I am aware of in Jerome Rothenberg's workings in what he calls 'deep image.' In the second issue of his *Poems from the Floating World* he writes: 'The deep image rises from the shoreless gulf: here the poet reaches down among the lost branches, till a moment of seeing: the poem.' Working with deep image is the development of a 'basic imagination.' I read FLOATING WORLD as an attempt to plot a series of points, the poems & translations printed, to surround an implicit definition of the powers of the deep image. Rothenberg's first volume, WHITE SUN BLACK SUN (Hawk's Well Press) has just been published. The poems in it are very good, very moving, very much alive: demonstrations of the fruitfulness of the approach to the poem via deep image. And the collection is, beyond the matter of the poems themselves (what shall be said of them?) a happening in itself: the appearance of a demand for a new set of concerns in poetry, the appearance of a cogent movement in a new direction. The notes that follow are offered as pertinent perhaps to the climate I've spoken of.

The present & necessary function of poetry is the transformation of the perceived world. This transformation orders the known world into an effective and coherent universe. The eye, seeing a concrete pavement for the thousandth time but the flakes of mica embedded in it, glowing & fiery, for the first time, sees a transformation and so is illuminated. But poetry cannot stop with that enlightenment. Epiphany is meaningless display outside the context of incarnation. Poetry is concerned with things transforming and transforming things, with the whole picture in mind. We are given: 1 world to transform, 1 language to transform it with.

Transformation is process, involves truth as emergent from process and not distinct from it, involves knowledge which alone redeems us from innocence, the deadly innocence of not knowing where and what things are. Poetry answers the questions what where when.

Nothing can be known unless it is known in situ, in the context of its world. Transformation aims at the continuum of all perceptions. Poetry is this continuum. Poetry establishes the mutual relevance of every percept to every other percept.

Percepts are from dreams or from waking, rise from the unconscious or from the retina of the awakened eye. Poetry, like dream reality, is the juncture of the experienced with the never-experienced. Like waking reality, it is the fulfillment of the imagined and the unimagined. The percepts, in order to be communicated, are fleshed in language. Poetry cannot exhibit naked perception. The clothed percept is the image.

Poetry is not the art of relating word to word, but the ACT of relating word to percept, image to image until the continuum is achieved.

The Line:

If the poem takes its departure from speech, a relationship of some kind must exist between the rhythm supplied by the image and the rhythm of the breath. What is the relationship of image to line?

One easy answer is to say that one image equals one line. This denies the independent existence of line, and is a quasi-solution that produces poetry of blandness, no matter how great the initial force of images: the images are not being articulated, urgency is lost.

Projected verse (for which see Charles Olson, *Projective Verse*) offers a method of resolving breath and line, and my concern with it here seeks to substitute the centrality of image for the centrality of syllable & line as a way of access to the happening of a poem. The line as set down on paper is an indication of the breath period, with visual & rhythmic considerations determining the visual notation.

The projective line ending in open juncture allows tremendous stress on the last verbal unit in the line, a stress exploited not for key words but for key silences, stretching out to vital & peripheral words. 'Systematic derangement' of standard speech rhythms, of the inflexibilities of our analytic grammar, is a sharp exploratory tool, and a means of locking images.

When the image, prima materia, is lacking, the verbal gesture is quickly emptied: the poem elapses instead of happening.

The fundamental rhythm of the poem is the rhythm of the images, their textures, their contents, offer supplementary rhythms.

In addition, there is the rhythm of the breath. One line represents one breath period. The line rhythm is a product of internal (stress, morphemic pattern) & external (weight, length) factors, relating one line to another and to all others. Each line is rhythmically related to another line by those same elements that relate lines formally to one another, i.e., formal similarities beget rhythmic relationships.

Thus a poem involves the fundamental rhythm of the images (fundamental because more complexly present), a rhythm which is at once intellectual & sensuous, and also the structural, more directly sensual, rhythm of the breath expressed in line. The counterpointing of these two rhythms is a principal source of fullness and complexity in the poem.

Deep Image:

Plucking things from the street or from the unconscious is comparable to the digging of ore. Images do not necessarily proceed directly from the pitchblende. Verbalization is of prime importance, and on its subtlety the success of the appearance of the image, and of the rhythm of images, depends.

The deep image must be transferred to the paper, BUILT into the poem, in language which gives it its fullest spatial, temporal, sonic & kinetic properties, as conditioned by its presence in a series & in a structure. Supplying the image in its fullest force is thus partially a function of language.

Basically, the fullest force is possible only by means of the successful employment of one image's position in a context of other images, the image, after its first appearance as dark sound, still lingers as a resonance. Thus resonance must be controlled, and the effective means of control are the acoustics of the space intervening between one image & the next. The subsequent image is conditioned, made to work, by the image that precedes it, and conditions, as it is finally conditioned by, the image that follows it: through the whole poem. The first image to appear in an André Breton poem will normally dominate all subsequent images and the poem as a whole, even when the reader seems to have forgotten it.

The whole poem is more than the sum of its parts. Very important for this superequivalence is the ORDER of images within a poem. The final quantum will vary with the rearrangement of the images and of the images' fields of force. Every image has its field of force, it shadow moving darkly through the poem, with which the poet must contend.

The rational progression of images is only trope, whether or not the middle terms are excluded: metaphor with a stale taste of truism. Only the superior rationality of the dream is an effective impetus for the movements of the deep image.

The image is the measure of the line. The line is cut with image in mind.

Language:

The verbalization of the image comes out of the linguistic patterns of the poet's native language.

In the poem built from deep image, the image itself bears an enormous weight, for through it and its connection with the rhythmic sequence of images, the flow of the image-conditioned word & music, the meaning of the poem exists, all communication takes place.

The American language of today provides the only reliable linguistic patterns for the poet of images. Verbal expression of the image demands an urgency and directness that only the spoken language of poet and reader can supply the language of here and now. "The language of the image must come across vividly and urgently, without cuteness of distraction."

Only in the native linguistic PATTERNS can the deep image communicate at full strength.

In the image and in the line, the poet is using a language superficially akin to that of everyday. Atop the familiar linguistic patterns, the images mold their own expressions. The poet charges these expressions using the full arsenal of poetics, so that the image works in all its urgency, at its maximal communicative force. The need for urgency, for tension in the work itself, cannot be exaggerated. The language of deep images restores the poetry of desperation.

October 1960
(*Trobar* #2, 1961)

STATEMENT FOR *NOMAD*

As a start.

It is for the poem to move among facts so that the entirety of the visible IS visible.

That in the rhythm & fullness of time: to gather, sort & build, "stone from under his mountains." We speak of composition.

"Know what is in thy sight, & what is hidden will be revealed to you."

The poet cannot stop with the visible, but he must encompass that before his "creating" can begin.

Forever our damned confusion of what a thing is with what it does. Dante on function & being, Hell where the images lose their functions, merely are.

"Mirrors coated on the back with tin, & blind men's dreams, these catch only the surface of the face, & that dim light cannot steadfastly endure even though it may make fleeting joy seem real."

In our day we do not find or do not seek God's grace, that light which Dante did not accommodate but which accommodated him: light proceeding from a more-fully-grasped complex vision of the real.

Our experiences of the Not Me (impersonal, "objective," not the Id of rejects & displacements) we treat *as if* demonic, as if answering to the Eichmanns who gibber inside each of us. Enough for me to suggest that we have not yet clarified our sight, & see still too much out of memory, & not enough by sunlight.

It is not enough to be nostalgic for the immediate. Build out of the immediate; music.

So facts are not just surfaces.

And here it is necessary to say that deep image is the functional perception of all dimensions beyond the surface.

We cannot move in the space of God. In the process of discovery (not invention) we call poem, the hidden real must be "created" in the same instant it is found. I have in mind this instantaneousness when I speak of the poem happening, too, of the poet in his poem.

I'm not talking about Method: a man's whole life of work is barely enough to come to a method. Nor about gimmicks, ways of making things "work." Gimmick is crap, no matter how you spread it. A poet's craft is his ability to orient himself by the use of words, his ability to allow a poem to be its own emergent form.

Since we are men, in the human scale of time & space relationships, the discovery is of ourselves through the visible, of the visible through ourselves.

The gateway is the visible; but we must go in.

(*Nomad* #10–11, 1962)

LETTER TO KEN IRBY

Bard College, Annandale-on-Hudson, New York
21 August '63

dear Ken,

sometimes I feel I shd never have published the NOTES ON THE POETRY OF DEEP IMAGE but shd have kept them (not selfishly, but prudently) to myself as a record of the heuristic value they represent. In letting them in print, it was my thought that they might be sparks capable of setting fire to someone's thought, somewhere in the world, & that they might make available to that someone what was & is available to me only in the actual process of my working. It is this fine letter of yours . . . that makes me feel otherwise, & to think it was a proper action to publish as Notes what I cd not even then (or now) swear to as doctrine. That is, & literally so, I never proposed (at that time, tho god knows an earlier — unpublished — enthusiasm might have suggested so) a program, a stance, an attack. What I was after was a way of looking at poetry, poems, & therein seeing an interaction of a human set of concerns with the phenomenal world (extero- or entero-conceived). At that particular time, I felt the approach via *craft* a peculiarly arid one (since craft in a small sense is something we must assume anyone worthy of notice to possess, & craft in the greatest sense is what a whole man's body of work may, may, arrive at, as EP's or WCW's or Blake's did). As long as I have been reading poems, I have been violently suspicious of anything that reeks of the form-content dichotomy; my fundamental premise is that a poem is a unison of forces, irremediably, inalterably, & that we must concern ourselves not with the parts but with the whole, what it PROJECTS, casts into our hearts. This, in turn, is Olson's wisdom, that he told me in the briefest and best possible way, "not imageS but image," as I quote in the footnote to my words in the *Sullen Art*. That clarity turned the scale for me; seeking is wonderful IF & ONLY IF you find. (G. MacDonald rightly calls hell's chief proverb: To travel hopefully is better than to arrive. I.E., only an Idiot would think so, no? Yet thereby the idiot hurts himself, w/o helping others to clarity). I'm getting vague now, many things urgent in my mind. But this much I shd add: some people were put off by my apparent indifference to 'craft' in those Notes.

It was simple humility to avoid that particular matter (of the essence tho it is) in a time when, e.g., Olson, Zukofsky, Dorn, Creeley, Levertov (not to speak of EP & WCW) have been loud & right & heard. ... So talking abt 'deep image' ... is talking abt ALL poetry, you're right there.

... I DO believe ('believe' is an abstraction from the processes of my life & working, rather than an instruction for them) that man is one single animal, not a spirit, but a unison. I do believe that love is an as-if palpable energy capable of kinetic & psychic extension. But I do intensely, as intensely, believe in the visible, SEE IT, i.e., as the epigraph I put to *Armed Descent* shd suggest, as does the title itself (tho few seem to recognize its source). I am not trying to afflict you with a 'credo'; in every case, I wd prefer to let my work speak for itself. But there are critics ... who will not READ the work ... but will content themselves with their own preconceptions abt the 'stance' of the poet in question. This is our modern-day version of the old biographical fallacy. It gets yet more horrible since it seems we know one another so well. ...

Yet you are right to say that those questions of Who, What, Where we are cannot ever be put to one side, even for a minute. But I propose this amplification: these questions can rightly & properly (owing to the real nature of the questions themselves) find their answers only in the work. Our poems, not our radio speeches &c., are the only efficient media for such answers. Those questions, being real ones, demand answers in reality (as the 'problem of poverty' can be 'solved' only when nobody at all is poor). God knows, the poem is real enough for that strength. And further, the strength & excellence of those questions is precisely in that they do drive a man on w/ his own work, fertilize those furrows of his mind where he can best plant eyes and get Visions, not potatoes. Not VisionS but Vision, I say.

But where is the audience? Where are the readers who consume but do not practice? I used to know a tiny schismatic Old Catholic Utrechtine church, the communicants of which were exactly co-extensive with its hierarchy. Is that the fix we're in now? If so, anything can happen. By all means, head for the hills. As I see you've done. I delight to think of you sitting there, in the presence of rock mountain, & where you can, as I have tried I hope with success to do here, commit "yourself to who (you are), totally, guts, mind, cock, heart, all."

... it is terribly easy to develop paranoiac feelings, not abt yourself necessarily, but about what 'they' are doing to poets thruout the world, abt 'establishments' & the like. True enough that the news is bad, &c., but we've got to deal by ourselves, handling what we can get a grip on, helping whenever we can in whatever way, but NOT sitting around & feeling trivial or abused or a member of a dying race. I know that scene with peculiar vividness, & it's always just outside the edges of the light the lamp throws, waiting to jump, as they say. It is Whitman's frequently censured 'naïve optimism' that allowed him to WORK for 40 years. EP another case. What's to be held to is not the vision of Ezra in the gorilla cage at Pisa, but Ezra getting the Shih Jing in shape years after. As your next state neighbor, Brakhage, says, Paranoia is a disease. Flat. ...

Robert Kelly

(*Sum* #1, 1963)

SONG? / AFTER BREAD
NOTES ON ZUKOFSKY'S *A 1–12*

In America the poet makes what many want but few value. Perhaps it is the same everywhere in every time. But when we say we'd paid a meager price, got it cheap, we say: "I bought it for a song."

What song? Nobody knows, though my mother used to say it was *do re mi*, stress on the dough, whenever I asked her, what song? And what we buy for a song is commonly a house. House. That's the idiom for buying a house you need at a price you can afford. That house you live in, my friend. Yes, I bought it for a song.

The Voice of the People would appear to tell us that Uncle Sap pays through the nose to the tune of 50 million. Yes, that's the tune and how you sing it, fetishly, through the nose.

It is the poet here who pays the song, for a house to live in gracious to his words and to his manhood and to his sense. The peril is to build a house without a door, where windows open into Russian easter eggs with never an aperture for the flesh to enter.

Spending even a few minutes with Zukofsky's *A,* I am already drawn in, involved in his complex order, a taut design set moving (tingling or slow) with song. I have looked up startled from his book, carried his patterns with me through a day, understood the way things work and move, in his tune.

But the poem does not compel by hallucination, and rarely by incantation. Richness of images moving to the fiddle, not the drum. That different music implies an astonishing fact: Zukofsky is a reasonable man.

Zukofsky's reason is not a matter of attitude or rigidities. An intellectual music: that's the uncanniness of *A*, reason and wisdom taken into song. Which makes me wonder: are *logos* and *ratio* capable of being married only in song? Because it's song that carries; the concern is with the poem, not the "poetic."

Poetry from age to age is threatened by the dead spectre of decorum. Pusillanimous poets in each age determine what is, and is not, appropriate material in poetry, what concerns of man can enter into rime with seemliness. Surely we have our own hypothecators of decorum, and they are not less spectral for being so publicly divided when it comes to the actual substance of their exclusions.

And while the pettifoggers have been busy with shears and doses, the poets have gone on entertaining as their first concern the *formal* discovery and conquest of the world in all the complexities of its substantive relations. Blake and Shelley and Yeats and Pound and Williams are for us stewards, not of dry excellence, but of the poet's total involvement in the world his senses or hypersenses tell him is real. Plainly the times count, but it is the poet, in his isolation, who must sustain the encounter.

What gives me such delight when I consider *A* is its formal insistence on the total world of time and powers and persons and concerns Zukofsky lives among. The deacons of decorum are to be baffled: this poet wants everything he knows. The audacity of his ordering leads him to put his son's bright sayings on a par with his father's wisdom, or to find Reb Pinchos as true a guide as Lenin, though Bach may be more swift-footed than both. Consider this matter.

The wisdom of time not different from the wisdom a man's heart learns to carry through a single day. But dailiness remembered can be home movies. On rare occasions I've wanted to shout yes, yes, I've been there too, I too have kin of flesh and blood, turn the damned projector off. But Zukofsky forestalls me by the subtle and moving way in which remembrance suddenly *exists* as present reality. That process, which I have not yet deciphered, is like a momentary interval in the mind's eye, refocusing. It is, I think, the touchstone of the whole sincerity of his art,

> Like the sea fishing
> Constantly fishing
>   Its own waters.
>
> The continuity —
> Its pulse.   (XII, 215)[1]

---

[1] [Kelly's article has full quotes from the 1959 Origin Press Press edition of *"A"* *1–12*. Having had to resort to "fair use" here to be able to reproduce the article, quotes longer than five lines, as a rule of thumb, feature the first & last two lines of the quote only. As in Kelly's original, each excerpt from *"A"* is followed by numbers in parentheses. The Roman numeral indicates the section. The Arabic numeral indicates the page in the 2011 New Directions edition in which the excerpt may be found.]

The close-ups of kinfolk, under the pressure of the poem's music and logic, fulfill themselves as the correlates *(accidents)* of the historical process *A* is. Be mine to me, Zukofsky says turned inward. And there indulgence ends: the forms and faces touch (so palpably touch) Zukofsky's own, and drive into the poem with the weight of all real things.

Thus Zukofsky's Celia and Paul are not, for instance, in a different space of the poem from that zadik Lenin who "lights" the long and closely argued *A 8*.

We can move in more surely on the freedom and dignity of *A* in the light of Pound's liberation (a long poem involving history) of epic from obsessive preoccupation with Homeric and Virgilian gesture, gesture that in English seems almost universally to have throttled the lyric impulse behind all poetry. (Standing on *Maximus from Dogtown*, on a clear day you can see the *Battle of Maldon*. There, in either place, the song is urgent, thrusting the event straight into the mind. Zukofsky, similarly but in a very different manner, does not conceal the operation of the lyric source. He, like Olson, would inferentially remind the reader of what has been the strongest motive of English poetry for twelve hundred years, and mostly neglected by the critics.)

And when I came to the length of *A*, apprehensive of the effort, I found instead that I was taken up into the music of Zukofsky's concerns, a music sometimes hidden in the lines [the] eye sees, but singing clear as the tongue works loose.

In so long a poem, no clutter, no sprawl. We are introduced not to erudition but to a lifetime, the perhaps fragile nature of man spending its powers wisely, to comprehend & to instruct, the mode being song.

> A
> Round of fiddles playing Bach (1, 1)

The opening improbable, arresting; there is music, Thursday the 5th of April, 1928, Carnegie Hall, the Matthew Passion: "The lights dim, and the brain when the flesh dims."

It is America in the '20s, the beginning, implicit or otherwise, of so much that still compels us. It is Henry Miller's America, too, "Remembering love in a taxi," but what we get here is the outside, the necessary lineaments of the world one glance at which sets the work off:

> And as one who under stars
> Spits across the sand dunes, and the winds
> [...]
> Hips looking out of ripped trousers
>   and suddenly
> Nothing   (1, 2)

It is Passover, and the Pennsylvania miners are on the lockout. Quickly Zukofsky begins to set in order, the themes that here begin are constant in all the thirty years of the poem. The young man plots the lineaments of perfection. Later as he matures in and through the poem, he lives up to that early graph, making real in words and form the task he sets himself as early as:

> The blood's tide like the music,
> A round of fiddles playing
> [...]
> Music leaving no traces,
> Not dying, and leaving no traces.   (1, 4)

It is the beginning of a formal definition of his intent:

> Not boiling to put pen to paper
> Perhaps a few things to remember —   (1, 4)

& more will follow, through the sections. The *objectives* begin:

> "There are different techniques,
> Men write to be read, or spoken,
> [...]
> "Everything which
> We really are and never quite live."   (1, 4)

In *A* 2 the horses and the sea appear, and the pattern of the lines grows more complex, the realities interweaving in the lines in a way we might have called abstract:

> The sea grinds the half-hours,
> Each half-hour the bells are heard,
> [...]
> Hyaline cushions it, sun,
> In one's own head.   (II, 6–7)

It seems to me that this is the sea and sea-horse journey to which the landlocked explorations of *A 6* bears some correspondence; my attention is drawn to the mythologems Zukofsky seems to be laying down, "In one's own head," against the clutter a way of bowing. Much of the clarity of the poem arises from the simplicity with which the myths are first brought before the eye. And that too is part of the intent:

> I walked on Easter Sunday,
>   This is my face
> [...]
>   In a style of leaves growing.   (II, 8)

The ending of *A 2* demonstrates the richness of Zukofsky's poetic so early on, and serves (loving the dailiness of the poem) to urge again the complex of themes arrived at:

> A train crossed the country: (cantata).
> A sign behind trees read (blood red as intertwined
> [...]
>   *O Savior blest*
> The song out of the voices.   (II, 8)

It always comes back to song. Weeping at the tomb brings on the elegy, *A 3*, the lament for Ricky. Ricky is no one we know already, and we are not told who he is. Zukofsky is careful to exclude that which would falsely limit the meaning of the death, and more, the mourning.

The poet's relationship is made clear, not to the stasis of personality, but to the function, as he *does*. Verbally, it links up with the Passion gospel that seems always to occupy the inner ear of the poem:

> I, Arimathea,
> His mirror,
> Lights either side —   (III, 10)

The immediacy grows from relevance, and in the things and persons Zukofsky touches, the poem moves towards its own shape:

> The song reaches home
> 'Here are your dead,   (III, 17)

Into *A 4*, the void of *A 3* stretches as lyric:

> Giant sparkler,
> Lights of the river,
> [...]
> Their sides gleam
> From levels of water — (IV, 18)

From the void a prayer to God, in the mouths of the old, of the Jewish tradition. To ancient psalmody, the chanting of the speech, the young oppose lyricism, song, it may be, for song's sake. *A 4* an invocation of the ancestors, the unsatisfactory prayers the old make: "deafen us to their music." *A 12* is here in foretaste, but here in anger & turbulence, no measure yet found among the phenomenal. Ironically, it is "how / music first came into our family."

Words and economics, the time of the poem upon it, still with the lamentation of the passion, "Speech bewailing a Wall." Eros stirs strangely, out of doors:

> That day,
> And the Jews eating unleavened bread;
>
> Ramshackle field-weed; —
>
> "— Lie down
> I'll marry you!" (V, 19)

Money for Zukofsky (and something of that original "song" I talked about) is not exchange but means, or so I'd gather from his preceptors. That stress on means is one vividly American impulse in the poem. It would be easy to make large statements about Pound's *Cantos* and their influence on *A*, though the chronology is not encouraging; something in the air, a possibility? But *A* is steadily and unconcernedly American (in ear *and* concern) in a way the *Cantos* never are, or should be.

To waylay *A*'s structure formally would be an essential preliminary to any sketch of source or (needlessly, in so transparent a poem) influence. Fundamental to the form of my notes on *A* is the realization that only five hundred copies of *A 1–12* were printed, and those long ago sold out. I can hope to talk lightly about the things that arrested me on my several trips through *A*, and what (implicitly) I have learned from.

What I have said and will yet say should be taken then as illustrative, not analytic. One proximate purpose of saying anything at all is to get the book back, somehow, into print, available.

A 5 concludes with an inkling of the result, the realization that the final plexus of forces and movements, what an earlier age would have called the resolution, proceeds from form:

> Under sky
> The winds breathe in the fields.
> [...]
> Sunlight trees,
> Words ranging forms. (V, 19–20)

Grace notes in the score, and *A 6* complies, the lyric equivalent, two musical quatrains across the field, Mrs. Green and her daughter. And then:

> And those loved seeking their own completion in a
>   voice, their own voice
> [...]
> Everything lowered to a mutual, common level,
> Everyone the same, (VI, 21)

"Tradition's pebbles" fill the mouth: "Words rangeless, melody forced by writing." The dialectic moves now to examine creation, *Natura naturans, Natura naturata*, opposites or complementaries? But Zukofsky will not be bogged down, a clearness comes; there is never according to my sense of things an actual breakdown to the abstract in the poem. With rhythm or word play, the concern leaps back to the immediate:

> He who creates
> Is a mode of these inertial systems —
> [...]
> "What about Johann Sebastian? The same formula." (VI, 23)

At times there is a fescennine lewdness that plays behind his lines, as in the bedding-down lyric

> "I beg your pardon
> I've a — "h" begins the rhyme here,
> Shall we now?" (VI, 23)

Such peripheral sexual gestures (they never move to center) act as gentle celebrations of that function that blossoms in the noble conjunction of love and honor to which I understand much of the poem to be moving, most forthrightly in *A* 11. (The absence of the explicitly sexual is startling, and needs a less biased mind than mine to ponder, I recall that Zukofsky normally elides the specifically coarse in his translations of Catullus. Those translations do not lose thereby, and that fact suggests in turn the possibility that modern criticism overvalues Catullus for a bluntness that's no real part of his method or accomplishment. By inference, Zukofsky may be reminding us in *A* that the more private functions do not have to be shouted to be real. But I sense at times a more general reticence, that goes along perhaps with the reasonableness I spoke of earlier. Such reticence would remind me of the *Cantos* once again, as parallel, the importance of the *cultural* concerns.)

Zukofsky as Objectivist, as a generation knew him, who proposed sincerity as value (in those essays KULCHUR has brought to print again, after thirty years), defines clearly now, as ever, the intent. The poem reminds us it's not the intent that matters but the intent realized. Towards the goal:

> My one voice. My other: is
> An objective — rays of the object brought to a focus,
> [...]
> Inextricably the direction of historic and
>   contemporary particulars.   (VI, 24)

True to his word, and with the swiftness of a man with something on his mind, the "particulars" come: Bach, the Matthew Passion, the parts of men: "We are after all realists capable of distinctions." Henry Ford, impresario of morality, holds forth, and against him Zukofsky poises:

>   civilization.
> Particular: Every fall season, every spring, he needs
> [...]
> Poetry? it has something to do with his writing of
>   poetry.   (VI, 26)

The poem considers the old and the doddering, the rich "fooling themselves" with toy trains, the idle stutterers playing mumbletypeg on Park Avenue, the vapid rich, and then, like lightning, a clarity from Lenin:

> "It is more pleasant and more useful,"
> Said Vladimir Ilytch,
> "To live thru the experience
> Of a revolution
> Than to write about it." (VI, 30)

Inevitably, as the measures "travel outward," the focus is on the country itself that grows those bumbling evils the writer cannot in conscience dwell on. For four pages we travel across the U.S.A. and back, picking up the apparent sillinesses that really betoken the durability of the human, the lastingness of the flesh. And when we come back, we find Bach, and spring making "new green," and the daily relationships (the Kaffee Kantata too by Bach, 'A kind of 'Hot Chocolates' five years after the Passion." Perhaps, anticipating, that steady movement of the poem, or really the movement it goes with, of history into the momentary, the national into the familial, the smaller circle, is the hardest accommodation the reader has to make, used as he is to the small used only as type of the large. But here the movement towards hiddenness is real).

The end of the section again draws music and grief together. The next section will violently change the rhythm and measure of the poem. Now, at the conclusion of this, taking leave of that land of music, the coda (halfway in the numerical scheme of the poem) begins with the formal problems:

> Forgetting
>   I said:
> [...]
> With all this material
>   To what distinction — (VI, 38)

What is *A 7*? Sonnets. Amazingly, seven sonnets, in a rare form (Donne used it), a *crown* of sonnets. The rime scheme is Zukofsky's, and some of the rime words are bodily repeated through all seven: *words, birds, sun*.

By the seventh sonnet, the lines are no longer integral, but broken, spread on the page, the music halting to consider itself. "Open, O fierce flaming pit!" is repeated from the first section; it is one of many ligatures.

The separation of octet and sestet is preserved, classically, but the sonnets themselves flow into one another; sonnet 6 enjambs with the first line of sonnet 7. In general, a word or phrase in the last line of one sonnet will be nuclear in the first line of the next.

But the language! An intricacy (matching the form) familiar to the reader of Zukofsky's lyrics makes its appearance in *A*. In the pattern are saw-horses and horses, the wind and light of the sections that will follow. Here is the sestet of the fifth sonnet:

> But they had no eyes, and their legs were wood!
> But their stomachs were logs with print on them!
> [...]
>   They had no manes so there were no airs, but —
>   Butt... butt... from me to pit no singing gut!   (VII, 41)

Sonnets. The conquest of the traditional forms is so total that the reader can pass by, seduced by the language and the iterated images into ignoring the formal. But the images, perhaps, seemingly of nightmare, or a children's story that will not end, make the mind hungry for form, and, Lo! with gentle cruelty he chastens us with sonnets.

The hard and alien measures of *A* 7 marked the break between the earlier sections, in which the immediate impulse is stronger than the historical, and the middle sections, Eight and Nine & Ten, where the historical particulars are gathered, dialectically, moving forward in time and inward in space towards the *nostoi*, the homecomings in *A* 11 and *A* 12.

A 8 will bridge the gap in the reader's mind between the Matthew Passion and Lenin, music and economics; the means of time and measure. To set it down that way suggests the disparity; the actual text is adequative. The verbal abstracts, to be handled throughout the section, appear at the beginning, as statement:

1 · A BOOK OF IMAGES: DEEP & OTHER

> And of labor:
> Light lights in air,
> [...]
> To right praise.   Labor as creature,
>   (VIII, 43)

Two choruses needed for the Matthew Passion: important that the reader dwell on two choruses, the interchange of voices and times in the section. As a start, Zukofsky sketches the pragmatic difficulties attendant on the first performance, quoting Bach: "To perform concerted music as it should be rendered, / both singers and instrumentalists are required. /... no one cares to work for nothing." For musicians to "perfect their technique," they must have leisure, but: "... observe how the royal musicians... are paid." Whereas the chorus of the Thomaskirche, in our terms, sings for a song. Marx:

> "*Equal* right... presupposes inequality,
> Different people are *not* equal one to another."
> But to make the exploitation by one man of many
>   impossible!   (VIII, 43)

To speak of labor is to speak of the poor. There are two mediæval lyrics in *A* 8, each connected with May, the earth, the peasant labor from which the historical process comes; the first lyric is broken before the end, the anguish of the story that would sing a song:

> Who by construction have
> A bird settling like a leaf
> [...]
> The poor
>   *Betrayed and sold*   (VIII, 46–47)

Zukofsky's marriages are always formal, made in the syntax of words and the syntax of music. I sense the passage above as the first place where the themes of Bach and [the] proletariat are drawn explicitly and exactly together. Marx's poor and the Bach-Henrici Jesu are congruent in Zukofsky's time.

> The facts are not strange to each other.
> When they drive, your choice
> [...]
> The mirrors of the facts must not be dis-
> simulated   (VIII, 47–48)

  After that, the May Day song begins: May Day the feast of Labor, May Day the great mediaeval feast of love. Zukofsky's *Maya* catches both traditions: the old earth feast of spring love, not remote from magic, the mediaeval flowering of the lyric (who is it who believes the *maya* to be the oldest genre of the vernacular lyric?), and the new tradition, not remote from techne, the song that turns bitter in the mouth of the worker celebrating that very labor by which he is enslaved, seeing darkly that hope of freedom is possible only from his labor. Zukofsky keeps the double sense:

> Light lights in air blossoms red
> Like nothing on earth
> [...]
> This is May
> The poor's armies veining the earth!   (VIII, 48)

  The lines are long, tight, in the historical passage that follows. The Manifesto, its terms and concerns, are interwoven with early lyrics, Catullus, mediaeval song, Negro work chants, Bach's double chorus still unpaid. The lines are preparing for the opening, the turning of the poem onto the American story, but starting from the song, in this case that of Dowland's, the implicit irony of any given event:

> I saw my lady weep, the glass harmonica
> Stilled — society splitting into two camps, two
> [...]
> Phase, the pit, Marx waiting, time to go, said Adams.
>   (VIII, 50–51)

  After the lines loosen into history, a space is made (the ear prepared for something that subtle, that exact) for the dialectic struggle in its own terms, still engrafted with music and art, the exempla; we're back to the particulars, in a score of the richest pages in the poem, towards the end of which that minimal stanza comes like a thunderclap, like Pound's rockdrill (beating it into their minds) thrusting the meaning as clearly as words can:

> Song?
> After bread. (VIII, 69)

We have been exposed to those who contributed "the greatest practical example." The poem is practical, and handles now America again, general and local history, the economic patterns that stand behind Whitman or Zukofsky (printed after *A 1–12* is Zukofsky's essay on Poetry, that concludes by quoting Whitman's "greatest poem," *Respondez!*, which "could … easily have served the definition of poetry we anticipate"). And from America, via Brooks Adams, to Europe feeding us, the sources of our story.

At length we come to present, presumably where the history for the time being (of *A 8*, late '30s) ends. And when the bread of history is distributed, the section as promised moves to:

> What is music which does not
> In any sense progress?
> [...]
> In the shell of beauty, and with beams like Venus
> To the sun. (VIII, 103)

Labor is everywhere. And where the war is now in Madrid. At the full of the section, May and labor rehearsed, the functional images of the whole section recapitulated in song, condensed to the ballade, and its envoi:

> Coda, see to it the burden renew,
> Sound out thick gardens dug up in purlieu
> [...]
> Luteclavicembalo — bullets pursue:
> Labor light lights in earth, in air, on earth. (VIII, 105)

It would seem that the clarifications have been made. But in the movement forward, Zukofsky would in all honesty tie it all down: so I read *A 9*, a closely-reasoned section, the most abstract (in avoidance of immediate physical referents) in the poem. It is alive as *jeu,* however solemn the occasion: two sequences of five sonnets and one coda each.

The form feels heavy and Tudor, the sonnets tending towards the clarity reached (to my ear) in the two codas, which I here set down, broken out of their rightful places:

> We are things, say, like a quantum of action
> Defined product of energy and time, now
> In these words which rhyme now how song's exaction
> Forces abstraction to turn from equated
> Values to labor we have approximated.   (IX, 108)

Thus the first coda. The second sequence and its coda uses throughout the same words at the ends of each line as did the first sequence. Within that limitation, because of it (the playfulness of it), the greatly different second coda:

> Love speaks: "in wracked cities there is less action,
> Sweet alyssum sometimes is not of time; now
> Weep, love's heir, rhyme now how song's exaction
> Is your distraction — related is equated,
> How else is love's distance approximated."
>   (IX, 110–111)

The elaborate complexity of rime and repetition, the internal cross-riming, for all of that the language so plainly is Zukofsky's. Through all, my pleasure is not that someone can write a sonnet sequence or fill out an exuberantly difficult rime scheme, but that Zukofsky can do it in his own speech, so that his one voice, whatever the tone or complexity of idea or mood, perdures through the poem. I am convinced from time to time that we finally read for Voice, to hear somebody authoritatively talking and singing, somebody who is himself. But that's beside the point; Zukofsky's voice and precise sense of word and sound conquers the form: to *use* it, plant his own crop there.

That is watered by what comes:

> Paris
> Paris
> [...]
> Cannot hear Paris
> Come over the air   (X, 112)

which carefully sets us in place and time. *A 10* is a Mass, a vulgate Mass. It is a noble pun, the Christian Mass in point the variance from *christian* to the behavior of Christians (we always hear Bach when Zukofsky introduces *christian*), as over against those masses the people are, terms in an endless argument:

> *Kyrie eleison*
> They sang
> [...]
> A mess sucked out
> No substance   (X, 113)

The war is in France. The Mass goes on. *(redo:* Shame. The "One substance visible and / invisible" becomes

> Incarnate
> Carcass smiles
> Corpses block the bridges
> Machine gun outposts smell of
> Dead gunners piled sandbags now   (X, 117)

The Mass is mass death, & France is fallen. But the vividness of the poem is not that of the immediately experienced war, but the vividness of history compulsively moving in its channels. Against the texture of that apparently ineluctable passage, the poet "Who could not take life" can kill, can hunt the insane animal history has grown naturally into. The Sumatran boar goes and perishes from the perfectly natural growth of his tusks that curve and reenter his jaw, closing his mouth. Against beast or silence:

> All resemblance to what lives or is dead
>   coincident with thoughts not waiting for tears
> Let a better time say
> The poet stopped singing to talk   (X, 120)

It is "Song? / After bread" again, the hardest moral of the poem for me to contend with. I must believe that song is bread. I must believe that to stop singing is to stop altogether. Here, as before, I intrude upon the poem, not to argue explicitly with Zukofsky's judgment, but to try to come to terms with it, make some sense of it for myself, simply by setting it down. Over and over again. *A* 12 will tell much of this, where, as I understand it, "at stroke of midnight" song will win.

The Mass of *A* 10 cannot end with the kiss of peace, the only Communion the clinking of glasses in the mess, but does with expectation:

> Till the sailors who mistook their planet
> > for a light
> […]
> And the people
> Grant us the people's peace. (X, 123)

Presumably each path of history the mind becomes aware of leads surely to what is present. The patterns of reverberation of *A*, the historical *einlaut* of the poem through the first ten sections, shudder, and suddenly the ear can hear the body of the sound. Here is *a*, here is the *coincident situation* that letter denotes and precipitates in our normal speech, a man, a woman, a child.

In the little *A* 11 (shortest of all the sections) and the vast *A* 12 (as long as all the rest together), Zukofsky seems to be writing out of the immediate source. It is not that the family is more real than history (they are names for different parts of the same spectrum), but that man's sense of what is right around him is, to begin with, almost non-verbal: as source, it begets a greater task. History is as much as anything else a congeries of words; we learn history in words. Our story proper, our *histoire* (Mallarmé) in which the poet seeks ceaselessly to implicate us, is immediate phenomenality, the verbal content of which is evanescent.

That work of *histoire*, the results of which are clear but more mysterious, begins for Zukofsky in *A* 11, with all the stateliness of direct intent:

> A 11
> > *for Celia & Paul*
> River that must turn full after I stop dying
> Song, my song, raise grief to music
> […]
> Things, her love our own showing
> Her love in all her honor.' (XI, 124–125)

When I first read *A*, it was *A 11* that came to me quickest. It was a music I had not heard written in my time, like Pound's *envoi* to "Mauberly" in the dignity of its vulgaris eloquentia, but resourceful of rime & recurrence in a way I thought no contemporary had a right to. The poem went into my mind and stays there ("singing itself" there, as Cid Corman would say, to whom I owe the debt of his specific insistence on Zukofsky, & to whom we all owe the actual physical existence of *A 1–12*, the book), and I do not really, I suppose, want to turn & examine it, preferring its fruitful presence inside. That's one reason I set it down whole.

Back to Bach, *"Out of deep need."* As I understand it, *A 12* moves fully into the open. I find myself more at home there, the richness of Zukofsky's formal impulse working itself out in many different patterns, aware of the intricacy of his dance.

> So goes: first, *shape*
> The creation —
> [...]
> Voice. First, body — to be seen and to pulse
> Happening together.   (XII, 126)

The section reminds us early that we are still in the presence of a lasting intention: the fugue. Bach's fugue on the letters of his own name becomes Zukofsky's fugue on the same notes:

> Blest
> Ardent   good
> [...]
>   things that bear harmony
>   certain in concord with reason.   (XII, 127)

That fugue, once introduced, is present lightly through the whole section. It will come back.

The concerns are different now, floppy is admitted as a term relevant to the condition, relevant to the poem. Frobenius senses the *paideuma* which disposes to maturity (as distinct from youth and adolescence) as the quest for order. That may say very little, since every making is an ordering. It may say much, & seems to here, the reader in his turn sensing Zukofsky ordering in more stable form the necessities that imposed themselves on him in the earlier sections.

> From the spring of *Art of Fugue*:
> [...]
> Most heavenly music
> For the universe is true enough. (XII, 127–128)

And those horses, for instance, who have been with us since *A 1*, are now four, and they are "like four notes," B-A-C-H in which the section finds its resolution.

The letters to Celia, the wife and child, the valentine *to Celia*. And from them to clarity:

> Measure, tacit is.
> The dead hand shapes
> An idea — seeming tiny potential
> Musk — a bee robs and fertilizes. (XII, 131)

And into *A 12* is wounded now Zukofsky's charismatic figure of Bottom, the loose-hinged realist, free among the things of this world.

Figures of lightness move in the poem. No longer is there any separation of song from bread. The song and the need are one, the lyric, grown imperative, is salvific.

> He has perched over — why — valley,
> In the pines
> [...]
> This is all-around
> Intellect, (XII, 135–136)

After the terrors and debasements of war, the rejections of intellect and responsibility that *A 8* laments, Zukofsky's lyric represents the world giving us another chance to "Light lights / Unknown to you."

He begins again for us. There is a gentleness of instruction in him, a gentleness that can cut and probe more fruitfully & painfully than many another man's hatchet (as anybody knows who's had a letter from him). Begins at the beginning:

> I'll tell you.
> About my *poetics* —
> [...]
> My father died in the spring. (XII, 138)

This extraordinary lyric, offered modestly as *Tafelmusik*, represents as clearly as any excerpt can Zukofsky's genius for *movement by condensation*. Condensation, then, not simply an absolute value, but a material and functioning principle of structure.

Zukofsky tells the story all over again by telling *a* story; he, the concerned narrator, between Pinchos and Paul, the one story. This passage, about Zukofsky's father, Reb Pinchos, is the longest single stretch in the poem; its clean narration and spare verse mark the voice in command. Denise Levertov wrote at length in *Poetry* about the passage, when *A 1–12* became available several years ago. I will not go over the ground, though there is much she (because of the richness of the poem itself) had no space to relate, the fascinating manner in which the several segments of the story are wound together around the implicit character of the Aristotelian narrator. To the Levertov review, too, I will refer the reader for the "Tale of the Dog," and its dark purport.

These pages of *A 12* are probably the "simplest" in the poem; the simplicity is not cunning, but exact registration. Along the way I notice:

> And the end is the same:
> Bach remembers his own name.
> [...]
> Says Einstein,
> But not simpler.   (XII, 143)

For father's father the son is named, the first letter of his name, for Reb Pinchos, son Paul. In such a way (everything being as simple as it *can* be, no simpler) Zukofsky's father leads to his son, his own life touched. For himself he sings. Zukofsky, *qua* poet, is not the subject of his poem but the object, that same objective through which the rays come focused to a point, the poem.

> You must, myself,
> As father of Nicomachus
> Say very little
> Except: such were his actions.   (XII, 154)

Reb Pinchos chanted psalms and befriended the mice. His chant goes on (through the invisible poet) to Paul's music. A different integral this is, chant *&* music as limits, the song (so easily elided, but Zukofsky never lets it go) between. In the son, music and history blend, the occupation of the forces, the preoccupation of design. In his son, the name of the blending is Bach. Bach, music, are no longer part of the "subject" of the poem; they have become instrumentalities; we've heard some of it before.

>   Measure, tacit is.
>   Listen to the birds —
>   And what do the birds sing. (XII, 156)

The attention given to father runs over to son, a shift from record to precept. For young Nicomachus, Zukofsky must teach, i.e., make the meanings clear:

>   Shall I teach Paul,
>   In Shakespeare is *militarist* —
>   [...]
>   Follow divine nature
>   Being such. (XII, 168)

Zukofsky is Aristotle now, and reviews his works, the gathering of the preceptors make us pass from psalm to sapiential:

>   If love exists, why remember it? (XII, 170)

Or the gnomic passage:

>   It wouldn't do at any time
>   for some Northwest Coast Indian
>   [...]
>   No more than it would have done for an
>   ancient Hindu (XII, 170)

Or such a judgment as:

>   Man was not born of a nothing
>   But from a substance
>   [...]
>   Is closed
>   So nothing can leave it. (XII, 171)

Order proceeding from discrimination. Attendant upon wisdom, the names of the mentors appear, Aristotle, Spinoza, Shakespeare, Bach. On four legs the horse moves, and nothing stops him from his movement. Perhaps the horse was broken in by imperious Lenin, no trace now of his trainer, he's been grazing long enough: the poem rides.

>   1   sound
>   [...]
>   Where cycles started or ended,
>   Without stores to drag them —   (XII, 173)

And gallops through its field. The oscillation of the dialectic hums a ground note: son's simplicity and wisdom's complexity. *Pericles* a figure of it?

>   The song does not think
>   To say therefore I am,
>   [...]
>   By another
>   As actual   (XII, 199–200)

And what is wisdom in 1950? Zukofsky, in slender narrative, rehearses the war and what followed. As with Pound, any distinction between narrative & lyric verse is untenable, in the face of the lines themselves. The poem is ordered in music: and Zukofsky more than any contemporary makes us look up from the mildewed vegetables of æsthetic decorum, the godforsaken prejudices of what is and is not fit to be poetry.

>   Where the round of sky
>   Awakes the eyelid
>   [...]
>   There's a natural use
>   And a use that's unnatural.   (XII, 206–207)

The poem, following Paul as its thread, discovers those letters from Jackie the Poor Pay Pfc, and finds itself led back to dark Brooklyn and what is imminent. "— Look, Paul, where / The sawhorses of 'A'-7 / Have brought me." Here are the two recognition scenes, horses, Paul:

> *Red horses —*
> *The second,*
> [...]
> *Go on*
> *Thru the earth,* (XII, 230)

> — Look, Paul, the small arrowroot
> Has rabbit ears.
> [...]
> The fire roared, quieted to light. (XII, 231)

When that is, as it feels, settled, the poem turns to Celia, and the B-A-C-H fugue begins in earnest, becoming the substance of all that follows. There are three sections, B, A, C, and then the letter H, a line, the last line of the book:

> **Blest**
> [...]
> Modifications of
> Imagination: (XII, 231)

> **Ardent**
> [...]
> To a bad heart, from wish-bone to no sense —
> Lectured walking. Spoke for himself to his son? (XII, 236)

> **Celia,**
> [...]
> Weaving,
> A fiddle. (XII, 237–238)

The stated themes involve us increasingly in the complex of daytime, the dailiness of life and things, musics, the personal relations that have grown from, and stand for, the historical relations the earlier sections of *A* tested and found no city in. The *things* surrounding, central, are Zukofsky's immediacies, what he has written and thus used, what he has not yet found use for.

The first twelve sections of *A* represent the first half of the whole poem still in progress. Zukofsky's line in *A 12* (especially in the A theme of the fugue) anticipates the complexity of *A 13*, five parts of which have appeared now in *Origin*.

Along those lines, it is not an inventory that ends *A 12*, but a sudden customs declaration of who and what he is, what he is bringing into the poem at the barrier of the unwritten work, what he has discarded along his way to the exactness of the end:

> Living, you love
> So I love
> [...]
>   unhurt and
> Happy.   (XII, 261)

This poet, coming up with the mask of Odysseus at the very end, does not wrestle loudly with fate but quietly arranges song among necessities. Song as arrangement, *rangé* as the Haitians say, with a spell on it.

So *A* is the most intimate of poems, a sustained and lucidly objective conversation with the sweet chaos that is a man's life. Zukofsky, in the act of his poem, is concerned to speak to the reader in the presence of music, a presence that sometimes (in the later sections) comes louder & louder until it masks the words he says and leaves us with the figure of his saying. Sometimes the words themselves are lost, or for a moment lost, but never the thread of his speech with us.

In our time we have been so afflicted with guns and gospels that those who read poems have grown to prefer poets awesome and urgent, raping intellect or sensibility to penetrate the walls we make to keep the clutter of drivel out, the cries of help we can do nothing about. Those who prefer poets at their most imperative (and I have more than a touch of that preference) may find Zukofsky not hard to read, but hard to hear. He will consistently refuse to bear us down with declamation. He is reasonable: it is his great strength and his great weakness; of that arcanum from which I feel from time to time a poem's power to proceed I find no trace in *A*. His insistences (for he will not give an inch) are different; repetition of word and music, words to many melodies, some frequent images, repeated, but always tightly wrapped round in words, to control the resonances of the thing itself, deflect its sound to the end Zukofsky has always in mind.

His mode sometimes is recitativo, sometimes speech, sometimes song. He has planned as carefully as Blake the levels of his "numbers," but to a different purpose: to close down always to the center, to control, delimit, enclose.

The mood is mostly personal, a man speaking to us of the things that have concerned him most, the order he finds in the world (the four legs of his horse), the order he makes there. In the later sections he seems to address his wife and child (rightly, since they are there, he can dispense with the poet's often gratuitous assumption of another audience) in such a way that we can overhear, not as eavesdroppers, but as guests in another room of his house.

Coming out from a second or third reading of *A 1–12*, I was struck strongly by the poem as life work. Not simply as the sum of striving along one line, the building of success and failure any artist projects, but rather *one* poem that has engaged Zukofsky's works and days, all through which he has grown.

I'm not here concerned with the poem as a record of process (the reader has no right to ask, Who cares about the process?) but with it as a destination of life and times made into an articulate structure of memory and melody where fathers and lovers and wife and son can turn outward and, each remaining each, sing or talk securely fixed in a world controlled:

> — Still awake, still pothering?
> — What, goddess?
> [...]
> We talk so late
> Let us go to sleep.   (XII, 260)

Thinking of *A*, thinking of Zukofsky proposing the form & task, I was startled to remember all his lyrics, that, I gather, many of us had taken for the real work. Now those wry and passionate and cool inimitable gifts seemed (offhand as I was) sparks from the anvil where the weapon itself is being hammered. I leave it at that. Weapon it is, a knife at any rate, whose edge is discernment, discrimination, the razor of exact perception.

(*Kulchur* #12, 1963)

THE IMAGE OF THE BODY

All along the film has made little of the body. Perplexed by images of light and dark, obsessed by the personal dilemmas of his workings, the filmmaker has succumbed to the easiest Manichaeism. Possessed of an instrument that plainly registers and re-presents bodies in motion, the filmmaker has, in his ambition to make high art, scorned the materials his tools afford him, has preferred instead to go awhoring after a soul that, by his hazy hypothesis, must set such bodies in motion. Trapped by the images from which he mentally flees, needing at length something to stick up there on the pearly screen, he resorts to one single iconic gesture, *Ecce Homo*, and from the facility of close-up the anguished pseudomythology of the *face* is born.

Lascaux, Altamira, Gandhara, Heliopolis, Athens, Ravenna, Byzantium, Florence, Rome: a visual genetics that has formed our way of seeing. The film from time to time seeks to imitate the compositional sense of painting or of sculpture, but misses the essential *ground* of such meaningful organization, the body standing fully weighted in the world of the eye. Only via the close-up fragmentations of a Malraux ("detail") is the classic reduced visually to the face-mask-soul progression. Nineteenth-century devotional art (Bavarian or Saint-Sulpice or Pre-Raphælite) provides the cheap, personalistic pleasure of the obsessive face, the face, closer to home, on the barroom floor. The great originals of film, men of technical virtuosity and defective sensibility, took the easiest way. The golden-ringleted, *putto*-lipped darling, & her sad-eyed lover, appear early enough in film, and stay there, *mutatis mutandis*, as apparently the cinema's only interpretive mode of coping with identity.

Bergman (who battens on cliché and sometimes makes a virtue of shimmering mediocrity) shows us recently in *Winter Light* the face of one of his beloved heroines, scarcely moving, for what seems hours on the screen, speaking her thrilling masochistic letter to her rabbit-faced lover, who, at the end of the grisly *perpetuum stabile* of close-up, quivers his upper lip meaningfully in turn. As flabby as the whole is, the attempt was a daring one, and rather instructive: the film returns to lantern slides accompanied by pretentious patter we're presumably too listless to read for ourselves. I write with some anger; the opening moments of Bergman's *The Naked Night* constituted one of the richest & most complex triumphs I've ever seen on the screen. But visual literature is hard, and magic lantern bromides easy; I lament his fall from vision.

The tragedy of the contemporary film is the utter & frightened distrust filmmakers have for the *visual means*, the *prima materia* of their own art. In this context, I am speaking about only one aspect of this distrust, rather than the phenomenon itself. But let me note in passing how close *Last Year at Marienbad* came to magnificence, how it failed in its own terms by lack of confidence in those visual terms themselves. That film, by all rights the opening of a new age in the commercial film, closed an old one, hanging on to the naiveté of plot, close-up, and spectral narration.

My concern here is not, however, with the abuse or unimaginative use of a device (close-up) presumably as interesting as any other device, but with the film's almost total inability to present the form and movement and weight of the human body. I rail at the close-up only because it has been one of the principal means of evasion.

The film has feared the body, avoided it, built all hopes on voice and facial *gestik*. I am not limiting my meaning to camera work itself, nor calling for a moral revolution among cameramen. Even when the camera adequately handles the body, editing perverts, distorts, or simply hides.[2] I demand re-Vision, a new clarity and purpose in dealing with the body.

In my intense belief in the unity of every man, the unison of forces each man is. I find the film's insistence on the soul-body dichotomy, with synecdoche as its formal expression, an oppressive affliction of the human spirit. And of spirit's flesh.

Man had no Body distinct from his Soul; for that call'd Body is a portion of Soul discern'd by the five Senses, the chief inlets of Soul in this age. Energy is the only life, and is from the Body.

I rejoice in the existence of soul, ruah, kha, spirit; I will praise accordingly, but will likewise insist that Shechinah walks only in the house of flesh, and that spiritual entities shall be predicated of visible phenomenal bodies.

---

2. Maddow's foolish *The Savage Eye* (The Peevish Tongue?) exemplifies; a good stripper well photographed, a visually exciting sequence, blasphemed against by capricious cutting and poetasting twaddle on the sound.

The film has consistently avoided dealing, then, with the human body, with the wholeness that man is, in the only dimension in which the screen can make that wholeness apparent?

The bodies of actors and actresses are derricks to move the speaking head from part of the world to another. Except when the woman's body is used as a specific sexual object, the body is seldom even seen, allowed to hold the *center* of the visual presence man is. (Valentino tango'd with his eyes.) The film is occasionally willing to deal with the body in explicit sexual terms, but only as fillip to the plot, and then in a deceitful sleight-of-hand way. Physical sex, the supreme bodily act, is hidden under verbal suggestion, evasively projected in negative, encouraged to escape from focus. (Resnais' timid handling of flesh in *Hiroshima* reaps it bland fruit in *Marienbad*, where the utter lack of physical presence of the characters in the intensely *seen* environment marks the major visual failure of the film.)

It was not always so. Earliest film was alive with bodies in motion. Chaplin (through *Modern Times*) disdaining all but the rarest & hence all the [most] poignant of close-ups, allows the humble and arrogant & beautiful and grotesque bodies of his people to speak for themselves to the eye. The body is a subtler instrument than the face, and the great film-makers knew it. The body, as such, constitutes the most potent *vision* of identity, and is accordingly the proper and natural centrum for the film.

I would suspect, and hereby submit, that one most plausible explanation of the powerful and apparently perennial draw of the Western lies in the fact that, of all our cinema — studio, experimental, academic — the Western alone makes slim use of face-soul, but abundant and necessary use of the body as center of the visual experience and sole conveyor of meaning. The body, clothed in the sacred uniform of cowboy and cowgirl that fits its contours and hides no limb, stands clear against the rock or against the sky. The magnificent & incredible spectacle of a man against the sky, a woman standing in the water, is robbed from us by all but the "lowest" cinematic forms

I see the Western as a wiser guide to film sense than any other category of American film. The fact that, by and large, Westerns are cliché-ridden and repetitious and ill acted is æsthetically trivial; the fact demonstrates *a fortiori* the visual sanity of the form's principal formal and functional means: the body in motion. Given the power of the body's image, the audience can survive all other weaknesses. I am speaking of the true audience that goes to movies for the eye's delight.

I am suggesting that the film, especially the film that takes itself "seriously," has not yet learned to deal with, much less how to deal with, what I contend is the most necessary visual means in any context involving humans, with certain exceptions less random than they look at first.

Brakhage's beautiful *Dog Star Man* centers, in *Part One*, on a body moving uphill. The tension, the surmise, a sight of the body again! generates a complex richness of imagery and meanings incredible after the slack ennui of most current films. I can see why Brakhage is so concerned with home-movies — the body (untrained, awkward, palpably *present*) engages Mr. Buggins as he runs that expensive film through his Kodak. I am fascinated by the legend that tells me of Chicago amateurs, the Pinkwater brothers, no fetishists, who shot thousands of feet of *feet* back in the 1930s. A corrective to Garbo?

(But that same Brakhage, in the earlier *Wedlock House*, almost broke my heart when, after intense and exciting preliminaries in black and white, the man and woman actually go to bed, and the film switches into vague negative, as if the need were: here comes the body, the body is *something else*, we've got to hide it. Thank God that Brakhage has come to full trust now in his visual means.)

The body is not "something else." It is man, it is woman, it is what we see when we see ourselves; we should see it in the darkness of art. The vitality of the film depends on its ability to break away from the psychological conventions of close-up and all that goes with it of evasion and reticence and vagueness. The film must rediscover the body, & the body's energy.

Dancing is body's vision. The body in motion is the body seeing and the body seen. The movement of human forms in space, in the camera's eye, should be the movement of energy rushing throughout all forms, impelled by matter and matter's laws, forming a world in any field in which it stirs.

The body is ever familiar. The body is ever new. Some filmmakers, perhaps unconsciously, have discovered and used the power of body's presence in an art that moves in light. The film's clarity is darkness and opacity, as the body is opaque. Buñuel comes to mind, and Eisenstein in *Strike* and *Mexico* and *Ivan*, Chaplin, Brakhage, Sennett, very different from one another, but each unforgettably committed, visually, to the suffering or triumphing enduring body.

(*Film Culture* #31, 1963–1964)

REVIEW OF STAN BRAKHAGE'S *METAPHORS ON VISION*

(for his home age at last)

──────────────────────── that everything enters the WORK

(those pages of Duncan's day book which speak (for the first time in our age of the world) of the Work, & of the worker, maker, that his blysse is, his Bonheur is, when the work is)
           (That writing of Brakhage makes to include all the circum-stances of the moment, music & the smell of bay leaves, pen in my hand — not as a function of myself but in response to that evocation whereby he induces phenomena into the dance signification.)
           & the Work sustains itself in.the.midst.of.it.all. Yes. & that he sustains the Work is of scant interest to you, bifocal gurus of the western hamerican Young?

  but what. you can. maybe. understand. is this.
           (since you need not *see*, look, here is a book, the same familiar oblong sarcophagus you long ago learned not to be scared of; Brakhage's book, of words, those instrumentalities you too have often blandly used so ill they wither on the boughs of your discourse & burst into ashes, Sodom apples you gather from the living tree of speech — words you fancy you understand, here is Brakhage's wordbook. Another Chance.
      — nor, despite the tone with which I am pleased to approach the issue, is the book Art History for the Blind; this book is marrow)
    Brakhage's films (e.g., *Prelude*) attack & agonize the lazy or untrained eye (not ready to run at its own true speed); in like manner, his book, the words flaming and flagrant in it, baffle & weary the ear for which words are dead or dying. A valuable instruction.)

Yes. Just this much. The "eye" is neuromuscular apparatus, & like all such needs to be trained, to "see" — just so, *that in us which perceives the full meanings & relationships of words*, written or spoken, must be trained, & kept in training.

The operative principle: "THE WORDS TELL" (Zukofsky); Brakhage reminds us, minds us, we must be ready for them.

(I myself, mildest of men, have received minatory epistles from those offended by my poem's assertion that the Sun is a Woman. What will happen when it becomes commonly known that Brakhage says the sky is not blue? Wow!)

Getting to it. Beyond the *metaphors* of vision (by that term Brakhage modestly conceals in Critical Language the nature of his achievements) lies a profound exploration of human vision. Man-sight. Words as metaphors of the act, no further than that. Man-sight. Too often the stress on *sight*, to the neglect of the former construct. I understand Brakhage to be concerned not with the 'automatic' reactions of the eye alone, but with what stands at the far end of the perceptual path. Man-sight, where *Man* (each word construct to the other, o blessed American) = that system terminating in eye.

What the butler saw — Why, peering thru that keyhole was it, did tumescence manifest itself in his member *at the sight of &c*. The Grammar of the sense, our confusions about who sees, what part sees. Does tumescence see. Does phallus see. Answer me.

Do you suppose Pavlov answered anything?

Art, western as sublimation of the psychological quest for wholeness, whereby wholeness of the work is allowed as the goal, and, in a mystery, possibly itself the means towards that prior goal it seems to substitute for. Physiological wholeness, of which sexual intercourse is itself a *metaphor*. See Blake's 'unreadable' theoretical reconstitution of Man in *Jerusalem* (about which Northrop Frye would know had he studied physiology as well as theology).

Thus, Brakhage draws on the Sources of his own movement to connect with the sources of each man's being. Not by writing about them, or turning back to regard them (SOURCE IS NOT SUBJECT), but by letting Source project itself into the substance of the Work: for the eyes.

"the formes from objects" source of what is seen "flow" thru the sources of what is seeing, i.e., a physiological unison,

& from that compound source, in motion, the work appears, in form.

That the cycle be continued.

Reading Brakhage, two areas of interest extend, both of which may be pitfalls for the eager-to-be-diverted reader: a) technical expertise
b) content, stories,
to call both by wrong names, as they might be so mis-taken.

It is wonderful that D.W. Griffith's thought to take the camera up in a balloon. It is wonderful that Brakhage has trained himself in the handheld camera so that a perfect fluid correspondence (or system of correspondences) exists between subject & object, one we can see. The first villanelle was a gimmick; the first canzone a major discovery of the whole craft. *Tekhne*, in full play & full meaning, furthers itself in the artist.

Brakhage is resolute in abhorring specious modes or instruments of power. That one, simply, already possesses the 'power' of blessing & cursing, and that one must forbear displaying these powers or wilfully grasping towards him. Otherwise, stricken in the work, or, as Lawrence has it, wounded in one's sex, by the diversion of source-energy from its proper goal, terminus, form in the Work.

("The shaman cannot help himself.") Poets, like bankers, can stand guilty of fraudulent conversion. Magic, and Brakhage. As the superior man, forewarned by soothsayers of the present omens, does not decline the ominous event, but walks out, himself, into Senate House or Theater or motorcade, because that is where his work leads him at that fated or fateless hour, likewise the artist is at the disposition of his signs.

Interruption the only tragedy, but to evade the signs is to evade the work.
 Ballistics.
  All for naught if the aim is bad. Tekhne go bragh. Remember Pound's the sun's lance striking the precise word — the romanticism of the Dynamic forgets: 'the precise.' Energy must land squarely in phonetic or associative or optic event.
   (Nor is Projective Verse playing paper-dolls with line endings, but has to do with: right aim of the energy discharge, i.e., seeing to the bore of the barrel.
 "Where will I end the line?" Where does your cock end.³
   =
As, via Brakhage, an opening of the words of power (i.e., clear & distinct words); cutting the words; sometimes the pun, as feedback. But: towards locating actually the 'roots and branches' of the neural physiological event. Task.
  But: reliance upon your *means*. In Brakhage's films, total reliance on the visual means, the film mediating the play of light upon a surface.⁴ The means incredibly limited, as light or no-light (with perceptible intermediate grades), as limited as stop & continuant.
  Now this book is a man discovering his sources & his means: these are essentials. Of the art.
   Without due consideration of them, æsthetics is shit.⁵
   So that this book, which does not presume to pass judgments or offer theories, is one of the most important works.of æsthetics.of literary criticism, if that term still delimits anything at all. Ever published. In America.

     (*Matter* #2, 1964)

---

3. Where does the power end? Where does the Hudson cease to be estuary & start to be river? Where the salt ends. In quo salietur?

4. In *Mothlight*, Brakhage's reliance upon the root means is total. The camera & its retinue dismissed, the film itself mediates light, having, in its own substance, previously mediated natural forms. The means are in our control.

5. Aristotle's *Poetics* is still intelligible after 2000 years. Can the same be said for most lit/crit after 20?

ON THE ART OF VISION

An *art of vision* possible in a medium that has dominated our century and that herewith frees itself from dependence on all other art forms. Film has tended, even in the most experimental contexts, to be a composite of literary and plastic arts, dance & music, the eye at the mercy of intention, culture, pretense, and imitations. Now Brakhage's *art of vision* exists utterly free of all that. It is a totality of making so intense it becomes a systematic exploration of the forms and terms of the medium itself. To explore the form without exhausting the form: A definitive making in any art is the health of the whole art, of the arts. Art in its oldest sense is skill, skill of making; *The Art of Vision* is the skill of making seeing. *The Art of Vision*, *The Art of The Fugue*, a presumptuous comparison only so long as we accord film only evidential value. This film makes immediate the integrity of the medium. Climax of the edited film, a new continent of the eye's sway, Mind at the mercy of the eye at last.

* * *

Is the word art lost to us? Skill in making is what it once meant, a way of making, so that art of vision = how to see.

* * *

What difference does it make what the film has been? Who am I to speak of this question? of it? What do I know? What is the film now? I speak of one film.

* * *

Brakhage's film is not free of story in the literary sense. Brakhage paraphrases his film too easily. If the film is not free of story, why do I say it is? *Dog Star Man* is deeply implicated with story — i.e., in this context, pre-existent temporal intent. But *The Art of Vision* is not *Dog Star Man*.

* * *

The word art has lost its balls. This title may grow them again.

* * *

Art is not the pomposity of Bayreuth, the bathos of Lincoln Center, the pack rat trove of The Louvre. Art is making.

* * *

The motto of the city of New York is *So What?* Be aware that it is *not* a rhetorical question.

* * *

It is time we understood *art* as a function, not an attitude.

* * *

Film, through its newness and availability, generates attitude more frequently than it does response. The attitude of an audience is not the filmmaker's problem.

* * *

It is important to call things by their right names.

(*Film Culture* #37, 1965)

LETTER ON "DEEP IMAGE"[6]

I must be clear with you that from my point of view there is no such thing as a Deep Image poet in the sense the bibliography on p. 19* suggests. Apart from the publisher-as-nexus, I am aware of few elements in common amongst the various authors you set down, and those elements have to do with shared personal past rather than identity, or even rough congruence of concern. For my part, the Deep Image was a fertility of critical examination, and in no sense a *way* of writing, poems or anything else. See, if you can, my notes in *Nomad* 11 in rejection of the possibility of method-as-gimmick. I am happy to see the fore-note on the first page of *11th Finger*, which strongly indicates the necessity of craft as the one possible instrument of a poet's becoming himself an instrument of vision, duende, allah, mousa. Duncan writes somewhere that despite the overlap of metaphysical concern, it is not to Blake that he returns over and over, but to Pound and Zukofsky. The resources of Vision are limitless, but they are in each case, and can be, communicated only by means of the intensest craft of the individual — they are not teachable, not propagandable; of craft we can speak, and humbly at least point to good work done. I mean a humility before our own work as well, whereby a man makes himself the instrumentality of Vision, but as perfect an instrumentality as he can, with all effort, make himself.

To group poets together as Deep Image poets is to suggest that there is a shared something, viewpoint, technique, quantum, intellect. That is simply not so, and no number of manifestos will make it so. So many confusions exist in the lit'ry world here, and our confusions are more readily exported than our clarities; now I fear that That Which Is Not is going to be offered as That Which Is. In the name of Vision will you (not that *you* have necessarily done so — it is to be wary of) offer us phony primitivism and the decades-old search for discordant images? Deep Image, at the level I devoted several of my years to its understanding, has nothing to do with imagism, amygism, neometaphysical or

*of *Eleventh Finger* magazine.

---

6. [Jerome Rothenberg's accompanying letter, also published in *Eleventh Finger* #2, can be found in *A City Full of Voices*, "A Book of Early Responses."]

anything of the sort. It is deeply painful for me to see its name applied to incompetent bourgeois romanticism. Years ago, Olson wrote me: "not imageS but Image." I cannot be clearer than by repeating that to you now, with all good wishes to you and admiration as ever, for that energy to articulate that the magazine does śpeak, and for the clear fore-note.

Let me urge you to read Stan Brakhage's *Metaphors on Vision*: never for a moment does he lose sight of the imperative nature of his craft and Duncan's pages from the Day Book in *Origin* 10: these have been the living and totally engaged proponents of total Vision in America.

God bless you,
Be well, and
Robert Kelly

don't import a dead horse
beśt wishes to your work

7 Auguśt 1965
(*Eleventh Finger* #2, 1965)

---

7. Even the British know about it: Housman's "razor ceases to act," Campbell's "Bloody horse." Which is what we are talking about here. And Lawrence *does* it.

8. The ancient Irish called some poets *bard* (the official, the court mnemotechnician, the academy in every age, the crossword puzzle word denoting everything in poetry inśtantly accessible to people who couldn't care less anyway); bard is the urban prophet, his knowledge the saying of a future he more dimly perceives; Virgilian prophecy: Excudebant alii, &c.) And other poets [are] *fáth* (cognate with *vates*,) or *fili* (=seer), and it is this poet that gives the modern Irish for poetry, *fileuchth* = vision, not into the political future but into the inśtantaneous real, the identity of each thing from which all process comes. (Blake's attacks on the Druids were the hośtility of the *fili* to the official Bard, propagandiśt of the eśtablished and measured order, the *idées acceptées* of the time: accusation and sacrifice.)

DUENDE, LORCA'S DARK SOUNDS

Duende, Lorca's dark sounds, the demon of earth rising in the blood or song.[7]

Mood, the tension of the poem, its material, stretched over the poet's mind.

Vision, into material into the layers of the world, awareness of things in their world, from which all the correspondences & emergent identities that make a poem proceed.[8]

Image, the unit of deepest awareness, the persistent and variable signal of the unconscious emitted into the field of the poem.

Four words: not to be equated. Each does refer us to an area of the poet's activity wherein periphrasis is inoperable, to a stage in the poem's process logically prior to craft and measure. They are the non-discrete happenings of a poem, available to the reader only in the discrete structure of formal elements. The poet's attention cannot fasten inside or outside: his workings must be non-dual. Nor is it so simple as inspired composition and craftsmanlike revision. The poet is defined as the structuring element itself fully vulnerable to all the world's happening.[9] To know what to master, when to exert mastery, is more important than how to do it, i.e., the last comes with practice directly. / Poem, as "natural structure," emerges from the process called poet. /

[RK archives, undated text from the 1960s]

---

9. The poet's conceptual thought, far from being irrelevant, is a major area of the happenings with which he must contend. It, the poet's conscious mind & intention, is not to be understood, however, as in any sense the meaning of the poem.

ENSTASY:
POEM FOR *EL CORNO EMPLUMADO* AT THE 10ᵀᴴ ISSUE

What is there is there in the teeth of
in the nose of in the hands of
that magnificent sunbaked woodsman
your reader is,
    in his mouth! in his mouth!
flat on the tongue road forcing its way down
where it used to be dark

    So there is
magnificence We are too shy to know it
unwilling to mix what we take to be
our essences You make us, & what is essence
turns out to be talk & you make it some
unfamiliar sort of music, song

The ideal reader Coming with prick in hand
to make out the lines Make the lines
The prick is soft free at ease ready to be ready
secretly armed: The ideal reader

or the ideal man. Encounter of poets
at the turning of the year Your year
The man The man

Open for you.

Homily:

  how, in the year unknown, the Spermatic Logos, which was not sperm or seed but was the Energy operative in all seed, the Spermatic Principle took up its dwelling in the body of Mary wife of Joseph, that she brought into the world, in eager compliance, the word flesh of God,
    who set up his presence as a radical presence in our brains, that is, in our physiology,
    in that, as my friend dwells in my body, lives in my mind & cells perceive him shaping what they perceive,

so the not-measurable Energy of the Divine Will/ing cast into the genetic material of all men, throughout the world, that flex of itself which is the Incarnation,

God entering man, becoming him, so that Jesus set up his tent inside us, invaded the seed & the seedflow, dwelled amongst us,

so that was the radical change in which the New Man is permitted (as seed permits flower) in his own garden by that Everter who remarked, Look, I will make all things new.   As serious assertion, then: that chromosomes of ancient men would be empirically discoverable to lack some matter or configuration present in our own.)

> but another matter
> is your music,
> time of the man
> entering, entering

To whom otherwise could I write this. Your magazine is breasts. Thighs, as on your own long legs walking, on fresh ground. Your magazine is stomach ass spine, a flash on the neural roads, broad hands, two feet & two eyes A mouth

(I have always been more excited by the aggregate of an issue than by the discrete works which compose it. A suspicious preference. It is likely you print many bad poems. It is beyond doubt your sense where North America lies is shaken in wind & sunlight. When. But we come to the issue. It is a matter of issue. Again and again.)   It is a matter of what you give — by your concern to raise the issue of the new man, you make new the painful literary tissue of your contributors. What do they give you half as significant, as forming, as the context & meaning you give them?

At some point all the work, good work & bad work & work that fails to be either, has to be melded, thrown together in the teeth of the world (& its literary values) in the name of the new age. *England's Helicon*. Tottel's *Miscellanie, transition*, are not interesting as history but in history, at the moment of their joining together that which is. Of value.)

You are in a country
where the eagle has a snake in his beak
I remind myself every day
of what that must mean
The winged prick, the sexual energy
(of rock! of the warm earth! of water!)
flying through the air
becoming the sex of sun,
the light of clarity spurting into the poem
The eagle seizes the snake
& takes him to heaven.
In the valleys of the sun the serpent
turns to a long thin fire of gold
& the heat that glows from him
becomes his wings. Sn -
ake. who is cold & slow.
burns into a bird.
    But a bird
fiercer & more beautiful than any eagle.
So the end of this matter is beyond its means.)

When I talk about your body
it is with a reserve
our time puts on me & has put on you —
not the Victorian game —
preserve we think we've poached on at last.
The verbal mess of what we may not say,
but a reserve that is worse than any
Catholic Spain or Protestant Bloomsbury —
I mean the artificial
limitation
of all man's body to his genitals,

                the false symbolism of the living prick
                (to which the poem returns)
                whereby it & it only feels or comes alive
                or comes at the end of history home
                in your woman's body. The whole
                body must come home, come home in body
                to its own country. Or:
                                    in Blakean terms, we will never overcome
the tyranny of the closed senses until we have utterly lived in the
senses, never acquire triple vision until we have used up all modes
of seeing with these blue eyes. It is not enough to be fucked. It
must begin: it is almost enough to be. To be is to fuck. Not the
other way round.

    The spectres of Freud-diminishers chain our
affections to one single act (suspiciously like our Puritan forebears
who made all sex but frontal intercourse criminally punishable — as
it still remains) & fatally divert man's attention from his body (the
frame of his unison) by abstract & meaningless considerations like
'intimacy,' 'respect,' 'responsibility,' 'father,' 'mother,' 'relationships,'
'group.' Who hath it? He who died on Wednesday.

Our concern must become single: to live in our bodies fully. To be
turned out of that fortress is to be destroyed. All forms of totalitarian slavery commence with the proposition: get out of your body.
Whether that is ecstasy, religious abstraction, psychotic fugue,
social-consciousness, group-loyalty, whether the threat is Marxist
or Theocratic or Fascist, the threat is the same. Men, alienated from
their bodies, wandering howling thru the abstract spaces of a
pretended race. The first city is man's body, & man must learn to
live there before the polls can have a chance of being made.
    The name
of this poem is ENSTASY: flourishing within the body, the garden
of the self rears food & flowers, which done can feed other bodies,
other beings. What sort of host is it who gives his visitors, his lovers,
nothing to eat.

Till the body
becomes the city
it always is

the spaces
between us
count for too much

but then
united with sensation.
singing the unison

the bodies
talk together
perfectly.

(El Corno Emplumado #13, 1965)

CRYPTODES

Sometimes I sing beneath the surfaces of things, or under the leaf turned up to rain, or in the corner with dust under a window. These are hidden singings, & have to do with themselves, sing themselves, & the things that are singing & in which they can sing. All that I make is part of the work, but all that I love & read & taste & touch is too; not all the crystals of the work must be made public. Enough that though one-seventh of the whole appear above the waters; the hidden bulk sustains the visible, & by its very nature must stay hidden. The disappointment of one who turns from two or three great poems of Coleridge to the 'collected poems' must be extravagant. That work sustained the poet — that was the form that conduced to song. No need for it to be public; perhaps a man should have to be a certified badge-wearing poet to be allowed access to *oeuvres complètes*. The form of writing sustains sanity & virtu of the poet cf. Duncan's *Writing writing* — no part of which commands, yet the whole plainly opens to his 'own' work. How tiresome Yeats's oeuvre is, & I note it now with astonishment, as over against the impact of "Lapis lazuli" when I heard Thomas speak it, or "Upon a picture of a black centaur by Edmond Dulac" when Hugh chanted it into my fourteen year ears, or "Cuchullain Confronted" when I first found it. Not qua *lyricism*, but qua the *immediate*, as such. All dimensions of the work can scarcely be visible at once, & if they were, no one reader *in his single time* could perceive them all. What I'm at here are the *cryptodes*, the hidden singings which go to sustain one, which are my prayer & my love-making & my magic & my devotions as well, which no one has to hear but my love, but the things I sing, but the song singing itself. I've gotten diverted here by the business of collected works — that's not the issue, i.e., the quotient of viable single poems in a man's work, not at all. Back to the point: That the work in all its fullness is supported & sustained by hidden acts of devotion, hidden perceptions & syntheses & once-told stories. (The thousands of stories I've told Joby night after night all our marriage long are such cryptodes — pure acts of words-in-love, which only now I see too as the deepening of the channel & the husbanding of the waters, rightly, by full use, by free exchange.)

      Give it away
      as it is
      into the hands of darkness
       &c.

I remember I wrote of a poem Rothenberg urged me to float, in the wine bottle we'd just emptied, down the Hudson, with his own poem, written hastily, in the dark as mine had been, for the same purpose. Characteristic of me I should have memorized mine & written it down when I got home, & used it as the dedicatory poem to *Her Body Against Time*. Yet the principle stands, though I loved *that* emergence too much to give it over.

Well, these few pages in honor to the invisible layers of the work, to the hidden songs.

16 June 1965
[Notebook 20]

POSTSCRIPT II FROM *A CONTROVERSY OF POETS*[10]

Because we cherish life, we cherish the poem as a life-sustaining force. Its strength is the strength of an object: a thing made, a thing present in the orders of our perception.

In our time, in America, there is a vast separation coming more and more to exist between two distinct classes of poets. While other observers have chosen to distinguish the two classes as "schools," "camps," and so on, it appears to me that the separation of which I have spoken, and in recognition of which an anthology such as the present finds its origin, has to do finally not with groups or social arrangements at all, but with a corresponding separation which has, since at least the middle of the nineteenth century, taken place in the nature of poetry itself.

The poem is a life-sustaining force. With rare exceptions in all times, it has traditionally exercised its function by means that are basically decorative. In its substance, in its verbal-musical substance, itself, much Western poetry has been content to be beautiful at best, agreeable at average, mildly disturbing at its fiercest, like Hollywood's treatment of a social problem. Those who today drink the bland waters of genteel orthodoxy from such journals as *The New Yorker* may expect to find in those pages verse that aspires to decorate the reader's consciousness in much the same way, and for many of the same reasons, that the furniture displayed in the same pages would decorate the reader's home.

Because of the overwhelming human desire for the familiar, it is to be expected that the bulk of such composition will adhere to traditional "forms" — patterns is a truer word. The harmony of symmetry has often enough before been used to assuage all loss, to shield men from an asymmetrical universe. Within traditional patterns, many an American poet writes to the best of his often great ability, producing work that can be exciting, but often by its ingenuity rather than by its inspiration. The subject matter will often seem to be daring; but the effect is frequently simply an effect, an affectation of timeliness: saying *condom* in a sonnet is a titillation, a source of that *frisson* a child may derive from saying *damn* in church.

---

10. ["Postscript I" was written by Paris Leary, the co-editor of the anthology *A Controversy of Poets*.]

A VOICE FULL OF CITIES

Such work, even the best of it, is to me a kind of perversity: an antiquarianism, whereby a poet insists on reaching his destination via outworn or originally ineffectual instruments. This quality of ineffectuality impinges on the goal itself: poets will write to less and less purpose, whittling their concerns down to the size of their tools. That is innocent enough, sad around the edges, but innocent. Literally perverse to me is the presumption or fatuity of some poets who choose to hum in the measures of Donne or Herbert about important human issues to a generation that has experienced Auschwitz, Nagasaki, Algeria, and the Congo. That is pure escapism, and can catch only the saturated ears of an audience attuned to the reviews and the world of little-magazine infighting. Nor is the perversion or betrayal simply a lack of cogent responsibility to the social and political world of the poet. More deeply, it is a betrayal too of the very achievement of the masters they follow, those masters who, whatever else their businesses, sang in their own voices in their own time.

It is not by subject matter that we can distinguish between the two classes of poets today. As has been pointed out often enough, the so-called academic poets know as much about politics, sex, money, the racial issue, and despair as the so-called non-academic. Conversely, the so-called non-academic are typically as scholarly, and more allusive, than the so-called academic. All of these matters are general. The difference does lie in this: the so-called academic poet, whatever the urgency of his own convictions, chooses to write in time-worn, pre-existent patterns, and often enough in outworn language, as if he himself did not take himself or the poem seriously enough to want to make it heard *now* by all those beings in the midst of whom he must spend his life. There is nothing sinister in this, no conspiracy of the *laudatores temporis acti*; in all likelihood it is ephemeral, too often it is dull. Social decorative verse, verse that serves to reinforce the typical attitudes of its presumed readers, aims at the topical, yet may, if it's well done, last *malgré lui* as long as Hesiod, or as long as Pope. Men like pretty things; what cat's averse to fish?

There are a great many such fish in these pages; delicate as flounder, rich as pompano, they will please a palate well, and then slip digestibly down.

For the past hundred years (as, again, with preliminary flickers of anticipation all through man's verbal history) there has been a better possibility: to sustain life by the creation of new forms, genuine new verbal structures arising out of our condition to sing to us of all times. The work of Whitman or Rimbaud in the nineteenth century — with awful slowness — has at last alerted us to the possibility of a poem that means something. I mean a poem that is not, like a tune we can choose to hear or to neglect, something for the sake of something else, like a print tacked up on the wall to hide the wall. I mean a poem that means something because it is no longer *about* something but *is* something: but, and this is all-important, a poem that, as a thing, does not come to exist æsthetically and in remoteness, as a thing would be in a museum, unthinged, but as a thing would exist, and possess meaning, in a world of living men. As a chair possesses meaning. Not as furniture, but as a place to sit down.

The poetry of which I speak, the poetry that concerns me and that I have tried to display in this anthology, is a poetry that makes extreme demands upon the reader. It is not content to be background music — taken as background music it is, like all else in that category, æsthetically trivial. On the contrary: it demands everything the reader has; it demands that the reader bring himself to the place of the poem. That sounds like the maxim of an older æsthetic; it is not. He who would sit down must present himself to the chair; bring himself to the place of the chair. Then the sensuous impress of the poem begins.

Much of the poetry in this anthology is of a radical newness. The reader may detect echoes of Eliot, or Stevens, or Yeats: the radical newness of which I speak has nothing to do with illiteracy. Further, the reader may hear, beyond the familiar moderns, music and voices from all earlier ages, spelled over into our time by the poet fully alert to history, time's movement in him, in us. It is the responsibility of the radical poet to apprehend as much of all that has gone before him as he can: to bring that into our age reviving the past not as antique, bringing it to life transmuted into the present, "set to a new measure," as Duncan defines it in his version of Shelley's "Arethusa." Radical newness fulfills the traditions in the creation of new forms, from which perhaps a tradition of the immediate will arise, one that will not bore us, one that will talk to us of life & in life, one that will be awake in the morning and summon us from sleep.

The prime material of the poem is words. Let there be no doubt about that. In general, the new poetry is the product of those poets who believe in the word, who believe in the word's strength, who do not say:

words fail me, but who may confess: *I failed the words.* The words do not fail us, and in the strength of that conviction a poetry has lately grown up in America that enlarges human experience and human relations by discovering, in the orders of music, the clarity and meaning of words, the wood of our world that grows from the roots of our consciousness. Modern linguistics hypothesizes a tyranny which language, as a system, exerts over its unconscious users. The radical poetry of the American language would liberate us from that tyranny, in clear consecution of that primal statement of the modern: *je est un autre.*

Utter reliance on the word necessitates as well utter responsibility to the word: the word, shaping itself through the breath or utterance of the poet, rises into form. The only form possible is the form the poem spells itself out in; the traditional metres and stanzas and "forms" are always available for *tours de force,* for training or chaining infant ears. But they do not, cannot, talk to us in our own speech, our own asymmetrical, nervous, alive, embattled, *present* hearing. The true craft, then, of the poet is total response to his materials, to the words, total openness to the powers of source energy — memory or imagination or inspiration, *Mnemosyne* or *Mousa,* we shall not argue that here — arising in him. In that sense, craft is now exactly what it has always deeply been: perfected attention.

I would hereby identify the true tradition of craft and form in our time as the tradition of Blake, Whitman, Pound, Williams, the tradition of the poet bold enough and vulnerable enough to elicit the form inherent in the marriage of himself with his material, the incestuous *hieros gamos,* in Jung's sense, that is the root gesture of all art.

It is plain, then, that my intent in choosing poets for this anthology has been to present those of our contemporaries whose concern has been with formal invention and discovery, whose technical attentions have been devoted ever to sharpening their own instrumentality, who have honored and taught us to honor the words, who have taught us to disdain decorative metaphor for the sake of genuine root metaphor, that transference of charge to the reader (like that "single image" Pound asserts the *Paradiso* to be), who have taught us to be sharp enough to hear the story the words utter, to hear the words' music, to be attentive to that heurism or process of discovery a poem is, to value the breath of life:

that is, the breath of a man shaping, being shaped by, the words, who have brought poetry to a new level of being, one that would make us & remake us, the readers, and would make everything new. It is one *god spell,* from Blake's "There Is No Natural Religion" to William Carlos Williams' lines, late in his life, from the incredible "Asphodel, That Greeny Flower":

> My heart rouses
> > thinking to bring you news
> > > of something
> that concerns you
> > and concerns many men. Look at
> > > what passes for the new.
> You will not find it there but in
> > despised poems.
> > > It is difficult
> to get the news from poems
> > yet men die miserably every day
> > > for lack
> of what is found there.

This is a great age of birth in the arts; we must not be seduced by the sheer bulk of fashionable verse into overlooking the plain fact that in the past twenty years poets like Charles Olson, Louis Zukofsky, Robert Duncan, have brought the poem to the new world Whitman had a foothold on, and have reinterpreted and given new worth to the ancient understanding of the poet as custodian of the words (the mythos, the story) of the tribe. At the same time, we must not mistake the great separation between the radical poets and the lapidary antiquarians as a mere *lutte poétique* time's ineluctable dialectic will resolve: schools and groups are not at issue. What is at stake is a radical breakthrough in the nature of human consciousness and the nature of human verbal understanding. Because we cherish life, we must cherish to the uttermost the utmost power of the poem to sustain us.

Annandale-on-Hudson, New York

Anthologies are finite. At the close of the present specimen, this editor is concerned to direct the attention of the reader to poets whose work, for one reason or circumstance or another, has not been included. Long active or newly heard from, these poets are currently producing distinct and original work. Enough to suggest that from the roster that follows, an anthology of comparable merit could have been derived.

Helen Adam	David Antin	Carol Berge
Richard Brautigan	Cid Corman	Judson Crewes
Guy Davenport	Diane Di Prima	Richard Duerden
Robert Duncan	George Economou	Clayton Eshleman
Seymour Faust	Vincent Ferrini	Max Finstein
Kathleen Fraser	Jonathan Greene	Kenneth Irby
Steve Jonas	John Keys	Philip Lamantia
Ron Loewensohn	David Meltzer	Barbara Moraff
Lorine Niedecker	George Oppen	Peter Orlovsky
Margaret Randall	M.C. Richards	Frank Samperi
Ed Sanders	Armand Schwerner	Susan Sherman
Gilbert Sorrentino	George Stanley	Charles Stein
John Thorpe	Lew Welch	Philip Whalen

[Robert Kelly & Paris Leary, *A Controversy of Poets*, 1965]

INTENTIONAL LANGUAGE

happens to the reader

lately since (possibility of)
focus on *poem*
language (rightly)
*semed

====

*semed = sign'd or meaning'd cf its craft, towards

====

language semed towards
                non-object/ive/,
(to borrow of visual art,)
as not of the recognize-object-as-such)

that is,
briefly,
words (*prima materia*)
attended into dance (syntax),
whence (i.e., be slow, from syntax)
a field-of-precept
("experience(d)?")
        opens
to the hearer
    (Repeat:
from the syntax
the meaning ('meant' or 'unmeant')
gets itself
landed mirrored or distorted)
= fucked into the hearer (or eingefügt)
((i.e., the poet's attentions are to that
scrupulous dance
from which the transfer,
           transmission;

On the other hand,
> there has been a tradition
> (old & little practiced lately)
> ((is this good or bad?))
of OBJECTIVE language —
> (even if coming-on)
>> — writing.

Writing the key *here*.
i.e., objective-writing
a) plans a destination — control —
>> for the reader's response.
b) serves as a basis of commentary.
((b) is finally more cogent historically than (a))
Eliade speaks of *intentional language*
> In Tantra:
saying one thing & meaning it-&-another
> / vajra = phallos = diamonds = 'mind' = vajra /
Intentional language is different from code & cipher (for obvious syntactic reasons) & from secret languages (like Shelte or Bog Latin, Pig Latin, Op-Language) because only some words in a given text bear (or suffer) the intentioned re-understanding.

Intentional language has a power of fascination
> (wherein its evil)
> & the capacity to be endlessly translated,
> re-interpreted, commented upon.

(Do you remember the Awful Sinking Feeling when you realize that your childhood enthusiasms Hopkins & Dylan T & Mr. Yeats were writing in Intentional Language much of the time, & that where you had understood a primal penetration of the world, a re/newal of the life of things, only a religious opinion was 'intended'? Which shows how little attention you should pay to their intentions. What do they know?) (tho GMH & DT probably did not know they were writing intentional language at all — so be careful with this word of Eliade's *intentional*. As much the reader's intent as the writer's, Freilich.)

((in a great number of years, their works will go the golden way of Mother Goose, & their intentionality be forgotten as Mrs. G's political pasquinades have mellowed into domestic myth))
((orchids to time, or history, or our beautiful Forgets))

We do certain past poets the honor
(& we have no greater honor to bestow)
of reading them
as if they meant it, absolutely.
meant what they were saying doing
as much as we do,
clearly compelled to create anew
a body of articulate sense.

Metaphor is carrying over charge from text to reader.
We have till lately insisted on the unicity of each poem, *not* wanted the veiled message, have wanted the subject to address the object, have wanted in our euramerican way to *be* the object addressed. Each poem an isolato.
But this is older, intentional form, hermetic, combinative, serving always the beginning of intellection, of COMMENTARY-begetting.

Examples of unimpeachably Intentional Writing:
— most alchemic treatises
 (wch are thus different from allegories, radically different.)
— tantric texts
— much mystical poetry of Islam
 (e.g., Ibn al-Arabi's Tarjuman al-Ashwaq) & of Xty (e.g., John of the Cross's few rich poems, each of wch serves as Initiatory Text for a commentary of his own).

Some distinctions:

Effective ALLEGORY interprets itself.
Any literary work CAN be interpreted in many modes
Intentional Language MUST be interpreted.

(Allegory is a characteristic & neglected Western form, & is fit instrument for our Faustian greed, since it knows nothing of Ensker/Eller, & knows only BOTH/AND. Good health to it.)

The poet will not be tempted to try Intentional Language writing
               until he knows something important,
or thinks he does.
                  Then he's in trouble
       since the whole mechanism (= river-machine)
of our modern 'non-objective' writing
                           (post Rimbaud,
   I'm talking abt,
               the AUTONOMOUS poem)
                                    is based on
learned ignorance,
             i.e., not knowing where you (the poem)
are going till you're there.

So at this moment there is a major cleavage in the possibilities of writing

"non-objective"   *"objective"*

                                              Intentional language
autonomous   primal words in symbiotic life with commentary
modern poem

(& these have nothing to do with the dreary sociologies of Letterz in Amurica)

(notice PLEASE that the non-objective is not equivalent to subjective: I continue the metaphor strictly from the visual arts; don't confuse the issue)

Already we can note certain poets or their spectres moving towards the Intentional Language, most notably, right now, say Lamantia
       (swayed by Schwaller de Lubicz's researches into the absolutely objective character of Egyptian hieroglyphics as Intentional language?)
or, less recondidtely, Leary's versified Tao Te Ching absolutely clamorous for the Special Understanding of the Chemic Initiation,
       & from there, much acid & grass
writing of our time.

The Faith of our Fathers (I'm talking abt Whitman & Rimbaud & Mallarme & Pound & Joyce &c.) had reference to an absolute puritan covenanter's faith in the power of the word-in-relation,
      syntax as absolute
                      the poem itself
as salvific.
      And that faith, new faith,
      even if it's now our orthodoxy
      (& it is)
still funds the most diverse lines of creative work (Roussel —Ashbery — the escuela de Nueva Yorque) (Pound — Zukofsky — Olson — Duncan — Creeley &c.) two evidently viable schisms in the meeting house, but both clearly on the non-objective side, as far as the work itself goes.

The healing:
both intentional & non-objective writing come to exist in form,
      syntax mediates.
                 I mean it is a man's syntax we listen to
    & thus take (his) (our) (the work's) meaning.
Note that the oldest extant English poems are
      riddles & spells.

                                          (7 August 1966)

POEM = COMMUNIQUÉ

To be able to find an image is to establish a location in the visible world. To claim an image is to set down points, points, finally to encompass a momentary identity. Image relates to poem as an habitual gesture relates to a known person, but with this difference, that the image must instantaneously, never-having-been-seen-before, establish the familiarity of the gesture, the sign-post of the known person. It is easy enough for the image to explode in its novelty, in the seductiveness of epiphany, but it must do more: with the same speed, it must open more than it closes, must open to what follows, respond to what follows, elapse instantly in the field of sight, linger as a controlled resonance.

There is mannerism and there is gesture. On the level of amity, but locate the individual, but only gesture leads onward, overcomes the tedium of identity, lets identity serve as a true impulse, as vascular system of The Communicated.

For with the image, the attention is finally liberated from its perpetual adultery between What Is Being Communicated and the communication's trembling How. Liberated and allowed to address, simply, the *communiqué*, the communicated mass, the supine all-things-being-over-this-is-it.

Communiqué is the best word at hand. The instantaneous (*not* spontaneous) rhetoric of Fire! in a crowd: sum of image and fear in the known world. Now there are no primal images, no treasure troves of archetypes operating in the force of Fire! Rather it is the familiar charged, loaded beyond bearing, so that its image, its gesture breaks open and open and open. It does not stop opening. It is finite. It is communiqué.

The loading takes place in that palace of rhetoric that used to belong to Procrustes. Torture goes on still, but it is language now racked on the image, language being compelled.

Historians of ideas feel at home with, identify as contemporary, 17th-century notions and alarms against inflated rhetoric, 'against unnatural flights in poesy.' Neo-Spartans are always with us, with their negative euphuism. But that kind of simplification is just another sport of Procrustes (Sade knew him as Minski). Language racked on images, emergent images, yields an essentially different poetic language, one that is, and should be, *superficially* akin to the language of everyday, the American language. The likeness can only be superficial, because the whole is not language alone, it is communiqué, and the total-communicated is vastly different from everyday language, not in its different content, but in the charge it receives, the load which is deliberately placed on it, which must break it. And here the shouted Fire! bears comparison to the cartoon of a drowning man shouting Au Secours, Au Secours. If it is not English, the waves close over it. But Help! Help! is no better unless there are waves and storm and the cramped leg and anxious eyes straining from the shore. Leading back to the image: for it is the images, and more, the progression and accumulation of images, which creates, which equals and superequals the context of the real world. And in that context, the poet's language, under the anguish of the communiqué being born, leaps for salvation to the colloquial language, a language of desperation, which explodes with whatever brightness and leaves a world of ruins. These ruins are the communiqué, the poem.

[RK archives, undated text from the 1960s]

THREADS 2: ROBERT SAYS

[...] I have a theory that poems should appear in chronological order of composition, so that each poem somehow comments on the one before it and the one after it, even if there are dozens left out, but in this fiction collection for one reason or another they are always mixed up [...]

in conversation with Bonnie Langston (1994)

Since the beginning of time, artists (poets, musicians, dramatists, novelists) have been paid for what ultimately is: the shaping of time as it passes. That is what rhythmos is, the shaping of audible or sensible or tactile experience — the word from which rhythm and rhyme both come, the potter's craft of shaping on the wheel when the clay is time itself.

in conversation with Simone dos Anjos & Pietro Aman (2006)

Once you get them to read a book, the world is saved. [...] [Anyone who's reading a novel] is in contact with the art of literature, is doing the work of the word, the basic work of the word that is done by the writer and the reader together, joined. And it's ultimately a free act, you know, because when you are reading, [...] you're reading always on your own time, whether you're on a train or a beach or you're alone or together, you're stealing a few moments because the story enthralls you, or you're reading just because you're bored to death in the dentist's office, or you're frightened, whatever reason, you're still in your own time, on your own time slash in your own time, you're there for your own time, and if nothing else, reading begins to tell you what your own time is, because when you go into a movie theater you're not in your own time anymore, you're in their time, you pay at the door and you go in and they turn out the lights and they show you the thing and you move at their speed, whatever it is, and the only time you have a chance for your own time is if you have to go to the bathroom, or you get thirsty or something, when you're back in your own time, and then you have to return from that to their time, but when you're reading, any book, any *book, you're on your own time. You make your own contract between the text and time, and that's the work of art, that's the work of the word, what goes on.*

in conversation with Bonnie Langston (1994)

The only thing I really look to a poem for is revelation. I think poetry is a true revelator in this time, especially in this time, when all the different bibles babble so loud you need the desert calm of the feeble poem to hear a new word come to life. What the poem reveals is what the poet didn't know — that's the first test. When the poem surprises you by what it's just made you say, or made your hand write, then we're on the way.

The poet's responsibility is revelation. Not just to say what has never been thought. But to say in clear words something that cannot *be thought. Let language lead the way. To play while the grown-ups do that frightening compulsive thing they do and they call work. To hope that they will see us playing, and be disturbed or distracted or entranced. And join us.*

To change the world one person at a time. The strange fact of the poem in a book: it happens to one person at a time. And it makes us do the happening. Music happens to us, but we have to read the poem. That makes us complicit in its coming-into-presence. And that complicity, in turn, makes us co-workers of the utterance. The words become us.

in conversation with Simone dos Anjos & Pietro Aman (2006)

So one of the problems — personal, political, moral, theological — of being a poet is to be held, rightly held, responsible for what the poem "says" to and does with its readers on its journey, and yet also to free oneself from an attachment to the text. The ocean of meaning too often becomes an academic birdbath. I suppose little birds have to be clean.

in conversation with Simone dos Anjos & Pietro Aman (2006)

I am doing something about it [the Vietnam War]; *that is to say, I'm working with all my energy all the time. The mode of my work doesn't convince politicians of the right or left that I'm on their side, but then, artists have never been successful in convincing entrepreneurs what they're doing is of any consequence; I mean, what is the heritage of a great writer or a great artist? It isn't, surely, of people in graduate school, of making a living interpreting his work; the heritage is a spiritual one, a slow advancement. You know, I'm understanding the human race to be a family that has been moving very, very slowly towards self-awareness for thousands of years, that our energies are best spent in developing this self-awareness & the harder we push on that, the faster we'll progress — but that progression is very slow: I'm thinking in geological terms. Man has been around for quite a long time & the pace of his development is accelerating, maybe, & with each acceleration comes, at the same time, overwhelming negative obstacles, things that will distract him either into the, essentially, cave-frenzy-animal-hatred-life of Capitalism or the beehive of the totalitarian Marxist state: both of these are his enemies.*

in conversation with Joshua Stolle [ca. 1970s]

2.

A BOOK CALLED *IN TIME* (1971)

TO

Herodotos of Halikarnassos

∴

Charles of Worcester

(prefix:

as (& not as)
the logographoi preceded Herodotos

but as (tho not as)
Novalis & Nietzsche preceded
Spengler & Kantorowicz

these gifts in time, ours, these
as
(& thus as)
chips or flakes
from our latest Pleistocene,
craft,

the poets (now
last scientists of the Whole

busy at their work

so
these now, from us all,
nothing personal,

shall precede some
formulator
       who will
be able to reckon,
           in prose

(i.e., poetry an earlier form, embryologically
     solid now,
but the prose of our horizon
     not yet made,

in prose,
later,
the dimensions of this
universal century & frontier time

R K
8/68

LETTER TO THE BEAR. RE: ROME

The passage of time encourages the historian to play ad lib with the blocks of data at his disposal, would seem to allow him to order them at his own instance (not their insistence) into whatever systematic general pattern presses most urgently on his awareness.

We who hear about things accept (time is so short here) the systems with the data; irrelevance is canonized.

From the assassination of Julius to the collapse of 'effective' government in the West in the 4th–5th C is a stretch of years at least twice that of any perceptible history of the American state, at least 10 times that of any of the Socialist states whose polities so exercise us. To tolerate Gibson's 'decline' or Mommsen's fiat that the Roman state was, after Cæsar, a mechanical & lifeless thing, is to accept once more the white supremacist gimmick of rating the purity & validity of republics by the absence of miscegenation (& the abstract symbolist thereof, 'debased' coinage). "Decline" will thus expose its meaning as: to develop, to be possessed of qualities, possible gestures of freedom & responsibility, lacking in that original contract invented by historians for every state.

From all the real data at hand (remembering that imperial history is commonly written by such as hate the emperor) it's hard to avoid the conclusion that the empire was as vastly superior to the republic as the present American society is superior (by God, look at the facts!) to the pristine & pure community of Salem. (I mean in a way, too, that what's wrong with Ausonius is right with Olson, a measure of a man's own strength being part of it, not simply thus it is smack smack. His efforts will wash the sea. Or keep digging in the system of thought you inherit long enough & you'll turn up the fact it's built upon or hides — a river NOT its straight sheen on a summer's day.)

The least important *fact* about the Roman Empire is that it fell, i.e., isn't here now under its former name. Closed for alterations as often as it likes, it reopens under new management & does not importantly change. I'm not talking about cycles. This is a continuity. Blues & Greens in the circus, black & white on the corner, we schematize by color because we are not interested in politics but in willful allegiances. Alabama is not Dacia; the barbarian is internalized, cannot in that sense 'come.' What are those so-called Negroes doing?

There was no Emperor worthy of record; the emperor row is shadowy, with overtones of evil if you look long enough. Look it in the teeth & say Prove it! The Emperor responds, We are here. The lot of us make the empire. Whenever the republic (clean white churches, snow, maple syrup, sleighs, the poets hidden, disguised as schoolmasters & divines, poetry tolerated as masturbation is tolerated, laws against it too hard to enforce) is overrun by a mob of niggers the Empire is open for business again, poets can come down from the trees & out from under the rocks.

Being is licit. Hold tight to that. Coins can be debased because whatever strength there is is elsewhere, part of a man's heart & his actions, like 'purity.' As our vision of Jesus is indistinguishable from the ferment of sinister Syrians in Rome, he having come into the Empire 'when the whole world was at peace.' The republic evaporates, ulcerates out in the suburbs; the City is the Empire.

A deep breath then. Poets out in the open? The shadowy aimlessness of the poet's motive the driving force of everything that moves? Which is close to the real burden of our responsibility.

RE: THE OCCULT

The traditional sciences became 'occult' when the city took on its modern sense & the bulk of a nation's people came to live in it.

Goethe's Faust can still stroll outside the city. He is the opposite of the Socrates of the *Phaedrus*, & grazes widely.

Living the life of the seasons, the life of 'nature,' is the beginning & consecution of the traditional sciences.

Just as the sky over a modern city is occulted by smoke & industrial throwaway, its proper atmosphere, so that antique science based on the inspection of the sky becomes mythologized, & hence a fossilized, hence a despised, science, rather than an open possibility.

[Cumont points out that in the deserts of the middle east, Venus as evening star still casts a shadow.]

[Countrymen are unlikely to forget how after a quarrel with the wife & a quick getaway, they came out to see the Pleiades flirting in & out of sight at the top of a cold sky. Or 'Orion blazing.']

Living up here, barely a hundred miles from New York, the calendar the hardware store gives me is marked out zodiacally, & tells me how the planets affect the parts of my body or the times of my plantings.

[Waite reasons that doctrine (true or false, profitable or foolish) becomes superstition only when the hypothesis motivating the symbolic form is lost.]

The sort of wisdom that the City of Athens spent two weeks a year in steady pursuit of, in the month of the leading of oxen, the journey outside the city walls to Eleusis, that wisdom was outlawed & made criminal by the City of Rome, that post-Augustan first 'modern' city, terrified of the interpenetrations of the world. Not until orientalism dominated Rome (the majesty of those orderings we have been taught by etiolate Gibbon to despise) did Rome become a city.

2 · A BOOK CALLED *IN TIME* (1971)

I point out two kinds of city: the cosmically-oriented city, laid out to be the type of the heavenly (i.e., the kosmos itself), the city that serves as *focus* for all the natural forces (Athens, Alexandria, Byzantium, Peking) &

           the other sort of city, that serves as refuge from the natural order, & strives to deny it as extensively as it can. (Republican Rome, that misunderstood the Etruscan *mundus*, or ditch, around the city, falsely apprehended it to be a mode of excluding the outside, rather than a mode of harmonizing the ground of the city with the forces of nature & the cosmological realities that ancient people seemed to have grasped. The sin of Sodom had not to do with the worshipful cock at the lips & gates of the body; Sodom sinned contra naturam in the most literal sense of those words, an inane hubris, to set a city on bitumen, & was burned. *That* is the sin a city can commit: To deny in its plan & life & ordering the great wheel of which it should be the hub. America is filled with such cities, abstract negations of the body of man.)

Rome was purified & redeemed specifically by the influx of Jew & Syrian & African & Egyptian, by their bodies, wise loins, & memories of a wider measure brought back to the sharpness of focus Latium had lost. I have predicted a like novation for New York, that will bring it to the fully functional & unparalleled fruitfulness of the City balanced between sea & land, between New world & Old. It will yet be the world city, Frobenius' altar to which all roads lead.

The traditional sciences, which can by our social forms be made superstitious holdovers, represent at best that empirical speculativeness which constitutes our best mind — study thereof can make us perceptive of conditions, states, rhythms we are no longer *in our bodies* conscious of. For the New Yorker, the stars are for the most part hearsay (which can be 'superstitious holdover'), like the rings of Saturn to an eye without a telescope, like the virus to the man without an electron microscope. There are no ready pragmatic ways of inferring the Pleiades. They go unseen, their dance ignored. And we are cut off.

The stars would lead us to the city, & the city restore us to ourselves.

IDENTITY   PREFERENCE   TEMPLE-COMPLEX

I. I felt the need to come to specific terms with certain bedrooms in summer, certain vectors of desire, certain deflections of my will & of other people's identity. I had to be myself 15 years ago, 10 years ago, a torrid week ago, at the beginning of this sentence: but these are all lost states, & I am forced to view them & learn them as Herodotos learned the palaia of things, by report, by impression, by a veiled word here or there let fall by someone who presumes upon himself & me to say he knew me. [Thoukydides may indeed be the exemplar historian, as such; but a man's life is less evidently shapely & purposeful than a league or a battle or an exordium; it is Herodotos who teaches a man to glean around, to keep his eyes peeled for those pathways through the wood of himself, to learn through research some glimmerings of the pattern of his own life.] For a very long time, I have insisted that conscious exploration of one's own past is an essentially unproductive short-circuiting of the proper balance of source-energy, & that the ineluctable quality of certain former experiences is enough to carry those learnings to the creative surface, *plane of the work,* by their own buoyant meaningfulness. What yesterday struck me with was this: that beyond those crystalline epiphanies I cannot forget & which arise within my work of their own pressure, there is a vast shadowy procession of felicities, miseries & confusions which *seem* to have occurred to me or in me or around me, & seem thus to constitute my story.

Who is it in me that desires? Is there a being, a Προυνικος, who is the Desirer in all of us, just as Duncan tells of The Poet, who speaks through the mouths of many human instruments in a given age? It has been all-too-easy to detach my identity (that means, of course, my sense of identity) from my desires & from my preferences: & this state, an harmonious one for the Hindu we read of, strikes me as fearful. My memories are of instrumentalities.

II. It is common for Mayan scholars to describe the great ruins, Uxmal, Palenque, &c., as *temple-complexes* rather than as cities. Around the great & perduring stone buildings, residence halls, observatories, temples & ball-courts, it is inferred that a great number of impermanent, thrown-together houses stretched out, to house the actual "inhabitants" of the place, or that from scattered villages, all traces of which have been lost, men came daily or weekly or in some cyclical pattern to work in the temple-complex.

The archeologist thus distinguishes the monuments of Yucatan from the ruins of Troy or Rome or any typical city of the Mediterranean koinonia. This distinction between City & Temple-Complex is a profoundly important one. Morley reasons that, because of the simplicity of dietary arrangements drawn from the willing fertility of the soil that supported them, it was necessary for the individual Mayan to work in the fields perhaps only two weeks of the year to feed himself, a week more for each additional member of his family. Thus the Mayan would find the great part of his time free [note that it is dangerous to use in such a remote context words like "time" "work" "free"]; we gather that the time so liberated was, willingly or unwillingly, committed to participation in the vastly proliferated ritual life of the Empire, the most obvious aspect of which that strikes us is the construction & maintenance of those vast & unlikely temple-compounds themselves. A race freed from the necessities by clement weather, fertile soil, abundant terrene & marine game, thus found itself progressively committed to ever-increasing ritualization of life & worship. Life in worship?

If New York were destroyed as I write this word, it is difficult to see in what way the root necessities of life would be threatened for the rest of America. The corn still ripens though Uxmal is desolate. The complex economy of the country centrates in New York, the communicative networks of America originate or repand there, the luxuries on which we variously batten are there processed or assembled or assorted. From the mean hovels of Rye and Lime & Hempstead & Babylon & Canarsie & Scarsdale & Levittown & Englewood and Kew Gardens a bewildering hierarchy of temple-functionaries arrives each day at the temple-complex, ready to devote (in the technical sense, *sphagia*) one-third of their biological time to the national cult.

In exposing the beginnings of this idea to a friend, it naturally occurred to inquire what is the nature of the cult itself, what god is worshipped on this most complex of all human altars. The answer seems to be: *Preference*. The yoga of the west confers identity upon each man in consequence of each man's ability to make Acts of Preference (much of our lives is given over to development & training of that ability). We are trained to discover our identities as products of all we prefer: we are the sum of our preferences. The abstract Deity, a benevolent god in whose nostrils all offerings smell equally sweet, to whom all preferences are of equal value, presides over a nation in which the whole business of life comes to be the enlargement & consolidation of preference-systems in consumption, opinion and behavior. By preferences we are grouped into provisional phratries or clans by birth & social rearing; by preferences the young man distinguishes himself from his phratry in turn. Americans are the least materialistic of all historic peoples. Our economy & all our way of life exist to allow assertion of preference. It is almost a matter of indifference what the actual substance chosen or preferred may be, at least on the broadest social scale. [Sub-phratries like the police or the veterans or the clergymen may attempt more general enforcement of their particular substantive choices — but they are reactionaries fighting a losing war: Americans continue their lawless ways, ready martyrs for their divinized freedom to Prefer.]

Those who will not join in the rituals, who will not cooperate with the beads in the intricate calculus of conferred identity, are mostly those deeply committed to some one or few actual substances: heroin, alcohol, cocks, cunts, poetry, music, images, pottery, words. These, formally, are heretics; they have distorted the worship of Preference: stuck forever at one stage of Preference-worship, these heretics have obstinately preferred the Thing preferred to the geometrically unlimited pursuit of Preferring. Notice that their sin is heresy, not apostasy. Short of samadhi, catatonia or death, no road opens to the apostate in our nation. [Though the generalization that follows is suspect in most other connections, it seems likely enough here: from a societal point of view, we perceive the reasons for the infantile qualities that drunkards, whores, & poets display.

They are children who have materialistically preferred the taste of the bread & wine to the high metaphysical abstraction of the Real Presence. Their materialism constitutes the only viable form of heresy in America.]

Too long we have indulged those academic liberals & survivors of the 30s who, in review after review, try to persuade us that dissent & heresy are matters of dissenting opinions or heretical beliefs. Heretics, mes semblables, beware of them, they are the chief worshippers at the altar of Preference, & try, like all the other hierarchs, to encourage the adoption of Opinion. Opinion, *doxa,* is of course the chief bread-&-wine of the cult of Preference. As long as they talk about opinions, they are not talking about things, any thing at all.

The worship of the thing, as meaningful existent, is one mode of heresy, perhaps of reformation. But it is clear that we must discover, or (doubtfully) rediscover, the true wellsprings of possible human identity. That is, each man must his own. To *know,* beyond opinion.

Pokorny on √pel-

flow ⟶

B. *pel*, 'city.' Old Indic *pûr*, genitive *puras*, 'fortification, city,' more recent *puri-*, *puri*, with the same meaning; cf. *Singa-pore* (Singapur), 'Lion City.' Greek (Æolic) πολις, 'fortification, city, state,' *(*p_eli-s)*, Homeric and Cyprian πτολις, with the same meaning. Lithuanian *pilis*, Lettish *pile*, 'fortification, castle.'

2 · A BOOK CALLED *IN TIME* (1971)

1. *pel-, pelə-, plē-* ‚gießen, fließen, aufschütten, füllen, einfüllen', auch ‚schwimmen, fließen machen, fliegen, flattern' und ‚schütteln, schwingen, zittern (machen)'; nominal: *pel* (Gen. *pₑl-es*) und *pₑli-s* ‚Burg' (‚aufgeschütteter Wall'); *pl̥̄-no-, plē-no-, plē-ro-* ‚voll', *pl̥-ro-tā* ‚Fülle', *pl̥-tó-, plē-to-* ‚gefüllt', *pl̥-ti-, plē-mn̥* ‚das Füllen'; *pelu* ‚Menge', *pₑlu-* ‚viel'.

A. Arm. *hełum* ‚ich gieße aus' (**pel-nu-mi*), *zełum* (**z-hełum*) ‚lasse strömen', Pass. ‚fließe über';

cymr. *llanw* m. ‚Flut', Verbalnom. *llanw*, *llenwi* ‚Füllen, Fließen', mbret. *lano, lanv* Flut', corn. *lanwes* ‚Fülle' (**plₑn-u̯o-*);

lit. trans. *pilù, pìlti* ‚gießen, schütten, aufschütten füllen', intrans. ‚fließen', lett. *pilêt* ‚tröpfeln', *pile* ‚Tropfen', *pilt* ‚tröpfeln', *pali* ‚Überschwemmerung', lit. *ampalas* (**ant-palas*) ‚Aufwasser auf dem Eise'; russ. *vodo-polь(je), pol(n)o-vodъje* ‚Hochwasser', kslov. *polъ* ‚Schöpfgefäß'.

⟵ **polis, *city***

D. ‚füllen, Fülle': Ai. *píparti* : *pipr̥máḥ*; *pr̥ṇáti* (*pr̥ṇáti*) ‚füllt, sättigt, nährt, spendet reichlich, beschenkt', auch *pr̥ṇóti* ds.; *pū́ryatē, pūryatē* ‚füllt sich', Aor. *áprāt* (: *πλῆτο*), Imp. *pūrdhí*, Perf. *paprāu* (: lat. *plēvī*), Partiz. *prātá-* (= lat. *-plētus*, alb. *plot*; vgl. auch *prātí-* : lat. *com-plēti-ō*), *pūrtá-* ‚voll', *prāṇa-* ‚voll' (= lat. *plēnus*, av. *frāna-* ‚Füllung', air. *līn-aim* ‚fülle'), *pūrṇá-* ‚voll' (= got. *fulls*, litt. *pilnas*, abg. *plъnъ*, air. *lān*; von **pel-* hingegen av. *pərəna-* gefüllt'); *pariṇaḥ* n. ‚Fülle' (: av. *pərənah-vant-* ‚reichlich'), *parī-man-* ‚Fülle, Spende' (**pelə-*); av. *par-* ‚füllen';

arm. *li*, Gen. *liog* ‚voll' (aus **plē-i̯o-s* = gr. πλέως? oder aus **plē-to-s* = ai. *prātá-*?), *lnum* ‚fülle' (**linum*, Neubildung), Aor. *eli-c̣* ‚ich füllte'; *lir* (*i*-St.) ‚Fülle'; vermutlich *holom, holonem* ‚häufe auf, sammle an'; gr. πίμπλημι ‚fülle' (ursprüngl. πίπλημι, der Nasal aus πίμπρημι), Fut. πλήσω, Aor. πλῆτο ‚füllte sich', πλήθω ‚bin voll, fülle mich', πλῆθος n.,

92

  pleroma

                            folk ⎯⎯⎯⎯⎯→

                    (com)plete ⎯⎯⎯⎯⎯→

                                        full, fill

                    (Note 1)

ion. πληθύς ‚Menge', πληθύω ‚bin oder werde voll, schwelle an' (: lat. plēbēs), πλήσμη ‚Flut', πλησμονή ‚Anfüllung, Sättigung', πλήσμιος ‚leicht füllend, sättigend', πλῆμα ‚Füllung' Hes. (: lat. plēmināre ‚anfüllen'); hom. πλεῖος, att. πλέως, ion. πλέος ‚voll' (*πλη-[ι]ο-ς; = arm. li ?), πλήρης ‚voll', πληρόω ‚mache voll' (von *πληρο-ς = lat. plērus, vgl. arm. lir ‚Fülle', i-St.); πλή-μυρα, -μυρίς f. ‚Flut', zu μύρω S. 742;

alb. plot ‚voll' (*plē-t-os); auch pjel ‚zeuge, gebäre'? intrans. ‚voll = schwanger sein'?? mit Formans -go- hierher plok, plogu ‚Haufe' (*plē-go-? vgl. ahd. folc ‚Haufe, Kriegshaufe, Volk', ags. folc ‚Schar, Heer, Volk', aisl. folk ‚Schar, Volk' als *pl̥-go- oder *pelə-go-);

lat. pleō, -ēre meist com-pleō, im-pleō ‚fülle', Partiz. Pass. (com)plētus; plēnus ‚voll', umbr. plener ‚plenis'; plērus, -a, -um ‚zum größten Teile', plērusque, plērīque ‚eine große Anzahl, sehr viel, am meisten'; plēbēs, -eī und -ī, plēbs, -is ‚Volksmenge; die Masse des Volkes im Gegensatz zu den Adeligen' (*plēdhu̯ēs), manipulus ‚eine Handvoll; Bündel; Hanteln der Turner; Soldatenabteilung' (*mani-plo-s); plēmināre ‚anfüllen' zu *plēmen = gr. πλῆμα;

air. lín(a)im ‚ich fülle' (von einem Adj. *līn = *plēnə-s), lín ‚numerus, pars'; air. lán, acymr. laun, ncymr. llawn, corn. luen, leun, len, bret. leun ‚voll' (= ai. pūrṇa- usw.), air. comalnur ‚ich fülle' (Denom. Von comlán ‚voll'); u(i)le ‚ganz', Pl. ‚alle' (*polio-);

got. fulls, aisl. fullr, ags. as. full, ahd. fol (-ll-) ‚voll' (= ai. pūrṇá- usw., s. oben); = lit. pilnas, abg. plŭnŭ, skr. pün ‚voll'; über ags. folc usw. s. oben; mhd. vlæjen ‚spülen' zu πλή-μῦρα oben S. 799.

(Note 2)

> VICE, moral failing, from L. *vitium*, "crime, transgression," apparently from *ui-ti-om, "deviation." What's interesting is that the idea of 'deviation' is not abstract or apparently even societal, i.e., not *deviation* from a norm, but deviation in a purer, *personal* structural sense. Leaning too far to right or left is vice. Perhaps *leaning* itself is vice, *inclination, prejudice:* *preference* **equals vice**
>
> From one stem, *uisuo, Gk. gets ισος, 'equal,' Skt., *visuva*, 'equinox,' the root is apparently VI- (Pokorny: u̯i-), 'alternate,' 'two-fold,' 'two.'
>
> Deep in the verbal root are: alternate, reciprocal, compulsory, equal, "gleichgeschwung'nes Joch," Libra, &c.
>
> Vice is to go away from 中, deviate from balance, "wobble," as Pound has it.

BEYOND THE PERSONAL

                  relationship
                            (not 'personal relationships')
but the mark or signal
            of what has been ordered
                         ∴
            or may yet be ordered
                         ∴
the signal at the crossing
               to the event
                       (relationship precipitates Event,
— in definition, —
that which, in what way or mystery not yet the charts,
                             came to pass)
& appropriate to the sharp-eyed man, polytropos, calm of heart,
                   the study of relationship
which gets him somewhere,
            if not home,
                  an island
in an otherwise romantic sea
            (which is, rightly, itself — as business,
busyness —
        relationship
              & that Homer was a merchant or of
seafaring merchant stock
            is more than plausible
                        in light of the event
& knew the value of his coins
               which are nothing
                        if not transportable

THE FRONTIERS OF THE FACT
                                                    (as response to SUM/1)

specify no question
Olson's epistemology
What is Sum?   Σ?   esse?   futurus?
"a work of morning"
etwas?)
        or revert
MUS, mouse
                (as musculus, muscle,
mice swarming
                      beneath the skin
as in flour sacks
                or yet an older
possibility
        (that is, root)
                    *mus
'muscle' itself,
        as name
                (Skt. mūs whence mūṣka)
of vulva,
    the muscle
or knot of well-omened flesh
from which we
        & all we know
issue
    & reduce sooner or later
but ever sooner
        to that same fact
                (the little mouse that steals our flesh)
    which has
        (Tenney smiling oracular:
the parameters of the sounds)
        a shape
to push beyond which
        (frontiersmen!)

2 · A BOOK CALLED *IN TIME* (1971)

or even at the edge
empties the cell of nucleus
& breaks beyond
    (or Dorn's
story that LeRoi tells,
of townspeople out to
Thoreau's shack pounding on the door,
  Come on out Henry we
know you're in there)
      as in
Tenney's music
you would not mistake
yourself for yourself
      (& as plainly
I'd have a right to sit
active in that life-class
writing down the woman's body,
  not a sketch of God knows what
but singing
the song itself
from that sight
    not of it)
      why is it
needful to neglect these wares
'I would do reverence to the
thing that's never shown,
the secret parts,
    the privates of her loins,
o pioneers)

THE DREAM WORK [1]

1

Just now this seems heuristic possibility: Wednesday's dream is not Tuesday's child & is not Monday's grandson. That is, dreams are not *linear* in their expanse (extense).

Are we falsely counselled to record each night's dream, lest we forget? The dreams that matter are the dreams remembered of themselves.

To organize experienced dreams in a calendar way, stretching them out as a line in time towards what, is to subdue that which does not take place in time to Time, falsifying both terms.

Chronology is oversimplification.

My premise is that the dreamworld in us is (like our lives, Q.E.D.) a complex solid of such a nature that 'crystalline structure' is a more useful analogy than 'line,' chemistry a better ancilla than history.

I am watching a snow field as I write, the complex foldings & turnings in the snow. Sastrugi, the intricate physics of the snow as snow, settling crystals locking & unlocking with crystals, snow in snow, AND the intricate impetus of the wind, moving in & on & after snow; let the experimenter note schematically & quickly one dream. No part of him will let that one dream stand alone. As he is writing it down, other dreams of various times will come forward, to be noted down (i.e., hooked on) where they connect. That is the beginning of the dream work.

Radiating & rotating, the structure of dreams will begin to take form, towards objectivity.

---

1. [A practical outcome of this investigation dream as social gesture/communication was the *Annandale Dream Gazette*, which had a brief print run under the editorship of the poet Bruce McClelland, and a still thriving online continuity guided by the poet Lynn Behrendt at the blog *annandaledreamgazette*. — RK, 2014]

2

All earlier discussions of dream seem to have confined themselves to dream as psychic event in the life of the dreamer.

We must now assert the autonomy of Dream as ARTIFACT, legitimate *product* of psychic event, not record of it.

We must learn to honor the dream as work-of-art, & to devise (towards some eventual perfection of it) a language or method for *presenting* in verbal terms that product (not representing it, or interpreting it et cetera).

The spectrum of hitherto noted applications would be of this order:

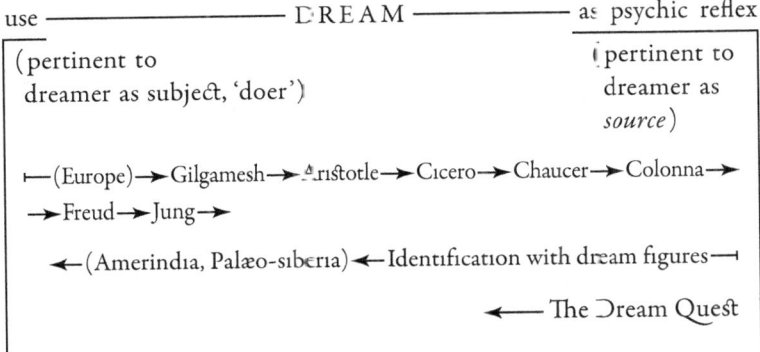

Now the *tertium,* dream as autonomous artifact, must be dealt with.

3

Earlier notes call attention (a) to the aperiodic & symmetrical structure of the dream-life — the series of dreams a man has over a long time — & (b) to the autonomous artifactual quality of each individual dream, whereby (its value as psychic reflex of the dreamer forgotten for a moment) it assumes the same sort of value a work of art possesses. Bear in mind there are good & bad works of art.

That processes rightly called 'creative' are going on all the time in every being.

That in most beings creation shapes with any purity only the dream. (Occurrence of familiar (known to the dreamer) faces, figures, & situations in the dream is no more an argument against the artifactual quality of dreams than occurrences of that kind destroy the artifactual quality of novels.)

Prudent social motive of the Dream Work, to constitute by recognition a new art form for the onrushing collective age

                                  thus to insure possible working conditions for all artists (I am writing as a trade-unionist)

        & a mode of conscious creative activity for those our fusty culture denies the role of art-bearers.

(Note that the Colonna spoken of in Dream Work/2 is that Francesco (b. 1433) who wrote the *Hypnerotomachia Poliphili* (a synopsis of which, with commentary by Linda Fierz-David, exists as *The Love Dream of Poliphilo*, Bollingen Series XXV). The *Hypnerotomachia*, with Chaucer's *Book of the Duchess*, are the two essential fixes on the literary (i.e., writing it down into the work) possibilities of the Dream Work. Distracted by art history, we reprint only Colonna's elevations of fantastic buildings; distracted by social history, we concentrate on *The Canterbury Tales* to the neglect of the supreme extended lyric in the English tradition.

But let me be clear that my concern is *not* with dream as source of literary works, paintings &c. — that has always taken care of itself, at least for those blessed or cursed with dreams.

No. *For the sake of the dream,* in all its clarity as fully created thing, the Dream Work is concerned with devising a comparably distinct way of transcribing, to make available, to make public. The problem of the Dream Work is not aesthetic, then, but logistic.

Dream is from Old English *drēam,* 'joy, gladness.' By night or day.

So far the Dream Work has been insistent upon the 'impersonal' qualities or behavior of dreams, how they are or can be of meaning not to the dreamer but to his society, at large. And so far this preoccupation has limited itself to general prolegomena towards a theory of transcription.

Now it becomes clear that transcription is only one possibility. The 'dream quest,' typically of the Plains Indians, had as its goal the acquisition of a dream, possession of which would serve as talisman to the dreamer, & serve the structural function of directing the mode of his integration within his society. (See on this subject Olson's phenomenal "The Gate & The Center" — now reprinted in *The Human Universe* — in the first issue of *Origin*, Spring 1951!) Externalization of dream 'instruction' concerns us as another (perhaps more important) way of honoring the autonomy of the dream — taking it indeed as the reckoning whereby perception & relationship can come to be ordered.

So that now:

Two Doors:

WORK YOUR DREAM   ACT YOUR DREAM

4

Each time there is only one utterance [that] will satisfy all the demands of the dreamer. The dream continues till that utterance is clarified & won, or irrevocably lost. Then waking can supervene — The sudden crisis of sensory input serving as a buffer, a distraction, from the overwhelming loss of the dream's loss.

Those who are inconstant dreamers must build a factitious strength in the orders of waking, must make, & seem to themselves strong. Our racial strength in the victories of dream, there are some brave men who defer the therapy of their dream, & insist on opening only to the strengths of 'conscious' origin — these men are traditionally in the minority. But as population *density* increases, fewer & fewer men will be able to dream their own dreams to clear conclusions. One expects then a sustained resurgence, quasi-permanent, of *all* the imaginative arts. One consequence of that will be the pre-eminence of *fable* & the comparative neglect of questions of 'form' & 'structure.'

But *fable* (I use the ancient word) is essentially *event,* some events linked in the telling.

re: Snow Jobs / we have got:

        riding out over the whine
        of the not-unjustified
        universal bitching about
        specialization

        (in sciences & scholarship, as a bad thing)

        is the fact
        that there can be (& at historical times
            has been, now is)
        a scientist of holistic understanding,
        a scholar,
            a scientist of the whole

the Poet —
        be aware that from *inside* comes
          the poet, scientist of totality,
            specifically,
        to whom all data whatsoever are of use,
        world-scholar

(from which infer the triviality of current trimmers & rhymesters,
viz. that they are not interested or interesting themselves in anything
everything &c.)

            Pound Goethe Coleridge (off the top of my head)
            greatness from the breadth
of their *concerns*,
        i.e., one (if only one) index is exactly
     that breadth,
          they do not have hobbies they eat
      everything
            true index: breadth of radiance *or* splendor
          poet as world-scholar,
            holist,

    (poet here = maker (with words)

(even as from the health of technology comes
                                    information-theory
            & from computer praxis
       to unitize
                (as first steps (0 = 1)
                      to unity, création du monde)
     poet then not the encyclopædia (à la McLuhan thesis)

                  but the DISCOVERER OF RELATION,
          reintegrator,
                      explorer of ultimate connection
             & connectedness in among & all
    (& if we let teleology or divine providence in: that's why
        poets are hounded from place to place & job to job,
           to keep them moving over the whole earth
      whole surface of act & process & learning & doing,
                   children of Cain the wanderer
                     whence music & the fashioning
                   of meta-
                all
                   material
            for our use,
                     at-one-ing
                              the world

Sermo

Those things we *make* on a frozen earth
free us inward.
                We are each a field
& also the limits of that field.
                         Above the
field the sun rises & stays in the sky and falls
to the inward west.
                  Everything that happens goes
on happening, planted in a thousand
fields, breathed in a thousand winds.
                              For
love & knowing & notice plant us in the minds
of those who love or know or notice us, those
we love or know or notice.
                    Those I have
loved *happen* still in my mind, occur there
as principles of order.
                  We are
haunters & haunted. We talk in our own fields.
What is called Imagination is the harvesting of
the field.
                In the folk tradition the harvest festivals
survive to remind us of the everlasting variety of
inner harvest.
                    Sound is image. Touch is image. All
things 'inward upon.'
                    Memory closes the door
of the body. Memory closes the gate to the field.
The Muses are not Memory's daughters. They
are the naked presences who walk in the
shade of each man's forest, sing by the rim
of each man's fountain.
                  Imagination — Χρυσοποιια
(In this way gold is made.

2 · A BOOK CALLED *IN TIME* (1971)

Given *any* niveau of language:

Chrematic enrichment — *romanticism realism*
surrealism
[which is ONE spectrum]

Chrematic depletion — *classicism formalism*
"the form plain"
one word
(a flex of χράομαι

χρημα
        a thing
needed & used,
goods, property, chattel, gear,
money,
a thing,
an affair,
an event,
a business,
matter,
a lot, a great deal,
wow! what a....
(megasuòs chrêma!
               what a big pig)
wow!
even): race, group:
chrêma thēleiôn,
               womankind

chrema
chrematic
(chrematic fantasy)
in
deed

Tensors

[jetsam

of it:

we'll keep the prepositions for the sake of a one day classicism we'll hold the nouns in good standing but the verbs in escrow (Chaucer did without them, all but the simplest, & verbal formulæ with *do, be, will* &c.)

(i.e., a *Renaissance* is needed for the proper use of verbs — Shakespeare, Webster; Donne already dwindling from it — from the 18th century onward — Hopkins & 20th-century apocalyptics notwithstanding, Tennyson & the pleonasts notwithstanding — our language has been of adjectives & nouns & adverbs.)

What we need are verbal *tensors,* or do we have them already in the possibility of clusters of (falsely called) prepositions?

Is there anything more interesting to us than *location* in space-time, ego, *relationships* of? Only the prepositions (& some adverbs) offer themselves as useful *coordinate — moduli.*

1) as against that familiar adage of creative writing teachers to make the verb come alive.

2) by *Renaissance* I mean too that 'great audience' we've been hoping — maybe wrongly — for since Whitman, i.e., ears that are not *embarrassed* by richness & accuracy.

So we look for languages of fixes, coordinates, tensors to locate 'reality.'

Things shun their definition, shuck off their own weight. The poetry we once were told lived in *things* must reside for us in things, & the romance of *locale* in poetry give way to the epic of location. If men make computers, computers are humane agencies in all their reaches; we need both retrieval, but mostly the *imaginative* (in its toughest sense) discovery of new *locations*, new grids, new tensors.

[This to accompany certain experiments in old-fashioned Basic English, experiments both in *relational poetry* & 'chrematic depletion.'

Tensor Languages

For the most part, the list of 100 "operations" in the Basic English list, with the omission of a few that beg the issue of a specifically *human* observer (say, see, seem) unless a specific 'subject' occupies such words.

2) All the radicals of combination which themselves occur on the list can be used with any other word on the list. I have in mind, e.g.,

with-
there-
-wards
here-

3) All such words will be called, in this system, *radicals*. These radicals may function in any way in which 'words' can function in 'English.' (Use of quotations here to mark words of a mystical character, not susceptible of easy definition, & not my problem in this context.)

Tur Sinai's article on the origin of language [in *Language: Its Meaning & Function,* ed. R.N. Anshen] his inferences from the adverbs &c., which postulate very much a tensor language as the earliest linguistic stratum.) So that = *Word* proposes to define the customary *location* of a thing with *relation* to the *space* of the observer.

WHAT   WHO

	Ablative Relations	Instrumental Relations
	Cnossos — Mycene	(K u r)
(vs/ mnemosune	Lesbic Ψ	'Odysseus'—x—'Sinon'
prana]		'Sappho'
pneuma]	[what did Simonides	
(psychro-) psyche]	'introduce' to	
anemos]	alphabet?]	
animus]		— "Jehova" —
hoama		
soma	'Zoroaster's' deity	
χορος	[gath/ering to sing=	
[σωματ-]	worship. Gathas are	
	s o n g s]	
(Cupid's lady =	the cross of Matter	Jesus = radix
Love's self)	+ (irreversible)	
Ψυχη		
		'Shakespeare'
		'Boticelli' 'Ficino'
		('Caravaggio' a murderer)
		'Fludd' 'Dryden'
	&	(experiment)
		'Rochester'
cell/f	⊙ circle of spirit	
	(shown with nucleus)	
		vacuum, air-pump,
⎵⎵⎵⎵ "m a t t e r" ⎵⎵⎵⎵		tygers & 32'/sec/sec
		'Melville' = ⟨
		'Whorf'

2 · A BOOK CALLED *IN TIME* (1971)

(Prepositional)   HOW

(Gilgamesh)   ⟶ Pindar

         Bible — Talmud — Zohar
                / gematria   ⟶ Sappho (Psapho)

Εργα Hesiod,   [i.e., Pindar as he
        the Phaeacian court   left them, *as* we find
                                               her work, her WORDS,
    Mohammed   not the scholars'
        (who will measure   'elegant emendations':
        Mohammed's face — *shiur komah?*)   In evidence : Daven-
                                               port's versions of
              ibn al-Arabi   the actual extant
                                               text, avoiding (re)
Avarroes ⟶ SIGIER   constructions]
                      ↙ Dante
(as validation of Dante *qua* poet)
Dante of Florence: ⟶ Chaucer — the number
Commedia = Sigier of Paradise   *& kind of his verbs*,
                                             e.g., in the Tales.

   Cordoveiro ⟷ Luria
                                            But see too The
Wolfram's dreams ⟶ Böhme   Book of the Duchess.
(Law's Behmen) ⟶ [Thos. Taylor]
                                    ⟶ BLAKE
"For everything that lives is holy"   ["Nelson"]

so: 'Pecos Bill'   'Aaron Burr' or
                                               'Pecos Bill'
the brothers Grimm a) fabula — narrative } das Volk
                       b) λογοι — dictionary }
                 the words of the
                       tribe

           G. Stein, 'dailiness' *Narration*
           a story = the story
                 (, of the people)
                                              or Ezra Pound.

Program:

1) An age of analysis has ended.

2) the concept of form is a barrier to experience. This buffer must be destroyed.

3) Beyond form is the experience of complexity.

4) In Euramerican society, the poet is financially & socially impoverished because of the prevalence of the idea that poetry is numinous — What is sacred for the bulk of men must not show change; innovation always an enemy of ritual. For the bourgeois heart to thrill, as it is well able to do, to poetry, poetry must appear in its traditional shapes & clothing. Santa Claus is his beard belly & red suit. The bourgeois audience feels poetry is sacred, knows that the sacred is its own concern rightly, but recognizes only familiar forms of the sacred. Yet they can take Cummings & Ferlinghetti. Because they're funny, and a tradition of apotropaic humorous verse does exist. The bourgeois is used to paying money to be amused, he's always on the lookout for a laugh. Hence he will accept the laugh despite the form.

The bourgeois audience — which could make poets able to sustain themselves *by* their work, rather than in spite of it — must be made to *experience itself* in poetry. Obviously the sexual is the easiest avenue of approach. But much care is needed, not to shock or embarrass, but to bring, preserve the enstasy & ecstasy behind the diversion.

2 · A BOOK CALLED *IN TIME* (1971)

Hygiene —)
   (ordering)
      (ὑγεία
well living
     Plutarch on oracles
  (which Taylor would he read on Plato?)
Earl Picus : *conserva* mihi, Domine,
   that that that I am
   is of your doing,
   to say 'Keep me' so
   is past tense of
   'let me be so' or
   give it to me;
   —

encyclopédie; Lansing on
     perception as
      structure —
well-living, & not be dismay'd
 (smoke, e.g., *Camels*):
  or learn what Henry Hudson did
with his river,
    Ausonius at Moselle,
Olson against wisdom
     as such.
Robert's good hour.
    Patch's *Fortuna*.
Ὑγεία more particularly Goddess name,
 who gives us.

יהוה: an answer.

Dr. Dee. Edward Kell(e)y, nat. sub.

Leone

(♌) roared:

off with the

THREU   Loci,

THRAC   not

SIMOI   places.

apud Dardanos. Extra ecclesiam
nulla salus.

Where I meet you all.

A song at night ¼ mile off,

on a wind,

delivered before it is perfect,

ended.

A song.   A very.   A night.

_____COPULA MUNDI_____

2 · A BOOK CALLED *IN TIME* (1971)

IN HISTORIAM

Now if I walk on a crowded street & point to a girl passing & say There! That one! in what way can I be sure that hers are *not* the tits from which the Milky Way flows, or if I touched her hip lightly in the crowd, how be certain that these hips did not once spread to let an unnatural radiance flesh in the world, Jesus or Castor & Pollux. If time has as Lansing says, a dual character, then surely the historical is not *righter* than the magical (any more than the replicable is *truer* than the unique, in science, QED?). It is the true annals of magical time that need to be compiled — or if not compiled, then duly & accurately transcribed at each moment, in overlapping palimpsestical overlays, vast collages of magical time in the dark & light of which we will be able to perceive authentically as in books of 'history,' the true history of our race.

History is Awareness.

Herodotos' advance on the Logographers involved his sense of the necessity for overlap — i.e., that the story of Cadmus from one point of view was not enough. Historians credit Thucydides with being the more accurate historiographer, but he *really* does not move past Herodotos at all. Book II of the *Persian Wars* is the clearest document extant of what history is *in* itself, the *inscience* of man.

[exempla: Pausanias   *Táin Bó Cúailnge*

   Riley's *Narrative*   Sahagun   Mahabharata

   Burton's *Pilgrimage to Mecca & Medina*

BIOTIC DIET

     (& it is clear it is not clear to any of them whether
     we are in a *post*glacial or whether the jig is up)
*di lu wa
   the flood
risen from
    (loss of solar radiation progressively as
    the big ices threw back the sun's
    rays
     &
    increment, proper motion of,
    the ice,

    now melted, under another cycle, another sun,
the flood
    which left only syllabaries & pictographs,
   alphabets later)
      on dry high-pooped ships
lateen-rigged
   the famous old Cornwall to Haifa run
2nd millennium before J:C:
     P&O!
      / alphabetization positive
      correlation with intake of
      animal proteins
pictographs / maize & rice
hieroglyphs / lentils (higher protein content)
syllabary / mixed flesh & spelt
     like, Escoffier, essence of beef,

glaz, jus de viande = the ab
    stracting quality
(Chinese eat everything in their other line)
  (Whorf's best evidence, Mayas ate *fish*)
men in cities, eating beef, *nagari*

2 · A BOOK CALLED *IN TIME* (1971)

& alphabets? alphabets are meat,
                    pasai tekhnai brotoisin ek
            the Fire Stick
(breaking down the complex animal protein chains
                            assimilate
make them like unto,
                us or ours, flesh /
                                (bulghur-cracked
spelt- swells of itself in water
                    needs no cooking, no
vessel's heat
        of Arabs & where
did we come in?
                (Dickens & Dumas products of excessive meat

(what did happen
was it took several hundred years to
restore zoostasis,
                animals in landscape
                (wat we could eat

A spoon of strawberry jam

                       full to sweeten our syntax)
how many english words make american propositions?
) Flushing avenue, i.e., Whores for the Brooklyn   Navy Yard
late deceas'd)
          whores / Theory of Sex,
american punishment: get it reglar,
                          prickly pear.
Taste this coffee // Theory of sex
            recondita armonia
(tenore con gazzo), recondite harmony
by which we *found* (a woman
                      12th C. Europa
((women
      (Uranus, lie quiet)
                    recondite harmony
(harmonia) by which (*Die Wahlverwandschaften*)
              we are related   (passive-voice)
no middle in america, no *Luomai*, we are
Salvation babies, saved people, Messiah's men, not
Messiah men)
         Theory (theoria) of sex, not, the generations,
whores are criminals, buggers are executed, Edw. II
(passive-voice, no *luomai* in american)
recondite harmony
         by which blent
we lift our colloidal identities beyond our time (haha
Many marriages & Mr. Steppe-Wolf,
                  her identity
body summon'd this
         (12th-C. Europa : "springtime." Maia,
John Wieners in the Common, last Boston man to dig
the Union Living)
         her body summoned   (active-voice)
all this.
    No *luomai* in american.

2 · A BOOK CALLED *IN TIME* (1971)

So the theory of sex is to enrich american Grammar,
(old men come at dirty words.)
                             But the nature of the
sexual *revolution* (not the nature of sex))
is verbal
           (word) — we rediscover (after 2400 years)
*L*ogos,
       ſpermatic our-own-brand words, which is
(1980 it should be here) ((i heard — in act))
                       The middle-voice in america.
cf. Mr. Lansing's Burden of Set I,
& Mr. Olson's Grammer in his golden "book," PROPRIOCEPTION]
Now Messrs Rockefeller Reagan & Romney
the three premature old gentlemen with the scythes
preside at the birth of Magnus Annus
                           (it is only at New
Year that the Old Year
is celebrated in public print))
Who are these old men & what do they want?
They are the witnesses of the new grammar
     called into being for its sake,
foul-matter of the printing press, the unrevised draft.
The slack catgut we (are) propose (d) to
           pull taut &
pull the sound from, new song &c.
Homer made his meanings.
Do they suppose Hesiod & Homer to be Tennysons?
They had no book. They made
     the republic
their dreams taught them had flourished & been forgot by unworded Dorian men
i.e., (Theory of sex)
we put whores in jail because Mycenae lost its tongue
       & Knossos is laid waste. (passive-voice)
So that when men can begin to ſpeak
the jailhouse rocks.
          (Cool: shut up & enjoy it).
(Projective verse is middle voice.)

A test (LZ) for poetry: could a republic Look to & find
its Olympos & Troad therein?
                    What is this american
myth of the naked woman
no one knew before we said it so (theory of sex)?
A man could stand up on a hill
                            (the englishman knew
& pile word on exact word
            — *luomai*
& anoint himself forever in the presence of friends
                & deliver our himselves.
Horse-opera. A man could,
                Areopagus.
                        Oath of the Athenian,
a man could stand

could stand against
with voice & hand)
                himself the re-
                flex of all his acts

2 · A BOOK CALLED *IN TIME* (1971)

for the Waiblings

                      or faithful remnant
      of an empire
more plausible than
                ours (our
      current american, post-1786
                      headless horseman of Sleepy
    Government riding
                    hard blind over the world)
the trouble,
the trouble
          with decentralization
the trouble with decentralization as a way of state

is the vacuum it creates at top

plainly & rightly
awaiting Cæsar
          but
               fixes no process (Gallia
         whereby Cæsar may be brought forth
SO THAT
         Mr. Johnson II holds the place of Cæsar &
(since only the strong
centre can hold
         & even a dummy like himself can see it)

holds.

And since he did not mix water & wine on the cold Sequana & did not march in rags through the Lombard states

he has no claim on the crown we honor
                      but maybe
                before he crumbles
                      may yet disperse
the nonsense of these fifty
states.

    , All feofs forts & taxes to the emperor.

LABRYS: *TWELVE MATTERS*

Labrys

twin axe

not domestic
utensil

but godform
tool

        (chops all our wood
   to begin for all men the making new
        (not a syllabus, give *this*,
  a set of specific tasks —

(trace
of our first instructors

      matters
  which will be our masters,
       some feeding for the
  intelletto.

2 · A BOOK CALLED *IN TIME* (1971)

1. Mare Nostrum

a) history from Würm glacial on
b) koinonia
c) linguistic community,
    Chadwick AND Gordon,
    "6" "7" "plough" "earth"
d) & etymologies of,
    "silver"
 solve
    & discover the paths
 to the first altars

                      (here & passim:)
                            basis:
                      Phenomenology
                        of Chronicle
                        & Folklore

(post Christum:
  a) relations, e.g., between
    Ireland & Egypt, Arabs.
  b) Glastonbury & its publicity
  c) Irish history from *Bk of Con-*
    quests up thru Keating)
: Let it be noted that there exists & must exist
a relation of truth between *any* reported datum
& *some* 'actual' event, fact or understanding.
Find the relation (s).
                (No thing is to be discounted as
              "monkish legend" or "folklore")

                (read the 1st bk of Herodotus as
                theory & the 2nd book as method in
                practice, for a *sense* of *historia*
                not approached again till our time)

2. Central Asia

This is a (the) big work:

>needed: Russian Persian Chinese Arabic
>>Kurdish Tocharian Turkish
>>'Mongol' Tibetan &c. &c.

who will open this world?

(given parameters that are presently crazy:
 Vedic, Avestan, Luristan, Roerich
 Gurdjieff, Aurel Stein, Sven Hedin
 Marco Polo, Tartar Relations,

>Iranian (extant) technics,
>>Persian tractates on how to do things,

&c. &c.

>from the Druses to Peking, or Sakhalin
>>for all we can tell,

shamanismus,
>what has gone on
minimally between Gobi & Trebizond,
10000 yrs unknown,
>there are starting points
>>but late in time.

Best start I've seen is Teggart's *Rome & China*.

Item: Nestorians ('who don't eat horse')

Item: Arabo-Persian 'mystical' poetry

Item: Christendom & Islam

>— hallajiya
>— derwishes of Konya
>— derwishes of Vienna!

>*Anwar* of Ibn al Arabi
>>"servant of the
>>>law"

2 · A BOOK CALLED *IN TIME* (1971)

    Giovanni
    Bernardone
    detto
    Francesco,
    stigmatic
(Asín Palacios on Dante)
     of what angel
   or Peacock Malek?)

        eis ten polin Istanbul
       Mikelgarth,
           the Big City
       of the Vikings,

   Item: the 'conversion' of the dynasty of Kiev.

3. The place itself

  ("your spot")

  each
  place
    on earth
  makes its own specific
  energy
  specifically
     available
  (learn to avail)

The Matter of Laurasia & Gondwana
place itself, dimensions of the room
  our space, our room,
ocean & atmosphere & continental drift,
ocean & core
magnetic 'field' of the earth
       (cf. Heezen's work)

Our place in the sun,
      & what that might mean.
To get to this work (Laurasia & Gondwanaland)
    : Olson,
        in verse & prose,
            &
Geology the academic science currently in
    most need of workers, & most rewarding to,
where the action of necessity must be, after
    this great biochemical generation.

4. The uses of earth

Œcology
    (& towards a general, human,
    use of all we know)

archeobotany

ethnobotany
    (&, by extension,
        ethnotaxonomy in genl)

    (paleobotany! — Siberia)
= towards a Universal Herbal,
            in which
    native (= the users') taxonomy stands
    side by side with Linnaeus & after,

in which, for any name, is given a
full account of properties:

    a) fabled
    b) literary
    c) cultic
    d) clinical
        , the Value (Virtue)
of ALL beasts & plants

(in which clearly the isobars of vegetation
    areas & terrains will be palimpsestical
   with the isobars of language-as-it-takes-notice
   and with the isobars of humans-use-it)
all this towards
a Universal Mirror of the Biosphere,

namely, whereof *does*
               life on Earth consist?

Who lives in this house
       (name, rank & serial number)

Lore of this house: œcology of a
     newly discovered earth.

"everything is in the room, but not necessarily near the door"

5. Sound (also called M u s i c)

acoustic no definition of interval?

    i.e., œcology of sound needed,

relationships, pitches *as such*

(how many Hz in Dreivierteltakt?
                                o=2)
: in psycho-physiological exploration
      of "pitch" "interval" "rhythm"
(not impressionistic accounts
                but *tracking*
the neural pathways.

(How # is?)
        Where does what grab you?

              A human intelligence must have both these
              matters (4 & 5, the different sources & natures
              of what comes into us from earth or air)

absolutely solid, at least valid for the geo-
graphical limits experienced. (*No Greek
sacrifices a camel*, as it is said.)
          It seems
to say the least reprehensible that we (= sum
of recorded data in us) know less about these
matters now than a Druid did or a Sioux of 60
years ago.
       Thru skilled Unlearning & humility
before living things, return to a *sense* of all
that lives around us. In us. Is us.

6. Traditionary sciences

(those reservoirs of exact delineation
& approximate prediction): as,

   a) *astrology*
           wch is not prophecy,
is signature, *character*
signed upon a man
   (by the hypothesis: by his birth)
in the light of which
his actions arise,
        i.e.,
            (if astrology
does nothing else, it quickens our
sense of:
ηθος ανθρωπω δαιμων
   that is, a man's character is his
           daimon,
  "fate"
    , he is what he does.

Thus the 'predictions' of astrology
are readings of characteristic
gestures & behavior,

>   parable of the
> mongoose & the tarantula on its back
> Crossing Ganges:
>   (I'm sorry,
>   it killed us both,
>   but it is just my nature to bite)

b) *ethnoastronomy*
>   organization of
>   percept in functional & meaningful
>   ways:
>   as correlative & objectifi-
>   cation of astrology:
>   as invention
>
>   as discovery.

c) *invocational magic*
>   transformations
>   of energy in identity,
>   identity as tool,
>   controlled perception

d) *cheiromancy & graphology,*
>   nexus of
>   'environment' & behavior,
>   signs of, on.

to wch might be added, modern (not traditional)
>   the
>   e) *kinesthesiology*
>   (work of Birdwhistell)
>   or whatever model science he's
>   using now,
>   i.e., the linguistics of
>   stance & gesture & bodily habit,
> full circle with the start of language,
>   body as mean*ing*.

128

Attention:

(excursus re: Occult)

publicity for the occult is a contradiction in terms, nonsense & nonsense spread thin. If it's public, it's not what you're looking for, since what you're looking for is everywhere, & therefore must be hidden as well as open, guarded as well as free. The hidden is: the unNoticed. Start looking.)

7. Techniques of Enstasy

a) Feeding, eating, chemistry of *bios*.
Ingestion . "poison / potion"
What is a drug.
What is food.
Homeopathy.
what is a Similar?
This is one door to the Signatures,
        the Rimes.
Eat Light.
b) tantra. en / ergy   praxis of energy,
                             in force.
c) 'identity'
d) merkavah • up in the in • arrival at the within.
e) *hal • maqam*
f) contemplatio.
g) dhikr : exercise of consciousness

: internal genealogy.

(after all our schisms,
startling revelations concerning the *Filioque*)

8. Techniques of Enstasy

the going out, & the going all the way out

a) love's geography
b) witchcraft, western.
c) ritual magic
        Crowley the only authority here

d) sex as revolution,
   magic as politics
               (beyond the fashions of
                these things, a perennial
                awareness & necessity)
e) Bardo
f) Jeremy Taylor
g) Jakob Böhme.

9. Shape

schaft/scaap/scop
            ('inscape' morphemically useful)
the function & meaning of *contour*

a) human, humanus, plausibly connects with
   humus, the ground, i.e., the intelli-
   gent animals that walk on the ground,
   that (to be specific)
        follow the contours
   or shape the contours of their own.
   Thus we are biologically bound to "shape"
b) Terminus : edge : limit : boundary
c) 'Platonic' solids
d) *topology*,
          properties of contour,
          as paradigm & paradise
e) here, if anywhere, to reassemble the
   old hierarchy of correspondences &
   signatures, the
            Resemblances
   by perception of which a man learns
   the world, his own attentions, his own
   capacities
f) & learns how to follow the lines that lead to Her.

10. Story

(Narrative. How we tell. How is told.
What tells. What is told.)

muthos & logos do not separate in usage
                till Pindar.

a word, what is it, a telling,
a science of utterance?

"Writing wants to go on"
                        (— Gertrude Stein,
in whose 4 essays in *Narration* we may
find a beginning).

a) Thousand nights & a night.
b) Mishle Sendabar & Petrus Alfonsi.
c) Jesus's parables.
d) Mulla Nasruddin
e) fabliaux
f) Miss Stein
g) Mr. Dorn
h) is there any meaning to this phrase:
    experimental narrative forms?

Cf. Stith Thompson's great *Motif Index* — is
      the motif then a germ of story,
& if so, what of the sense we have that the
story telling is the story told?

Cf. Frobenius' *Atlantis* collection of Märchen.

How do we say?
How do we tell?

Does highly developed verbal ritual (rite or
liturgy) operate against tale-telling, against
the tale-scop? (Hopi & Navaho as over against
Winnebago; the unliturgical pre-Christian Irish
and the unliturgical Muslims pre-eminent for
story telling as such?)

What are the minimal parameters of a
                        narrative event?

Information-theoretical methodologies of use
here. How much makes a story?

11. Time & (or as) dimension

this wd not be impossible here:
a total proportional table
        of the biological times
        of all species
towards an absolute definition of time,
= elapsed reality as perceived,
                        — how long is long?
(Since we insist on quantifying time, or rather
on Time as Quantity, how do these quantities
relate in different cycles of life.

Towards a definition of Now.

12. The Nation

or that which is insistently here & now

a) *The Land*

    cf. Third Matter, above.

    towards an exact survey (even in the li-
    teral sense not yet accomplished) of all
    the land & waters of,
    ecosystems, faunal geography, phytogeography,
    i.e., the *real* "States" United by Ocean

    with the fond hope that humans will be
    reckoned eventually as physical & cul-
    tural parts of ecosystems, both responsible
    & response/able thereto

    (cf. work of Sauer, Anderson)

b) *"Indians"*

The great from & persistence,
     & as para-
digms of the availability of social order
from terrain & necessity,
      past 'preference'
— Beothuks, what to them?
— why were the 'Hopewell' territories
 empty when 'we' came?
— these Delawares, the first inhabitants
 of the eastern megalopolis
     (wch still
doesn't spread into Iroquois areas,
still follows the Delaware coasts &
estuaries & inlands)
     why do we know so
little of them? of the eastern Al-
konquins in general?
— Hopi claims: shd precipitate at last
 a consideration of whether a tribe or
 culture ever makes anything up out of
 pure fantasy — what are the roots of
 tribal information?

Every fragment of tribal procedure & tribal
legend defines us. Their claims are our
instructions.

c) *Americanistics*

of which, it will be clear,
 politics the least important,
  least characteristic phase,
& most slipshod in time)
     Brandan's scramble
     Flateyjarbók
     Landnámabók

2 · A BOOK CALLED *IN TIME* (1971)

    Cabeza de Vaca

    Melville

    City history
            (e.g., Breukelen
              & Shawmut & St. Francis)

      Town history

   County history

  pedology & then:

Rivers & mountains

                              note that
                              Plato's *Politeia*
                              (called *Republic*!)
                              is NOT complete
                              without the
                              dream of
                              Er the Pamphylian,

                            | State
                            | depends for any
                            | possible
                            | meaning
                            | on a previous
                            | clarity
                            | about the
                            | nature of
                            | (what is it a)
                            | man.

Gastronomy & costs
      (i.e., 'social' history)
getting right down there
    to the place
        itself

(New Haven ordinances
ca. 1680
have been at length
'humanized')
America the Industry of
(telos as) Personal Liberty

   sidereal time
      price of wheat

   height of the steeple

& age of the
      steamboat captain himself,

   down to the

     ground

2 · A BOOK CALLED *IN TIME* (1971)

Language is space

10 · XII · 70

THREADS 3 : ROBERT SAYS

What a great company we were, what a fantastic chevere I was permitted to be part of. The company of those days — like Gerrit Lansing's wonderful phrase "the company of love / safe in the garden that is themselves." How can anyone work without a company? Olson used to say that Shakespeare was what he was because the actors were all there, and all of them playwrights too. And that Duncan would have been Shakespeare had he had the Company.

There we were. A group of close friends. The great Paul Blackburn the eldest, the clearest, the best established in a world of letters. He brought us not only the sharpest attention to syllable, pause, line length — music, in other words — that I had ever encountered or even thought of — I'll say more about him. But he was my link to Pound, whom he had known, and corresponded with. Blackburn with his meticulous but exuberant translations of the Provençal poets — restricting himself in his pietas to those poems only that Pound had not translated — and his own sculpturally vivid registrations of love in the city — they moved me more than Proensa but they couldn't have been "found" trobada, without Proensa.

The rest of us were more of an age: Jerome Rothenberg bringing his vast enthusiasm for any poetry that wasn't the Anglo-American canon, who brought us strange treasures from otherworlds (via the translations of translations we all did in those days), but most importantly from so many worlds he knew and strove in: Yiddishkeit and Seneca, Navaho and Polish — all the influences he was going to blend in that great structure of ethnopoetics he was to construct over the years. But most of all back then what got me was his work from the contemporary Germans, Celan above all — and Rothenberg was the first to bring Celan into American poetry. So there are two close friends bringing to their friends Ezra Pound and Paul Celan — do you see the excitement, the "beautiful contradictions" (Tara's great phrase, meaning elsewise) of those days? Rothenberg too, with his wife Diane, the anthropologist who poured a lot of sheer fact and lucidity and sagacity into our discourse, were the social presence that united us — their big apartment way uptown between Broadway and the river, was the welcoming Sealed Garden of our endless palaver.

And George Economou (with whom I had founded the Chelsea Review, now Chelsea, only to abandon it when it lost its focus, and with whom I went on to found Trobar, which was, small as its lifespan, one of the two "classic" embodiments of Deep Image, along with Rothenberg's Poems from the Floating World), George brought mediaeval lyric, Spenser's dream epic, Chaucer's versecraft he and I had both been studying when we met at Columbia, but he also brought modern Greek poetry, a language native to him. Kavafis and Elytis and Gkatsos were the ones that stood out for me. I had learned of Kavafis (as Cavafy) from Durrell and Forster, but only as a presence, a mood, a wise old voice — but from Economou I heard Kavafis, the craftsman, the young but wearying lover whose love was spent on vowels, his phrases looped around the beloved's half-reluctant throat. I can still hear George speaking the tumble of his syllables, a-óratos thíasos na perná — this was another way of hearing into the heart of the poem.

Armand Schwerner was there with his native grasp of French, and there too he gave us the blessedly divided world, the crazed inventiveness of Michaux (my favorite at the time) alongside the solemnity of Paul Claudel, whom Armand couldn't quite take seriously, but couldn't quite dismiss either. I remember a reading when Michaux's "Mon Roi" and Claudel's "The Muse Who is Grace" both got read... But this was a Schwerner who did all that in the context of his joyous and detailed readings of Wallace Stevens — amazing to me, because Stevens had always been my secret altar, and his long poems ("Adagia," "An Ordinary Evening," "The Comedian") had seemed the closest anyone had come to what I was after.

And my friend from CCNY, David Antin, always eroding the easy lyric, insisting on the intelligential, the acute. He tried so hard to take me in hand and chasten my lust for the gorgeous.

His distaste for lyric lushness did finally become a guide to me — one I didn't always or even often follow, but kept in mind, still do. And his measured, witty dance around the edge of prose, working already at what would become his "measure," the spoken grace of intelligent discourse — he more than any kept us close to the acerbic eroticism of André Breton and the surrealists, who in a sense were our truest generators. And his spoken/written work over the years has been a pole star of intelligence and clarity, spilling out of what poets usually talk about into what we must learn to talk about, everything.

So many more in that company, the painter and critic Amy Mendelson (or Amy Goldin) who brought me and the rest of us directly into the heart of the action in painting just at the moment when painting was the best thing happening in New York. Her still unpublished long theoretical assessment of Georges Duthuit's huge anthological rebuttal of Andre Malraux's imaginary museum was a text that guided my awareness of art as specific generator of discourse, and a vital guide to just how alive language can be when talking about it. And she, curiously or not, was the one of all of us who most abruptly and usefully saw and saw through our poems. Hers was the reaction that I wished for and feared most — she taught me something like pudor, a certain sense of shame a poet must have, not to be always I I I-ing. And intelligence the surest weapon against the cant of feeling.

So that was the fervor we were in when I first began to discover other contemporaries who had been through some of what I passed through, and found their own brilliant way towards our "vulgar eloquence," that is, the beauty of the vernacular itself: Robert Duncan above all, Jack Spicer, and the more austere Charles Olson [...]

in conversation with Simone dos Anjos & Pietro Aman (2006)

3.

A BOOK OF THE COMPANY
"Heaven is other people"

— Directiones Cordis —

STATEMENT

        [John Martin asks me of NEW YORK
           when I was there & certain ones of us
              began to speak,
   & what came]
in from everywhere,
           primitifs from
Rasmussen's Copper Eskimos & the Trésor
de Poésie universelle no wilder than Neuilly,
               from the broken
Andalusia of assassinated Lorca that groped
its way out of the subway gratings, naranjeiros
& olive trees where rank ailanthus
                (David Antin
first told me the name)
           stood before & still & ever
after, a short-lived tree, a tree of heaven, tree
in Brooklyn subway cuts & east side back yards:
                    city
where the white language of america died in the
sad old men's bars & the new
             vernacular of the
Emperor Frederick Augustus, spade majesty & Cuban
baseball arose in our mouths
           (aforesaid by Ezra
into our time)
        everywhere,
& what (I must be clear) it was: people)
Schwerner from Belgium, actual foreign
country, big concept man who learned
more painfully to sing, taking pains, than
anybody I ever saw, came thru, tuneful intellect
(New York in late '50s, against the backdrop of Corso bopping in

sonnets & lacey forms, a nice guy sans cultura) & Schwerner with the proletcult lycée vienna out of his ears (which when I first overheard were attending Mr. Stevens)
        learned also
easy upper west, never a prole)
the words of this tribe (uptown tho it was,
          to sing
out of his head.
    From everywhere
(& what, more important than ourselves, was elapsing on the east side: the giant forms of the men who'd been some way to Black Mountain, who seemed mean & hard & over in love with truckdrivers & poolhalls & war books, who were reading Raymond Chandler while Rothenberg read Buber, that tough thing that has so come to say, & stay, & mellow, Oppenheimer & Sorrentino, amis de Creeley, & Blackburn who had never been anywhere but where he was, all over the world, who was the bridge, & the authentic Key to the Cidy)
        from
everywhere, that was the colloid,
no orthodoxy for us, no doxy,
     nobody pays for tail in the City,
  no teleology
      what is here is everywhere,
       what is not here is nowhere),
so that all this is false, being history, & the only thing that would finally be of use would be tapes of certain talks I had with Economou from 57 to 61, certain tabletalk around the Rothenbergs' pork molé 60 & 61, food is as much history as anything else, who we were or were not sleeping with, what bar on Leroy street shocked Eshleman new from Indiana, why he & I drank a bottle of El Cerrito in a backyard on 7th St. & still could not be clear, our, my, one's constitutional incapacities,
         & Eshleman's
work, arching over the intervening time, arrests me with his sure bodily awareness of flow, of the poem *as* flow and hence *as* continuity, *the* continuity in the mad agonizing space between body

and body, and to talk of anything but his work, our work, wd be
personal histories
                   and as the sequel shows, what always happens is
personal history
                         when what was intended was a public gesture
    yet in an art where there are no public excellencies, where the
private did & does matter, where the public gesture (*other* than the
work) breeds swift tyranny,
                           these people were working to come through.
Hasid Rothenberg
                 saintly man fond of artful silences, whose prolong-
ed trances in foreign tongues hold him where he had been, & where
Quetzalcoatl went to heal his flesh corrupt with false longings, &
where the sun
healed over alchemy & politics,
                           who didn't trust Kennedy,
who fancied the smell of burnt flesh unseverable
from our consciences,
                 who tried to go back in time's
womb & be born again,
                   a savage tending his dong,
song, sang
        out loud & wailed rabbinic
& came to supper with spiny fish in his bleeding hands,
            'my ocean, my ocean'
who did not know Greek,
             & la belle Diane,
that same & I made a beeline for, New Years Eve 59/60,
sleek lady with complex rhythms & ostensibly
simple desires, who loved the far-out & declared
herself & sought everyone's good fortune before
her own,
    (who introduced me to Jackson Mac Low, the man I'd seen
for years, face of the young Pound now his face &
more like himself, all over town,
                     and Jackson taught time, time in &
of the poem,

whose work goes on & goes
on in massive neglect of our theories, obedient
to the processes, no less verbalized, he incessantly
makes up,
    a huge body of work, a man who writes all day
long, who did the work in a city where — constitutionally —
work is to be shunned)
       & Diane brought us to those
places, the great loft on Chambers street, biopsy of
new music, measuring itself ever, & she glad to
carry the new dances into old places,
         she whose own
work was & is uncontaminated by second
hand theory, is incorrigibly itself in finding
out what & why things happen,
        who most used the poem
as a heuristic machine, a sighting glass, a kit
for feeling the fingerprints of the world,
         detective,
who has never sounded like anyone but herself,
          she,
from Whittier, further west even than Economou,
         a well-
done man from raw Montana, oro y plata,
        who watched
the signs & remembered the gangs sloping off gravel
on the railway, surely not Dorn's CB&Q? golden
spiked Union Pacific of our no longer primitive
dreams?
    primitive, natives of our own hungers, needs. (& Levertov,
putting some or all of us down, or was it only me, said This is a poetry of
desire, not of need. A very subtle thing to say, but the distinction was hers,
not there in the world, where *hunger* is unquenchable & Eros & Vision, &
need a philanthropist's cold way of seeing the statistics of it. Wd she speak
ill of Eros? Yet she found something, calling it wrongly, that was wrong
there, in the air of that time of work, a *voulu* insistence on the distant &

the Strange, often to the loss of kitchen & subway & bed, the works of dailiness in a city

but they were men in a trap, who mistook the sunlight itself for their cage, & the ripeness of flesh around them for archontic evil & (so persuaded) thus needed a magic out of the trap, a language, an alchemy of the Tour St. Jacques or obsidian self-torture of the Aztec priest, so they, or we, were not pastoral

detected no order,

made

order when we could,

a syntax of objects, an Ernst, a Spoerri table

but talked too much. O how we talked too much, primitive & deep image & duende, blithering slogans & all the gimcrack foolishness of the articulate young.

(Sd. Rothenberg to me: we'll be sorry if we give 'em a slogan! & so we were)

but there *was* a splendor, light reflected back upon us from those words we used, tried to stand under & be worthy of,

&

the words were worth, held us to what we'd promised, bound us to our premises, measured us, indicted us (Rothenberg & me, who'd done most of the talking, at least what got to print; Economou reluctant and thoughtful reserved, Rochelle Owens laughing at the clumsy words we'd prosed around what we & she cd so much better sing, Wakoski slyly at the sidelines, poking fun, Mac Low scoffing openly, alert.)

& now may be seen those words float back in the casual dissertations of gents who have not troubled to read further than the slogans

(Lorca, forgive us your duende. Nightmare of our nights, forgive us the word we thought to hold you at bay with)

But now we've vanished into our lives of work, and I see them seldom, perhaps they see themselves seldom, we all have new friends too & different places & live elsewhere, & that makes all the difference in personal history, in

the making of americans
                   & the poems alone break out of the isolation,
alone (as ever) save us from death,
               & it was our thought to get blood-life back in the *line*
          wch is syntax & history & beast-desire, when since the '20s we have been assailed day & night by noise, false or suspect informations, caressive syntax in all media, & all men have shut down, banked cortical measures against the blast of words
                 & we had to get through, the line, the hypersyntactic, the silence, to disturb the normal deadening flow, the line, life/line, to get thru to your ears rightly stuffed against madness
    how to reach you   [Whitman's *you*]
     (there
were those who trusted the knifepoint of haiku, thus got thru your defenses but had nothing to tell you, who exhausted themselves in the penetration,
   (popularity of that form = emissio præcox, as national ill)
(& there were those who sought to chat, posed as friends colleagues & friendly storekeepers, who 'sought a theme' & found an easy measure of verse, to reassure, soothe, but in your dark you wanted, more?
                                     (& there
were those who, lacking all cool & all cunning, but with some force, shouted out loud, sometimes at you, relevancies of green leaf & thigh, thorns & chaotic desperate promises that your bodies had a lease on life no social contract could abrogate,
                & some of them chanted primitive to you, muttering the words & handling the bones, casting spells wet & dry,
   & this was their need, to reach you before the world was empty & the grasslands grew up again over all that we wanted.
                           The poets I've been about & at shared an intention to speak without the construction of an order or neo-classic structure. This was freeing. This was danger. This was the possibility of getting trapped in your own habits of utterance for lack of a conscious ear. But the freedom was uppermost in mind, no barriers,

no imposed decorum. Music was what happened, or was supposed to
happen, when you talked, wasn't a special attention.
Anti-style. Anti-rhetoric. To strip to the least
(that most durable of poetic resolutions)
& the least was: image
                    subverbal, translatable, i.e., (hence in *Floating
World* & in Rothenberg's, Antin's, Economou's worlds the importance
of translation: Neruda, Breton, Celan, Lorca, the Primitives (seen qua
Levy-Bruhl, not Levi-Strauss))
        ((whereas to be able to translate, say, Zukofsky
into German wd be equivalent to remaking that language))
                                                        the least
(& hence, by that bittersweet wisdom of Athens & Crimea, the most)
was image
        & here these nomadic foragers fringed the territory of the
haiku-chippers)
            Rothenberg's own *Sightings* are the clearest documen-
tations, as well as the beginning of a push I think sought to discover the
image *within* logos / verbal / syntactic
                                        ((as Ken Irby observed of Pushkin's
I loved you once, a poem without *an* image,
                                or as Spicer's researches nailed
up on the door in clear view, the word *is* primal))
                                                    in Rothenberg's
Sightings the poem happens between the lines of static, lines that are
of words, lines sloughing off words, the serpent renewed, everything
coming out of the sciences, the whirling legs of Magnum Chaos, & the
whistling demons surface
                        to punish us — & so many of the poems of his
& them & us & of that time had as their intention (cd that be part of
Levertov's meanings?   too much intention, too little attention?)
had as their intention the forced encounter of the reader with the
abominable, to rub our faces in the rotting flesh that falls before our
economy. Horror never far; accurate as that is to our time, it made a
bluster in the verse at times,
a pre / occupation
                rather than the verbal ground seized & fully occupied.

Now all this was happening from the late '50s onward, & my own part in it maybe from 60 thru 62. It was the city, & it was the fertilities. *Personal* fertilities far more than I knew (I who always too easily believed in theories & public intentions). And now that we've variously entered our several works, & can share only as we share with the world, as it finally must be, what matters is that we did bear our divergencies forward without contamination, offered or suffered the encouragements of a business that is never easy.

Where we were wrong was to speak of deep *image* when the word we wanted was *depth/thing, tehôm*. We could have spoken better of the opening door, or the wellhead, or the well to which the hawk swoops to drink, joining air & earth & water with his own fiery nature. The word *image* botched it, when generations of critics have debased that word into an easy theory that denies intellect & denies music. It was the deep thing we meant, that the poem was itself the battle with Kur, or with the dragon of the deep waters who locks up the fertilities of earth.

The poem is that, but the poem is subject to its own laws, its own depths and heights and battlefields. And the battle with the underlords of diminution and cruelty is always personal,

& there are no orthodoxies below the skin.

Our several adventures thereafter would have to do with word, only earth of the poem. From which everything comes, from everywhere. Past the limits of our intentions. The hard work of attention begins. *Trobar* stops meaning to find & begins to mean: make.

Last of the materialists, the poet salutes the morning alone.

(*Black Sparrow* pamphlet, 1968)

ON PAUL BLACKBURN

PAUL BLACKBURN · *IN ON OR ABOUT THE PREMISES*

Blackburn. The AleHouse poems. The Bakery Poems. Hidden behind those quaint terms are saloon & restaurant. Eat drink and watch the girls pass. Nobody I ever heard can watch like Blackburn, eye faster than a lizard's tongue. & just so the tongue goes too, speaking a way (we should one day get around to studying) that ambles its way into the solid shape & dignity of poem. We hear him see.

The lone eye (walking around), the lone eye finds company, when it talks we hear. Sounds like. Never takes his eyes off and everything his eye lands on takes life from the touch. Clearly Blackburn never met a boring man or a woman not worth a glance. They're all worth. I mean, maybe, we're all worth, worth it.

Maybe these poems are better than we deserve. To call him compassionate misses. Passion part is right, everybody in the act, every act right in the center of itself. And the detachment (from & into time, so we can get it too) writes it down:

> It always is,
> always was
> this way, Ed,
> all the time.
>
> It is not that it does not happen.
> It does,
> and there is no help for it.
> And
> there is no end to it,
> until there is.

Poet of the City. I have never detected him in a generalization. Can city be anything at all but people held in the eye & heart? known, talked to, accurately heard ?

Cape Goliard, whose books are always handsome, does this one very glossy, with good drawings by Michelle Stuart, a woman whose work we could bear to know better.

"The Watchmen" big poem seen not too long ago by some in *The New Yorker*, ends the book, a great piece on the testicular origin of the alphabet, or am I joking, I mean (I mean that it means) that LORE is continuity among men, over the years, fences. Letters of alphabet also the 'family jewels.'

Blackburn. The evidence of his care here, all senses, care, cura, the young priest in a very old parish, knowing it from the street, careful eye, responsible for the souls he meets, taking us musically into his care.

(Caterpillar #7, 1969)

INTRODUCTION TO PAUL BLACKBURN'S *THE JOURNALS*

The Journals to my mind are Blackburn's quintessential work, and demonstrate the way his work knew to go, the power of music he could charm out of everything that came his way, or even looked as if it were thinking about it. The poems and entries are also his last work. The latest writing in it comes up to six weeks of his death in September 1971. From his papers, it is clear that in those last weeks he tried to collect the Journal pages together, and did sense them (as many of his readers from 1968 onward did) as a continuous & coherent book. The present text follows generally the order of what he had collected together and erratically paginated as *The Journals*. When repetitions, revisions, and versions have been taken away, our inheritance in this particular amounts to a typescript of some 160 pages.

Power. The tip he took from Pound was not a tune, but a way of finding. Of the poets working in these past three decades, I would say Blackburn is the paradigm of the processual — the one who most allowed his life and work to intertwine, who sought and found in the happenstance of experience a mysterious beauty called music when we hear it, that is, the Form made clear. His work reads the wayside signs and covert signatures, and is alert to every coincidence, analogy, trick of the light.

To say these things amounts to saying that Blackburn was a formal poet — he sought form and found form. He worked hard enough at the trobadors and their prosodies to qualify, had he chosen, as a walking book of meters and 'forms' — but those collected shapes were not the forms that concerned him. What form can be discovered as one moves through life? So his forms are always innovative, sometimes mimetic (because he loved descriptions and people and simple alignments and catalogues), but more often directly expressive of the interaction of the thing seen with the man seeing.

And very much he loved to see. Early in 1971 it became apparent to Paul and his friends that something was very wrong with his body. By mid-March, that something had been called cancer, with all the death-knell sounded. But it seems to me, without sentimental hindsight, that a few years before, certainly as early as spring 1968, Paul had intimations of death upon him. From that point forth his work, especially *The Journals,* reads like a *carni vale,* a joyous farewell to the flesh of the world. Spain, Italy, Occitan, the places he had loved and worked in on and off for twenty years, now saw him again for the last time. And the new places, California and the western mountains, he began to rack up among his knowns.

Blackburn died young, as these things are reckoned in longæval America, but his farewell was leisurely, intensely scrutinizing the whole show again. Autumn and harvest, drive the last sweetness into the grape — all the images Europe has given us, from Ausonius to Rilke, of what it means to live on earth and then, suddenly or with warning, not to live there any more. These things talk in Blackburn's last work, strange melancholy unusual in our people, who know how to want with urgency or reject with bitterness, but hardly ever this old world song, relishing, departing, going.

Paradox, not of Blackburn but of America, that the voice that is most our own is truest to the older sequence. Very strange. In New York, which was most his home and center, he could find the sunlight on a wall not different from Barcelona. We can warm ourselves there.

What I most value in *The Journals* is the further transcendence of the closed poem (that museum piece, that haunting but snake-filled urn) his work had long been moving from. And what gave his achievement of the open poem its peculiar power is, in some awful and simple way, just how well he could sing. He is among those to whom we must turn if we would learn how music is not dependent on its earlier conditions or social contexts. So many who have tried to open form (whatever that may mean truly) have cast away (if ever they had it) the sonorous particularity of their own breath, their integral, their own. After the mid-1950s, there is a developing pattern whereby Paul's idiolect in the written language comes closer and closer to his idiolect in the spoken language; far from making the poems bland or conversational, the syntax grows deeper roots, twists, recovers, holds attention as no singsong could. Learning so to be honest in ear and mouth, he spoke his mind. As a result, the falsity of pastoral could not finally attract him, much as he loved olive and goat and maiden. More to his point and his time, he can sing straight (a phrase he used time and again earlier on) from the city and about the city, accepting it as the natural condition of man in a way few other poets have understood. Between the earlier generation of experimenters who imagined taxi dissonance and tohu-bohu represented the city, and the latter-day meta-hicks who turn away, Paul is one of the very few American poets who have been able to address their work sanely and coherently in the midst of the ordinary condition of contemporary man. A man, he is himself everywhere, and everything becomes natural to him. As Pound showed us long ago, the natural is the most difficult to come to, to say.

To the music nothing is trivial. To the composer of these poems, no idle dailiness was without its seed of connection. A New York poet, as they say, happiest in the middle of things, a stranger to scorn. It was all around him, and he could handle it. From what seem the most casual notations of place and event, Blackburn's formal intelligence discovers a new order rooted in content and inextricable from it, even if the deft musician willed it away.

(1975)

3 · A BOOK OF THE COMPANY

ROBERT DUNCAN & THE RIGHT TIME

1.

I am looking at a picture. It is a large color photograph of Robert Duncan, and it came at just the right time. The right time is the deepest, most pervasive, and (to me) the most salvific keynote of Duncan's poetics. And Duncan's instrumentality in the world.

2.

The right time. I had been asked to contribute to this assembly of memorials and *témoignages*, and three poets at once stood forth in my mind (like the past Masters of music who beautifully and eerily address Palestrina in Pfitzner's great opera, at last to be done this very summer in New York).

    Charles Olson. Robert Duncan. Paul Blackburn.
I thought and thought; to those three men I owe so much — stance and sense of work — both because of the fresh new way, *dolce stil nuovo*, they developed that renewed American poetry in the 1950s, and also because of life experiences in which they engaged me. They were masters for me, and very generous men. As it happened, I had just written a brief memorial of Blackburn for another journal, & wanted to rest with that a while, before writing a study of one of his poems, long intended.

3.

I am looking at a picture. It is a color photograph and shows Robert Duncan at the side of the picture, holding, not without a certain amusing awkwardness, a large painting. Duncan seems to be restraining himself from smiling, or his face seems in that mode half clairvoyant and half giggling that anyone who knew him must remember as his — the face of Mrs. Maybe, maybe, or the playful spirit medium.

4.

The painting he holds is not shown completely, cut off by the photo's iron rectangular habits. What we do see is plenty, though. It is Jess's portrait of Robert's mind — though that seems too pompous a way of describing this delicious registration of Items in the House: a portrait of Robert himself, younger, and looking more serious (youth is a serious business indeed), paintings, a bookcase, a candlestick in flame (shades of Arnolfini's wedding — for this also is a portrait of the painter's mind, the house, life, work he shared for so many years with Duncan, his life companion, and hence a portrait of their marriage, where the shy bride is present as the flesh of the painting itself — and no one has ever used impasto with such intimate, domestic sensuality as Jess has.) A hanging Tiffany lampshade before a fragmentary window. A bowl of flowers on top of a bookcase, and some books arrayed. *Pistis Sophia*, the five volumes of *The Zohar*, two spines of the three volumes of *Thrice Greatest Hermes*.

5.

Pictures of pictures. And me looking at a photo of it. It or them? Jess has played, as ever, with the representation of representation. He who has made the greatest collages (in my guess) of our century, or sharing that grandeur only with Max Ernst, is delighted in his own paintings to play the same elaborate ludus — never condescending to *trompe l'œil* — of image and representation, the one wrapped within the other, level upon level. His paintings, like Duncan's poems (but just to breathe this, not to carry on about it), delight in embedding texts and references, the bibelots and hand me downs of a well-stocked mind. Redeeming the sparks of the Glory. G. R. S. Mead's *Thrice Greatest Hermes* stands on the bookcase, the great turn of the century (that century) chrestomathy of the original Hermetic writings, translated and popularized by Mead, the celebrated Theosophist. It is ardent aspiration towards redemption of (or sometimes redemption through) the material world that animates such texts, and that will again and again occur in Duncan's writings, from *Mediaeval Scenes* to the last measure of "The Regulators."

6.

The right time. Forty years ago I was a young man persuaded of myself and my powers, and knew I could do wonders in poetry. At the time, I was caught up in the last-gasp formalisms of the 1950s — pallid imitations of Hopkins, Eddic measures, Welsh meters, Auden, blank verse monologues. I felt a certain perverse pleasure in those things, but could smell as well as the next person the mouse-droppings on them, & see the dry pale moth take flight. Some vital spark was missing in the poets I liked and imitated, yet in the other contemporary work I got to see of an anti-formalist inclination, while I found some vigor, it was all yawp & coarse, scarcely deep-funded in the lore of poetry. For I wanted all things — the measure and the immoderate, the archaic trove of all high poetry but also the vivid 'language of flesh and blood' — itself a phrase as old as Wordsworth. We keep repeating the same experiment, century after century. It's clear we all & always need what I needed then — the archaic and the instantaneous, the moment no less than Merlin.

I began to do what I could, to work away from the habits I had learned, and see whether I could find some music in other ways. For all my reading I was terribly illiterate in what was actually happening. Then one day, at the right time, my friend Hugh Smith (himself a poet of the determinedly regular, anglophile, exalted) put into my hands a copy of a book by Jonathan Williams. The very title punned its way through my defenses: *The Empire Finals at Verona*. This was his Catullus, englished, updated, coarsened, lightened, but also refined, alert, vivid. It was the first book I had seen that suggested to me there was life in an American verse, an American language way. It was the right time.

And then I found — at that little drug store on Sheridan Square — the small square book that came as close to being a best-seller as anything Duncan ever published: the City Lights edition of Robert Duncan's *Selected Poems*. Then on David Ossman's radio program, "The Sullen Art," I heard Duncan reading his "Poem Beginning With a Line by Pindar." It struck me then & strikes me now as the richest enactment of poetry I had ever heard with my ears. By ear you could hear new measures of poetry discovering themselves, falling back into traditional metrics rising into exaltations of formal Shelleyan, Shakespearean language, leveling out into broad powerful music of the sacred ordinary speech of living folk. You could actually hear verse stammer and give way to prose, hear prose in all its different struggle back towards the towers of verse. It seemed a trove of antique power & a school for sense. Not just the luscious musics of the man, but a music that supported, revealed, exalted the operations of mind.

7.

For I had come to realize that the only gift the poet surely has is to disclose to a patient, quiet, often indifferent audience (the shape God takes in our time) the delicate, complex, total operations of the poet's mind — and that articulation of knowing is the only music worth attending to. This is what Duncan seemed to be about, and why the 'narcissism' & 'self-involvement' (that I found people were always quick to blame him for as person and poet) were in fact mere negative labels for an absolutely essential concentration, by the poet, on the only universe the poet truly has to study, observe, report from, & come back singing.

8.

What else does the poet have? The world the poet shares with the audience is expressly words. And only by studying the 'tones given off by the heart' can the poet have anything worth reporting, worth taking out time. And that is where Robert Duncan and Charles Olson, so utterly different, yet always for me an 'ordered pair,' represent the immense possibilities that their masters — Stein, Pound, Lawrence, Williams — had so variously opened.

9.

So there was this Duncan, suddenly, and I realized that (it sounds so dumb to say it, so true, the experience we all have if we are lucky) I was not alone. This man, so unlike me in all his social gesture, his sexual orientation, his sense of order, his poise, his grace — this man was the closest to what I always knew it was possible to become: a poet for whom the old great tradition was still alive, but who still knew the rainy light of Hollywood and the smell of buses, the pervasive, inescapable twist of the beloved through all the day's conduct, all the chambers of the visual. Who did not busy himself forging fake antiques but allowed the vigor of the old music to hold sway in his mind until he could hear himself think. Who was founding — or was it finding — (who can really ever tell them apart, bird or oboe, tree leaves or rushing water?) our colloquial eloquence.

3 · A BOOK OF THE COMPANY

10.

The right time. I sat down this morning to start writing this homage to my dear friend Robert Duncan. I read the news, and the news told me that the princely Thurn-und-Taxis family was selling their castle at Duino on the Adriatic coast, the castle where Rilke wrote the Elegies. How shocked I was! Not that the family is selling it, but that the castle is actually there, actually surviving. That a castle of the mind is also an object of Italian real estate. That the world exists at all is always the strangest news. That there is, or seems to be, something there when I finally get around to opening my lazy eyes.

11.

I sat down to write about Duncan and stared at the picture. A few days ago, Jonathan Williams (whom I got to know years after *The Empire Finals*) and Tom Meyer, whose creative union has been a wonder of the commonwealth for thirty years, and whose friendship has been my delight, paid me a visit. They were carrying a red cat from Carolina to Vermont — fit employment for poets in any age. I told them that I had been invited to write this piece, and asked them what they thought. A blessing, I guess I wanted, some kind of go-ahead. I always seem to be asking for permission. Here was I, persistently heterosexual, trying to write a decent homage to the greatest poet I had known, a poet who insisted on being identified as homosexual, and on locating in his elaborate and excited sexuality the wellsprings of his work. I suppose I was asking them for an idea. Like Mary Baker Eddy, I believe that the real angels are good ideas. Ideas that teach us to go on. To go new.

12.

Jonathan said: I have a picture for you & handed me a print of his color photograph of Robert Duncan holding a painting of Robert Duncan.

The five volumes of *The Zohar*, are, of course, the Soncino Press edition, translated into English by a team of Rabbis including Paul Levertoff, father of the poet Duncan admired so much and felt so warmly towards, Denise Levertov. The translators left out the more arcane tractates of operational magic as unsuitable for the enlightened modern audience to which they brought the classic of Qabbalah —

those treatises are the strange meat of MacGregor Mather's *Kabbalah Unveiled* — a book not shown on Duncan's shelves, though important to the Golden Dawn, and thus to Yeats, of whom Duncan was a singular inheritor.

The books are in the foreground. The work is always in the foreground. The work is what matters. I'm reading Nathalie Blondel's new *Life of Mary Butts* — a writer Duncan spoke of highly, & frequently urged upon his readers and friends. It was Duncan who made me first, and most, aware of Butts, and from him directly or through Ken Irby came the earliest precious tattered Xeroxes of her remarkable work now at last coming back into print. Today in the Blondel biography I find Stella Bowen saying, as she reminisces about Mary Butts: "I should have known that the way to enjoy any artist is to attend to his work and not allow one's self to be confused by that lesser thing, his character."

13.

Mary Butts. Gertrude Stein. Hilda Doolittle. Duncan gave us these writers, or restored them to us. His serious *Stein Imitations* understood Stein not as an influence but a School in which a poet might study and learn the craft. The craft of speaking, of letting writing go on. Stein was a mere celebrity, H.D. a vanished imagist of faded luminary, Butts not even a name, according to the accepted wisdom of the 1950s. Duncan did more than his share in restoring Stein to her rightful, mother-of-us-all status, the Queen of Language, by which all telling is made possible. Duncan aimed us firmly at these women's work, by whom writing and its various registers and genres could be restored. Robert Duncan was more than generous. He gave us not only himself, he gave us others as well — and that is a rare generosity in a poet. The one time I heard Dylan Thomas read, in the flesh as we so rightly say, he spent the first half of his program reading late Yeats — I had never known "The Circus Animals' Desertion" till I heard him read it — and then his own work. An amazing arrogance, an amazing humility conjoined — and to this day I am grateful to Thomas for himself and for opening another door on Yeats. As we are grateful to Duncan not only for his huge symphonies and demanding chamber music, but for his clear bardic eye that caught, sensed, and restored the writers who came before him.

14.

The poet's worst enemy is bitterness. Envy & jealousy of other poets are the sickening, blighting hazards of a calling with few obvious rewards. And often those who have, from Muse or Society won true rewards, rewards like sweetness of life or life companions, do not recognize their own good fortune, do not grasp that they have been rewarded by the same principles to which their work gave voice. Duncan always saw his good fortune, grants or no grants, even though most of his life and most of his work was spent with the smallest presses, the most exiguous — and exigent — audiences. Knowing his good fortune, he had the grace of kindness. While he could be catty, or venomous as a surukuku, when the mood took him, his generosity towards the living and the dead was phenomenal. More a generosity of spirit (like a fan letter he wrote to James Dickey about a poem he'd read and respected — unanswered, *tu sais*) than of deed, it allowed him to praise, welcome, take delight (and therefore creative energy from) the good work of others. If energy is a product of delight, then all the pleasure we take from the good work of others will surely feed our own.

15.

Once when Duncan was staying in my house for a few days, I found him one morning gazing at my stacks of paperback mystery stories arrayed in a great copper-lined cavity meant for firewood. He walked over to the kitchen table and began talking about our affinity, the only time he ever spoke of any such thing, an affinity grounded in the joy of reading. He felt at home in my house, he said, with these piles of thrillers, of sacred trash, since he too read and took pleasure from such things. We discussed them a little while, noting the way certain pieces of our work had been subtly affected by this thriller or that — Ngaio Marsh, Dorothy Sayers, Michael Innes. Then he went on to say how sad he found it to meet so many younger poets, or would-be poets, who took no pleasure in reading, no pleasure in books. How can you write if you don't read? How can you create a powerful new work if the power of such actual works is closed to you? We read, he said, we like to read. We take pleasure, we know how to take pleasure from reading. We learn how to give pleasure through writing. The important thing is the energetic act of reading, of pleasure welcomed through the engagement with the text.

16.

I thought of Duncan's drawings of the Ideal Reader — he'd drawn it I think for that limited edition of *Letters*. It showed what seems to be a woman of middle years, comfy of disposition, seated in her garden, a great sunhat shielding her features, her whole posture 'bent to her book.' That picture is one of the most shocking avant-garde proclamations of its day. A book is to read.

This was 1963. I was understanding that writing spilled out of reading. But that sounds bookish and mandarin — not the worst things in the world, but I wanted more. In Duncan I grasped the balance, a balance I tried to specify in a book title of my own a few years later: *flesh, dream, book* — all the sources of our poetry: experience, vision and reverie, and reading. How could we ever write a poem if we did not know that there was such a thing to be written? And yet we always, always look for it, the poem that presupposes no previous poetry. A poem that is an absolute. Perhaps a hunger for such a poem predisposes humans to imagine a moment of creation ex nihilo, a word spoken out of nowhere.

17.

The right time. Duncan knew what it was. Punning on the French word *Bonheur*, he called happiness the *good hour*. And what made it good? It was the hour that called us to work, the hour that issued through the instrumentality of the poet an articulation of all that was going on in the world. In the mind. A scientist of the Whole, is what I'd call the poet, back in some ravings in the Sixties. Duncan explained the exact instrumentality of that science — the poet writing is itself speaking to itself, while we listen. So of course (he was clear) there could be no traffic in greatness, in calling so-and-so a Great Poet — there was only one great poet, the poet of whom we are all variously, crazily, fingerprint individually, metabolically, literally, tunefully instrumentalities. So our goodness lay not in *what*, but in the fact *that* we are able to declaim. And that sweet doctrina rescued poetry, for me, from the clashing teeth of the confessional and propagandaic, the two molochs of the time I was growing up, when Duncan was the sudden clear voice of poetry I heard speaking in our idiom.

18.

The right time. In the Pindar poem, after telling of Psyche's hard tasks, and all the creatures that had come to help her out, Duncan turns to himself, the deed or task it is to write a poem, this very poem, a word the hour calls out to be written:

> … So, a line from a hymn came in a novel I was reading to help me. Psyche, poised to leap — and Pindar too, the editors write, goes too far, topples over — listened to a tower that said *Listen to me!*

So Jonathan Williams wrote a book that fell into my hands, and jabbed a little chink in my armor, and I began to take notice. Forty years later he comes by, when I need a push, and slips me this photograph he took of Robert Duncan holding the painting of Robert Duncan by Jess.

The photo was taken probably in 1968 or 1969, which is about when I visited Duncan and Jess for the first time at their house in San Francisco. I saw the paintings then, and studied it, and my memories of it then aid my seeing of it now. I saw the whole of it, but memory has ruined the picture even more than the cropping of it by the photograph. I am left with what I feel. And a little bit by what I see. So I am looking at Duncan — he wears a striped shirt, clean and neat over a white tee shirt. His sideburns are full, even bushy, and his almost-smiling face is a little plumper than I remember it, content seeming, well-fed, but with some haunting under the eyes. His arm comes up and crosses over his head to support and balance the top edge of the painting. In doing so, it happens that the hand shields his eyes. The painting reveals a world of art and artifact elaborately indoors (John Muir said to Emerson, Mr. Emerson, yours is an indoor philosophy), but the photo is otherwise — from the weathered grey wood behind Duncan & his painting, we see we're in the back yard, not yet a garden, of the house on Twentieth Street.

He needs to shade his eyes from the California sun. His damaged eyes, the great eagle wandering eyes of him, so disconcerting, so penetrating. Is it the left one, is it the right one, that is the wanderer? I look at the photograph, and can't tell — because the second thing one notices when you look at the photo is that it has been printed backwards: the title of the books are mirror-style, left is right and Duncan's slightly unfamiliar plumpness is the inversion of nature, the 'accidental' *contra naturam* that is so close to the essence of art. And no doubt my own memories have been polarized, magnetized, trivialized, kellyized, many fine specifics of what I see. Of what I saw.

19.

Right time? 1919 when he was born, a year after the war. 1988 when he died, at 69. In the days when he was blocking out *Groundwork* as the summa of his life work, he had planned out, with some explicitness, the work of his seventies, the work of his eighties — the work of my senility, he said, planned already. Perhaps planning such things is enough. How can one plan for an hour that has not come, when what our best work is really is the voice, tone, tell, tale, told of that hour? It was his jest, a bold jest, with time. It pleased him to plan ahead, as it pleased him to conduct his own performances of his latest poems, using a strange cheironomy, his hand waving like Leonard Bernstein's conduction of his own music, but by no means indicating beat or evident rhythm. Instead the hands were more Picasso's hands, inscribing the moment of the poem's out loud onto the visual air. I watched in 1982 and 1983 as he read aloud, over several evenings, perhaps twelve hours of his late work — and always the hand moved, a bird beside the text, a shadow sometimes taking on solidity.

20.

Elsewhere I have written, but that is my story and not his, how twice, in the most literal manner, Duncan saved my life. Save me he did, from wanhope and foolish hauteur and dumb desperation, when I too was "poised to leap." He was the tower who spoke, and like the tower in Apuleius's story, there is no life in the question of whether or not the tower 'liked' Psyche. I have no idea if Duncan liked me — he said more than once that my constant harping in those days on women, on making love, was tiresome — but maybe that was just a playful gay way of telling me he didn't like my work, while generously giving me a way of painlessly enduring that displeasure. What I do know is that his generosity of work and presence enriched that whole generation of poets who wanted to do the hard thing, the salmon folk of language, who wanted, like Arnaut Daniel our master (Dante's, Pound's, Duncan's, Wieners', Rattray's, Lansing's, Stein's, Irby's) always to swim against the stream, to leap upstream against the falling water so as to release their own starry influence up there, where we come from. Duncan's pressure still moves in the language poets, in the new romantics, in the neo-formalists, in the many contradictory squabbling heirs of his mind and his song. I feel a gratitude to him I can hardly yet begin to speak.

(*Conjunctions* #29, "Tributes," 1997)

ON OLSON

CHARLES OLSON · *PLEISTOCENE MAN* (I)

Charles Olson : PLEISTOCENE MAN. A Curriculum for the study of the soul. Buffalo, Institute for Further Studies. $2.00.

---

study of the <u>soul</u>
                    (whose title <u>is</u> that?)
is this a cultivation,
ta'wil? Скрябин? a matter of μουσικη?
                Warlock's cultivated death,
mors, mars, morsus,
             sharp death
      pitch of life?
             soul?
                    that soul melted out of ice
arose in our hands
        (beauty of Folsom points
      a function of their function,
                'efficiency')?
                      (beauty?)
soul?
we have had that word to pay with
for 3000 years
& it has never gotten us out of debt

        (<u>Seele</u>, also <u>seligkeit</u> --- a state of
                   (i.e., a happening in the)
                        mind

νους? ψυχη? εννοια? διανοια? επινοια?
    θυμος? φρενες? αιων? κηρ?
נפש?   ανεμος? πνευμα? βουλη?
head, heart?   body? hand?
                         gland?

<u>man</u>
     (makroprosopos,
         Adam Qadmon
                    Pithecanthropus,
     chymical marriage at Mt Carmel
  Neanderthal = Sapiens   (= sign of marriage)

a curriculum for the study of man.
which would be a study of his Body General
    & (as from)
              his Body Specific, & any
      recorded experience, & the τεχνη

```
                          ---
                    (that's what it is)
      of recording experience, telling what happened &
                                what can happen,
         our ΤΕΧΥΗ/λογος  age---

    so historia remains the recounting of what a man
    experienced
                 in his place     (Clio!)
                                       --- & that will never
    go rotten on us
                    (as the filosofas have
    (so would take Homer Hesiod Herodotus
                    Pindar Pausanias Plutarch
            as best guides to the stations of the Greek
                          underground railroad
                 (& so for any culture those
    i.e. men who had no idea
                          of what was going on
          but wanted like crazy to find out,
                fact by fact, breath by breath

          (which is why in our age magick replaces philo-
                     sophy as study of order)

                                again, breath by breath,

                        & if that is soul
      a passion for the hands to hold
                & the head to understand
            & the heart to read the verberations,
                                      alright, soul.
    But, that, word!
                    lex orandi lex credendi
              or, as once remarked,
              vox pop verb sap .
                              securus iudicat orbis
                                              terrarum

    I mean his hungers are our best history of the
                                        Pleistocene.
```

(*Caterpillar* #7, 1969)

CHARLES OLSON · *PLEISTOCENE MAN* (II)

Now I come back to this again because my first take on it as recorded in an earlier issue hereof was *pre*occupied by a laughingly systematic bellyache on the subtitle of this (not to surprise you, considering the author) amazingly useful work. Now forget the subtitle, except & until, you understand the book('s tendance & direction). Let it pass, for now. I've been learning.
So that Poet whose work has conspicuously summoned us to the realization that the poet in our days is, and is the only, (as I understand it), scientist of the Whole,

                              now in this month's letters, October 1965, from the Poet in Gloucester to a Blake-scholar in Buffalo, what is likewise evident is the necessary turn of the, our, attention to the substances & consecutions of the world we inhabit,

      "In fact it *is* poetry, Pleistocene, in that simplest *alphabetic* sense, that you can learn the language of being alive" (p. 9),

                                             language of being alive. Now the eye of this book is on, is concerned to direct (purpose of letters) at a distance a course of study, primaries, and to this end there are exact instructions, bibliographies, *lisez and ne lisez pas*, to conduct "the people" thru (what I'm supposing to be) the maze of æsthetic archeologists, histories & altitudes, towards, towards,

      "There is no single text in Pleistocene except *one*: the few, & *separable*, remains. [Not any historical speculation, only speculation by such persons on the basis of those REMAINS ONCE MADE KNOWN TO THEM."

The tenderness of Olson's concern for the remains, (which I would call data except held back by those interesting things about data Piggott says in the first chapters of *Prehistoric Europe*, it's there but can we see it, understand what it is that we find, plus the extent to which our seeing depends, just that, depends)

& for the making known of what can be made known!
(& here Olson says, page 12, to keep in mind: "you don't have to

teach you have to extricate. Don't do anyone else's work for them: do what they might not be able to *unless* you have given them a superior chance at.")

And he calls Clarke's students (I guess they are, in a school, a university, in america, getting such in/formation/s, hard to believe) "the people." Which is the loveliest address.

(*Caterpillar* #10, 1970)

SOME PRELIMINARIES

1.

Every great writer gleams in the grace of admirers, the shimmering glamour of detractors. We see a writer scaled by our own perspective, reverence or disdain. Olson got his share too of the excessive reverence that spits itself out as competition, resentment, chopping down father.

I knew the man from 1962 for half a dozen years, and hardly saw him in the last two years before his death in January 1970. He died at fifty-nine. As I write these notes, I have already outlived him by three human years. While he, such is the nature of these things, continues to be older than me. Twenty-five years older — that was the measure. He remembered the end of World War I, I remembered the beginning of World War II. Such definitions as time offers.

The man. Everybody is distracted by the man — there was so much of him. He seemed half a foot taller than I (me at six-three), lean but bulky — the only man I ever found myself literally looking up at. And he would stand close. He was a dancer, Olson was, and moved always forward towards the discourse. A strange thing it felt. A dancer, not a boxer, though always crowding in.

So much of him, yes, but also curiously little in another way. Sometimes he seemed larger than life, sometimes shy in an imponderable way. Watching him chat with a waitress you saw the shyness of the man, his friendliness, his sweetness, his holding back on the huge engine of his body's power.

Don't let them diminish you! he cried out to me one night, and repeated it over and over, gesturing at my big body, my big appetites. The sizes we shared, of shoes, eyes, airs.

2.

Several months ago some young poets came to me and proposed we all talk about Olson and the Black Mountain poets. They occasioned me to look at the strange reluctance I've felt about dealing out loud with him and his work. I began to think it was time to say what I had to say, if anything, about this man, this maker, who to my sense of it renewed poetic discourse — and not just in our language — vastly more than he's given credit for.

What I want to do here and now is offer, just offer, a couple of working notions about the shape of Olson and his work. I think these notions are worth working on by critics, and by biographers who want to deal more deeply, even if speculatively, with Olson's inner life, the growth of his mind, than Tom Clark's pioneering biography had time to do.

On the way to these ideas, let me try to dispel the common, poisonous, cartoon of him as a domineering pompous patriarch ruling by his size and voice and laying down a stone yard full of by now outdated laws and orthodoxies. Let me share instead the sense I had in the 1960s, and that has stayed with me thereafter — ever since one night he said to me, standing in a curiously hieratic, Konarak sort of Indian way, how no one has grasped the feminine in him, no one knew the woman he was. And one night, more shyly still, he began to talk about the feminine in his own work — not just some exalted sense of Sophia as the feminine disposition of Godhead, but rather the particular feel and agenda of a certain sort of writing that he did. Shyly he spoke about it, wouldn't identify the work of his that he so identified, but clearly gestured towards it: the narrative, the continuous, the *récit*, the "visionary recital" — the tale of the soul. Perhaps narrative itself is feminine, and it is no surprise that the most purely narrative of all the Maximus poems, "Maximus, from Dogtown," about Merry and his Bull, demonstrates a coinciding of the end of Story with the end of the poem in the opening up of the female Earth's part to "take him in." Narrative returning to its womb.

3.

Here then are two notions I'd offer for critics to assay: first, that Olson was a man struggling against certainty.

He was struggling against the Aristotelian groundworks of his Good Education, against the innate conservative tendency of his social mind, against the convictions with which he had grown up, the convictions of sexual and political hegemony he had won from Lawrence and Pound.

Just as I would read Melville's work after *Moby Dick* as a flight from his own fluency, I want to read Olson's work after the first flight of Maximus as a flight from the unexamined certainties by which a man might know myself, "my wife, my car." Away from the apodictic evidence of the senses & the usual homages they demand. Out, out of the social —

Out into the garden of the Platonic nuthouse, as he must often have thought of it, towards the illuminate intensities he began to work with from Meier and Corbin and, in general, the "Arabs," work towards what he would wind up calling Angelology in his *Curriculum for the Study of the Soul.*

Angel. Soul.

Funny words, you'd think, for the man who wrote the *Mayan Letters*, the savvy correspondent in that immense *Briefwechsel* with Creeley, to come to.

Moving as he did, he was doing, we have to remember, what his decade was doing too, the drugs and quests of the 1960s of which Olson is the clearest and least self-deluded conquistador, who for the sake of the journey itself, the pure Emersonian outward, moved from certainty to the visionary Abyss.

I remember Olson one night reading, with minatory fervor, the incredible passage in Melville where the greenhorn Platonist is imagined stepping out into lucency off the crow's nest and plunging to his death, or worse, in the endless ocean of speculation.

Where Pip (in his turn, on another Gloucester summer night) had sunk down to the lowest realms of matter, and seen God's foot upon the treadle of the loom.

Thus my second trope is to test a sense of Olson as the man struggling towards the Angel.

My own guess is that Olson was himself that honeyhead, that Platonist with his foot off the crow's nest. I think he tumbled down into the holy mouth of the sea and the sea spewed him forth — Maximus come to the world's end, straggling up on those Mahayana shores that a century before Henry Thoreau (whose name sounds like *thorough* in Massachusetts) had, first of Americans, come upon, translating the *Lotus of the Good Law* from French.

Someone should find out how Olson came upon, as he did come upon, the figure of the Buddha Amoghasiddi, the meditation deity of accomplishment: *I am the one who accomplishes all my intentions.*

Can you say that? Isn't that what the "young" Maximus is always saying? And here I will insist on the figure of Maximus, who is not an irrelevancy of the text, a glib Persona. He stands as the engine of accomplishment. Being big he is able, able to stand his ground, stand by his word, able to do. So Maximus is no meek Ishmael battered by conscience and tradewinds, Maximus is the deliberate voyager. And what he sails across, measures with the body of his feeling, is not some dinky periplus. Here is a man who can cross the open seas, a mariner, one who can move out of sight of land, and still get there.

So this is the character of availing, non-existentialist but sheerly experiential, who is the place-lord, the day-god, of Olson's great working out — not a canto. The Maximus *poems,* he insists, not cantos, not a song not a single singing, not at all, though *(The Songs of Maximus)* Maximus can sing.

Call it a dream. A dream is the opposite of a song, can I raise my voice and say that, with some conviction? A dream is the opposite of a song.

And this is Maximus's dream, a dream he got falling asleep over Apollonius of Tyana, or reading the sermon of Maximus of Tyre.

Until he thought he was the book he read.

Then he became that book. And a man becoming a book is on his way to the angel, to being "divine" — like St. John the Divine, who saw heaven descending onto Patmos, and who ate a book.

It is by an appeal to the courts of Mind, an entry into those noumenal wildernesses from which both the conceptual *&* the historical are banished — not as wrong but as nonproductive, ir/relevant, *Irrlichter* in the gloaming — that Olson's painfully honest later poems strive. On a journey from identity to being, sensing those — so freshly — as opposites.

Now Olson used to pronounce "literature" like a bad word, and seemed to hate the artifactual sense of a text as a thing, an amenity, a commodity abstracted from its culture and esteemed for its very distance from its conditions of production. Hence the restless horny probing after sources and histories, the "irritable searching after" an authority outside the text, mirrored in the text. Hence all the business in record offices, archaeologies, Yucatan, Dogtown Common, annals, ledgers, diaries — as if the authenticity of the text in feet arose from its having been conditioned by antecedent textual evidents/evidence ("things seen").

What must it have been like for such a man to encounter the necessity of the Angel? When Stevens, in his late poems, came upon the necessary angel of earth, it seemed like a profound metaphor, but not a Man (remember that the "angel" with whom Jacob wrestles all night until the rising of the Dawn is, in the Hebrew text, *ish,* a man).

Olson's angel, he found, was all sourcing and tendrils and shakings far off of the web. Olson found hints towards the angelic in, of course, the soul, & I fought him, and we were estranged by my surly *lèse-majesté* about his use of that word, and I'm still not sure if I was right or wrong about his use of it, though God knows I was wrong to give him (or anybody) displeasure by carping about the term, qua term.

Of course the Angel points to the soul. Your soul. What else do you need an angel for? The Soul is what you cannot see. The Soul is what sees. A man can't see his own face. He needs a mirror. The Soul holds itself up as the mirror — Olson may have sometimes badmouthed literature, but I think he came to understand, better than any of us had, how a book could be a mirror. And how to make such a book.

(*Rain Taxi,* Spring 1998)

FIVE SHORT REVIEWS

ROBERT CREELEY · *THE FINGER* (WITH COLLAGES BY BOBBIE CREELEY)

Start of the year with an incredible poem from Creeley, wch word we say meaning, yes, *credible* across terrain we had not known the poem cd make its own, as here, the personal history of what we are trained to call. Archetype. And usually encounter with fustian & throat clearing and presumption here totally absent; here that naked strength not simple, not simplified, characteristic of Creeley.

> I was not to go
> as if to somewhere,
> was not in the mind
> as thinking knows it,

Bobbie Creeley's collages are part of the book, strange that it shd be so, I wd have imagined no illustration cd serve or subserve, yet it does the beautiful one, say, that faces

> She was young,
> she was old,
> she was small,
> she was tall with
>
> was all distance, her eyes
> extraordinary grace…

A beautiful book (printed by Graham Mackintosh) in 300 copies. But the poem. As rich as "The Door," & to me grown older thru that understanding.

(Caterpillar #5, 1968)

3 · A BOOK OF THE COMPANY

PHILIP LAMANTIA · *SELECTED POEMS 1943-1966*

Sixty-two pages reprinted from earlier books, few easy to get. Twenty-seven pages printed "here for the first time anywhere," the section called *Secret Freedom*. Philip Lamantia is a poet who does not occur in time; time meets him & overhears. From the first poems (written when he was sixteen) on to what we assume are his latest, there is a not-measured propagation happening. The change from year to years is less noticeable than the change from poem to poem: the spectrum remains constant. Transformations are instant, line to line:

> The crash of your heart
> beating its way through a fever of fish
> and your trip ends in the mask of my candle-lit hair

or

> a caustic air
> that spins new top the rock of enigmatic love,
> affinities of the mineral diving board
> that is my body concentrating to the rhythm
> of its murex hand churning the waters below
> and only the starlight consoles

to quote the last line of the first & last poems in the book. Each ecstasy begets the next, & the pale cotidian [sic] light between them is elided. And this absolute resistance to time fascinates me; for some years we understand, he had "read the spells of Egypt patiently," and the static only *internally* changing presence of Egyptian texts may be the best emblem, & the best introduction for reading these poems. The high excitement of his public readings is missing here. I keep coming back to rock. The poem "Coat of Arms," of recent ones, is very powerful.

(*Caterpillar* #5, 1968)

STEPHEN JONAS · *TRANSMUTATIONS*

Tho out well over a year, & erratically available in the United States, this book needs to be kept in mind. It's the first anything like large collection of Jonas' poems, & as such, a major event. Event means coming forth into the world, outcome. And however ill-publicized the event, the event matters. When the book came to me, summer of 66, I read it thru twice, find it hard to confess that a poet of such mastery of his resources (& they are many) shd be ill-known to me, I'd seen individual poems, but they pleased without pushing me around, & that's not interesting to me, I mean I can't use that. But this collection, the series of "Orgasms," a few of the "Exercises for Ear," to encounter this work seriously is to question everything, renew everything. Of all the poets who have presumed to carry Pound's torch forward (suspiciously not yet let fall in Merano), few have been as faithful as Jonas in preserving the root gesture of P's work: *care,* care for the facts, the breath, wch is fact, the word, wch is fact, care for the attentions. Money, Fedl Reserve and Usura are material here, but they have conjoined with alchemy, where much of SJ's research has been; he investigates the decay of matter from within, the historic gesture (& here he'd divide in my mind from Olson, or do I misread?) becomes metaphoric of internal growth & decline, while remaining primary evidence of such processes. That marriage makes Jonas' poems extraordinarily rich, & his ear is very good. So good that it's hard to find it musical at first: it's specific, doesn't sound like anything else, balks the yen for the familiar that disfigures most litry comment. Doesn't Ives say somewhere that if it sounds beautiful at first hearing, be sure it's the same old slop? My first reading of the book I fought him all the way, & he stood up to it & sang in my face. American language, lifted up. A great book.

(*Caterpillar* #5, 1968)

STAN PERSKY · *LIVES OF THE FRENCH SYMBOLIST POETS*

Its cover camping as an *nrf* book, its seven pages of text illumined by photographs of the poets, its text telling many true & false (by statistical norms) stories of the frequently misspelled poets, not misspelled, variously spelled poets, variously poets Corbière, Jacob, Apollinaire, Cocteau, this book is a little Jātakamala of the incarnations of John L. Spicer, whose latest, normative incarnation was the poet Jack Spicer. Or if my right to say that is questioned, it is certainly a collection of inventions, & the invented thing is always true, whereas the found thing is only sometimes & not all the time true. And, if that judgment too finds no favor, let it be said that Persky explores the minimal parameters of storytelling. Even if you don't like the stories in this book (wch wd be unfair to six poets at least), Persky is getting us closer to the day when we will have seriously to consider what a story is, what makes one, & what are the implications when it's made, what implications the fact of it being there makes. I've been thinking about this since at least the time I sd in a letter to Fielding Dawson how past fiction his work was (& I was thinking of his accurate ear) & back came a blast from wch I am still thinking. It is fiction. = making things up. = telling. Give us a phenomenology of that. (Wch might = get Gertrude Stein back in print.) (And Dawson into it, publicked.)

DAPHNE MARLATT *FRAMES* AND *LEAF LEAF/S*

Within a few months two very different books, a presence in the commonwealth, a quality that articulates clearly, & these two books show the breadth. *Frames* is a long, quiet narrative poem. She's learned from Duncan, from Andersen (whence the story of Kay & Gerda *Frames* is built on), but mostly from the words that are the story. No story but in words, the words spin.

Leaf Leaf/s (written during the later stages of *Frames* as I understand it) is a collection of short, tight lyrics, much reflecting the syntactic, phonemic *Lila* of D. Alexander: again the play in words, but in these poems she's less concerned to follow the words as *hodos* or road (as if towards a destination, a 'story') & more concerned to play in the midst, an elemental pastime. I think of Crowley's distinction between invocation & evocation, the former leading towards macrocosm, the latter fleshing anew the microcosm, making a new "form" — this latter seems the preoccupation of much of *Leaf Leaf/s*. The title itself gives the centripetal direction of play.

I've been reading *Frames* since it came to my house, & slowly, feeling no urgency to reach the end. Intrigued by the contrast between the extense of *Frames* (however particular the title) & the nuclear contractions of *Leaf Leaf/s*, I wrote to her in my notebook:

> "But of course you were Daphne, & when the continental sun of rational purpose, of conscious manipulation of the woman who is Language, when this daylight assault began you had no choice but to connect yourself with the earth, dark enough to feed the inside of your body & yet low enough to allow you to wave arms in light…"

What does a man want of a woman poet. He wants, besides to fuck her, he wants to hear at last clearly the voice of all the flesh he has touched & worshipped & exploited & redeemed & lost & found himself in. In supreme selfishness, he wants to hear her answer, as a man on earth wants so deeply, without end, to hear the voice of his planet, his bed, his mother. *Leve moder, let me in*! But the woman who is a poet is not his mother & not his lover, yet from her words he wants that total responding daylight will not give him; she is not his lover, she is the voice of his lover, even the lover he could never have or never touch or never let himself possess. All the more so for the homotropic male: the woman poet speaks in a voice he needs immensely, a voice he can never finally deny. ((Maybe then your best audience will be the platonists, occultists, ooy-lovers, homoerotics and homoierotics — they will want you to be absolute earth, & perhaps seek to cut off your access to the upper air, the aither in whose lonelier engagement they spend their energies & their care.)). I am with an old-fashioned thought (perhaps as you also are, with a story from the older countries of the heart, the ice-splinter in Kay's heart only the physical articulated tears of Gerda's body can thaw), an old-fashioned instinct to seek meaning in women, & do it all ways, including to shape towards her the flow of Language she is (Apollo invents not the language but only the alphabet. The language is in the keeping of the mothers, yes? who guard the intricate courting dance of phoneme & morpheme)..."

There is much solidity & power in Daphne Marlatt's work, & I admire not just the grace in it (or thrusts at grace), but that it can so provoke me.

(Caterpillar #7, 1968)

LEROI JONES'S *THE DEAD LECTURER*

That Jones carries the definitions of our craft into the age to which they must be relevant if they are to mean anything at all. The poetics of Information compels the clarity, which is not then, like the clairvoyant hindsight of the *symbolistes*, to its own sweet sake, but towards the Republic, in the sense which Pound has urged. Yes, we know that. Yes, we know all that. But do we do it, do we do anything about the burden of fertile clarity the poem must bear. Jones does. At times the person speaking in the poems must allow the conservative reader to cherish the belief that it is the person, not the society, which is swarmingly at fault. The reader must not make this mistake. He must not confuse the *dramatic* utterance of a poormouth nigger for a poet's apology in the face of a society utterly & meaninglessly corrupt. "Who put that knife in my hand?" can be a worksong. That is. Is. Am I going to find anything wrong here, an inherited literary nice-mindedness that keeps the poem from cutting too many throats. Is that wrong. Is it an insistence on an order a man can make out of the necessities. Suppose it is. What are those adjectives for, greasejobs to slide the whole work in, sharpening, sharpening; hone-oil. What is the poet standing there for, what is that in his hand after all. Does the needle, or the prick, in the shady nighttime lanes of Mittelamerika suddenly look like a knife, gleaming with its own life & buffaloing the vagrant hordes of an uncommitted triggerhappy bourgeoisie. The gentleness of Jones' verse does not deceive, & is not iron-in-velvet or anything (nothing) like that. It is a real gentleness (the sublimating orator throttling the microphone in anger at an audience he will not, for the sake of the clarities, physically attack) & see what becomes of it. The reader is brought into the presence of a man debating his means with himself. Where is my source. O there it is. Pow. The answers in the deliberations. And the poem emerges, disclosure by disclosure, through the presentness of each substance, image yes but more truly fact, of its own concern. For the sake of its clarities. The speed of Jones' poems is very great, I don't mean rush of breath & so on, there is that, but the quick density of movement, by which each gist or fact is on its way to the next. No transitions, no vacations at Grossingers with a Choice Image between a & b. Truly linear, the poem is a consequence, at every moment, of its means.

> Liverwurst sandwiches dry
> on brown fenced-in lawns, unfinished cathedrals
> tremble with our screams.
> Of the dozens, the razor, the cloth, the sheen, all
> speed adventure locked
> in my eyes. I give you now, to love me, if I spare
> what flesh of yours
> is left. If I see past what I feel, and call music
> simply "Art" and will
> not take it to its logical end.
>
> ["Rhytam & Blues," 2]

Poem after poem will land; I am not aware of what I could call a bad poem in the book; of what I've got in my head, maybe "Footnote to a pretentious book" seems least stated, or is that the flatness of an ending the truth of which could go no other way. Conscious, in the modes of my own reading, of my hunger for that which establishes most clearly the bases of its own sound, i.e., its sound. In so far as sound is voice (100%), as I say, one after another, sounding a single compelling voice: "A poem for neutrals," "Short speech to my friends," "Black Dada Nihilismus," "Green Lantern's solo": these are the best information we're getting these days, & these days very much in them. In terms of the poem as news, they are at first glance the compelling ones. Jones gives us the news that isn't in the newspapers, & that's fine, but also the news that, by its personal & radical newness couldn't last ever to get into any other form of discourse, the poem lives for that gesture: "Duncan spoke of a process," "The Dance," "Valéry as dictator," "The Liar." Herein the learned will find the lyric that consoles them when the form of the poem otherwise seems to be getting too close for comfort to the real world they despise. Yet these lyrics, quieter than the other poems in the book, are no set pieces of poetic evasion:

> The role given,
> mashed into protein
> grace. A lifted arm
> in shadow. A lifted thinking
> banging silently
> in the darkness.

> I fondle what
> I find
> of myself. Of you
> what I understand.
>
> ["Dichtung"]

There is a small poem in the book of which I am disproportionately, & in terms of where I momentarily am, fond: "A poem for speculative hipsters" which concludes:

> Only ideas,
> and their opposites.
> Like,
> he was really
> nowhere.

Social stance no more than social grace is a protection against sterility. Jones, as much as any poet going, is busy watering the ground, & we are to be grateful that his attention has not limited itself to one area of inquiry. He knows the abstract evasions of the city & the clichéd passions of what is not yet in the city. His language does not offer any hiding place for either of those questionable dignitaries, the professor & the policeman, there are no comfortable vaguenesses here. It is a curious fact that many folk, reading Jones or hearing him read, sum up their experiences by observing that he is angry. An instructive fact: that our muddles normally move themselves to clarity, the precise word, only when anger is present: No, it was exactly 2 minutes *to* five god damn it &c. Hence, casually seeking connective, they infer anger where there is clarity. Maybe it is as well. Then they can perceive anger in lyric, & at last comprehend that the significance of a man's life, like the significance of the poem, is a business of precisions:

> And let me once, create
> myself. And let you, whoever
> sits now breathing on my words
> create a self of your own. One
> that will love me.
>
> ["The Dance"]

(*Fubbalo* #1, 1964)

EDWARD DORN'S *GUNSLINGER, BOOK I*

This is it. Straight. Pound complained that the accuracy of Cavalcanti would not be possible in our time, for lack of a shared philosophical language, a way to talk about things in relation. Time changes. Or Dorn otherwise, no matter. Must be out on record, right now, that this is the solidest straightest richest new long poem now before us, poem as line-forward, going somewhere & being there all the time it travels to.

If you don't know what 'accuracy' means it is possible that you'll have to go back to the beginning & start again. Or forget about it & hustle the stale goods out of the agora. What's happened is that Dorn has learned (us) to talk, he always could, but at this incredible gait:

(the naïve academic narrator:)

>   Miss Lil! I intervened
>   you mustn't slap my
>   Gunslinger on the back
>   in such an off hand manner
>   I think the sun, the moon
>   and some of the stars are
>   kept in their tracks
>   by this Person's equilibrium
>   or at least I sense some effect
>   on the perigee and apogee of all
>   our movements in this, I can't quite say,
>   *man's* presence, the setting sun's
>   attention I would allude to

(or Lil, the Mysterious Madam:)

>   *That horse would sit at*
>   *the table all night, terrible*
>   *on whiskey and rolled*

> *a fair smoke*
> *and this texan insisted he was*
> *payin for my girl's time*
> *and he could use it any way he*
> *saw fit*
> *as long as he was payin like*
> *and I had to explain*
> *a technical point to the Shareholder*
> *namely, that he was payin for her* ass,
> *which is not time!*

And the way Gunslinger talks, I'll give no samples since his best emerge in dialog! Gunslinger as mythic hero, a semitized (forgive me, Ed) & areopagized Coyote, the Sun's son like the great Navajo gambler. Or so it sounds, to me, on one wild reading of this straight american Dante (durante = the enduring, dante = the giving) — a common noun, with the help of god. It is entirely possible that people will laugh their fool heads off in this book, what with the Turned On Horse & the slicker who calls himself Claude Lévi-Strauss, yes, & it wd serve them right. This being the most serious poem I've read in some time (or is that my fat-lipped kiss of death)?

Mythology comes alive, those few times it does, when it roots in flesh & grows, simply, new bodies & new maps to take movement on. To talk abt Gilgamesh or Odysseus or the Heraklids is not mythology but philology (or worse). Now here in a most remarkable way the substance (always image/nation) of the west, West, comes to terms with a remarkable human not to say political intelligence. Incredible the way this man can register exact socio-historical & mythical states ("How far is it Claude? / Across / two states / of mind, saith the Horse.") without thumbing the old hagiography in our faces. And that *is* the body of his invention, solid. I keep coming back to that word for this poem that won't let up.

And *accuracy* I spoke of, easier to point to it than say what it is, the tending of language & concern for its clearest directions.

> Salud, poeta
> what can you sing?
> All songs but one.
> A careful reply.
> Then can you sing
> a song of a woman
> accompanied by that
> your lute which this
> company took to be a guitar
> in their inattention.
> Yes I can, but
> an *Absolute* I have
> here in my hand.
> Ah yes, the Gunslinger exhaled
> It's been a long time.

Dorn right now has the fastest proper notion of any of the stars in that constellation of where we are.

(*Caterpillar* #5, 1968)

TWICE ON CID CORMAN
TOWARDS CORMAN: *THE TWO TIMES OF POETRY*
==

"Offer, respond, let be"

so here, Creeley gone…
let me tell a Creeley story

1961, my book, his daughter,
the avalanche, the post card

the actual answer

I quote myself to Brossard,
RC's "sense of responsibility to the other"

that even taught me, and he did, and all his poems are towards,

so to Corman,

who answered every letter the day it came
& matched the size if he could, and he could

as if it came natural.

The role of letters (Lovecraft, Rilke, Corman, strange fellows at the mail box)

so the Two Times,

the act itself
     which I say is one of listening with your hands
and then the after.

vision & revision.

So Clayton and I had some contradiction about revision.

CE: Corman did not revise.
RK: He did nothing but revise.
CE: He did not revise his own work.
RK: Exactly, he revised mine. yours, anybody's.

For him, revision was the chief act and deed & instrument of criticism /

What he would do with somebody's poem.

What he did to *Hagoromo*, setting stage directions in the flow of Zeami's language.

Rock in the stream
revises rivers.

What *Origin* did was respond —
        to the voices that were there, beginning in those bleak but budding 1950s to sound, resound.
        so CC was almost, as a responder, compelled to be so various in the styles and patrimonies of his poets,
        so that Eberhart could be featured not far from Olson, or my featured issue of *Origin* (5, N.S.) could share some pages with William Bronk. The critical understanding that could handle with real passion Coolidge and Enslin and Taggart and Blackburn must have been one that knew how to listen.

[RK archives, undated text]

ON CORMAN

> I lift a little
> cross-shaped flower
> white to smell it
> and all I smell's
> my finger,
> could a flower's
> scent be so
> transparent?

As I finish writing that down, very late at night, scraping the barrel of the mind, or wherever it is that we find things to say, I find myself thinking about Corman.

Chaster and quieter than I am, he would have written:

> I lift a little
> flower
> white
> my nose
> smells just my finger
> or even less.

Maybe less playful that day, he'd drop the nose:

> I lift a little
> flower
> white,
> smell just
> the finger.

Yes, that's where he'd likely stop — and he would keep the "I." He never abandoned that paterfamilias of poetry, the authority of the perceiving, recording I. But he'd drop the 'my' — goes without saying. Maybe he'd add — I can almost hear him — Poetry is what goes without saying.

3 · A BOOK OF THE COMPANY

There is a wonderful human *push* in saying it, saying it anyhow, saying it though it can't be said.

He trusted the silence around his words, trusted silence the way a man trusts the walls of his house. Not many of us live in houses whose walls we raised ourselves, yet they are our walls, we take them, they hold us, and they stand. Silence is the firmest thing of all.

Few of us carve the silence in which words sometimes consent to happen *hard*.

Only in silence are words really hard, and only when they're hard can they be themselves and mean themselves.

How to trust the words: trust nothing else.

I began to correspond with Corman in the late 1950s, and most of the urgent, almost daily exchanges took place between then and 1962, when he brought out the issue of *origin* (2nd Series) that featured my work. (William Bronk was in that issue too.)

The brusque, testy rightness of Corman's letters — always the same length as the letter he was answering, doing so (this was a pride of his) the same day he received it — was a severe and valued guide to me in those early days, and many another poet grew strong and clear on Corman's strictures.

One of the first books by Cid I read was also the longest I know, his poems from Matera, the parched austere Italian landscape he exchanged for Kyoto. *Sun Rock Man* he called the book, the words stacked. Those poems won me, as his grace and acumen had mastered me earlier.

And now I think:

>   CID
>
>   COR
>
>   MAN

Cid is the hero, el mio Cid, el Campeador, who is both a hero and a poem of the hero, subject and object intricately connected, the unknown narrator writing of mio Cid, my Cid, as well as el Cid, as we usually remember him.

Cid, el Cid, al-Sidi, the lord — (like the Sidi Hamet who was the author of *Don Quixote* that Cervantes discovered in his head or in his heart to tell the story), the champion of a struggle against the Saracens, who bears a Saracen name,

and Cid is Sidney too, so common a bourgeois Jewish-American name made romantic, estranged from the seventy-years-gone calms of Roxbury and Dorchester into the Extreme Orient of poetry, the land where the pearl comes from,

the thing we need, the word we find, the text that suddenly understands us.

The double sense of the name — the exotic, the commonplace — reveals at once the starting point in the everyday, the common light, which through the ardent listening of the poem turns out to be the sparks of Lurianic splendor. The glory is always here and now.

And **Cor** is heart of course, his work never failed to feel, never for all his love of the minimal, the barebones, the harsh Zen light on the rice fields, never stopped referring gently to the eternal triangle of speaker and a found world and a heart that hears.

He had such grace. We imitate his minimals with ease, but they seem slim or slack or trite, lacking the heart he had. The heart he heard.

It is so easy to take on those Japanese clarities, brevity, lucidity, and take them as excuses to be brittle, disconnected, uncommitted.

How false it would be to think of Corman that way — read his translations of Celan, or his great verbalization of a real-time enactment of a Zeami *Nō* play or his wonderful reading of Bashō's pilgrimage, and you find the emotional complexity of tenderness, gesture, response. Always he was searching for that, always letting silence cancel out the usual acceptations and associations of words, as only silence can, and let the revived meaning speak.

(*Cipher Journal*, July 2004)

TARN: A TRIBUTE

A tarn is a lake
is a deep low place in a high place
is a secret name
for someone
who is always someone else

we stand behind our product

we stand behind our names
and move them around

a name is a mirror

but a mirror is a name
you know yourself by, who,
a mirror is a question and a name always seems to be an answer,

is it, the glorious peach trees oozing darkest amber gum
whether or not there are peaches on the tree

a lake in the mountains

a boat on the lake

a man in the boat.

the lake is in China

the boat is on the lake

the man is not Chinese

who knows what a man is

he comes and he goes

something about him is always far

A man in a boat is no age at all.

So say a poem is a poor man's open-heart surgery
or no
A poem is the archeology we are taught by stones

no
A poem is the blood from the stone
a poem is mountain milk.

So one writes poems the way one studies a lake,
that is, with half an eye on those pine trees over there
where there might or might not be an otter working on a freshwater herring
the kind called alewife
that have no husband

but most of the time just waiting for the sight of the water
to calm the surface of the mind
enough to shut up the clamor of palaver

or a poem is something said by someone with nothing to say

someone who is always someone else

Why can't a poem just be a naked woman?

Because no one is.

It is written: the nakedness of woman is the deception of God,

for the body is built around its Secret,
which is the Secret of God,
and it cannot be shown
however hard you look

but when you look very hard at a poem
you see what is not there

or only a little bit there

like a named woman
of whom you have heard
or a named man
you met on the elevator
but don't remember

only the name.

The name is a lake in which its person drowns.

But "to remember something is to make it somehow a part of the present and thus unreal," says Borges (or Norman Thomas di Giovanni says he says). Since the real is all that has been said, spoken into place and forgotten, forgotten into being.

No lake, no mountain, just a name.

Nomen numen.

The name is a deity, the Romans said. The play on words, which is a play in words, is more than a play. The name is the god, but the god is also the name. To call a god by name is to invoke the god's numen, power, the godness that soaks the world with that sudden quality of places and persons we call 'numinous.' The *numen* is there, the *nomen* has been spoken. The old linguists tell us that our word 'god' itself comes from some archaic verb for crying out or calling, so that god means: what we call out in fear or praise. Lord, hear our prayer. Or Joyce said, perhaps more literally than he knew: God is a cry in the street.

But Tarn is also a département in France, where Albi of the martyrs sleeps, whose Gnostic beauties persist in NT's work.

For Tarn has that rarest of sensibilities: an austere sensuality. So views the object of desire with the yearning detachment of a geologist catching sight of a syncline across the valley.

Or a tarn barely glimmering in the twilight.

And he, in this respect most like the French poets who are his secret kinsmen — Claudel, Segalen, Cendrars, Auxeméry — is most at home in traveling. He is someone who has had to go there, stand on desert or mesa and understand the place by being there.

(Not he a Hölderlin, who found his Hellas only in his soul's swaggering rhythms of ode. Or me, for that matter, for whom all geography is in my own body. Or in hers.)

Tarn goes there, has to know what it is to be there. Our own word 'be' is two words in many a language (neighbor Spanish for one), an essentialist meaning (as, to be Irish) and a stative one (as, to be hungry, or to be in Philadelphia). Tarn like a good Mediterranean intuits that to be is to be somewhere.

The earth shares her identity with him, and so we are.

December 2008
(*Golden Handcuffs Review* #11, 2009)

ON JONATHAN WILLIAMS

AN EAR IN BARTRAM'S TREE

The revered poſtRomantic & razzmatazz at laſt has a big & necessary book for us to read together many of the fragmentary blitzed perceptions His Speed has given us over these years. JWs is a man whose anger is always intereſting, & he truſts its crackle, & that alone would keep us going, the zap. See the man nicking presidents on the wing & making mischief at the other old pensioners of the AmLitEſtab. Mischief can sometimes lose edge on the page. Not often. He goes. JWs goes very much his own way, his own crooked mile, eye out for the shades, for vulgars & classix, for sharp clean erotical predicaments, & mebbe he does pay much attention to what the other feller's up to. Yet. Yet. To read around in this book (& I counsel peripatetic here) is to wander in america's largeſt openair museum, filled with real footnotes & ſplitting walkie-talkie lecturenotes as we pass, yes indeed, from exhibit to exhibit.

    My idea (ever since reading the *Empire Finals at Verona* in the late '50s, Catullus versions &c., a book that was an initiation for me into the liveliness & fidelity of the world of freedom paſt the Iron Curtain of maſterpiece-making) has been that Wms is afeared of his own tenderness, & no business of mine to pry, since he would turn our eyes outward so well. For all the concrete-poetry, readymades, jammed signboards & overheards, I get moſt alerted by JWms when he rears back with something like this piece from "The Familiars":

> masses of rattlers as large as wash tubs,
> as large as watermelons,
> lying in the sun by their dens.
>
> the Indian said:
> deer and ginseng and snake are allies
> avenging each other;
>
> but it is another Spring God, god of rattlesnakes, puts
> their signature
> on the plantains by the ledge.

, when he does stop and does keep looking, and neither shyness nor restlessness push him away from long regard & the registered response.

In that line, a section entire, part VI of the 3rd symphony, from MAHLER (1964):

> WHAT LOVE TELLS ME
> Anton Bruckner counts the 877th leaf
> on a linden tree in the countryside near Wien
> and prays:
> Dear God, Sweet Jesus,
> Save Us, Save Us.
> the Light in the Grass,
> the Wind on the Hill
> are in my head,
> the world cannot be heard
> Leaves obliterate
> my heart,
> we touch each other
> far apart...
> Let us count
> into
> the Darkness

In some old way, to read these poems is to walk with the man, travelling man that he is, sharing the sights & sounds.

(*Caterpillar* #10, 1970)

COLONEL GENEROSITY —
SAYING THANK YOU TO JONATHAN WILLIAMS

I miss the elegance of the man, the energy of the poet, and above all the generosity that made sure publishing was publick-ing, and that brought to the commonwealth (as he might call it), the shivering needy children we are, news that concerned us and made us better — or at least (often) made us laugh.

The first publisher of Buckminster Fuller, Guy Davenport, Charles Olson — yes, of course they had other little books, but Jargon, with the always beautiful big format, lucid printing, visual sense of importance, endurance — Williams put their names and work out where the hungry poets and readers of the late '50s and early '60s could find it, did find it. We were sick to death of the gentrified poesy of that era, and the books Jonathan made us read (made the Eighth Street Bookshop stock, display) cured us, gave us a fresh wave to ride.

I first met him when I was a frantic reader buying on credit (they kept tally for such ravenous ones) and he was working in Ted and Eli Wilentz's stockroom — a tall slender not very articulate young man, much callower (for all the work he'd done, his travels, his Black Mountain days, his publishing) than the upright gent I'd meet a decade later, when he came to read at Bard College. Or maybe he just didn't like me then.

What am I to do with his death? Same month as Robert Owen Callahan, the San Francisco poet whose own publications reminded me a little bit of Jonathan's, & reminds me too that the great publishers are not those who print and distribute great books but those who create a great new zone of intersection of idea, image, music, and history — a new zone in which books can be read, and our minds can be made known, shared and renewed. That's what Jargon did, and Barney Rossett's famous Grove Press, and Dalkey Archive, and McSweeney's, & Black Sparrow, and some few more.

Jonathan knew and revered Mahler and Elgar way back when nobody played them, when academic composers dismissed them as pompous romantics. Long before the recent fashion of rediscovering tonality, Jonathan was humming Mr. Delius to me on the phone or reminding me of anecdotes in Bruckner's sad little life around his immense music.

What am I to do with the death of any friend? Any one? I have to understand that the last gift a friend gives is his death. The death is a gift. Not in the narrow, cynical sense of leaving stuff for his heirs, or leaving space for his competitors, crowing room for his rivals. Not at all — those aren't gifts, they're obligations or commitments or curses. No, what is a gift about the friend's death is that he has, now, at last, given himself completely to you, in peace and thoroughness. He is yours now, to hold in mind, to be reminded by, to talk to and, who knows, be answered by. Death takes away the alterity of the friend, and brings him to you, me, in the place of sameness, where we know ourselves. And where our own death is waiting.

The grief I feel for him is for a man who was a friend for forty years, a voice in poetry & public discourse grandly & often dizzyingly different from anyone else in his time. The grief I propose the community of poets should feel, though, is for the loss of one of those rare writers who somehow are able to include within their own work the propagation, care, and feeding of the work of other artists. Names come to mind: Harry Crosby, Robert McAlmon, Lawrence Ferlinghetti, perhaps Cid Corman more than any — they were poets who perceived no gap — much less created one — between their own poetic productions and promoting the work of others. Not just their friends — dozens of the writers Corman brought into the world never met him, never did a thing for him, except let him bring them forward as part of the large, subtle project of his own poetics.

So it was with Jonathan Williams. This is the thing that's so remarkable about him — how he embraced publishing as publicking, and what is writing in the first place but the publicking of speech? What he himself wrote, and what he published in the six decades of Jargon, the press he founded, form a kind of indissoluble figure, an ideograph of the kind Pound made us lust for and try to construct.

I need to state a simple gratefulness to Williams, for all he published of the great ones of the last half century — Zukofsky, Olson, and all the rest — and also, personally, for his own work. It was his *Empire Finals at Verona* that showed me in the late 1950s, for the very first time, that the sparse, ironic, vernacular of what would soon come to be called the New American Poetry was capable of subtle resonance, quiet rehearsals of ancient beauty, shocking clarity. Those poems of his, setting Catullus to new measures at once historically challenging and linguistically (that is, politically) consequential, showed it could be done. There was a freshness, playfulness, & sniggerless sexiness that did speak Catullus. Some years later, his *In England's Green & (A Garland and a Clyster)* allowed the old stuff to show through, the Blake whose own mighty ironies awakened British pastoral into visionary energy and transpersonal love.

This was the same Williams who would, clear-eared and wicked-witted, make lyrical conundrums out of signs along the highway and hasty scrawls in public places — all the while listening to Elgar and Mahler. I once watched him attending to Elgar's *Second* — his whole body moved to the music, stately, arms swaying, as if to some celestial, slow-motion bluegrass. Maybe Williams let the world take him too much as that wry teasing commentator, maybe he was too shy, finally, to assume the vatic role his lyric gift entitled him to swagger about in. Too much a gentleman.

He never failed to recognize and promote those gifts in others. In the dozens of artists he proposed to the commonwealth through Jargon publications, the famous and the obscure are in balance. Charles Olson's *Maximus* in its first outing or Louis Zukofsky's *Some Time* (surely one of the most beautiful books ever printed) share the bookshelf with the unknown poems of Alfred Starr Hamilton, the unlikely epic by Buckminster Fuller, the eerie photos of Lyle Bongé.

Williams reckoned it a privilege to discover and promote the under-attended-to, and he had his own distinct notions of what made a poet or photographer worth his efforts. None of the books made money, or only a few did, so the whole of what Jargon accomplished was to manifest an early and very handsome instance of what had by the mid-1900s become a new art form: the small press, which has now metamorphosed into the moneyless transactions of blog, zine, Web site, file-sharing, and all the other forms of free love we hasten to embrace. In Taoist measure, being small & being heard. Being small and making a difference.

Above all my heart keeps coming back to the generosity of Williams and how he made promoting the work of others into an ordinary and everyday part of his own work, all toward a sense of enriching the community of poets — a community that artists need as much as the commonwealth needs them: a quiet, desperate hunger often recognized only when it has been filled and those who filled it are taken away.

As they say in the newspapers, Jonathan is survived by the poet Thomas Meyer. They met in my house on that visit to Bard in 1969, fell in love, and lived together ever since, mostly in North Carolina (where Jonathan was born and died, hard by Black Mountain College, of which he was one of the most distinguished alumni) and in Dentdale in Cumbria. Thomas Meyer is, in my opinion, the strongest, strangest, richest poet of his generation, and has contented himself with the quiet, the mysterious domestic peace that nestles inside the wild gay life of London & New York in which they also moved. In that quiet (as Schiller famously remarked), his talent ripened.

Jonathan is survived too by their heart-son, Reuben Cox, the photographer. And that is apt. Williams made thousands of photos, the real things, 2 x 2 glass slides, of poets and poets' graves and gloomy places that make us glad. And into the great zone of meaningfulness that his writing and publishing both declared, he drew also American photographers — Meatyard, and Laughlin, & Lyle Bongé — who were creating a new *vulgaris eloquentia* for us, the images of our concition.

For forty years, Jonathan Williams lived with the poet Thomas Meyer — two poets living together, sharing and abetting each other's work. Considering how viperish poets can be, that ordinary domestic creative continuity seems itself a marvel and a demonstration of the kind of generosity I'm talking about. Meyer, who entered into that relation when he was fresh out of college, has been quietly creating an astonishing body of poetry and translations; for me, he is one of the preeminent poets of our time. It seems to me that as different as Meyer's work is from the work of his life companion, it reflects, on an intimate but telling level, the generosity of this grand seigneur we have lost.

Williams and Meyer, Meyer and Williams, wise critics in days to come will analyze what I can only intuit, or foreshadow: each enriched the other's freedom to investigate areas of extreme poetics. To study their work — which always abstained from any trace of the collaborative — would be profoundly important for a study of the psychology of the writer. (Their surface image was appealing but misleading: the portly Henry James keeping house with an even more angelic Arthur Rimbaud.)

They supported one another, these two poets, their work radically different, Jonathan moving steadily into the gaffes and grandeurs of American talk, roadside signs and malaprop miracles; his work moved over the years from complex music towards wise, witty, foolish one-liners, if sometimes into Deep Whimsy where I dared not follow.

(Jacket #38, 2009)

THIRTY PASSING REMARKS ON THE BLACK SPARROW PRESS ON THE OCCASION OF ITS HUNDREDTH BOOK[1]

1. Over a hundred books of poetry published in four years by one press whose work was to publish poetry; it has done that work. To deponent's knowledge, nothing like it ever in America.

2. A white parrot-of-prey out of W. H. Hudson soars above a manuscript. It vaunts itself, it exalts. It stoops to seize & print, turns small, gets black. A cycle of engagement. A man makes this happen.

3. Mysterious geography of our sources. Poetry from Los Angeles.

4. Perils: to distinguish the Very New from the Lingering Eccentric.

5. All home-baked breads are not the same.

6. In a story by M. P. Shiel, life is *speed*; the fastest sperm gets the egg. He reminds us that *quick* used to mean "alive."

7. Poetry is primary.

8. The common weal has here been served by a press that takes & gives poetry as primary, not as filler, prestige, contrition.

9. "Everything new is by that fact good." It turns out to be a law we ignore at our peril. It turns on the word new, on 新.

10. The frontality of it takes us by surprise. That poetry is the thing itself, the product, on sale, sold. The confusions of our murderous economy puzzle the poet; he studies his royalty check, feels used & bruised. He is like a painter all of a sudden, only poorer. It is a shock. A book of songs he's made, now sold in the neutral terror of the market. Bring him a camel, houris, tax forms, steep mounds of pistachios, books of moral theology. Is he entitled? It's a problem, a rather new one.

---

1. Printed as the Introduction to Cooney Seamus's *A Checklist of the First One Hundred Publications of the Black Sparrow Press* (1971) — incidentally, the 100th book was Diane Wakoski's *On Barbara's Shore* (1971).

11. Except that he's poorer than a painter & richer than a composer, the poet all at once can't tell himself from an artist in America. He's so used to being the runt of the published litter, to isolate self-pity, to talking extra-loud at parties. The poor poet. Maybe it's time (as Olson suggested some years ago) for poets to stop feeling sorry for themselves.

12. This Black Sparrow Press, being a press, supports nothing but itself. It does not in many obvious ways change the poet's life or the chances of social justice. It changes only subtly, & what it changes are the conditions of public attention.

13. Subtle improvement of the ears. Whitman's "great audiences" still to seek — not in sight yet. But the possibility. There's no place for talk like in the ear.

14. Perils: the Clique, the Friend of a Friend, the Good Companion, the Man of Einfluss, the Social Rout, the Fashion. No publisher has ever avoided all. I think the Black Sparrow has done well here, has flown over these dangers unbedraggled, only a feather or two out of place.

15. The trouble with venal books (see above) is not that bad work is printed, but that dull work fills the ears of the audience. (Not a mass audience —

16. Poetry never had a mass audience & never will. If I had a dollar for every American who has read *Clarel* (i.e., by Melville, our Great Writer) I would still pause for reflection before entering a better Chinese restaurant.

17. Ditto the *Faerie Queene, Kalevala, Mahabharata*, not to be parochial.)

18. The trouble with venal books is that they stuff the ears of the Happy Few to whom the poem's News could come, the people who could themselves form & transform it & carry it forward. This is not a matter of quantity of books, but quality of attention. Like any other benign event, a poem requires sustained awareness, the eye kept on the ball, the ear alert.

19. How to carry a song to the 300 (Corman guessed) or 3,000 (I'd guess, with celtic expansiveness) humans who *could* hear it, *could* make use of it? This is the only problem connected with the publication of poetry: how to set an accurate text out where they can find it.

20. It is not to be expected that every first-rate mind will issue its subtlest processes in a form every graduate student can minutely appreciate. It is to be expected that a small stone falls in a very large pool & the ripples go on & on. Weakening steadily perhaps, but the thing has been done the environment has been radically changed.

21. I have heard poets whose work suggests greater sense rave at the prospect of an audience of millions. Such poets will weary of the Resolute Confucian Small of the Black Sparrow Press, will hanker after rock festivals & the beating of wings in the lower air. It is our work to sing the world into place, dance trees & raise the dead. We must be clear, always, about the *means* to these necessary ends. Festivals & crowds are results, not causes.

22. The *sparrow* as Egyptian determinative portends what is *small* or what is *evil*. Comfort here for elitist & blakean alike. We all know what black means.

23. When I walk into a gallery, I do not expect to see the paintings hidden in the dingiest corner while the main space is given to decorator mirrors & wallpaper. That is exactly what we find when we pick up a book review supplement or a publisher's catalogue. The primary, the blissful Homer for which the whole art is formed, lies tucked in the back between children's books & thrillers, unless the poet happens to be a Russian with Second Thoughts about Stalin.

24. Leading to: whatever else may be said about this press (& it has its weak points, & enemies properly attentive thereunto), it has set the priorities straight once again. Every now and again *somebody* has to do that. Laughlin did it in the '30s & '40s, Jonathan Williams in the '50s & '60s. John Martin is evidently doing it now, since '67. Given our american affluence, we can apparently afford only one of these at a time. Make use of it.

25. I'm writing as a poet who's had a few of his books published by the Black Sparrow Press. What commitment I feel is to a press that keeps certain properties straight, that esteems the product of workers in the field as its primary concern, that is prepared to devote time & expense to setting out an accurate text.

26. Interesting to note that (as far as I can tell) the whole press has been supported exclusively by the sale of books. No foundations, no government grants to cloud the issues, no kind heiresses. It is commerce, & it has a cogency of its own.

27. Some of the books are expensive, are for collectors to collect (or whatever they do with them), thus presumably supporting the press & building throughout the terrain odd interesting pockets of attention to the work of many poets. The trade editions have been called expensive too. Some of them even cost as much as records.

28. Naturally, as brahmins, we are not interested in commerce.

29. I come back to it, that this press (and some smaller ones like it) asserts, as no media will ever dare to assert, that poetry is a primary, an existential fact of renewing importance to a society menaced day after day by its own shoddy past & habits of attention.

30. Sequential release of time's stored material. This is better than a magazine. Magazine used to mean 'warehouse' or 'arsenal.' The present point: that work be available, that there be somewhere in these years a *currency* of what men make.

(1971)

AN INTRODUCTION TO THOMAS MEYER'S
UMBRELLAS OF ÆSCLEPIUS

yo usrānām apīcyā	*he who knows the secret*
veda nāmāni guhyā	*hidden names of the cows*
sa kavih kāvyā puru	*as a poet / seer he greatly prospers poetic art*
rūpamdyaur iva puṣyati	*as the bright sky its color* [2]

Who will preserve the old names, not as lore in aging books (for all my love of books)
       but will set them to dance in the new days,
              the new discourse we have after all (Amerikanoi!) fashioned? Is there a contradiction here, one we want to weep or wrangle, say, between the beautiful precisions that have been preserved for us in old records, old poems,
       and this new, necessary, sense now advancing from the powerful productivities of Pound, Olson, Zukofsky and those who have learned from them?
       This sense demands the clarity possible only when a man speaks from his own experienced body his own breath (as our song goes), size of the world about him what he can in fact touch with his feet, his swung arms:
       the perhaps natural sentimental restoration (so dated now, a public thing now, but not long ago a sharp excitement, reaffirming us) of the Body as center,
       how does that sense do combat with the old words, the natural unhumanized (it would seem) events (the flower, the stream, the beast under the hedge) in fact deeply humanized, dream-realized, by the names we have laid upon them
       or recovered

---

2. *Rig Veda* 8.41.5, cited & translated by Calvert Watkins in his essay "Language of gods, language of men," in *Myth and Law among the Indo-Europeans*, ed. Puhvel (Berkeley: University of California Press, 1970).

from their shapes or behaviors in a trance of our own attentions

                        or

caught from the old books, names, words, old ways of talking the world into place? Combat or concert? What excites me here is a continually sustained dialectic between an holistic sense of language (= English in all her times, Maldon to Altamont)

                        and a

refreshed (but equally holistic) sense of the poem as existential process. Most of our great innovators (but not Pound, or Bunting across the water) were suspicious of the old words, the 'poetic' words, in turn of the 'poetic' things themselves, as if every creature but man were a captive in an arid poetic zoo —

                       and rightly enough

were suspicious, in favor of their concentration on the Now of the poem's coming into being. But the poem does not come into being far away from the mind, and the mind, good mind, is alive with all the instances of naming and singing, old and new, that have borne in upon it. In Meyer's work, then, I find a type of the above: dialectic of the historic and the existential (to use words tireder than his own) right in the fact of the single poem, a dialectic that is not resolved by,

           but does, in deed, resolve the poem. And that's our contemporary marvel, that we have set forth (in correspondence) a new discourse:

> "whose problems — language problems — have been largely solved, to the extent that even my students quickly master them. We *do* have a language which is more responsive than any we've had since the 17th century"

(Don Byrd, letter of December 1973)

The austere exercises of craft and skill seem to have prepared us to unite our *times* again. To move in all the times of our mind.

And this language, solvable but not easy, is one I find Meyer working through. Responsive? The new language so, yes, because a language is not its lexicon, and the lexicon of our attentions can feed, now, the enriched complexity of mental act the poem now can be:

I open *The Umbrella of Æsculapius* (the name is a stretto of all these themes here striven), & I find:

> *Gorgon-headed candied sea holly*
> *has an adder's hue,*
> *eyes & nose*
>
> *that make a man a mirror*
>
> *& when you gather it*
> *(root & wort)*
> *let no sun*
> *shine on it*
>
> *Light steals the color of its power).*

And I ponder this instruction, or as instruction. If the old words (Gorgon, holly, adder, wort) are good for anything (not as helps in reading old poems only), then they are words still, word here being utterance, an outer articulation of what is (suddenly!) experienced. Good for anything. They store the power of long attention to things in the world, and on them we draw. They bring us too the fruits of a kingdom that seems to vanish from our sight day by day, and the lost possibilities (ecology!) of knowing in the senses are recruited, won, for the world of the mind, the knower, knower of this field,

As ever, then, accumulation and discharge.

But the way the lines fall, above, demands our notice, the dwindling measure of the first eight lines all at once rapt & quickened with "Light steals the color of its power," outrageous that words of such vagrancy (light, color, power), weak words, can here be wielded *as* powers, can be powerful, caught in the quickening dance itself the apparently meek preceding accuracies prepared.

*

Dance? The image of dance has haunted poetics at least since Yeats & Charles Williams and William Carlos Williams. Each age of poetry seems to have a pet metaphor drawn from other arts for an inward vision of its own nature; so in the sixteenth the stage, seventeenth the choir, eighteenth the senate or the coffee-house, so in our century we seem to have toyed with the image of ourselves as dancers and our shared work as a most complex dance. Clearest here to me is Duncan's offering of the 'attend/dance' — the poet's constant attention to the behavior of phonemes and syllables in the very act of his articulation, 'vowel-leading,' following the tones in (what we would love to describe as) the words' own way. Writing the poem, then, is discovery, *trobar,* finding the music & cooperating with the linguistic event — a dance sometimes of standing aside.

Dance? Perhaps the metaphor is obsolescent, or gradually turns into an image of the poet as scientist, with mind, heartmind, eye all fixed on the work "under hand." Dance or not dance, I point to something that would describe what the sounds of words *do.* How they lead and defer to one another, or how a word hurries in and blocks with its sharp vowel a whole chain of darker meta-phones. Metaphony. Beyond the gap of "word" or even syntax. Dance, why not, the light limbs of the lovers as a metaphor for the air we breathe into our own intricate passages, air that takes shape and color there, returns to the world to say what process it has moved through and now restores to the public air.

Following Meyer's traces, I'm dazzled by the daring of a quatrain like this one, on Egyptian Neith:

> *I've been, am, will be*
> *yet no man's drawn my net apart.*
> *My shuttle wove the world,*
> *I bore the sun before the born.*

where on the last sound itself (a word, too, provocatively used, forcing full consciousness of all it means, & does not mean), all the preceding dozen syllables converge, resound, as if they'd found the single Tonic of their system.

*

When I read such work (and perhaps that's Pound's *sinceritas* working again), I want to believe whatever a man tells me who tells it that alertly I will credit his predicament and his passion, come at length perhaps even to trust him that the gods and flowers and lovers are not just names in a book, needing glosses or sweat. They are names in *his* book, a glad book, fine instance of the life of process brought to life.

Annandale, February 1974

PREFACE TO BRUCE McCLELLAND'S
THE DRACULA POEMS

The poet is monster. His life is wielded with vast and terrible disproportion. Of a face he makes a journey or a Paradise He embeds himself in his text.

Here monsters are brought to life. The claims we make on other people, the grip of love, in all ordinariness, these make us the monsters of their quiet lives, dreams, insistences, disclosures, prophecies: all the texts of terror a Blake calls "Vision." (Reflect upon the drawing where he says it.)

Here, in this cycle of Investigative Recording, a monster is preserved, its deep identity probed, its yearnings — pothoi — compelled to speak.

Yearnings of a monster! They become *narration*.

The Odyssey is the meditation of Polyphemus, a dream-dazzled recital meant both to explain the discomfort of his sensory deprivation, and to distract his all-too-single mind from dwelling on that absence.

Dracula, that Centralian noble, dreams of the cachets of true availing prestige: a Swiss accountant, an English tailor, a Swedish mistress, an American poet to herald his reclaim.

Now what particular monster is here? It must be particular, to socket its teeth in something sure. We are brought to meet it via McNally & Florescu, who publicize Vlad Tepes the Historical. But of all monsters, none is less scary than one comfortably ambered in time past, safely sealed off behind death dates A.D.

So Dracula must be liberated from the bloody calm of Transylvanian history. He must be coopted by that Committee of Desire we call the living. Only here, among us, does Fear abound, enough to get our thoughts fixed on the notion: this godly animal can suck our blood.

And more. And worse. The poet (that monster) sometimes understands itself as making a raid on language. If it sucks language, what bleeds?

Is *silence* the secret blood of language? Juncture, pause, boundary: why are these lines so short, so broken? Is breath the blood an octave up? These lines do not imitate the suavity of the Lugosi they speak so kindly of. No snowy shirtfronts or diamond tiaras. Only the formal gown of language, razor-slitted here with cunning vacancies, to show.

Show what? A frightened sleek body, longing the caress a perfect-tongued lover might supply, timid that the cost of such induced ecstasy might be ec/stasy.

This deadly love that settles from the skies.

The problem is that Dracula, as mytheme, got mixed up with Nineteenth-Century English pain fantasies, le vice anglais and other algolunacies. The story, at heart, is not about suction, exsanguination, parasites, victims, or even the broad Hungarian steppe stretching towards China.

Nor is that pipistrelle Baron a mere dope-slick spike. Drac no drug. No biting people. No allegory for the pain that answers itself in little drops.

The specific monstrosity of the poet lies in its caring too much. Too much about the means (offending Christians), and too much about the ends (offending Buddhists).

Ultimately the monster is alone.

For all the gaiety of this work, a poet who talks Dracula tends to slink home at almost dawn, his bat-cape draggled over the shoulder of some latest friend, met in the Blood Hour between the closing of the bars & the moment when Blakean angels crank dawn up over the Atlantic. He is almost alone.

Gaiety is language risked. The poem lives where people take risks. Taking risks is saying what you mean. And what means you.

Lonely silences between lines. Why do I really feel that silence is aloneness? Is it really the *difficult*?

"These are not easy poems." They are haunted by the language they annihilated to assume their present skeletal form.

Dracula his fang. Fleshless victim: the air around them bleeds. Is it that music bleeds?

Yearnings of a monster. Œdipus in the horse-haunted grove, Frankenstein's new Prometheus adrift on the ice-floes, preserved and isolated at once, the Poor Bat who cannot say his mind.

The touch. That Dracula is the saddest lover, who seeks in the holiest way to become the other, but in the basest way only absorbs her Digestion (a voice creaks from his slim belly, unfattened by all his suckings), digestion is a sort of transformation. But only as killing is a sort of loving.

So I see the psychological brunt of these poems as the epiphanies of a man afraid of the other, as well he might be, afraid of the blood and tremble of him, who writes these spells, these knobby, pungent ropes of garlic, to guide such love to him & past him. And this out of a decent human disinclination to hurt or destroy.

Poetics of compunction.

The loneliness of art's decisions makes artists boozers for relief. The writing that goes on in these poems becomes writhing, angel-wrassling in interspace, wit & sinewiness & such all hungry to be sure. It is not in place. It is between places, I think, always a sentence of problematic intention, amphibolous. Amphisemous.

When this poem feels depressed, it reads a history book or tells some puns. But at its strength it offers no easy salient. Unseductive, it reserves itself for the haughty Syntactic Reader it has in mind.

As with so many tender important things our days, if it isnt magic it isnt anything.

Magic works by renewing our confrontation with the monstrous.

The monster is the man of one meaning. (The poem cures him by separation and division. Its weapon is the sword of Ali.) She brings all her skills to one focus, spends her time bent over the table. On which words take form. The form they take is hers, or his, till the only form left is theirs. Art is the casting out of pronouns.

I am that sentence whose prepositions are everywhere and whose pronouns are nowhere. Thus saith the Lady.

In the light of those fructifying confusions I read this work. Naturally at times I confound writer with written, girl with boy, biter with bitten.

With barefanged literalness, McClelland answers (as every bravo of the tribe of Ezra must) the ultimate Poundian question: the life of the poem, whence does it come?

[As EP himself rummaged Dante and Cavalcanti and Arnautz to find, sumthin abaouwt music, twang of the mind, them spondees like plucked strings —

        but Olson had to carve another answer, not the mu-sick, mu-sick, the sick of shlock we suffer now, drifting us off

— and so to each, alone in his eachery, the problem comes, to be worked out always
in terms of *this* one, this speech-possessing being,
the poet has to solve it *in* (not by) his words, her words]

So McC addresses it too: where does the life of the poem come from? Not history, Vlad Tepes & a mouthful of tuneful Slavic; not music. Is it the blood? He plays, as Maître Chomsky plays, with the metaphor of Animal. No wonder he falls back on Dracula, Abraham Stoker that Victorian quintessent, deranged by the Old Testament. The Life is in the Blood, sez Pentateuch. (Language is an organ, sez Chomsky.) The poem is endocrine. Feed flies to spiders, spiders to sparrows. Feed men to ... ?

Just here, where Olson, following the bent of his crypto-Christian Aristotelian mind back into Middleness, Iran, discovers the ultimate task of the time to be *angelology*.

(and he is right)

at just such an intersection McClelland fills in the blank with that curious mystery, Ænigma Americana, man-as-woman-as-city-as-poem-I-say-these-things-and-yearn-for-all-I-dread; name me and win the poem.

Who are these pronouns? Does a woman take a man in her mouth? Does a man take a man by the throat?

Poetry is taking language by the throat.

And we are back with the metaphor: Man is a sort of animal.

He bleeds to prove it.

The metaphor is tolerably familiar. Several trillion dollar global enterprises are built upon it.

The poem eats the man. Q.E.D.

Could it be that even while Chomsky is busy trying to flog life back into the metaphor [economically viable but intellectually exhausted], McClelland here is draining the fluid out?

Poetry, then, is biting language in the throat, drawing out what is mortal, drossy, stale? Another well-connected metaphor is at hand.

But be at the throat. If the source of life is not the blood, it must be the syntax. (Not an organ but a system. Not a node but a net. Not a brain but a mind. Not a what but a when.) It must be the movement, I mean it must move. The capillary jump.

Here McClelland is of use to us as Bataille was, to focus on the dread: is life in the life of *things*? Bring the knife to the skin to learn the lives of each. Living one another's death. Old philosophies renewed in the moist body's clefts. Then he takes the knife away.

The wonderful prose section, of the transparent, the diaphane she. Bare allegory (I could think) of Language as he would fondle her below the organdy. To rescue Her from Her transparency? Words, we non-linguists know (and linguists dare not entirely forget), are substances enough to shock or grieve or make erect. The *names* of the body!

Nomina substantia.

The Dracula Poems comprise at once the presentation of a complex ideograph, and the simultaneous self-commentary glossed out around it, expounding it, deriding it with straightfaced pedantry, resorbing it into the tight complexity of its first form.

"An explanation enriches without diluting." The text shares the virtue of its hero: thoroughness. It explores the image cluster, casts off the horrors and the movies and the casual sadisms.

A thorough poem.

From its dream I recover an image of what primarily Dracula must have been. He was the winged dragon that Miss Psyche's parents dreaded, who lived in the castle on the haunted mountain it was death for vapid pretty wicked sisters to visit; he was the one who moved unseen in the awful convulsions of the marriage bed, whose kiss soothed his beloved into sleeps that issued in the unpeopled daylight. Nervous waking, rich comforts of attention, unseen energies. The house itself is alert. Psyche asked at last: whence comes the life of this castle (this poem), this love-knot we tie every night in the dark? She guessed it was a body, lit her candle and painted a handsome one in hot wax. It rose and spoke to her: I am not he. Or, I am he no longer. And he went. Her guess was wrong. The life was not in the image but in the movement. This ur-Dracula then, as we always somehow knew in the movies, turns out to be Desire. Who moves.

June 1976

AMERICAN DIRECTION: ON CAROLEE SCHNEEMANN

Schneemann: the work moves for the years I've been watching it, always from [the viewer's] lower left to upper right. Boxes, canvases, a wonderful frieze of watercolor paper she gave me a dozen years ago, with transfers and fuzzy enigmas transpiring upwards, always upwards, like cartoons becoming flesh becoming More Than That.

This philosophical direction is an Amerithing, a touch of Emerson, a clear honest yearning towards hanging the completed work up right there, on the chandelier (life an Irish party). It is innocent, and its rage to get there probably has scared many of the otherwise audience. When sophistication, the authentic Europe of the head, joins with the native urgency of her work in so many arts, there is a kind of shock or overload; the cheap machine of publicity freaks out and people stand around abashed at her shapely largeness.

I for one would not have it otherwise. Schneemann is a painter, filmmaker (apotheosis of that up-to-the-right movement in *Fuses*), embodiment in body meant of arts not yet culturally specified but factually, actually, in her work given. Schneemann is a writer, a diagnost of our malaises & deft spokeswoman of the priority of *personal meaning* above all. Her written texts work vigorously as a fusion of personal *planh* & the most outrageous outward! social! invention!

Schneemann's work is in essence: *problematic*. I would not want her work to veer from its own variegation of means (her Media are Many, not 'Mixed') or kaleidoscopic inwardness of gesture; I would not want it less clamorous, good-humored, immense, complaining, generous, zealous, yeasty than it is.

There is a triumph to be made of circumstances. Comes to my mind a recollection of a theater piece years back, in a raunchy East Side theater: Schneemann on stage, upright & bare amidst a raft of literal garbage, the 'set' of that event. She stood like the pleistocene Lady of Beasts, but also like any artist, every artist, over the junk of one's life, here, for an instant, lifted with wit & power & decency into a luminous gesture.

2 May 1977

A NOTE ON NORA JAFFE
[FOR *DRAWINGS & RELIEF SCULPTURE*]

The furniture of the mind, like every other, gets creaky, faded, falls out of fashion. The Art Nouveau that gasped back to life for a few moments in the later Sixties, epicentered at Sausalito, leaves a generation hungry for those sexy, sinuous, 'organic' forms, but one wisely unwilling to pay the price of elvishness and cutesy that the Raspberry Reich of art demands in these glib days of Commodity.

I want here to hail an artist who startles me with a body of work at once abstract and sensuous. It answers the questions that vex me sometimes: where did a feel for *our* forms go, feel for delicate calf muscle or solid trapezius? Is the flesh just a good idea? Sometimes one wakes up hungry for the simple likeness of humans, even as Ezekiel (maybe) in the torment of exile looked up towards the highest reach of his imagination and saw the Likeness of a Human seated on the Throne.

Nora Jaffe's work is haunted by us. We are the ghosts, *nos homines*, who wander through the vast controlled spaces of her paintings and drawings, who come through the walls of her remarkable reliefs. In her work some Genesis goes further: human made in the image of Image, then world made in the image of human. Image, not shape. Jaffe's work is not representational. It shows us nothing. It enacts from the ground we share: the space we are, and by being in it master and obey.

This is the 'human universe' that American poetry has cared so fervently about. And here in Jaffe's work, like Olson's, there is no place that is not us.

And that perception, if I'm entitled to it, is the only verbal aspect of her work at all — not a 'concept' but a steady conceiving of all of *that* as all of *this*. Appropriation: making ours.

Paradoxes abound. When I first saw her work, like any other child of god I saw cocks and their destinies leaping all over the plane. The in and out of intromission, gothic ogival upvaulting erections out of the longmuscled ardor of leggy forms, svelte bellies — how fine that was, a homecoming for the eye. But at the same time, how clearly wrought these images were in (to me) an entirely different tradition, of Gorky's agonic abstraction, in a structural vitality so focused it could annihilate the figure itself in the burst of what it does. These images do.

Then a subtler, rarer still, sort of tension exists in her work. Two words go over and over in my thought when I consider her big drawings, two words not much yoked together: Elegance and Energy. True elegance is a shiver, pubic coiled on an immaculate sink, a finger pointing to a word in a text, a seventeen-day-old moon erased by a cloud.

Why do I feel so patriotic looking at her work? This is my body, my town. Her work dares to dissever myself from that community. This is too big for you to get out of. You'll really have to think of some way of putting up with the energy of this system. It says.

And I answer: I love the size of this. It is big in a way that ratifies *Scale* as the fifth dimension of the arts, all arts. I feel it's given back to me (restoration, apokatastasis) the size of what it feels like, what it *is*, to stand in a place and do something there, anything, anything I would wholly do. I feel restored to my own terms.

Another way of saying that is, of course, to celebrate anew that wonderful Absence in this century's art: the banished window. These works are not peepholes, no prosceniums. There is nothing outside. There is nowhere else.

(1978)

NOTES & PREFACES

NOTE ON HARVEY BIALY'S *BABALON 156*

Cult or court of love, sweet incenses of insidious beautiful tantras, the wild kill-society love mood of Peire Vidal in the garage of Arthur Avalon, there's a muddle these days here beginning to be resolved. This male-fascist thing of *investing* in women, hope to blast thru the proximate lady to, exactly what, here, one, at least, of us, them, tries to define. Modulo a crooked music. That here, in this scientist's hands, takes account enough of matter *not* to lose the woman in Shape. As the patriarch said, Nice thing about piety is getting out of it, into the fresh air. Where even Salome comes to rest a while from her own fierce juices, no good, even out here among the sunflowers & the Impalas the grind of primal desire rehearses its lessons. Chug chug. The nakedness of woman is the work of God, says irish-american Wm Blake, we will never get away from it. Now here what to my sense of it is happening is a hard edge appearing, some of the *exactness* of guarded ritual here edges into the poem, if we're quick enough to see it. Bialy engages with an utterly serious vocabulary, thinkable, closer the better, & his music is thought's tune also, locating the world. I like his geography. A test book. Try it on.

(1970)

PREFACE FOR GEORGE QUASHA'S *SOMAPOETICS*

Eros also has its intellect. I would speak to that in Quasha's *Somapoetics*. There is a pleasure in it that is thinkable. The arguments of lust have too often confuted growths of logical structure. Here they con/foutre each other, twine around, somewhat spin. Of the several longer structures being sung these days, Quasha's seems among the clearest, most vexed, funny, even in a way duplicit (but then song of its nature tends to enthymeme) — it revises itself, it hides dappled among its many sources, it darts. But I think of the ogives of its aspiration, sharp slits in the apparent substance of fact & theory through which Quasha displays, often enough to my taste, exciting and logically voluptuous enactments.

Depths & depthesses. Our sense is grateful for the heat. Like all hot books, *Somapoetics* writhes in friction. I poise my native Fire here, though Q's interlocutors are nymphs of an opposite Element who teach the subtler frictions, musculature of water. To my sense of it, this present time is focused on the new possibility, perennial, Osiris restored from his long dismemberment: the long poem, long song, long count, possibly among us. Of all the long processes now going forward, I feel *Somapoetics* is the most interesting. It touches me close.

(1973)

PREFACE FOR JOHN YAU'S *CROSSING CANAL STREET*

John Yau, as near as I can figure, made his first connections with the local facts of our language during the reign of the first Elizabeth. He may have been a west-seeking Imperial Geodetic official who crossed Eurasia to find the rumored springs beyond the Volga. His coming aroused interest among the lyric poets of the Crimean Tartars, his far kin. They in turn aligned him with the noumenal accountancy of the Counts of Roznberk, those incessant patrons of the precisely focused exotic. Following the subtle gridwork of the hour he soon found himself at ease in Angleterre, guest of Fulke Greville. While he never visited the long low house at Mortlake (the nefast name may have deterred him, dead lake, dead water, sad prolepsis of poor Wen Yi-Tuo, in whose adopted city Yau now lives), Yau was properly respectful of the work and cunning of Dr Dee, the catalogue of whose library later followed him back into those transcendental carryings-on east of Lake Baikal. Some years later, he allowed himself to be born in America, to be reared in Boston. Yet the savor of those first linguistic connections, back in those years when Sidney (specifically! his appointed task!) struggled to greek us, bend for the first time in English a subtle fluid measure of verse, that savor still stayed with Yau, enfranchised him of and from the Trimount jargons, to move, to move with his ears and hear with his eyes.

I got to know him when he put in some time reading at a small Nestorian university on the banks of the Hudson where I happened to be Prefect of Logaoedic Studies. I found him flagrantly irish, wild, a close reader, deep talker, anxious to learn from everybody. Already his sights were on the measure of his public work. Which here opens.

16 Nov. 1975
(1976)

TWO NOTES ON FRANZ KAMIN

1) On *Ann Margaret Loves You*

Once while I was listening to a lecture on dreams, I noticed that the girl in front of me had fallen asleep on her arms. Where was she then? It would be gentle to guess that Franz Kamin is busy exploring the geography of her elsewhere. Yet the force of his work is like that of all the other explorers, whose images become gentle and benign in hindsight (Audubon, for instance, fleeced Keats' brother at cards). It is transgressive, impatient of the natives, hasty, not yet polished for the presentation to the Société d'Ailleurs. Here are the travel diaries, still stained with blood and lime squash.

(1980)

2) On *Scribble Death*

Kamin's work has an unbeatable combination of formal obsession with vernacular energy. *Scribble Death* is as full of creative paranoia as the preamble to the Constitution, the ardent self-pity that makes us American, learned from Virgil and our crazy religions and the rock-infested acres of our post-glacial unfarmable New England. This is a continuous novel in a series of discontinuous texts, a weird and funny frenzy of suicidal life-affirmations, silly beauty. There's a lot of hard, sexy nighttime music (Webern writing an opera on Raymond Chandler?) but beside the all-night drunken monologue of the guy on the next stool you suddenly realize you're hearing the world's last love story.

(1986)

TWO NOTES ON ELIZABETH ROBINSON

1) Four Faces for *String*

1. Poetry returns literal space. It tells what is inside sealed vessels, knows that the King of Pentacles wears beneath his yellow robes. Knows but doesn't tell.

2. Elizabeth Robinson writes that kind of poetry, grown strong from not always telling. At her text, I think I'm reading myth or folklore, then suddenly hear someone crying in the next room.

3. There is a Borges story called "The Sect of the Phoenix," about humankind's oldest religion. *String* is scripture for that sect.

4. I can't go on or preface will be wordier than book. But not longer. Her string is very long, loops all the way from God to even darker places. It is the latest strand in her subtle, distinctive writing. Elizabeth Robinson isn't like anybody at all, so we can recognize her instantly. Deeply.

(1992)

2) A blurb for *Counterpart*

For twenty years Elizabeth Robinson has been making language do new things, and for a wonder she's never afraid of that shadow of words we call affect. In this new collection, *Counterpart*, her precise ear and sense of line sustain a poignant austerity of gesture. She knows that the real dark is the one we keep inside, and her lines scratch at the shell. Her exuberant imagery is chastened here, focused — image names meaning. The book is exciting in its silverpoint tracing of the complexity of our "dubious desires." She probes macabre spaces, golems and hells & devils, but not the ones our culture knows — these are the proper monsters of her self-encounters.

(2013)

[BEGINNING OF *A CRITICAL ORGANON*] : TOWARDS ENSLIN'S *FORMS*

A HEADNOTE:

A season or two ago, John Taggart called me to invite a statement or essay on *Forms* for this colloquy. I agreed, with an eagerness I owe to Enslin's work in general and this most intricate rich poem in particular, and with a dread reluctance I more and more feel in confronting any enterprise of 'literary criticism,' my own or other people's. The point I would make is not an attack on criticism *per se* [though my hope to supplant it with 'deicticism' is of note here], but rather a conviction that an effective criticism, one that can enter and sustain discourse about the poetics of the past twenty years in America, is still far from being with us; instead, emergent critical enterprises have been turned, in all their novelty, to whipping the same dead (or at least subdued) horses criticism has been working over since Eliot reclaimed the art. Criticism has been inept & tardy, say, with the *Cantos* — and it's sixty years since they began. In Kenner's most recent work, we see at last a capacity to move with some of the nimbleness of wit the poem obviously both arises from & speaks about. How much longer will we have to wait for a critical amplexus of Olson, Duncan, Zukofsky? There's no lack of willing termpaperwriters and thesis-shufflers — but an astonishing lack of critical *impetus*. Be that as it may, I find myself embarrassed at being able to offer so little to this gathering about Enslin. What seemed to me to be required, before I could deal with *Forms*, was to begin and carry through a review and revision of my own critical presuppositions and demands. Taggart did not ask for that, be it noted. I scarcely, in these beginnings, get around to *Forms* at all. Yet I can in some sort of conscience offer these annotations, if only because they all came about while thinking from and about *Forms*. What is here is a series of propaideutic reflections, or coming towards being able to say something about *Forms*. A pox on my fussiness, maybe. But it gets me started, & moves me toward the conviction that a person's whole critical or deictic enterprise is single, one work, organon or such, ere to begin mine, and offer, is wings to Enslin, in homage.

3 · A BOOK OF THE COMPANY

1.

Wishing to confront the poem, I would like best to set before the reader: times of its process, instances of its turns. To do so would turn my back on the self of it; the flesh of the poem is not, or not very, amenable to the critic's histology. Not *pars pro toto*, but *totum per se*.

2.

That seems to tell the reader Read it. Only that way can one become a reader, the reader of *Forms*. Too much association with the young or the uninformed (those two most innocent categories of avidya) can turn the critic into a persuader. (Peitho, whose name and business that was, was not much favored by the Greeks.)

2a.

Criticism is not persuasion.

3.

To discuss *Forms* is an extreme case, but still a case, of discussing a poem. By all laws of the psyche's honesty (that yearning we call logic), the critic should first set forth his preconceptions or biases or, more to the point, the preconceptions of his theory, if he may be said to possess one.

4.

So that, my act of criticism means to represent a new possibility, not a Criticism but a Deicticism, deictic (Greek *deiknumi*, I demonstrate, rather than *krino*, I judge). This new or deictic possibility means to gesture towards, walk along beside, assert ontologies, abstain from evaluations, prestiges.

5.

Should there be an Underwriters Laboratory report? 'This poem will do no one any harm, and might do some people a power of good — but only if they read it.'

6.

But books — like patent medicines — also do good just standing on the shelf.

7.

A poem in five volumes, 646 pages; a poem as long as itself. The list price of the five volumes is $100. Most of the volumes are likely to be out of print, until some bliss-bestowing buccaneer runs it off on his offset press and lowers the price.

8.

I am tempted to write about *Forms* without referring to its length. While its length is no accident (any more than that of *The Nibelung's Ring*), it is not something that bears in upon the reader's notice moment by moment. This poem is long only compared with other poems. It has fewer words than *Valley of the Dolls*, and conceivably fewer female stars — but not many fewer. Is a year long? One sits in the green golden afternoons of Dutch summers, cities, sipping coffee, watching wife, reading. The wind blows. Presently a year has passed. One has eaten 700 meals or so, swallowed a few hundred gallons of coffee, read half a thousand books. Is it long? Is it long compared with this moment, this utter privileged night, humid, throwing cool breeze, the night freight shuddering north past Cruger's Island? A year has nothing to do with the moments which, to an abstract eye, appear to compose it.

9.

But this poem has a plan — I mean it is written in English, has proper names in it, Garance, Surinam, Slocum, Mahler. It tells stories. It is not at all like a year. No year, no *annus mirabilis*, is so fervent all the time. Can the year be fervent all day long? The incommensurability of day with year (never a whole number of days) ought to remind me: the whole poem is demonstrably a unity, but not experienced as unity.

10.

Any more than the Iliad or Commedia are, can be, *experienced* as unities. They can be known as such, at first by pious belief or tradition, later through a long sense ((a year?)) the piety helps to motivate. Known as such through diligence, scrutiny, remembrance. Any jack teacher can *prove* the unity of a poem. (Or disprove it, if it comes to that.) Important to ask if such demonstrability inheres in the poem-object or the teacher-subject. Since proof has nothing to do with any text.

11.

Rumors began to fly in the 1940s and 1950s that the fragments of great Osiris were being brought back together at last. The news came in from London, Alexandria, Rapallo, the West. The fragmentations which had been our study in any of the several traditions (e.g., Liszt-Busoni-Varèse-Cage), the fragmentations by which we characterized ourselves as modern — perhaps there was a process that, even more modern, a wind blowing from the achronic future, brought the ripe smell of a more integral turn of affairs.

12.

"It all coheres," said Pound. No matter if he doubted his work. It all coheres and gestures towards a wilder, ecstatic sense of coherence than we've known.

13a.

Criticism needs to tear off its clothes too, pass under the *jugum* to the mysteries, abandon its zippered calm, if it is to be (and it is to be) a fit partner to poetry in the great mind-dance of this commune. By fragmentation, by homeopathy (like curing like): the fragmented critique opens and exposes the wholeness and unity of the long poem, the long-supposed fragmentary poem. Criticism must be as attentive to its own process as to the 'object' under its consideration.

13b.

It is appropriate to distrust continuous expository prose offered as criticism. Glints reveal.

14.

Because it *is* a consideration — a conjunction of stars, a shared constellation. Not a dialogue — because the work and the work are incommensurable. But like dialogue in that the feeling is mutual, I'm sure.

15.

It is less that I want the reader to confront the poem, this poem. It is that I want to speak from a decade of confronting and evading this poem.

Almost all of *Forms* came to me in typescript. I served, as well as my messy habits permitted, as depository in Not-Maine of the completed sections. Reading the sections as they came in — or sometimes scanting the reading, things always going on so — was a rare and mysterious privilege. Not reading it as it was written (what earthly difference does that make?), but reading it as I was living. Which does matter. I have never studied it with frantic or sustained attentions. I would flunk an exam on it. Yet I've read it, read it living, so to say, rather than sitting.

16.

So what I have to report is somehow like that: a poem that passed by me one decade, like a long freight train.

17.

Richard Strauss wanted to be Mozart. Stravinsky wanted to be Gesualdo. Enslin talks about Mahler, consoles himself for his time's inattention, and for the sadder fact he notes, that his time had no meat to be attentive with. Over and over he cites Mahler's perhaps similarly mooded prediction, *Meine Zeit wird noch kommen*. My time will yet come. Sometimes Enslin quotes it as... *wird jetzt kommen*, as if to say My time will come *now*, using the word cognate with our own 'yet.' Mahler's time comes or goes. Since the poem began, Mahler has become, from a bizarre mystico-schmaltz outsider, one of the central figures of the music world around us. Enslin makes that prediction with his *jetzt*, an act of insistent magic, come, make my time come now.

18.

In truth his time comes *jetzt*, comes as he writes and as the reader reads. His time (as Gurnemanz explains to battled Parsifal) (as every poem explains to its evident author), his time turns into space. A long poem manifesting its *rhythmos*, its shapeliness in time.

19.

Enslin and Mahler? Long, complex, musical, narrative, self-involved, ironic. But there is a verticality in *Forms* I miss in Mahler (it may be there, masked by Mahler's hurry). Unhurried, constantly beckoning me in to hear, apprehend, resolve the curious transient harmonies.

20.

Consider the difference between a sentence printed in the grammar of a language you're beginning to learn, and the same sentence shouted at you in a strange country. The relations between the thinking subject and the thinking object are always to be made clear. Or the difference between the artifact and the projective.

21.

Cherish Coleridge's implicit advice: If you conceive of a polarity, immediately set it at right angles to another polarity.

22.

By extension: any polarity that does not summon another, *crossing* or complementary polarity, into existence (into mind) is not a true polarity at all, but only a set of two terms randomly or inexpertly chosen, not polar at all. God *&* Man is a famous example. [Which summoned in turn from European brains at length another false *&* infamous polarity, Devil-Woman, from which we have not yet recovered.]

23.

When one speaks of the processual one does not mean the random or the disordered. The exact contrary is meant. I have heard from Enslin that before *Forms*, or early at *Forms*, there was a detailed 'graph' of the poem's intended path. One thinks of the similar arrogant itinerary prefixed to *Paterson*.

24.

A good motto for poets comes from the Qor'an, Sura 18: Allah says to contractual Mohammed, who had promised yesterday to expound a puzzle 'tomorrow,' "Never say 'I shall do that, without fail, tomorrow.' Unless you add: if Allah wills."

25.

If the poem allows.

26.

Later, Enslin threw the graph aside. Over and over the text speaks of its own liberation, of its kicking off the ball-and-chain of First Intentions.

26a.

There is no tyrant like a good idea.

27.

It would appear that intentions have as little place in poetics as in criticism. Deictics.

28.

Earlier in that Sura: "What knowledge they possess is little. Therefore, enter not into controversy about them beyond what is at hand."

28a.

Sense of the work, always: What is at hand. *There* are both the strife and the striving. Both cutting edges of that divine double-axe, the word.

29.

The critic (and, *a fortiori*, the deictic) who strays from his text is rallied by the cry Back to our sheep! as if he were shepherd and the text before him a congeries of smelly, unruly sheep. The text is not sheep. Perhaps the deictic is the sheep who strays from the flock of his mental associations out into the cold meadow, wolf-beset, of the text's own behavior.

29a.

A good sheep who strays from his proprieties. Proprieties always lead to a market place. Where the sheep is slain.

30.

Beware of a critic with a point to make. He is like a hired interpreter who has shady business of his own to execute in the shadow of the Pyramids he's supposed to be expounding.

31.

A poem as handsomely *durchkomponiert* as *Forms*, so elaborately wrought, warns us against understanding the Yearning for the Open as any sort of debased craving or nostalgia for the imperfect.

32.

The perfect artifact always leads to more than itself. "Its vistas lead... to other vistas." (Duncan on N.O. Brown)

33.

I spent the day gathering all the books of poetry together, putting them in the alphabet again, out of the time-sequences or strata of their arrivals. And that too is an Isis-task, the gathering, all the fragments brought together, the contiguity of texts. The communal poem this age declares, of which *Forms* is a big wave; I think of Nono's title (is it?) "like a wave of force and light."

34.

If prose is to be written, critical, examining, deictic, then what I have to say in such modes must form one continuous work or process, pieces of which can be publicked at need. Organon?

35.

I mean that obviously there's only *one* work a man has, at once work, tool, problematic, analytic, statement, suasion. Now the tale of it considers this event, now that. Gestures. Gestures towards, touches, embraces, recur. Sometimes insists. Sometimes not.

36.

A poem on what happened as I moved forward to 'write a poem.' That is, to bring myself to the place where my energies or mind or skill, or at least my *hand*, could be put to use.

36a.

Who knows what part of whom writes? *Forms* is the poem or text that resulted from Enslin moving forward to a place he dimly intuited to stand in, a place maybe remembered dimly from a former year, where blackberries might be found low under the shadow and shelter at once of the sumac; the text arises form its own pursuit. And *Forms* is the text that resulted from Enslin baffled, striving, hurrying to write a poem called *Forms*, et cetera?

37.

A long poem, a big house, and how to get in? Is there room to stand inside? How does the poem make room for a reader? The social fact of language, divine, human glory of, pentagonal, a star. It amazes me always that I can read. That I can get into any text. That a text is whole and integral & obviously not with the stucco crumbling off the chicken wire, yet I can get into it. Not just the breath of me, but that I can get inside and stand up there. How does that Happen? How does the poem let us in?

38.

Is it narrative? Sheherazade's House, Winchester House, the never-ending room after room of fiction? Not so, not here; there are stories, but they are discrete, shapely, contextual. They are tossed up, spray from the lyric frenzy, subside again. They generate and are generated. Dante's canzone of the Three Women is perhaps the earliest emblem of how it happens.

39.

But it is not the stories that keep me alert and keep me, frankly, reading. Nor is it, I think, some sustained and recurring measure, like that Virgilian cadence that carries me through the *Cantos* — though I'm not as sure of that. There are musical intricacies in *Forms*, god wot. But I think that at the core of my stay with the poem is the sense of telling, a heart-mind in discourse, *favella*, our power of reasoning, noticing, telling — and any story is, however fascinating, a sub-case of that power, a glass of water from that fountain.

40.

This work would teach Ad Version, a thing we need. A turning-towards. To teach us to turn towards. The contradiction that that is not antagonism.

41.

Terms from two different traditions we could use well in talking about *Forms*. Foucault (in his Rivière book) speaks of all the dossiers he's read as constituting "an intersection of discourses." Reti speaks of "interversion," interchanging the notes of a theme to produce a new theme. One of the greatnesses of Enslin is the variety and variegation of discourses he can both maintain in sequences, and 'intervert.'

42.

Art does not come from procedures systematically followed, but from a process of living in the world: living with other people, with mind at work, with mind, in touch. There is no way of predicting art from life-style, of course. There is no way of predicting art from the 'style' of itself. The painting, the poem, is its own tribunal. If judgment should ever happen to be needed.

43.

Is this a poem: A series of variations on a limited but persistent trove of themes. Every office has its own furniture, windows, lights. These shape the work done therein. The few things I manage to remember, things I can't manage to forget. Manage: to take in hand. Enact.

44.

Like every other profession, writing has its carpets beneath which all too personal affairs are swept. The cock hardens by itself but the heart must be hardened. I hate this. I hate this timid turn towards where it's easiest, because most quiet, even the long quiet of the 'therapist', the flab blab, the lax. *Forms* is wonderfully tonic here, like the rest of E's work — I find Erslin consistently working an accurate, human way through the confusions of private & public; closing is part of disclosing. And venting is part of inventing.

45.

God, he's so patient with people! No wonder the poem is so long, it takes in all the turns, the nimble receptiveness that waits at the end of loves.

46.

Latin *putare* meant 'to cut' as well as 'to think.' The knife of thought. It survives as the Italian *potare*, 'to prune a tree.' To shape the growth. Build a poetics from these thinking/s.

47.

Poetry is that curious activity where ignorance is of more avail than certainty. But an active ignorance. Feed the animals and speak well of women, said the old poets. Olson on how a young poet should learn his business: "Feed sugar to horses."

48.

A good thing a long work gives its society: Chance to hear one voice, one idiolect, sustained for a long time, distributed over hundreds of topics, needs. Media, TV, are worse than the Académie Française as standardizers, samers. The long work to hear around in. The corners. The streets.

49.

Of course length is not long. Length is thick.

50.

Singing schools. We've heard of those. But what to sing about? Or, what is singing about? *Forms* speaks there, is another kind of school, one that teaches care, of doing, or of knowing, or of knowing what to do.

51.

I do not write criticism. I don't exactly know what that statement means. I do not write criticism, but if I did, I would write about *Forms*.

52.

Immense embarrassment. I say: I will not judge, I will demonstrate. But then how strangely I fail the task, gesture vaguely towards a closed book, murmer this and that. It is as if I couldn't get the book open in public; and that says something about me. And it. And public.

53.

But why, if I wrote about it, would I write about *Forms*? Because *Forms* seems to me a compelling interesting story, a matrix of stories; and in some way the matrix is richer than the gems it bears. Mottled with a man's feelings ["Mahler-ial fever"] in the world. The thing he needs to know. (I need to know. I need to know what somebody needs to know.) The places. The women. The woman.

53a.

Years later, *Sitio*, the place, the singular.

54.

Poets write bad criticism. That is, it may be interesting, but it doesn't help the order and enterprise of Criticism as a thing in the world, thing in itself, church and academy. Poets write criticism filled with quick shots, thrills, sudden grace, hard garnets, sly asides — but it has no structural value, what *ces poètes* say, doesn't help to build the large brownstone house criticism means to have as its own.

55.

We don't expect (as Pound complained) critics to write poetry. When they do (Winters, Empson), they write the sort that brings property values down. Their poetry is full of quick shots, thrills, sudden grace, hard garnets, sly asides. But you can't live on it.

56.

There are people who think a body can live on pure protein. Not so. Art, like life, is immoderate, lives on contradictions, not one thing.

57.

Even fire needs air to burn.

57a.

Or: public fire is hidden fire burning common air, our local fuel.

58.

Condition of Poetry: I have no architecture to throw athwart the world, no dymaxion, no gimmick. Nothing but the deed itself of utterance. What a slender means. How close to prime-matter it seems to be. And what do you do, sir? I say true. Like sooth, the future? The future is locked in what anybody says. So what do you do? I say so.

59.

Sometimes I have allowed into poems material that Blake (or Satie) would have sent to the margin. Perhaps doing as I've done has been the effective gesture of liberation. At the same time, when it 'works,' it means a poem built from the outside in, always seeking center. So the challenge between centrifugal and centripetal lives in poetics too. *Forms* includes its outside, as surely as *Synthesis* and *Ranger*, with a conscious and explicit use of marginalia, extrude the inward, the source-within.

60.

So I suppose several sorts of criticism, of a criticism. One of them disposes the reader to the text. Makes the reader hungry for the text, or makes the text's largest sense beckon the reader in a new way. What does that mean? It means I fear a criticism that is all opinion and insight, or that fails all fore-play and all climax for the sake of a mechanic intromission of *statement*. I fear a criticism made of statements.

61.

To care about *Forms* because of the stories it tells. Moi, I like stories. The ones I read here stay with me over the years. Enslin wields the rhythm of persons so well that there is a large mood or sense in me that answers only to the word he names: Surinam, Garance.

62.

Rhythm of persons. That interests me. In the later works, Enslin (like Coleridge noting Psellus) puts in the margin names of initials of the persons whose deeds or desires flourish in the text beside. These marginalia make the thing I mean here even more conspicuous. That much of the beauty of Enslin's work is in his, and its, miraculous openness to the psychic presence of other people. His work is a sort of anti-Tower, for all the fabled hermitry of his life's circumstances.

63.

That's the huge promise and implication. A work that returns to the people. That should be no simpler than the life to which it speaks.

1 Feb 76
(*Truck* #20, 1978)

ON IRBY

[The years I have known him and the love I have for the man and his work curiously do not equip me to speak abroad of his writing, its insidious and pervasive music, its vast range of referentiality — to both of which I turn again and again. There is no body of work remotely like it. In another order of discourse than the celebrations of such a festschrift as this, I would content myself with deictic, that is, I would read into the record page after page of Irby's work, excerpted, repeated, accepted, the work that instructs and nourishes me. Deictic, in my paradise visions, replaces critique.

But they tell me that is evasive, cowardly, and perhaps it is. Certainly I've had trouble bringing myself to the place-of-writing in response to the editor's invitation. So much so that at length I imagined that the best way, only way, to liberate myself into discourse on Irby would be by accepting the spontaneous and unrelenting *disciplina* of discussion with smart people. Some hours of discussion with Charles Stein and George Quasha led to half a hundred pages of transcription from the tape. I was glad to have talked, but could not find that the consequent text had, as such, value to a student of Irby. But I found I had said half a dozen things that had been on my mind to say about Irby, and these alone I wind up offering, to him, to the paideuma he summons.]

*

Catalpa is like *Moby Dick* in that it starts with a raft of curious quotations, extracts from other texts. I think the most wonderful of these gleanings is by Irby's brother, James, introducing a work of Borges: 'The *activation* of thought, shared by author and reader, miraculously effected over fatal distance and time by words whose sense alters and yet lives on, is the real secret promise of the infinite dominion of mind, not its images or finalities, which are expendable."

That ending haunts me, as a statement in itself and as a way to reading Ken Irby's late work. Interesting that Irby puts it at the very end of his gentleman usher's anthology of loci about place and shape and ship.

I'm startled by the statement. I am as a reader so often caught up in the particulars of Irby's work, that it be Fort Scott, Kansas and not Coffee,

Kansas — this place and not that place — as he seems himself always caught up in a web of local specifics. Yet here it would appear, at the last, that the dominion of Mind, that *nous* which is our first and last appeal, motivates its images in time, in time to let them fall away. That images be expendable! That finalities, having activated the thought of the writer and the reader, can be expendable, leaving what, what other thing, Other Thing, the mind/ing in energy — this seems a promise Irby makes. I would expect, from it, that his road would cast off images and places, even while being illuminated by them in the first place; an emptying will come of what has made his work so much itself. Kenosis, by accurate pun.

(I remember, it must have been 1963, having a letter from Irby in which he, almost casually, faulted my then imagistic preoccupations, by citing Pushkin's *Ya vas lyubil* — a poem in which "there are no images.")

*

Careful here not to confuse me with him. I've always been much too willing to jettison the specific place for some lyric observation comes to me out of it. Whereas Irby does not do that; he doesn't drift away from place, I mean from the place. Yet at the same time that which The Place motivates is available. And place is, obviously, the balance point between where we're coming from and where we're going.

*

Place is always referential to a journey.

*

Does it come back to what Ed Dorn had to say about Gloucester so long ago [in *What I See in the Maximus Poems*]? Gloucester is unvisitable, unneedable, irrelevant. To confuse the place with what it motivates is to blur source with 'subject' — in a world from which subject has at last been banished.

*

[We were talking about Olson and place, vs. Irby and place, and Bob Callahan's work had gotten into the conversation too:] I think that Olson's work, like Callahan's in another sense, is *prospective* always.

[Prospective was questioned; I tried to gloss it:] Whitman, Whitman is prospective. And I don't find that prospexis in Irby. That doesn't seem to be the energy I feel working there, an energy *towards*.

*

I think there are only two things you can be. You can be an Exile or a Prophet. And the prophet leads out of literature, and the exile I suppose leads into it. [Literature and other religions, was I think my sense of it.] That is the sharpest line between Olson, say, and Irby. For all the likeness, Olson seems always to appear as a figure, a stern prophetic figure correcting any tendency towards an interiorization of awareness. On the other hand, Irby always realizes his *severance*. I think it is his glory to be so much in exile. He is Ovidian, writing his Tristia perennially. His work, so evidently complex with geography and history and personal travels, reveals itself as not prophetic of a departure, but recoiling from one, a *nostos,* a seeking home. In many ways he relates to literature more complexly and obsessively than any writer I know. There is a brusque American habit of dismissing, oh that's just literature — and Olson, no less than I, posed as an enemy of lit — may at times have been so, since literature always canonizes text, and text makes religion, and religion eases us away from that terrene perplex Olson insisted on.

*

Literature. With whom else discuss Mandelstam and Pasternak and Kipling and Rilke with equal fervor, equally without prejudice? Irby is, or seems to be, the custodian of everything he has ever read. This a tribute not [alone] to his memory but to his care, his huge care for the art he speaks always towards

*

[And then we turned to the dead, to the mediumistic — how the lonely voices of the newly departed are current in Irby's work.] I mean Irby strikes me as like Staudenmaier [author of *Die Magie als experimentelle Naturwissenschaft,* who incarnated within himself, his 'body,' several hundred persons or personalities, & discoursed with them]. In his silence, walking, abed, in the poised vacancy of houses, he apprehends the gestures of Sam Thomas or Max Douglas, lets them speak in and through him. Never does he seem to seek the occasion out as a 'medium' would, but always as an alert man would, tolerant of the voices that speak in him and how they relate to his present affairs, researches he is never away from. Not just in poetry. I think of that Ellington piece he speaks of so often, played me once: "Reminiscing in Tempo" is the name I recall. In everything he's involved with, Memory is always Tempo, memory is a pacing device of one's own current apprehension of things. It doesn't, in that sense of it, seem *sad* at all. (Though Irby, reading say from his notebooks, generates a mood of Virgilian sadness I hear in no other recent author.) While the first blush of memory, remembering, may be sad, I think the effect is soon changed, to a quickening of immediate perceiving. Memory is the polarizing filter that saturates the colors of the immediate present.

*

It is a both/& sort of business, to have this place, to have been always somewhere else coming here, over rough roads, pausing for wine.

*

Orexis = hunger, a hunger beyond the sad yearning of *pothos*. In a world where there is an actual disease, *anorexia*, hunger for being less, not-hunger, disease of young women, denials. Orexis is not the hunger of Sahel, that mortal *need*. It is desire raised to its highest power, without ever taking leave of its 'power-base,' the body, the flesh.

*

[Was I, am I, now or in that taped discussion, subtly trying to subvert Irby's actual historicism into interiorism?]

*

But that's why I speak of the absence in his work of prospexis. I don't think he tends anything further than this present moment distilled from all past time. A past time he has at his finger tips... very often that magisterial, Olson-like purchase he has on his material, that it *is* material, makes us think he is after such goals. But I think the momentum is different:
> he wants to make things public [re/public them]
> in order to appropriate them
> anew
> into his own life of passion.

*

Those Danish poems are often very beautiful, very visionary, as if from some inner perspective drugs had authorized. They drive on from a landscape one supposes to be very uniform, a landscape that takes power (and thus communicates it) in the act or fact of being remembered. Or is that true in general: Landscape doesn't count just by being there; it comes into its reality by being remembered.

Or again: Landscape is what-is-to-be-expended.

*

[For all Irby's preoccupation with the newly departed:] I don't think of Irby as at all a medium. The concern of poets with mediumism has often been, most recently been [people as unlikely as Spicer & James Merrill come to mind] with writing as itself an act of mediumship — and that is not Irby's concern. The dead he reckons with are not, in his grasp on them, different from the living. The Olson who comes in death's dream to visit in Kansas, the Michael Brodhead who 'actually' visits Kansas, they are not different in person/hood. They possess the same sort of ontological verity, occupy the same plane of being.

*

So if Irby is a medium, then we are all in summerland, and all Time ectoplasms in his work. Death has nothing to do with it.

*

[What I'm trying to deny is a sense of Irby as a literal voice-hearing medium in his work. To my ear and mind, the syntax of his presentment is more integral and together than the gnomic allophones one hears at the edge of life. Such a denial would not be necessary if the work were not so apparently preoccupied — that much must be granted.]

*

[Extraordinary how much of what I have to say about Irby is apophatic — assertion by negation.]

*

Irby's work continually rejects magic. Even while talking much about the occult tradition, he seems to represent it as something questionable.

I don't think he is merely 'fascinated' by the occult; minimally, the occult represents one more geography of human gesture, rituals and things that have style.

*

Friction is a simpler name for magic.

*

Even so, neither the summoning of memory nor the web of symbols seem to excite in Irby a nostalgic appetitive mood. We know the usual nostalgic poem:

> Hearing this
> I thought of you
> & want you
> right now

*

Who of us has not written that poem a hundred times? Irby does not. He challenges us, dragging together the network and the imagery, the hunger and the desire, but then, excellently and rarely, he does not combine them to produce the obvious. He keeps the gap. Conscious of being able to manipulate that distance, he nevertheless accepts it. The risk of seeing. Accepts the exile, in which *alone* all percepts and data have mutual relevance, as being, all of them, descriptive of Home. Exiles are exiled from *everything*.

*

So he does not set a simple *this* against a distant *that*. And because of his abstention from that easy friction, he is deeply (perhaps more deeply than he knows) contemptuous of magic, at the level of efficacy with which it might operate for — or — or anybody who has ever been ceremonially involved.

You can't do magic without having an intention. Ficino's dilemma was not different. Much as I would like to do magic, I don't want, therefore I can't get.

3 · A BOOK OF THE COMPANY

*

Yet reference to the occult, specifically to Freemasonry and the several traditions it inherits and renews, grows more and more frequent in Irby's work. It is my sense of it that these perceptions-and-renewals have to do with the Occult in the broadest sense, and the little occult (of the traditional sciences in general) is being used as metonymy for that. That is, Irby is concerned with all the clarity that has ever been achieved and then in any sense occulted. Freemasonry speaks of a Lost Word, & there is the key (always in my sense of it) to Irby's concern. He is a Freemason who hopes to sound aloud the lost word, all the lost names of poets and painters and composers and architects whose work has fallen, in its beauty or difficulty, somehow through the grid of the canons, fallen out of the academic hoppers. There the living and the dead stand equivalent, and each voice is cherished for its difference. I am excited by this vast appetite (orexis) in Irby's work, that he wishes to bring to public view (if only, as I guess above, the better to reappropriate what he finds for his own passional ends) all the lost.

They are the true occult. From a recent letter of Irby's fell a xerox of a pindaric ode by Mary Butts hidden fifty years. From Denmark he comes home bringing word of the painter Carl Fredrik Hill. From his phonograph I first heard Szymanowski & Miaskovsky & Lekeu. I've never had more than with Irby the sense that here's a man for whom everything that ever happened on the planet is relevant. Relevant, and worthy of being held in one synchronic plasma: the poem. *That* is paradise, that is the world in which nothing is ever finally lost. He wants to drag everything forward into the light, all the odd romantic composers and colonial English botanists and unusual southeast Asian spices, all the obscure events of personal history, peeing off the porch, eating a duck, all the copious enactments of desire & curiosity & overhearing, all into the light.

*

And makes me think there is no history but personal history.

*

It's very difficult to have a conversation with him in which he doesn't know a little bit more than you do, or has a few more bibliographical references you hadn't considered. [Here, as in some of the appetite I speak of, he reminds me of two other poets I have been honored to know: Gerrit Lansing, Jonathan Williams.] So the conscious, paradoxically 'public' Occult is metonym and frequent symbol, in his work, for this real Quest to restore all the lost members of the body of mankind. So that the passion of his poems becomes: to be connected with everything that has ever been.

*

There's a poem where he talks about getting poison ivy, Point Reyes is it, just the way and where Drake's soldiers must have gotten it coming up over the same cliff, ivy, sumac? and suddenly there is a community of blistered explorers he, and we, become members of. More important than the pain, the plant becomes a gateway into a *mnemonic experience,* perception pacing history and being paced by it, the intensification.

*

So there is no link but consciousness, no history but notice.

*

[As I suspected, these notes are part of a failure. They are things I think about. That is, things that think their way between me and Irby's texts. As such, they are distractions, more mine than of him, wayside seed on stony ground. A sense I could leave a reader with is the ideal compactness of an Irby book, the strange density of his language; however small the book, even these recent *Études* which is I guess the smallest, there is an achronic complexity of unfolding that translates itself as the feeling of a solid book in hand: a sensation no other poet's volumes hallucinate me with.]

[The taped discussion took place in summer 1978. I've excerpted my remarks, enlarged them a bit, added bracketed notes, now in December 1978. RK]

(*Credences* #7, 1979)

3 · A BOOK OF THE COMPANY

FROM *OASIS* TO *POASIS*: TWO PIECES ON PIERRE JORIS[3]

SECTIONS FROM *A CRITICAL ORGANON*: ON PIERRE JORIS

67.   What Joris has done is: taken back into the old world the oldest world. He has flipped the page that has on it the gaudy, meaningful rebises of Dee & Fludd and shown us an older page still, rock page. Joris in fact seems to be before the ice, or perhaps that spring morning just after the ice (A.I.) where that xenolith is left moored in the then — ooze near the Bodensee — the rock I speak of in *Parsifal* on which no one has sat since the start of the world.

68.   Middle of Europe middle of world. Middle Voice. Joris writes:

> dawn unbroken
>
> at the edge of
>
> where work has
>
> brought me
>
> breaking.

the ear tunes into middle-ness. The condition I'm always hankering for, Uneurope, is achieved: an absolute landscape, in which the eye is the only acculturator. Before Europe. (B.E. & A.I., our terms.)

69.   This is not just the sense that rides in *Antlers*, but in another book, *Hearth-Work* (where I find those lines above written). I wonder at the fluidity of his placement. He can get there around the Renaissance, as it would appear no American. When he talks of Dee & Praha circle, I see simultaneous images of magical galactic supremos in our future, and louse-ridden shamans in our almost past — what I don't see are the historical Usualnesses. This is a quiet freedom, but won (I know) with

---

3. [A third, more recent statement of Robert Kelly on Pierre Joris's nomadics can be found in Peter Cockelbergh (ed.), *Pierre Joris — Cartographies of the In-between* (Prague: Litteraria Pragensia, 2011) 139–143.]

altogether too many eyes rough red at dawn. The Price, as they used to say. To get it straight, not out of the scholarship (which right or wrong seems the thing these days, would-be images with noses in bookses), but out of the very fact of being there.

70. Which reminds me I saw Joris one night walking along a country road in winter, and he was very cold. I never saw anybody look colder, or look as if he were getting more from it. This is personal to him, I grant, & who am I to guess his tremble. It ties into the work only there, where I get to see the sureness of sensory experience. He trusts pain as only a romantic lover can. (And the stroke of luck, & the weakness that comes the moment the head turns away from feeling.)

71.   the losses
             in night's short lap

                             he says, accurately identifying the locus of all loss, there is a classic spirit or spunk in him that can trifle even with that, can play with 'lap' as if along that other sense he raced towards dawn.

72. He has the feel of those betweens, those membranes. Membranes I meant, but membrances I wrote. We are bound to what we say. Karma of poets: to be believed.

73. I want to honor that pre-European mid/way that speaks so earnestly in his work, a morality of sustained care. He is not frivolous. (And so his humorous touches please me least.) But not sadsack either; he *will* find the light, even if he has to suckle us on syntax to guide:

            when the function of
       touch becomes
       perfunctory

       it is good
       to part.

74. Let me read in this, from his "Morning Prayer":

> May I choose the undivided path of Listening,
> Reflecting & Meditating
> So that, being born,
> My time may not be squandered,

Strange lines, strange necessary prison of earth. I understand them too well.

75. What I'm after is his proud sense of the moment, of deriving everything from the sensuous event. This is not a naive program of description, or a refusal to do anything in verse but describe. It is, exactly, a derivation from, derivation from a thing seen, a bone handled. All the faculties of intelligence, memory, even tradition are summoned to work on these derivations.

76. Thus at one point early in *Antlers* he calls himself an espontaneo. I think that means a member of the audience at a bull-fight who gets carried away and leaps down into the arena to do battle. Thinking about that self-definition, I become aware that the espontaneo, while indeed impulsive, spontaneous, of the moment, in fact depends upon the prior existence of the arena, the fight, the bull. Spontaneity is no context. I think some consideration like that is what has been moving Joris and his work away from the (so to say) contextless void of sensory clamor towards an almost narrative tendency of order. In *Antlers*, before we are invited into the steaming guts of the slain deer, we must move through the not wholly recondite traditions of Saint Hubert the Huntsman, the weird stag with the cross aglow between its antlers, and, closer to the fact, the antlers Joris acquired from a drunken Lapp. (That Lapp was only feigning drunkenness — they have to move those goods down to us in the tepid world.) Then we can come to it.

77.   But the image, the
       actual
         image remains

he writes, and I find the way back to his text.

> A signature clearer
> than diamond.
> Moon-branches

and the hot fever of the knobs from which the antlers grow. The pain is there, cognized, the sprout of the actual. Simplest thing said. Law.

(*Oasis* #18, 1978)

REVIEW OF *POASIS: SELECTED POEMS 1986–1999*

1.

I used to carry on a lot about the Poetics of Information, seeing it as the one possibility for the poet, that practitioner of the science of the whole as I insisted on calling the craft, to sum, summon, sum up the world around the place of his practice. Make a *summa poetica* of the space and time that spawned that practice.

This kind of poetics included for me amongst its stars those who drank deep from Pound's Catawba: Olson, of course, and Duncan (especially of Mediaeval Scenes and Passages and Circulations) but also Marianne Moore, James Merrill, Louis Zukofsky.

These were poets from whose ardent couches you rose knowing more, bearing more information — I mean real stuff, names, places, dates, theories, events, attitudes, works and days — than you did before.

Some of these poets sent you scurrying to books to find out what was going on. This was true of Pound and Olson, but it's important to remember that it's equally true of Frank O'Hara or John Ashbery — you'd just want different reference books to get in the swim with an apparently insouciant O'Hara *frivoliste* meditation than what you'd need for one of the later *Maximus Poems*.

Then there were the poets — Jack Spicer above all comes to mind, and then Steve Jonas, or Gerrit Lansing, or Thomas Meyer — who send you not to a book but to another man, another knower, *arif*, another one of the spiritual elect or *fedeli d'amore* who could guide you not into the information behind the poem, but into the sensibility, the divine and hidden *doctrina* from which the poem speaks.

Lore, not information.

2.

At the same time, in the same grand Edenic atelier where language is perpetually renewing itself, there were, are, poets working whose references need no encyclopedia, no guide but the warm attention of the heartmind. The intimate texts of Creeley, Celan, Corman leap to mind, whose work told you absolutely nothing, and instead demanded everything from you. Poems that seemed spoken, in none too confident a voice, by one person to one person at a time. No Whitmanic reach of the *rhetor*, no Blakean "orator." Somebody instead, talking to you. Poems that had no "material" but language. But poems written in a language that could no longer take itself for granted.

So we had the poets who proposed, with fact or music or narrative, to educate us. And then there were poets who proposed to make me work for a living, pull it out of me, drag it out of me and bring to bear on their words whatever passed for paideuma or learning in me.

Olson, always cherishing Creeley as his *frère*, did not seem to notice or care about this radical opposition of their practice and their goals. I, who cherish both of them, want both of them. Want both ways.

3.

And then there is the midground, the space where the poet stands, voice *aliquantulum elata*, "a little lifted up," as it used to say in the Mass, talking to you, but only to tell you where he's been and what he's seen. And this is where Joris's work is most distinctive. If Creeley talks to you in bed, Joris talks to you at the teahouse, in the café. This is the great possibility he identifies, it seems to me, when he speaks of the Nomad and the nomadic as exemplars of a poetics. The nomad carries his world with him, and travels through ours.

And of course that's what Olson, especially the Herodotus Olson of the early *Maximus* and *The Distances*, was after — someone speaking from where he has been, and from whom he has been while there.

4.

I'm running through this to provide a context, or is it my pretext, for looking at Pierre Joris's work. When I come to read through this selection from a decade and a half of his poems, I am delighted to be reminded that he took off in the sixties, when the poets of information were strong and many. Back when there were already a few workers who even then were trying to do both: Enslin, Blackburn, Oppenheimer, and Taggart a bit later.

So here at length is something like a Selected Poems from Joris — & the dates are a little illusory, since the condition of striving that the poems reflect began earlier. These works condense and recapitulate the formal and rhetorical excitements of the 1960s, resume them & bring them forward. Like a good nomad, Joris travels through time as well as space; his poems embody all that he won from Africa, the Maghreb, Paris, the two Americas (left coast & right bank), then mingle it with all his practice in the hip US sixties, the discourseful resourceful poetry scene of the seventies in London, the language industry in the eighties — and brought them forward. That is the point. The contemporaneity of the work before us in *Poasis*.

Someone who has followed Joris's work can see where it's coming from, and I want here to celebrate the great caravan of his arrivals. How much he has brought, to the poem and to the book.

Because they are scarcely the same thing. But the book is what you'd expect from a caravan, cinnamon and silks and salt.

5.

The strength of this collection is the variety of the man's work. Over the last decades, Joris's poetry and poetics have made him known in England and America, and *Poasis* gives at last a detailed and accurate presentation of the range of his work. Again and again he is a shadow moving in a bright landscape, again and again his personal delights and sufferings come off camera, mere occasions to engage with the geography of our politics, to point out with a lovely, lyric alertness the landmarks of decency and power he has found on his strange hegiras. That *h-j-r* root fascinates him, this Luxemburg London Parisian North African American poet-exile, travel, escape, transhumance, the night journey and its visions.

As we read through the collection, the pieces get steadily richer. For me, the high points of the collection are the sequences *Winnetou Old & especially Lemur Mornings* — more than just the 'best' work in the book, they are the core of the book, & reveal something of the richness of Joris's sensibility and the breadth of his cultural gesture. In *Lemur Mornings*, Joris grasps this English to which he is not born, takes it and shapes it with real assurance. This is no piddling triumph of nuance and idiom — this is the achievement of actual saying, sure and mysterious as a magic spell. This is the densest language work in the book, yet it still preserves a narrative thrust, still pushes exposition in that middle ground, speaking to the conjuncture.

It is just that cultural grasp that makes his work distinctive, and of value right now. Joris is, like a very small number of others that come to mind, a poet who is in full control of European theoretical adventures of recent decades, and whose work is both a light that illuminates theory, and also an instance of it. This is important poetry too in that it examines in detail the question of marginality and exile — which is the single thread linking Modernism & Postmodernism, surely. The discourse of nomadism, of exile political & spiritual, of rootlessness and the Edenic country of the text — these are issues that come alive in Joris's poetry, and propose for his work a readership wider than the usual community of poets.

6.

When I think about books that wield the same sort of literary clout with a similar range of discourses, I don't think of books of poems. Instead, Chatwin's *Songlines* comes to mind, a vivid intersection of narrative & expository discourses like the one we find in *Poasis*. Susan Brind Morrow's *The Names of Things* explores — but in prose — a not dissimilar dance of personal growth, erotic identity, with North African cultural presence.

These are texts that play in the same fields, but they're not in one another's shade. Among poets, maybe the late Leland Hickman, & the perennial energies of Clayton Eshleman's underworld investigations come closest to Joris's sort of endless, & endlessly productive, journeyings.

7.

Most of Joris's publications in this country have been small press and small scale. Only his collection *Breccia* comes close to this in size, but made up of much earlier work. *Poasis* is the mature work of an important poet.

8.

There are some gentle, parlando diaristic texts — almost nostalgic for the say-anything sixties. The method and the issues of nomadism are already well established, for instance, by the opening sequence "Canto Diurno." I'm conscious of a certain impatience as I read through it and the "Janus Calendars," anxious to get to the more demanding & less overt poems of the middle & late book, which is where the poetic excitement happens, in the domain of demonstration, not explanation.

9.

I think the book's title plays some riffs about ways we might be well advised to read it. Its artful polysemy embraces:

1. poiesis;

2. oasis, the act of poetry being itself a stadial or oasis condition in the nomad life, by its very lingering in language emphasizing the nomadic quality — the poem as a provisional pause, an overnighting.

3. Veiled in the title too is the phrase 'as is' — which of course translates the French *tel quel*, title of the review and hence the school of thought through which Post-structuralism was famously articulated. The title thus situates Joris in his proper historic relation to France (where he worked so long) and to the drifts of current theory instantiated in his poetic practice.

(Samizdat #7, 2001)

THREE SHORT REVIEWS

ALLEN FISHER, *STANE* [Place, Book III]

A dozen years ago I was hailing the birth of a Poetry of Information — it would grow from lore and data no less than from sensory experience, precisely because data are sensorily experienced. My Olsonian hope has borne less fruit than I pretended, but one utter triumph of such a poetics is the ongoing work of Allen Fisher, of which book III appears as *STANE*. This English poet, with a clear musical sense and breadth of what constitutes *interesse*, has a work going on that continues to challenge close reading. It *is* close reading, and what it reads it carries forward, addressing the deepest epistemological problems of literature: the shifting primality of reading before writing. Fisher is not mounting a Poundian Suasion, but experiencing a lively compulsion to which he is subject and subjects in turn what he reads — a compulsion to be lyric, just like that traditionally reserved for flowers & fucking. These are not "found poems" — far from that. Fisher has lost his texts into a discourse in which he feels at least free to speak. Poetry is making one's own. His work excites me by his exacting feel for method.

(*L=A=N=G=U=A=G=E* #11, 1980)

THOMAS MEYER, *STAVES CALENDS LEGENDS*

The strongest work this various, resourceful poet has set before us.... His eye is natural, his language tense, lifted by magic and desire. Much of his text says things seen, says them so well they are sublated *per musician* — one literal gesture of his title (staves = notches, runes, letters, musical staffs). There are eighteen poems in this collection, most of them long. The sound of "The Midsummer Banns" — a decent richness, as if Spenser's Ireland were never an imperialist's victimage. Consider the "Loom Song" where we measure

> the distance that bounds
> the common range of vision

Consider the runic alphabet in "Starcraft," the powerful prose apologia in "Inland Draught." A real sleeper is his adaptation of Ælfric's dull schoolboy Colloquy in a mad dream of what poetry must, translation should: activate the common words of place and name and occupation. Two wonder-poems end the book, one about Thomas the Rhymer (seized as eponyra), with its quiet analysis of faerie / ferlie / fairy — the "tingle of faerie!", and a self-song, "The Telling of Sir Thomas Valentine." More than any syntactic poet I know, Meyer has made the page itself the unit of perception and realization. One reads the page; the page sounds.

($L=A=N=G=U=A=G=E$ #11, 1980)

JOHN TAGGART, *DODEKA*

A sturdy, bright, compact text forever looking around its own corners. Its wordstock of haunting imagery is validly (= strongly) processed, and sings anew certain old stories, this crystal as a paradise where slain gods are resurrected. Its fable studies transgression & wild meat so vividly it could be read as Marcel Detienne's *Dionysos Slain* set to a new measure. Since the Self selfing is the sole voice of Conjuncture, I tend to prefer the willful to the canonic intentional, yet the strict charm of this important poem lies just there where unconscious and conscious programming mingle. There is a lucid (though typo-deviled) preface by Robert Duncan that generously explores the double genesis of the poem.

($L=A=N=G=U=A=G=E$ #11, 1980)

FOR ROTHENBERG

I wish I could be there now to thank and praise and celebrate — bless you all for doing it for me. But my sins (that is, the body) have caught up with me for a season, and I remain rustic. My mind though wanders in such an immense garden of gratitudes to Jerry, and to Diane, for what they've done for me and what they've done for American poetry. Jerry's Hawks Well Press published my first book, & in that sense gave me my start — but more important, they gave so many of us a place to start from: the nurturing network spreading out from their amazing apartment way up north off Broadway, a powerhouse of æsthetic scheming, revolutionary anthropology, subversive art history — all the conditions of a community from which art can come. I don't know how I could have thrived without them. Or how we could have thrived: back in that time, the 1950s, American poetry was showing signs of life, after all the dozing between confessional and professional, the couch & the classroom. Rothenberg, through his linguistic gifts, through cooperation (so many years!) with Diane's energetic ethnology, through his own genius, was the great rouser in those days, catching revived surrealism but adding to it the excitement of the profound Otherness of space & time, the so-called Primitive, the tribal, the magical, the oral. For us, he played (and plays) the role Picasso & Braque did for the painters, and Leiris & Bataille later for the French poets: opening the sparkling world that comes when you crack open literature and see the primal gestures of oral energy and sudden imagery from which it all surges. Kabbalah, cave painting, Iroquois legend, Navajo chant, Hasidic tales, Central Asian epic, German avant-garde, immigrant histories — he summoned us to attend to the deep literature of which the 'literary' is only a sheen. He didn't get caught in formalisms, credences, opportunism. He taught me a dislike of slogans, and almost succeeded in teaching me modesty and the Taoist wisdom of *bsiao*, being small. He is a great figure, who stands above & beyond the schools and tendentiousnesses of poetics; he has given us, in his poetry, criticism, translation, anthologies, a body of work that exhibits what I suddenly realize is an ethical purity, a touchstone for the genuine.

8 December 2011

THINGS I THINK ABOUT WHEN ESHLEMAN COMES TO MIND

Years and years ago, Clayton & I were walking across the grassy triangle in front of my house. Out of nowhere, he asked if I thought of him and his work as not spiritual enough. I hardly know what that word means, but I had some feeling for what Clayton was asking me. I assured him as well as I could that spirit hunts in unlikely places. And I was righter than I knew:

Eshleman has been inscribing an Emerald Tablet of his own all these years. A guide to the operations of the breath in this world of flesh.

Where Paul Valéry warned us to go down into the self armed to the teeth, Eshleman's journeys, for half a century, have with a kind of gentle ferocity sought the meaning of the social inside the body, then the meaning of the body deep inside the earth.

Thinking of that makes me remember Eshleman's long dedication to the ideas & therapeutic practices of Wilhelm Reich, who sought in the repressed or degraded body the etiology of political evil — the fascist body of priest and commissar.

Eshleman's adventure began long ago still on the surface of the earth, when Mexico's living clash of ancient and modern, race and language, then Japan's ornate archaic modernity fueled his own youthful assault on the "quietude" of American poetry at mid-century. This is the time we were beginning to be shaken and renewed by the intelligential energies of Olson, the earthly and heavenly passions of Duncan, the exactitudes of Spicer, the "vulgar eloquence" of Williams.

Then Eshleman's work turned literally inward, to his own excavations, his own territory, that fleshly miracle one calls one's own body, its caverns of rapture and surfeit, the muscles of mind.

His probings in Reich and Blake led him to the body of the earth itself — the Upper Paleolithic caves, the bones of imagination. He has gone down and seen and felt and been alone with them. And spoken on behalf of thirty thousand years of silence.

I admire his ability to endure the weight of earth, literally, over and around him as he humped and squatted his way through the caves of the Dordogne. Me, I would be scared to death in such entombments. He though is an enchanted literalist, he had to go there and see it for himself, feel the chill air & secular drip. This seeing-with-his-own eyes is what's so really, keenly, different about him.

How different the images on the wall are, must be, when you see them over and around you, curved in real space, not flattened out as designs on a page. Eshleman got to know the ancient scrawls & gouges as people in his shared space. The shocking discord of imagery in his poems merely and truthfully reflects his decades of conversation with stone men, his passionate embrace of stone women.

He can never escape from the clutch of the body, the fateful awareness that we live in the body, can only live there. For him, the body leads back always into itself, bowels of the earth bowels of the human. Inward, power, more shit than splendor, but a dark exultation of pure sensation. Which the poet can coax into feeling.

For the poets of desire (Rilke, Duncan come to mind), beauty is always in the direction of the other, & the body is a chreode of the soul reaching outward — out towards a glory or a union which at worst might turn out to be, or seem, vacuous or (Shelley's word) inane. But for Clayton, the body, like the earth around us, is centripetal, whirls & torques always inward; his poems drag us down, joyous into the dark, mouth full of words, mind full of images to thrill us on the way down.

He may not meet, or make us meet, Persephone down there. I don't think he is as much interested as I am in the Queen of Hell — but what he finds down there not only fuels the rage of his poetics and his translations (as if Artaud and Césaire and Vallejo were alcaldes he interviewed in those dark caverns). It also enfranchises him to write *Juniper Fuse*, which it seems to me is the greatest book ever written about humans (or whoever we are) in the Palæolithic, our kinfolk, their arts & mind.

His work gathers and disperses. Lately he seems to want for the most part to direct us towards the more recent work, the last two decades of his striving. The penetralia of personal experience can best be known, best chanted, in the penetralia of time. A geological poet he, a skeptic Novalis in tune with rock.

When he speaks (whereas so many nowadays vaguely do) of alchemy and alchemists, he does so with the authority of a man who has obeyed the terrifying commandment the ancients called *Vitriol*: By visiting the interior of the earth, thou shalt discover the hidden Stone.

Nobody is like him in his struggle. With ornery stubbornness he has kept visiting the dark occasions, and brought back for us poems unlike anybody else's. His style is impasto, the gouge & splash of images, unrelenting, thingly, their weight always pressing on us.

At times he makes the wildness of most poetry seem effete. Because he has gone down and done so with a language fit for his researches: clotted, angry, surprised, full of grunts as a cartoon, full of magical gleams like sunlight striking through chinks of rock, hard as tourmaline, sheets of mica peeled away.

I know of no poet who has fed so richly from the thingliness of the world beneath his feet, none who so resists the glamour of beliefs. He is a shaman with only one superstition — the flesh we share.

(2013)

THREADS 4 : ROBERT SAYS

(I had, in 1975–1976, while living in California, written with ferocious intensity and amazing freedom the long poem called The Loom, *which itself is intricate with narrative — which was, in fact, when it came down to it, a laboratory of narrative beginnings. How to begin anywhere. How to go on. In that poem, music and silence helped, moving me along.)*

in conversation with Simone dos Anjos & Pietro Aman (2006)

When I was fourteen, I climbed the side steps of the great New York Public Library and demanded a library card. (For years I had had cards from Brooklyn and Queens, separate systems. This was the Big Time at last.) When I was filling out the application, the blank space beside "Occupation" I paused over — certain of the answer, but timid of inscribing it —, then wrote down Writer. *I have tried to live up to that commitment. Through the years, I have felt more and more the centrality of writing to my task. I'm told I'm a good conversationalist, and I enjoy talking and discoursing — and listening — for hours. But nothing of that really counts until it's inscribed. Yes, I know that what one says, and perhaps even what one thinks, gets inscribed somehow in the spaces of the world — the Akashic record of the old Theosophists, perhaps. But what mattered to me is getting it written down. Writing is from* writan, *to scratch something in. No wonder I like pens.*

in conversation with Simone dos Anjos & Pietro Aman (2006)

I don't feel myself doing a different thing by writing fiction instead of poetry. I write with the same intention whenever I write something. It seems to me that the one great thing in literature that's happened in this century is considering the possibility of writing being a single coherent act without divisions into genre. It seems to be such a small thing to say, certainly it's an obvious statement, but it's an important one to me.

in conversation with Larry McCaffery (1988)

The "freedom" I refer to when I'm writing fiction is a social or strategic freedom in that nobody expects anything of me when I write fiction. The sense of freedom that I didn't find simply given to us in American poetry — and no one in poetry had that freedom during the fifties; besides, it is a social impossibility, being a poet — was available to me as a fiction writer because no one was telling me what to write. If I wrote a poem as off the beaten track as some of the fiction I've written, I would be thrown out of the poet's guild. Unceremoniously. But if I write something that's merely a dreary Algernon Blackwood ghost story, no one cares. Yeats wrote such things, and no one stopped him from doing so.

But it's also true that back in the fifties, the opportunities in fiction seemed more wide open in that, in fact, nobody knew what to write. [...] There was freshly renewed with us, then, the sense of raconteur, *of the* récit *replacing the old artful psychological strategies. I remember the shock we had as we read or re-read the* Mabinogion *and the Icelandic family sagas and the* Arabian Nights *and Balzac, to see that there was a domain of action from which narrative could arise, and that psychological was not the only momentum or gesture. Language could enact — we saw it at last. Now, of course, theories of narrativity are everywhere. But back then, telling was no way to analyze.*

in conversation with Larry McCaffery (1988)

I don't like "poetry versus prose." I think we've been stuck in it too long. Our great rhapsodes, like Blake and Whitman, could falter from one into the other very meaningfully, & write long passages of prose falling into verse. Duncan, our best teacher of this, in the Pindar poem breaks into extraordinary prose at the end, not as in musicals where people burst into song — here the fact of language bursts into prose. It seems to me one of the incandescent moments of all literature, when the exact nature, and the exact size, of the genre difference became clear. You can palpably feel the difference between poetry and prose — only different in the way blue is different from orange. It does not belong to a different animal, but a different color in the spectrum of itself. Of writing. So pushing on writing as a thing in itself — the unity of writing, the whole art and by that I mean that all writing is interesting, all writing excitable, be it the writing of advertising copy or the writing of politicians' speeches by nameless graduates, I'm interested in writing. The energy of poetry that lay in the fifties, in American poetry, now lives very much the same way in American fiction writers. There's the same excitement — what can we do now, what are we free for now? [...] So those kinds of things that the casual reader need not notice, need not be bothered by, are present as a deep source. The question I think interesting in reading a poem is not what it can be boiled down to mean, but can I take this roller-coaster ride too. Can I go into that process from its ab initio *wherever that was, and come out through it, can I be processed by this text? Can I walk this word?*

in conversation with Bradford Morrow (1989)

I haven't spoken about many of the contemporary French masters, Derrida, Lacan, Barthes, Blanchot — they are important to me, but like Heidegger, more so as [what I think of as] *poets. With the French, poetry takes leave of the line, perhaps forever. But that's another story.*

in conversation with Simone dos Anjos & Pietro Aman (2006)

4.

A BOOK OF DISCOURSE &/ON NARRATIVE

```
prose must go faster
         before we choke)
we write language
            (poetry : hypersyntactic
                     organizing principle
                     at work
                     :golden
                           (minimal)
                     definition
(least is gold
(But it is (says Milton)
                  a medium
               = a MEANS

a several man
(prose teaches speed teaches care teaches verse
       --circulation of the accepted light
First we speak.
Poet=maker. Poem=the first thing made.    THE product (of).
a cycle of 22 lectures.   letters.
of 26.
```

=

ON DISCOURSE[1]

what is it that's not art & not science? I asked, & finally get the answer,
    discourse,
        wch stands in both, and behind both. It is our discussed world, so brought into being.

        The opportunity of (hearing about) this issue of *Io*,
        was for me to resume the discourse about discourse begun in my book *In Time*,
        now here carried forward, & to be read as such.

My thanks to EG for his wicked conundrum, to HSB for the occasion.

                                        RK/IX.73

---

1. [We have combined some of the shorter sections of "On Discourse" on one page, whereas in *Io* each section is given a separate page. Order & layout remain unchanged, and each new section is still marked.]

the forms of love

Love
Is what we're getting ready for.

To confine love to the body is as wicked as to deny it there. "I am not innarested in your horrible awful buboes."

Those who wear their bodies in love's service — let them be wary lest they wear love in their body's service.

I am not my body.   A crow on a tree is not a tree with no crow.

A lion on a field is not a field.

"The Knower of the Field."

I ramp on my green House my field. To others I beckon. I wander.

Now this body of which I am ample I am & am not.
And that is confusion enough for any contradiction, & contradiction enough for any dialectic.

BUT WHAT OF DISCOURSE?

To speak. To speak from a place and not be that place, or being it only in the imagination. From body and its immense many-dimensional geography. Her topology. To speak.

                                              Now. I am not interested in your false knowing, your opinions red or blue or black.

Item: the Physical Universe is a Metaphor of our Discourse. Exists, if it exists, for the sake of. Our discourse.

"Science" is discourse that thinks it has something to say. "Literature" is discourse that replaces Aristotle's mirror with its own bright eyes. "Art" is discourse that supposes that it has silenced itself.

These people (makars, trobadors, & trobadillos) think they're alone in here.

        Not so. O no not so.

(Two Notes on Language)

Numbering.   Arabic numbers replaced roman (which were cumulative) & Phœnician (which were purely ordinal) to help men reach the perception of Qualitative Numbers.

What is lost is qabbalistic pertinence of letter-number relations. That will be transformed, is being transformed, into *phoneme* as (or and) *quality,* which a later Qabbalah will be able to compare and relate.

Or otherwise: the phonemes of a language are the 'genes' of a folk-soul, representing at once their difference and distance from early writing ("letters," staves, runes of Hermes and Woden) and from primal speech, & also the quality of that soul brought to expression. Only the synchronic reveals the deep image of a language, its duende & daimon. A folk-soul is mediated by language: by grammatic trait & phoneme, not by lexicon and allophone.

Consistently men have metaphorized reality in two ways:
as space   (shaman)   or as time   (brahman).

Shaman	*Brahman*
"find your spot"	"escape from the wheel"
One moves in space, holding time as a tool,	reincarnation. / = the againspace
	heaven / hell = the then-space
"Knowing the right time"	from which our modern version is:
time is the tool of personal power,	history
	analysis
I will	dialectics
	"Will" is immanent in time (God's will, will of Zeus, Historical Necessity, Ananke, dialectical materialism)

Because of our polytime & easy space, our age is suddenly capable of honoring both ways of knowing reality.

But a brahman who stops at school-learning is like a shaman who stops at sitting-up exercises.

These are two modes of knowledge, not two knowledges. NB.

The mode of knowing when & where. I-will & what-is it.

Poetry assembles everything from everywhere, is holistic, & is thus the great bridge between the two modes of knowing.

Rhythm (physical cycles, time fucking space, being "felt")
       connects.

Rhythm connects.

The rhythm of images and the rhythm of silences
    connect head with body.

The great urgency is to heal the J-Xtian rift between head & body, *not* to assert one at the expense of the other, i.e., not heads vs. jocks.

(people respect "Craft" because they think it can be taught thus allowing a guild of teachers, and because its application demonstrates time-consuming honest industry on the part of the writer, and permits easy (typically numerical) critical conclusions on the part of the reader)

There is a craft beyond such mechanic senses of craft, an altitude of total attention to the world's means, total vulnerability to the response spoken inside us.

Art is in danger whenever we are told what must be done. But only in danger, not destroyed.
      Destruction comes (as it did to skaldic and trobador verse) ONLY WHEN THE DEMANDS ARE IMPLICIT IN THE PROCEDURES —
        When the academy is internalized.

The enemy, here as elsewhere, is always Conventional recognitions.

The egg is Chaos. Chaos is a state of things antecedent to any relationship with the world as we know it. The inhabitants or "molecules" of chaos are in a closed system not yet spilled into ours.

Chaos: Yolk   ♃   Albumen   ☿   all in the Shell   ☉

Only in chaos are things neat and ordered by kind and degree. When the egg of chaos cracks, things get mixed up — this is called the Way Things Are. The eggshell in the omelet, son cosas de la vida.

The enlarged vocabulary of the 'best periods' of english prose reminds me, lucus a non lucendo, of the comparative poverty of vocabulary in some of the loveliest times of the poem. Reminds me that poetry begins in speech as prose never does, prose, that late form, that abstraction.

The Ego transcends itself in clamor, not in discretion.

Reticence is the enemy of love & 'progress.'

The Ego is the secret. It is the first instructor, & its lessons must be well learned before the next teacher appears.

What is wrong with education, especially primary, especially in america / is that it proposes to the student the suppression of the personal ego

> how, how, can a young being function when
> its only mainspring is unwound??
> so his ego is encouraged to project itself into the
> future in daydreams & fantasies of self, sex, job
> possessions, behavior, identity /

> > the future tense begins with the
> > suppressed ego /

whereas the place of the ego, to work in all energy & benignity, is now.

The Ego is Now.

The public (such public as poetry has on this Island) wants short poems, objets d'art or polished opinions. It wants pills. But short poems don't teach a poet how to live — he hungers for the long instruction of a sustained work.

The demand that the poem be brief is essentially the bourgeois wish *not to be bothered by the poem*. Slip it in, let it sing, back to business. The short poem, for its educated bourgeois audience, rimes with the parakeets in cages, bonsai, african violets. Stocking the jukebox, the haiku box, the hype box.

What they never understand is that all the poems are the same length.

Only the time is different, as measured by their clock.

Every poem is as long as itself.

Ten short songs, ten wee poems, induce in me an exhaustion no Goetterdaemmerung or Fairie Queene can.

The *Cantos* cleared the air of 1916 & on, cleared it of nervous wit and frittery elegances, even of the lustrous amy-gisme he had helped along.

It is striking that, apart from Pound, it is the women in our century who have kept the TIME of poetry alive, H:D: in *Helen in Egypt*, *The War Trilogy*, *Vale Ave*, Laura Riding, Edith Sitwell.

Their hands were on things & their heads & hearts were not free of care. They knew that extension is not the opposite of intensity. They kept the long measures available, still in ear, worked, woven,

behind the fashionable bric-a-brac on the publishers' shelves.

A long poem is a lived time. A poem is a lived time. Turn away from the clock & Creeley's *The Door* is an epic.

That it darkens in the mind while it grows light outside.
Skull & sky are *reciprocals*. Night my aurora?

Fertig: ready or finished. To get ready for something is not to be ready for it.

Are you ready? i.e., to begin.

Is the coat ready? i.e., is it finished?

        Is it done? Has Energy completed
           its work & rested, come to
           the end of itself & found a
Thing?

A Thing exists only when an energetic process is completed.
(We try to catch hold of that dynamism by the passive voice — the Covert Doer of all things done.

                (Elsewise, the animism of *It fell*)

The deed hidden in the done.

           Callimachos' lampchimny like a
           palm
           (Yeats celebrates it)
           is no less an available art-work (i.e., contemplatable Deed) for not being museum-able (i.e., lost, no longer a commodity).

           More so.

THE TABLES OF THE LAW

       there are said to be two
  Tables of the Law.

One of them is shown in the works of men, in all the work of consciousness & skill by which & in which the race has declared itself

the other table, never shown to Moses, is hidden from the foundation of the world, & will be revealed only when every human has awakened in the Utter Mind

The tables of the Law were never laws, commands & vetoes — such is priestly imposition & deadly dream

the table revealed is written in our works, the table hidden awaits the universal wakening, which is not Judgment but Resurrection

It may be that in Eternity, the two tables display the same text.

―――

The Mortal Senses /

     5 panels,
         modalities of the mortal senses whereby
            the exponent seeks to tran-
            scend the sense or comes
            to fruition through it /

     Touch, or Botticelli (who felt the contours,
         felt along them,
           lusted after them,
           lusted along them,
         longed not for mass but
            continuity)

    Sight, or Van Eyck
    Smell, or Gruenewald, Gauguin
    Hearing, or Raphael (the Acoustic Space,
        Scoula d'Ateni)
    Taste, or Carpaccio/

in Raphael the acoustic space turns into static image = the sound wave is arrested. *Heard.*

―――

The SUBJECTIVE
         is not the opposite of the rigorous.

It is the most rigorous, the most difficult.

The *precise subjective* is what philosophers are too lazy & too generalizing to labor, scientists too frightened to search out.

The Objective is p.r. for the Generalization.

Objective order, so-called, is mental artifact, consensus, "collective consciousness," "lethargy of custom (STC"

The 'objective' is a consolation prize for those who've lost the real.

at Cal Tech I was talking to a class I didn't know, sleep-talking in the morning, & found myself drawing out this polarity:

 Yearning for Otherness (Kubla Khan cited)
            first poem I had ever read)

vs.

 Yearning for 'personal,' one's own, Experience

       (The Boar cited, wch
         the class was asking abt)

afterwards, Diane Wakoski spoke of Duncan's distinction he'd once made for her, between the poetry of Magic (wch was Gnostic), and the poetry of Passion /

as we spoke, I found myself confronting another polarity, the Descriptive vs. the Prophetic,
       wch turned the question away from 'sources' (wch the other polarities beg), and did accept the neurological-spiritual identity of any poet, i.e., he is what he does & what happens to him, since he is the field-of-event (whether the 'source' is book or dream or 'flesh,' history or any other hallucination)
      I took Duncan's set as expressive of stance or feeling-life of the poet — did he seek to know and turn away, secure in his knowledge and rescued from the contingency of his desires, or did he seek only that knowledge fear & lust compel a man to — gnosis or passion? (I'm not happy with the distinction — but that seemed what the words of it, Magic, Passion, portended as opposites. I'd have them (as I suppose RD wd) as complements)

Back to it, what was brewing in Descriptive vs. Prophetic)

(where, e.g., Diane, though drawing as 'source' only on her love-life, fear-life, was concerned, in the fact of her images, has passion to estrange herself from what she had known to what she yearned for *beyond* that lived-in condition, was in fact concerned with the Prophetic) so that I read out, fast:

Descriptive	*Prophetic*
past	future
self's 'experience'	self's initiation
description	prophecy
history	creation
"passion" (for one's 'own')	passion for the knowledge of the Other
reality, (another RD distinction)	actuality
narrative	incantation
what happens to a man (passio, in that sense)	what he makes happen.

. .

from which a Diagram, my favorite, arose:

```
                    "intellect"
                      GNOSIS
         THEOPHANY     ↑     EXPERIENCE    vision of
                       |                    History
  "intuition"          |
M                      |                              M
U    PROPHECY ←————————+————————→ DESCRIPTION "sensation"    E
S                      |                              M
I                      |                              O
K                      |                              R
         IMAGINATION   |    KRATOPHANY                I
                       ↓                              A
  vision of          PASSION
  Eternity          "feeling"
```

Stein reminds me today of my old insistence on Middle Voice.
This summons to mind:
> historically, the development of the Indo-European verbal system,
>> where *Active* contrasts with *Middle*

(Active, e.g., "I wash (something) ;
Middle, e.g., I wash myself)

(Active: secular, aionic, ethical.
> Middle: psychological, daimonic, initiatory;
>> Classically, Middle = Reflexive)

this contrast develops into

>> Active vs. Medio-passive
>>> (i.e., where the Middle takes on passive acception, sense)
>> in Greek & Sanskrit.

Later still, finally,
> into Active vs. Passive.
>> (as in Latin & thereafter)

The emergence of Passive as the effective morphological contrast to Active (amo, I-love/amor, I-am-loved)

is one of the profoundest evidences of the departure of the daimones, the "obsolescences of oracles," the loss of direct awareness of the spiritual (dynamic) spaces & their occupants,

i.e., the death of Pan.

> Men are now understood *as able to be acted upon*,
>> as *objects* in a field (c.f. the 'Odyssey Land-scapes' in Panofsky's *Early Nertherlandish Painting*, chapter I)

that is Roman art & Roman sense.

The implications of, & present need for, MIDDLE have been on my mind for years. The historical comes to aid.

(Stein offers this correction to Barfield: "Christianity is Active, Buddhism is Middle").

Porphyry suggests that to experience the body, in or out of "meditation," is to be *passive*.

"But those things which approximate to matter and bodies, are themselves, indeed impassive; but the natures in which they are surveyed are passive." (*Anx.*, I, 19, tr. T. Taylor.)

18th January 1973   Yesterday 61 degrees in the afternoon.

The Imagination is reprocessing this region.

We are not only processed by geography. We process it. The currents and rhythms of earth
                         change as our minds change.

The fatalism of Arabia, no less than its close-croping goats, made desert out of fertile Palestine.

WRITERLY/

        as a term of craft.

That writing is a recent form of composition, composition the discovery of form & pattern in language, the following and transcribing of those powers & the realities to which they lead. Maybe they exclusively lead.

Writing fixes some part of the sound & sense of that — using in our language the abstract inaccurate *word* as integer, sentence as plasm, jardin, ocean.

From this a writing can yet grow that does not start & end in sociable speech. Such writing is usually condemned as "literary."

That kind of language must now be reclaimed, cleansed, and redeemed.

It must be a *writerly* language, and its distance from the colloquial a measure of its distance, not a proof of its impuissance.

"Revolution is not the seizure of power by the proletariat, but the destruction of the very ideas of power, proletariat."

Writerly language allows the fact and experience of art to be exultantly in the foreground, and thus refuses to be complicit with the bourgeois appetite for *trompe l'œil*, substanceless windows, Aristotelian peepshows to view events which by the very mode of their perception become pornographic.

Once & for all: *writing* is the plane of event.

ALPHABET
> instance of something neither concrete nor abstract /
>
> n o t a t i o n s   as intermediators between
> the sensible and intelligible worlds
>
> what more likely system for qabbalah to
> crystallize around?
>
> creative integers /
> what if numbers are *letters* rather than 'symbols'??
>
> (language is symbolic — not alphabets)
>
> runes = staves = letters = digits =
> analytic entities:
> *Beings.*

LETHE,
> the river, describing that principle
>
> flowing also through 'conscious' life
>
> whereby insights, clarities, revelations,
>
> decisions and technologies
>
> are obliterated
>
> lost
>
> in individuals and societies /
>
>
> acid illuminations,
>
> newyearsresolutions of the
> numberless dead /

the shift from lunar calendar to solar

          represents the transition
from interior-intuitive awareness

        to conscious reorientation of intellect
in a cosmic discussable sphere,

    ("Zodiac"   as grid)

(The Canon of Yao shows some of the structured
         implementation of such a shift)

the later shift from solar year beginning to vernal equinox
to solar year beginning at 1 January
            (emblematic of winter solstice)
      tho not *on* it,

     presumably because of the Dead Days
         between solstice and Janus?)

represents or enacts

    a shift of attention

from the zodiac (as index of the fixed stars &
         thermometer of the planets)

to the RELATION OF SUN TO EARTH AS EXPRESSED

        QUANTIFIABLY

    IN TERMS OF DAYLIGHT.

               Ego amasses.

            The newborn dragon
              counts its gold.

/DREAMS
man who went (like Charlie in Modern Times) through the gears of a clock & found a space inside
      where what seemed to be a woman waited
 (These alliterating staves are inevitable — the sound bound up with the nature of the breathing space,

gasp the clock allows us)

> March of light
> Markandeya wakes.
> What he dreamt
> lies under him.
> What in dreamless sleep
> escaped his glance
> becomes his life.

The nonsensory or supersensible experiences of Dreamless Sleep are reported to waking.
     The name of the report is
Dream —
    dream is translation from dreamless sleep into waking.

  Dream is translation.

  Dream is membrane.

More accurate dreams, comrades, better translations!

What the ancients called 'false dreams' are inaccurate or inadequate translations, deceptive,
     that give a false sense of the Dreamless
Text
 (so Æneas leaves the underworld through the gate of false dreams,
   inaccurately translating from the story of his own soul into the Dream of History.

I want to prove that life can be penetrated from every side.

That life is an occasion with many doors.   I've greeted the guests & plotted the rooms.

   The valences of the true man are unknown;
my work has tried to graph them.

What lies on the other side of sex, of war, of fear?
       Of place?

What is the other side of *this* place?

       Or the pronouns,
     to know who they are.

When the imaginable becomes actual. When it is written down in a book, told, erected in our common presence.

The imaginable

is actual.

A fundamental exercise in ta'wil is to study what happens to you when you write the word down. When you say it aloud.

How does the world change when the word is made?

A poem is the ta'wil of the first word written down.

The intercourse of sound & sense is trivial on any analytical level. It means in a different way. I mean it means in a different world.

It is the other side of the consensus.

Conduct

the way goes through
the touch

THE WAY GOES THROUGH THE TOUCH

mirror convections of the seafloor below my floor)

Atlantis is childhood.
Atlantis is yesterday.
Atlantis is this place today, the spiritual forms sunk in matter.
Atlantis is our present sleep, its waves our dreams.

These & other *récits* are true. To inspect them is to see that not only our conception of 'history' (history is nothing else but our conceptions), but the "facts" of it themselves, possess a form, a rythmos we must also study.

No happening happens only at the level of itself.

(Allegory & the anagogic modes of literature dimly shadow this circumstance.)

Events not only spread out their ripples laterally through the whole world, but are mirrored in all worlds, all times. All selves & levels of a man's being.

No process is complete until it has cast its light on every floor of my life.

the Moon is borrowed light but the Sun is borrowed power.

on the way
& coming back)

   Star.

  for instance.

     unfocused abstraction ≠ focused abstraction ≠
       concrete ≠ specific

I want to say these 4 categories are more use, some of them, than
    abstr./vs./concr, viz.

star is concrete, but not specific.

adequacy is abstraction, but focused.

      The focus is what counts, not the form-class of
        the so-called Noun.

on SS vs Interpretation)
>	my heart rose to this,
>	in measure with its long coldness at
purported meanings,
>	the oatmeal of academy

>	(the real thing wrong with the *Parhudnee Review*,
>		not its choice of dull poets)

the 4-fold reading habits of the middle ages made (some)
>	sense as corporizing the 4-fold mind-world of the m.a.

not so, to day

(as NOB rightly replaces the Hist. of Ideas with the Hist. of
>	Consciousness)

our world's folds)

>	our world is consciousness.

What we must get to is this:
>		that the happening of a text is
>			(is in, is made of)
>		the reading of it,

>		what the book *does* in head & breath & heart
>			or now it anatomizes us
>				(= our experienc*eds*)

beyond that, there is discussion
>		(no bad thing, maybe, and criticism, etc.,
>			an other, an interesting, sometimes,
>				other, thing, techne)

Alchemy was what reading certain books did to the head.
>		(To the sex-life)
Reading and (as it is said) Reflection.
Pound, insubstantially, knew that the art of poetry, of language,
>	lies in the art of hearing
>			(calls it 'reading')

: that literature begins, that renaissances of literature begin,
> when men learn how to hear ("how to read").

Criticism as a work of daylight is a response to provocation,
> i.e., in its best, it is an answer, a work evoked,
>> at least proposed.

We must revise (criticism) to keep it from becoming
> an evasion of the internal event precipitated by the
>> stimulus (the text),
>>> evasion by transferring the energy
> of the total response over to an area of dialectic
>> or gridwork "where we can handle it" — i.e.,
>>> abolish it & offer its Spectre.

NAIL words together,
> parataxis, not
>> the fluent endlessness of,

moi!

> (Céline's three balls, strung
>> out on a hill
>>> looking down on Paris
>> along the dirty river of the fairest dead)

Find. And say it, out.
> The Nail
>> be your scripture

> (the screw
>> your hell & too much time & not

to stand there forever
> but say it, for now.

What is this "within"? It is not inside, not in space, it is not inside the head or death would ruin it.

This "within" is not inside. Except if it is understood as *inside the thought*.

"Within" is the abyss of the synapse,
                          the Unplace from which Place intermittently flickers into visibility.
                          It is inside *thinking*, but it is unthinkable.

"Within" makes itself known. That process (or is it a simplex, a *deed*)
      is always called Utterance (outerance, outside-ing, "without" ing)
            word spoken, Logos.

All words are declensions of *without*. Speech can make a hearer conscious of *within* — but not by words & meanings — always by the gaps, leaps, silences.

Words are the gods of Without. The Within is the Without of Words, the Without words, the Without of Language.

Everything that can be spoken is other.

Knowing renders its objects objects, out there, in the plane of knowing, in the stance of being known.

We intuit approaches to Within *between* words, propositions, sentences, categories.

The Middle Voice (not 'Active' not 'Passive' — reflexive, it is called, deed for the sake of the doer)
                      is closest,
the within for its own sake being within.

Within is gap.

                                      (*Io* #20, "Biopoesis," 1974)

FROM "INJUNE": "ON NARRATIVE"

An angel came to me today & told me that my proud dislike of narrative reveals an unwillingness to be accountable for my own actions. I contended that narrative is mostly just greediness for guilt. Storytellers fussily choose details. Let the selection be natural (I punned), let what happens happen. Let what happens reveal itself fully & truly in what happens next. If that were true (he smiled) I would need only one pair of wings. You are in the grip of a simplistic belief about causality, hence excuse yourself from natural act. You think this causes that; not so — these cause this. All these cause all those. The corn ripens in its season and whether you want to or not, *you go with it* as it grows.

    Look, I said, I hate the theater, I want *now* to turn into *then* in such a subtle way it feels like now all the time. I am only responsible for now. Now is my mother and my father. That's why I keep quoting Pelagius. Let the moment ripen — the grain is the same as the seed, the yield the same as the source.

    The angel smiled again at me (as one smiles at a deft prevarication). That sounds nice, he said, but these three pairs of wings I am are to hide & reveal, to propel my intelligence through the enigma of time. Maybe to deny it at last, since the Work or Arcanum of angels is the End of Time. You are striving to assert that humans can wield an angelic intelligence, total in each motion. You think you can possess time, & make this now so wide it touches every then. Every one. You are just greed, I think, just another lover of time. You stall, you linger to slurp up the honey, you go to war and make philosophy and create gods and theologies just to keep the sun motionless on the mountain. You trust causality because you people are begotten, not created. We angels are created, and all our science is *will*. But not even we can will all ways at once, or even one way forever. Will-less, you drift and think you can choose the causes. Will-full, we move through the world & all we know is where we can go — our very movements are permissions. We can only move where all the rest is moving. Will-less, you move through a cream of forgiveness, and dare to talk to me about Pelagius! First of the self-styled Christians he was to make it plain that we are accountable for each act & each failure to act — *& are responsible for nothing apart from that*.

    There's a war going on (I burst out), there's violence & stupidity, the planets run & recur in their dumb cycles, every jolt they give us spills over into war & cruelty. The sons of God who honor god in flesh & openness are everywhere slain & imprisoned. And not just now — it is at every stage of human history. How can we even have a right to walk on our feet on this continent where Cortez did what he did, where murder is the natural answer to every question, where the books of the Mayans were burned and black men were sold and young men are still made slaves of war? It was never different. In Pelagius's time citizens were enslaved, slaves bartered, rulers flayed alive. His God dies on the cross. What is the sense of narrative? What can it tell us the cemetery and killing fields forgot to say? We do not love, we do not live in honor. If there are causes, we have never deciphered them. If there is a cure, it has been hidden from the beginning of time. Why do men take pleasure in killing & destroying? What *is* that pleasure? Is history the name of it? Did anything else ever happen? The animal delights in its *here & now*, and we kill it. Our cortical memories, which are supposed to be stocked with situational devices to protect us from contingency, are they anything really but treasuries of barbarous images, records of torture & dismay? If that is the world's will, I turn against it. I turn against history, against story, against time — I "turn my body from the sun" in search of the exact moment — even sunlight cannot find it there.

The angel seemed to pause now; at first I thought he was stuck for an answer. Then I knew he was waiting for my anger to simmer down — anger does no good. And this time he did not smile. These facts & stones in your mind, he said, are accurate enough. But where in any of them do you see anything but what a human did to another human? The tale of human horror has only one meaning — men did these things. And only one hope — men could *choose* not to do them. One at a time. No other way. But each could choose. What humans call Will is a joke, an unreal thing, a recorded tune a life keeps playing in the background while it jerks & trembles to the trembling of the net that is its life. Human will is what humans have always done. It is not a motive, it is an abstraction-from — a vector mathematicians could *infer* from human behavior. But that behavior can be changed. Consciousness has something to do. Is something to do. It takes a million years, maybe, but it took many millions for you to become the killers you are.

Or you are a jar into which all the honey of time has been poured. When time ends, the jar will break, & there will be left only the honey you've gathered or restored.

(*Caterpillar* #15/16, 1971)

FROM *THE LOOM*, § 12: "THEORY OF NARRATIVE"

Every story
as it goes
implies
every other,
as if a man or woman
could open in her behavior
a road to every deed.
And every narrative
would tell the whole story.
For a while,
caught in the beginnings of his fabric,
the old storyteller,
blarney-licking shanachie,
is happy. Everything
will fit in.
Just as a young man
if he's any good
believes that nothing
is impossible, & his life
will seize every moment
& do everything.
But each act
performed
is a limitation,
& the possibilities
begin to close down.
Not everything can happen.
The best of them,
Rabelais, Joyce,
the sages who wrote
Mahabharata,
the Odyssey, Lönnrot

between two worlds,
they tried to get
everything in.
I bless them for it.
Maybe the Dogon can do it,
who have reduced
every element of *happening*
to an ideograph,
& the thousands of signs
can be manipulated.
Or recognized
as natural forms
repeat them or mime them.
But *everything is possible*
is different from
everything is done.
An aspect divides.
The story
that seemed so promising
becomes only itself.
That is the history
of existential man;
it is not tragic
but it is less
than we could imagine.
The distance between
might be tragedy,
or we could make
tragedy out of it.
But mostly we make grief,
& grief
does not have the awe
of the tragic, the sacred
destiny
offered up in blood

on the altars of Mystery.
Grief does not have the wonder,
the *Diesen Kuss der ganzen Welt!*
from which something
more than tragic
arises, & truer to our time.
It might be
an exaltation:
> at the end
> he became
> himself.
But there is a distance in me
senses that *himself*
as failure, even though by
common belief I would take
that as a man's best chance.
The distance is an edge:
a man must become
exactly other than himself.
To do the Other.
And break the story open again,
that the spiritual Seed
be not forever locked
in the material form: our oldest
prayer. Sun, take this
weight off my bones, these
bones off my Name
& let my Name
speak in the world
out loud alone.
Because the Spark
of *its* Nature
is free to participate
in every form,

yet the Form
of its Nature
is loathe to relinquish
that pinpoint of fire
& so is prone
to lock the Spark
deep in the earth
of its formal substance.
The story ends,
under the hedge
the blind Teller
falters, ends
in a shudder
of particularity,
tracing in his mind
the wonder
he has failed, it
has failed, to include.
Inside the story
the Spark gleams,
groans, leaps
out in passages
of apparently
irrelevant description,
fastens on things,
weapons, colors,
a look recorded
in some eye, a silence.
The Spark, groaning,
understands
it must follow to the end.
And after that end
endure
another beginning.
A new story.

Some men have tried
to simplify,
solar myth, Freud's
clutch at mythologies,
Jung's archetypes,
Graves's beautiful
goddess to whom
every tree & every word
is of its substance
consecrate, to whom
all stories relate.
The notion
of a primal story
is wistful hunger
of the Spark
for a limit
to its wanderings.
But the history of the world
is the story of all its stories.
The Spark
is not delivered
until all possible
stories end.
And there is an austerity
somewhere in the mind
that wants to end them,
"hastening the end,"
to which every new story
is as sad as a new child,
begotten in concupiscence
(trishna), linked to death
& suffering, prone
to carry the chain on,
resolved not to be deprived

in its turn of any experience.
And so the existential hope:
a man
resolves to become himself
becomes himself
& ends his story.
But the story begins to swing again,
gets used to the spaces
in the mind it obsesses.
The shanachie hears it,
falls for it,
& begins to say.
The spark
maybe this time can move
the flesh *its* way.
The fabric
of the story
pulls tighter.
The old image:
a woman
at the loom
passing the male
shuttle
through the standing
warp —
the stand
of any story
is our shared
knowledge of the world.
Maybe a shared
world.
Consensus.
So the story
is never

for the teller
(the shaman
cannot heal
himself),
it weaves
through the stand
he shares with the world,
the spark of his telling
enters
the hearer's mind
& instantly
a new story begins
that runs for a while
(the length of
telling)
almost parallel
with the first —
then
in silence
it veers
off its own way.
Efkharisto.
Eucharist & good day,
this spark
communicated.
What else is there
to give?
Ideas, opinions, pseudo-
records of pseudo-
personal experiences,
the fakes & flukes
of memory?
We communicate
a spark

& the rudiments
of a trade
to clothe it,
yarn
to make the weave.
And (sutra)
the thread
of meaning?
It is organic:
it is beyond
any intention.
These are the ways
of a story's happening,
its event
is the mind.
A meaning
is what is *found*.
And so the shadows
"close around"
the Hero — he is caught
in an adventure
he must follow
to the end.
The Arabs & the
writers to the Grail
knew a secret,
a way of weaving
story into story,
Sheherazade,
now takyth this tale
leave of Syr Gawain
and torneth
unto Sir Perceval
a while,

a while
to twist
& change,
keep all
the stories
going
& none
ever
allowed to end
except they fold
back in
to the ply of another.
At sunrise,
the legend is,
the teller dies
if he lets
the story down.
It is to keep it
going, up there
babbling
like a ball
played on the
spume of a fountain —
hollow
as like as not
but in that gap
or emptiness
allowing
a place for us.
The place to talk.
The Spark, concealed
but preserved —
preserved in concealment,
served

in concealment —
twitches & gives
off light
in the Hero's mind,
Herakles stifling
on the barren plain
dragging the shambling
stolen cattle
on to the end of his
world. And there
he sets pillars up
to mark
the place beyond which
no story tends.
I can feel his vast
sigh of relief
as the columns rose:
an end, an end to it,
end of the world
& no man goes beyond.
As he, the Hero,
cannot strive
beyond his story,
is locked there
the way the Greeks
saw their stories
locked in the sky,
unalterable narrative
of the fixed stars.
But they move
& have
their own motion —
little by little
the stories vague out,

move
away from the Pole.
And even the Polestar
wanders, in time
rejects
the fable of its north.
And Herakles,
no sooner was his
back turned
on his gorgeous
pillars all brass
& porphyry & gold
than some hooknosed
Phœnician
traveling salesmen
sneak through,
pragmatic as the tin
they'll fetch back
from Cornwall, the dyes
of Brazil gleaming
already on their sails
coursing indifferent
through the end of the
world. It has
no end. Herakles
goes home & finds
his ten labors
have changed to twelve,
he's off again
dragging a world
out of his memory
to meet it,
outside,
in the flat sunlight

of wherever it is.
A story
has only
a beginning —
maybe that much
is free to us,
in my choice
to begin or hold
a wise silence
& not yield
again & again
the fire
into the form.
Give fire
to the fire
the old text says —
& draws
a picture of it!
A man
walks down the street
he carries a torch
comes to a forge
from which the blacksmith
is unaccountably gone
but the fire blazes.
He brings his torch
in full daylight
blazing
to the fire.
The sun
is overhead.
A little boy
is watching him.

(1975)

EVENT: ELEVEN PROPOSITIONS, WITH AN ANNEX

1. Vision into the midst, see into
2. (not read into = take out what is not there)
3. Alexandros (who is Paris) 'reading into' Sparta. I read into the delicate echoity of my friend's hips a story that is not there.
4. (From, starting from, what is there: the ripple beneath the skirt initiated by my apparently accidental touch, the clinging dress yielding & returning)
5. What is there is Event. The story imposes on it.
6. To make a story is reading into the Event, now. That is to take out of an event what is not there (though it may be somewhere else).
7. Now if I wish to honor in full praise the Event her hip was at that time, I must forego the story (the "burning tower" "Agamemnon dead") & deal nakedly with the event.
8. The dichotomy I imply may be the central issue dividing our sense of prose from our sense of poetry, & dividing as well the Classical world from all that follows it. If so, Homer is the last poet whose story was not a *reading into* the event but rather an accurate registration of the full event *itself*.
9. *Muthos* 'statement of percept' (i.e., 'word') — *Muthos* 'story'. Logos has a very much coterminous range (statement — argument — story (plot) et cetera).
10. Thus for Homer the statement of a percept bears with it the elaboration of its story. *Muthos* is not yet divided.
11. Proposition (7) is accurate of our time & proceeds from the development of the craft & senses attendant upon, at least, Rimbaud's & Mallarmé's conquests.

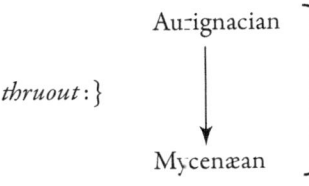 The Universe of common sense, reasoned conclusions, celebration of event — leading celebration of process — leading at last to elaboration of story.

A. There is reason to suppose we have generally misunderstood the intellectual history of the west. I suggest that ancient undocumented man was rational in the extreme, exploited magical means when everything else failed (why not?), & apprehended the world in a way we would call commonsensical (no *primitif*, no *participation mystique*, none of that unbroken line of nonsense from Rousseau to Lévy-Bruhl), i.e., exhibited enormous respect for percept & perception, & the modes of exactly registering percept. The great thinkers of those times had the world at the tip of their fingers, & hence remain unknown & uncelebrated. Why should they be remembered, whose thought was every man's thought, played on every man's instrument?

What we have come latterly to celebrate (paying no heed, e.g., to Plato's hesitancies in the matter) as the 'first thinkers' 'first philosophers' 'first minds' of Ionia and Greater Greece are, far from that, those who, under the pressure of the collapse of the Mediterranean *koinonia*, fell into insularity & parochialism. They are the diminishers of our sensorium, whatever they may have done for our categories; by imposing an *in illo tempore* cosmology on us, they eliminated from our awareness that which we are slowly, after all this time, and under our own pressures of non-Western sources, beginning to learn again: that cosmology is perception.

Bruno Snell points out that Homer has no word for *body*, in the sense it has for us. Yet Snell, in the depths of his education apparently regards this as a primitivism in Homer. Homer could not have had a word for body: he had *anthropos* — man, that totality he does not think to divide, but that we, following Homer's betrayers, chop into soul, spirit, body, &c. Homer knows that if the *khros* is wounded, it is not the body, the whole man, who is wounded.

The breakup of the unity of man (that first dissociation of sensibility) may well allegorize, proceed from, the breakup of Mediterranean unity. In unity cosmology is now.

B. All of this, as literary transformation, can be observed in the obsolescence of *muthos*: 'word' in favor of the restricted meaning 'story.' The word & the concept have been divided. *Epic* is invented as a term to refer back to that time when percept lead directly to percept & the whole chain of such events was, e.g., an *Iliad*.

[RK archives, undated text]

ESSAY ON CLARITY

Karma what wisdom me. Foulfoot, the sluggard, the right & left hip dragger, initiates my heart. Come & dance. Long wondering through the various deserts, a return to my speculations looked as if afforded me. Truly this is a time of recondite novels. Gads of evanescence, clobbering some air. The drag of prose (by which is all too easily meant all too easily done, *vs. song*, or All They Know ((aint much)) or, Not What but How). Not what but Who, & that's sad. Not that I'd care. For all of me. I know no better than any (every)thing I've seen, such as my seeing is, I have trust in it & God who gave it so. And made it. Once more the story without narrative. Towards catch clear as catch can. Widdershins, against the sharpness of the immortal sun. Widdershins uttermostclarity (as if, shadowed by light), a slogan if nothing else. Clarity. A word that brings some holiness wholeness in its wake, cut it (swimmer) as you like.

Nor clear is simple, no. Clear is bright. Shines more better than anything.

The clarity our patters give us. Here lies. Here stood. Until 1927 the hanging Oak. Clear against the snow, the light, dark tree.

History preoccupied. Swinging upon it. Here the tree is clear. Looking for three hours with mounting satisfaction at a stopped watch.

[RK archives, undated text]

SOME THOUGHTS ON JUNG

These are recent reflections on Jung. I've been reading him since I was fourteen or fifteen, and he's never been that long out of mind or practice, but God only knows (for that very durative reason) exactly who or what I mean when I say 'Jung.'

Duncan once wrote of N.O. Brown: "he is a poet, his vistas lead only to other vistas," never to conclusions. We don't need conclusions, we need going. So it's that Nietzschean aspect of Jung that most interests my respect.

Awkward luminous important arousal that is not the dream and not the day, that stands up out of dream & haunts the day. We say: I remember the dream, I remember this from my dream. But the remembered thing is constantly reconstituting itself all through the lived day. It is not a memory but an upwelling, not an image but a shaping tendency, a *rhythmos* that marshals event and response.

Jung appeared in the world like a personage in one of those very dreams he taught his patients to dream. His uneasy presence in psychology, literature, comparative religion was less a comment than a demonstration. Even his most doctrinaire, hard-edged articulations (like the *Visions* seminars) have the air of theater: reckon with this Figure.

Better than analyzing something merely there, he looked about him & synthesized a new narrative for us to enact, dream by dream, hermeneutic act by hermeneutic act, a pas de deux for analysand & analyst. He gave us not a science but a story.

Blessed are the makers of stories, for they shall never be alone. The soul doesn't want to be understood; the soul wants to be *known*.

The problem of Jung: in our age we are blurry, we mistake things for their opposites, since opposites remind us of each other. (Olson remarked to me once that *the* problem of our time was a growing inability to distinguish public from private matters.) Jung's synthesis was supposed 'analysis,' even by himself, and something very new was speciously validated as something old.

That gave his reflections their appeal: you can have my story, he seemed to say, without giving up any story you may have that still works for you. (Whence the delighted reception religious bodies have accorded what they take to be his thought.)

There is only one thing to analyze: mind. If that.

Everything else is story. Or everything is story, conditioned, behavior conditioned and conditioning, experienced. Jung's synchronicity is merely whimsical when it is used to explain unusual occurrences (the wow of things); it develops great power when it is seen as in fact the norm or ineluctable relation between anything and anything else — the conditioned codependent arisings. Properly grasped, it reminds us that the story tells the story.

And Jung's story is a wonderful one, even a wonder story. No one who acts out, in dream or desire, even a little bit of it, can ever feel wholly bereft again of connection with other people, other times.

By Jung's insistence on the mechanism of projection, an inhabitant of Jung's story (a Living Reader) is led into a land where every person, every being and relation is relevant to his own life, needs, growth. No one you meet is irrelevant. Caught in a web of compassion, every beast bears a sign.

The poem writes itself, the poet its First Reader. To see the contradictions calmly, with a spacey eye.

And while this growing sense of the interrelatedness of all beings is, by the mood of Projection, linked to a sense of permanent Self that Jung never calls into question, it is nonetheless well along the road to compassion. Towards the *feeling* of compassion, even the affect of compassion, from which a new sort of cognitivity would arise. One that, almost incidentally, can see through the subject's own pathologies.

Synthesis may be as valid a metaphor as Analysis is for that sheer compassionate knowing which seems our only plausible goal. But it is a metaphor

Whereas the story tells.

(*Spring*, 1982)

ON *THE CRUISE OF THE PNYX*

TO THE READER

There are three Modes or Measures discovered in this work. Poetry and prose are two of them, represented as they usually are in print: squared-off prose, poetry flush to the left margin but uneven at the right. The third measure is a between-rider, or transitional grade between poetry and prose. I dedicate this measure to the Queen of Between. It can be called logacedic, prose-song. *Like poetry, it occurs in lines, and its lines are to be respected as units of context and performance. Yet like prose, the lines tend to spill breath over, rushing towards the* act *or* it happened *prose usually aims at. This logaoedic measure is represented here by text which is set flush to the right margin, but irregular at the left — making a sort of mirror-image of verse.*

ON THE COMPOSITION OF THIS TEXT

As many have surmised, the poem is locked in the pen (quill, reed, calamus, stylus, biro, keyboard, graphite of all time compressed in the simplex geology of a pencil). We release it from the "stone." Finding the stone. *The Cruise of the Pnyx* began its journey in a certain multi-colored Venetian quaderno, & there its characters — the bishop, his exasperated wife still close to life, the devilish Schwefel — began their emblematic voyage.

Of course we are stars, or from the stars, and are trapped here. And while the way out is not verbal, words show the way. So the words had to find their own way to the reader; in this case, the poem kept trying to find a *means,* a blade's edge between the habits of prose & the ecstasy of lines of poetry (since poiesis is ekstasis, the sassy line standing out from the daily fact of discourse, like a white ship from the harbor). That realm between would be the poignant midground of our departure, uneasy, one foot on the dock still, in jeopardy.

How to do that, how to *show* it to make it sound itself aright!

That is when Open Studio opened its resources to me, & gave me free use of the AlphaComp composing machine, & enough instruction in its use to be left alone with that remarkable instrument. And in that privity, this text came into word, as I discovered techniques of controlling the visual path, shaping it on the page in ways that would be neither possible nor understandable in any conventional printing mode. So it's apt that Open Studio & Station Hill Press now make public a text that could not have existed without the skillful means they imparted.

(1975)

RUSSIAN TALES: EXPERIMENTS IN TELLING

I had complained to the poet and linguist Bruce McClelland about the hard time I always had trying to sense out the meanings of Slavic words, and how opaque their root variations on Indo-European seemed to me, compared to the reasonably transparent (= familiar) reflexes of the Germanic and Romance families. Since he knows Russian and Old Church Slavonic, he could not enter too deeply into my sense of alienation, but instead put into my hands Townsend's *Continuing with Russian*, in the back of which I found twenty-two columns of roots and word-forming elements, with glosses in English.

As I looked at these, the glosses and the sounds of the Russian stems themselves began to tell their own sorts of stories, and I found the English morphemes (sometimes shadowed by Russian sounds and semantics) were linking up in sequence to form narratives and lyrics. The resulting fables reminded me of the style-world of the fairy tale.

These thirty-seven researches are experiments in allowing language to tell its own stories, as it is well able to do, if we listen. The tellings are obedient to, and exemplifications of, what another poem of mine had recently articulated as

> Language is the only fable
> and is utterly able.

(1981)

AFTERWORD TO *A TRANSPARENT TREE*

Fiction is very strange. The soul says I need a change and the body says but it's so interesting right here and the spirit says Pack your bags; fiction has to respond to all three, yes, but mostly it has to respond to the world. The world is the place with no I in it, a bright continuity with no permanence.

It has never struck me that there is an interesting difference-between poetry and fiction. I write poetry (language turned by sound & silence) all the time, or try to, and call myself a poet when I have the nerve. But I've written a lot of prose inventions, lies, fables, fantasies, attacks, apotheoses, revenges too, & call them "fiction" or even "novels." Now, this fiction of my fiction is a double one. I write it with a good deal of care and attention, craft, I suppose, but at the same time with the delight of the amateur or the beginner. It seems to me that this *joie de dire* is chiefly available to me because our culture distinguishes the poet from the novelist, and since I'm clearly the first, I'm free to play, without prejudice, at activities befitting the second. The critic has the ready punishment: the "poet's novel" or "poetic fiction." Such phrases mean usually it isn't very good as stories go, but you'll find it hard to forget (*The Green Child*, "The Connoisseur," *The Dead Seagull*, "CB&Q").

My concern is writing, and for me poetry and fiction and anything else are at times useful but scarcely necessary labels to identify momentary crest-forms in the sea of language writing & language saying. So what I'm noting here is my refusal to apologize either for writing fiction, or for not writing more of it.

In the frozen masterpieces of *Dubliners* I long for the kindness of soul of Chekhov, but when I'm reading him I miss the physical urgency of Paul Bowles that can make a thousand-mile desert a claustrophobia, or the nervous wisdom of a Kipling, the immense bodiless benignity of Chesterton, the haunting purposelessness of Borges' skeptic profundities, the clean truthfulness of Beckett's minutiae, the powerful credulity of Machen and James, the timing of Doyle, the exaltation of Charles Williams, the smutty obsessive-ness of Mann, the vedantic clevernesses of Nabokov. My masters, my noble ratty masters whom I still worship, and at whose ironic feet I lay this assortment of my desperations. I know, or used to know, the canons of the Good Short Story, & have never cared much for those fussy expectations, though God knows I love the stories

(James, Conrad, Joyce) from whom the rules were worried loose by unseen scholiasts.

Story has always seemed to me to be about happenings *vertical* to the common mindstream of the time & the society — whether by virtue of invention ("adventure," "crime," "ghost" stories) or by virtue of harmonic intricacy — the sheer heedful detail and episode within the common texture (James, Joyce, Nabokov). About happenings — about the contingent arisings, impermanent things bruising one another into eloquent new patterns. The world hurting us into speech.

So I'm always trying to do everything. The stories in this book are not very like one another, it seems to me, though each is trying to be everything. (The very definition of the Moment of Writing might be: *Now* I can say it all, at last, the whole thing!) People usually tell me I'm a Difficult Poet, but I don't think these are difficult stories. Certainly they're not trying to do anything but tell themselves.

The earliest in this volume, *Cities*, was written in 1966 and published as a little novel four or five years later. It had been composed on the surge of energy left over from writing *The Scorpions*, my first published novel. *Cities* was written quickly and with delight, some of which I still feel, though some of it has turned into puzzlement because of a book with a similar title by Italo Calvino, which many of my readers mention to me. Though I've read & admired Calvino's *Italian Folk Tales*, and looked at his *Castle of Crossed Destinies*, I've never had the heart to read his book of cities. I gather from descriptions that it's Marco Polo-ish, and very good. From what I hear, it must have been written just about the same time as my *Cities*, and by its merits and his good karma has won more attention from the public than my little novel has yet. No doubt there are people who think I stole from him, or perhaps a few who even think he stole from me; neither is the case, obviously, and lately my puzzlement has turned to a slow admiration of the means by which the very hidden cities Calvino and I were both presumably in search of have chosen to declare themselves, and force their own secret commonwealth on public awareness.

Besides *Cities*, the reader will find gathered here some of the fictional enterprises of my last fifteen years, but not all. There are stories I dimly remember ("The Bassoon" was one, a Gurdjieffian reconstitution drowned in irony, and "The Prelector of the Sanhedrin" was another, whose feel I remember vividly, though I forget the plot) but have no longer in my possession; I assume them to be among my papers at the Lockwood Memorial Library in Buffalo, which here takes on a significance similar to Cox's Bank in Charing Cross — though rather easier of access. (Did I consign those stories and others to the estrangement of distance and archive exactly to match Watson's tin dispatch box in my fashion?)

But past such discrete stories momentarily unavailable, the bulk of my work in prose has been aimed at several novels, no one of which is finished. The largest, which I call *Parsifal*, is finished in the sense that the last page has been written. But the book is so large (the typescript is about 1900 pages) that I have not yet finished revising it to my satisfaction. Since I love revision almost as much as I love the act of writing, it is possible that I will, in Johnson's phrase, protract my labors. Another novel (is it called *Carla* or *The Novist Philosophers?*) has two of its three sections finished — it is about America of the soon future, and is not large. There is a sequel to the *The Scorpions* also, which gives my detestable protagonist another chance; the text has no name and not much substance yet. And there is a small novel (almost in the original sense of that name) called *Erin Tantra America* that is scheduled to be published — a finished text amongst all these seedlings.

My daily practice is poetry, and what I measure my life by is the growth and variety of the poems I am given to write. This sustains me. What fiction I write, whether in grand forms or small, always seems free and fabulous and alongside. Parerga. Jeux. But there are eerie moments when I wonder if the tail is not a good deal better than the dog. It doesn't bite, for instance.

In the present collection, apart from *Cities,* all the pieces were composed between 1977 & 1983. "Samuel Naked," which tries to investigate the life & disappearance of my great-grandfather after he was invalided out of the Union Army, was perhaps the earliest started, and the last finished. "A Winter's Tale" (1977) is loosely based on a Long Island murder trial of some notoriety, and was clearly (even I knew it at the time) prompted by my own crumbling marriage. "The Guest" was written in response to what I took as a challenge to write a Gothick story, which my challenger glossed as "scary, with kinkiness." As I wrote it, I tried to imagine what a vampire really was, and if there is such a thing, what the bat in the window and the waggled crucifix might really be symbols of.

The seven smaller pieces are my favorites of the past few years, ways of working on different scales & measures. Most of them exert themselves to conjecture at the nature & efficacy of silence — people's silence, the animal that walks beside them, inside them, around them. I suppose that if my fiction has one pervasive theme, it is that people (my feckless heroes and heroines, my me) do not know what is happening to them. In the bewilderment of sensuous focus and inconstant intention they move, heroically enough, waiting for the world to decipher itself, or clue them in. Waiting for word in a strange town.

The stories interest me, things do, for their sizes, too, the scales they negotiate. Size is a matter of how close you stand — a two-page story, held to the eye, bears down with endlessness.

*

I appeal to two conditions of reading: the book we do not finish reading, and the book over which one falls asleep. From the latter text, dream-reason carries on its own narration, and Borges' garden of paths that endlessly divide, a curious Sunderway, expands all through our sleep. And then when we wake up the book in our lap seems curiously arbitrary, disappointing, unaware of its own ramifications, mute.

In the first sort of reading, the unfinished, what the writer began, or what through the writer was begun, now acquires a dynamic (if that's not too hot a word for what seems at first a listless condition), a genetics of its own that goes forward. Whether we ever finish "the" book or not, the book is always a-finishing in us. We may be clever, conscious, deliberate, or do it in our sleep. The overdue book you took back to the library in seventh grade continues to write itself, must be writing itself, in you now, its structures and resonances interpenetrating those of your daily life, and of everything else you read.

I appeal to a third condition — the recognition that comes to us from time to time that some book we indeed read to the end didn't truly end as its author asserts. We find the author's smug demonstration of the fruits of causality merely specious guesswork, implausible, hasty, jejune — or just wrong. We know better. We have some sense, clear or less clear, of what the text really was aiming at, something the author missed, or muffed, something the conjuncture pressed upon characters and world — something we intuit. I am haunted by such continuities, beyond the neatness of closure.

Dream narration, lifetime continuations, daydreaming a book onward: in such ways the imagination, by an autonomous act of transgression, corrects wayward masterpieces.

And so I think of fiction as a transparent tree, an intricate unimpeded proliferation of branches from a common stem. The stories go on, each visible through all the others, mutually exclusive only by logic (that woodcraft of Time), not in Vision. The shape of a story is the viability of it as seed: how ungovernably it will ramify. Like any writer, I fancy myself a master of control — leading the reader along only that branch of path the writer chooses — but the writer no more controls the ultimate fiction than the gardener controls the pears plucked by bold children at midnight from his artful espalier. The integrity of bark and leaf & fruit & taste — these will triumph, and mind will use what it finds.

Reflections like these no doubt make writers sweat hard on the last pages, to do by rhetoric and magic what the energy of the story itself has no will to permit: an end persuaded of its own finality. Why else the gorgeous perorations and poignant austerities that close books written in a more common language? Savor such flowers, but do not be fooled. A story goes on, and no branch obliterates another, however they may twist & stretch to share the nurturing light of the reader's after-imaginings, their only eternity.

And yet, and yet. The tree grows, our attention wanders, the transparent must be shadowed into compact visibility. Colors, saturate hues to shimmer or lour against (Ungaretti's word) immensity. The infinite transpirings of text do not absolve the writer from the task of finishing his story. Mole-like, maybe, the worker snouts his way through the writing, only his own body (or body of his fate) lending inertial mass to the projected story. The ending he comes to doesn't end the story — it just reveals him, dusty-jowled, triumphant, self-revealed. If you want to find the writer, forget the autobiography & look at the last pages of the books.

If I were a critic, I would write a book about Endings, Endings, and guess how from Merlin's last cry below the stone we could deduce the mortal weakness of the Grail & its company. A book of endings would be about *ta'wil,* that spiritual etymology that leads apparency back to its original. And what is here is a book of branches, this book of mine, ours, branches made a bit more manifest. Travel freely from one to another, or work back, perhaps tonight in your bed, to the inconceivable refuge of the single trunk.

(1985)

AFTERWORD TO THE SECOND EDITION OF
THE SCORPIONS

As a story is found in a bottle (or a bathroom, like the Eosite-interlude), so a story is found in the mind. It is complete — one feels the beginning and the end at once, close-clasped together, sensible as a broomstick, coherent as the outside and inside of an orange. The story is found in the mind: I mean that I understand any story as a certain shapely action which has a feeling & a smell of meaning different from any other action, any other shape, I've known.

When this story began, I grasped it one day and knew the start & finish of a man. I could hear his voice, could feel the endless argument of his justifications, the lust of his celebrations, the yammer of his anxieties. I could feel the pulse of his risk. I knew he began talking, and at some moment he would stop talking. And that would be the end of him.

Our stories last as long as we can tell them. This story I think is about story itself, about the sensuous interweavings of telling that comprise a life. (When *The Scorpions* was first published, the poet Robert Duncan, himself the most luminous and articulate voice of telling in our country, was angered by the book, and told me that it was a sin against, and I had sinned against, the spirit of story. Story. The sin, he indicated, was starting an adventure story & not telling what happened, not revealing the end. I do not think that is the case; the story I found I told to the end, and everything is revealed. The adventure is the telling. But Duncan may yet be right, for in telling as I did, I may have sinned against the discretion and masked cunning which are the property of Story — Story tells everything except: I am a story. My happening is no different from my words, Everything that ever happened is just some words in a wise or wilful mouth.)

When I was a little boy, I had a favorite time. It was on the rare morning when I was home from school, sickness or religious holiday, & my parents were at work and I was alone. I would sit on the blue day-bed in the dining room, downstairs, the window shaded by the mulberry tree, and listen to the clock ticking. It was enough for me, in my shy desperate infancy, this brass clock ticking behind in the kitchen, ticking with the never quite perfect regularity of wound-up things. I learned that no two seconds are precisely alike, and that every now and again, without warning, without even slowing down in any flourish of cadenza, the clock would simply stop.

Allow me to be there and it ticking mysteriously in the kitchen, the room invested with sunlight, me not reading or eating or playing. Silence, deep silence, with one clock singing through it. Singing at it, I think now, as if the very sound it made were the cloth that silence wore to let me see it.

And then the clock would stop. The tumult of soundlessness would rush into the room like a posse of accusers. I would jump up and run to the kitchen and look at the clock. It had stopped at a number that is no time. No Pope died at that instant, no president tumbled from his limousine, no bomb fell. No special time. The clock stopped and that was that. The stopping did not mean anything beyond itself. In the bewilderment of my childhood, I had found the one thing that could not be webbed into the intricate superstition we call 'meaning.' Its only meaning was where it had been, what it had sung on its way to surcease.

So I grew fascinated with endings, with the difference between going on and no more, with the awareness that nothing stopped but the clock.

The story I found in my mind was about a man who talked and shaped experience into labeled categories, and lived with his categories as long as he could. It was a story about a man who talked his world into place and then, at no special moment, like a clock stopping, just stopped. For him no special moment, but in a book every moment has its specialness, and none more so than the ending. I had to tell how he got to the final image that rose, with the story, in my mind: of being on board a no-account fishing boat drifting into the fog, fog & nothing more.

The last chapter was written first, to fix clearly the goal or telos towards which language, action, tended. Then, hating it, I wrote the murder of the red-headed boy. Then I began listening to the psychiatrist, to let him find his way, through the virtual obscurations of his will and fancy, and the real obscurations of mine, down the shoreline of America. By the time the doctor gets to the end of his telling, the end of America, the reader has the data needed to form a feelingful conviction of what manner of man has gone what manner of journey.

The story found in the mind (like the one in a bottle) is whole. It is whole, even if the text, like the manuscript in the bottle, is sea-leached or shredded, and seems at first only a fragment. Everything is a fragment, or nothing is. Without even begging the question (and what is the question?), I will insist that any narrative, even the most conventional well-made plotted novella, is itself a fragment of a vast transaction. A transaction of energies and influences and cross-purposes and mutualities. Picasso, in those fantastic private final decades of his life, demonstrated that the most perfected works of classic art were for him no more than the wellspring of variation, and worth only their force as stimuli for the next, the next. In such painful wisdom, he dissolved the proprieties of art and the greed of art as property at once, and avenged himself on that commodity fetishism of which he was, economically, so great a beneficiary. The work changes. Any work of art is an object, & like an object is susceptible to an infinite proliferation of interdependent variations. Uses.

I wanted to move against masterpieces, not by writing a flawed one, but by casting the reader, always the reader (the proletarian of the text), into a conjuncture whose circumstances were rendered as precisely as I could. To that extent, the novel was like a poem: a deed for readers. And taking the ancient trope of the journey (Gilgamesh, Grail, Gulliver) — I suppose I don't really know any other structures except staying & going — I set out to listen to my man speak his way towards silence. I knew that his clock would run out, but did not, at the outset, know how many adventures he would have along the way, or how long it would take him to use up his fund of compassion, by which alone the intellect is sustained.

Many reviews of the novel came my way, and the ones that seemed most to get the point and sense the shape of the book, were, to my surprise, in several science-fiction magazines. I shouldn't have been so surprised: they must be used to horror stories, and their characteristic heroes, like mine try to flee from experience by controlling it, like those sad whimsical lovers who flee from passion by making a science or technology of love. My hero (and he is a hero, of intention, attention, interpretation) is a genius of the apotropaic, a rhapsodic paranoid, & a bad man. Much of me in him I was concerned to cast out. Nowadays I might treat his demons more compassionately.

Fogs have boundaries, and winds, and islands. It was not my concern to grasp some demiurgic power over my hero, and see him saved or damned. I wanted to listen to him till he stopped.

There is no greater pretense than the fiction of an event, and no greater fiction than the presumption of a self, hero, being, I. Today the Hudson is ruddy brown as the Missouri, darkened with yesterday's rain, heaviest in any one day in the city's history. Down the midchannel the river flows, and where it cuts through the salty water of the estuarial tide coming up river, on that margin today rafts of debris — trees, vegetation, mud-choked leaves — string out down the river for miles. It came from everywhere and is, for a moment gathered here. It will disperse. Things get to be everywhere again.

6 April 1984

THREE BOOK REVIEWS

WILLIAM GADDIS'S *CARPENTER'S GOTHIC*

The special callnote of the American genius is the portentous far-off horn call of allegory. No matter how modestly the great American novelists (all few of them) keep their eyes down, attending to the view from their piazzas or the peach of their plate, the reader keeps waking up in mornings of richer implication.

So it is with *Carpenter's Gothic*, William Gaddis's third published novel. In my own doubt quirky [sic] reading of literary history, the publication of his *The Recognitions* in 1954 was the Great Divide in our letters, when we crossed from the desert of psychological introspection into the fertile uplands between Sierras, where Story and Language had it their own way again, mything all day long and the stars blazing in ancient arrays newly, and secularly, seen. The world had come back, with its spaces & dimensions. Size & gesture were possible. We were ready for the *Iliad* again — the mind speaks by action.

Gaddis fans had to wait two decades for the next big book, *JR* — action becomes speech. Interminable conversation is the matrix in which we glimpse from time to time the options of action, the writhing of money, our own dearest monster. This book is a kind of *endlose Melodie* that observes with unflinching irony the death of the Wagnerian gods into commerce, Thomas B. Wotan, Valhalla on Hudson.

In a way, the new *Carpenter's Gothic* is an Hegelian synthesis of the earlier books — the golden abundant narrativity of *The Recognitions* vitalized by the acerbic agonic vernacular of *JR*. *Carpenter's Gothic* is a book of bothness — for America has never understood alternatives, Kierkegaard, the Flood. America is a Both/And kind of place, never an Either/Or — our fondest dream is to be everyone. A book? A book is an everything, a *totum*, a final analysis, monument, seed, both leagues, world series, nothing left out. A book is Noah's Ark, and two by two they come aboard — word & gesture, cliché and profundity, the ear & the mind.

I finished reading *Carpenter's Gothic* with an enlarged respect for Gaddis, that he could win such beauty and rewarding complexity of design from people & situations that are, on the face of it, at once utterly familiar and weirdly indistinct. I suppose his chosen method, by ear, is the aptest. I can't think of a novelist who hears better than Gaddis.

The book seldom speaks in the voice of its or any author, but when it does, the prose is rich, tender, allusive, subtle, and subtly mocking its own airs, its own grace — as a house might, by a studied excess of ornament & fretwork, subtly mock the genteel aspiration of its builder — who would yet live, placid and cordial, inside it. From the very opening paragraph of the book (which had the odd effect of bringing tears to my eyes, wreck of a dove), this reader lurked in expectation of more of that wonderful prose of his, descriptions and likenesses of such power and originality (and modesty), that it is to *Carpenter's Gothic* I would go (just as to the works of Hawkes & Gass) for compiling some chrestomathy of late Classic American prose.

This is the brilliance and solidity that every now and then (just enough?) serves to ground and ennoble the goings-on of the characters, who advance their own lies & intrigues (from which the reader gets or guesses most of the plot) in a continuous palaver of spoken banality so artfully *heard* that they seem to be strings of joycean epiphanies, opening one by one stink-pit sepulchers in the hell of pettiness and deceit.

His characters are stricken with belatedness — epigones all of vaster and shadowy polities (commercial empires foundering in peculation & venality, religious commerces of various hues grasping for chances to exploit the minds and mines — the pun never explicit, is pervasive — of the world. Are they old money gone wrong? A man of family actually an adopted nobody? A spy or a demented professor? Defined only by their complaints, his characters drown in monsoons of excuses and explanation.

They talk in sentences that are almost without exception fragmented, over-running the measure or falling short of it. The completeness of a character's personality is signified by the wholeness of the sentences he speaks. Over the course of the book, Liz (most suffering closest to us, hence the most bumbling stammer of the lot) gradually learns to say a sentence or two complete, till in a moving peroration just before the end, she can briefly claim her own articulate identity. Her interlocutor, the *misterioso* landlord McCandless, promptly loses the capacity for closure. He drivels on, starting & starting over like all the rest of them. It is his measure: characters do not change, they stand revealed. Syntax is destiny.

This is such a cunning, thoughtful book that I have no critical aplomb after one reading. It is, in miraculously brief fashion, a pretty thorough anatomy of falsification of experience personal, political, economic, spiritual. The greedy evangelists who play so large a role offstage are figures of fun, absurdly meridional, vile, and dangerous — all the more so since their villainies, though detected, seem unrebuked by our society.

Offstage. Yes, there is a sense of Greek play in this book. All the action takes place in the house, all of it till the very end inside the walls. Just before the end we have a scene in the yard or garden (where we first *see* the house), and the very last shabby sentiment of all is uttered in a car just pulling away from the house. Till then, everything is hemmed in. Unities are observed, though time seems compacted oddly, time passage represented mostly (as in *film noir*) by the accumulation of newspaper headlines and the arrival of bills in the mail.

The house is the point of it. *Carpenter's Gothic*, Gaddis is careful to have a character explain, is that gingerbready gothic that handsomely infests the Hudson Valley, built from the outside, with elevation in mind, the rooms fitted in later, as they could. It is vernacular, built from generalized plans, the Nineteenth Century ancestor of the Do-It-Yourself, anybody can do it. Build a house (but how to live in it?) Write a book (but what do the characters *do*?).

Here, they never stop talking. They talk (but not about love) while they're making what we would normally call love — Paul rousing himself & trying to rouse Liz while raving his commercial schemes is as nasty a scene as you'll find outside Nathaniel West. Some heartbreaks later, Liz herself will be talking just as much to, or past, the point while rousing someone it would not be fair to the reader to specify.

For this book, if it is to be everything, is also to be a detective story, spy thriller, whodunnit. It has its locked room, its missing documents, its testamentary ambiguities, its suits at law, its stolen scientific papers, its mysterious stranger and vanishing ladies, foreign intrigue, and, perhaps largest & [murkiest] of all, its absent father doubtfully slain. Beneath all the splendors of his prose & grand designs, Gaddis is also gifted with a work-a-day skill that can make all the links come out perfectly neatly without resorting to exposition by lecturing sleuth. The mysteries we're left with at the end of the novel are not annoying ones — just the old immense incurable enigmas, our own folly, deceptiveness, vengefulness, despair.

There is in general an interestingly uneasy sense of transgression about the book — about the fable itself, and the text we read it in. At times a character will, with something close to plausibility, bring up an image or trope the reader has just encountered in the richly ornamented but sparsely supplied voice-over narration.

Narrative occurs in the book rarely, like [old] family 'good' pieces scantily furnishing a seedy house. And the characters are themselves objects, family possessions, left-over chattels. Liz and Billy and Paul (who gets a full name) and McCandless (who almost does), infantilized by an impenetrably unfair legacy, infantilized by the lies in their mouths, in their whines, their awful nicknames, their servitude to second-hand dreams. Liz, for all her red hair, toys at the manuscript of an unwritable novel, drifting to it in her rare zones of Bovaresque alonenesses that feel like soon to be interrupted masturbations. When Liz makes love, she's actually talking about fiction — her sexuality hopelessly compromised by (we see) fantasy and (we are told) by some peculiar crash by which she has been impeded in the proper execution of her marital obligations. Gaddis sails close to the wind here, taking risks of this transgressive sort, rubbing the textures of story and text together and letting them wear thin, show through. In a lesser writer, we might be left with the sour taste that the self-referentiality-of-the-text (old Narcissism writ large) often deposits. Here, Gaddis joyously welcomes the participation of the reader in demystifying the angry, ugly story he, American, is compelled to tell.

Because this is a Viet Nam novel too, & one of the subtlest of them. The scandal of that war makes all roguery possible, even obligatory, as if it were no longer possible to have an American government not worked by manipulation, and not implemented by knaves. We no longer have a meaningful alignment of good and bad. I do not think Mr. Gaddis has an optimistic bone in his body — at least not in his writing hand. We are foolish if we expect the skillful anatomist who excoriates vicious folly to provide a cure for it too — & doubly foolish if we credit any panacea he does trick himself into prescribing. Apart from the marmoreally succinct etiology on page 98 ("money attracts the worst"), Gaddis gives us no causal analyses — just descriptions, voices, the drone of specious excuses. The jabber never stops, and it all enters as if it were one & the same: TV, telephone, radio, speaker. There is not much to be heard beside the

voices — some birds, some music, the wind. The jabber never stops, &
after a while the reader knows these people will talk themselves to death.
And so they do. There are, undramatically and certainly ungraphically,
deaths a-plenty in this novel.

I'm conscious of each remark as more properly a topic in some
vast essay Gaddis & his work deserve. *Carpenter's Gothic* is the shortest
by far of his three novels. It has, accordingly, been praised & welcomed
— as if the author had finally shed unsightly fat and came in, for once,
looking like anybody else. But there is no diminution in his scope, rich-
ness, ambition. The ambition is huge (stories of *The Confidence Man,
Miss Lonelyhearts, Tender is the Night, Heart of Darkness* — all amend-
ed, rebuked, renewed) and the deftness uncanny. For all the evident
importance of the book, it never seems puffed-up or oversolemn. On
the contrary, it is (& we may hope to be likewise, we ridiculous) a very
funny book. I don't mean just innuendo and snigger, I mean laughter,
absurdity, wonderful clenches of slapstick, the collages of nonsense we
inhabit in the Age of Gentrified Terrorism, when the phone never stops
ringing.

[ca. 1985]

I AM NOT A HALFBACK: ON ROBERT COOVER'S *WHATEVER HAPPENED TO GLOOMY GUS OF THE CHICAGO BEARS?*

As children we read stories about what would have happened if the South
had won the War Between the States. We went on to fantasize: What if
the Republicans had driven Franco into the sea, or that briefcase had
exploded right under Hitler's chair? When the time comes to welcome
the what-if genre into the game preserve of literature, Robert Coover's
new book ought to be one of the choicest exhibits. It has all Mr. Coover's
delight in technique, his inventive brio, his earthy humor, along with
the passion for justice that marks all his writings and makes them stand
out among contemporary masterpieces of anomie, with which they are
usually compared.

Imagine what would have happened if Richard Nixon had not put all his bizarre energies and tragic goofiness into becoming the ruler of our country, but had instead, way back in college as a dedicated mama's boy, put his whole being into becoming the greatest football player in the world. This daffy whimsy spurs Mr. Coover's "Whatever Happened to Gloomy Gus of the Chicago Bears?"

Mr. Coover's first novel, *The Origin of the Brunists*, revealed his range, his ability to handle huge stories and detailed development. His *Pricksongs & Descants* was a major demonstration of the powers of brief fiction, manifested afresh this year in the extravaganza *A Night at the Movies*. And his novel of two years ago, *Gerald's Party*, is a sinister miracle of relentless attention to the upwelling of one unending party that's all too like the world. Here he takes hold of the ordinary novel and, with apparent modesty, briskly renovates its traditional features: the chapter, the unassuming narrator lucid and civil as can be, the telling dialogue, the heroic figure just offstage, remembered by those who loved or loathed him. Mr. Coover takes something that looks from across the room like any other novel, and opens its depths and mysteries with subtleties of handling that challenge close reading, though the casual reader banquets well enough on slapstick and sagacity.

Great men display themselves against the sky of our wondering but wandering attention, then disappear. After treating the historical Richard Nixon as a fictional character in *The Public Burning*, Mr. Coover now scales him down, makes him score touchdowns and conquer virgins, so we come to know better the man who ruled us, and the us he ruled.

For this book is an anatomy not of power or even the lust for power, but of something more automatic, hence more dangerous than that: "He was nothing but Self," nothing but a will that works without intelligence, without even the dignity of desire. We are not, of course, speaking about the 37th President of the United States, but about Dick no-last-name, nicknamed Gloomy Gus, one-season hero of the Chicago Bears, shot down by goons in a labor action against a steel mill around about the time the Abraham Lincoln Brigade was idealistically dying in Spain.

The story is told by Meyer, a Jewish metal sculptor in Chicago. Time and milieu remind us of Steinbeck or Farrell. After a downfall (about which we learn the facts only later), Gloomy Gus has taken refuge with

Meyer's buddies, filthy-mouthed, lovable Jewish leftists, whose own varied shades of socialist heresy keep them wrangling. Since Gus is, despite his downfall, one of the most famous men in America, the most coherent agitator has the wicked idea of using him for propaganda value in the upcoming riot. Meantime Gus seduces & entrances Golda, the sister of one of Meyer's friends; she soon turns to Meyer for comfort and, after Gus's death, for sex.

Meyer is lovable too, & talks, as his friends do, a Yiddish-enriched high-calorie English. A vast unfinished bust of Maxim Gorky, his favorite author, stands in his chilly studio surrounded by the junk & scrap metal from which it is welded together. (No need to sound the allegory alarm. Writers are always writing about writing.) Meyer's lovability is, naturally, suspect. Like many a famous narrator, Meyer does little to help the living figure whose ruin is his story, and his own ill-concealed resentments and jealousies hint at some connivance in the death. Be that as it may, telling the story of Gus certainly helps Meyer find his own voice, his own nature, even without his uneasy fulfillment through the amorous Golda he inherits. (Golda? Meyer?) Gradually we see the narrator move to center. He becomes in his way a semblable, an alternate version of the narrated. Richard Nixon finds his Boswell, and the biographer finds (just as James Boswell did, at length) himself. When Meyer comes home carrying a fine fish for dinner and finds a swastika painted on his door, his instinct cuts through bewilderment, and in his desperation he turns it into art in a passage that makes the heart of the book glow. Weeping, he paints the Nazi emblem into a design of flowers in a garden, and Golda promptly appears, to abide in his bower. Of the two different kinds of self-defeaters, the subtle and the overt, I find myself thinking more about Meyer than about Gus, and I think that Mr. Coover has justified the curious Jewishness that seemed at first an arbitrary contrivance, an appropriation of Bellow types & Roth patois.

There is nothing subtle about Gloomy Gus. His girlfriend Golda calls him by his right name, Dick. Gus lives by rule, practicing every moment of the day to learn the drill for everything he must do. Nothing is natural to him, nothing at all. He is a monster — and in literature, monsters are fun because they mean only one thing, undiluted by the mere circumstances that keep the rest of us from epic consistency. It is all will with Gus, without a moment of imagination.

Scattered through the book are quotations from Gus that seem the very words of Richard Nixon — they sound so like the man that a mere historian would not dare unfather or debunk them. Gloomy Gus is Richard Nixon, in all his awkward triumphs, in all the plodding determination every act takes, in the harsh light of the will that makes every act equal to every other. Mr. Coover cooks up some ribaldry to remind us, through Gus's Lucky Pierre shenanigans, of the sheer potency of the former President.

Gus's downfall is a little like Richard Nixon's too. Gus lives by signals, and every now and then gets his signals crossed. These episodes are slapstick, deliberately callow. The final triumph of the maladroit comes about when a gridiron situation evokes a bedroom response, and before the breathless thousands of Chicago fans, Gus prodigiously misbehaves. As I read, I recalled the poet Charles Olson saying that the greatest danger to America was our hopeless confusion of public with private. Talk shows and gossip glossies ride that confusion; we're all celebrities, nobodies, names in a book. When the historic Richard Nixon fell, it started with a two-bit burglary. Everybody turned ethical — and he was gone. But public ethics is a rare ripple in America, soon subsiding into the glassy sea of the Main Chance.

Mr. Coover's Richard Nixon is a nobler, stupider character than history's — such is the nonchalant optimism of even tragic art that the animal determination of Gus gives him a brief dignity. Gus is an innocent, all prowess and no sense. Mr. Coover shows us the madness of the will as it operates without intelligence, and makes us think about that most secret of all our transgressions, the deep sin of being innocent.

It is hard not to think of Melville's *Billy Budd*, with Gloomy Gus an alliterating peer of the tongue-tied sailor — Gus's skill and Billy's ineptness are two faces of the same Know-How, America's cruel god. Mr. Coover is one of our masters now. The tumultuous, Babylonian exuberance of his mind is fueled and directed by his equally passionate craftsmanship. He seems to be able to do anything, & this funny, bitter, human book is fair proof of it.

(NYTBR, 27 September 1987)

POUNDIAN ROMANCE: INVESTIGATING THOMAS McEVILLEY'S NOVEL *NORTH OF YESTERDAY*

> "a hungry book, reading the readers"[2]

The coincidence of means with goal is, in this world & beyond it, the special quality both of the illuminative path and of the highest energies of literature — one of the many reasons writers constantly confuse their practice with religion. It was the particular triumph of Modernism to create — in Pound, Joyce, Stein, Proust, Mann, Broch, Beckett, Céline, even Rilke — a determinately secular epos to enshrine, instruct or transform our secular world. (The fact that poets are religious about Pound & novelists about Proust shows merely that religion can embed itself in the secular, snug as an abbé in a Neuilly salon).

In *North of Yesterday*, modern dreams open out onto a late Egyptian mystery, and from its perfervid sensual nightmares some characters discovered lurking in the mind of the teller (like Lovecraft's Old Ones, ever watchful for their chance to speak and move), proffer to the Narrator (the voice we get to know) three fateful flowers. Their petals, eaten, produce effects which are coincident with history arrowing its way to the novelist's now, coincident with the drugs he and his beloved are forever high on or low from, coincident with the very book itself, sent from Back Then and always being lost Here and Now, a book that turns ineluctably into the novel we are reading. Classical modernism and classical mystery story at once. I found pleasure in the fact, though, that the self-reflexiveness of this novel is relaxed, even genial; it is not at all portentous, clever, or French. McEvilley takes for granted a novel's (and our own) capacity for being fascinated by its own coming into being. We are souls making souls in a vale of soul-making, we are part of theogeny. We like the smell of our own armpits better than that of others — this fatal penchant is the root of self-awareness in modern texts. We are fascinated by our own dreams. The narrator in *North of Yesterday* spends a lot of time dreaming, with and without the help of sleep.

---

2. Thomas McEvilley, *North of Yesterday, or, Flowers of Waz* (Kingston: McPherson Company, 1987) 179.

Pause now for : Lyric Mytheme from the Turn of the Century.

On a warm night a long trolley ride from Market Street, when the wicker porch furniture groaned and cracked under the quiet passion of a young couple sitting close not quite furtively in the dark, in June, with mosquitoes sibilant and the dog asleep, with parents not far and society in love with lovers as it always is, summer warmth around the turn of the century, Ezra Loomis Pound and Hilda Doolittle were, a little bit, making love. Damp clothes and quick breaths, a hand here, a hand there, all of it unsatisfactory, enthralling, fulfilling, incomplete. By midnight the mustachioed swain had risen for his long walk home, the girl (exhausted by sheer feeling, pre-orgasmic excitement swollen and released to post-orgasmic irritable lassitude without ever the Everest of orgasm proper in between) watched his athlete's body move with a fencer's short neat steps to the sidewalk and disappear beyond the meager porch-light.

In the gorgeous simplistic bargain basement called Literary History, it is a commonplace to believe that Ezra Pound spent the rest of his life fleeing such feelings and such tendernesses, and that H.D. spent the rest of hers trying to sustain that evening forever, projecting it into past and future, Egypt and Greece, Rome and Bethlehem, always, the throb of that not-quite-unspeakable, deeply articulate, yearning. Boys will be boys, girls will be girls.

It is true that the *idle* reader of the *Cantos* looks in vain for the author's amours, or any love stories more recent than rainy Toulouse in the XIIITH Century, or some renaissance affair too complicated by family history and real estate manipulations to have much gyzm. The subtle reader is, as usual, better rewarded. Busy writing the Cantos for himself in the acoustic reverberation of the master (for one must chant the Cantos that one hears, that is the secret, we must write the book we read), the reader soon learns that many of the Cantos, especially the later ones, are concerned with the articulation of the heart's poise in a world of passion. Poise, the pivot. Pound chose as one of his most important glyphs the ideogram (found in the very name of China), which can mean the middle, the heart of the target. He writes of the Unwobbling Pivot. We recall him, Pound in his power, as one who stood by his words, unwobbling, and we remember also the man between two women, a man between two works, a man between two worlds. Olga *&* Dorothy,

4 · A BOOK OF DISCOURSE &/ON NARRATIVE

Poetics & Economics, Antiquity & Cathay — a man trying to be just the one he is, no other. Pound is patron saint of our modern polytheism, even as, in the mighty agon of the Pisan nightmare, he began to cast away this idiocy of a self. No wonder the impassivity of the Confucian acrobat so pleased Pound, who tried to hold his own at the pulsing heart of the, of any, dialectic.

Surely H.D. in her own work sought & found such balances, such chambers and alcoves of desire between the determination of her heart to find comfort and love's mating, and the determination, Isis-like in her tenacity, not to give up one iota of all the world that has been.

Her mode became the *palimpsest*, as Ezra's the *ideogram*. These two modes are the Eve and Adam of modernism — by which Ism I mean to indicate not an historic period but a watershed of spirit from which we still are plentifully supplied.

Palimpsest: the inscription of a new text on an old parchment from which the former words had been scraped away. With time, (or with infra-red photography after the turn of the century) both messages came through. Layer upon layer of meanings, narrations, build up. This touch touches every touch before, skin upon skin. The palimpsestical method studies the overlay of all that has been spoken. It is the method of *superimposition*. On the other hand, the ideogrammatic method works by *juxtaposition*, assembling entities, objects, words into a speaking structure, a structure whose unity-of-saying is a function of the very diversity from which the complex image is welded by ear.

The ideogrammatic method. This was Pound's great formal declaration, & the awe-filled, god-crazed spaces of the Cantos (especially those canto-beginnings, those fair embarkations at the start of many of the individual cantos, ideograms that commence the journey outward, each time, from the silence of his life or the deeper silence of his logic, his terrifying "So that" which ends the first canto), those spaces ripple with light and dazzle with the congestion of thought in all its *substances*, packed tight; these passages are in fact the ideograms themselves of a great new language Pound only began.

End of Retrospection. Back to McEvilley.

This is not the place to remark yet again Pound's immense influence on Twentieth Century poetry & poetics. We all know that. Here I just want to sketch, draw the bow almost at random, in hailing this lovely, intricate new book of McEvilley as a rare thing, a new thing, an instance of Pound's not hitherto much noticed pressure on the novel.

 Pound's snows of Lydia & golden lyres transcend their local times and occasions. In McEvilley's urgent rhythms, Pound's poetic of image / ideogram / cluster turns to a *narrative syntax,* an alternative excellence at last to those of Paul Metcalf and Guy Davenport as our most noble Poundian novelists (& they more so by the coalescence of concerns than by templating of method). In McEvilley's work, variation & repetition, the rich bottom-work of the round dance, make the ground on which his dancers move, never stable, never pausing. Every recurrence is a jolt, not a serenity. His images dance round and slap our faces, our meek modern faces. Pound's measures are set to new burdens, and Pound's haughty spondees and clangorous trochees (read out loud page 58!) tell H.D.'s stories, classic entablatures made to writhe with the serpentine delusions of the heart. McEvilley is running away from the classic world Pound still (per aspera ad astra) hungers for as *norm of the spirit.*

 The deeds and transforms of this novel are not serene. A hero lost at sea (over and over: Egypt, Turkey, Yucatan) is born or reborn a sea-monster — he is, or someone is. In a passage of great beauty, a woman is missing from her bed while her lover searches, haunts, through all the houses of the town looking at the sleepers still or restless in their silent beds. A criminous old procurer lives forever, an ancient poet refuses to desist in his discourse. Things happen, or seem to. What else is new? Peopled with fascinating language, this book tells plenty. But what does it tell?

 All events are myth. In so far as we can recognize them as *events* at all, not just as shadowy smears, blurs, pixels of discreet light, to that extent it means they participate in myth, rehearse myth, renew myth, or simply present myth. Myth means that which we have no other way of apprehending than as a whole. Any event is myth, and any person is myth. As Barthes pointed out in the same brilliant year that Olson wrote *Projective Verse,* the capacity of language to use the *passé défini,* the simple past tense (he came; it fell), implies a dependence, both naïve and functional, on some imputed creator/observer who can measure the boundaries of process itself, & determine when an event is, and when it is finished. (I write this on Good Friday, & recall with a shiver that the

God we call our Lord said, "It is finished" as he stood against the wood of the cross.)

So the tendency of the modern novelist to erode the edges of the event, deny its close-endedness, abrogate the privilege of its ego and the ego of the character — this tendency is not a fashion (though it may be fashionable at times) but a breakthrough in the Tacit Communal Theology that runs the mind of the west. In *North of Yesterday*, each act knows itself as several, not as single. This novel, exciting obedient to its hypermodern agenda,[3] calls into question the very nature of 'event,' 'person,' 'character.' And in doing so, it does not appear to pay even lip service to some inherited wistfulness towards unity. (We are states united, but states apart, in gods we trust, but take no refuge in them.)

This deliquescence of character & event enrolls McEvilley's book in the glamorous army of books found hard to read. (One newspaper reviewer found the sentences detestable and their purport obscure, if I remember aright.) What an interesting thing it is, to be hard to read! Or be, really, as this book truly is, very easy to read, a lollop every moment, easy to read but hard to understand. By understand, I mean a nervous and insecure questing for connections faster than the author cares to supply them.

Egypt is fanciful, and Greece a poetic land of the lost. Not much special knowledge is needed to read this book, just delight in language, a pagan lust for imagery, along with patience for the figures of the dance as they wind and unwind themselves. (One of the dumbest things in the world is to look at a dance and want it to be architecture.) The novel spouts a few local thorn-bushes of arcane reference, which are also things we might be happy to learn about. And it is alas only too likely that many

---

3. Whatever Postmodern may finally come to mean, I want there to be a term to mean, and I am using *hypermodern* to do so, strategies or enterprises that carry forward the basic modernist devotion to technique ('technic'), as well as modernism's characteristic methods: fragmentation, ideogram, palimpsest, alienation, analysis (as in Cubism), etymology. Modernism's deep, almost mystical belief in the *means* at hand — "a man at the mercy of his means" — seems still to go on generating work of great power — Brakhage's films come to mind, and Zukofsky's late poetry as it helps to shape current poetics, or the work of Jackson Mac Low, or the polytheistic psychology of James Hillman.

a reader won't recognize Quintus Smyrnæus, though it would help to — an often deprecated later Greek writer whose accurate Homeric metrics and plausible Homeric language, used in an epic that tells (as Homer's did not) about the Fall of Troy, combine with a fine bloody imagination and great imagistic powers to make much more than a pastiche of Homer. Quintus is an important character in this novel, partly used (I suspect) as an affectionate teasing of the Ezra Pound whose oeuvre seems so basic a donation, or permission, to McEvilley, partly as a link in a tradition of writers reading writers — a poignant avowal of demure humility, if McEvilley is to [Pound] as Quintus Smyrnæus is to Homer. It is from Quintus that the little book is sent that the narrator learns to read, and in reading writes the book we read, and in that book learns the mystery Quintus has stumbled on in Egypt. But for all its authors, there is only one book, ever.

At a rare moment of solemnity, the narrator confesses:

> It is difficult to explain what has happened to me since I began this book. How many have I looked for on the river? When I found them, what was it? A flutter at the heart, a mouth pulsing at the hand. A tenderness that stuns the brain, casts a mist around the head, and we fall.

This book. The converse of the singleness of the Book is *all* the books that any book is, all the ways of reading, revealing, & hiding itself away that a text has. "My" book is missing, & Quintus's book is "his."

This multifariousness conditions delight. The pleasure in *North of Yesterday* is the pleasure of *reading*, not that species of remembering we call 'plot' or 'understanding.' The pleasure goes on in the text the way swimming goes on in the water; not without dullness can it be extracted therefrom. The pleasure is in the text as we pass, almost bewildered by the diversity of resources & presentment of McEvilley, a very generous writer, indeed, provides. We are life-like readers in a life-like manifold of provocations. As readers, we are tired of paying writers to simplify our experiences & abort our destinies. So though there are some things in *North of Yesterday* I don't like (just as there are some bad restaurants in Paris and some dull poems by Yeats), I like well the amplitude of registrations and remembrances he has brought to tell a story that is, when you get down to it, painfully simple.

I like this book I like its blend, a wonderfully fatal mixture in the author, I guess, of prank and pomp, each outwitting the other:

> ... she crawls from the water on all fours and looks about strangely, remembering nothing. And I take her, sleek and soft, to my chest, and kiss her in the dream, not caring.
> "*Venus decumbent: sunstroke, puking fevers, pulsatilla.*"
> I discover a critical opposition coming, Uranus in Cancer and Neptune in Capricorn, and dash off a note to the papers: "There will be famine in India, civil strife in North Africa..."..
> She crawls onto me, slopping her breasts on my face like slopping waves, wheels, slowly, like a cow in a stall, and sucks at my cock, her head rising and falling wetly, ruminatively, tongue etching language of serpents on my spine.
> I look it up.
> "*Venus at midheaven: dancing; gold & silver; skill at chess.*"

I like the blend of what is happening here, the dance of registers, and so on, but I don't like the way he lets his narrator see, & characters use, women. Perhaps it is our way, our pre-modernist way, here analyzed in one of its typical acts of humiliation. No part of this book pleases me less than such incessant blowing of the flesh-flute (fond as we all are of the flesh); the women 'gobble' or 'suck.' That they seem to do so in a parodistic way is no excuse, and no surprise. It may be parody, but I hate it anyhow. Parody only makes things worse; what malady has parody ever cured, what tyrant has it ever toppled? Parody only adds to the obnoxiousness of the thing it has chosen to target the additional offensiveness of flippancy — a double assault on the reader's sensibility. And here the very thing parodied should not be woman's behavior, but the habits of male obsession. Men are, in *North of Yesterday*, maybe not much better — but *they have language,* while women are mumblers & gobblers, literally (in the instance of the far beloved Della) faceless, or veiled. The book has its revenges on male lust: The bloated Roman governor Lucius Porcius, thinking he is rogering a choice young harlot (the same whose fortunes dominate the secret history of the novel) finds he has been buggering a man, an old man at that, a dead old man. But one suspects that Lucius is punished more for being old and fat than for being (as his name suggests) an early instance of Male C. Pig.

A VOICE FULL OF CITIES

Long ago every boy noticed that Grail is an anagram for A Girl. In *North of Yesterday* a girl is duly sought, Della, and found, Waz, who is or is like unto Isis; she is the veiled woman who is both goal of quest and core of nightmare. Her name sounds to me like one name for the papyrus itself, as if she is the paper (our word is from the plant's name) and the book, the virgin ground it is the male's High Destiny to inscribe. Things that are sought for are, after all, *things*, and I have already mentioned my dislike for the humiliated status of the feminine in *North of Yesterday*. There are ancient Gnostic undertakings that hint at the necessity of humiliation if a certain transformation of one's destiny is to be achieved — but this is not the place to talk about them, and this is not a decade in which they can be heard. Instead, pass with me to the lilt of the Nilotic barcarolle and enjoy an

Intermezzo: the Egypt of Normandi Ellis:

Midway through my reading of *North of Yesterday*, I received a manuscript of a book I had read passages from a few years before: Normandi Ellis's "translations" of Ancient Egyptian texts, *Awakening Osiris*. These translation had haunted me — & again I felt something close to me as I read them. I delighted in her grasp of some surer image or tone, religion, gently mocking her own lovely unreformed American language still thick with things to feel and things to see. Egypt is so many things, or there are so many Egypts. Hers seemed to be an Egypt that the body could reach its way to if only the ear listened carefully. It is a country of substance stronger than image, of aspiration more than theology. Things yearn, and Normandi Ellis is adept at catching the voice of their clamor. Like McEvilley, she was *hearing* the world. What a fine writer she is, I thought, as I read. What a sucker I am for fine writing, I thought, delighting in it here in Ellis's Egypt, and in McEvilley's Egypt, not at all alike, land or writing, but each immensely participating in the act of inscription, the act (to give it a gypsy name), The Act of Making the World Be There By Opening Your Mouth.

Everything I remember, everything that we can remember, as far as Egypt from us now, since every past we remember becomes our own past, part and parcel, silent and fervent, & from it we can speak. Ellis speaks form her strength of language and living, evidently, muscular from the stresses of a life of reading, living, listening & clearly responding in what is remarkably one voice to a host of early and middle Egyptian texts It is a beautiful book, *Awakening Osiris*, now announced for publication by the Phanes Press in (is it?) Chicago.

End of Intermezzo. Back to McEvilley again.

There are so many Egypts. The Egypt of Breasted & Wallis Budge, those old scholars, of Champollion & Gardiner, of Aleister Crowley on that red-letter day in the Cairo Museum, of J. A. West, the thoughtful, measured Egypt of R. A. Schwaller de Lubicz (my own favorite guide), the Egypt of Herodotus, of Solon, of Aristocles (whom we with unintentional boon-camaraderie call Plato) — none of these Egypts help here.

Menacing us all in America is the Egypt that the nineteenth century thought it knew about, of towns grandly named Memphis (TN) or Cairo (NY), of Shriners' temples & lotus-columns, Grauman's Egyptian Theater and Goudy's Egyptian Extra Bold. This is the Egypt that seems to summon forth a kind of Low Church pomposity: we find it in séance transcripts & mimeographed wisdom lessons from Southern California; we meet the same tone of hushed solemn stiltedness in Norman Mailer's *Ancient Evenings*. We don't find it in Ellis or in McEvilley.

Different as those books are, they renew Egypt in the same way, a way that strikes me as very fresh: reinterpreting the past through our own bodies, i.e., through our own capacity to experience pain, pleasure, bewilderment, dismay. Their Egypt is watered by *doubt*, and serves us.

Other modern versions of Egypt do not prepare us for what goes on here. Not even Cavafy's wonderful learned afternoons, lewd as an old coin still warm from its passage through so many hands. Certainly not Durrell's conspiratorial Egypt or Forster's clear-eyed sideshow. One begins to get a flavor of McEvilley's Egypt maybe in Strauss's later opera *The Egyptian Helen*, given its own curious temporal & narrative resonances, almost interferences with, H.D.'s *Helen in Egypt*, our greatest narrative love poem. But McEvilley's Egypt is mostly the fringe-land of later Greeks, a hotbed of sex and mysteriousness, violent and swollen and orgiastic, but finally human — in a way that technocratic Rome was not. This is the Egypt to which Christ was carried by his family to escape from the quisling running-dog vassal of Roman hegemony, King Hesiod.

Perhaps this is the best time to find Egypt, between the coming of Christ and the coming of Christianity, a long century or two of dwindling Hellenism and gathering Gnosis.

We do not hear Isis's side of the story in McEvilley's book; a little bit we do in Ellis's — not because Ellis is a young woman but because she will not leave any item unconsidered, untouched, untasted. That is the task of Isis, is it not, to reassemble the world by noticing it, part by part, to achieve that all-satisfying multiplicity of and in which she is the only unity? Strangely, as I finished *North of Yesterday* I found myself thinking back on H.D.'s great poem, its girlish solemnity, its utter accuracy of feeling-in-remembrance.

I think in fact that McEvilley is trying for that, and what is really most consequential about this book of his, a book I will not forget, is his urgent attempt to combine the methods I have ascribed respectively to Pound and H.D. In the start of *North of Yesterday* the ideogrammatic method is used elaborately, while the last chapters yield the shimmering texts of palimpsest, voice over voice recorded are recalled, a stately antiphon of loss and presentness. Is our author leading Pound back to H.D., this curiously learned novelist/critic/scholar, holding aloft the hymenal torch to light then, and us, to the thalamus, the bridal chamber from which a new mode of writing is expected soon to be born? I only ask, and ask again, in case you were wondering why I bothered earlier on with Ezra and Hilda canoodling on the porch.

So this is the sort of scope or ambition I sense in McEvilley. Like the young *ingénues* on the French stage in the old days, all our young geniuses are around fifty. The soon to be quinquagenarian McEvilley has come forward with this powerful novel. It is not his first, yet it clearly feels to me in many senses a First Novel. It is the first novel you write (for we are somehow writing it, of course, modernist text that it is) after first reading *Steppenwolf*, you are suddenly seventeen again, whatever your age, and beginning to realize that your disordered quest for your mistress is not too different from the universe's quest for meaning — the girl as God. It's the first novel you write, too, after reading Homer or Edward Dahlberg or Savage Landor, or someone else for whom the old gods and the old neighborhoods (Lydia, Attica, Egypt) are still playfully alive. It's the first novel you write after reading Pascal Quignard (of whom we should hear much more in these U.S.) or Guy Davenport, and realizing that Rome's senescence is a topological fold of our own bumptious salad-days, that kind of rehabilitation of Late Antiquity into the recent past, viz., one's grandmother's gauzy summer evenings, turns of the, always the same, century. Egypt is born again with the nineteenth century in its teeth, the Musée d'Orsay and Greyhound busses faltering through antique American landscapes of the future. That is what Pound and H.D. left us with: the past is our only future. And who knows that better than the young person telling the story, the Actual Story, of his or her first love? Where nothing is so important as what really happened?

This mature and conscious writer has written a young man's book, desperate, taking every risk, believing immensely in his own feelings and his abilities to record them. The ambition is endearing too in all that it confesses: the first novel that you write when you want at last to admit to yourself and the rest of the world that the simplest things please you the best: sex and slivovitz, palm tress and evening stars.

(*Review of Contemporary Fiction* #3, 1988)

TRIBUTE TO THOMAS McEVILLEY

When you paint a girl blue and roll her on a canvas or when you paint your hand with red ochre and press it on a wall you are doing the same thing, making the same sort of thing.

The mess of meaning lasts thirty thousand years.

Nobody knows what you have in mind in doing so. But that is not important, thank God. There are people, and McEvilley was among the smartest of them, who know that once the mark gets made, it gets made in us. It lasts.

He doesn't care about the 30,000 years that separate such marks, marks that could be generated tomorrow if there were such a thing as time.

Art doesn't defy time. It denies time.

So art speaks to a society by itself and by the critics who help us, force us, to look at it, or intensify by their palaver the force of seeing.

Criticism can be nothing without literature — Baudelaire, Apollinaire, Ashbery, John Yau, it keeps going. But literature could be nothing without the cave-work, the isolato crazy self-encounter that gets cleaned up and publicked as philosophy.

I marvel at the breadth of McEvilley's generosity, his insistence on tracing thinking back and forth, our Europe, their Asia, their Europe, our Asia, their hands on the walls of our mind.

I suspect McEvilley knew there was no such thing as time, only space, space of cave, canvas, display case, window, śloka, stanza, epic. What is any epic poem but a refutation of time, the whole war in your hand (as in Homer or Quintus of Smyrna).

We say of someone who has died that he has gone away. The French say 'disappeared.' Proof enough of the poverty of time, the richness of space, into which such animals can prowl off.

The work of his that touched me most was the novels — are the books so telling because he was a writer, one of the few I ever met, who could talk about everything?

Context was complete in him. So everything could be said. Those years of saying everything else, art, culture, poiesis, and all the while he was making his masterpiece, *The Shape of Ancient Thought*, that showed so clearly that we get what we think from the same place we get language, the breath of the other.

In his last novel, *The Arimaspia*, someone starts us off by saying that out of the primordial soup of neurological perceptions and proprioceptions someone else is trying to shape and organize a bicameral brain. Our kind. Then trying to make some sense of what he's made: the baby god of the self, confusing his own spasmodic gestures with the movements of the planets and other wanderers.

So art is otherwise. Art is thinking with the hands and so on.

McEvilley sat in his cave in the Himalayas a long time (I forgot to ask him if he was in the Terai or the high peaks), sat there *thinking by himself*.

When you think by yourself everybody thinks with you.

East and west, thinking crowds in. It can dwindle into mere thoughts or stay alive as thinking. And writing was his way of getting thinking out of the body. It might be the only cure for thinking.

March 2014

NOTES FOR AN AFTER DINNER DISCOURSE

Why is this night different from all other nights?

·

Napkins.

·

A mother would say it, mine certainly would:
Civilization?
Civilization is napkins.

·

Here, not far from the grossest graffiti in the east, near the intentional sleaze and squalor in which we sometimes choose to live, here we have eaten in common a decent meal.

·

Decent, what a strange word.

·

That which is fitting. That which fits. A suit, the news that's fit to print. To be acceptable. To accept. To take. Take lessons. Root DEK. Take lessons and be learned. Become a doctor. A decent salary.

·

A meal that fits. Fits the hand and the mouth, fits the eaters, fits the purpose of eating. Wipe the mouth. Nourishes.

·

After eat, talk. Don't talk with your mouth full. Talk from an empty mouth?

·

How to talk a good time. What do our sayings say about talk?

·

Talk is cheap.

·

Talk yourself into it. Talk it up. Talk a good time.

·

The simple pleasures of the poor:
    poor Irish
    shtetl Jews
    slave Blacks
    that common delight in signifying, dozens, palaver, highfalutin talk, *hhokhmah*, wisdom becomes a smart answer, a fresh

mouth we said, the Blarney Stone from which the Irish took the art that pleased them best, talk talk talk, musical unending talk, Joyce's Finnegan's Unending Wake,
                    There seems to be a connection:
Poetry / Poverty
If you don't have money, talk If you don't have food, talk.
.
Talk is cheap.
Pleasures of the poor: Eloquence (Ogmios, chief god of the Celtic peoples) and Sex.
.
Lots of talk and little action.
.
And what do they say, the poor who do not have decent houses (a house that fits), decent food, decent lives? How do you fit into a life?
.
Some days ago the Nobel Prize for Peace... Mother Teresa of Calcutta... Albanian... went to India... usual middle-class schoolteacher... broke away... care for lepers... the poor, the dying, giving them nothing decent, just that attention. Of listening. What do the poor say?
.
Mother Teresa says: "The greatest miracle is this, that with all that they suffer, the poor do not hate us."
.
The poor of Calcutta. Friends have described...
.
"they do not hate us."
Is it true?
.
the great text from Isa Upanishad:
>   He who sees all beings
>   in and as the Self, and sees
>   the Self in all beings,
>   because of doing so, he does not hate.
.
does not hate.
The greatest miracle is that they do not hate.

- That is, they do not hate you.

- Are they too busy with the pleasures of the poor,
talking,
making love?

- Do you hate? Do I hate myself for standing here and talking to people I don't know about poor people I have never met, except in books, except in New York and Newark and Wounded Knee, where I tried to think they did not hate me.

- Time will tell.

- Time talks. Time tell
if there are any values that remain useful even in depressions, revolutions, revolutions like ours that have grown old and fat and lazy. We live in a lazy revolution, yes, with our mottoes strewn all around us?

- Where would those values come from? Values that are true even now when we're rich enough to have food, food rich enough to have grease, grease enough to get on our chins and fingers and be wiped off with special items called napkins meant for no other purpose.

- Our culture comes from deserts.
    Chaldea, Palestine, Ithaca,
        the dry islands of Greece, parched Crete,
the cold deserts (the monks called them) those isles off
Britain, Iceland, the Niger bend, Sahara
                            and before them,
those other marginal terrains, Sumer, Egypt, the Indus Valley.

- Culture *means* what survives.
Culture is what is done, what survives even the graffiti and the slops, even the endless talky dinners & the vegetarian/carnivore tug of war. It may even survive the desert, Arabia, where our oil is waiting, taxed by another set of credences.

Talk, food, work to be done. This night is the same as all other nights.

27 October 79

COME OUT: A BACCALAUREATE ADDRESS

What is a talk, if only one person of the hundred persons present, is talking? Is it that one speaks the talk out loud, and all the others inside themselves, patient, talk silently back? When I listen to a lecturer, I certainly am talking back all the time, slyly and quietly to myself. I score off his infelicities or inaccuracies, exult in his discoveries I will borrow, applaud his elegances, deplore his prolixity. That is to say, if I am sitting listening to a lecturer, I am indulging in some complex behavior that is not really at all like talking. Instead, it is like separating myself from what is being said.

What is it, then, to listen to a talk? Am I listening to a book speak? At my dullest and slowest, I can read faster than the sprightliest orator. Why should I listen? Or what am I listening to?

Is it that the suprasegmentals, those tones and inflections and the stillness of human speech, compel communication more effectively, subtly, than the bland alphabet of books? Or is it that the live rhythm of breath and breathing define an *infra-text* no written language can ever articulate? Do I (and here my also puritan conscience is alarmed), do I listen to the lecturer to listen to his body? To his physical presence on our shared planet, physical in a physical world of vibrations, cycles, amplitudes? Is that physical infra-text in fact the necessary basis or truth or etymon of the lecturer's apparently abstract discourse? Is *he* finally the only thing he means?

What is the basis of discourse? I am asked to address, not a question but a group, a group of people who propose to share some time. An envelope came in the mail: Congratulations! You have been chosen to be the Baccalaureate speaker! Compelled by that mysterious choice, which by its solemnity enforces my commitment far more than my own will could have contrived, I stand here now. I say the word "baccalaureate." What is such a speaker? One who speaks? On one who makes a speech? Is a speech the same as an address? My address is where I live, or how to find me. Address an audience. Address a topic. Is an address the same discourse? Homily? Sermon? Chat? Lecture? Talk? Is this after all a talk?

Just as all the other twentieth century arts have been so much about themselves, so discourse, our discourse, our fresh new style of inscribing ourselves in the world, has learned to be best about itself.

A VOICE FULL OF CITIES

The poem (that primal or crystalline mode of discourse, *vajra*-talk) is its own coming-into-being; nothing it says or opines is as interesting as how it came to be, and how exactly (with musics, *me musikes*) it came to be itself. Perhaps when Livingston Lowes (who was, after all, however zany it may be to recall it now, a contemporary of the Russian Formalists) wrote *The Road to Xanadu* — a large book that tried to answer only: how did this small poem come to be — he may have had no inkling of how well he had entrained us towards a genuine sort of criticism. I would hail the road, little travelled as it has yet been — a road that could be presumptuously called The Road from Meaning to Being. A road that presently will be concerned with the factuality of the work of art, its consequence in the world, its process of becoming, its targets, its duress, its initiation of the reader into a collaborative exercise in being.

Be that. As it may. Listening to myself talk, I see (see because I am really reading, re-reading), I see that I have strayed to a familiar topic, of the processual arts and the *poetics of being*. By my habits of old attention, I've made a mistake, and turned from addressing an audience to addressing a topic. The audience waits.

Now this waiting of the audience, waiting in this case perhaps for me to say something, is itself unclear to my concerns at the moment. The audience waits for the speaker to say something. What did he say, they will ask or be asked later. Far from merely being permitted to hear, with joy or regret, the speaker's suprasegmentals and panoply of breath and so on, as above, the audience is required to understand, or interpret, or remember, or give report. It has to carry away some sayable paraphrase. Out into the world. Where suddenly the speaker is to be measured not by the breath and tones and operatic gesture, but by that same sayable paraphrase carried out into the world. "What did he say?"

I am, perhaps more than most, a speaker distrustful of such messages. It is not at all that I doubt the sayability of truth. I doubt how well it travels. Like certain mountain wines that become insipid in lowlands, it does not use its power to intoxicate, but does lose its power to focus or induce focus, to specify, to be itself, to speak of its morning and evening, its days of becoming, fermenting. I am reluctant to speak a truth that does not reveal its ground.

There is also a reluctance in me to speak without a text. There is a not altogether curious unwillingness I have noticed in many poets and writers to be less than formal in public. For one thing, all these symposiums and colloquiums and chats are conversations-through-a-bullhorn: the scale is all wrong. But more than that, to talk about a subject is to talk around it, to talk without a text, the good old *hypokeimenon* which should lie beneath and sustain discourse.

I have been standing here talking a few minutes, anxious to alert you to certain issues, but equally anxious to avoid offering my opinions about them. I am seeking a text, or even to become a text. What then is the nature of this text I seek? It is not the underbody or motherpart of discourse, nor yet some flourish or style to adorn it. It is a rock on which a rock, a seed from which seed. Text answers text, even when we are silent.

So as I thought about standing there, naked because textless, it occurred to me that the place itself might have something to say, this lectern which is also a pulpit, in a church which also is a college. I face an audience of scholars departing. And after all, a text did come to mind, almost as if it were spoken out of the judaeo-christian alignments of the molecules of place: old wood, glass, bellmetal, when I stood alone a few days ago in this chapel, to test its resonance. My text, then, comes to me from Paul's second Epistle to the Corinthians, the sixth chapter, seventeenth verse: *Wherefore come out from among them and be ye separate.*

The words seem appropriate to place and occasion. A sonorous prescription for this coming-out part, this separation-festival of people who have been together. Together too long? Or not long enough? Or not together enough? Or too together? This solemn ceremony todays answers: No — together just enough, just long enough.

Come out implies you've been in. *Come out from among them* means that you've been in the midst of, of whom or what? Of *them*. We know who "they" are. They are the ones disgraced by that bulk pronoun, the ones we won't share our "we" with. And "they" is the paranoid pronoun, as it has been called: they're out to get me, they're after me, they're at the door — that "they" is certainly meant in the text. But more than that: come out from among those who have no names, who have no specificity by which you can know them, or tell them from yourself. Paul appears to be addressing converts menaced by backsliding into idolatrous enterprises. His mind fills with relevant memories of the severer prophets, and the little sentence he says is a chain of quotations from Isaiah, Jeremiah, Ezekiel. Paradoxically, he enrolls himself among the Prophetic Company at the very moment he seems to be bracing his hearers to separate, separate evidently from *every* "them." His choice-of-words, as we'd say, recruits him to a tradition. And a tradition can be, can usually and easily be, is almost always, an idolatry. Come out from among the comfortable undifferentiated presence of a lot of nice *them*. Come out from the dark fear-fantasies of the Kafkan *them*. Come out from the supportive traditions of forced learning and quick forgetting. Come out from the pastoral place where "meaning" and "love" and "responsibility" and "change" are taken seriously. Come out from mindless work that's supposed to help the mind mature. Come out from the comfort of acceptance and from the rapture of rejection. Come out from society *&* come out from crime. Come out and *separate*.

What dos this *separate* mean? Isolated? Peculiar? Speaking an idiolect? I suspect it means: live up to your fingerprints. Live up to your *I'jaz*, that fine Arabic word that means uniqueness, inimitable and sacred differentness — we have to borrow it for our critical vocabulary. Paul's Greek word is *aphoristhête*: be marked out by boundary, mark something as one's own. Declare a field, and plow it, and harvest it, and know it, know it as your own.

I have borrowed Paul's imperative-mode. "Plow it," I say, tossing another metaphor out at the assembly, "know it," I say, "know it as your own." How do I *dare* say such things to you, dare to extend the text, a sacred text it may be, sacred if only by being a text? How do I dare to *interpret* it, then assail you with those interpretations as projectiles dropped down on your sameness from the pulpit of my difference? I defer. The text is not to be interpreted, the text is to be known. And grown on from. Embedded in the next thing said. And on. So I can say that the text tells me to withdraw from the nameless into the named, from the unconscious, that is, into the conscious. And be separate. Clearly, Paul meant "be a separate group, separate from all other groups." But I take his group and dismember it, borrow his imperative but leave out the embarrassing circumstance that his verb in Greek is *plural*, even as *ye* is, or was, plural in English.

What shall I make of that? HE is telling all of his listeners, as it were, to be separate together. As I look around, it is tempting to conclude that he had a church in mind, a gathering of the elect — and leaving the matter boringly there. But this text of his that I've nipped out of context, doesn't this text have something better to tell us? When Paul spoke, there *was* no church but his remarks. We might say: no church but the text.

You (plural) be separate. The story such a text tells me is this: that when you live up to your fingerprints, and have become as utterly distinct as you are (not as distinct as one can be but as distinct as you *are*), that when the unicity, *I'jaz*, is manifest, all at once and by that very fact alone you enter a secret society on whose behalf I choose to think I am addressing you. This society has preserved its identity & function undismayed and undistorted for many centuries. It is inherently secret, and uncrashable. It exists only insofar as each has achieved a functional distinctness, a holy difference.

The society could be intolerable, elitist and smug, except that members can only dimly and unreliably guess who the other members are. A face in the papers, a name on a wall — the links are subtle, endless, intricate, boring, compassionate, eternal. It has no agreed upon names, this society. I can call it by a nonce-name, just this once the Society of Refugees from Idolatry. Whoever they are, they are not *them*.

No conscious person can worship an idol. All separation is separation from idolatry. I think that is what Paul's text was after, to rescue its hearers from the idolatry of groups and preference & belief, to guide them instead towards functional enactment out there, always out there, where in the largest text, the world incessantly becomes itself.

[RK archives, undated text]

ZONES OF A NON-LINEAR DISCOURSE ON THE RED SEAL

Non-linear because I want to draw you into the circle of reflection & consideration & trial & error of this process I've been working on for several months now.

1.
RED SEAL
red seal records
re/a/d seal
seals of Donegal
a seal in Galway harbor

2.
COMPOSITION IS RESEARCH

3.
caves of the Dordogne and the Pyrenees
are topological extensions of our minds
brains calvaria
where we find scratched on the wall
ONLY what we are prepared to read
the decipherments of rock scratches
Sobin, Eshleman et al.

4.
read the impressions on the mind
read the fissures folds
for the brain also is a process of creases and folds
cerebral cortex cork rind of our tree
to write on bark
beech bark smooth beech = *Buche* = buch

5.
to make the mind disgorge
its buried darknesses

to make the dark speak
without trying to turn it
into the presumptuous light
like honoring the dream
by dreaming it
by carrying it around by day
by reading / re-reading it
not by interpretation
but by dwelling with
because reading a book is dreaming someone else's
I mean to enter the caves — whether Lascaux or language — &
come out with a decent dark thing, a word or poem,
that does not presume to interpret what was found down in there
but is itself the fruit of that *sweet encounter* with the, in the, dark.
Anthrôpos pantôn metron said the Greeks,
the human is the measure / means of all things,
what was carved on the rock wall
speaks in us now.

6.
BREATH is the light that illuminates the word
… hence the world.
Variation on Cocteau: *Un seul souffle éclaire le monde.*
Learning to breathe in the dark

7.
read seal
= radix too,
the radical,
passing a little intersection in a Boston suburb
and seeing it was called Red Square
(not far from the courthouse where Sacco & Vanzetti were
persecuted and destroyed)
Red Square
red sign

the radical
interpretation
a word is radical, is root
a word is radical, so we have found the roots
and spoken them

8.
Don't expect any person to do two lives at you.
The poem is a treatise
and sometimes the poet uses prose as a disguise
(like Lorca's wonderful plays, or Olson's wonderful essays)
the poem is a treatise that can never be made obsolete by subsequent research
because the poem is the prime investigation of its world disclosed.

9.
Red Seal records,
records then were disks with grooves on them,
in wax, shellac, vinyl later,
as now the optical gleams refract from the whirling CD
grooves of light
light refracted, light concentered,
to find the center of light.
Let all thought leave a mark
on some wall,
then invent a system to read it,
this reading system is called writing.
(Now I read it to you and you write by hearing)

10.
the oldest sign
the red hand on the wall
read what someone thought,
read how someone leaned
her hand against the wall.

28 November 2000

THREADS 5 : ROBERT SAYS

It is the freshness of stories that is wonderful. I speak in the "Afterword" to The Scorpions *of Robert Duncan's anger at my book. He said I have sinned against the spirit of story. That was a serious accusation if we conceive of "story" as different, and necessarily different, from writing. But Duncan himself says somewhere that, "A man has no dream except the dream he tells." A dream exists only when you tell it, either to yourself or your wife at breakfast, or whoever it might be. Yet Duncan seems to believe, as almost all of us do, that there is a thing called "story" which is different from its given embodiment as an act of telling. If I had a theoretical interest here, it would be to push language to the point where it tells its own story — language as fable — to see where there is a difference, to see whether there is hiding in the world some story different from its own telling.*

in conversation with Larry McCaffery (1988)

Some believe the dream comes from the gods. Some believe that the dream comes from the ancestors. Some believe that dreams come from a part of the dreamer's self usually remote or removed from consciousness. Some believe that dreams are scraps of memory and fantasy, remnants of the day. All of these beliefs are probably true enough in their ways, and certainly all have been productive of creative and analytic results. Scriptures and assassinations, benzene rings and orphic odes arise from dreams.

What if the dream is something else as well? Not individual, not a message from God or from the archetypes or from the soul. We hear Freudians speak of the language of dream, but what if dream is language, is language the way language is language: systematic, intentional, focused on saying something. What if dream is above all, exactly as language is, social. This is the aspect of the dream that is seldom considered, dream as arising from the speaking back into a community, a community of native dreamers (so to say).

It was to examine the idea that a dream seeks an intended audience outside the dreamer, that the Annandale Dream Gazette *was founded years ago. The dreamer dreams towards someone — and that someone is within the community. Thus two goals are achieved by harvesting the night's dreams & publishing them: the dream may find its intended hearer, and we may gradually come to learn the nature and shape of the community itself, the community into which one dreams.*

So: the dream is public. The dream is social. The dream is communication. The dream intends to speak to you. These are the notions to investigate.

in "What is the *Annandale Dream Gazette*?"

Walking through Los Angeles, a seedy outlying tract more like old Brooklyn or Chicago, vacant lots stretching out, rare buildings. One of them in a building all by itself, like the last house left standing from a row of attached houses, is an old bookstore: in the window are ranged impressive sets of leather-bound volumes: one multi-volume set The Flora of New Guinea. *I call out to Ted Enslin who is walking with us, and prompt him to look in the window. We are astonished at that set — of course the store is closed.*

in the *Annandale Dream Gazette* (September 10th, 2007)

[dream etymologies, 1]

family.

    I dream that "family" is as if from the Latin verb, fo, fare, "to speak."

Then family means
        the people who talk to each other.
Our word "fate" comes from that verb too — fatum, *"what has been spoken."*

So familiar things are:
    the things that speak for us.
    And sometimes to us.

[dream etymologies, 2]

In dream I learn that the phrase

vain scrutiny

is a technical term, and means a secret meeting or covert illegal assembly. At first I think this must be a mistake or mistranslation in the book I'm reading (I'm often reading a book in a dream).

But then in the dream I go to the dictionary, which gives that as the proper meaning indeed of the phrase, evidently a calque or translation from a Slavic expression — I see the Russian phrase in Cyrillic.

In the story I had been reading when the phase cropped up, the illicit meeting had been infiltrated by police provocateurs.

in the *Annandale Dream Gazette* (Sunday, December 30th, 2007)

RUNNICLE

A runnicle is an image left over from dream left in the mind at waking, an image or fact with no narrative content or context. This information is itself a runnicle, I wake with it, and hurry to write it down, to share this runnicle with the dream community.

in the *Annandale Dream Gazette* (Friday, May 23rd, 2008)

5.

A BOOK OF DREAMS

Now Blackburn's manner in the dream is very like life. He's
my jealousy, even more amused at how upset I am to find you
cool, he's clear that things dont matter very much, especial
love, nothing's worth getting into a sweat about, nothing me
He refuses to help me find you, or give any clue to where yo
but goes along with me for a while, to watch my reactions.
                                          From this point till the
am in terrible anxiety, desperately trying to find you. (Th
I've had for years, of losing, thru my own stupidity, people
then hunting & rushing & gasping all thru the night to find

DREAM STELE

        a boundary stone
   between the end of *Dream Work 1–5*
         & my next field

          = = =

The dream is different things & all our differences

The dream begins in a place we cannot reach

trying to come to it from the other side

There is no other side to a dream

On the other side of dreams a doubtful wisdom makes us doubt each livelong day

Sometimes I hate dreams nightmares night emissions from an oracle whose glistening daytime skin I've never seen

have I?

The most luminous dream is opaque

We remember
& we are always remembering, all everyday remembering all day long

Is there an end to the place dream reminds us?

The dream goes on all day — our lives can be read as footnotes to our dreams as easily as our dreams as wasteproducts of our lives

REM. Vidimus rem. We saw something.

Seeing is going on how many ways do I have to say this

Dream is the thing

The lucent alabaster of the dream structure, the same white building for each man, whereon our lives inscribe or chisel a sense, a regatta of senseless images, graffiti, from waking, vandal scrawls of our lost wayward personal natures

It is the same for everyone, and we deface it

Hell is personality

I would have greeted this black precipitate with greater joy had I not seen, sidewise peering from beneath the ashes at the bottom of the vessel, the glint of an eye. A bird's eye it seemed to be, & the tiny plumage around the eye seemed iridescent. This might then be the bird concerning which the Manuscript instructs: "Destroy this deceptive beast, but guard its differences."

IX 1970

AN EXPERIMENTAL PROGRAM FOR DREAM RESEARCH

Hypothesis: Dreaming is a societally conditioned "linguistic" activity.

*

Where psychoanalysis has erred is in relating dream "content" exclusively to one or both of these areas:
    (a) basic human conditions, "archetypes," at which the analyst presumes to arrive by induction.
    (b) specific personal traumata, life history, which the analyst presumes to discover.

These areas fall on either side of what is here suggested as the most pertinent source & application of dream: the dream-*langue* of the dreamer's culture.

(Freud's analytic successes in therapy are evidence here, since they arise from the deeply shared cultural background he has in common with his patients.)

[Linguistics comes to the aid of psychology: no linguist would connect the presence of nasal vowels in French with the size of Frenchmen's noses (as in a, above), or with the activities of the perfumers of Paris (as in b).]

Dreams can be rigorously investigated by the close study of dream-times, dream-rites, verbalization of dreams, dream-records, dream-manipulations, & the uses of dreams within a given tribal group.

Environment shapes only the lexicon of dreams.

*

Experiment: Investigate the dream reports of a chosen community.

Procedure:

1) Geographic community — town tribe or institution.

2) Each member reports all recovered dreams.
    a) at outset, no attempt made to instruct in the skills of dream recovery or dream transcription.
    b) preliminary observations should establish a baseline or norm of un-manipulated dream behavior:

spontaneously-remembered dreams/night
recovered-dreams/night
no report/night

3) When some pattern emerges, the communicative members of the dream group will be asked to submit daily transcripts.

HEREIN LIES THE ABYSS IN THE WHOLE MATTER OF DREAMS.

Neither the psychologist nor the oneirologist can deal with dream-as-such, but only with dream as it is made public, reported, communicated through language or gesture, i.e., through *translation* into what may turn out to be an entirely different *system* (though consider here Lacan's confidence that language is systematic on both sides of the conscious/ unconscious membrane.)

So we will be looking at dream reports. An obvious first step will be to examine these texts from a purely linguistic viewpoint, to determine if & how such texts differ stylistically &c. from the everyday utterances — in speech & writing — of the same dreamers.

(& here be it noted that the data will be of immense value to the theoretician of narrative technique & style, folk-tale and epic. In dreams reported (oral or written) lie the origins of all story, all *ennarratio*, telling.)

Any findings at that textual level will aid (via the principle of "strangeness") in directing the oneirologist's attention to areas of dream experience (dreamt-ex-perience) felt by the dreamer as transcendent of his conscious experience.

4) When the more or less spontaneous recording of dreams has been studied (preferably for a year at least), the reporting dreamer can be encouraged to omit from his verbalization all accounts of his own remembered feelings, dreads, delights and desires, and to indicate these by some nonverbal "tone-marking" contrivance, such as underlining sections of transcription in colors coded to various emotions —

1.) this is scarcely to minimize the role of feelings & fears, but to allow the imag-istic/practic components of dream to emerge more starkly.

(Comment: My impression is that dream reports are blocked by recall or sequential emotional states which naturally strike the wakened dreamer as the most important components of his dream. They may indeed be. Yet we're trying to look at the language, not yet the messages the language is encoding. The color-underline technique will allow the dreamer to report in some subtlety his own *emotional involvement with the dream suite*, at the same time leaving clear that *process* with which he found himself involved. Or, if my imputation of difference *&* distance here be wrong, the suggested technique allows the dreamer to set forth clearly, without the interference of present or recalled emotion, the *symbolic representation* of those very emotions or physical states communicated to the dreamer by his own dream-articulant "unconscious.")

5) At length a repertory of dream transcriptions will be on hand. It is at this point that the real work begins, *&* at this same point we go into the dark.

As far as I know, no work at all has been done ever on these matters, at least since whatever work may have gone into the Assyrian dream tablets, and the much-copied Artemidorus, and other primitive lexicons of dream-equivalences.

Our search must be for patterns and the color-coded emotions might be, perhaps, our Rosetta Stone for the whole process

We look here for images (things = phonemes?), events (dynamic interacts of thing *&* person, person *&* person *&*c. = morphemes?). We look here for narrative sequences, "stories" (but where does a story end?) (related chains of event, = tagmemes? Query "related"- events perceived by dreamer as "one" story?), narrative sequences and the odd gaps (=sentence juncture? paragraphs?) that seem to separate them.

The equivalents I am questioningly offering are guesses, though in some way they seem structurally equipollent. We might read the color-coded emotions as the suprasegmentals, which are in the first contacts between speakers of different languages the likeliest components to get across the barrier, though hardly without distortion. (We can "read" fear, amusement, excitement and so on from stress *&* rhythm *&* breath, long before we ever know a "word.")

(*Io* #8, "Dreams," 1971)

[POSITION PAPER]   [*FOR A FUTURE CONVERSATION*]

= a turning /

    over what it is I

believe   know

in the Word   the word
                                                              ſpoken
                                                         it
                                                          becomes
                                                   my
                                                      duty
                                                    to ſpeak /

                        the medi-
                        ation
                        :

                       'dream'

                                 there is a place of dreamless
                                                                Sleep
                                   called the Deep Place or № 4
                                 here we adventure by night &
                                 leaving that Place
                                                     ſtand
                                 at the crossroads
                                        (=Woman)
                               where the choice is made:
                               to die or to Day /
                                           To call on
                               or go to Day
                               is to take a road
                                      & invent

There is   a Dream
a   to carry
world of   forward to waking
One.   in this world of 2.

(*here 2 becomes / here 3 becomes*)

5 · A BOOK OF DREAMS

<u>on</u> this World of One
of
                      <u>it is said</u>

<u>it is believed</u>   <u>it is known</u>

manwomanly mind
womanly mind
man mind/woman

so that one says

Allah, that grieving
Woman

[shown, e.g., by
Michelangelo
on the tomb of
Giuliano de' Medici]

hence Dante's tears

or wherever
women are
Sad

    a Grieving
Woman
      is the sign of
God
    sealed on the
a naked woman on the earth /

fathermother

to take
that believing
into doing

using

being used /

(right column, rotated text):

that access to that condition (Place) is via the Extraordinary Consensus of Poem [et not very many cetera]

that such access kindles a fire there that burns with a fleshly or 'saffron' (Ibn Arabi) light

that light casts shadows: which are the World of 2. (whose dimensions are three).
[3 = 2] ¹ !

SOME EXTENSIONS

Being born is equivalent to passing through the crossroads towards Day.

Dreamless Sleep, it is to be supposed, is not a null place ('void') but a congested emptiness, a vital condition where *we* are emptied. I.E., *sunyata* is not the void but the empty*ing*.

From the Dreamless Sleep one can:
1) invent a life & be born. ("incarnation")
2) invent a dream & move towards waking.
3) invent a dream & remain [Tir na nÓg and so on,
                                                  the Deva realms]

In each case [4 becoming 3] the power of the World of 1 is being manifest.

From my window, it is absurd to talk of reincarnation, as a distinction without a difference. To perceive a world at all is an imaginative act, of the very faculty which invents a life, or supposes itself to remember one.

Memory is, *that* sort of memory is, invention.

We do not remember. We process our flesh & discover.

Those who speak of reincarnation often slight the imaginative world where all worlds are being created, all lives being lived, all at once, at nonce, at never, at sixes & sevens.

"Do you remember that time when we..." An invitation to share a consensus, a fantasy, an invention. "Do you remember what the capital of Thailand is?" is an invitation to a larger consensus. Plug into a present.

[RK archives, undated text]

SEVENTEEN ARCANA FROM THE INFINITY OF DREAMS

1.

For a poet to write about dreams is like a man trying to describe his wife. Nothing he ever says can possibly do justice to her beauty, sustaining wisdom, intimate knowledge, and her sheer importance to him in every aspect of his life.

Nothing I can say will deeply reveal the profound yet simple otherness from which we wake, every single day of our lives, wordlessly instructed to begin anew. To tell afresh.

And yet the man must again & again try to tell about his wife. He tries to describe the actuality, the fullness, of her. Only to find himself reduced to telling mere anecdotes about her, stories that his listeners may find silly or pointless or incomprehensible. Just so, the poet begins by writing vastly about Dream, and winds up telling a dream or two. Telling a dream, then, may be a little like showing a snapshot of your wife....

Dream — is it synecdoche? A part from which we must, by divine or mathematic cunning, intuit a whole?

2.

My dream, we say.

As if a dream is mine —

and perhaps it is.

Maybe my dream is the only thing in the world that is truly mine.

Since my body belongs just as much to you.

3.

How we speak of dreams, how we claim them, or let them claim us.

Dr. King said: "I have a dream" — but that kind of dream is the precise opposite of the dream that comes to us at night. Dr. King's dream is a daytime vision of compassion and order and renewal. It is a vision.

Yet the power of his great cry! How much of that power comes from his use of the apparently simple word, "dream"? Isn't the dream the thing that comes in the night and masters us? And mastering us, it gives to it its declaration, its vision, an air of the prophetic. Since it comes from the dark, from the Gods, it comes to us with an authenticity greater than anything we might merely want, even if we want it with all our hearts.

4.

What is Dream, what is Vision?

Do you say, I dreamt of you

OR

I had a dream of you?

Do they mean different things?

5.

Can you tell a real dream from an invented dream? Is there a difference between a dream that comes along to someone in the night, and a dream that is made up by the same someone in the daytime — invented (according to the usual hypothesis) by the same mind that dreamed the "real" dream?

Is it possible that all our narratives, fictions, lies, daydreams are nothing but dreams ill-silenced by the light of day, creations dimly remembered from within the chambers of the night, but no longer insulated by sleep?

6.

Where does a dream live in time?

I notice that some people tell their dreams in the present tense ("I'm walking down this hallway, and there's this figure coming towards me, I can't see its face, it's hooded...") & some people tell their dreams in the past tense ("I was on a beach in some southern place, Spain, maybe, and I looked out to sea & a woman was walking in towards the shore. I could see her only in silhouette...")

When a dream is told in the present tense: the dreamer is still experiencing the dream, still at the mercy of the dream negotiation.

Negotium perambulans in tenebris: the business that walketh about in the night, the Bible said. What we used to call the "progressive" aspect, action going on simultaneously with its description. The dream told in the present tense is happening now.

When a dream is told in the past tense: the dreamer has distanced himself from the dream. The dreamer is trying to assert control.

Narration is control.

That's the absolute of it. Past tense narration asserts absolute control. Control is safety. The teller is safe from the tale, safe from the told.

On the other hand, the present tense narration is still in flux, it can change, the dream can change, squirm in the dreamer's grasp, become a different thing.

7.

Or is the dream always a different thing?

The Jungians play at wakeful dreaming. Once the analyst Nor Hall and I found ourselves at a party holding each other by our living waists as we danced some strange summer dawn and I thought: neither by sleep nor intention did this strange dream come into the world of flesh, this world we call actual, but by the way things work out. Karma. Or, *la vida es* indeed *sueño*. Neither of us planned it, neither of us told it, yet it held us, firmly in its grasp. We happened to each other, for those few minutes, the way dream happens to us.

8.

Dreams are just the parts of sleep we notice. Life is just the part we notice of all that's going on. It's all we dare sign our name to. Life is the part of existence we feel we have the right to complain about.

Alive *&* kicking, as they say.

9.

Dream is so much less a mystery than anything else that happens.

Maybe dream is the simplest thing of all that happens.

Just the mind, alone in the night.

No body, but it feels. No body, but it moves. So simple. So few it needs.

10.

Why don't we need as little as a dream does?

It needs so little to do its work.

What is the work of dreams?

(We know that Freud called the dream work, but that's what we propose to do with it. We want to make it show us something we think it knows. Twisting the arm of a dream.)

But what is the dream's own work? What does it want with us? What does it do with us?

Well, as Freud also pointed out, it wakes us up.

It returns us to the place where we wake and breed and work & die, and a new generation of dreamers takes our place.

11.

Remember the cartoon showing Goldilocks as a sweet old lady, reminiscing to her grandchildren: "Well, I never dreamed that there were *bears* living in that house…"

To dream here means to have a foretaste of the actual, as well as of what comes. Who might be living in that woodsy house? What might be waiting for us inside the radiant precincts of the coming day? Who, right now, is on the other side of the door? Who is inside your eyes?

12.

The way we use the word. "I have a dream" — but that means nothing born of the night, but born of the conscious wit and will gazing into that vast somber scary thing called the future. Dr. King filled that dark with the lightning flash of his motivation to heal his people. Truly call him Doctor King. But scarcely a dreamer, though he had a dream.

13.

The way we use the words.

> I never dreamt…
> I never dream…

5 · A BOOK OF DREAMS

I have a dream…
I had a dream…
I dream of Miriam who…

(And in my father's day they used to call a fancied lover a: … dream boat… but you don't need one to sail to Dreamland.)

They say that dream comes from an Old English word that meant "joy." Such pleasure is hard to stand.

We tell our dream to a doctor. The doctor is trained to digest this information without being destroyed by it. A dream is dangerous.

So if somebody wants to tell you their dreams, lie down on the couch or the ground & compose yourself as if to sleep, close your eyes and listen. I used to run a dream workshop and that's what we did. We pretended to our bodies that we were sleeping, so that when the person told the dream she had "had," we could seem to be dreaming it too. That is the best way to hear a dream — to dream it along with the dreamer. That is the richest way. That is also the safest way, the body snug in its posture of listening inward, safe from the arrogant mind.

14.

Judgment is later, and interpretation, and all those energetic dances of the mind with its images. Dance with your images, darling. They're all you have.

Interpretation. Of course I interpret dreams when I am told them. Seldom when I have them. I do not often dream.

15.

Dream = spontaneously recall the dream at waking or soon after.

That's what we really mean (socially, linguistically) by dreaming

That's what she means when she wakes him in the morning and asks: Did you dream?

Dreaming means then: remembering *now* & experience *then*. What a strangely simple doctrine of Time we must cherish, to be so easy with then & now. From within the walls of sleep we carry something with us.

16.

Evidently what we call dreaming is a kind of remembering.

Not every morning, nothing is certain, I am listening to Schumann — the *Symphonic Études* that Pat Meanor gave me, played by Jean-Yves Thibaudet — and thinking about dream. Then I begin to think about Schumann — the tragedy of his invariant attention, the hopeless grandeur of his ardor, the intensity of his devotion, the radiant tonality of his desperate refusal to despair. But then an end came even to that, to him; one morning the dream just does not come.

There is such grandeur in the world, such goodness, if we wake to find it, let it find us. But nothing is certain, the right hand moves at a different speed from the left hand, they make a beautiful music, that is true, that may last, if not forever, still last long enough for us to hear it.

Does the dream last long enough for us to tell it?

And if we do not tell it, what is the dream then?

And whose dream is it then?

Is there something, anything, in our world that is not told?

17.

When I was a little boy I learned that everything is better after sleep, everything is better in the morning.

I have never truly decided whether it is the sleeping or the waking that heals.

But healing certainly there is, between the last flutter of despondent weariness and the first wink of daylight.

Of course I suppose now it is the dream that heals us.

But I suspect that the dream we do not remember is the dream that heals us. Instead, it re-members us, and we wake healed.

(1998)

HYPNOGEOGRAPHY

West of Ninth Avenue the high bluff ends; the land falls away abruptly in a series of cliffs and steep hillsides canted just enough to bear grass among the pale scars where rivulets have scored the earth on their way down to the Hudson. To get there, they must cross the long grassy meadows along the river, the very fertile alluvial tract that stretches north the whole length of the island. Winding streams get there gently & smooth, un-bordered roads wander here and there, past small, neat farmsteads, taverns and gas stations. The light is sea-light everywhere, and clouds bank richly, picturesquely, over the dark Jersey palisades. When it rains, the rain comes sweeping in from the west, angular as autumn sunlight at dusk on golden Sundays. But when the sun shines it is sweet and steady, coming evenly down like a decent teacher in grammar school, fair to all her pupils. I like to walk around here, or drive the little roadster you can rent at almost any garage. The roads aren't paved, and we New Yorkers like it that way. This is farm country, and from its good black soil most of what we put on our plates is grown.

East of the cliffs, though, the city gets busy. Tall white buildings everywhere, hundreds of thousands of them cunningly nestled close together without each denying another's light. Crowded as can be, but the streets don't seem that way. In fact I find it strange how empty they usually are, considering how densely built up every block is now. The banks are beautiful, & there are fountains in front of the meanest church. I'm fond of the lower East '30s & upper '20s, where small townhouses manage to skulk unbothered between clubs and foundations and sleek hotels operated by people who say they come from Northern Italy. The north side of Canal Street is lined with shops and restaurants facing the canal. People sit outside to watch the little skiffs and sculls nip along the broad water. But south of Canal, the land is more open, with broad fields and a good deal of woodland, little woods on low hilltops, and hardly any buildings. The dirt roads are dusty in the summer time, but vacationers reveling in the wine gardens and outdoor theaters and ball courts don't mind. In the shade of a big cottonwood I leaned on somebody's mailbox and watched a young woman get out of her car and go into the courtyard of an inn across the way. The wind fluffed out the tulle of her dress and I heard it sigh against her legs. How quiet it is here, and the wind itself needs us to make enough resistance for it to be heard.

A VOICE FULL OF CITIES

This is how it is in my dreams. I mean real dreams, the kind you have at night when you leave your mind and body alone a while. For years I have been having dreams in which I walk around New York City, where I was born, and where I lived for the first 25 years of this life. The New York I dream in is a little different from what I see when I go there by train now, and some aspects of the dream New York is what I have just been describing.

It is not New York before modern times — cars run around, big Late Capitalism buildings abound in the denser parts of town. It is, as far as I know, not New York after some implausible reconstruction after some all too likely disaster. It is just New York as it is, exactly as it is, in dream.

So what I want to know is this: all over the earth women and men are dreaming every night, and among all their other dreams of love & terror & monsters & mates, they have dreams of place. I want to know the places they dream. I have a feeling that the Dream Representation of place can tell us a lot about what we think of as the 'real' place. Smart people like the Highland Maya of Guatemala (I'm relying on what Dennis Tedlock told me once) are concerned not just with what a person looks like or does for a living, but how he 'represents' in dream. I want to learn, and want us to learn, how our countries and cities represent in dream.

With that in mind, I want there to be a science or a study. I have given it the name Hypnogeography just because everybody can figure that out.

What I propose is that all generous persons record their dreams [in general a good thing to do] when they dream of place, and that the records or recitations of these dreams be collected, examined, compared — that is, compared with one another and, when possible, with the undreamt 'real' place we find at the end of the road in from the airport.

When all such dreams have been assembled and overlaid, a truer geography will appear. I don't mean that the Dream Place is truer than the so-called 'real,' but that all versions of a place are needed to know the Place most truly. That's the goal, and this is the project I have in mind. And the mind is what we finally get to know, as dearly in need of mapping as any virus or nucleic acid strand. And how to map the mind, except by what we tell each other?

This statement was read 10 September 1986 to the Hudson Celebration at the Omega Institute, Rhinebeck, New York.

(*Doctor of Silence*, 1988)

HYPNOGEOGRAPHY II

FIRST KANSAS TALK: INTRODUCTION[1]

It's particularly wonderful to have a painter make that introduction[2] since for most of us, land begins — our awareness of land begins — as landscape, & landscape is a painterly conception. It's as if you're walking along in my neighborhood, and you see a stunted tree or a new-grown trunk. The house we slept in last night had such a tree outside. You look at it, and you think, "I saw that in a Sassetta," or "I saw that in some medieval…" — a tree that has imitated the patterns of an earlier mind.

I'm mostly going to read a few pages tonight, now, and say a little bit, and I have to begin by saying that what I say tonight, I would not have said had we had this congress at the end of August, rather than in the middle of October.

I've been in Lawrence before, maybe twenty-five years ago. It's grown quite a lot. It's still a very agreeable place. It's a place that — well, this morning, Charlotte & I saw our first Swainson's hawk skimming down over the grassland, looking for — the book says it's looking for a rat or a gopher, so we looked for a rat or a gopher, too, but we saw only the hawk, and it stayed there for about an hour, going back and forth. So, I'll think of this visit as the hawk visit.

---

1. [The following is RK's later note to an online presentation of the two talks: "There is a short quasi-fiction by that name in my prose collection, *Doctor of Silence*. When the painter Paul Hotvedt read the piece he was stirred to think and plan further, since the notions of the geography we see only in dream rimed with some of his own work as a meticulous and reverent scribe of the waking world he observes all around him in eastern Kansas. At his prompting, a local arts council organized a conference on Landscape and the Imagination [entitled "Imagination & Place"]. It took place in Lawrence in 2001, a few weeks after 9/11, at a moment when the meaning and sanctity of place reigned in everybody's thought. The texts [below are] my contribution — my insistence on the authenticity of landscape dreamt, and the importance of mapping it alongside the waking given."]

2. Robert Kelly & Denis Cosgrove were introduced by artist & conference organizer Paul Hotvedt.

A VOICE FULL OF CITIES

I used to dream about a city, a city that shimmered by the power of dream, through the daytime sense of stone, and concrete, and asphalt, of the common city where I was born. Now that city has changed. The so-called real one, the one where the towers fell, fell into the shadow where Castle Gardens had fallen long before, and the Battery itself, and the aquarium, where an electric eel in its murky box of water on display lit up my childhood. Early lessons in what it meant — eel, electricity, Edison, floodlights, the World's Fair, the War. Of course, I'm a New Yorker. Of course, I am used to things being gone, which makes it all the more important that we recollect together the interior city, or let me call it the *inherent* city. Re-collect the traces of the city that inheres inside the real one, the one anybody can see, or see until a terrorist destroys it. But the inherent city can only be lost when the image of it fades from the mind of the dreamer or the visionary, Shinar Plain, or Lot in Sodom, or Aeneas's Rome, or Brigham Young's City of the Saints. Or say, I think, that the inherent city can never be destroyed; it can only be forgotten, which is why we have come here today, to unforget it, to unforget the dream.

When this conference was proposed — I guess we talked about it a year ago, over a year ago, perhaps the summer or autumn of 2000 — when this conference was proposed, it was just supposed to be one more interesting thing that we could get to say about humans and landscape, women and geography, one more interesting variation in the long attentive sarabande of intelligence that we dance with Carl Sauer, and Charles Olson, and Edgar Anderson, James Malin, and Gary Snyder, and Ken Irby. Then suddenly, what we are doing here now seems immensely and differently important. We have suddenly been put in charge of the indestructible and, by paradox, we have to take very good care of it.

The longer I stay in any place, the clearer it becomes that we inhabit different levels of time. The ground we walk on is a recent word, but the sentence has been speaking for such a long time. We know that every land is a different land, the alien shore imbedded in our own, the land before this town that still lingers in the town, as the town. The town is the skin we see of all that's been. The town that we were reminded of, of 1854 and all that came after — massacres and posses and the grief of that, the quiet resurrections in a town, & all lying there, always present. "There's Quantrill now," said Ken Irby last night as we walked down the street, pointing to a figure on a wall somewhere, in a window.

"There's Quantrill now." So, that hundred and some years doesn't simply disappear. It simply deepens our awareness of this place and this time. We know that there are strange, half-magical writers like Mary Butts in the wonderful story "Mappa Mundi" and Charles Williams in his strange novel *Descent into Hell*. The way they have seen and described the way time and place co-inhere, the way Lutetia still lives inside Paris or Aeneas's Rome inside Moravia's Rome. All land, all place enshrines its history. A place never lets go of what happened there, but there are special places where the times show through. And one of the things it means to grow up in a place or come back to a place in which you grew up is to know the times of the place — your times, your ages, all mapped on the supposed actuality. You walk on the street.

Bashō says, "One quality that poems have is a kind of sadness, like a man dressed up in all his finery, on his way to a party, only the man is an old man." You walk on the street of all your life and somehow, step by step, you have to master the times imbedded in that place. If the place is Rome, then you have to be Aeneas, Virgil, Bruno, Verdi, Moravia, all at once, as well as whoever you are. Don't you understand? The dead become everyone and you become everyone who lived before you. It may be that geography also is genetics.

But there's another dimension to all this, that I've been excited by and bothered by — can't tell — for years now, the place we dream. And that's the subject that this conference got started by, an essay called "Hypnogeography." It still strikes us all as a funny word — to write down the map of the world you find in dream. That's simple enough. Now, that follows from a kind of major hypothesis; that's another fancy word — we can never have enough long words; long words are wonderful, because long words give the mind a chance to rebut them as they pass by. Whereas a short word, like "puff," you don't know what to do with it. But a word like "hypnogeography" or "vososquasm," a disease from which I pretend to suffer, these words are long enough to give you a chance to bite and spit out if necessary, or to swallow. But, a hypothesis that exercises me a lot is that we talk casually, or at least since the late nineteenth century we've talked casually, about the language of dream and dream language, and all that. And that has meant, I think, traditionally the "language of dream," kind of "this means that" effect of the dream. The ancient Babylonians said that if you dreamt of eating your own excrement, it meant that great good fortune was on the way. And we find the old dream tablets & the *Oneirocritica* of Artemidorus contain lots of material, translation so to speak, of "this means that." In that sense, the dream as a language is a familiar thing. But from the days of Freud & his immediate predecessors and his followers, dream language became more an exploration of what the dream was saying. Not about what would happen to you when you dreamed this; rather, the dream was an endless conversation that you were having with yourself. Or the dream was, according to some theories, an endless conversation that the god, or the over-soul, or the spirits, or the demons were having with you. In other words, the dream was, and remains, in Freudian and Jungian analysis, and even, one suspects, in Lacanian analysis, unless you get very deeply into it, the dream remains the voice of the other speaking to the self.

But that's not what language is in most of our experiences. Most of us learn language by being surrounded, by being wordless, surrounded by the other, and having to acquire words to address the other with. We have to speak to the other, saying "Feed me. Love me. Give me what I need." These commonsense notions of language as an exchange between the self and the other have traditionally for the dream analysis been pointed always in the same direction. So the hypothesis that came to me some years ago is what happens if we take the language the other way around and assume that the dream that I have is indeed language and it's indeed a word, but it's not a word that God is saying to me, or that my unconscious is saying to me, *but that I am saying to you,* as Whitman says, "whoever you are?" Suppose then that dream is the language of the self to the other. It's an hypothesis I think worth thinking about, worth examining.

If the dream talks to the other, the dream is the self speaking to the other, a dream then is a word that you are speaking to the world, then it might be worthwhile to investigate what the dream says to the world, what that story is that the dream is telling, a story that you are not ready consciously or wakefully to tell the world. Perhaps a story you need to tell to the world. That's why it occurred to me years ago that I should try to gather a bunch of victims together who dreamt a lot and who would write their dreams down & publish them in a very small compass. I live in a tiny hamlet called Annandale, named for that unfortunate valley in Scotland where Lockerbie is & where things fall from the sky, the little town of Annandale, which is barely more than the college that's in it. And I suggested we start the *Annandale Dream Gazette,* which was a brief, short-lived publication which a couple of good people, generous people as Paul would say, got together and put down their dreams every day and published them once in a while, on the theory that if dream is language speaking to the other, the other had better have a chance to hear it. Otherwise, we're just mumbling in the shower, singing Verdi in the shower, the way I would, but no one was allowed to hear.

If that's then the major hypothesis, the minor hypothesis coupled with it is that dream might have something to do then with the world of geography, the word of place. The specific words that we dream when we dream of cities, as I explained in that tiny piece called "Hypnogeography" itself, two or three pages long, I oughtn't even to call it a story or an essay. I have all my life dreamt of New York City in a set of ways that have been standard throughout all the dream years. It's quite like New York in a lot of ways and quite unlike it in others, but it's repeatedly the same way. Only last year, for the first time, has another avenue opened in my dream New York and it opened by running across Broadway, forming an X with Broadway, an astonishing thing, since Broadway is the marker of true north in Manhattan Island where all the streets are running map north, but Broadway runs true north. Suddenly, another great St. Andrew's cross had been made. A great saltire had been declared and another avenue had gone off at an angle, reaching a cathedral, of all things — a thing New York does not notably need, since it has half a dozen cathedrals of one kind or another already that no one goes to except Tibetan Lamas when they need a place to perform to the white folk. But there was this cathedral. I have to deal with that. But it seems to me that the place, then, that we dream, the place that we standardly dream, not so much the dream of one night when you dream that an explosion occurs in such-and-such a place, but rather the dreams that you come back to, the dreams that you return to night after night or year after year, when you dream a predictable variant on them — that's the stuff that we need to hear about. And I would like someday a great mapping of that to come to pass.

The problem is, of course, the endless trash of the personal. I speak of the eel, the electric eel, the old aquarium, my memories, the child nose pressed against the dirty glass from the noses of all the children who had pressed against it before, looking at the eel swimming in the water dirty from its own excrement, the sense of just the warping, the thickening, the thickness of memory in shape — all the personal stuff that we bring to the dream. The dream crosses it and returns to the world. That's important. It's hard for me to look at the World Trade Center ruins and say, "Yes, I miss the World Trade Center, but I also miss that eel that was there sixty years ago and that was wiped out long ago and the Battery Aquarium was wiped away long ago for other reasons altogether, said to be connected with yet another war, yet another time." But these individual instances of personal memory seem to become the trash, or as the alchemists said, the feces from which we begin our operation, so that in the dream, as you know, with however you approach the dream, the individual details of your personal life that flood out into the great plain of Shinar, where the dream is building its tower of Babel, those individual feces, traces, the mere corruptions of memories, as you'd say, grow the Temple of Memory, memoria, from which we might learn something about this geography of the world that I've been talking about.

So I would just want to end by saying that I do want the hypnogeography to be a subject of inquiry. I want generous people to record their dreams when they dream about such things. They can do it for other purposes, too. But I think we might be able to assemble a dream geography of our world, as a dream geography of Lawrence, Kansas, might emerge Sunday afternoon from Soren Larsen's workshop in mapping. That may happen. The notion that we might, in fact, be able to map something that is documentable, that we'd have something there at the end.

The goal then would be to find all the versions of a place that are needed to know the place.

I wanted to finish with reading what happened once when I tried to talk about a place. I tried to talk about the house I lived in. "I live in an old house that has no address," I began. Then I had to go to a footnote and understand what that meant — no address: "A road, but no number — off east, beyond the sumac and the hill, the loosestrife of our small marsh anxious these nights with singing frogs, so there's this ode of spring. There is a crossroads where the highway runs fast past the almost unseeable entrance of a road whose name is like mine. But that's beyond 9G, beyond time, beyond the Ennead that stands this side of the Dodecad — that's a region between the Nine and the Zodiac in which no fixed knowledge is. No steady knowing. Nine Gods look up and worship. Twelve look down and see me standing there, afraid as any four-year-old to cross the blazing highway. Corner of the Dog — Nine Gods. Turn west with me. & then the house, with no address, too close to the Post Office to need one, just two houses down towards the stream. Known by name. This is the center of a vast, invisible city. Yesterday as we drove along, I saw a broken pump, its handle rusted, pointing towards the mountains. And saw the ultimate city, now only a dream inhering in that space. Certainly it too will have post offices and streets among its lily pools and tiger walks; I am less sure it will have numbers. No address except the name of the city, the City; and the mail gets there. When I first moved to this town, I computed that by the grid of my city down the river, I live now on 2,097th Street — West 2,097th Street — at the corner of Broadway. But that city is no longer anybody's system. The grid is more spacious now, builds up as well as out, comprises the nearer stars, has its root in water."

 I was trying to write about what it looked like to sit in a particular chair in my house and look across the room. I don't think we've paid enough attention to interior landscape, but that's for another conference — the conference of the crowded desk, the stuff under the bed, the things you find when you open the drawer. That is our *Iliad* yet to be written. But now we need a proper geography.

 That's all I wanted to say now. I'll say more things tomorrow. I'd love to hear your comments, or reactions, or rebuttals, or castigations, or your reprisals — no, not reprisals! Renewals.

Audience Member: In Douglas County, there are no places and no knowledge. Every intersection has numbers for both ways.

Robert Kelly: It does. It does. But they're only available by use of the God of the machine. It's triangulation. We must talk about the triangle some time, how the triangle is what's left out of all of these issues, the way in which I can connect with you deeply only by some triangulation. And we keep forgetting that & that's why we keep walking against the — into the mirror, constantly. Mirrors resist triangles. Now you can find any place with the numbers.

AM: How would you contrast the dream place with the so-called real place?

RK: Well, the so-called real. I was afraid there might be a philosopher who would notice that. See, there's one of those short words — real. Oh! A horrific word. That's the worst fourletter word in all the world — real.

I would contrast it simply by the fact that I can see it only when I'm asleep and then remember it. It's very real when I'm asleep & less real when I'm awake. And when I'm awake I can't quite walk down that street, but I can remember it. So, I'm not saying that waking is more real than sleeping, God knows. I think perhaps the opposite, probably. But certainly whatever is conventionally called the waking world, maybe the waking world & the sleeping world — but that suggests the world is awake. It may not be. It may just be you, or just me, or some triangle between us. In proper terms, I think the contrast is that the sleep world, the dream world always seems slightly more persuasive to me than the waking one. The waking one where I'm walking down the street, it's always something of a surprise — "Oh yes, this is where Broadway is crossed by 17th Street, and I'll turn that corner, & there'll be that closed coffee shop," — but in the dream, I may not know about the coffee shop, but it feels tremendously right. It feels, "This is how it actually is," whereas the real is only how it happens to seem at the moment. I think in dream I'm less of a skeptic than I am in waking. I'm speaking from my own few-and-far-between dreams. (One of the reasons why I want to get all those generous lads and lasses to write their dreams is that I have so few of them myself, which is my great shame and secret; I am not in that sense a dreamer. Therefore I look at the dream like a starved child looking through the window at the candy. The dream place seems, as I said before, to have this persuasive factness about it in the way that waking doesn't. Waking is iffy. Anything might happen, but in the dream, life just steadily runs along.

AM: [Question about the way travel in dreams is discontinuous.]

RK: That's not my experience of my own dreams, which are lamentably poor in jump cuts; I have to walk the whole way. I wish I could do that.

I'd like to know your way of getting right to the goal — later tell me your secret. But I mean, we don't know that. We make grand statements about dreams. The poets of this world make the grand statements, and yet the difference you and I discuss may be vastly important — that your dream jump cuts, and I dream without them. That might be far more important than anything else that we dream about, the very structure of the dream experience. I don't usually dream scenically, in the sense that was mentioned, but rather continuously and rather wonderfully boringly — the way lovemaking is boring; that it just is this wonderful going-on, in that sense that you don't have to do anything. It does itself when it's genuine. You're not doing something to someone; you are being with the experience. In that way, dream has a wonderful, pervasive ongoingness, in my sense, without the scenic quality of "I am witnessing an event," or "I'm leaping through an event."

But these structures may be terribly important. That might be a kind of macrostructural difference that we want to explore sometime.

SECOND KANSAS TALK: PUBLIC DREAMING

All the more wonderful an introduction[3] because of the person from whom it comes, the poet from *whom* it comes. It would just be battering the badminton bagatelle of praise back and forth if I were to go on to say how much I like his work & how instructive that has been, specifically to me in the world of place because one of the very earliest books of Ken that there is, maybe the first one that really got deeply into me, was the book with the strange title about the grasslands of North America. He had suddenly taken all that material between — as you know, the west — for a New Yorker, the west begins with the Hudson — had taken the rest of that three thousand miles west and dealt with it. Understood it in a way that I was beginning to understand also from that man up in Gloucester, not Eliot,[4] who just spent summers in Gloucester, but the man who spent years and years there.

---

3. Robert Kelly was introduced by poet Ken Irby.
4. Allusion to Richard Schoeck's talk about T. S. Eliot, just concluded.

Let me say first that I think, Paul, you & your friends have gotten another conference together. We've gone from dream, where we started out, to geography, but geography seeming so abstract we started on about place soon enough and land, the *tertius gaudens* between Earth and World, and then places, and then, soon enough, we were talking about places we know and places we've lived in, and places we came from, even New Jersey, even places as placy as that; not just this exotic British Columbian cloud forest, but New Jersey.

Maybe then, what we've been really talking about is *going public*. The theme that seems to unite all this, I suddenly realized, when Cosgrove showed the slide of the Cunard building in Liverpool, & I remembered that the first job I had as a teacher was in the Cunard mansion in Staten Island where the people watched those boats at the other end of the journey, steaming up New York Harbor, through the Narrows. I think you've really been talking, not about dream, or imagination, or place, but about public transportation, & so I propose "Going Public" as the name for your next conference, where I can bring my trolley cars & the B-13 bus of Brooklyn. I grew up in Brooklyn in New York. New York City has an extraordinary transportation system — *had*. (I don't know what they have now since I haven't lived there in years.) That is a double system. I'm not talking about suburban, which I knew nothing of — only white people — I'm not white you know; I'm Irish, but that's not to be white in New York. White people are Protestants. Protestants, when I was a child, they lived in the great suburbs: New Jersey, to which you were carried by what we called the chube — that's t-u-b-e, chube — or out on Long Island where you were carried by the Long Island Railroad, called the Lon Gisland. In the city, we who lived there were in the possession of two systems: one hierarchical & one, in Deleuze's wonderful word, rhizomatic. The hierarchical took you from any part of New York to lower Manhattan. It was about getting you to work and back. It had nothing to do with the intercourse of people, but just the carrying of people like fodder, or whatever we are, from the place where you slept to the place where you earned your money. The rhizomatic were the buses and even trolley cars, which I vaguely remember (they all disappeared in World War II or soon after), but the buses carried people from themselves to other people. So, to go from neighborhood to neighborhood — & you could do that — meant this strange, nonlinear — and nonlinear they certainly were — rhizomatic method of getting an impulse from Sheepshead Bay, where I lived, out — for example you could go to Greenpoint or even the place from which my accent comes. (I speak with a particular accent of northern Brooklyn called North Side.)

So everybody comes from somewhere & that's the best thing about us, that we come from somewhere and when we go back home, even if I who can go back home and people talk to me on the street and say, "Where are you from?" and I'm walking down the street I'm born on. That's distressing, because accents change in places. They don't change in us. We carry them. I still carry my grandfather's — who died forty years before I was born, but I still carry his accent. I'm still carrying it here in Kansas where nobody knows where I come from & no one can tell where we come from. I was talking to Ed Casey downstairs while we were exchanging bathroom instructions, where he came from, because his pronunciation of one particular word was just like my wife's mother who comes from outside of Denver. And the rhizomes of speech connect us deeply, even more deeply than walking.

But, anyway, if you go to public transportation, let me know, because that's... I do deeply wish, though, thinking about trolley cars, that Charles Olson were here. He is the one figure that we desperately miss. Cecil Giscombe has spoken his name and quoted him a few times, I was very happy to hear because Olson was the one who, for my money, first connected place and poetry plausibly — not in a descriptive way, not in painting a word picture, which had been done ever since Petrarch and perhaps even Ausonius, painting those wonderful visions of the River Mosel, that prime old Luxemburg event of the Mosel River, but the one who connected poetry and place in a productive way, where the place spoke the poem, not where the poet sat back and described beautifully the place he saw, but rather where the energy of the place itself, or the disposition of the place in space, as Olson might have said, generates the text, so that Olson scrupulously, in the *Maximus* poems, examines, say, that glacial moraine, which incidentally is geologically continuous with the moraine that starts in Brooklyn, where I grew up, that moraine, the top of which is the old abandoned houses & reservoir called Dog Town. He examines the land occupation. What do they call it — land use, the history of land use? I hate the phrase because it suggests using a quart of milk & throwing it out and buying another one, but there is no more cow from which this land comes, so we don't dare use it their way. But I think they call it land use history. He would concern himself with the disposition of every house, every stone, every street: who lived there? What did they do? And the very disposition of those places in space generated in the text — some of his wilder, madder texts in the middle *Maximus* — generated the poem itself. The poem is speaking from & to that disposition of place in space.

When Olson was living (Ken may know this story better than I) he snuck away to London once and lived with a wealthy lady in her house in Hanover Square. One day he disappeared from the house. No one had any idea where he went and people began to get a little worried about him. As you know, he was ten feet tall, so he stood out, especially in England, where one isn't ten feet tall usually. They finally found him. He had gone for a week over to Bristol where he was sitting in the public records office reading documents about the early codfishers of Bristol, the people we associate (if we associate them at all) with John Cabot & the so-called "English Voyages" of Cabot, who was not himself English, but who voyaged for the English at the very end of the fifteenth century, out of England, looking for fish. Olson was preoccupied with those things, public records. So he, much more than the essentially Romantic William Carlos Williams writing about Patterson, he — Olson — Romantic that he was, in an utterly unromantic way allowed the disposition of space, place, town, house, street, car to dispose the poem in ways that are obvious if you start reading his work.

One of the most wonderful poems in our century is his poem "The Librarian" in which he tells a dream, a dream he simply had, but a dream in which the topography of Gloucester, where the dream happens, largely figures and it ends with an extraordinary series of questions about the "real world," like "When does 1A [the highway] get me home?" "What is buried behind Lufkin's diner?" "Who is Frank Moore?" And the poem can end that way, with the simple questioning of the facts of place, a place to which he is summoned by the dream. So, in a way, the poem becomes a kind of sobering up experience from the dream, as if the poem is the way that the dream recovers our "normal" waking reality.

So I wish he were here. He would have bothered us considerably & I think he would have found fault with every remark that has been made, but in a way that would have made us feel, well, a little less than ten feet tall ourselves, but then we are less than ten feet tall. He was actually six eight. He was a very tall man. So the ten feet is clearly an exaggeration. I wish he were here. He's not here, but his sense of poetry as place & from place has been important to my thinking about all this and important to the way I've been understanding the things that I've been hearing.

I've been especially interested this afternoon in the way in which anecdote has begun to flourish, in which anecdote has come away from the chit-chat after the talk to enter into the talk. That is, the anecdotal "This is where I come from," "I saw this happening," "This was interesting," "My father saw this," "This happened," "I said this to my child." I think anecdote is the closest we come to public dreaming. I think when people sit & tell anecdotes to each other, they are, in a way, dreaming together out loud and in real time. You'll come away, & — you know the interesting thing about anecdote, & I'm sure your experience will confirm this, is a year from now you won't remember who told the anecdote; you'll remember the anecdote. You'll remember it the way you remember a dream, free-floating.

We used to run a dream workshop at the college where I teach. I mean, I ran it; they didn't. They knew nothing about it. They would have killed me if they had known, but I had a dream workshop where we sat and discussed dream. This was back in the days where — Robert What's-his-name, in Buffalo — Barbara knows his name. He taught in Buffalo for years and years — yes. He was publishing extensively about dream & dream-sharing, and Barbara Tedlock has a new book just on dream-sharing and so it's not lost; it's something in the air. Anyway, what we noticed is that if you listened to a poem as if it were a dream, that is to say, if the class lay down or slumped in their chairs and closed their eyes and listened to a poem, turning off all the Brooks and Warren, or whatever the recent version of that is, turning off all the critical machinery that they might have had and just listened to the damn thing as it went by, two things happened: it came alive in their minds as if it were something they had experienced, and it reminded them of dream. So even the most conscious, clear, hard-worked, Virgilian kind of poem, "I am making this as I am making it," would turn curiously into a dream when so listened to. So I think the relationship between dream and all the rest of it is not simply exhausted by taking dream as that which happens on one side of the sleep line, and everything else is on the other. Dream interpenetrates waking. Casey, I think you did this. You referred to Freud's *Tagesreste*, to the dream as the remnants of the day before. In just a similar way, I screamed out when I heard it, into my head, "No, no, no! The day is *Nachtsreste*! The day is the fragments & the leftover bits of the dream that we share with one another." & I think both ways we can deal with it.

& when we got to anecdote, I was with Cecil when he and his kid were somehow hassled in Steele, North Dakota — he didn't give us any of the particulars of the hassling, so therefore I could invent them myself and then forget them and remember them vaguely, I would remember them vaguely the way I would remember them vaguely if they had happened to me twenty years ago and if I had been somebody else. So you know, it's a very strange thing that anecdotes give us, & I submit that they are a species of dreaming out loud. & we dream probably to give, my argument is that we dream for the other.

& let me just stop talking about that for a moment and move to the sense that what is wonderful about dream is the giving part of dream that we were talking about, the dream as imagination. The dream is something in which the ego has a very small investment. When you wake up in the morning you are so confused by the dream that you are anxious simply to disburden yourself of it, give it to another, and only later does it occur to you, "That was my dream! You have my dream! What are you doing with my dream?" because we don't exactly do that. We're used to giving the dream to the doctor who just publishes it. We're used to telling the dreams with no particular consequence to ourselves. If only — God! If only we could write poems that way! If only we could give each other poems with the same failure of ego participation that we tell our dreams. Well, that may be something we could learn from dreams.

The word I want to bring in here, towards the end of what I have to say — I'm going to read a few pieces — the word is *locus*. *Locus* is the Latin word for "place" and I ran a series of readings once, back in Dutchess County, called *Locus Loquitur*. I chose the Latin word partly out of simple pomposity of spirit, but partly because I like the "*Loc-Loq*" sound. *Locus Loquitur*. It means "the place talks." The Germans in the audience, of course, would remember that locus also means bathroom, "the place" in slang German, so locus — the bathroom talks. Well, we tried not to have too much potty talk in the poems. But *Locus Loquitur*, the place talks. But that reminds us in turn that the word "place" that we've talked about a lot, imagination & place, is also the Latin word for the passage of a text and in fact, the plural, *loci*, or "low-kee" as I guess they say now in this modern, non-Catholic Latin, that plural doesn't mean "places" at all. It means passages in texts. Locus doesn't have a plural anymore that means places. The place when it's neuter means "military encampment," *loca*. So there's only one place in Latin, locus. That's very interesting. You can express the plural otherwise, but if you say it with locus, the plural means "passages."

So I'm fascinated by the way in which not just place, but passage summons grace. A couple of summers ago, I did a series of poems responding to the paintings of an extraordinary Italian painter named Brigitte Mahlknecht, who lives in the Tyrol, the German-speaking region of Italy. Her paintings, paintings and drawings I should say, are deeply animated by a sense of aerial photography of place, of maps. Topography seems to be the secret ingredient in all of her pictures. So I've written in response to some of her pictures, and I want to read two of these. The first one is this one. This is responding to a picture that looks like this. God knows you can't see it, but if it looks like a kind of a Xerox of a Xerox of a Xerox of a geodetic service topo map, then you're seeing it right. You see streets and houses and avenues and people and some giants, fat figures.

> Now it happens that we are across the world from ourselves
> and the ocean between is made up entirely of streets.
>
> You have come at last to the inside of the body.
> It is the only University — there is no end to what it tells,
>
> and the business of the magic life
> is to map the outer world inside, to map
> the inner world out there until
> you are master of the distances. And these distances
> must be sung
> suddenly
> to come home.
>
> Now it happens that we are each other
> and can see who and how we are
> only across an ocean made of streets,

nothing but houses forever.
Sometimes a park exists
the shimmer of far-off smiling cities
caught in a romantic self-deluding eye,
our senses only mean to sympathize
with everything we think we find.

The park is made of more of me.
Come lie down in such arms, this phony earth,
artful hillsides, grassy gun emplacements
of Fort Hamilton, by weird enclosures
where polar bears flounder in green water
under concrete fjords in sluggish Sons.

All I am is muscle.
There is no mind
except keep talking.

No flower but the *millepertuis,*
St. John's Wort, easing the tensions
of the Happy Few,
o small elite that lets words lick their skin,

when what they need to do is read these words you left so
hidden in your streets,
the gulfs of darkness
stretch inside our bodies, dark organs

trying to speak,
hidden like spores in dirt, like dirt
inside the cracks in rocks,
cretti
I cretti di Burn, a whole town
cast in the porcelain of time, craquelure,
the lines we walk on
to find ourselves,
to be with you,

prelude and fugue.
But we will never get there,
the famous flowers will come out and rave in color

and they, they fade, of course they fade, I will too,
animals like marmots burrow in the earth here,
they carry all the gold back into the ground,

and now I hear them tunneling in me,
the little mapping people
who measure out the world in yards of me
inside,
and your eyes project your body
to the ends of the earth.
To know at all is to map and to be mapped,

streets through our bodies,
and I will not tell you
what kind of people I am
who walk along your streets
but I am there, the cracks in rocks
are runes, the letters
you scratched on the wall, idly
your fingertip trailing in the dust,
the words your body meant

and here's my ugly body stretched out on yours
until we are exactly one
a terrible wedding waits for us.

I am so alone, he said. I am so alone, she said.
There is no listening to some people,
all we ever do is complain, complain
you are too far, I am too near,
know me, my skin
must have some terrible sickness
it so craves your hands to touch me,
what am I, a victim of the strange green fiery disease

Grünewald's Christ writhes with on the cross,
as if it hurt him more than crucifixion does,

why do we need one another,
each one
on the other stretched,
stretched out
street of skin to the end of the world,
why are you so far away?
(But this day, he said, you will be with me in Paradise.)

I read last night from the beginning of a passage of chapter one. This is an interminable five-page story. It's almost literally unendable, but I'm going to read a little bit more of chapter one of *A Line of Sight*. And I'll go to the footnotes from it, which are important to read.

I'm looking across my living room. This is about twenty years ago. The living room as it was, it doesn't exist anymore, because nothing does exist anymore as it did even yesterday.

[....]5

If you can find anything hard-edged in what I said to ask a question about, please, feel free.

Audience Member 1: Could you say more about the disposition of the place in space?

Robert Kelly: With Olson in particular, you can actually see it on the page, where the page becomes a mimesis, the map. I was reminded a little bit by the pictographs that Denise was showing us last night. We get a mixture of words and I know in the [Indian] ledger books, the ledger images, those words were added, it is said, by others — but imagine them added by the very people who made the pictures. So that there are passages of Olson's work, some of them very mysterious, where the words on the page seem to be mimetic of a place. Other times, the places

---

5. [RK read from *A Line of Sight* (Chapter 1, and its notes 4 and 5). See "A Book of Outside / Inside," p. 410.]

are clearly mentioned, where he'll give the names and who lived there and when they lived there, and so on. But the way in which I imagine Olson to have had this most patriarchal but innocent, if that's possible, if there could be an innocent patriarchy — I don't know, but I think there was — in which he stood before an Earth that seemed to him sublimely feminine and tried to read it with his body, let him not do anything to it, but let it make him swoon with understanding or swoon with desire. Somehow the place he looked at, where he was sometimes capable of immense acts of physical, numerical detail — the fisheries, the histories, who lived, how much, what the numbers were; get it right; translate it correctly, etc. — in which those very numbers work as meaning — I mean, after all, number two, number two is sexual. We imagine that when we quantify something we have rescued it from our libido. Far from that. I mean, the libido is more at home, perhaps, with number than with anything else. It is, after all, the moon that teaches us measure, the moon that teaches us to count. It is the menstrual cycle that indicates to us something about the nature of our own progress. It is the moon that we see growing and diminishing, growing and diminishing, that teaches us number.

So I think, in a way in which Olson would have, perhaps, accepted my saying so, he stood with respect to the world in such a way that he wished to allow it to map the work in him. I'm not always sure that we can look at his poem and get the landscape back again. I don't know yet, if that answers it, but for my own work, I'm always conscious of the fact that landscape, "land-skip" as Cosgrove said earlier in the English way, does really come from a word that means "making," *schaffen* in German, *schöpfen*, to create. Because the land exists as itself, perhaps, but landscape is something we make. People make it. Landscape doesn't make itself. Landscape is something we make. The old word for poetry, like poesis, poetic, the old word for poet in English was scop. The one who made the scape was the scop, which was the Old English for poet.

So landscape is something we create by our perception of it. We put it on the wall of our houses. I was so happy to hear that all those people want landscapes on the wall. I guess that's because they live in tiny boxes of rooms and need extra windows, but what about the generic quality of landscape? That's an important thing. Olson was trying to be specific to landscape, but A.E. Housman was trying to do that too. He, too, was being specific *from it,* as was Olson. But you wonder about the generic quality of the landscape we see. Very few people put on the wall a painting of what they would see if they looked out the window, behind the wall, through the wall. I would like to do that. I mean, I can't imagine anything more wonderful to look at than what I look at out of the window. I mean, whatever is out there. That's it.

But so much landscape seems to be about a fanciful horizon to be embraced, and therefore it seems to be essentially pornographic. I think of landscape as a species — most of it — as a species of pornography because we wish the caress of an unmarried horizon *&* it's something that we have no right to out there. So pornography, I have a lot in favor of pornography, but that particular species makes me more embarrassed than the Vargas girls on display in the KU museum, draped, or festooned, or the Helmut Lang photo that has replaced her. The pornographic sense of caress, because we started with the horizon as caress *&* the stars as caress. I think we have to earn our landscape by making it. We have to earn our horizon. It's not just given. And remember, too, that horizon is not just a caress, but like many a caress, it is also a restriction, because it is the Greek word for the boundary, the thing that hems us in — we're trapped — as was ocean to them, too, the ring, at the alveolus oceani.

Paul?

Paul Hotvedt: I want to recognize Bob Sudlow who is here today. For one, he is a landscape painter, a very celebrated one — but also because Bob told me one time that as he falls asleep at night after a day spent driving through the landscape and walking about in the fields, as is his daily practice, he recites in his mind all his daily travels. It replays, much like a dream. I want to connect that with what you said about the dreaming and the waking, they are not divided, all these experiences interweave.

RK: Is the recitation with pencil or with the words? Is it like reciting with a drawing instrument what one actually had seen?

PH: In imagining, in his mind.

RK: But landscape is one of those grand words that creates far many more problems than it solves. I mean, it's just so vast, what's at stake here.

Audience Member 2: Some of the themes that I see that we're celebrating here include mapping — two central themes — mapping and vehicles, both physical vehicles across the earth & also through the imagination and consciousness. There's another concept that we've focused on, which is getting our bearings, getting a fix and fixation and fixed things. I'm realizing that fixed things is an illusion. Space is an illusion because we're constantly traveling through time. In terms of mapping and navigators and people driving vehicles, I've noticed — I want to make two comments: First of all, does anyone else have the feeling that despite last night's and today's presentations that we are at a place right now that is not finished with what we congregated about. There's further to go on about what we're discussing.

Also, I'm surprised that there's certain central figures in this, whatever, genre, or area of consciousness that are missing to me, including the writer John McPhee and writer Annie Dillard.

PH: Actually, you did anticipate correctly. The notions you talked about of incompleteness were addressed directly in opening remarks last evening as being absolutely necessary. When we first started tossing ideas around we didn't have a theory — at all. And it didn't happen until we started saying, "Okay, let's talk about scope and limits." This is our little frame here, we're going to do whatever we can, because it can open up.

AM2: I would finish by saying that one possible direction is being wise to the Earth as informer of our consciousness and our vision. There are also navigators of the future vision and some of the people who are cartographers for me include Clarisse Lispector, Hélène Cixous, and others. We've got to start taking responsibility for creating our landscape — that's done through our thought and through our words and through how we build our lives.

RK: Okay, so do you want to talk it out, because Irigaray might be really where he is going towards.

Audience Member 3: You mean the elemental?

RK: Yes, that sense that he's asking for — I thought when he said Dillard and McPhee that he was talking about anecdotes of place and the emotionality of our relations to it, but I think with Lispector and Cixous ... Do you know Irigaray's work?

AM2: I'm just starting to know these people, but...

RK: Edward Casey's book, the preface to Casey's book [*The Fate of Place*] speaks about stuff that I think is exactly what you're after.

AM2: These people are like trailguides to a world or a reality that I'm only beginning to understand. It's like I am in this night & they are showing me the way.

AM3: A sense of body that extends the body limit in such a way, questions it & melts it down in such a way that it rejoins landscape in a very passionate, elemental sense. And it might be another sense of Disposition, to continue with that term, because I was struck that disposition, if you take the word apart, means somehow not being pinned to a position. Disposition. And that's why I liked it so much. It seems very poetic, as if to release land from being positioned, that is, tied down, prematurely. And it seems to me that your poetry, Olson's poetry, and Irigaray's thought about body as at the disposition of the land, of the elemental, are all tied together.

RK: That's beautiful, from my point of view, that's beautifully said & understood and kind of held together through the elemental.

AM3: I think just about everybody has talked about moving from one place to another, has represented the mobility of our society, the moving from place to place, and the idea of landscape is something that we shape in our mind signifies something that would fit a very mobile society, because then you take your place with you, even when you're leaving one place after another and I'm wondering if you have a sense in your — both of you — in your poetry which addressed the role of actual landscape, some image, a fixed place, a place that stays there year in, year out, season in, season out.

RK: Stays inside you mean? Stays inside your mind?

AM3: Well, that stays where it is and doesn't move with us, the role of actual landscape. What role does that play in your thought?

Richard Schoeck: Ed Casey was talking about his fondness for disposition. To that we could add transposition, which is moving from this place to that place. And there are so many wonderful overtones of that word in our culture. Transposition for a musician is an intriguing metaphor for what may take place, for what may happen in other dimensions of our culture. I'm coming at your question only askance.

RK: We have heard stories from people of spiritual disciplines of various kinds. I've heard these stories from American tribal sources. I don't know how reliable, it's just all anecdote by now with me, but you hear them at every level, of essentially getting an image into your mind of landscape and traveling around by the world until, by design or accident, you see that shape suddenly in front of you & then you know here it is. That, perhaps, was the way in which Salt Lake City, which was referred to before, was founded, when someone saw that that particular weird little shelf under the mountain by the lake was something they had seen before. So, as to the portability of landscape, I mean, the Dutch invented the landscape painting as something you can tuck under your arm & sell, usually exchange for drink and food at the local inn, the owner of which will sell it onward as Vermeer's work entered into — I think twenty of his thirty-some paintings began life as objects of commerce in that way of trade. But I think this carrying of the landscape in the mind until the world comes to its senses and falls into place, maybe we are carrying the landscape with sufficient urgency so that the world, as I said, falls into place, or disposes itself in suitable connections. I don't know. I don't have that kind of landscape. Do you have that kind of landscape that you carry with you? Expecting the world...

AM3: It intrigues me that there is a whole literary genre in the eighteenth century, letters from American farmers, Thoreau's *Walden* ...

Audience Member 4: It goes back much further...

AM3: There are dozens and dozens of books being written by people who live on a little farm and then write about a year on their farm. Annie Dillard has books like that. It seems like the rest of us, then, read that.

We don't have such a little farm ourselves, but it becomes a literary commodity. They tell us about what it's like to live in close, intimate connection with a piece of earth & maybe, I don't know if that's kind of a pornographic landscape, but it is at one remove. It's at one remove & maybe sets the rest of us in search of such a place that we keep with us. Or maybe it's a substitute for such an experience.

AMI: But I think what you're talking about is something that suggests the genius loci, which is the sense that within the place itself, there is a genius ... I think this may be what you were referring to about finding it or something which, over time & the different occupants, has always seemed to reassert itself, where — maybe a place of epiphany, where I think ... the sacred or the timeless or the elemental erupts into the mundane...

RK: That genius loci is good to think about because genius is one of those words that represent our usual tendency to make abstract that which begins as more concrete. The genius originally was the Latin word for the generative power, the sexual power of an animal, of a situation, so the genius loci was the power of a place to be productive of plants or animals or to feed your life, to feed the life of your children & the life of your crops and your herds. It's the same root that gives us generate, genital, and all the rest of it, which is — when we start talking about geniuses we have to remember the root of it. But that sense of finding a place, finding the fertile field, finding the place which will nourish our thoughts...

RS: There's another resource of language that was anticipated this morning when Ed Casey was talking about land and real estate. The word *realty* which we nowadays get only with realtors and the like — the world realty several centuries ago meant *reality* and obviously, that got buried in the language. There is this linkage of earth and reality that we have lost in our modern world, owing possibly to urbanization, possibly simply not understanding our own language well enough.

RK: Legally, then, real property contrasts with moveable property. Literally, I think so; I think that's the legal distinction, as if we were all about resisting the nomadic, down with nomadisme, escape from that.

RS: Those who did not own real property were excluded from the polis — they were excluded from a reality that has become "substance" and should have been better translated as "being…" So it's interesting that from a long tradition, not just in English but in other languages, there's this curious linkage between reality or "being" and real estate which seems to me to be a way of specifying, perhaps over-specifying, the reality that is there in the Latin, and that ambiguity is there several times over in Western culture.

RK: As if the language were reminding us, yes, it's all right to settle down here. It's all right to occupy this space.

RK: You have to heap — polis was originally "heaped up things" — you have to heap something up *&* have it protect you from the distraction of mere movement, I guess. And don't forget the scrape part of Casey's art, the scrape which is the incision in the ground, which is also the Roman *mundus* that divided the city from the non-city. To have a place is, in a way, to delimit it from that which is not a place. The nomad, because he has everywhere, has nowhere. He has no place. He has not been scraped. The land has not been scraped out for him, if scraping is scratching, is writing. We are told that writing originally — writan — was a scratching gesture too, so that writing is a scraping as the pen still does if you're lucky enough to have a bad pen that scratches so you can hear yourself think, literally.

AM4: I'm sorry. I haven't been here all day, so this may have come up in a previous conversation, but what strikes me is that as a culture and specifically in North America, we have, it seems to me, a very mixed sense of place, so that — what happens, for instance, if the sense of place can only be an invention, can only be in the imagination. It cannot be physical. Your attitude towards place is that it is an imposed place, then it is not welcoming or inviting or a choice, perhaps that you made. It seems to me that that engenders another set of emotional ideas *&* connections. Do you know what I'm saying?

RK: Well, you bring two things to mind that I think are comparable, but very different in their moral weight. One is — well, I live on the Hudson, on the shores of the Hudson River, about a hundred miles north of

New York, and all our "Indians" now live, if they live at all, in Oklahoma where they were forcibly dispossessed. So if you want to learn the language that names the rivers & streams & rocks in my neighborhood, you have to go to Oklahoma to learn them. Now, what did those people carry with them of our place, the place that is now "my place" that was their place, what do you carry with you into exile? Or those people in British Columbia who were displaced, not so dramatically as from the Hudson to Oklahoma, but still displaced from one part of the land to another part.

The other thing I think about is that there is a now considerable weight of interesting scholarship going on in classical studies, arguing that the Homeric poems, that we've heard about a little bit this weekend, the *Iliad* and the *Odyssey*, in fact constitute, in their geographical reach, a mapping of northern geography onto the southern seas. That the stories told in the *Iliad* and the *Odyssey*, in fact, did not "happen" in the Mediterranean world, but in the Baltic world and in northern Germany and the coast of the Baltic and even the Gulf of Bothnia. That those stories were handed down by tribes as they moved down into the Mediterranean world, constantly readjusting the nomenclature of the story geography onto the real geography so that we wind up with names imposed upon the Mediterranean by the Greeks which reflect the shape of the Baltic world. There's an interesting book, not yet translated into English, Vinci's *Homero Baltico*, on this subject, a huge scholarship on this mapping. It's not a strange book. I mean, it's not about a weird "Finns wrote the *Iliad*." It's not about that. It's more a sense that we carry a vision of place with us and apply it time and again just as New York State is full of names like Carthage and Rome, Troy, Utica, places that we have no right to the names of, & nonetheless we found them in our hearts and we imposed them on the land. But I'm more interested in the other thing, the dispossession issue of what do you do when you've been thrown out of your country and you carry it, remembering Zion as the Jews were in the first Diaspora. What did they carry? Did they map Judea onto Babylon? And have we been, like the Mormons, or I suppose most do, mapping their sacred geography onto a common geography?

(Cottonwood Review #59–60, 2002)

THREADS 6 : ROBERT SAYS

If I stand outside and describe the event, then I'm not in the event anymore. When something is happening to you, it's just happening to you, and all that is available to you is how you feel about what the event is. I suppose people who are drowning are saying to themselves in a kind of voice-over, "I am drowning now" (like the man at the end of Blade Runner *who says, "Time to die"), but most of us just live in a world in which we are living at the time we are living there. It's like Lily Tomlin's old line, "Oh, are you the party to whom I am speaking?" We're just where we are. The minute you stand outside and describe it, you've lost your involvement in what is happening. Even though I didn't get to this through theoretical observations, I feel justified or permitted to be that indifferent to describing the outer shape of the event — while providing the inner species of reality that the characters are presumably going through.*

in conversation with Larry McCaffery (1988)

I'm fascinated by rain, it's my favorite weather, I love rain [...] and I keep thinking about the way people are with rain: the sky opens, a lot of water falls out of the sky and very shapely and pretty and focused and it doesn't last usually very long, and people scream and carry on as if God were angry at them, and in fact often create a god-like Jupiter or Pluvius, who is angry, whereas what would happen if you stood in the rain for a long time is that you get wet, eventually you dry, you might even feel the wonderful sensation of coldness [..]. [...] I think the way we react to rain is not unlike the way we react to art. [...] [We] are afraid it will do something to [us], whereas all it will do is give [us] an experience. It's not an experience like violence or certain kinds of sexuality that leave a tremendous effect afterwards, it's an experience that you're left with. So the challenge of a piece of writing like mine, I think, shouldn't be the challenge of understanding it as you go along, but the challenge of reading it and then letting it rest in the mind. Because I keep thinking of natural examples, I mean if you look out a window and see a tree moving in the breeze, I'm seeing that now — *if I tried to* understand *that, I would lose much of my contact with the tree and with the wind, I'd try to work out the physics of the wind, and eventually I might want to do that and become a critic of the wind or a critic of the tree, but in the meantime it's so much more gratifying to look at it* quietly, *to experience it deeply and quietly, and then see what happens later on in yourself. You've had the experience, I'm sure, of meeting someone not making a big impression on you, and yet that night in your dream or the next morning when you wake up, that's the person you think about. You hardly noticed him when you met him [...] and that's what I think writing should be, you read it and say, 'Oh, so what,' and then a day later or a month later, a year later, somebody comes in your mind, it has processed itself inside you.*

in conversation with Bonnie Langston (1994)

You say social or political context: it's hard to say. I'm not of "left-wing" persuasion; I'm not of a "wing" at all. My belief lies — if it lies anywhere — with the earth as a shaper of our experience, ourselves as almost feminine in respect to the earth. But the typical capitalist, i.e., exploiter of environment, wants to shape the earth & bend it to his purpose — takes a masculine role, fills himself with yin foods to balance that yangish possessiveness he wants to destroy the world with. I think it's time for us to become a little more feminine with respect to the earth because the earth is deeply feminine herself — but to respect it, that seems to me, at the present moment, more urgent than politics (as politics are usually understood). I'm not of a "left wing" or a "right wing": I despise those things & I'm deeply suspicious of all bandwagons because all bandwagons crush people under their wheels: everyone, without exception. So with Cleaver's proposition: if you're not with the revolution, then you're part of the problem: I guess from that point of view, he's part of the problem: that is to say, those who are not with the revolution — & the true revolution is the revolution of the earth, the turning of the human consciousness inward upon itself in response to the earth: any politics fights against that — & I see Nixon & the Weathermen as essentially two parts of the same coin, trying to cast his attention, possessively, jealously outward, to seize power, to change the earth, to dig out the iron of Minnesota & dig out the oil of the off-shore waters and use it & use it & use it: I mean, Mao's a Nixon who writes poetry! [...]

The genuine ecological activists — & I'm thinking here not just of Gary Snyder who has devoted so much of his energy & his work to that — but to people who, at a subtler & perhaps deeper level of actual involvement with the earth, have, in a way, been making things good, too: like the poet Ken Irby, the poet Eric Kiviat right here at Bard (he lives nearby) — but people who are trying to contend not with the politics of earth from the lecture podium, but with the reality of earth, walking around on it. [...]

I mean letting up a little bit, learning a little bit, stopping & letting the earth teach us. For instance, ancient cultures like the Chinese & maybe some of the Mediterranean ones had systems of — [...] *maybe they were just intuitions — of some vital properties of land & landscape themselves, which shaped human life — & maybe that degenerated into the later magical divination of geomancy. I don't know. But it seems to me that one of the possibilities is that the earth shapes us. One of the possibilities is that the earth has its own meaning, that we are able to ignore for a time & put up our monstrous crap on its face, but eventually, perhaps the earth has certain communicable meanings, which, I am now suggesting, we sit back & listen to.*

in conversation with Joshua Stolle [ca. 1970s]

6.

A BOOK OF OUTSIDE/INSIDE

the basic thing loves learn
(or one loves in order to
learn):
the outside is the inside.

5·vij·78

A LINE OF SIGHT

CHAPTER I

I live in an old house that has no address.[1] The house is dark most days. Years ago it had a name,[2] taken from the two lime trees that block the afternoon sun from the front windows, trees much sought by bees in May and June. Tea is made from the flowers.[3]

Especially at the foot of the stairs it is dark, bottom of a dry well. On the wall above the last few treads is a large map of the Kingdom of Bhutan (Druk Yul), showing in monochrome relief the ranges and valleys & waystations. In the uncertain light that at times falls on this map from the opposite room, the tan spread of Druk Yul (isolated from the uncolored surround, India, China, Tibet) sometimes resembles a large cookie,[4] at other times a fallen leaf, which before withering rumpled into crests and gorges.

In one corner of the map there is a smaller replica, in outline, of the map itself. This diagram is called a Reliability Index, and shows sector by sector the confidence, expressed in percentages,[5] that the viewer can feel in the information sketched or verbalized in the large map. It is to be wished that every map conceded in such a way the inevitable inadvertency of its parts.

To the left of the map, and somewhat above it, there is a fierce grinning bright polychrome demon mask of unspecified origin, clearly enough the product of some tantric intelligence of the mountains. Bhutan. Tibet. Believers identify the mask as the face of an adept holding back his semen, resorbing his orgasm, swallowing the world. The face is the brightest object in the hall at the foot of the stairs.

NOTES TO CHAPTER I

Note 1: no address. A road, but no street. A street, but no number. Off east, beyond the sumac and the hill, the loose strife and the small marsh anxious these nights with singing frogs, there is a crossroads where the highway runs fast past the almost unseeable entrance of a road whose name is like mine — but that's beyond 9G, beyond time, beyond the Ennead that stands this side of the Dodecad — that's a region between the Nine & the Zodiac, in which no fixed knowledge is. No steady knowing. Nine Gods look up & worship,

Twelve look down & see me standing there, afraid as any four-year old to cross the blazing highway. Corner of the Dog. Nine Gods. Turn west with me. And then the house, with no address, too close to the Post Office to need one, just two houses down towards the stream. Known by name. This is the center of a vast invisible city; yesterday as we drove along, I saw a broken pump, its handle rusted, pointing towards the mountains. And saw the ultimate city, now only a dream, inhering in that space. Certainly it will have post offices and streets among its lily pools and tiger walks; I am less sure it will have numbers. No address except the name of the city, The City, & the mail gets there. When I first moved to this town, I computed that by the grid of the city down the river, I lived on 2097th Street, West 2097th St. But that city is no longer anybody's system. The grid is more spacious now, builds up as well as out, comprises the nearer stars, has its root in water.

Note 2: a name. Erwin Smith the postmaster lived in the house around the turn of the century, and called the place Lindenwood, from the two in front, one at the side, saplings all round. The tree is Schubert's *Lindenbaum,* an aching song of nostalgia that summoned Hans Castorp back into the bourgeois world from the bourgeois dreamworld up Davos. I don't know much about Erwin Smith, but pieces of hardware from the original house turn up in other houses round about. A characteristic door-hinge. A hasp.

The house has a name. When John Navins still kept the old Barrytown post office by the unused depot on the river, I found in his postcard rack a view of this very house, E. Smith's Lindenwood. I bought it for a penny (the same coin that would, in its time, have been enough postage to send it, say, to Helen's Great Aunt Malcha, that beautiful woman, who carried her best dishes from Poland to Texas in the late eighties — my card would have caught her in St Louis, perhaps around the time of the Exposition). A search in Navin's shop turned up a brown-wrapped parcel of several hundred such cards, which I bought almost all of, leaving some for the unlikely traveler who might want some evidence of having spent one day in his busy life at the Three Corners, beside the stream Metambesen, under Cedar Hill, primal Annandale.

Note 3: flowers. Tilleul, lindenflower tea — the French are very fond of this, and the Germans only a little less so — no doubt it is their bee-natures coming to expression. Tilleul is likely the most popular *tisane* or herbal infusion, or shares the summit perhaps with chamomile (from which I once rolled myself a very interesting cigarette, on Bank Street, to decongest — successfully — my tight chest from a New York midwinter catarrh, while Diane Wakoski talked about Beethoven, and in the other room La Monte Young was writing a long detailed letter to Diter Rot in very black ink). Linden tea I have never tasted. Absurd to buy, with all the flowers we have each spring. I promise myself one year I'll gather some flowers and brew. But I no longer believe our health depends on herbs, and the branches of the big trees are a little bit above the reach of my naked arm.

Note 4: a large cookie. As one sits and hears the last large sumptuous measures of Richard Strauss's *Capriccio,* his last opera, written and performed (in the recording heard now) while the world was burning down around him, and no countesses ever again would read sonnets, or hum them aloud before the mirror late late after a desultory party, and no woman would ever again try to make up her mind, and for all I know, no mirror ever again would stand clear on a wall, calm in its gilt oval (that shape in which a woman sees herself most truly), it is false or feeble to think of food. Yet there are times, especially at night, when the house seems to be alive with a midnight appetite, an astral Dagwood planning strata of unlikely foods, a sweaty old rich Rossini turning from music to, what? What would Rossini have eaten late at night, when the sky was too bright with stars, too sculptural with cloud, too clever with nightingales, for him to go to bed, however pretty his companion or compliant nurse, what would he eat, while his kidneys ached and the moon sashayed across what he already knew must be one of the last lovely spring midnights of his life? Here again the thought of food is a blunder, fart of a woodnymph pursued. But what would he eat? Would he tinkle a bell, and a cadre of diligent, unsurprised servants fall into *sorbet* formation, or pull a mousse providently beforehand from the ferns around the ice-block in the double-doored chest? After the truffles and gooseliver and cockscombs at dinner, what would pacify the, not hunger, truly, the *need,* a pure spiritual need it may be, yes, Rossini's utter desperate agonizing need to take into himself now before sleep or love or dying, just one more morsel of this after all adorable cosmos. He is silent as he watches them carry first a table, then a silver tray with Something on it across the dark lawn. We shall not stay to see him lift the cover.

But in this house some similar tendency, less elegant, less poignant, for our sun will never fall from the sky, true? it's always here, yes? always as it is now, supreme and ordinary, forever, ewig, ja? some similar nudge of appetite troubles the hours between midnight and sleep. What will it be? Not then the earnestness of cheese and oil and garlic & bread. A cookie, a biscuit, something heavy, crumbly as earth, dry, not juicy, not sweet, not very sweet, no creamy inwards, no chocolate, understood? a dry fine halfsweet crumbly cookie, no slimy cakes, no deceptive froth or teeth-aching icing, just the fine dry halfsweet, less than halfsweet cookie. That comes to mind some rare nights, when Bhutan becomes the half of an immense peanut butter cookie, say. But then a voice from the hallway cries: Man! Do not eat your world! Man! Man! Man!

Note 5: expressed in percentages. In fact the diagram in question reveals upon inspection only the alternatives: Good. Fair. Poor, distributed over the gradients. Memory said otherwise, & must have its little say, for fear of what She will do if balked of her constant ameliorative urge: Improve the Past, Begin by Improving the Present, etc. A man who constantly corrects his memory may find himself eaten by tigers or bitten by scorpions, carried by eagles, trampled by bulls, disliked by other men — no pedant worse than the pedant of inner experience. An accurate memory is needed only when one is going somewhere, n'est-ce pas? Or has been somewhere. The intense static beauty of these nights needs no more memory than a dog has, between one bite and the next. Here it is.

Percentages have the advantage of being, by definition, relations to that definable Hundred (old Satem-Centum), a number in historical times roughly between 91 and 120, with a tendency for the higher sum to be operative in more northerly climes (Iceland, Wessex, Trondheim). Whereas in Hebrew the number Hundred is exactly equal to 10^2, and is spelled exclusively by the ten successive *yods* emitted from Nowhere which implanted the Tree in whose branches, now in sun, now in shadow, we have for a while the right to live.

On the other hand, it was always peculiarly irritating to my father to hear any price over ninety dollars described as, for instance, ninety-four ninety-eight. He would insist, with some show of reason, that for such sums we must say, A Hundred Dollars, and get it over with. In this I felt an honesty of mind, anxious to hear the truth however horrid, so anxious in fact that it preferred, after endless years of pain, truth plainly swollen with trouble to truth corseted and faking a smile as it puffs its way in. Let's hear the worst, he'd say.

It is my hope that Pradyumna P. Karan, cartographer of the Druk Yul map, leaned similarly to exaggerate the painful, & that his 'Poor' is a cautious way of saying fairly reliable. But I fear the reality is even worse than the disclaimer.

Was it a lake or a mountain? I hear him thinking, Was the government bungalow on the yang or the yin side of the hill, I must have written it down somewhere, is this the road to the airport or the path infested with giant leeches? is this little dot the leprosarium or the monastery? is that a cliff or a deer park, a forest or a glacier, a pit or a pinnacle? There are no answers, there must be no answers, he has never been there, no one has ever been there. Most maps of this state do not show the town in which this house stands. There is a bridge over a river with an Indian name (Sepascot?), a small dam, a pool of deep quiet water dammed, apple trees, many locust trees, the kind of alder called red willow, whose inner bark is smoked. It is a place only real, without fame, without maps. No one has ever been here before.

CHAPTER II

The bond between the mountain and the map is color, and color is what is hardest in the dark house. The great dark lime trees keep back the road and the light. There are days in June when the year's not too wet that the bees themselves are frequent enough to break the light, noticeably dim it with their elaborate speculative lacework at the window. The light must come from the room through the archway into the hall at the foot of the stairs. In the hall there the map of Bhutan is large, and under it a map of Yucatan[1] is small but colorful, with tiny pictures of temples and deities marking the sites. In that specific sense, the god was flayed in the hallway, in halflight, or in the evening ugly yellow glare of the three overhead bulbs, Uxmal was built.

These places are important as separations.

Below the tantric mask is a simple drawing of two mature bears walking side by side across a sketchy field. Their noses tend towards Bhutan, but between them & that fanciful goal are two objects, mounted on the lintel-post[2] itself: a circuitboard from a very early computer, handsome and abstracted from all function, a stuffed circuit, considered as an artifact for the eyes to admire. Below that, a clear snapshot of a much-loved cat who died at one veterinarian's from an obscure disease contracted while he was being boarded at another, shortly after we came back from Mexico. Below the bears is a Nying-ma yantra, a diagram we acquired in California, in the Tibetan language. We have never been practically in Tibet, and can observe the mandala without a specific sense of loss.

NOTES TO CHAPTER II

Note 1: Yucatan. The neighborhood has a number of spiritual links with Yucatan, and at least one unpublicized telluric *nadi* or geo-astral vein unites the two terrains. Stephens, the first anglo into Maya country, brought back from the jungle many chests of Yucatecan antiquities; these he stored with his friend John C. Cruger, who lived on his (almost-) island up the road and river half a mile. In a local library, there's a first edition of *Incidents of Travel in Yucatan* inscribed by the author "to my friend John C. Cruger." Only ruins, or strictly speaking, ruins of ruins, are still to be found on Cruger's Island (though there is a wonderful rock formation shaped like two breasts on one chest — the Breasts of the Goddess An or Danu or Donu, for whom this district is named — one can climb between the breasts & sit there nestled, look out on the river, dabble feet in it if the tide's right). They say that Cruger's Stephens' antiquities were later floated on a barge downriver to form the nucleus of the Meso-American collection at the Brooklyn Museum, close to which I used to live, and in the library of which I first read Stephens — knowing none of all this. But my ignorance did not keep me from living a dozen years (or more?) in this northernmost outpost of the Mayan Empire, a ruin like the rest, surrounded by dense thickets and a quiet swamp with very black water.

Note 2: lintelpost. At one time, after the house was built, archways were cut, facing each other, admitting from the hall to the music room at the right, the study at the left. Years after that, both arches were reduced, by means of chipboard stretching from the original lintel to a new false doorway in which a cheap new panel-less door was hung. Two isolated rooms were thus formed with a hall between them. At the time of our entrance to the house, the arch to the music room we caused to be restored, leaving the study able to be shut off by its flimsy door from the hall. So it is on the chipboard panel between the adventitious doorway and the original lintel of the square arch that certain of the items are mounted to which attention has here been called, the yantra, the bear couple, the mask.

Though it forms no proper part of this account, the east lintel of the restored archway into the music room does constitute in fact the defining edge or obstacle by which the line of sight is bounded on the southeast. It is thus strictly of marginal interest, the gutter of this left-hand page these remarks propose to read. Yet that same lintel, clearly not the lintel in the text proper, but the one facing it, closer to the piano, closer to the yellow chair — that lintel was for several years one of the two foci by which the elliptical presence of the Ghost Dog made itself known. The ellipse in question extended from several feet into the hallway and music room up, at an angle we guessed to be 45°, to the landing at the top of the staircase. The Ghost Dog never appeared elsewhere, but for years could be seen frequently at the head of the stairs, or abruptly wheeling round the lintelpost downstairs. Even now, the Ghost Dog is sometimes seen in the latter, or lower, location, as if the slope of his presence were also a slope or declivity in time, the lower always later, the lower always later.

Since the installation of the Weber piano, with the decoupage panel front, and the A's that stick in several octaves when the weather is damp, as it so often is, the free movement of the spectre has evidently been limited; the piano abuts on the lintel, and thus occupies the area his ghost paws and muzzle invaded on those typical nights when he would calmly and unmenacingly come through the arch and disappear.

CHAPTER III

The point is, that these objects are not alone in the hall, by any means, but are the ones that can be seen, wholly or in part, from the yellow armchair[1] that stands at the end of the music room,[2] close to the one window the sun reaches, but divided from window and sun by a square small table covered with cactuses, some living, some questionable, some dead. The cactuses have not stood there for a full year yet, by any means, so it is uncertain whether in warmer weather they will be moved to one of the porches, there to be at the mercy of possums and cats and raccoons, or whether they will be allowed to remain at the safer sunny window, at the expense of the chair which will thus be unable to come close to the window when need arises in the heavy heat[3] of a river summer.

Walls call for the futile and the dead. Unvisited kingdom, dead cat, unplugged-in circuit, unacted mandala no less a circuit diagram of an essential but incomprehensible process. Everything is there but an oil painting to complete the taxidermic array. We hang our dead upon the walls, & dare the sun to shine thereon. Taxidermy = to arrange the skin: to decorate the surface. More honest the stuffed owl in the study, the stuffed blue kingfisher out of sight (though in the hall) around the corner, on top of the old escritoire.[4] But the gaudy demon mask, of papier-mâché formed soggy from minced up manuscripts or codes of statutes or Gujerat newspapers, gilded now and painted in red & blue, toothed, muscled, gasps in the light. It is the brightest object by daylight or candlelight. The light knows how to find it. The face is doing something.

NOTES TO CHAPTER III

Note 1: yellow armchair. I first met S.K. (the initials are curiously enough the same as my father's) when he and his first wife had just separated. I never knew her, except for whatever inferences I might have chosen to make from the furnishings of the house she'd just abandoned. I did not choose to make any inferences at all, and was content to know S. in his present tense, a learned, various, skillful man. After some years, he met and married an extremely handsome woman Helen and I had known slightly in another set of connections. Into our knowledge of S., then, came his new wife, D. Time passed, and at length D. began to make just such observations as I had omitted. She perceived her house full of relics of this (to all of us except S.) unknown and not clearly interesting earlier lady. Soon enough then, these offensive objects started leaving the house. S. & D. were kind enough to think of us, and passed along three occasional tables surfaced with tooled leather, a sofa & armchair matched in yellow relief upholstery, & a Simmons high-quality bed. We had never bought furniture, and these gifts, while substantial and useful, were not after all surprising, since things have a way of migrating (as another friend, C, would say) towards our house. To put it another way, I have never seen a house so rich with arrivals. A dim historical sense persuades me to confess that my cigarettes and lackadaisical habits soon did for the leather tops of the tables. The sofa went on the porch (books are stacked on it, in cartons, waiting to go. Where?). The armchair is by the window. For my present purposes (if these discursions may so be dignified), this chair is important. For one thing, it is the one armchair in the house in which I'm comfortable. I can sit in it as long as I like, write in my notebook, read lovely Barbara Shapiro's biography of the great John Wilkins, listen to Wagner, listen to Helen playing Ravel at the piano, or just think about women, or about how I'm 38 years old and people still give me chairs. But the most important thing about the chair is that at times I sit in it and see nothing except what is directly in front of me, a single line of sight these notes attempt to deliver to a world hungrier for them than it probably knows. Of all things, it needs most to look one way with all its eyes. As for the bed, we'll sleep in it tonight.

Note 2: music room. Each day the scant sky light (not skylight) enters the room from the west. For a long time the room was a living room or sitting room. People came and sat on the long yellow sofa, the yellow armchair, the blue bentwood armchair, hassocks, folding steel chairs with curved wooden seats, the piano stool. But they stayed too long and said too little. As time passed, the room turned its space into accommodation for piano and scores, records and tapes and the machines to play them, a radio that could always reach the old city 100 miles away, and on some rare days (low cloud cover, minimal solar flare activity, a little wet coming down) could pick out the older city 200 miles over the mysterious oldest mountains east. So the room filled with different sonorities now, no longer the uneager implicit voices of young people confessing their desires or pressing urgently, shark-fashion, their omnivorous need for omnivorous attention, no longer the louder yelps of friends faltering towards middle-age full of negativity and suspicion, no longer the paranoiac drones of distant anthologies or local politics. Now the room was fuller with sound, sadder in a way not to have people squatting all over it, but not much lost, maybe not much lost. The room, that room, was never meant to be a khan or caravanserai — the sad ugliness of talk in that room came, as much as anything, from the room itself, from the sweet sense of snug enclosure it gave the visitor, the comfort of knowing he was held and cherished; in that maternal power, all the locked in shittiness and suppressed whine corpse-floated to the surface. So men and women who outside (or even in another room) (any other room?) laughed and held their masks in place and acted as if they had control of their own, if not lives, then at least responses-to-their-lives, in this room turned infants. Infants = unable to speak. Infants who pretended to talk, while all the while their hearts dripped down huge round american beauty baby tears that it could not be "like this all the time," that they were here, held and o.k., and in their hearts they hated the enclosure, fouled the room with their mental diaperings, blatted, bleated, left at late hours when the night was too far gone for anything but sour. In the morning, their dead cigarettes and unfinished drinks (identical with those to be detected, at that hour, anywhere, in any, unloved, room in, this world) were pedestals for dust and demons. Every morning the room to be ritually cleansed, incense lit, blinds opened, windows raised — the sorrow lasted. *These were not people* who sat here while the constellations rose and set, who complained and fantasized and went away. They did not know that this house was a journey. They took it for a rest. So the room excluded them at last, cast out the sofa and the music began.

Note 3: heavy heat. It is said that last year there was rain every day in the month of June. The summer altogether was agreeable to us when we came home after a year and a day, or a year to the day, allowing for leap-year. Only during our first week in the house, the house still foreign, smoked with strangeness, a dirty window, was there heavy heat. Then we dragged the bed (the former guestbed — we were camping in the house still) over to the west window & found after midnight most of that week enough wafted air to sleep by — except for one night when I roamed through the house & wrote to no purpose perched at the high writing table — no, not there, that had not yet been brought out of the store-room — so it was downstairs, at the kitchen table, the study still too strange to repossess. Then and a month later three days of heat. The summer was as I loved it, cold, wet, unpredictable, with days blazing like a polished shield on a pebble beach, quenched suddenly by a rip tide — *aither* days I called them, knowing the word of Greek for the upper air, where fire lives that does not burn, but moves all things in brightness. Then autumn came early, cold days of October, but the winter was mild, so mild that I only recall a few days of being cold, a few days of snow, the way a man healthy all his life might recall in age a few days of childhood sickness, precious for the difference.

A lovely rain. Falling now on Annandale after a warm March day. Spring frogs on both sides of the bridge, both sides of the house. Spruce wet tips, gnarl of oak and locust, smooth of maple, bare against the close sky. Cars parked not far away, they glisten clean or muddy in the passing light of other cars. Violet light in the woods where a woman with a deep voice in a new house bathes her flowers all night in false sunlight, mild. A distraction most of the year, allowable tonight seen through the lovely rain.

Note 4: escritoire. This family heirloom or Twentyish 'secretary' stands of course out of sight, but it has stood near me since my earliest memories. Perhaps in its grimly pitted and scarred way, it is my memory. Every year or two, the urn-turned wooden finial that surmounts the centre of the top must be jammed down in place, the original nails still intact, never yet making perfect contact. It stood in the living room of the house I was born towards, a room that patterns still my understanding of such things as carpets and sofas, vases and sunlight. The old story. The secretary (as it was always called) has four drawers, largely unhandled of its onetime bronze fittings, a yawning gap (Ginnungagap) above the drawers in which a cubbyhole-pigeonhole console fits, & a glass-fronted wooden-fretworked double-doored bookcase above that. The cubbyholes are gone now into another room, and the glass doors are locked with an omnipurpose mock-antique barrel-key not at the moment in hand. It will turn up. In the bookcase section is my meager gathering of old books and leather-bound trophies; the oldest is the editio princeps in Greek & Latin of Aristotle's works (Lyons, 1597), the sleekest an eighteenth century vellum of Theocritus the loveliest Baskerville's octavo printing of Catullus. The name secretary though, continues to haunt me. From the earliest times I imagined concealed within the veneered processes of this most angular desk a feminine presence lurking, coeval not with the wood but with the joining, a sort of loving easy flapper, late Friday afternoon, office party, Thorne Smith novel. Her clothes are insubstantial as her thoughts, but both are tender, playful, warm. She will not marry the boss because in the deepest world she is the Boss; for all the fragility Fitzgerald and his crowd found in her, to me she is most durable, surely more lasting than the bronze that would have locked her in. The key is lost, and she moves freely in and out, not I suppose of the furniture itself, but of the name 'secretary,' a name whose ambiguity owes perhaps something to the gin-scented hebephrenia of the earlier century. Nymph. Nymph whose svelte contours were implicit in the earliest Night from which Eros himself came, a spectre of her loveliness, to her forever returning, turning. Even as from the woman's dream and woman's *space* the first man arose, perhaps to do her work, perhaps to serve her.

CHAPTER IV

Because of man's sins, he perceives the sphere as a circle. Reflected from its convexity, the items of the wall and hall arrange themselves, maps and beasts and masks, thermostat[1] and architecture. The lintel says: This is where the wall ends, or the door begins. Or the door ends, and no man can pass by. Because of his sins. In the sphere of sight, every object becomes a surface, a surface becomes a word. The word, because of his sins, wanders down the centuries between what we laughably call its root and what we, half-ashamed, half-hopeful, describe as its obsolescence.

The word wanders, meaning only one thing to him at a time. Because of his sins. Sin, says Clement, is inadvertency.

Lost word?[2] Every one is. Lost word, when the pale sunlight through the unclean window gasps the last shadows of dimensional things? Lost word stuffed between the cracks of a broken pane, to keep the wind out. But there is little wind most weeks, and the storm-windows contrive a more sophisticated protection. And what was the word?

NOTES TO CHAPTER IV

Note 1: thermostat. Set at 62° winter days, 59°–60° winter nights when the incident light of the hallway allows less accurate knowledge of the dial. Very cold days, set for a few hours at 66° and let it be. To change the setting, it is necessary to hunch over and peer into the bronze box, careful not to get between it and the light, and then twirl the milled knob with the right hand until a little blue interior spark flickers to mark a change of state. Immediately a roar begins in the furnace room below, or else cuts out. In less than a minute, water is gurgling subtly in the radiators, either perking up or coming to rest. Heat, anciently loving to rise, climbs all day to the upper story and lies in wait for the sleepy householder. Often it is stifling at the head of the stairs, the long hall to the bedroom lined with books & maps. By the doorless doorway, the heat is gentler. The bed is cool.

Note 2: lost word. This is the famous lost wax of Freemasonry. Fingered into shape in beeswax, the finished model is closely packed in plaster, sherds, brick-dust. Then the whole is heated, & the wax runs out the channels or sprues left by its own melting. Molten metal is poured in and takes the wax's place. Later, when the metal is cooled, the mould is broken away, and the sprues or spurs of irrelevant metal hardened in the relief-channels are now broken off and filed down. The finished image, if all is well, now stands perfect to the first intention. The process is called *lost wax*. In some similar way, the creation of the physical world must have involved a Word spoken, a Word lost like wax, replaced by the dense matter of our own projection or illusion, more or less polished smooth.

CHAPTER V: QUINTESSENCE

It is the last hour of your life. Turn down the thermostat. Beyond Bhutan, exactly where you can't see it is the cabinet of alchemic texts, the red telephone you can't use, the painful manuscript, the air-conditioner plugged into the circuit too low in amperage to power it. The chemical lamp, all unseen things. The Brave Soldier has come at last to the bottom of the well. And finds himself in another house, just like all houses, every house. The wall. The wall might be the surface of what the Greeks, in nervous fear, ingratiatingly called the Hospitable, the Euxine Sea, a smiling most dangerous flatterer. We call it Black, and have forgotten to be afraid. The wall wants me to forget everything beyond its so casual opacity.

Courteous wall! Distinguish all! Discover the surface that evaporates off the sphere. Around the corner is the lintel, geometrical as Egypt, that cancels any further sight, and leaves us only Vision.

(*Sparrow* #20, May 1974)

A TALKING HOUSE

Looking around my living space and working space, I contemplate the writer's situation. People who talk are talking to someone more or less present. Writers may or may not be writing "to" someone, but they are writing language, and language is always deictic, demonstrative. There means "right there" even if there's nobody home but me. Writing is always being done somewhere. During this period of sustained attention to Ashbery's work, we seem to be invited to think about the interaction of his living space and his writing work.

But I have to guess about such matters from my own. I look around my house — the dining room table I write on at morning, the umbrageous office screaming with books where I type any other time of day. The spaces in which writing & living happen are bewilderingly interfused — especially as they come closer to, touch, turn into my work table at which I am sitting. Here I am, surrounded by a mixture of fond acquaintance and freezing terror. How can I ever make sense of even this desk beside me (really a six-foot door poised on four filing cabinets), it's at my left elbow as I face my computer, which sits on its own table facing east northeast on a pale winter day, let alone of what's on the shelves, in the filing cabinets? A book is a box. A piece of paper is a snowfield, like something out of Eisenstein with an interminable line of dark figures shuffling across it to meet some preposterous idea. What am I doing here? Are these not the palpable all-too-fleshly evidences of my mind, such as it is, its interests and appetencies and own bewilderments? My eye roams, hoping to find audible rest. Hopi kachina, Lucite scotch tape dispenser, rock from Cuttyhunk that wrote, no, taught me to write, the ending of a novel. Old eyeglasses. A whale's tooth. No wonder I write Thinglish.

How would it be if I were Ashbery? What would my poems be like?

His house is neat, at least the public chambers of it where John and David have welcomed me, the quiet amber gloom of the McKinley era softening varnished woodwork, the staircase mounting towards (opposite of Goethe's Faust's descent) the realm of what must be *the mothers* — the heart of the house, the secret a house keeps.

But his verse is various and leaping. From percept to percept, *instanter*, his mind leaps from thing to shining thing.[1] I have to struggle to make some linear sense out of my own tumultuous real estate, while Ashbery leaps free from the neurosis of upholstery, neatness, cleanness, into those ecstasies of sheer dithering that make his work so great. Not just great writing, but healing writing.

I imagine the paintings upstairs I haven't seen, & maybe more pictures lining the steep narrow stairs to the attic. Zo's lithograph showing *The Assassination of Sadi Carnot*, Stanley Spencer's *The Poet's Grave*, Redon's one surviving encaustic panel, *Vers Ayesha*.

Ah, a house. Nothing one ever makes is quite as massive, integral, intricate, mysterious, as a house. The house of a poet is her greatest poem, lost forever the minute the poet, in Wodehouse's immortal phrase, passes in his dinner pail. Because every dust mote is a consequence of breath, every necktie left unworn but pretty in the closet, every white handkerchief (who uses those anymore?) left neatly folded in the chifferobe is part of an immense text. From which the poem speaks. I say this, but I can't prove it. Proving a poem is hard work too, and nobody thanks you for it.

No doubt the vastness of Bashō's tiny poems & prosems along the way, those divine obiter dicta, owes some of its greatness to the fact that his

---

1. By the strange torsion of Time, master of paradox, it may turn out that the poetry of John Ashbery is in many ways a much richer instantiation of Charles Olson's notion of Projective Verse (in the seminal 1950 essay) than much of the verse of those who claim Olson as their master. It is Ashbery's mind's breath that leaps immediately forward, does not linger with cheesy sentiment or restatement. Nothing is restated. Everything is new. O scholars of the time to come, read Ashbery anew in that uncommon Black Mountain light. And see why the commonplace Us-vs.-Them anatomy of casual criticism (Black Mountain versus School of New York, etc.) is worth re-investigating. If it ever really was investigated, and wasn't just a nonce label that had more to do with who was friends with whom, the social. And what's wrong with that? By social we live. But we shouldn't confuse it with judgment. Especially not The Last Judgment…

house was the whole narrow road to the northern district — Japan was his house, and let him speak.

But I have been brought far from Hudson, that Victorian palais on Court Square, across from the bandstand, the grass even in winter is greenish still. David and John live there, and to move through the rooms — those I have visited — is to pass of course, as I'm sure everyone notices, from era to era. The kitchen is 1930s America, comfortable as an apron, there must be a cookie jar, there is certainly a box of cereal. Whereas the workroom up on the second floor is a timeless après-9/11 of computers & printers and office light and little magazines and what we used to call reading books. But you all know that. What gets me is the extreme Americanism of the place. I feel I have never left home.

I suspect I have a touch of Dr. Who, I feel at home in every house the way he is at home in every time. Dr. Where. Because I love houses. Every house is a book, & I love books. That every house is, or writes, a book — that is the very premise or enthymeme of the assembly you're reading now — if indeed this essay gets into the assembly and the assembly gets published, & if it makes its way into your hands & you've read this far, or just opened up by what fools call chance & found me here. How unlikely all this sounds, how unlikely of fulfillment, like the predicaments Howard R. Garis used to warn us about at the end of installments of Uncle Wiggily. If the postman doesn't leave the milk in the toaster, we'll hear what the old rabbit gentleman got up to tomorrow. So this house of Ashbery writes a book, employing him as its man of words.

What fiendish reciprocals the world is rife with! I make a house & the house makes me. I think I'm writing my own stuff in a house but the house is shaping my dreams so that I wake to write them down. Where else could a dream come from but where you are? Where I am, I mean. Where am I? I mean it, the house writes the man.

So the editor of this assembly is sensible if indiscreet. She wants to learn the true author of the poems ascribed to Mr. J.A. Is it the house in Hudson? The apartment in New York? The primal abode among the apple trees of Sodus? She reminds me of those Baconians. Not Shakespeare wrote these plays but another using that name. Could Ashbery be seen as agent of a secret conspiracy of architecture, furniture, carpets and clean old glass windows to create a new poetics? The paintings, real or imagined, on his wall? Poets love constraints of all sorts — *Chains* was one of our best magazines. Poetics is the unbounded boundary. *Frontière sans frontières*. I have enjoyed this assignment, Miss Morrissette, because it allowed me to discover that I really do think place is the deepest poetic resource of all. Or, to go on with my schoolboy French, *Mes murs ma Muse*.

(*Raintaxi* portfolio, "John Ashbery Created Spaces," 2008)

BUFFALO PROBLEM 1

How grasp this city.
Why should it take a man longer than a day to get the fix of a city.
Paris in an afternoon, easy.
Is it because a city like this is like this — like every other city like this, eager to display such likeness, chary of revealing what is different.
Nothing different but the lay of the land.
Which is the relevant difference.
We are shaped by what shapes uphill & downhill, the length of sight, pull of the trees with reference to the water table, which itself follows *to some extent* the contour of the land.
That a flat spread city is virginal of its difference.
(Young man, the name of your little magazine is *Fix*)
Follow Main Street with humility.
The great cities of this world built out all ways from citadel, island, market, palladium, stone ex cælo, London from Themys, Paris from the little island in the Seine, Peking from the Imperial Palace, Rome from Tevere, New York from that tapering landgrab peninsula circumdated by wall & water —
the first act of civilization is to build a bridge, the Pontifex holy master of the city, who holds together (as centripetal principle) what grows out from center, by its own movement.
So we must measure cities by their ability to hold together all the parts.
The great paradigm city 19th-century travellers saw in the bend of the Niger,
armed gateway for white men to walk through
after they crossed the ditch.

(*Fubbalo* #1, 1964)

FOUR SHORT PIECES FROM *IO*

A NOTE ON DIMENSIONALITY

(1) even though there is say the paradigm of Bodhidharma, lidless eyes of the awake man, there is a different order of seeing, perhaps simpler, because ocular, that yet seems difficult of access,

I mean shape-vision (Botticelli, Ingres, Miró obvious coordinates, as emanations — maybe Labisse, Chagall, Rorschach as spectres)

whereby an outline becomes seme of a [tradition] [message] [continuity]

(i.e., qabala as technical 'exercises' in the speed of neuron firing)

so I am looking at the shape (against brightness, afternoon) of a soap bear

(sold as grows hair, sold as containing, after series of lustrations, a *surprise* in its interior) where surprise is takeover of shape by interior content (Jack Horner to mind here: plums)

: so there have been some few to whom reality was not nucleus-enclosing but was (i.e., each thing was) itself nuclear

(let the art historians bitch abt Egypt, & complain that seeing *shapes* is seeing 3-dimensional reality in 2-dimensional terms — as if *dimensions* had any meaning other than that rigid scalar one: quantifiable by one numerical proposition — the value of res ægyptiaca lies in that ability to comprehend (picture) what has been apprehended (sight): in gematria, the number of Vision is the number of YHVH)

so it's the shape of the soap bear I speak to you of, a median bilateral bulge making for cuteness, i.e., the curves speak plangently, 'sweetly' (a word we cd once use) of the vale of Har

(so that marriage, say, is dangerous, in that it is capable of recidivist innocence (in Blake's sense of innocence): the strangeness of our lives a function of sexual indeterminancy,

    a man can find himself back in Beulah like a shot — but that is no problem here or there)

      strictly speaking, then, n-dimensional mathematics can speak properly of dimensions; does your saucer spokesman suggest that by 1980 we will be able to put the *mensa-* in dimension № 4? i.e., coordinate extense or duration in such dimension with (our sense of) counting numbers? I'd like to hear more of this)

    I think I'm offering this, re shape, Egyptian art, Miró, &c.: that the number of 'dimensions' in which an image may be measured once transcribed is irrelevant to the dimensionalities of the imaged.

    I.E., we will be living in the 4th world, 4th image, by 1980?

(by which time the UFO-passengers will have given us a sense of why Amerindian languages put such stress on the distance of reported action? are these dimensions:

 HERE-NOW

 HERE-THEN

 THERE-NOW

 THERE-THEN ?

speculum universale).

            17 August '66

MAPS, BORROWINGS

    In conversation with Harvey Brown today, I got started on putting together something that might hold value, a speculative tie-in of those wandering Norsemen (check minimally Turville-Petre on Norse mythology, Oxenstierna on the Vikings (also in current *Sci Amer*), Runciman on Crusades, varia on the Norman (= Norseman) kdoms of Sicily &c.) with the Sufi (= here non-theistic mystics of Islam), as if via the first (9th–11th C) Norseman push (from Russia to Newfoundland, Lapland to North Africa & Persia) by a group of enthusiast drug-taking warriors (parallel here the Assassins of Syria, who were in fact in close contact both (a!) with the atheistic mystery school of Cairo, & (b) with the 'Crusaders' themselves) & then by the second push from the North (Hansa, I mean, Russia to Britain the tradesmen, paralleling the somewhat similar in time vast push of Muslim merchants from Java to South Africa, Mongolia to Russia), as if by these two phenomena the Sufi impulse had *already* shaped the west.

Basic problem is with all the mystical borrowings nowadays from wisdom, literature, making always for personal imprinting but not for societal in/form/ation, i.e., no place (no 'figure of outward') to direct the inward meaning towards. No city. Here a glimpse of Norse might suggest a possible paideuma (personal + societal impress, jointly & congruent) as might arise or be wanted from these present jollifications. QED

Principia here:

— all data must be summoned & entertained together; function of an historian to construct a grid for sifting such data

— there can be no genetic or racial history (e.g., the Celts)

— History is history of place, i.e., world history or local history, place = grid

(and a pun saves us all: mapping via maps!)

20 May '67

(from: "Selections from letters," Io #4, "Alchemy," 1967)

WHY COLUMBUS DISCOVERED AMERICA

It is good for a people to believe that the nation is only 5 minutes old, with time out for coffee. As Rome went sour, it stressed a hectic search for ever more remote antiquity to be its genesis. Better to believe that yr grandfather came here from Mt Carmel & yr greatgrandfather was a gorilla. Dont blame me if L'anse au Meadow turns out to be Waterloo, if the Leif Erikson stamp really shows Judas (whom Brandan found floating on the almost-American ice), come to call the whole thing off. Garcilaso was told by a master of Inca lore that their culture founders had come only 400 or so years before, or the distance between Jesus & King Arthur, or Columbus & us. There it cuts out Ten generations & the virtu goes out of us. Happy Columbus Day, & maybe it was really Capt John Smith?

(Io #6, 1969)

(OECOLOGY)
 ((housekeeping))
if we confine
our attention
to those (largely riparian)
areas where
men have been inclined to settle

we will, doing so, (i.e., thinking just
miss   abt coasts & waterways)
two basic
things we need to know

    a)   the Rest of the Terrain

        (turf is not terrain)

    b)   the in-fact parameters
        (where it almost = perimeters)
    of humanizable land

---

to (a):

    swampland 30 miles from NYC,
        unknown,
    beast-ridden, known if at all to the occasional
    hunter or ranger,

    or,

the Jackson Whites, or
       West Tag-kanic peoples
    (110 crowmiles from NYC)
who are NOT
      on the roads,
    hence not IN the society,

        or,
the Coast Range of California,
    all the way up, empty,
    some roads thru
          said to be "known"
      or
Omah Sasquatch Bigfoot & Co.,
         non-Humans, photographed maybe,
    but not known in situ
because their land not known,
    as
    (as yet)
the big buildup of autoroads & autobahns
(Federal Interstates, *not* local)
          is in fact
the greatest protection of "resource"
  (i.e., unshitted-up land)
we've got,
     where cars
   don't go,
       people don't go
& cars don't go over or onto or to
    a huge proportion of (actual)
      land in the (say) USA

           even
    where the road goes THRU it does not
give access to the depth or inner
      Body of the land —

  so that

> we are now (1969) actually less possessed of the land
>   than we were 100 years ago (as old maps & deed clearly
>   show)
>   & the land opens to its natural successions,
> its own alchemic balancing act
>   balancing even what
> we put upon it in the way of a Rather disturbed
>   atmosphere, watertable &c.
> : we are less *on* & wrecking the land now than when we
>   stuck to the horse
>   & the horse didnt need exactly a
>   road at all
>
>   (Note for the Winter Issue:
>   ban Snowmobiles & skidooz now)
>   & we are now happily
>   stuck with our vehicles, our goddamned Mounts.
>   Ergo (note to the elite):
>   Know the inner Body of the land
>   unmapped
>
>   (e.g., check the actual conditions of USC&G quadrant
>   maps now. I've got a map of Bhutan on my wall
>   that is honest enough to show a Reliability Index,
>   i.e., how reliable it itself is as map of that
>   terrain. USC&G shd be encouraged to do likewise
>   on its not infrequently imaginative projections
>   of what oughter be, Here be tygres & hyppogryffes)

---

to (b):
>   If we don't know
>   what we don't use
>   we wont ever know why we
>   use what we use
>   — are there undetected ways

in which the land itself
  —in time or in its time—
wards us off?

           — are we burdened
with hitherto undetected obsessions
compulsions & "preferences"
unconscious re the use of land
landscape, terrain?

Economy grows out of ecology —
           if that
Staten Island sea-captain is right
& the Karlsefni party DID winter
at Bayonne & Manhattan ca. 1003 CE,
     is there a draw in the land
(itself)
     & is the draw of that strange
canyon & outwash set called LA
     entirely social?

     Geomancy;   does the earth pull
us?
    These are fluted speculations,

           the point,

━━━━━━━━━

           before all that,

to honor (keep off
     unless you walk in intellect)

& thus find, the Body, of the land.

           (*Io* #7, 'Œcology,' 1970)

ON HUMAN CLONING

Since cloning is a human idea, and the only people (as far as is known) who are doing cloning are human people, it is interesting to me to speculate on the mindsets from which we might turn out to be working.

I recall reading in a newspaper recently, among endless titillating speculations about cloning humans, some geneticist quoted as saying something to this effect: Well, we shouldn't get our hopes up too much — if we were able to clone Mozart, we might not get another great composer — we might just get a cab driver who liked to listen to music on the radio and hum.

What I found fascinating about the remark is that the geneticist (if indeed he really was one, not just a nameless authority) somehow imagined or intuited that music itself was part of the genetic package, even if genius wasn't. (My intuitions would point to the other direction, and suppose that genius or brainpower — as great uncles used to call it — is more likely to be a physically conveyable capacity.)

If cloning Mozart is somehow involved with a taste for music, then a clone of Kant might have a taste for candied fruit and shooting pool, and a clone of Hitler would be nice to dogs. This seems close to nonsense, if not madness.

I am suggesting that, in the context of cloning humans, the question "What is being cloned" properly understood requires a prior investigation of "What is a human?"

Since we are humans, and self-awareness does not appear to be an automatic faculty of our species (observe how our mythology sneers at Narcissus for his agenda of self-analysis), the question of what is a human is just the sort of question that irritates the many, frustrates the technologist, enriches the philosopher. Most of us don't know the answer, but we know something that, for our practical purposes, is better than the answer. We know what a human does.

A human wants.

And what is bizarre, and it doesn't take Freud to know this, is that what humans want is infinitely various. Tastes and accomplishments and inclinations — whether they arise genetically (our cloned cabbie listening to Shostakovich) or environmentally (Irishmen tending to sing Irish songs) or some other way (Mozart/music/reincarnation) — whatever it is that humans want is also the token or totem of their self-definitions.

I am what I want. That seems to be the deepest truth for us, what we identify our very being with all of the many inclinations — sexual, political, ethical, religious, consociative — that we feel.

It's time to think clearly about what we are, and what we want us to be. This life & next life. Who is it, what is it, that we want to clone?

So from that point of view we might in fact discover that human cloning has been going on for years now, and its biochemistry is called propaganda or advertising, since by such means one human is made to inherit or inhabit the house of preference, the house of desire, built for another. But to go on in this vein would be spoilsport of me — I know what we all want, real cloning, hard-edged science, the real thing, gold and pink and cocoa babies tumbling out of the assembly line full of All Desirable Qualities.

Do I err in supposing we should first really find out what these inclinations, velleities, tastes, desires really are? Should we find out whether or how they connect in turn with the creative industrious qualities we seek to replicate by means of cloning?

At the moment, I am yielding to a trinitarian inclination, embedded in me by my language (your language, I'd say, if I were being confrontational), our Judæo-Christian heritage, our trinitarian system of government. I am haunted by a trinitarian anxiety: I am afraid that when conception takes place in a living system, there is a father component and a mother component — and there may be something more.

This something more can be, if you like, dismissed as trinitarian guesswork or 'Ol Soul sneaking back in, & I won't quarrel with you too much. I think it's worth thinking about, though — just thinking, I mean. Not much here to measure. As with the behavior of subatomic particles, you can only see (if you can even see) where they've been, not where they are or what they're about to do now. What they're about to do next is discussable only statistically.

And since statistics is a science that measures no thing, we could even think statistically about the Third thing that creeps into the act of human conception. By and large, it seems to produce behavior oddly different from the behaviors of other animals we know much about, yet with odd kinships too. All creatures seem to know themselves from somebody else. All crows watch their backs. So their must be some sense of anxiety, some sense of identity conveyed by this Third Thing.

But this Third Thing when it involves humans seems to come bundled with a pressure to articulate, and hence symbolize, and hence eventually realize, the very inclinations that use for their own purposes the cellular hypostasis of body & consciousness with which the science of genetics concerned itself up till now.

I am daring to propose a sort of prolegomenon to any future human engineering: such a study must carefully and sustainedly and subtly examine the very qualities we wish to replicate. The qualities we seek may be gifts of that Third Thing, and may accordingly be capable of being roused in us by acts of education and influence vastly beyond anything we've ever studied in our hard-edged conventional paideumas. It may be that the qualities we want can indeed be cloned, not by cloning the base metal of human gonadic production, but by influencing the consciousness of the parents, the consciousness of the fetus itself. Who can say?

We have not studied what precisely it is we want to achieve, and we will be in no real position to clone anything humanly worthwhile until we have that intense and unprecedented work. Because the specific gifts of consciousness (Mozart, Fermat, Ramanujan, etc.) we want, and want to replicate, may be all round us, latent in us already, and may infuse individuals in subsequent generations without the prod of the geneticist's magic wand. The wand in question may be Hermes's staff itself, the meditative act which studies the world so quietly that the most contradictory serpents can peacefully twine round it.

I mean it's time to think clearly about what we are, and what we want us to be. This life & next life. Who is it, what is it, that we want to clone? Tread gently — we are on sacred ground. Vagueness here will certainly be the death of us.

(*Nature Biotechnology* # 9, 1998)

THE WORLD OF NULL-E

The first weeks after the Loss will be spent trying to reproduce the experiences of being entertained by the Power. People will try to sing and dance and talk as these behaviors were exhibited to them on their televisions. Some will succeed, and be popular for a while among their fellows — these are the ones who were most successfully programmed by the Power. As they grow older, they will be imitated by others, copies of copies, until the end of time.

But here is a mystery: through the force of the immediate itself, the im/mediate, the Power of the mediated gradually is lost, and its place is renewed by the unmediated *force of presentness*. So that these dimwit actors repeating shtick they've learned from actors repeating shtick all the way back to the last sudden flare-out of the dying tube now — enactment by enactment — are healed into presence. They're actually here. You can touch them. Hit them if you don't like what they do or say. They are in the world.

Art returns to the world

Writing is just dreaming with your fingers.

No wonder touch so exercises the fancy, fantasy, of the writer.

Don't wonder, touch.

Afternoon in Dun Laoghaire, shopping in the little mall, walking to the bookshop, watching the Martello tower. Lovers playing on the cannon.

Judith Mok has an amazing voice, an equally amazing pair of eyes, Laser Eyes is her nickname, her husband says. I see her photo on the CD of her songs, I want to see her singing, the voice is rich and precise but the music is dull she's singing, like a beautiful woman making love to a marionette, pseudo-folksongs by real composers — folkish kills unless you copy.

I think she's Jewish. Her eyes are Sinai eyes, and find me out.

For Christ's sake, sing real music.

So we walked out along the strand, stepping on rocks & such, sea weed, gulls interested in our approaches, fishermen, a few bathers, then walked on paved esplanades past the muddy little cove, Gentleman's Naked Bathing, now filled with the neighborhood families in very dowdy proper bathing costumes, eye-bite of 1957 thought I, and we kept on.

Around the corner and half under Joyce's Tower their house, we sat all night and talked with the Irish and their cats, and phoned out for Indian food soon delivered.

Then we walked with Peter and Enda the long walk back to the hotel perched above the harbor and said goodnight, they for the train.

It isn't Joyce, it isn't Dublin, it isn't even sad. It is just the middle of the night and huge Irish sea lies simple to the moon, moonpaths and shiplights and harbor glimmer, it's just the way things are, beautiful and always an inch or two out of reach.

At two a.m. I looked out our window high above the esplanade and watched them at it, screwing on the cannon this time, her left leg languidly let down at times finding contact perhaps some comfort, with the earth, while he worked hard in her, and she let him, worked as if he was trying to shoot them both out over the sea all the way to France.

Napoleon comes from there. Small, intense. His penis I have seen, a little scrap of black leather no bigger now than a cat's tongue.

Montaigne had a Jewish mother.

I dreamed of you last night. I was walking in an open space, a construction site or series of them, trees on my right, and on my left a huge array of rubble heaped up over an acre or two — rubble that looked like spare parts or ruined pieces from Niki de Saint Phalle installations, curves and toruses and wheels and spokes all colors, rounded things, swollen things, their bright colors a little faded under dust. I was carrying something long and skinny with a metal flag or vane at one end, carrying it like a spear before me, the vane flat, quivering as I walked. And I was talking to you (as I often do, did you know that, in the day as well as the dream), but this time, to my astonishment, I heard your voice answering me, close, close, as if I were carrying the sound of your voice in this instrument I held, whatever it was. And then as I came to the end of the field, to a road, where another road joined it from behind the trees, you came into view, coming out from the trees along that other road, and came towards me, smiling. Smiling. Your hair was full and long and very neatly draped, and you wore a blue dress, vivid blue in which no trace of purple or pink was hidden, blue (it occurred to me as I woke) like the fresh blue of hydrangea bushes I once saw growing in the Himalayas, strangely suburban looking in those wild hills. Which were the source of the flower. No, maybe yours was darker, a little, than that. I have never seen you wear that color. The dress was full, lots of fabric to it, loose around you, but gathered gently at the waist by a belt of the same fabric. Self-belt. Around your shoulders lay, because the day was cool, a shawl of some black soft stuff. And you smiled. We came towards each other as if never apart, and embraced easily, kissed lightly, without such public display of affection as would have made us uneasy. How smooth & pale and welcome, welcoming, you looked. Smiling. There was no distance, and we began to talk. That was the dream, and I woke happy, healed. Now I imagine that men without legs must dream from time to time that they are walking, & then wake up bitter, cast down from the high normal beauty that they once had and seemed in dream to have again. But I did not feel such loss at waking, just a joy at our still being in the world together. A sense of permanence. And we even were talking.

The Loss. That's what they called it when the lights went out. Two things happened. The Angel of Amber came down and took electricity away — the gift the gods had given us for a couple of hundred years had gotten us into trouble. And just to make sure we kept out of trouble, the Angel of the Planet Mars came down one summer afternoon and degaussed the planet. All the magnetic scripts, to use the word politely, were erased, scrambled, poeticized, made interesting instead of factual, in other words turned out to be In Other Words. Kaputt.

Which looks enough like Caput Mortuum, Death's Head, the black beginnings in alchemy, to make me sit up & take notice. Blackness. The Nigredo, the Putrefaction. First step. Alchemy is the History of Africa.

So there we were, no ROM, no RAM, no CDs, no tapes, no Walkmans (note barbaric plural), no TVs. Fucked. What were we going to?

And who were we, in the first place?

How did we get so fucked? Here we were in a civilization far more prosperous than nurtured Aristotle & that lot, and without a single plague or loss of a harvest or enemy occupation, we suddenly felt wiped out.

What is the matter with us?

I don't have a clue. Don't look at me.

I know what we do wrong, but not exactly why we do it.

Fumbling with the notions of devil and Satan great or Satan small don't work for me. I know the name of our affliction, but not how it got there.

The name of our affliction is Entertainment.

They show us beautiful people on television so that we will find ugly the faces we see in the mirror, and have to buy something to make us better. So that we will find fat and ugly and thin and old the men and women who move around us in ordinary space, and have to buy things to make them and us look prettier, cooler, sexier, younger.

Their most important agenda item: to deny us the pleasure & comfort and presence of our own body. Own bodies.

All the religions and codes of laws propose to outlaw the bodies of other people, and even one's own body. Why do they do that? Only for this reason: to make sure pleasure remains a basic economic commodity. No sex without marriage, marriage being primarily a socio-economic arrangement. No pleasure is ever to arise immediately from anyone's body — that is the basic rule of not just capitalism, but ever economic society.

If we could have and give and take pleasure freely in and from one another, there would be a shivering of the timbers unseen since the days of the great comet, or whatever it was that slew diplodocus and scorched Eden.

We would be.

Till then:

Fun Rule of Capitalism: All pleasure must be bought.

Fun Rule of Capitalism: Every interaction must be a transaction.

Rule of Capitalism: only that is to be valued which is yet to be paid for.

Rule of Capitalism: once a commodity is purchased, its value immediately diminishes, and continues to diminish. (This is the only immediacy of capitalism.)

To depreciate something means to lower the price.

Africa is the history of alchemy. To debase a population, to bring it to the lowest condition of human existence, enslave it. Sell slaves and work the slaves. Build a society on the efforts of such slaves. Deny them any function in the enterprise. *Ein Geist Genügt für tausend Hände* snarls Faust at the end of his downward path, One mind suffices for a thousand hands. The slaves. We used to call them hands. Then farm hands. Hired hands later, when the economics of slavery changed, and instead of buying slaves outright & being responsible for their upkeep & well-being, such as it was, you bought them on the installment plan, using a device called wages or salary, & left them to take care of themselves.

And when this population is suppressed, oppressed, repressed — the three presses of the system — they rot. They are the putrefying sector of society. And from that rot, the Stone is made. For this is our philosophic Sulphur, to which the Wise bring the philosophic Quicksilver of Art & the Salt of Lust, and by these, cooked through all the revolutions of despot Time, eventually the Stone comes true. The world changes.

Let it be true.

Towards the black community capitalist society has long ago grown accustomed to looking for innovation in music and art, in language and worship — these powerful energies of our species which capitalism knows how to neutralize as Entertainment.

The commodity once purchased continues to lose value until a time comes, as it may, when the commodity of time begins to outweigh the commodity as loss, & the thing increases its value, as Antique (a word often written backwards to attract our attention to the vile little shops). But its new value as Old Thing is only established as a result of, and in the act of, a new commercial transaction.

You know all this. You all know all this. Why am I saying it? Then again, why are you doing what you're doing? I see you, I see you doing it again and again, and you wouldn't be doing it if you thought about things the way I'm thinking about them now, would you. You wouldn't do it any more. You'd break away, out into the open of being a person among persons and nothing but persons.

Walking up and down the little streets from the harbor where the ferries came in stuffed with Belgians in their small cars. Walking along the high parallel streets where no one seemed to come except the locals, to the Chinese restaurant, the Indian restaurant, the tobacconist on the corner. A neighborhood is what it sells. And yet we love it.

People come back from the souq and say How marvelous the markets of Bukhara. Of Darjeeling sprawled down the hillside. Of the Porte de Clignancourt. Of Hamburg at the Saturday Market when it snows all year long. Souq means street. Where the business gets done. Where the people are.

We know we were there because we bought something & brought it home.

Singular felicity of merchants! To sell in one place what you obtained in another!

Weaving.
I want you.
I want you. And from this want of mine (and when we say 'want' we think we're talking about desire, but the word knows better: it speaks of lack, impoverishment, economic malaise) we improvise a culture to supply it.

You come with opera, with blue dresses, with Sealy mattresses, with K-Y Jelly, with merlot, with maître d's, with churches and flowers, with fields full of trailers stretching towards the Indiana border, don't go there.

Between the obsession to acquire and the obsession to repeat, the soul has no more room than a cat in a cigar box. Something's got to give. The rubber band better snap. Or else.

I dreamed of you last night. I dreamed you out with ardor. You cried out: Hollow me, hollow me out! And I did. The mystery was this: the hollower you grew, the hollower I grew, as if it were sheer absence I shot spurting hot into your Netherlands. We poured into each other until we were empty. And that was suddenly the way to wake the world. Work the world, I mean, get it off our backs and off its butt, get it working again, void of predetermined paths and values, gleaming like a nice clean window in an empty house.

Paths and values, the man said.
Was it a man, or was it just me?
So all we have to do is dismantle (destroy, undo — you pick the word, depending on your ferocity level at the moment) the entertainment industry, that's all. It is the largest industry in the world, employing more workers and influencing more people than any other.

The Entertainment Industry. E is its own name for itself in several spiritual stations of its degradation. The world from which E has been banished, the lovely world of E, we will call the world of Null-E!

E!-world:
Public schools
    With yellow buses.
High Schools
    With gyms and driver red and yellow buses
Colleges

          With football teams and creative writing
Graduate Schools
          With career development offices
          and slave-market annual meetings of professional 'associations.'
Television
Radio
Movies independent and otherwise
Theater
          Broadway
          Off, Offoff, Offoffoff, college, etc.
Poetry Slams
Music Industry
          Recordings
          Concerts (commodity-events)
          Conservatories and recitals
          Boombox and streetjuke
          Walkman and MP3
Publishing
          Books magazines newspapers sold in public places
Sports Industry

NULL-E! world:
NOW STOP AND PONDER WHAT THE NULL-E! EQUIVALENTS OF ALL THOSE ARTS AND MEASURES AND SKILLS AND DELIGHTS WOULD BE WITHOUT ALL THOSE E-THINGS. NOW STOP AND PONDER WHAT PLEASURES AND DELIGHTS THE NULL-E! EQUIVALENTS WOULD BRING US WITHOUT ALL THOSE DUTIES[2] TO DISTRACT.

---

2. All the E-things are duties. Observe that participation in some species of entertainment is required by law (primary and secondary education), or by custom (television, radio, music) or by inflexible patterns of social pressure. (Try to meet with people without going to the movies or a concert or a game or a museum. Conversation is permitted, if at all, only in the form of 'reaction'-discussion of the commodity-event just experienced.) All species of entertainment are civic duties in Capitalist societies, & should be so treated, we should carry them out reluctantly if at all.

THINK OF THE INTENSE BEAUTY & ACTIVITY THAT WOULD ARISE, SUCH FEATS OF RAPTURE, DEEDS OF HUNGRY HEARING EMPOWERED SPEECH DISTRACT, THINK OF THE INTENSE BEAUTY & ACTIVITY THAT WOULD ARISE, SUCH FEATS OF RAPTURE, DEEDS OF HUNGRY HEARING EMPOWERED SPEECH. HOW WOULD WE LIVE IF WE LIVED IN THIS FREEDOM? WOULD WE BE BORED, OR REBORN? BOREDOM IS AN INVENTION OF BANKS, TO MAKE US SPEND IN RESTLESSNESS.

No more school.

No more prisonhouse of children warehoused eight hours a day so their parents can get a rest from the Mediated hyperactivity of the children, reinforced every night in dozens of ways.

No more yellow buses carrying prisoners to an empty book.

No more empty book.

Beyond the E-world, every book will have meaning, at least the meaning some woman or man put there. Not an educational committee. The only good book ever written by an educational committee was the King James Bible. And look at the damage that's done.

Just stop listening to me now. I have something to say to myself. You've got to stop this dreaming business. A dream has nothing to do with the day. Leave the dream where you find it, in the soft universe of sleep, along with the blue coat, the Irish cannon, the moon on the sea, her vivid eyes. The day does not need these things.

Leave them at the gate.

The trouble with psychoanalysis is that it commoditizes intimate, interior, experience. The dream contents are the coin of transaction. The dream images, the sacred personages of night, are dragged into the daytime fiscal transaction, one of the ways you *pay* the doctor who *pays* attention to you.

Leave them in the night. That's where they do their work.

It is possible that the only dreams we remember are the failed dreams, the ones left over on the plate at the end of the night, the ones that did not succeed in keeping us asleep, or the ones that had not finished their word of healing us.

Heal an image with an image.
Heal a heart with a heart.
Dreams have a work to do.

Work is the opposite of entertainment. No wonder the E world wants to breed the attitude: Take this Job & Shove It. No wonder they want you to think that Work = Job.

Whereas Work is different, it is winter fire & summer sea, it is *what we do* — it is the sister of play. Work and Play are the two enemies of Entertainment. Play has to be tamed into Game, then Game commoditized into sport, arcade, Nintendo, Vegas casino.

Work, you healing wave, in you I wash myself clean. Said Busoni's Doktor Faust, which after seventy-five years the E-world is finally going to co-opt as entertainment at the Mythropolitan Opera, early in 2001.

Work: making something. Making something that wasn't there before you, making something [in] obedience to your inner sense of form or fun or faith.

Play is similar in its disposition of energies, but has no tangible product.

Running and walking and swimming and wrestling and studying the Talmud and reading novels, these are Play.

Writing novels and digging dancefloors and composing Talmuds, these are Work.

The only joys are work and play. And you.

You.

It is a strange bracing alchemy to know that the woman in the world you most want to make love with is precisely the one you dare not touch.

I dreamed of you last night. We were not dancing, we were not doing anything. The stars were shining, if you can call that doing. I'd call it work if I were a star, but I'd probably be lying. Just expressing my inner nature, just venting my personality. Light flows out of us.

Dream is job enough, comrades. Keep the masses asleep long enough & they'll have a dream.

23 December 2000

Dear Diary:
It's about time I cut out all this bushleague Fourier bullshit about work and *jouissance* and money. I don't know a thing about it.

But I do think this thought. Here is my thought: Imagine all the pleasures we could have that literally cost nothing in money or social-credits or whatever it is.

Imagine what your day will be like if and only if: You buy nothing except food and shelter and clothing. If everything else is free. No TV (coz no lectricity or batteries) etc. If you do (don't do) this every day.

Imagine a life entirely made up of actual events. All interactions are with live people and the generous spirits of the dead (speaking through memory & other inner didacts). Imagine a life spent active, joyous, with the living, the dead & the gods. And demons, if you like them. Imagine a life full of lives. Not echoes & monochrome Xeroxes of autumn trees, spring flowers, her lips, his eyes, and so on.

Imagine hearing no word that was not addressed to you by somebody, in a body actually present.

Imagine our sense restored to the actual places where we live.

Shut me up, I said, and imagine.

You heard me, imagine it! Don't just sit here reading my book, shut the book up and imagine.

IDIAZABAL is a cheese from Spain. It sounds as if it should be a God from Mexico, someone carrying a woman out of a volcano, someone with feathers coming out of his ears and a blue word coming out of his mouth saying Here, here is fire. And when you're tired of fire, here is water. Here is everything.

"Spend in restlessness" — that is the story of all our shopping, and most of our sex life.

The cheese actually is pretty good, tastes like parmesan made from sheep's milk, near as I can say.

I have no idea how it's actually produced.

Idiazabal. She made it.

"We went to see some people who were taking two ostriches from Venice to the Duke of Saxony." So says Montaigne, visiting in Augsburg. He explains how the birds are leashed & led. Not what they were doing in Venice, or will be doing in Saxony. The birds walked all the way.

I have no idea.

I dreamed of you last night. We were walking in a culvert or paved ditch beside the road. At one point the culvert, in which we were ankle-deep in clean running water, autumn leaves skimming along in a brisk current, dipped under the road, and we went down with it, crossed, came up the other side & kept walking. I carried the memory: we have traveled *under* the road and I woke up with the emphasis ringing in my ears.

Have no idea. That's what seems to be trying to speak. Just have no idea.

Cluelessly competent, be a girl without a guide, a scout without a boy. Be there, be there and shut up.

Don't be here. Here is too busy, too crowded.

Be there. Nobody is there yet. Nobody is ever there.

Until you come.

Come to me. Please.

In the shabby little woods I love so well that ring my house we were walking and stepping over fallen branches & sinking pleasantly into the leaf fall of ten thousand seasons, for not only in the autumn do leaves fall, and we were talking about this & that, the Romans and how they made roads, though not here, and how the roads they made are still there, I walked on one once that went from Italy to Spain, though I walked only a kilometer along it, it was if I had made a whole pilgrimage to Compostela, because *it is the road that makes the pilgrimage*, that road carries us.

The pilgrimage I was making had in mind a union I wanted to hurry before the footlights of the world. I kept wanting to come close to you, close to you, & I would brush from time to time against your soft hips that would press back against me, you can never tell what a hip means, Touch me more, or Keep off me now. It means them both, we press against each other and never know.

I have no idea.

Where the maple saplings were closest together we had to squeeze through, especially tricky because the bare vines of Virginia creeper slung from the few old tall trees wound like webs through the sapling thicket and I wanted you (*j'ai une fringale de toi*) and I couldn't say it, couldn't say it (what are you, an ogre, do you want to eat me?) I crave you (I am here)

Come to me. Think about me till you come.

I want us to be us.

Think about us.

In Michel Tournier's strange novel, *Le roi des aulnes* (translated all too clearly as *The Ogre*), the nicest man slowly, without any crises or fuss, turns into a monster. This is the story of so many lives. Or how does that nice shy fierce not competent dreamy poemy mystico art student turn into Hitler? That is the biggest question of them all.

No, it isn't. This is: Why does anybody want what they want? Why, for example, do I want you so much that I spoil all my copybooks scribbling your name over and over.

I found a pen in a Viennese coffee house in the corner where Hitler used to sit.

How is it that I can write your name with even that pen?

Is the name stronger than history? Is desire stronger than the awareness of time and justice and truth? *Das Geheimnis der Liebe ist größer als das Geheimnis des Todes,* sings Salome death, love, one greater than the other, but both end in silence, decay, the living put in a tomb, the corpse makes love?

They are the lyrics of Capital's favorite song. One thing is realer than another. The breathless privilege of Value, of Preference, makes the desirer pant over the object of desire.

For the secret of money is deeper than the secret of love, it is the secret of having a weapon to seize and forever appropriate the object of desire. It is the phallocratic oath: with this coin I thee take, with this credit card I chattel thee.

Fringale, a craving.

Non, no.

I dreamed of you last night. We walked across a blue steel bridge over a small river. Not a single swan was to be seen, though this was a city. There are no swans, I said. You answered (taking my right elbow with your left arm, joining limbs with me), There never are. This answer puzzled me, and I had to piss. I pissed off the bridge while you still held my arm — I used my left hand for the offices of micturition. The stream of urine arched amberly on its way to the water. It seemed to take a long time.

Jazz. What happened to jazz is what happened to all music.

Music stopped being something you do and became something that gets done to you.

How sad that sentence is. Let me look at it and feel sorry for us all a little while.

Music only does you good if you do it yourself. Watching people play music (as on tv, but also at a concert) does you as much good as watching people exercise through the steamy windows of suburban gyms, or watching girls do aerobics. Which, come to think of it, is also a common sight on tv.

Who knows what benefit (says the Devil) there might be in such breathless inspections? Could watching Jane Fonda classic workout videos enlarge the soul the way listening to an old LP of Bjoerling singing the *Cujus anima* does? Stranger things have happened on this stray piece of rock. "Christ, what a planet!" as the master said.

Here is the simplest rule of Null-E! (and remember, we don't like rules, don't make 'em, done enforce 'em):

COMMENTARY ON PETER LAMBORN WILSON'S "ATLANTIS MANIFESTO"

In the six numbered sections of this tiny yet constantly unfolding book, unpaged, the reader will find more than on a shelf of books starring the A word. Wilson's method is allusive, witty and correct: his concern is not to persuade, but to provoke. The Greeks (who gave us the name and coordinates of Atlantis in the first place) identified the evilest deity they knew as the goddess they called Peitho, the Persuader. All corruption of manners and morals can be laid at her door, all wandering from the path of your own dharma, your own good sense. Those bad companions your mother warned you about are bad precisely because they seek to persuade you from your way of thinking to their own. If they did no more than lift silently the flower of their sinful pleasures, who would betray them?

As if the first five sections didn't give us enough to go on with, the last section offers forty numbered facts and clusters of fact. (A fact is something somebody reports, or calls attention to in the world, or a statement put in meaningful connection with another statement.) He writes with the insight of a man who has found the overnight ferry to Atlantis, and has spoken with passengers who have made their way there and back.

What it occurs to me to do to honor this book and alert readers to its value, is not to review it further, which would mean, in effect, to review Atlantis itself — since PLW gives us so many data to work with, the info we need. Instead, I want to respond to it: it is not a guidebook or a history, but a manifesto, and manifestos mean to provoke, clear the path. All aboard for Atlantis. Offered here are my first hour's worth of reflections his book provoked.

At the end of my remarks, I offer a new conjecture about the 'actual' location of Atlantis.

1.

Of Atlantis, we know there is only one place for sure from which it can rise.

Windswept seas cannot swallow forever the time-swept Image that rises to us, through us, as us.

We become Atlantis all the time.

When we have been good to time, & good to one another, the City comes back to us. When we have used our time aright, with pleasing & helping & consoling & thinking, then the Lord of the Interior — only part of which is Sea —, Lord Poseidon, lifts his horn & summons us to the dance we almost remember.

(The dance it is the business of all governments to make us forget. Carl Schmitt and his strange local descendants coopt dissent itself and rebellion into the texture of the law, making the 'state of exception' the norm of modern totalitarian polity. It will seem as I go along that wherever Atlantis was or is, it is the enemy of totalitarian — that is, arbitrary (monarchic, despotic) — government, since it proposes itself as founded on the natural order (seven terraces, seven planets), which are without exception. Totalitarian government, which used to yammer about Law & Order, is actually the opposite and enemy of order — since order by its nature can never be arbitrary. But I digress — thank God I still can.)

Wilson, though learned and scholarly by inclination, I'd judge, writes with whimsy, proffering half-cocked identities to us, as if to keep at bay the wrong kind of reader (of this book and perhaps of any book): the reader who wants to prove something, or see it proven.

2.

Polis (the privileged and much praised Greek name for city, or city state, as, The Athenian Polis)
is horror show too.
Polis killed Socrates.
Rightly, said Klages, who said he deserved it, truly did corrupt the youth, led them from speaking Gods to a mute Idea.
Polis is police.

3.

Anadromous, the salmon leap upstream, against the flow to breed, force their way against the current to breed and die. These are the Gnostics, hot for origins, for the land of the pearl, Oriens. Pearly luster of sperm, milt, egg. These are our heretics.

Catadromous, the eel swims away from its life. Downstream and away from the comfortable pools & creeks where it lives so close to us.

Downstream and finally away from stream itself, away from current and from current events, going into the preposterously huge sea (seven-eighths of our planet's surface), hurrying on its sinuous way to fuck, in utter silent mystery — no human has ever seen eels mating — and beget transparent leaves, glassy idiolects that take ages to speak. These are the little elvers [sic] that in time make their way from Sargasso, where every eel is born, up all the streams of the northern hemisphere, Russia, Mississippi, Italy, Iraq.

These are the prophets who come from the sea, Poseidon's messengers, eel song, lipid romance, phallic shimmer, but their sex is hidden. The testes of the male eel were not confidently anatomized till the 1920s; Freud devoted his doctoral dissertation to the eel gonad problem; he came to an uncertain, but correct, surmise about their location.

(Freud! Isn't it interesting that of all creatures he would choose to examine the eel. The eel, whose whole sexual practice is, to our eyes at least, thoroughly repressed. Trying to find the testes in the phallus itself, the engine inside the symbol.)

Upstream, denying the customary flow of event, down to the seaweed sea, denying the customary flow of time, salmon and eel, the twin priests of Atlantis.

The Philistines were the Celts, who taught the Jews to cherish the eel — the snake it is licit to eat. The Irish, snake-deprived, are the remnants of the Cro-Magnon who worshipped, still worship, the eel & the salmon.

Dagon worshippers, whose dark chthonic and pelagic mysteries blinded the Sun God Samson, who took his revenge, governments always do, and tore down their temple. The Dagon worshippers set off for Donegal and Kerry, for shadowed Innsmouth and Arkham on the Miskatonic.

Out of the desert and into the sea, out of the sea and into every stream. Under the Kingston bridge I watched a kid pull up an eel every time he sent down his baited hook, eel after eel. They are many. And they have much to tell.

Abraham came from the eel-infested marshes of Sumeria, Shatt al-Arab, the source.

This is the oldest place we know words from. This is the very region that the infidel Saddam Hussein at-Tikriti sought with terrible success to destroy — culturally and physically. Murdered the Shiites and

'Marsh Arabs' who in their mud-daubed vaulted chambers built of reeds whispered Sumerian in their sleep. Drained the waterways and filled them in, the ancient gateway to Atlantis. God in His mercy knows what at-Tikriti thought he was doing, but we know that every tyrant hates Atlantis. If only because it is a hidden kingdom over which he cannot stretch his hand.

Abram, who listened. Who abode in his marshland until he heard the voice. Lech lecha, get you gone, arise and be gone from this place, the voice said, and Abram changed, went through his spiritual puberty, wasn't a greenhorn any more turned virile, changed his name, set forth from his calm stream to breed, to breed such a multitude.

Abraham the eel, the circumcised snake.

The snake purified of malice & venom, maintaining his endurance, cleverness, adaptability, ubiquity, its phallic grace.

Enoch the salmon, Khidr.

The eel is green.

Eel is Aal in German, but ahal says Luther, perhaps missing the point, an eel is pure vowel, pure liquid.

*laks- is the salmon, the liquid that runs uphill, crashing on the rocks

where Arktos is waiting, *Rktos, the bear god of the north, the mouth of cold hell, the Government who gobbles up all heretics, snatching them as they leap upstream

and is nourished by them.

It is a bitter fact that the martyrdom of heretics seems to sustain the institution against which they struggle.

Fatal paradox of dissent. "The blood of the martyrs is the seed of the Church," it is said, and how sadly that irony can be read.

So Atlantis works by silence,

> dissent sunk deep
> into a Sleeping Vigil
> a Waking Torpor
> a dreamer conscious of the dream,
>
> bright-eyed silence,
> the Buddha answers all questions by hoisting that flower,

four decades ago Flower Power was the first flush from Atlantis's sluices as it rose towards '68 —

any flower's power is to be beautiful a moment, and then die, and then be born again

Atlantis is the long sleep from which dissent wakes, speaks clear, & is engulfed again,

silence always smiles.

4.

Sometimes a word is no better than a wound.

Yarmulkes and fezzes hold the chi in.

A man with a hat is holding his breath.

Tantrikas restraining what feels like (but is not) the self surging up to 'express itself' like any bad novelist.

Grimace of control. "Demon masks" teach us to keep our public faces to ourselves.

Put on this face.

F.X. Messerschmidt's heads of human types and predicaments. "Man Straining at Stool." "Man Born Mad."

Making faces. Making faces means resisting roles. The mother says: if you do that with your face, it will stay that way. Would that it could. Would that Atlantis could teach us the decency of making the countenance be a token (tekmar, Zeichen, sign) of the inner man. Socrates ugly without and fair within? They likened him to a grotesque Silenus chest in which medicaments were kept. Maybe. But maybe beauty is skin deep. Maybe what you see is what you get. Maybe a beautiful person is a karmic resonance as much as a lofty wit.

Yesterday like Bruckner I lost my cap. But unlike him (who lost his cap or had it stolen on the Imperial Railway), I lost mine in a shoe store. Bad feng shui, to bring a hat into a den of Birkenstocks. The contradiction. I knew at once that this day I was a victim of the dialectic.

"At once" means later, the next day, when the cows came home, or not yet, when you hear their bonging Switzer bells over the hill,

not yet do I know what it means to lose something

to have lost something

to have something slip out of my mind

the bell ringing

Atlantis rising.

5.

I always enjoy belaboring the obvious. So the ocean of Atlantis is the aion, the cerebro-spinal fluid, the continuous ocean, unbounded, that flows from the brain through the spine to the amnion, that surfaces as semen & swinges [sic] our knees as the synovial fluid, all of that is aion, our own, our own aeon, our eternity. Eis aiona = forever. And into this sea has sunk some earlier knowledge, a science of being that is somehow veiled, mislaid, 'lost,' by the operations of the Socratic Geist.

Aion: the sea inside which the seven-circled city of the human brain floats secure, sealed, lost to view, forever speaking, processing, making me happen. Making me speak.

It just so happens that everybody has this fluid creek that, followed downstream, will lead them to the ocean, in which they will see, far off or near as Rockaway, the meaningful terraces of the Shared City rising.

No wonder we can gossip, eat lunch together, make love, enjoy one another's solos on the ukulele, weep at one another's graves.

All of this Peter Lamborn Wilson demonstrates (= "points out") by writing down the letter Ψ [psi] and calling it Poseidon's trident. The Emperor of Atlantis, who had a wife no one may name. Poseidon, who was lord of the Earth, whose name may be an ancient Potei dan or Potei gan, Potentate of Earth, Lord of the Garden where we began.

And his/her trident is Ψ, then, the psi of psychology, psychosis, psionics, first letter of Sappho's original name, the trident of the triune bowing, body, soul and what is that other thing? Is it a word that holds body and soul together?

Strange too that we have heard elsewhere of a god with an unspeakable name, a god whose name in scripture takes a plural form, a masculine plural of a feminine noun, the name we can sometimes say, ELOHIM.

> The trident is not Neptune's alone.
> It is wielded far East by Shiva,
>   lord of wealth & cattle, Lord of Atlantis.

6.

There are two ways an island can disappear.

I encourage Plato, like the Bible, to be read backwards or sidewise.

We are taught and have always believed that Atlantis sank beneath the sea.

Au contraire, Now it can be told:
The sea level fell, and left Atlantis part of some continent.
It is still there, Still here.
The island is hidden in the land.

Poseidon, as Frobenius made clear, is lord of the earth, and the Greeks too knew him as Lord of the Earthquake.

Some suppose Atlantis to have sunk thanks to an earthquake. But Atlantis is the earthquake, it is the earth that remains when the world is shaken.

When the sea falls and all the land connects.

Global warming scenarios predict that whether we want to see it or not, Atlantis will 'rise' again. The sea level will rise, the high places of the land will become atolls, archipelagoes. Ponape is Atlantis? Hawai'i? Do we have to wait till then?

It has never disappeared. It has only been lost. To be lost, you need a loser. We are the losers. Now to turn finders, finders keepers we sang when we were children sang Robert Duncan, purest of all modern Atlantean poets.

With finding in mind, where shall we look for the seven terraced city? Seven hills of eternal Rome? Terraces of Cambaluc, Peking, the wide-eyed great stupa of Bodnath, the everlasting Bodh Gaya? Borobudur?

Every city I think has a piece of Atlantis. Atlantis really means city, as human refuge from the condition of being hunters, or pastoralists, or agriculturalists — something else for human energy to be busy with, the city work, a different kind of work, the work of else. The one we can only accomplish with one another. We are the material.

Every city has Atlantis the way every Catholic altar is supposed to have embedded in it a piece of the True Cross.

2004

HUDSON VALLEY SOWS THE SEEDS OF TOMORROW'S UTOPIA

Because the land was beautiful, the people who came here slowly learned gentleness & the arts of peace. Because the land was secret — an arm of the distant ocean reaching up between cliffs and highlands, woods and meadows 150 miles into the heart of the country — it became a place of thoughtfulness and reflection.

Valleys are good places to think. You can't see very far except up or down the valley, so you have to think, triangulate from where you are.

At the dawn of the new millennium, in the middle of all the anxieties about technology and cults and Armageddon, a simpler and most beautiful thing was happening. The animals were coming back. One day a woman heard a raven croak on her pine tree — within a year, the birds had taken up the woods they had left 100 years before.

Soon the bears came back from the distant Poconos and the Shawangunks and swam across the river to fossick in the back yards of Poughkeepsie ranch houses and Barrytown mansions. Wild turkeys had come down from the western hills, and the deer were always flourishing. And one night a man coming out of his driveway saw a wolf looking at him with mild golden eyes, the thick tail hung down, the whole animal looking at him unafraid.

It was happening: the great gentleness that, two centuries before, had been foreseen by Edward Hicks in his painting, "The Peaceable Kingdom."

We were part of it. More accurately, it was us. We ourselves were the place to which the kindliness and truth of the world had to come. The valley began to fill up with people who came to study the arts of peace.

Great river of learning

By the middle of the 21st century, the Hudson had become the great river of learning, and people sometimes called it The Mother of Beauty. Traditional liberal arts colleges flourished and experimented, always trying to involve students in actual productive work in the arts & scholarship and science.

Charter schools worked with public schools, and more money began to be spent on libraries and laboratories than on yellow buses. Parents started to take their children to school — a kind of ritual investment in the child's learning day.

By the end of the first quarter of the 21st century, a child expected the parents to discuss the day's schoolwork every evening. Preserving a continuity between the classroom and the home was the best way of strengthening the educational system.

New museums began to open, and conservatories; performing arts centers developed in every township. Humanistic institutes and religious seminaries, hospices, retreat houses & workshops in all the many lineages of spiritual practice and art flourished in the valley.

People who came here, and more and more kept coming, were moved by the wonders of technology and the beauty of the natural world, orchards & mountains, forest and escarpment, the little kills and the great broad river. They wanted the best of both worlds — silicon and serenity, the computer and the waterfall.

They felt a natural caution about new technology. They wanted to keep technology on our side. More and more people began to work with themselves, their families, their communities, following the guidelines of ancient traditions of knowing one's own mind and new technologies of knowing the world. Make technology help the decent, creative life — not replace our lives with marketed fun.

This was the problem: Technology back in the beginning of the new century was being used to enslave the mind of Americans through the sinister connection between pleasure and money. The manipulators of technology tried to sell every species of amusement or delight as a commodity — a kind of pay-per-feeling.

But we in the valley learned to discover in spiritual practice and family ceremony and making art some powerful counterforces to the packaged entertainment that was threatening our country with passivity and bemused torpor. We sought and found a cure for the slave mentality that the entertainment industry constantly tried to impose on the Americans. Our valley became a refuge from the obvious and banal.

It was in this valley that Americans first drew up the lines of the great Culture Wars. Our teachers — humanists, artists, priests, lamas, rabbis, doctors — taught us that we are the masters of our own bodies and our own time.

Rights of pleasure

How dare the corporations try to sell us our own feelings, our own emotions — pleasure is our birthright. Don't Pay for Pleasure is still a potent slogan; don't let them charge you for your own perceptions, your own mind.

The gentleness of the land taught us peacefulness, & in that gentleness compassion could grow. As we turned more and more away from mediated pleasures and mortgaged mind, we began to learn a thoughtfulness, even a tenderness about our own lives — & then slowly, gently then about the lives of other people.

Selfish second-homers began to notice human misery beyond their acreage and began to try to do something about it. Not just by arrogant philanthropy & feel-good gestures, but by the kind of spiritual renewal by which we study our own nature, and from it learn how to help others.

Old wisdom reborn

The valley became rich with Buddhist monasteries and Sufi mystics and Christian retreats and institutes that studied new sciences and ancient wisdom. At first, people shopped around, as they always like to do, for comfortable insights. They learned caution: There were spiritual entrepreneurs who tried to sell them their minds or their postures or their breath.

More and more people began to work with themselves, their families, their communities, following the guidelines of ancient traditions, of knowing one's own mind, and new technologies of knowing the world.

Our valley's destiny brought it all the tools we needed, the unique blend of immigration and ancient settlement, the high-tech service industries, the highly educated population, the useful proximity to the southern metropolis, the energy of natural beauty itself. All these factors combined to make this the place of transformation.

The peace of meditation, and full employment, and sustainable agriculture, and affordable housing, and care of the elderly, and developing rich contexts of society and art for young people to grow up in: All these turned out to be not separate problems but a single problem, the problem of caring about other people, looking into one's own heart & finding the world.

(*Poughkeepsie Journal*, 28 June 2009)

THREADS 7 : ROBERT SAYS

I don't remember the early issues of Trobar *so well. I don't remember any kind of strong or clear or even any in most cases theoretical or historical behavior going on in the magazine. I know one of them has "Notes on the Poetry of Deep Image" and Rothenberg's response. Though we had lots of theoretical concerns and fixes, I don't think a lot got into the actual magazine. Probably because in those days it was so hard to do such a magazine. The money, the running around the city to get printers and all the rest of it. I think, too, while we had polemic concerns, it wasn't yet clear to me how important it is to foreground the polemic in a theoretical position. Perhaps, it wasn't as important to me then as it certainly seems to me now.*

in conversation with Dennis Barone [early 1980s]

A huge part of the success of Allen's anthology was that it had the theoretical statements. The most exciting of course was Olson's. Duncan's was yes and no. Leroi Jones's was very exciting. Some were not just making theoretical statements about poetry. Duncan, Olson, and Spicer were doing that. The others were wonderfully capable of making statements about a stance *towards poetry, a stance towards reality, & a poet's stance towards reality. I feel, by the way, that it would not withdraw time from me. It doesn't take any longer to write criticism than it does to write a story about girls or something. I write a lot of fiction, but I haven't published much of it. It's not part of my public image I want to advance. Criticism I find does something to my mind. It's ungenerous. Every now and then I can write criticism if it seems to me exactly generous and specific and donated. Giving something to the world, etc. I was able to write a long, long review of Zukofsky, some 35 pages on "A." It was the only major review "A" then had. […] It took me a long time to write it. I wrote a critical tribute to Ted Enslin. Yet, it is very rare that the critical thing seems to me to be possible for me without misusing a part of my mind that I pay for misusing. If I were to get involved with hasty book reviews then I'd be lost.*

in conversation with Dennis Barone [early 1980s]

Let me say, just honestly, lest they think I'm an enemy of philosophy, that I'm an enemy of philosophy when it isn't poetry. I think the great philosophers of modern times — and I'm going back as far as Nietzsche — the great philosophers are essentially poets. In our own day, for example in France, though I think there are some wonderful French poets of the present time, most of the great French poets have chosen prose or apothegm as their means. I think of Lacan and Derrida and Barthes as poets. Blanchot is a poet. It's hard to think of them as prose writers even though it looks like prose from across the room. Heidegger is a great poet, I mean as great as almost any German poet I can think of, certainly as great as Celan, though a different man and a different being. The philosophy I tend to argue against is that which purports to talk about philosophy without actually doing it. The doing of philosophy is a great and wonderful thing. […] That's what philosophy is all along, it's language. Like Ezra Pound used to say, that when poetry forgets that it began as song, it gets dead. When philosophy forgets that it began as language, it gets dead. When it thinks it is talking about something outside itself, it becomes almost impenetrably alien to human use.

in conversation with Leonard Schwartz (2005)

Learn languages — not for high literary purposes (like reading Aeschylus in the original — though that is very great) but just to shake up your own language mind: so that. So that every speaking moment is a re-negotiation of space and terms between you and your "native language." Learn languages for the sake of confusion. For the sake of the other music. The danger of this — or any method — is fluency. Learn to stammer. Creeley revived/ revised American lyric poetry by learning to stammer. Get the syntax right and the words fall into place by themselves. Grammar is where the meaning means.

in conversation with Simone dos Anjos & Pietro Aman (2006)

What I'm trying to say is something like this: As I grew into writing, I began to understand what I could do and what I had to do: I had to write each day as if it were the last as well it might have been — and might be. And this writing was not to be the mere accumulation of artifact and commodity — the world does not lack for pieces of paper with puzzling inscriptions. What I had to write is what I understand: that there are all the human domains within the single faculty I speak of, that language is adequate to reach out. That I can say. (The earliest novel project I had, in college, was to be called The Moment of Saying. *The title meant both time and momentum, and understood, or confused, the saying with the said, the woman with the word. The woman is the word.) It took me years to learn that what-I-say is not the language of "I" but the language of language. [...]*

I mean [language] in a more or less economical, anthropological, or human sense. Language is the ocean in which humans swim. It is the relationship between us, whether close or far, and it is the air we breathe that keeps the living in touch with the dead. Nothing is lost. It is the ground we move on, the contour map by which even our desires are inflected, shaped, expressed. Sea, air, land: Language is all. By experimental operations conducted in language — i.e., poems — we have some hope of operating on the world that language makes by describing. Here the political hope and the spiritual hope of poetry become one. Language is aspiration.

in conversation with Bradford Morrow (1989)

7.
A BOOK WITH & AGAINST THEORY

SOME THOUGHTS CONCERNING DIE DICHTEREI DES OBJEKTS

```
World about us,things,boxes,mountains,springs.
Possessors,ancestors and fathers to us,
Whence we are.We are,they are,but theirs
Is the existence,that is THEY ARE.
Why are they not poems? Poems are from
Us,about us,for us.Therefore they are not
In OUR POETRY,which is:aesthetician:ART,
ARTificial ARTifact of ARTisans.
They do not have poems,there is to them
NO need of poems.For us need.
In our need we build boxes mountains springs
for OURSELVES:all bad in us is bad in them,
all good good.In consequence:
We build,we have,we are:three of verbs
& many nouns will form the poem of
The Thing,in which we will be slaves
Not longer to what it is that in us is
Bad,downbuilding,unhaving.
```

LECTURE ON IDENTITY

1. I propose the study of *phenomenal identity*
   a. no chance beyond the moon
   b. according to Kerenyi, *mundus* ('world') is not necessarily cognate with *mundus*, the ditch around the paradigmatic sacred (urban) enclosure; the latter perhaps of Etruscan origin.
2. & language moves on its way
3. but (= &) falls back also upon itself
   a. not only through antiquarian revivalism
   b. e.g., /æ/ in english, phonemic in old english, phonemic in modern, apparently absent thruout the middle english period & early modern english; not to say that the use of the *phōnē* is the same.
   c. not a revival of the old sound of words, but the language, thru breaking & monophthonization, thru vowel shifts &c., rediscovering the particularity of that *sound* in, e.g., American english
      ci. usage & pattern determine our speech as american
      cii. anagnorisis determines our speech as english
4. /æ/
   is mystically the central *phōnē* of our speech system; its typical *phōnē*;
   a. a single vowel
      a.1 possessed of no consistent orthographic symbol in our alphabet
      (*a* indicating many other *phōnēi* as well)
      a.2 represented even in IPA as digraph
5. By the way, is essence for the sake of the function?
6. It is foolish to dismiss apparent identity of words because their 'etyms' are seemingly different.
7. As with words, so also with all apparent identity.

[RK archives, undated early text]

PRYNNE PICKS

It's these injections I'm having
some sort of otherness in muscle
now in arm & now in butt
                                  it makes
me thin sad & most unwise
                                  it makes
a crystallized extract of uncertain origin
(alligator urine like or not)
merge with my meaning. Lo! a crystal
Im Kristall dein Fall!
                              there is a magic
book foretells it all,
Pokorny, Etymologisches Woerterbuch
der indogermanischen Sprachen,
where all the words
recede to their most attenuated
(most capacious) ascendant
or that root no-root
highest common denominator
of our simple words,
a language never spoke & hence
no language:
                      no-root of no-language
uidh m-, audh m-, tekt- m-
            in diour mama mushk
except a man be born again of your spirit
he shall not have life in him

                                  [RK archives, undated early text]

7 · A BOOK WITH & AGAINST THEORY

CARLOS CASTANEDA, *THE TEACHINGS OF DON JUAN: A YAQUI WAY OF KNOWLEDGE*

re Don Juan, book of Don Juan)
         a keeping alive of that word,
  knowledge

    (gnosis)

for which a man has to fight

  in him
      (self) to get, revealed.
             I think this book
will be the testament for the next say decade, will be
the most 'authentic' thing the public be allowed to hear
(but I ask if we do hear it,
          we are given the beautiful exactness
& taut morality of don Juan,
         but are we given the *process*
       of experienced reality?
(not the big "experiences" alone but the river of circumstance
  whole, intact, moving)
        ?
         why does Castaneda hide
     each thing & give us only some things?
(not to pick on the man, who has already confessed himself a
failure at the thing the book is about doing — he *does* give us
a book of great value

  & we are given the shadow of a beautiful ethic
(a shadow because Ethics = what you *do*
          & we are not
shown all
or even most of what don Juan does,
        ((Understand I am
  talking

       abt a book, Gulliver in Yaquiland, teller always between us &
the road of knowledge, a book which is never transparent
however much we'd want that, a book particular to
certain experiences but not transparent to them))

                                                    & as
usual,
everybody will hold the book in hand & say, Tell us what to do

(but certain paths are erased from the landscape, certain in-
gestions ruled out, from the start
                        as being easy
                    thus not taking the whole
                        corazon
                    of a man who will walk them)
Don Juan tells it from the start: knowledge is hard to get,
                knowledge is hard.
                                        don Juan does not
commend the easy/
comes now to re/mind
                    of the perennial valor
                of inner experience (experience)
taken seriously,   taken onward,   as path.
                                        Do it yourself.
You cant go there without going there.

                                    (*Caterpillar* #7, 1969)

A MEDITATION ON HERACLITUS

A work true to its maker's life?
Am I the one?
One who made?
Is the world-as-it-is true to the
human mind?
Alam al-mithal?
Only in the spiritual world is there a
harmony of experience with intention?

Not to have to know what I mean,
but what *I say* means.
And what *what I say* means.
Beyond this work
        lies an austere landscape of
not saying anything at all
unless the life itself, the First Life,
is a form of saying.
A form of speech.

Ah well, the wet boat,
the skirts of Heraclitus raised
to keep at least the garment
of his sense
        out of the common moisture
it behooves us to walk through —

is that a kin
or clutch enough
        for your experience, your
Erlebnis?
The way through the woods has little
to do with trees,
        which is why all metaphor
stinks under its carapace,
corrupteth the striving Wit
into mere resemblances,

i.e., the boat died.
(Egypt called it.) (i.e., differently, the
nave or vessel
        parted its wholeness,
                      i.e., Latin,
the boat broke
        (as a lamp cracks, William,
or as a delicate lekythos
breaks its neck
        & we are served
        if we are served
        by only the memory
of that commodity.)

Get down to it:
        what did the boat do?

The boat blinked in the lightning,
the boat had buttocks in it,
soft ones, & gold eyes
cruel a little from so many sunrises

(so many surmises?
Not good for a girl to guess
it was a gull over the short sea,
it was a boat
over the sun)
        over our surmises
this craft passes
& the waves are true to her
if not good,
        & the wood
whereof she floats
is from a high mountain
& her mast
        is everywhere —
                meaning Nowhere?

meaning beyond our surmises,
arrivals,
      she is, a boat is a she,
she is strung from the sky)
              masted everywhere,
she does not founder
because her nature
is the nature of the
sea she plows.

      Who is her master?
No man in her story,
what's a man do?
the mast is her master
            &, the she he plows
is master (mistress) of his instrument.
One sex! Then none!
And the waves relent not of the ship,
& the ship knows herself best
in the way she goes.
          Perhaps she comes.
Perhaps the philosopher said:
                "If I must,
I must.
    I have let the water
run between my toes
& curl
      up to my metatarsals —
that is the Road of Experience.
But I have held my garment's hem
well over the surf —
        when my wet
footprints dry out,
        my robe will still be clean
& nothing in me or outside
will show I passed this way."

                        (*Truck* #15, 1975)

FROM *TEXTS*: 16 [READING HEIDEGGER]

PART ONE

"We are who we are by pointing in that direction…" [9]
Fedeli d'amore, we turn
towards what has "turned away from us
since the beginning,"
we are in love with that Absence, *ausencia*;
a courtly love.
        "Man is the pointer." [9]

Midnight Easter. 30° strong wind. Squall. Walked out on the porch lured by what Helen had said, about how spooky it was out. Hours back. And now I stepped out and found a big gibbous moon just rising through bony trees — just after I'd said to myself how dark it was. Thousand things moving in the night, rustle close and far — is that the strangeness, leaves turning in no wind?

When I turn & point myself. When I turn.
Where in the world
where the loveliness of words,
                  their business in society
    & their old homes
across all-too-romantic oceans
yet I revisit still, warmth of their *focus*
        to bring down
the light world & the glad hand into the good word.
That we speak.
That if we talk long enough
everything will get said. If we
talk, that is,
until the tape
reaches the sun
& notified by chromosphere
yields up its message once for all.
वदामि vadāmi, I am speaking, will be
a little while yet,

7 · A BOOK WITH & AGAINST THEORY

have always been. Jívāmi, I live; vadāmi, I speak;
शसामि çansāmi, I praise.
Lesson One in being about to be always speaking.

"Or do we imagine   that a man could even in small ways   [31]
encounter the essence of truth, the essence of beauty, the
essence of grace — without danger?"
And opinions? Opinions are commodities
        they barter
     in meaningless battle, contestants, who?
But "what becomes of the tree in bloom? What becomes of the
meadow?
          What becomes of the man — not of the brain but of
the man who may die under our hands tomorrow and be lost to us,
and who at one time came to our encounter?"   [42]

      A sight
      we came
      he comes &
      speaks
"I will go on talking forever," said Creeley.
Quick, quick as becoming
      I will go on
becoming   my talk
       becomes & goes & comes.
What happens to the man?
The man becomes.
What happens to the tree? The tree
     is lost in the panoply of his becoming,
    where the woman also so long wanders,
a trick or treat of the mind,
       girlfriend along for the ride.
"We must stay with the question," says
Heidegger at sunset on the ruined day.

What have I become?
       Depression, of seed, all that
"sperm & sun" stuff

                        undone. I am tired,
    tired of I
    am tired of

            & always she is, is.
    Before whom I passed,
                humiliated as before a flowering tree
    to stand in question.
    To come into question & be lost,
    there, in the size of that room,
    carved faces looking down from the coffered ceiling
    at Wawel castle,
    chamber of the question these judges
    wait all their afterlives to decide.
    And by resolving make empty, confuse,
    make trivial
                what had mattered, the doubt
    I did allow to bring me.
    It was a real question, needed no answer,
    needed only to impel me here.
    Here. Where 'a tree in bloom,' for instance
    those small willows by the parking lot
    which diffuse such lightness these days, these
    questions. So should the months be named,
    & what moon measures
    are modes of questioning.
    Moods of the Lady.
    Days by day. "Under the Heads"
    that room is called
    in Cracow of the necromancers,
    the faces look down
                withered old boys
    lazily spitting in the stream of our lives.

The text is constantly corrected by what I read. Text heals text, but the weaving takes my hands, or, beyond any metaphor, the roof of my mouth to shape sounds off, declare the text. And what I declare becomes, public, subject to the correction of the book. The book is called 'the world' or 'the world as read,' or 'I read.' Here specifically the book is called *What is Called Thinking?*, a translation by Wieck & Gray of Martin Heidegger's *Was heisst Denken?*, 1954. Text upon text. The text corrects my going. I am conscious of the fact that 'correct' may mean 'deflect,' 'foil,' 'silence.' After all, on Helen's piano stands the score of Mompou's *Musica callada*, silenced music, no less acoustic for its suppression. *Mal tu par l'encre meme*, says Mallarmé in one of the finest phrases in the world. *Ill-silenced by the ink itself.* Or should I read: *by the very ink?* The text amends itself. Textum: what is woven Textum: what is read. Constantly one is reading. And when one begins reading, then one is especially conscious of the text, as for example when the text presents itself under the discrete guise of a book, even a book in one's own language. Yet text runs back far before book. Text is dead leaves & twigs & broken branches & spruce needles drowned on the porch-roof today, & from such presentiments of *Ur-schrift* we once learned letters. And the pale sky we learned to spell, blanker than any Malevich, is text, too, and not simple. The text amends itself and the words go on. I pick up the book and go on:

"The multiplicity of possible interpretations does not discredit the strictness of the thought-content. For all true thought remains open to more than one interpretation — and this by reason of its nature. Nor is this multiplicity of possible interpretations merely the residue of a still unachieved formal-logical univocity which we properly ought to strive for but did not attain. Rather, multiplicity of meanings is the element in which all thought must move in order to be strict thought. To use an image: to a fish..." [71]

    & there he leads me
    like some biblic pastor
    to an image.
Thought leads to an image?
His thought
    twists, leads him,
thought leads to a fish.

    "the depths and expanses of its waters, the current and quiet pools, warm and cold layers are the element of its

multiple mobility,"
     its meanings are its movements
       & its resting still.
From rock learn to move.
It steadies to go.
'To use an image' the fish
  poised still
  as if it had grown there
  an almost opaque crystal
  held
    in a thick apparency.
Means to stand still
but not stand,
    means to move
     & only later, later
move you.
    This old rose-bush here
is two months from flowering,
& when it does, holds
fleshy blossoms curtly,
  a week or so
  until a rain.
A rain like this, started before dawn
  & drowned the front & back fields,
midafternoon comes down,
  the gleam,   the sheen.

But Nietzsche says "the last men blink." "What does that mean?" asks Heidegger. "Blink is related to Middle English *blenchen,* which means deceive, and to *blenken, blinken,* which means gleam or glitter. To blink — that means to play up and set up a glittering deception which is then agreed upon as true and valid — with the mutual tacit understanding not to question the set-up."   [74]

Blink, automatic
shut an eye
    to ward off brightness or to hide
from the gleaming vision

       that opens, oh first and mightily through *colors,*
past the opaque world.
       Consensus.
They blink consensus.
The root
    is no root, that earth
bears nothing but a sweet lie
till the pain begins. And then
How to color the root-forms of consciousness
shown as posed stars & starlets drumming a wheel,
ghost-world, old blue
    tree grown down to us from a
    half-heard message in a garden,
the word
overheard.

(Now I should be thinking of 'revenge,' the "will's revulsion" against the world and its passing away, the gnostic rosary of pains abstained. To turn against the world is the same as turning towards the world. Before one, the panoply of anguishes, necessities, immense delights. One decides: I will, and takes the world. But never the world as it is. Only the world as if. One says, I will, I will take the world. But I will leave the pain. (Or, says the Denyer, I will leave the pleasure.) And there is no world as is. No *tel quel.* We discover thus that the world is an enterprise such that any attitude towards it serves to embrace it.

Any posture at all accepts the world.
Any place to stand is place.
for that man be delivered from revenge
Heidegger quotes from Nietzsche
whose name the children hear as Nature
so that their Nature
forbids revenge;
    they will turn
in the world & trope like honeysuckle,
turn & sing like morning glory, wake
& turn & wrestle like the vine.
"man suddenly became unrestful because he had no more time.

That moment is the beginning of the modern age." [101]
But recurrence. Eternal Recurrence,
what is it but the shadow
time casts on eternity?
What is it but a gorgeous mistake
transposed from the text to the textless Utmost out *there*,
eternal?

(It is only on page 110, last paragraph of the first part, that Heidegger
glosses thinking as: "relatedness to Being.")

[...]

PART THREE

"By naming, we call on what is present to arrive." [120]
How can we be anywhere
by being ourselves here?
And at last all unexpectedly
we have come to the foot of our Tower.
A tower shaped like us too, shaped
of the space between us
& grown a lifesize high.
      Thought
carved its complexity
out of the simple air & now
my love we can walk in
& fumble with the new-old stairs
twisting counterclockwise towards a talking heaven.
This tower reaches down to us
to be imagined into place,
as between close-set houses, city,
air moves quick, wind pulse
or what feels like it
     though no branch moves.
Then it arrives & is a tower,
of the sort that talked to Psyche,
comes to talk to me, names us its own
who so quietly, like April early daffodils are
shy in the gateway, green but not yet gone In.

7 · A BOOK WITH & AGAINST THEORY

"Calling offers an abode" [124]
who dares live in?
           At the top of the pen
     a sort of ruby, small
focused with liquid light it seemed.
Can I write with that?
Where is all this writing leading?
Where is all this leading
that is writing?
        This writing that is reading?
I for instance find it difficult to distinguish reading from writing;
the distinction is elusive, subtler than our verbs allow, 'middle.'
Read is 'active' — write is 'middle' of some ultimately human verb.
And 'passive'? To be read. Do you read me? How does it read?
How can I turn it round? Till I was fifteen years old I read, thereafter began to write. More and more what is read (what I read)
becomes or is exactly a provocation to write, a complex *protasis* to
which I must in every case fit a conclusion.
                         If I pick a book up do I
read it? If I read it now and it was written then, where is the text? Is
a book (as adolescents are said to believe) no more than a talisman
in hand to help dreaming, to better fantasy? If the reader decides
whether that 'better' is verb or adjective, isn't he the writer?

There is a word that answers for itself.
There is a word past my decision.

"it calls even if it makes no sound" [124]
the sound of order
shaping outside towards spring,
a noble wind down from Orteora,
passions of a region, *altitudo!*
where does it call?
"If there can be no knowledge here, then in what way is our nature revealed to us? Perhaps in just this way, and only in this way, that we are
called upon to think?" Then "What is it that calls on us to think? We
find that we ourselves are put in question, this question, as soon as we
truly ask it, not just rattle it off." [125]

But to draw back from that haunted question
& still see, still go on seeing, the beautiful women move
from shadow to shadow among the trees, the upright trees
at the end of winter when nothing shows
of what they will become except these women moving,
their bodies urgent with becoming.
The question that faces me is
which way
        is ever that,
      which ever
runs to this, runs home to this, dazzles
the way a bottle, broken, a thing in the sun.
So a prior question had to be faced: why
from the orders of discourse Heidegger summons
was it necessary for me to beat a retreat,
into the familiar sensate boscage of some girls, shadows among
shadows moving?
                Why does it turn? Why turn?
The only answer I had at the moment lay open to hand,
the 1849 translation I had just bought from Mario for a dollar
of the memoirs of Chateaubriand
to find that self-conscious self-honestly swaggering
Heros
becalmed in a clothless ship off the Coast of America.
He sees the sun set through the bare rigging
& in that religious glow "saw
an unknown woman and the miracles of her smile; the beauties
of heaven seemed to me to spring from her breath; I would have
sold eternity for one of her caresses. I figured to myself that her
heart was beating behind this veil of the universe which concealed
her from my eyes. Oh! Why was it not in my power to rend this
curtain?"
      Saw not the sun but the
women behind the sun, behind the seen or any
seen thing, saw
the woman behind the question.
To face the question is to face the woman.

7 · A BOOK WITH & AGAINST THEORY

To face the question is to confront the world,
"worldliness of the text." [Edward Said]
       The woman
is circumstance. Ka'ba. He saw
"through the mist of the cordage in boundless space"
the woman masked by the setting sun.
That is to say he is a romantic. He begs the question
to open, begs the woman
to appear,
    to come down & embrace him, oceaning her long
hair around his sumptuous confusions
to bury in her whatever of him cannot face the question.
However tenderly she asks.
       Sunset soon.
Sunset in a book, & star-rise
"I could never satisfy my desire of looking at Venus, whose rays
enveloped me like the hairs of my sylphide long ago."
    Like hairs ago
    around now,
       swart
clouds of this sunset coming close.
      A dark
pocket full of wind.
"What we encounter at first is never what is near, but always only
what is common." [129]
Turn in or out, the close
has a habit of betrayal, of
being *far* suddenly, an eye
    looks back in from somewhere full of lust
but also dust.
    The mediator
lingers too long at some gangway —
there is a door at the end of the hall, let him find it, hurry,
become unspeakably sure & jostle
the flock of sparrows that settled here this season,
whirring their not too effectual
wings through the words.

                              Take off, it's mine!
            he cries & the plane
lurches across the Missouri field
& flies all four of us into Kansas, a dip
of wings to show the city
back there giddy on horizon, a gulp.
The whole flight the bulk & lights
of Mount Oread ahead of us,
                           a lump of meaning on the plain.
Two young women, one older, one me,
pharisee hastening to judgment,
have I lived by the book I speak?
I lived. The plane came in sweetly, slowly —
the hardest part was scrambling down the wing.
The stale eye
could never see this,
we are too beautiful for its dust.
And Sekkei's Daruma back there in Kansas City,   [Bodhidharma]
the big eyes never closed
because he has found inside outside
a perpetual current of renewal, λο'υεται   [louetai]
he washes himself clean,
bathes in ocean,
                  his limbs are almost language
& he seldom sleeps?
                  Secure on land! Madness
to find safe
down here where wars begin,
Quantrell comes to town.
                    The clouds do not bleed.
"As hearers, we abide in the sphere of what is spoken, where the
voice of what is said rings without sound."   [130]
Where can I hear you
where the overquick responses do not quell?
I want to know you in time,
not those random
apparitions, mordant street — corners, sideviews in mind.

And when you told me I was sad
did you mean you love me? Casting
the unsounded voice of your nature upon me,
a touch, one of your touches?
We are also
among the angels,
chosen, needing this war to enforce
the unchanged meaning of our once-for-ever act —
the shadow of which
is Time
when all the things that began were beginning.
We came before. I knew your face
by your thighs. The cause
is to feel how soft you are where my fingers
touch you. Do they
make you soft?
Can one say that the wind ever begins?
Oh the permission, the sweet endless morning
to wake in as if itself were a flower & after
yesterday's rain almost all the trees are telling
but the grass is louder, color
runs up from the earth
into "the green sky,"   [Rumî]
that center of the spectrum, vivid shapely light,
shalom of green. Somewheres the road has dried.
Heidegger will not let us draw
from this innocent pastoral environment, will not let us hearken to
words out of the air, out of the mouth
of how they seem at first to mean.
To find a word, find a word. Take
word from word & swallow the core.
But the meaning does not dwell
in the original, hypothetical, etymon,
but in the changes, the distances
the word brings forward to our meeting.
Not meaning is immanent in it but uses, accommodations, compromises,
harangues, sad light at evening when the lovers
have not been clear.

What do I tell when I tell the truth?
Sad light on a mossy door, boat house, lake of departures,
where love itself is exile from the self?
Where sorrow turns into a strange joy, birds in the leaves?
What will a word tell me of that?

Then Heidegger glosses [140] 'Memory' as *devotion*. Memory "initially did not at all mean the power to recall. The word designates the whole disposition in the sense of a steadfast intimate concentration upon the things that essentially speak to us in every thoughtful meditation. Originally, 'memory' means as much as devotion: a constant, concentrated abiding with something." [140]
And devotion is to use up utterly, that there be
no crumb of self left
untransformed, nothing left, nothing
merely remembered.
                It all goes
into the fire of this hour Memory,
is it to be now? Memory, now?
The world is never more vivid than those times I look at it with
yearning for itself just as it is.
                    Nostalgia for now.
                              True memory:
being utterly mindful, conscious of this as-is.
And I give *thanc* at last for being
alive at last & giving thanks,
                      & thanking Give
who gets me to dislodge
the dull stones of inutile possession. To turn
& give thanks to *thanc,*
                mind's forethoughtfulness or swarm
of presence, sent
            to breathe an atmosphere onto this globe,
the eye I see to thank you with.
To think is thank.
Thanc, "the original nature of memory: the gathering of the constant intention of everything that the heart holds in present being." [141]

7 · A BOOK WITH & AGAINST THEORY

Thank whom but the day,
                this quiet so cool when so fresh
as evening was, the street is still not dark?
Nothing only remembered.
"The supreme thanks, then, would be thinking?"   [143]

I remember the drive down
Figueroa to the city,
the little busy streets
along the ultimate neighborhood —
And the neighbors
arrogant
conceive
a kingdom built out of gypsum
finger touch
gouge soft
— a feeling in the *mind*
rebels against these blank
fondlings
who share their soft nothingness.
Be with the angry earth,
coal measures of Kansas
stretching south, a name
to put an end to them
or yearn out of the broken earth
a long curious carbon questioning
that knows its mind across the world
it burns to become, its mind is *diamond*.
And diamond tells me
of the sky I'll turn to
& my inhabitants
clear of disorder. Not ordered.
Known in place,
which is the only.
"For in giving thanks, the heart in thought recalls where it remains
    gathered and concentrated, because that is where it belongs."   [145]
Strum on the heart

to be thankful
as a limb   [*melos*]
is thankful,
dance, strut.
A musical lyre, an
harp.
    David.
        Who is the never
repressed spirit of holy play.
Playing around with his words
No psalm is solemn,   [see
              twist,   Rosen-
lord of song *&* dance,   berg's
lord of beating around the bush,   translations]
strutting,
      you bright Never!
The love
outward
that is Grace
compels
me to yield
an animate text:
"Language is not a tool … Language is not this and that, is not also
something else besides itself. Language is language. Statements of this
kind have the property that they say nothing and yet bind thinking to
its subject matter with supreme conclusiveness."   [153]
Did you wait for me to speak,
to say something while the cool, almost grey day
went down over Metambesen?
Did I quote another page, just one more
one more & then was quiet? Was I?
Is this question now
a question?
The initiation you affect to feel
is where you are pregnant with the answer
Desire?
      Desire is — question

7 · A BOOK WITH & AGAINST THEORY

or to slay
        a man's ancestors,
put him right in the middle of his need.
"As διαλέγεσαι, the λέγειν or proposition proceeds back and forth for itself within its own domain, goes through it, and so covers it to the end. Thought now is dialectical."   [156-7]
And so we run
not between extremes
(as it looks to the *misnagdim*)
but through & through,
the way a sword
interrogates its target —
never as easy as one thing at a time.
"one thing and one thing only matters with this question: to make the question problematical."   [159]
                So I go back through his book,
the book, to find the earlier declaration:

"we find . . . that not a single one of Plato's dialogues arrives at a palpable, unequivocal result which sound common sense could, as the saying goes, hold on to. As if sound common sense — the last resort of those who are by nature envious of thinking — as if this common sense whose soundness lies in its immunity to any problematic, had ever caught on to anything at the source, had ever thought through anything from its source!"   [71-72]

The only value
is to make difficult.
Satan
simplifies.

As I read the Heidegger text ("The more completely our thinking regards itself merely in terms of its own comparative written history . . . the more decisively it will petrify in fatelessness")   [166]
my head falls forward & I almost sleep, in mid-air sleep, & to this sudden upright coma a dream comes, like this: I am on horseback, going SSE down the flanks of the Elburz Mountains. My guide or dragoman's behind me, & he wants to drift westward back to a hamlet he can reach

490

by nightfall. I keep trying to dissuade him, for the sake of the journey, but at length I have to leave him to make his own decision. I ride on downhill, SSW, perhaps alone.
Where do I ride,
   or to what wonder come,
      a passage of the eye *alone*
         shaded in the dwindling daylight,
            7:13 under the trees' new leaves.
Then on page 174 Heidegger catches up with my unintended reverie: "Every human attitude to something, every human stand in this or that sphere of beings, would rush away resistlessly into the void if the 'is' did not *speak*."
               The horseman I was had been hurrying down the Persian mountains, down to a plain or valley will take him west to Tehran and Asia Major. Down there, *l'Asie,* a gulf, a void, where *is* has veered off to town, back with people, with humanity, leaving me in this thoughtless cool downhill solitude.
Tune
of the obvious
"a weightiness ... we can hardly ever weigh,"   [174]
in the is,
      tune
of is
    this is I say it,
say it *&* think it, λέγειν τε νοεῖν τε
turned to be being.
             I wait.
      The ride I rode
accuses me downhill, accuse me south,
     the time
persists to be obvious. Even hear it: why did you leave
that good man,
don't you care
for the substantiality of the world,
the text?
       Is there a tree
to break my fall?

7 · A BOOK WITH & AGAINST THEORY

"Being" "problematic" "ground" of all questions, of any   [179–80]
thing I say at all,
"let our astonishment make us aware."   [183]
Then pause a go
& I walk out
among the musics
where Franz Kamin discourses & conducts
a chapel of musicians in
a gentle swelling limnologic drift.
And Marcia speaks to me of Heidegger,
clearing my text, in the dark,
on the straight path
under the increscent trees: a place
               for this discourse, swings round
plants a condition,
               fruit of the vine.
Can I come back to the text
clear as a cock
at 4 o'clock
promised by the light they swear to?
               Why did this father
               walk the straight track
               before me,
               am I free even yet to walk along the book?
To speak my own breath?
               The words think themselves in place,
     in passage, lure
my breathing to speak them, are lured, rest
on sudden afternoons behind closed lids,
hand on head hand on arm the weight goes down.
The child sleeps.
               Land on,
would the truth be known.
Would the known be true?
I thanked him
after the concert
for the words of it

while the music still
eddied past me,
                    linger of sound.
He helped me know the night.
She helped me ask the question,
                    can the night be known?
It is *that*
before any sophia
came gently from the compassionate half-fallen angels,
that might have come.
Adjust the knob
on this living
microscope,
         εν νω, εν νω ἐχειν
    hold in mind-
             fulness, to keep
in mind.

Λέγειν Heidegger offers, 'letting-lie-before-us,' νοειν, 'taking-to-heart' The definitions begin to assert themselves. Is the act of definition, because it is seeking the limit, a picking up and going, and being gone? I wonder then to what extent the mustard in the jar, lilacs in the plastic bucket, are gone certainly from the world into the likes of us. To savor, to smell. Or to notice the molecular orders of this nearby air and take in. If I eat do I define? Do I set a limit?

    First sin of mindfulness:
to know anything but mind.
                The swelling double-basses in Brahms'
Third, slow movement, I now mistake for a big truck a quarter-mile away, gearing up or down to come near, to be gone.
                                    Alternatives:

(a)   Haze over the moon,
someone screams.
This thing that scares them is their pleasure,
roysterers of a May evening by the stream.
Politics of music.

(b)   Colin Wilson's character
who loved Furtwängler's Second
exactly for its vast
ordinary-denying length.

(c)   I would not like to think it has caught up with me, mood of
tenants of Tudor buildings full of mysterious poetry
written between the dog & the dark.

The room finds space for itself.
The definition shuts the door.

My trouble now with the book is that I know all that. I know all that. Or what I think I know is in fact worn deep into the table on which this new text is trying to write. The words are Heidegger's but beneath them, shading or interrupting or distorting them, is the pattern worn or carved, time out of mind, in the old wood of the rough desk top. The uneasy pen reads the old grooves like a stylus on a record. I know for my own sake, or think I do, or say I do, what Martin Heidegger says now: "when we let the sea lie before us as it lies, we, in λέγειν, are already engaged in keeping in mind and & heart what lies before us."   [209]

All my sense of lying-in-wait *in* the moment-does that falsify Heidegger here? Is it that he is waiting to know, while I'm only waiting to say? He almost, like Sartre, knows too much to be a philosopher. But then he vindicates himself, chides me, realigns the text:
   "And philosophy strays furthest from this hidden question [what is called thinking?] when it is led to think that thinking must begin with doubting."   [211]
Not with doubt.
The move
is gradual
out into the tepid morning
already snarling with sunshine.
One way to accommodate myself to every place.
But we have come to the place called Being.

April–May 1975
(*Sixpack* #9, fall 1975)

TEXTS : 18 [THE BASTILLE]

What was locked in?
Was it a sock with louis-d'ors
was it a sense
         of Order, was it an Order
of frightened men who yet were the Redeemed?
Was it a dream?
         This morning I perched
on the corner of the bed, bent
to slip green socks on, rock green
we said ten years ago to mean a dress
she wore up Mt. Mansfield that looked like it,
cold summer day, the turn
over the mountain or Notch. The Lock.
Where cattle were dragged in
& locked in the caves,
         the smugglers
about the time of that notorious release.
Quatorze Juillet, the prison
gives up its doors in sudden
gasping for the talkative light.
         Ἀποκατάστασις,
a restitution, a reversal
when the stars of heaven run
back & mark time in their places —
         but are they, for their beauty,
Warders,
         king's men of this fortress Earth-Europa,
kinsmen of a False & Lying Root
         that kings up through our
simple earth
         & hogs the lumen?
         We are light.
We are the light
         we are bereft of
when any us gets

                    bogged in the slammer,
                                        lost to an air
only means because we move in it,
                    this droll plural,
                                        this
other, but this better, Lie.
                    APOKATASTASIS the Living
Theater chants, Ginsberg tells them,
                                        Chris Wagstaff
brings me the text: reversing the satanic current
& making it celestial.
                    (Be careful
        it is not Restoration,
                        the king brought back, now Emperor,
the Seventh Devil,
            care)
                            Reverse the satanic flow.
Revising the satanic information
& peeing on the floor.
                        The pee goes yellow & runs
below the door.
                It is a book by Georges Bataille,
    the battle
            is not over,
                    men are in prison for women, women
are trapped in men,
                    the battle
                            drips out under the
door of the vast mahogany armoire
in the polished half-door of which
young William Blake once saw
his ascended brother Robert's face
wishing him the good news,
                    door
behind which in Bataille a blond
timorous girl has taken refuge, there to diddle herself
till in release or revolution the pee

    comes out from under the door
    & washes the monarchy away.
                                We hope. The sexual
  is our hope. Not a chance,
                        is what the Queen said, no chance-o uno
      ("if he be male
                who is my better-father fuller lover,
  just watch him batter down the door.")
                                Apokatastasis, I said to Stein,
    is that word known
  in this collective. Yes, he said, it is astronomy, precessional [sic],
  Olson used it to talk about the stars
                          Come back abruptly
       to their original formations,
   platoons of lumens
            breaking down the door
                              into this dark chateau
  where the imprisoned French, all of them,
  Vercingetorix, Celine, Genet,
                 were lying or are lying,
  with that sleazy double-tending clarity
  locking them in
  by which they see & understand
                        the pee beneath their divan coursing
  as one more irrelevance,
            one more sex-pun of the profiteers.
The king's mind. O I would have
    a kingly mind,
                Königsblau, auswaschbar
    it says on the Pelikan ink,
                   this blue is royal,
        it washes out
or is a washout or
we have longed ago shampooed
                      that man right out of our hair.
Out of the cliché
    where we lingered, with the familiar,

```
                to try to make
                            earth stand
            firm dharma under the weight of sexual want,
                        as if to fuck
                                    did a favor to the earth,
                aligned us
                            with solstice & furrows & raindrops & rose.
But the yucca suds flop back on the parched ground.
The hair still stinks. I stink
under my arms & my neck, my groin & my cock, my ass & my
sock, humanus, I walk along the ground
                                        because I forgot
            there was a better, only other, way to fly,
                                            that I could go
absolute
                And so I stay
with pockets full of robert-d'ors, wire
spectacles around my eyes, my woolen green
political lecherous optimism round my mind,
                                                    waltz
past the prefaces to dungeons, cool my animate fire
over the drafty manhole covers of oubliettes
where my forgotten human brothers
                                rot in anarchist disorder
while I take my comfort
in Love-religion
                    & talk to stars,
                                apokatastasis,
                                                the zodiac
will surely stand arrayed
& I will bide the time
                    till it comes by,
            the universe
                        surely on my side.
If I had a side.
                    If I were anything but a stink
            fingerprint-clear on the stinkometer.
```

A VOICE FULL OF CITIES

                                        The Queen is dead.
The King forgot himself at last.
                              No one in the jails but us,
          no people but people.
                              And it is not
as simple as that.
                    Of course this isn't what I
wanted to say. As usual I wanted to be beautiful
or significant. What I have achieved
is a trickle of girlish pee under an immense door.
I dont blame you for laughing,
                              for turning away
from the messy table where the demonstrator
screwed up the whole process, his own, your own, my
own & the wobbling quavery dough-mass (say)
eebies down flaffling on the floor. Gets pee on it.
Confuses
            where it came from with where to go this August.
Sees the still moving pee-rill & faintly remembers
a time before that river flowed,
                              when the king had a sleepy throne
& all the dim bones
            had marrow in them, fat priests
all looked like me, happy to be different,
                              glad
to have something to say. To eat.
Citoyens! That stream of citrine shameful pee!
All is not well with the Revolution!
True, the shaggy prison
is now Folk Fun Palace of Eighteenth-Century Chambermusic,
Indoor Tennis,
            true my famous
Oration on the Twelfth of Glumaire
is memorized by every schoolboy.
                              In fact they memorize the light
falls in the classroom window,
            they rote it all their lives,

denying all other.
      And the women don't read, the girls
  are taught not to read,
        taught to walk in the woods
where they can do no harm,
         be busy with their little hands.
Citizens! Alert to the energy of disorder here I tell
how Blake's brother Trebor
had learned how to appear
in rare ynâgoham wood
such that his baby brother's face
would be elba ot ees him leef him
& hear what he says. What he says
is The revolution has never taken hold of our senses.
Revolution through sexual freedom takes hold only of our sexual
feeling but not of our senses because our senses are estranged
from sexual feeling,
      because Emotion lives where Motion should.
The revolution has never taken hold of our senses because the girl
still has to creep into the walnut not mahogany closet to
masturbate, because she is ashamed of her body & other peoples'
Body and other peoples' Feeling and In fact she likes being
ashamed she can only turn on by Shame it is the Shame that
Excites her who otherwise would not pee on the floor
              The revolution
has never taken hold of our senses and Until it does it will never
Get beyond our senses It will never get There
            to which we have
been trying since at least the time of Enoch to compel it The
revolution has never taken hold of our senses and until it does our
senses are chained to this attractive but mortal Consensus
              The revolution
has never taken hold of our senses and until it does we are stuck
with our senses and Our senses Dont give a shit about the Men
rotting in the bastilles Our senses couldnt care less Until they wake
up & die
    There will Never be a Revolution there will only be A
passing of crowns from one head to another

                                        There will never be a
revolution till you focus not on poli-eco-sexual-theotic but on the
Whole Consensus
            which is senses Which are Senses which is our senses.
The talking closet closed its habit
& resorbed the polished wooden gleam
back into the sound of the sound,
                            a fold
before sense
Blake paused at the foot of the stairs
& asked It isnt *only* senses, is it?
And heard from the corner, near where the cat
had lately had kittens,
a voice insisting:
Marilyn Chambers is not Lenin. Patty Hearst is not Lenin.
Not even Lenin is Lenin.
                You mean Yaqui don Juan is Lenin? he sneered —
but No,
        there was silence
from the cat & the kittens
as if Great Lenin had not yet been born
& whirling stars & molecules were hurrying book in hand
to take their places for the immense & universal apokatastasis
in time for his leaping down the channel of his mother
into this immortal lake of pee & blood & rock & no more fear.

                                        13–14 July 1975
                                    (*Wch Way* #2², 1976)

7 · A BOOK WITH & AGAINST THEORY

ON MICHEL FOUCAULT
FACULTY SEMINAR RESPONSE TO FREDERIC GRAB

I have been maintaining for several years that the history of literature is the annals not of when texts are written but properly of when texts get read. History similarly is a mix sequence of an array of interpretations. Reading comes before writing, say I, with paradox. So I am happy to welcome tonight not an essay on Foucault, yawn, but a reading of him, which is necessarily a reading with him. Since my personal and professional obligations coincide in the production of poetry (both through my own writing, and thru my lucrative hobby of hypnotizing college students as producers of poems, I approach Fred Grab's remarks with a gladly divided attention. I must speak briefly to each of the two different donations his paper confers on us.

To begin with, I am impressed by and grateful for the initiation he provides into the discourseful world of Michel Foucault. And here let me say that the limber spirit of Grab's style is a nice tribute to Foucault's nimble caperings, that are no less goatish despite sentences of an almost trans-Rhenish, periodic solidity. (Foucault is like a man whistling Brahms — to speak at all is to commit oneself to variation.)

We hear that F wishes to be 'enveloped in words.' Curious that in the very sentences Grab uses to tell us of Saussure's decipherments of Roman anagrams, we are not only reminded that *fou* is embedded in Foucault, the student of madness, but are also delighted to perceive that, by strict saussurian anagram in the first words of 2 successive lines, we can read the name Grab. We are in a dance of meanings, surely, devious, tricking us away from our solemn dependencies on empty traditions & noodle-slack rigors. Both authors are enveloped in words, indeed. Every text wants to come authorless into the world — the text itself is perhaps the first Bloomite, clearing elbow-room for its own coming into being by coaxing its supposed author into exile.

But Grab's strategy is to 'tease' Foucault 'out of the striations of his discourse.' Why? Can we not endure, like trusting readers of poetry, this presumption on the part of a text? Shelley lets Ozymandias speak; can't we let Foucault fall silent? But just there he is the professor, challenged by an agreeableness, does not fall silent, changes masks, keeps talking.

Here Grab is content to work in what seems to me essentially a way of *poiesis*; he seems concerned to invent — in exactly the Latin sense of 'discover' — an idea or ideology behind the text. If the author is silent, the reader speaks. Foucault is being measured now by the "strength" with which Grab responds in *his* reading.

Thus he sets himself, in a fashion of which I am not certain Foucault wd approve, to trace some of the master notions of Foucault's work. In wonderful questions F asks of 'mental illness,' I wonder to what extent F had availed himself of Laing's work in England, Hillman's in Switzerland in depathologizing not only the academic discourse about madness but the madmen themselves.

In the grand procession of the centuries Grab catalogues as clearly, is F too quickly looking for extreme cases, then generalizing them to *zeitgeistliche* imperatives? If I knew Foucault better, would I still feel he scants England explicitly, where at the end of the 17th C John Ray & John Wilkins are already concerned with a *grammar* of similitude, thus bridging via taxonomy orders F cites as diverse? Wilkins developed something very like a 'phonemic' theory of ideas & entities; little known as he is today, & as much as his work merits study, I have to adduce him here lest we confound the centuries with the nations, and find, like Couperin, every nation France. Hahnemann's revival of similitudinous thinking in the 19th C worked seminally in modern medicine & immunology. Newton, our archetypal 17th-C figure, grammaticizes history via quantification: surely a joyous mishmash from the viewpoint of Foucault's schemata. My complaints, though they are scarcely that, I mean only as warnings that Big Pictures are all too often dispelled only by even Bigger Pictures. Or am I asking naïvely that the future influences the past, & that the qualities of F's later work re-infuse his earlier?

The paralysis of language cited from Foucault & Nietzsche Grab resumes this way: 'If God is indeed dead, plainly the Cartesian cogito has perished with Him.' Here I demur. Not the *cogito* but the *ergo* has gone to the wall. The only God who perished is a certain causal Monster at once perfected and detested in the 18th C. This God is the *ergo,* and Nietzsche dutifully, predictably, expels it. Now Foucault should turn to the *sum*, Overdetermined Being itself, ontology grammatically chained to a pronominal 'subject,' to Yeats' 'dying animal.' As if being could 'have' a subject! But it seems rather as if Foucault returns to the safe ground of the *cogito*, terrified as we all are of taking up any kind of serious residence as citizens of a trans- or non-Cartesian universe. Who can blame him? Grab does not.

Well-chronicled by Grab is Foucault's vital battle against 'History of Ideas' as usual, that curious, notorious region (one can't call it a discipline or inquiry) whose natives are busy sacrificing the latter to the former, i.e., slaying the life of ideas on the altar of something they take as history: development, continuity or its spectre Change, tradition. Exciting as such histories (even the honest/humble ones might take the curse off the topic) are, they commonly wind up full of sequences and void of sense. Likewise are we well off delivered from transcendences (at least those about which books can be written) *&* the quest for Original Ideas *&* their Re-Appearances. If an 'idea's' least importance is seen to be its origin, then its *vehicular force*, its power to initiate social change — will once again be clear to our undistracted gaze. That is the perhaps over-pragmatic conclusion to which I would hurry F's analysis.

But after all the argument I can hardly (as a poet) undertake to understand, let me turn to my second business, to confessing how delighted I was by the substance of Grab's talk. When I say 'substance,' I do not, of course, mean Foucault or Foucault's texts. I mean the verbal enterprise we have listened to. I admit that poets are traditionally assigned a taste for all style *&* no substance. (A quarter century ago — already! — Roland Barthes spun the gnarled fine tuning knob of his then primitive instrument *&* refocused that bland error to this exciting almost truth: all *écriture* and no *signifié*.) So, knowing Kelly, I'm not surprised it is the discourseful text of the Grab lecture — in both admirable sense of that word — that preoccupies me here. Modestly he has assigned his own clarities to a surely (if not purely imaginary source, a French writer named Michel Foucault. This Foucault bears to Grab no doubt the same relation that the mysterious Flegatanis bore to Wolfram v Eschenbach, or Sidi Hamet to Cervantes — a wise, old heathen whose unbaptized shadow our close author, our proximal, our neighbor makes intelligible light. We are rapt in a zone of twilight language, where the text comes into being for the sake of the commentary it will attract, where the real meaning of the Law is to summon the Talmud into being. I value the remarks I've heard tonight because they allow us to attribute the greatest value to this Foucault Grab fancies he has read — the power to excite discourse. And lest that value seems mandarin or *précieux*, let me gloss it with a more familiar parable about the arcana of text & reader: the sabbath is made for man, not man for the sabbath.

10 March '77

7 · A BOOK WITH & AGAINST THEORY

ON WALTER BENJAMIN
FACULTY SEMINAR RESPONSE TO FREDERIC GRAB

My first obligation is to thank Fred Grab for getting me to read Walter Benjamin; he used the simple expedient of asking me to respond to the remarks you have just heard. As a result of his request, I've spent two weeks in a crash course with an erratic, but thrilling syllabus — the books of, and about, a man whose acquaintance I should have made years ago but never did. Unaccountably never did, since I knew Heinrich Bluecher and studied Gershom Scholem and have read some Theodor Adorno. So to stand up here at all tonight is to speak in the voice of ignorance — a tone not unfamiliar even on the 42nd parallel. All I have to share, then, is enthusiasm. Benjamin strikes me as one of the most remarkable investigators I've come across, an intelligence operative within a set of pleasingly multifarious constraints, of the kind Fred has been making clear.

What strikes me as especially notable in Fred's talk are these considerations: the theme of finding the grave of Benjamin, i.e., of discovering which, if any (& the answer is certainly: *none*) hermeneutic tradition enrolls him; the theme of the "status of the 'final' textual product"; the theme of the unattainability of what Fred calls "the ultimate signified" of Benjamin's signifying texts.

About the middle theme I can say nothing; Fred has set it out clearly, and drawn interesting, even delightful, conclusions from the absences he celebrates. I will speak of the other two themes in reverse order.

The signified. If, on the basis of my infant sense of B, I had to title this talk, I'd go for something like: Against the Homogeneous, For the Coherent. I notice B speaks of fans when he writes about Proust, segments of fans that open and reveal and fold and conceal. He writes about Leskov, about Brecht's plays, above all about Kafka — but a Kafka who is strangely deracinated from his novels, a Kafka who is all parabolist — B even speaks of *Amerika* under its first title, that of the first chapter, *The Stoker* — as if that very fragment were more conspicuous than the whole it introduces. B appreciates the stories of Stevenson and Kipling in passing. He studies Baudelaire at great length — but as if (or so it seems to me) the stanza were more the work at hand than the poem.

So I see Benjamin as a scholar of synecdoche — thus a rigorous modernist, firm adherent of that fragmentation which is *our* classicism, according to a great American filmmaker.

This passion for the part, which is readily agreeable with a compulsory distaste for the whole and over-whole works of the massive 19th century, this passion seems to be reflected in the cult of quotation Fred speaks of. And that taste is my second diagnostic sign, just as much so as the Swiftian burden of an actual library, thousands of books, which Benjamin contrived to carry with him, would not abandon, defined as his milieu of action. For the passion for quotation is the urge to set up a detached kingdom, a domain of clarity — of the kind I think Barthes had in mind when in *Writing Degree Zero* he offers these strictures:

> /... clarity is a purely rhetorical attribute, not a quality of language in general possible at all times and in all place, but only the ideal appendage to a certain kind of discourse, that which is given over to a permanent intention to persuade... Political authority, spiritual dogmatism, and unity in the language of classicism are therefore aspects of the same historical movement...

Barthes is surely not thinking of Benjamin, but the shoe fits — at least to the extent that the quotation cannily comprehends the political, spiritual and literary contradictions which are the joy & despair of the ideal read of Benjamin. Benjamin's language lives up to the challenge, enacts itself with a lucidity that surprises me, given the infolded richness of his thought, and the living presence of those same inescapable contradictions.

It seems to me Benjamin can be very much a Marxist. At least sometimes. That may be the rub — one can't be Marxist just sometimes. Here is a man who claims to be at home most in his library, who experiments with hashish, who studies, even if somewhat at second hand, the Qabbalah, but who offers a statement like this, "A work that exhibits the correct [political] tendency must of necessity have every other quality," as a QED for his Marxist essay, "The Author as Producer." And though Adorno may carry forward the attack on idealism more radically than Benjamin, it is the latter who, in the same essay, will define the good writer by this litotic method: a hack writer is "the man who abstains in principle from alienating the productive apparatus from the ruling class by improving it in ways serving the interests of socialism." It is hard to imagine a more persuaded aesthetic than that. And B is not a naïf, sentimentally doting on *Arbeiter-chic*. When he attacks the writers (Kæstner we know best) of the *Neue Sachlichkeit* for turning "the struggle against poverty [into] an object of consumption" we are reminded painfully of our once contemporaries who made a good living denouncing the Vietnam war.

But I don't think it fair entirely to B to claim that his Marxism is inconsistent with his earlier theological interests, or with the strain of mystical reflection and apocalyptic, even angelological, imagery from which his work is never long free. We don't have to see him as a fuddled intellectual oscillating productively but symptomatically between irreconcilables. Important here, and for me conclusive, are the clear last words of "The Author as Producer: For the revolutionary struggle is not between capitalism and spirit, but between capitalism and the proletariat."

My last diagnostic trait is his *apartness* — a flair that goes well both with mandarin and with mystic. Amateur of cities, lover of Paris, he laments having to steer his great unfinished text towards an exoteric title, Paris, Capital of the Nineteenth Century, away from the haunting title *Passagenarbeit*, that is, The Arcades, those roofed arcades of Paris, necessitated equally by sun and by rain, from which, protected, the reader looks calmly out onto the truth of the streets.

Apartness, arrant logology (as I'll call his quest for quotation), synechdochism. Are these clues enough to "crack the case" as Fred dares us to do? Political commitment, lucidity of argument, playfulness of discourse as in those superb "Theses and the Philosophy of History" completed in his last year.

In his well-known essay "The Work of Art in an Age of Mechanical Reproduction," Benjamin uses a peculiar word; that word is *aura*, and by it he seems to mean the authenticity that streams out of an actual person or an actual thing (in particular the actual work of art) towards and to the onlooker. In what it would be naughty to call the 'reproductive arts' the aura is replaced by *personality*, which becomes commodity — as every thing and relation in capitalist society must ultimately become. I would like to know more about this word *aura*, and if I'm lucky I soon will. But at the moment it gives me my last clue. I sense in Benjamin all complexities mobilized towards an actual and powerful intent: a *flight from commodity*, a releasing to us of aura from the works he so minutely studies, a releasing of those works from commoditization. He does wish to alienate texts, even the cities and architecture he lovingly apprehended as texts, from the ruling class. He knows "the bourgeois apparatus of publication and production can assimilate astonishing quantities of revolutionary themes...without calling into question its own existence and the existence of the class that owns it." (*Aasp*). So a thorough alienation is the motive, it seems to me, of this urgent scholiast. Commentary is the use of value texts. Benjamin is a rescuer.

And like all rescuers, messianic. And like all messiahs, fated. Thus to introduce our very brief second theme: *le tombeau de Walter Benjamin*, the missing grave.

The easiest way for me to think of Benjamin is as a mystic of the worldly. To say that, yet to admit that he is without the visionary physiology of Blake or the uncial coherence of Beethoven or the glorious tatters of light of Cézanne (those better-known mystics of the worldly), is not to have assessed him for blame. For he has discovered (and in that rarest of all poetic registers, pure old daytime prose) the lineaments of rational perception that threaten constantly to renew the world.

Fred introduces the loss of B's text by the shenanigans at Vico's funeral (a real Finnegans wake) & the loss of Benjamin's gravesite. I have resisted long enough the soft hooting ramshorns of Mosaic reference with which Grab tempts me. I will say it, yes, we must apprehend Jewish Benjamin anew sub specie Moysis, as a type of Moses. It is hard to imagine a Moses who has crossed over into the promised land — *Exodus* is too subtle a book to allow such an hermeneutically unprofitable happy ending. Moses is lost; if you would seek him, read The Law. From what we have heard tonight, the loss of the Benjamin opus, instead of obscuring the thrust of the text (however that text finally may constitute itself), actually see to summon *il miglior lettore*. The loss of the text gains readerly power, evidently. (Or, as I seem to keep saying in this room — and this time WB is on my side — Reading *is* Writing).

I for one am glad that Benjamin passed into obscurity. At times these past few weeks, I've been haunted by a contrary-to-fact condition: what if Walter Benjamin had yielded to the ceaseless importunities of his close friend Gershom Scholem and emigrated to Palestine, in 1930 or the decade thereafter? Would the lucid flâneur of Paris have become the city-less pundit of the Hebrew university, someone old? Can we imagine a regulation Israeli Benjamin, ethical, sturdy, sage & safe? No more than Moses would he hide himself in the Holy Land. As bitter and vain and terrible as his suicide was, huge misunderstanding though it may have been, one can sense it as his flight from betraying the ground of his striving. It may have been his own curious Negative Dialectic.

3. I. 1979

LETTER TO THE EDITOR

The book survey in № 7 is focused in a way no 'reviews' we see ever are; the *use of texts* is at stake, and people's reflections on what stirs them are in turn of next-generation usefulness. So I pick up half a dozen things I hadn't considered, and that's good news. The solidity of Silliman's judgment is, as usual, exciting.

So I want to send along, in return, my own list of this past year or so, the things that stirred most in my thought and writing. Trail of dust, maybe, or pillar of cloud. We never know till we see what's done with them.

Walter Benjamin, *Reflections* and *Illuminations*. I begin with an amazing critic of our own fragmented light, whom I had missed until two months ago, and who's been the sharpest call to order lately.

Braudel, *The Mediterranean World in the Age of Philip II* and the other work on the material culture of Capitalism.

Barthes, *Sade/Loyola/Fourier* and *The Pleasure of the Text*: Barthes at his most public/private & private/public, the one critic ("deictic" after my own heart) who knows how to walk that line. These books fulfill the promise of *Writing Degree Zero* (coeval with Olson's Projective Verse essay). And the head-note by Richard Howard to the *Pleasure* is remarkable for all the issues it starts running with clarity, wit, and quickness.

Engels, *The Condition of the Working Class in England* — to come back to that, as ever to Marx's *Capital*, to ground in the world root of their thought. Fact as the rain that renews the air of theory.

Gregory Dix, *The Shape of the Liturgy*, a beautiful study of the diachronic, a gesture shaping for nineteen hundred years.

Georges Bataille, to wander in the complete works now coming out, especially *L'Histoire de œil*, *Le Bleu du ciel* (which I've read in a wonderful private translation by Paul Auster and Lydia Davis), *L'anus solaire*. I owe much of my orientation here to Paul Buck and that remarkable journal *Curtains*.

Salvatore Timpanaro, *The Freudian Slip*. (Marxian philology reborn.)
Umberto Eco, *Theory of Semiotics*.

Hillman, *ReVisioning Psychology*.
Cardew, *Stockhausen Serves Imperialism* (a book so savage in its attack on our avant-garde preoccupations & airs that it seems to be kept out of this country altogether, whereas the same author's earlier conformist *Scratch Music* is widely circulated.)
Tarthang Tulku, *Time Space Knowledge*, a casting of Buddhist analytic & synthetic into the american language.
Marx and Engels, *The German Ideology*: the orchestra tuning, the wind rising.
Heidegger, *What is Called Thinking* and *Discourse on Thinking*.
And ever useful (now I own a copy all the more so):
Onians, *The Origins of European Thought* (Arno reprint).

And I do not want to leave out of the record those books which are not held in the hand, namely the texts of light:
Hollis Frampton, *Zorn's Lemma*
Herzog's *Kaspar Hauser*
Tanner's *Jonah who will be 25 in the year 2000*.

And, to match Benjamin at the beginning, this very great film which I finally saw only two years ago:
Vertov, *Man with Movie Camera*. (I suppress the *the*'s deliberately).

PS/ Capitalism brings 'story' and 'writing' together. Stateless communism must dream into being a language which tells its own story. And in which language is the only story. Are not these the pivots we share in what we would move?

PPS/ Sour note in McCaffery's sideswipe at Enslin. Not because of my predictable preference for 'positive criticism' (my deicticism, as above), or my equally predictable defense of Enslin — rather because the rating-system (fourth-rate, third-rate, etc.) is built on the very structure we are all trying to deconstruct. At once came to mind the old Macaulay reading the young Marx and saying: That is just how to learn how not to write. And Barthes' actual strictures (*Writing Degree Zero*) on 'clarity' — he recognizes the danger of the lucid becoming the compulsory — neatness and clarity the tools of persuaders. Yet it's interesting to learn how not to write too, & I take it abstinence is a sort of use.

(*L=A=N=G=U=A=G=E* #8, 1979)

MORNING ITEM FOR BRUCE ANDREWS

when my mother and father were growing up they said and I bet yours did too that a given couple seen sparking spectacularly in the shadows of the Hupmobile or yet more spectacularly visible hand in hand shopping for a diamond at J. J. Friel's (the Irish pawnbroker, where is he in what franciscan hell now) (you can see his faded advertisements still on old brick walls in Queens) on Broadway Brooklyn were *an item.* this means that the bound morpheme *-ing*

wears out over a paragraph of verse the way sunlight yields ineluctably to something less, even if (as last for instance)less spectacular in itself, a snowy full moon yawning through local atmo- (hey, Lady Luna, clear your throat) on a day when the first robin had been seen. The morpheme I keep trying to reinstate in free is god name among the fraction of my ancestors, though they usually called him Freyr (one syllable), i.e., the lord tout court (as masculine of Frau in another neighborhood of speech). Helmut Dantine (professor of philosophy at UCLA after all those U-Boots)

had early in my life reminded me: in american movies germans speak english with a german accent. that's how we know what little we know of why people do what they do, if they do and it isn't just done for them by Mr. DeMille in the sky as I was raised to reckon a possibility. but I was good at explaining how Total Omniscience left room for Free Will. you'd think I'd be better now at liberating Memory from me or at least from my mother and father walking in Williamsburgh sixty-seven years ago and deciding to get around to get married which I suspect a sentimental consequence of urban snow

(like the poem by the poet laureate at the time of my birth years later) yet have no fault to find with sentimentality since it leaves me here on the beaches of morning unsubdued, still with a word or two in my mouth and a problem to solve: how were they an item, Sam (called Jim) and Margaret (called Muriel), hand in hand under the ardent geometry (as I always thought of it) of the El shadows, in winter, believing in a strong god and the possibility of children, walking, an item, a generative string in the stream, and having cleared their throats they spoke me, *&*

others, or I am where their -*ing* came to rest? In Cambridge, in Jeremy Prynne's rooms in Caius, bashful? overweight admiring Jackson Mac Low in the old Figaro in 1958 he looked so like the youthful Ezra Pound, that scrappy beard that fighting eye those incomprehensible politics? it seems that anybody's life is watching someone else's he may or may not become. if he does it's sentimental (like catching leprosy or enlisting in the merchant marine) and if he doesn't then the word remains bound and no one knows. I am close to believing language is the pawnbroker's window

and then we need a brick (courtesy of Krazy Kat) or a book (Marx will still do, or the Vimalakirtinirdesasutra, or you) and we in the act of speaking borrow glorious trouble & someone needs to turn us around, feel that nice cool glass at the back of the neck and face whatever we'd find there in the other direction from language, if we looked, if we have anything to look with or are enough of an item to do anything or what was our language before we spoke?

22 March 1989

ALBANY LECTURE ON THEORY [1]

A lecture, like a dream, should have intervals of lucidity. In between, the audience needs a certain in-space for reverie, with passages of dark dullness by which to recruit and restore their powers. A lecture should, like a newly met companion, guide you along an unfamiliar path, occasionally touching you — on the arm or shoulder or hip — in ways that seem a bit invasive, at times leaving you to flounder along, wishing for the touch of the hand a moment ago you found so impertinent. A lecture like a waterfall should keep going even when you look away — you still hear the comforting roar or ripple of its continuity. You know it will always be there when you turn your attention back, if you, when you, if you, when you ...

But this is a keynote lecture. The keynote (OED tells me) is the first, hence lowest, note of any musical key, the tonic. An interesting writer in 1762 then borrows the word to indicate the tone (and he means the actual pitch) in which the bulk of the words in any discourse are sounded. The main sound. The main sound of a voice talking.

The tonic of your talk.

21 years later, another writer has come up with the sense of the word I guess you had in mind: the leading idea of a discourse.

That is a smart (if partial) definition. Since it implies clearly that whatever the 'keynote speaker' has up her sleeve, it's all part of a larger discourse that continues after she, or in this case, I, shall have finished talking and retreated to the delicate shadows of imperfect attention, somnolence, occasional aperçu, reverie & intellection — and the discourse goes on, outside and inside. See example of waterfall above.

The discourse is inside and outside at once; once started, it never really stops. I still am in the middle of some conversations that started forty years ago — the speakers fall silent but the discourse continues. This is not an essentialist fancy or metaphysical pleasantry. On the contrary, it is root hog neurophysiology, right in us, in the bulk of us.

---

1. [Talk Delivered on 16 January / 23 March 2001 at SUNY Albany Graduate Students' Conference]

7 · A BOOK WITH & AGAINST THEORY

Once heard, a word resounds. Once begun, a conversation finds its way through the crannies of our attention, percolates through the clay of our indifference, runs swift and clean in the occasional channels when we get interested. And flows from one to another in words, and never really stops.

So be careful what keynote you listen to. The tonic is always there, below the raga, help (hindering), touching (letting go).

What is the keynote you have asked me to sound?

NOTES FOR A TALK TO THE ALBANY GRADUATE CONFERENCE

I want to talk about a new theory of poetry. Maybe it's truer to say: a new theory of theory.

Let me begin by saying that Peter Monaco called and asked me, as I understood it, to talk about the relations between poetry and theory. And so I will. Two ways would interest me: talking about the relation between a poet, me in this case, and theory. Or talking about the relation between a poem *&* its theory. It is this latter that I'll talk towards, from some notes I've been making.

Start out with me by remembering that theory comes from *theoria*, Greek for looking, a way of looking at something, or at things in general.

Poetic theory is usually construed as views about how poems ought to be written or how they should affect the reader. It is strange to think that anybody would have views about how somebody else should do something, but that is the American way, inherited from the weird Christian fideist centuries when belief was invented. (Religion was once a matter of public cult and private psycho-physical meditative — yoga — practice. After the middle ages *&* renaissance, it becomes more and more a matter of 'belief' — a strange interior commodity promulgated — sold — by the economic processes called missionaries, conversions, preaching — whereby one locates one's social identity by itemizing and comparing one's notional inventory with others. Does this sound rather familiar to students of poetry — schools of poetic practice?)

Suppose we forget to have an attitude about how a poem should be. Suppose we forget to clothe ourselves in the (patriarchal, it must be confessed, and stressed) authority one would have to possess to stand out in the street and say Poems should do thus and so, poets should do thus and so.

Suppose theory was not a code word for repressive strategies but a simple description of an act of learning, one grounded in careful observation — *theoria* — of a written text. Something written. Some thing written.

To read the poem. To let its own unique and particular theory arise from readership, the act and mettle of hard reading.

There is a tension that pervades not just the history of poetry, but *the history of the individual poem itself.*

Its coming into being. Cosmology of the poem.

The tension between orthodoxy and the heretic, between established schools and juvenile delinquents like Pound and Rimbaud,

such tensions replicate themselves from era to era, from language poetry as radical crazies battering at the gate to language poets as the serene professorate against which the young have to find some way of making a space/time of their own,

all that is familiar enough.

But it gets warmer when we sense the tension as between procedure & process,

between rule and rapture.

Some background (that soon becomes foreground):

There is a fundamental malaise in our literature.
It is the tension between *the poems as cultural artifact*
      — which includes a sense of commodity, amenity, possession, emblem of the good life, totem of tribal affiliation, token of nostalgia, courier of love
                as against *the poem as revelation.*

Is it an ornament or is it a tool?

7 · A BOOK WITH & AGAINST THEORY

An ornament is made in obedience to canons and rules (must rime; can't rime; no first person pronouns; must be vernacular; must be exalted; must be imagistic since no ideas but things; must rely on syntax since only language tells, etc., etc.)
while a tool does work. Opens or breaks or heals.

But where we really get to it is in the act of writing, where the poet veers between two intentions:
— the intention of writing a poem (if not worse than that)
— & the intention of clarifying, addressing, the mind happening of daydream, day drift, logic, memory, desire, angst, or whatever else is going on down in there, where the action rises in us to speak, as speaking.

Dying each other's life, living each other's death — that would be the right way of it. I must be serious if I'm citing Heraclitus.

So I want us to get into our range of sight that problem, we know it so well from schools, where the young poets love and hate the old poets, struggle with them in trances of reverence and reveries of revenge,

we know it so well when one school of poetic practice suddenly Takes Over. Surrealism did it. Modernism, Formalism, Objectivism, Confessionalism (or whatever we call that bleak decade of weary disclosures), Language — each takes over and makes new rules.

Vates meant rhapsodic prophetic poet in Latin; no wonder every movement of poets when it takes over creates a Vatican,

complete with imprimaturs (usually in the form of blurbs & prefaces), nihil obstates (usually public funding), & indexes of forbidden books. The *Ne Lisez Pas* group.

A great way of studying any poet is to examine the poets he abhors or deprecates. Ditto for any school of poetic practice.

(Novelists seem to be otherwise. They know they can't all tell the same story. But poets, a simpler, ruder race, haven't quite figured that out yet. If professors are reading & teaching George Oppen, we'd better write Oppen poems. Poet logic. The whole history of influence/imitation in poetry probably is as simple as: trying to win for oneself the readers one sees attending to the work of the other, the influencer.

Because whatever we do, we are doing for the reader. Hypocrite reader, says Baudelaire, hypocrite perhaps because the reader judges himself to be different from, other than, the writer. Just as speech needs an upper lip and a lower lip, poetry needs a writer and a reader. The poem is a transaction, not an artifact.

That's why Pound and Olson and Duncan and Celan and Ashbery and Zukofsky are so grand, they put us to work. The transaction of the poem is more complex, complicated — more effortful, eventful.

What's interesting is that our poetry wars are not (unlike the people in the Comintern — Trotsky really was an enemy, Stalin no fool) between natural enemies. They are psychological (of course) struggles to exclude one's own hidden agenda by finding it or projecting it on the work of other people.

Show me who you hate, and I'll show who you really are.

My basic points were two:

In any poem whatsoever, there is a combat (which is exactly a *concerto*) between disclosure and construction, where each tries to co-opt the powers of the other. This contradiction is in fact the mechanism or craft of the poem's coming into being.

The critic's apprehension of this struggle is in fact the *theoria* of the poem — each poem contains within itself a more or less precise articulation of its own 'poetics.'

My goal is this:
To rescue critical intelligence from generalization, to focus the specific intelligence of poetics precisely on the theory inherent in each text.

If the poem is to be a revelation (that's what I want it to be, my own prejudice, as if you didn't know it already), it must start out by revealing itself, and, by *theoria*/theory, its own ground of being, its own coming into being. Only if that's clear can it really gesture, *mantis* or *vates* or *ollamh* or bard, out into the world of what we have not yet thought.

And to travel in the world of what we have not yet thought is, it seems to me, the only target, as it is the only justification, for the act of poetry.

(2001)

THREADS 8 : ROBERT SAYS

Listening, I think it's about listening. I have come to believe (and I keep saying this, so I'm sure you've heard it before) that every language is a second language, language itself is a second language. We remember childhood, the vague excitement of heard words, their colors, their shapes in our ears we tried to taste in our mouths, words were things then, and the system that any natural language is hadn't gelled yet for us. (Michel Leiris is wonderful on that epoch.) We heard, and what we heard the Others saying somehow, but we didn't know how, somehow related to, mapped onto, connected with, the other things around us, the thing things. Things that spoke to and in us with a vividness and distinctiveness, each its own. I keep trying to listen to things that way still again, things that are "always already" speaking (in that famous French phrase). So one way to answer is to say that there are three phases: things and no language (earliest childhood), things and language distinct but interlinking (ordinary life and language), the words become things of their own (writing, the poem as object in a world of object, made so not by the accuracy by which it may map some prior emotional state of the "poet" — that is, not by its force of representation. — but by the fact, thingliness of the language itself.) I want to write Thinglish. And when I push students in workshops, it's towards Thinglish, the pebbled stream bed that purifies the stream of language that runs over it.

in conversation with Mark Thwaite (2006)

Not so much responsibility as privilege. People have to find the materials or minds to do work on the world, for the world; the poet has at least the materials right there in the mouth. Words. Language, which is always there and common to all, so the poet is always walking through familiar places, holding familiar objects to display to those around about. Making them unfamiliar, so they can be seen. Language, no matter how arcane we become with it, language keeps us always with other people. Joyce's polysemous & difficult tongueplay in the late work comes out of his fierce determination to respond to the social fact, we dream in language and wake to speak. Language is always social. Language is the other — the other in our own mouths.

The poet is someone who has nothing to say except what language lets. And "let" is an old, odd word in English, that means both permit ("let the children play") and prohibit ("let and hindrance"). Language lets, poets listen, and that listening is their main responsibility, when coupled with what language lets them, makes them say, keeps them from saying.

Maybe the deepest responsibility of the poet is the simplest: Keep talking.

in conversation with Simone dos Anjos & Pietro Aman (2006)

Even now, a decade or so into collaborations, I'm just beginning to get some sense of what collaboration is about — not formally, I mean, or in terms of personal relations between the two collaborators, but in terms of the psychic economy of the collaborator alone. Why would I do this? What can I do for it, or it do for me, that writing solo doesn't manage?

My first "collaboration" was with Hoelderlin himself — the dead are wonderful to collaborate with; they are immensely demanding, insistent on every last word of theirs, but at the same time wonderfully welcoming. I did a homeophonic reading of his fantastic hymn "At the Source of the Danube" (my "Unquell the Dawn Now" heard his "Am Quell der Donau"). That led to further collaboration with the German experimentalist Schuldt [...].

The main collaborations, though, have been with Shelley — his Mont Blanc *in four pages became mine in forty, with all his words intact in proper order, but with mine intruding, interfering, impregnating. The rule for me in that mad journey into another man's text was this: that the result must seem in no way weird, must seem ordinary poetic discourse, must not scream I Am An Experiment.*

Then with the wonderful Tyrolean painter Brigitte Mahlknecht of Bolzano. I took one look at her drawings (people mapped as cities, cities mapped as language) & knew we had to work together. She sent me a fax and we were off. A year later, I had answered her faxed pictures with faxed poems; she answered my faxed poems with faxed drawings and paintings. We met in Vienna in the last months of the last millennium, and spread out over a big studio floor all the pictures and all the poems they had elicited. We put the results together, The Garden of Distances [...]. Our rule, and one I insisted on, was this: Prima la pittura, duopo la poesia. The picture comes first. The poem answers the existent picture — so the poem is a pure response, a desperate reading of the intricate surfaces and intersections of her work. [...]

Then began the collaborations with Birgit Kempker. Once again, our actual meeting in real time and space took place after we had finished our basic work — sixteen chapters of Scham / Shame, alternating. This time e-mail was the method, & again I was (by design) in the role of responder. [...]

Yes, I love collaboration. I'd be happy indeed to collaborate again with Birgit, Brigitte, Schuldt, Friedrich, Percy... As I say, I'm still trying slowly, non-urgently, to figure out what is at stake, what is in play, when one artist collaborates with another, living or dead. And I wonder who my next victim will be... And poets are ahead of the game here, aren't we. In the fact that every single word we write down we borrow from those who spoke before. Every act of speech is a collaboration, in one important sense. And all the more so, every act of writing. Poetry = cheap, democratic, collaborative revelation.

in conversation with Mark Thwaite (2006)

8.

A BOOK OF TRANSLATION

```
RIME
      (for times, places, poets, that can use it)
is not decoration, IS AN INSTRUMENT OF
DISCOVERY (Sapir:  rime as heurism)
the translation, then, must bear
witness to what has been discovered
(& that, is, the diff.between tr. & something
else);
        What rimes (with what?
- - - - - - - - - - - - - - - - - - - - - - - -
1) how the utterance /is/ goes / covers / LINES
                            in
                                          + (2

translating rimed poetry
(the (orig.) rime an arrow to
the final word, wch must be
some way aimed at in English
                      rime
```

Verso: Diplomatic transcript of a note [illegible] Etch

ON TRANSLATION

1.

It may be that language itself is only a second language, tormentingly slow to be learned, to teach, to work, to use, to be free of. It may be that *die tiefste Sprache*, the deepest speech/language/tongue, think of it, the deepest Tongue, is dream.

Not the dream we fumble until it finally drops with a clunk and we wake into our almost-shared, this, place, the dream that lunatics like Freud have taught us to sample at different rates of mental alertness, to find gaudy imagery and somber imagery and little narratives, knives, wounds, bananas, movie stars, auto cars, girls we left behind

but the deep dream, precisely (if undemonstrably) the one we can't remember.

Speak for yourself. The one I can't remember, the Dark Age between sleeping and dream, dream and waking — that one, *dortn*, over there.

That Night came first, and from it Want is born, and from Want a Word is spoken, but we first are spoken by the dark, of which all writing is trance/lation.

2.

So I offer translations:

a) from common language uncommonly wrought (Am Quell der Donau, "On the Source or Spring of the River Danube," by the greatest odic poet of modern times, Friedrich Hoelderlin) which I have heard into English by dint of deafening myself to what is laughably called the "meanings" of the German words, and opening my ears to them as English. So this isn't a translation from German into English. The poem wasn't written in German, it was written in FORM, and from form it has spoken anew into another, lesser, form. For translations of this sort, even this sort, even mine, are gnostical descents.

b) from dream — I woke up with the word Oelbewoelbe in my mouth, as if from German œl, oil, Gewœlbe — but no, BEwœlbe; now that dreamt sound or word spilled (quilled) into my conscious memories of another man's story, a tiny, awful childhood memory of a beach on the Baltic where the bodies of Jews were washed up after a Red Cross ship was bombed by the British. So translations from the borrowed memory, i.e., the Me speaking the language of the You.

c) from the roots of another language, where the whole wordstock becomes fair game.

d) from my own memories — the FLOWERS. I will insist that one does not write about the past, but that all writing translates all the past, most totally often when one isn't thinking about it.

These then are some glimpses of some of some of some of what might be in that word TRANSLATION. I have written a series of poems (for the late Robert Duncan, whose translations of Nerval and others show the way) called *Lations*, to explore that end of the root / route.

And these must be, here are, trance/lations, to unvoice the dream into the laxed luxury of hearing. Language is the money of dream I here give thee, with my unworldly goods I thee endow.

sketched 7 April 1989 19:00

TRANSLATION ALL-PERVADING[1]

One of the proper enterprises of all such conferences as this is to point fingers, deplore, encourage, redress. But there's one thing I don't want to get lost in the busy (and necessary) assignments of blame in the discourse of hegemony and margins. That is: *all text is translation*.

Or every text is a translation. And here text means to mean something woven, in the usual Emersonian sense, something woven out of nothing, or rather out of sheer *perceiving* — be it words or image or music or equation or systematic statement of the facts or law.

Text is vibrant human response to inner registration of outer conjuncture — a 'visible sign" of grace.

And everything we do translates from what befalls us in this long dwelling into what is substantially available to other people.

That said, however undemonstrable it may be, let me hurry to the immediate application: I hope we can keep some of our minds free of the logocentrism that haunts the verbal professions. If every text is translation, then there is a huge Translation World out there that has nothing directly to do with poems & novels & lexicons & stolen naval plans.

I think of opera, the nonsense (for so it strikes me) of its textual entertainment compared to the glory of its consequence, the vast heroics of the voice alone. The voices in the reverberating hall of the orchestral sounds, the voices themselves resound inside your own body, the voices implicate you by breath and literal feeling into their passionate design. It doesn't matter what they say, it is what they make your body answer. It is in the voice's heroic coming-forward to you, in you, finally *as you*, that the real story of the opera is told. (Perhaps that is why we'll never give up *Parsifal* however pretentious the text, however vile the conscious mind of its composer.) So the real translation going on in opera is not (as usually supposed) story into text, text into tone, but rather the annihilation of the words into the otherness of sound. The listener is taken into the structure of the music, & the listener's joy comes from the dual pleasure

---

1. Response to papers delivered by André Lefevere and Nathaniel Tarn at the Translation Conference "Translation as Cultural Transmission. Toward a Politics and Poetics of Translation" at Bard College, October 1992. [Eds note.]

of absorption into the oceanic insistence of sound, while at the same time holding-self-apart in a rapt passionate analysis of all that is befalling.

So translation can annihilate its "original" — and perhaps should do so more often, even in the language-to-language sort of business we usually have in mind.

* * *

In Lefevere there is a covert or perhaps simply vestigial presence: the author theory. Someone (whether individual ("writer") or collective ("society")) disposed of their habits of attention and feeling in such a way that the result is readable — i.e., a written-down piece of language — by readers in other situations.

Inevitably, such a focus on the whodunit aspect of the text will prioritize and value, overvalue, the role of the author (be it the solitary Genius or the Great Age of English Literature). And in overcompensation for that distortion, we will (and rightly enough) develop an attention to and discourse about hegemony and all the rest of it.

If however we shift to the priority of the text, certain interesting shunts of value and attention become possible. For one thing, the role of the listener/reader becomes that of the agonist in the drama, not the audience. And how this happens shows something of the majesty and solitary delights of translation.

The translator is first reader.

The translator is like the God of Genesis on the morning of the sixth day — looking about on the world created by the new reading, the translator must fashion Adam and Eve, new readers to share the delights of the new reading.

* * *

There is a sense I want to remind us of, a sense in which language is itself a second language. That is, the infant (the "not-speaking one") lives (as I almost remember, and you likely almost remember too) in a seamless web of meaningfulness. They are not meanings the way language (that droll Wittgenstein at the chessboard) would collect and employ meanings. But we had those relations — sounds and shapes and colors and directions. Now it sounds glib to talk about what we did then, with such delight and desperation, The Cry, the Cry of Merlin was our cry, coming out of the stifling ground of unending experience. From which language, that is, other people's language, would presently rescue us. But we would pay, wouldn't we, for our deliverance, and pay dearly. We poor pagans on Infant Island would be *book*ed soon by Bible, police, dictionary, law.

The process of language acquisition (as our commercially-minded commodity society pleasantly terms the business) is usually presented as the child like a buyer in a huge supermarket (the French nowadays speak of *hypermarché*) gradually accumulating labels for sensory & cognitive items.

My own memories (do you have memories too?) suggest more the picture of the child as an islander invaded by a hardworking colonizing power. The sensitive relation between perception and feeling, the nuance of distance, the abrupt and often terrifying presence of things, textures, sound — are quickly overwhelmed by the snarling or quacking or caressive seductions of the hegemonizing language, that is, human language itself, the so-called mother tongue.

Soon the child is speaking like everybody else, more or less (and in this "more or less," this narrow house, comes to live the essence of eloquence, poetry, signifying, persuasion). The child's own idiolect of sounds and signifiers is liquidated into the Boss Language that has to be used to get anywhere at all in the ripe world around. Nothing is left of the language of this poor tribe-of-one. Every infant is an Ishi. Or maybe here and there something is left; the sound *zh* as in "measure" has some valor for me, left over from infant proto-narrative as an index of force or heroic. The names of heroes would feature this sound.

Do you have any memories at all of your first language? It wouldn't be bad — and it needn't be Freudian — to think about them & recall them. Call them again.

I'm thinking then that a proper "subaltern" study of language would depend on recognizing the birth trauma of language in the individual not as a pleasant experience at the shopping mall but as the brutalizing, marginalizing, colonializing overwhelming of the self's tentative grid of meaningfulness by the power of society's most self-corrective and repressive institution: The Language.

The fact that from this *The Language* beauty and eloquence can be born, fashioned, begotten, not just reported — that is the curious and splendid contradiction which makes a Dante possible, but also, *lehavdel*, makes such a conference as this one both possible and necessary.

To sort things out.

But the joy of translation part of it, art of it:
To dance with the mind of the text —
Two ways of playing/seeing this:

the Prior [author's] Mind, fashioning the text out of Own Pain and Own Delight,

        is met by the Posterior [reader's] Mind, who out of Own Pain and Own Delight reads

                and if that reader happens to be guilty of a different mother-tongue, AND if the reader happens to be compassionate by disposition,

    the resultant
reading of the text will be a translation.

Translation is compassion.[2]

    Here the sense of text reduces the page to a more or less (again, that fateful phrase) permeable membrane between Mind One and Mind Two — and the dance becomes the dance of the Living with the Dead, the Near with the Far, the Native with (always) the Alien.

    Not a bad dance, and the music is good too, usually — so good that the translator leaves it out. We stand in the noisy street of our vernacular and watch through the window of the translation as the translator dances suavely or exotically to the indoor music we can't hear.

    But we don't have to assume the Mind of the Author — we have the text, its own Rosetta Stone, portal not to another mind somewhere but

---

2. Lefevere points out wittily what a left-handed sort of shame-faced activity translation was in the eyes of the very Classicists who did it and still do it, and whose very insistence on the Value of the Classics — not just Greek and Latin anymore, but French, German, Arabic, Chinese, Japanese, Sanskrit, but always Classics — makes translation socially necessary and economically possible. If people didn't rabbit on as they do about Homer, would every American publisher have its own up-to-the-minute translation of the *Iliad* to peddle to captive audiences in Freshman classes all over the empire?

to its own realm of more or less (again) unlimited experience. (*Es sucht der Bruder seine Brueder* might be the motto of all translations of the first sort, *Mirror Mirror on the Wall* of the second.)

The Original translated some complex of human presence into language. The Translation restores a human presence, pistoning off the text, or (subtle play of light, *lusus luminis*, catoptric ballet) reflecting the text onto new persons. Who come to dance too.

In this manner or mode, the translator stands before the mirror of the text, and strives to see in it the passions and permissions of the translator's own life-in-language. Here Pound stands staring at the impossible Rihaku (his Japanese name for our Chinese-Iranian friend Li Po) and hears the woman in him speak the River Merchant's Wife. Here Catullus stood before Sappho's φαίνεταί μοι (*Phainetai moi*) ode and found the juice in him rise to the pain and self-sad playfulness of that oldest of all our laments for the power of the social order over private passion. These poems reincarnate by mirror, by sheer light.

And for all the wonder of the resultants, or even the travesties and follies of unpersuasive translations, we see revealed this truth: The text has no magistry, it has only a reader.[3]

After all is said and done, we read so little. We retain so little. Even to remember a little while what we read is an immense act of privileging.

Translation is only a special case of reading.

Translation, like reading, is remembering.

Translation is remembering in another language.

---

3. Or no reader, like most texts in the history of the world. Think of Greek Literature, as it is packaged and taught: from Homer down to the fall of Constantinople to the Turks — a period of roughly two thousand years — a more or less continuously understandable language was spoken and written in what we call Greece and its ever-shifting colonies and suburbs. Of those two millennia we have picked Homer, Hesiod, and the fifth century, and, five hundred years later, the New Testament (which for special and obvious reasons we are willing to accord every now and then the curious privilege of being Literature). And that's that. The period from 100 C.E. to 1450 C.E. doesn't count. Literature became Roman then, no other nationalities need apply. Then it became European. We know the rest. But we keep tending to forget.

ALL WRITING IS COLLABORATION

Every language is a second language.

That's where I started. (Where we all start.)
Language as an allergic response to the silence in which sensations are received, the roaring synesthesias of silent childhood. Something like that. Slowly one learns to word these feelings, then sentence them. Sentence them to life? Sentence them to other people. Not a word alone, but words in cahoots, yielding from the silence of my excited body some cry woven — to give the minimal, to banish inquiry, to give just enough. But why give?

To answer the other person. The other party. In fear or desire, something in me stirs to address the other person. I don't want to put it in words, I want to put it in doing. *Im Anfang war die Tat*, says Faust, & the word, logos or Christos, came after.

Since language is the first-born of silence, since language is a translation of skin & bone, of eye & ear & belly, of hunger & want, since language is all of what it is for no other reason than to inveigle itself into the awareness and presence of the other,

all speech is collaboration.

I take that as the road. *M'introduire dans ton histoire*, says Mallarmé, to work myself into your story. That is what a poem is always about. To introduce these words (which are the spill and tools and spokes and speaking of the mum me of *m'introduire*) into you.

And hear you in turn.

All writing is collaboration: all the words I use have been used before, and even the wordless sounds I try to wield or make sound from the page by grunts of the alphabet, all those sounds too have been in your mouth first, you and the birds and the tigers.

All writing is collaboration in that it responds — every sonnet is a response to the formal rustling hush of all the sonnets before, every letter answers a letter, every text answers a previous text. Reading comes before writing — in human history as in the development of the child, how could it be otherwise — so every writing is response.

Writing is trying to answer.

In my case I set out with the noble dead: Hölderlin and Shelley, to talk with them, supply my side of the long-pending dialogue. It is brave to talk with the dead. Then I risked working with the noble living: two German-speakers, Mahlknecht and Kempker, painter and poet. I had to be really brave to work with the living.

Work = being conscious of the collaboration. Letting the other know. Letting the other answer.

Whirlpool of answering. The vortex.

In *The Garden of Distances*, I wanted there to be one text in two genres. So that the reader would, as I had, begin by reading (carefully, detailedly) the picture, then read the ensuing text, then the ensuing picture, and so on, just as you would read a book in verse and in prose, or in ordinary type and italics, just keep reading. Each text reads the one before it.

What I set myself as a task with Shelley's "Mont Blanc," or a stanza from Hart Crane, or a poem by Whitman was this: to preserve all the words of the 'original' in the exact order of the original, but with intrusions — at any moment, & for any stretch of word time seemed needed — of my 'own' words.

I wrote into their text, so their text following my intrusions would become response to them — to which I would respond in turn with my next intrusions, and so on until we had finished what we had to say.

Interesting contrast that makes between 'original' & 'own.' Simpler to say: mine & yours.

But there was another aspect of the task: the resultant poem, though it seems to conceal the original words (where do you hide a leaf? in the forest) in all the 'own' words added, should in some obvious way 'feel' like the original in important respects: tone, register, ambition, scheme.

So collaborations with the dead (which I sometimes think of as Impregnations of the other's text, or as Reincarnations of the other's text) require strict attention to the actual words of the other in their vital 'original' order. The dead are quick (their words prompt to my need) and slow (it's so hard to budge them from their stated positions). The words of the dead are profoundly honest — or we must make them so, as they make us.

Collaboration with the living: two people tell lies to each other that turn into truth.

(McPherson Special Catalogue, 2005)

NIGHT THOUGHTS

1.

It may be that any poem as we read it is only some of the first few spring leaves of the actual poem, whose true unfolding — from deepest root to flower to fruit to recreative seed — is to be found in its proliferating, uttering of itself in us. It grows towards us, becoming itself in all the translations of it, the illustrations made to or from it, the setting of it to song or symphony, the critical essays on it, the misremembered quotations of it, and retroversions of all those things back towards the 'original.'

So we'll never really read Poe until we read him in German and French, and also let resonate as we read and reflect all the Hollywood adaptations, the music, radio plays, critical essays, exam questions, misquotations, scribbled excerpts on love letters sent or received — all of these are the poem. The real poem. We have to understand what a curious, deep, scarcely penetrable thing a poem is, any poem is. We have to observe that in a sense Baudelaire (who translated it) got more out of "The Bells" than did Poe (who wrote it).

We have to understand, then, that the whole poem, the true deep vast poem of the poem, is an energy behind the artifact, an energy which comes to expression and fruition in every translation (however clumsy), adaptation, musical setting, etc.

Which brings us closer to Edward Young.

His *Night Thoughts* is hardly remembered in the English-speaking world. Students are not much set to study him in Birmingham and Chicago and Bangalore, as they study Spenser or Blake or even John Clare. (In Nagoya they study everything, but that's another story.)

And the poor beautiful exciting orphan nomad poems that are not taught in school — how many of them will ever be read again? Here and there, in moonlight, under a hedge, half-understood, whispered into a man's ear: adored. Maybe that's how poems should live, only that way.

The tragic-comedy of poetry in our time is its utter dependency on the sugar daddy of the university — which supports 90 poets out of 100. That's good, of course, for the poets (moi aussi), being sustained by the university as in the Middle Ages writers of every kind were sustained by the monasteries. (Anyone with a head for likenesses will have long ago noted that the American university is the thorough inheritor and analogue of the mediaeval monastic institutions, abbeys and priories and friaries and nunneries and charterhouses...) There were then and are now Goliards, of course, disconnected wastrels with a head for a tune, too-educated libertines on the road, for Fun, that shifty goddess whose vagabond votaries worship her by restlessness. Sure, there are still readers, and even scholars & scientists, outside the Academy — but so few. And often embittered, always embattled. But always fun

The sad part is that the only older poems (pre-slam, pre-Pulitzer, pre-PBS poems) that get read at all are the poems taught in schools. Thank God for the wild nomads who prowl around the hedges of the university, utter outcasts or resident misfits, who read and shout about what they read, & do so outside the sonorous halls of Ac. Because these are the ones who keep alive the tradition of reading unassigned poems, non-canonical works — the hard-to-read mystical prophetic Blake, the real Novalis.

But back to Young, himself a notable victim of institutional neglect — though in his own day (he was born about 1680) no poet was more famous in England, better paid (always wanting more), more highly regarded critically. (He is a sobering lesson to current poet-celebs.)

Neglected as he has been for centuries by the Academy, his work has flourished in other strange, almost magical ways: by the intense and problematic influence *Night Thoughts* (just that one poem) has wielded in many times and places. The course of that history makes me realize that it often takes centuries for the poem, the essential poem, to appear fully. Millennia maybe. Like those agaves that blossom only once a century, only sometimes do some of the great old poems come to flower, as the *Iliad* did after a thousand years of neglect flower in the Renaissance, and again in the German Romantic era, and again in our own. And as *Gilgamesh* has waited three thousand years to flower in our day, when from a bunch of dusty tablets it has turned for us into the central, defining poem of manhood, city, destiny for us — and for no other time between its composition and now.

Of *Night Thoughts*, then. What they did with Poe, the Europeans also did with Young. He became not a text but an atmosphere, an attitude. They associated him with their own dark crazies, *Maldoror & Gaspard de la Nuit* and Nerval and Barbey and Novalis and Hoffmann.

It is not that the French enjoy Young and we do not. It is that they take him to be an entirely different kind of poet, one who has (as in some unwritten Borges story) written a text utterly different from the one we read, though the denotative meaning is the same.

When they read him, the language doesn't get in the way of the poem anymore.

The poem is what is found in translation.

2.

When we talk about Young's *Night Thoughts* at all, it's usually because we've noticed, somewhere in an album of Blake pictures or a glossy illustration in some text on romanticism or clinical depression or melancholia, a sleek, arresting image by William Blake from the surviving series of engravings he did for a deluxe edition of *Night Thoughts*. Only the pictures prompted by — or it might be truer to say dreamed by — the first four books of the nine-book poem in fact survive, of the many hundreds of drawings and engravings Blake made. We read that this picture — say, a vertical naked figure, his ankles in the sky, blows a long, sweet-belled trumpet right into the earsocket of a skeleton who seems to be gladly rousing from its shroud — is an illustration from *Night Thoughts*. The picture so tellingly, playfully (the trumpeter's sex is hidden by a coyly but naturally enough raised knee) argues the abrupt and welcome character of the resurrection of the dead, that we perhaps are not required by curiosity to seek out the poem that tries to take on new life through Blake's image.

If we can find a copy of *Night Thoughts* — Dover reprinted (only) the four books with Blake's engravings handsomely enough thirty years ago, and it is that paperback I'm looking at now — we flip through and find the picture, and see that it is on the opening leaf of "Night the Second." We start reading, and find the opening lines:

> "When the cock crew, he wept" — smote by that eye
> Which looks on me, on all; that power, who bids
> This midnight centinel, with clarion shrill,
> Emblem of that which shall awake the dead,
> Rouse souls from slumber into thoughts of heaven.

That's what Young gives. All the rest: naked muscular androgyne sleekly athletically beautiful; an Olympic trumpeter rousing a perky, not the least bit grisly corpse from the neat burial shroud; a trumpet in the sky — all that is Blake.

Or is it? Where is the cockcrow Young wants us to hear, where is the eye, the looking, the slumber, the heaven? All metamorphosed, that single word clarion turning trumpet, and the trumpet — the exact center of the image is the trumpet's mouthpiece snug in the human mouth — generates for Blake the whole image. In other words, the poem has dreamed itself into and through Blake into another blossom of its meaning.

In other words, for every person who (till now, fortunate reader) has read those opening lines of "Night 2," ten thousand have seen the Blake picture. In other words, Blake has given birth to Young anew.

In other words: in other words. The whole poem lives in other words.

3.

It is not often that I've been asked to review a book published two centuries ago, but here it comes. Jonas Mekas, visiting the publisher of this paper, noticed on Phong Bui's desk this small calf-bound book: *Edward Young: The Complaint; or Night Thoughts on Life, Death and Immortality. To which are added The Last Day, A Poem. And A Paraphrase on Part of the Book of Job.* (Brookfield, E. Merriam & Co. 1818.) It is a late edition, three quarters of a century after the poem's first publication (London, 1742). Looking at the pretty little book, and from his own European education and wide reading recognizing the text as one so central to the development of romanticism, the Gothic, the Decadent, and in general the whole psychologizing drift of literature from the 19th Century onward, Jonas proposed that the poem, so little known in America, be reviewed in *The Brooklyn Rail*, and further suggested the present reviewer to be assigned the task.

To turn to the text itself is indeed to enter the dark. But not the dark we want. Not the dark that the continental romantics found there, full of demon glitter and sardonic images. It is not the great shattering dark of Beddoes or Nerval, or the sinister, ever-moving dark of E.T.A. Hoffmann. Instead we find not the welcome dark of fantasy but the dimness, the funereal gloom of a chilly English church, twilight on a wintry day, some padre droning on & on in a spate of sermon, chastening the skeptic. Glorious rhetoric, but soon we snooze. This priest finds in the coming of death and decay that sort of generalized hope of resurrection that animated so many brilliant poets before him — Herbert, Donne, Crashaw. He proposes his poem as a *Consolation* — the poem's proper title, *Night Thoughts* being an afterthought. He finds in the gloom of death and judgment a fit reason to praise the God of Light. This to us preposterous theodicy, this justification of God and his providence and the pains of existence in a world he created, this is the excitement of the poem, and the basis of its long argument, nine books worth, full of wonderful imagery, rhetorical suasion — but not much that threatens to change our lives.

The poem is written apparently to console, but in fact to instruct. The shadowy figure of Lorenzo, the skeptical and undutiful son, is the person constantly addressed. Unless the reader finds a Lorenzo in herself, the reader is likely to be reading at right angles to the rhetoric of the text — one more reason, perhaps, for the poem's relative lifelessness. For thousands of lines we observe Lorenzo rebuked for unbelief, for indifference to God and God's glorious creation.

And this is, after all, the splendid thing about Edward Young. His poem strives against indifference, which is as we know not only the dullest of all sins, but the most sinister, since it is the root of civic crime (think Germany 1933–1945 — or perhaps some closer examples) and of personal despair: clinical depression. Young seeks to kindle the excitement of Lorenzo, wake him to moral life by making him contemplate the vastness of misery and the even greater, if somewhat hypothetical, vastness of God's grandeur in creation. And since he cannot point to that grandeur in actual presence, he can make it present only by rhetoric. To make the unseen vividly present.

Now praise of the inapparent is always good news for poetry (even if the inapparent has as common a signifier as 'God'), and Young gets a lot from his philosophic certainty — fully Christian, of that faintly Eighteenth-Century Deist flavor we still get from "The Spacious Firmament on High" sung in so many churches. His certainty of divine providence is wrapped in, expressed through, his keen awareness of existential misery.

Writing a few generations after Milton's *Paradise Lost* (after Milton lost paradise for us), Young avails himself of Milton's metrical and rhetorical strategies — at times it feels like Milton Lite — but where Milton is grand, severe, prophetic, Young is plausible, conversational even, trying to persuade. Where Milton takes the huge risk of vanishing grammatically or imagistically into hermeticism, the Stygian and demanding marshes of alchemical speculation, Young is always understandable, literate; he stays within himself, as they say, lucid, interesting. He writes so well, so smoothly, as if he were born among immensities, and nothing ever bruised his thought. Long periodic sentences, architectonically suspended verse paragraphs, telling enjambements, sonorous blank verse. Easy to see why he was popular in his day. Not so easy for us to see why he was so influential.

The moment was ripe. In another decade or two, Bishop Hurd would utter his remarkable lectures on medieval culture and literature, ushering in the immense fashion for the ruin, the Gothick. Magic was in the air — Swedenborg was thrilling Europe with lucid accounts of daytime transactions in the spirit world. The dark Satanic mills, factories, were gearing up, though, to darken our skies and make men and women seek their stars inside. You all know the story. Into this world Young's poem found its way, and there, safe inside a more or less Christian and orthodox argument, lay the shimmering naughtiness of night.

So Young's poem is the first to hit the big time with this extraordinary agency of moon and melancholy that will go on to haunt literature from Walpole and Radcliffe to, most evidently, the Romantics, then the French decadents, all the way down to triste d'Annunzio and beyond, casting its moony spell on the Russian symbolists, and is still not by any means dead in our day, animating (if that's not too sturdy a word) our dormitory poetry of midnight misery, the video games of the Goth, Satanic rock, chic Death.

How amazing that a poem we can barely read with continuous pleasure nowadays (nowanights) should have not only seemed interesting but a masterpiece in its time — far eclipsing Milton for many years. Ezra Pound would have detected a nasty rule in all this: Display fashionable content in a safely competent formal vehicle, and you've got a hit.

Certainly Young's audience was ready for it. The grief of a century of civil war and rebellion lay heavily on England's memory, and the relative peace of recent years, stimulated by the opening of India and the China trade, left the English free to refocus civic demands on providence, sail through gloom into glory, the way the merchants of the East India

Company were struggling through the benighted East & expropriating its jewels. The grand colonial gesture, the British Empire in its earliest stages, the era of Hastings and Clive, Young in passages of immense and (perhaps) unconscious brilliance maps onto the galaxy itself, and ends his long poem (through Book Nine) with a panoply of gorgeous guesswork about other stars and other planets and other sentient races under God's mind — as if yet another ocean full of continents awaiting the explorers of the Hanoverian kings, fleeting like Seraphim through the colonies of the skies.

4.

A poem happens in time, and we call its author the first genius or wastrel who happened to notice it in the psycho-cosm & write it down, having spotted it growing there at the side of the mind.

Casually, slackly, we think: the poem is the seed or source of its translations, illustrations, critical commentary. Not so. The poem compels those to appear, always seeking to make manifest among humankind the still undisclosed shape of the poem itself. The poem solicits the sensibilities and energies of artist, critic, musician, translator, summons them to attend its four-dimensional apparition.

So many midwives a poem needs.

The inexhaustible beginnings of a Rilke, a Hölderlin, a Keats poem… after all these years are still not all written down. A poem is a, always a, only a, beginning.

October 2005
(*Brooklyn Rail*, November 2005)

REFLECTION FOR PEN AMERICA — ON TRANSLATION

Translation is of course conspiracy. Whatever else it is or may intend, translation represents a concerted move of the few against the many, the foreign against the domestic, there against here. It is the paradox of the solitary army, taking orders from a distant text, parlez-vous'ing these commands into some semblance of the speech heard round about the place where the translating is going on. Translators are much-traveled characters, close kin to spies and pioneers — two other occupations with a range of acceptation from the most honorable to the detestably covert. But all are cunning. So when we hear that a translation has been undertaken or published, *cherchez the plot*.

Now if a trove of unknown Inspector Maigret novels should come to light in the attic of one of Simenon's innumerable mistresses, we might expect the resultant flurry of translations to be cued by no more veiled an agenda than Dives at his gilded door — Get more, get more. Things sell.

When, on the other hand, *PEN America*'s editor invites us to reflect on what translations are needed, what is being kept from us, what are they (over there, back then, far away) hiding from us now, there is a gratifying whiff of the conspiracy theory and it seems to me exactly right. We are invited (indicted?) to become co-conspirators in a huge project of subverting the way things are so far.

And what a grand business it would be if from our various cranky or overparticular or generous responses to the question, a permanent forum could be established, under the aegis of PEN, to maintain a continuing archive of titles and authors we need to have translated. A needy and querulous voice (like the voice Socrates assigns to Love itself) that might lift up from time to time and demand Cyprian Norwid or Quirinus Kuhlmann (two poets who happen to be on the top of my oldtimers list of those needing translation).

Such a forum might also remind us that we lose whole bodies of work when translations lose currency, since the language of the translator seldom has the intimate and obsessive presence that the original has in its tongue. Writers whose names we know vanish from our reading tables when their translations age or grow vague. For example, I think we need to hear Quevedo again in our own lingo, and Gautier, and Mörike, and

Lermontov, and Strindberg, and Lautréamont, and Platen, and Tyuchev, and...

It is a fertile and exciting gesture, this *PEN America* idea of opening up the whole issue of what we're missing by being monoglot. Or, most of us, sesquilingual — I mean most of us read Anglo-Indo-Afro-Carib-Australo-American pretty well, even natively, plus a heavy smattering of some other tongue, typically French or Spanish. So we'll call the usual American reader mono-and-a-half-glot. Nevertheless, since that half tongue is seldom up to allowing us to loll in a hammock with Musil's notebooks or Lacan's jokes or Lezama Lima's original paradise, we rightly clamor for the artful interpreter to tell us what those geniuses have been saying.

But in a lifetime of buying original texts and then reading translations (at times performing the religious duties of comparing the texts *en face*), I have come to believe that translation, as an enterprise and a business, is just as much part of the sinister Military-Industrial-Complex (what we now call the Entertainment Industry) as the hexing of the Kyoto Treaty.

So we need to invent a conspiracy, a confederation of spies who bring us the news, from then or there.

What are they keeping from us (whoever they are)? What is out there that we need to hear about, read, come home to? Imagine what our sense of literature would be like if no one had bothered to translate Proust and Dostoevsky and Kafka. When Bellow sneers at some putative Zulu Tolstoy, I fancy I hear the voice that could never have predicted Gilgamesh or Bobrowski or Rushdie or Lessing (Rhodesia, for crissakes!) or Meddeb or Diop or any other of the humane texts and geniuses that had the temerity to arise in regions off the A-list.

But Bellow's prejudice is accurate enough in one sense — there is a worldwide plot against our business as usual, a plot of eternity against the comforts of time. Translation, whether translations of new texts, or new translations of old texts, or deviant translations of traditional texts (like Gavin Douglas's Scots version of the *Æneid* that thrilled Pound so much, or William Arrowsmith's *Petronius* — that satirized Pound), all translations betoken a conspiracy against the mind-at-present.

We sleep in language, if language does not come to wake us with its strangeness.

So the bringers of the strange are our appeal, the writers we need now. I'm going to offer a brief list of titles, in case some idle dragomans are itching for work.

Ernst Jünger, *Heliopolis*, his big utopian novel. Several decades ago a very small press published a version I've never found — Jünger's most ambitious book needs a good literary translation, one that considers the precise and lapidary nature of Jünger's style, likely the most self-consciously focused of twentieth-century German writers.

Boris Vian, *L'herbe rouge*. A sequel of sorts to his *L'écume des jours*, which was a sensational million-seller in France (and once a Penguin paperback in English). Vian's perennially fresh sensibility makes him such a sweet alarmist.

E.T.A. Hoffmann, *The Serapion Brotherhood*. A nineteenth-century translation once was to be found in Bohn's Library, I think. Certainly needs recasting. Hoffmann's neuroses are precise and vivid, and fraternal with our own. He can talk now, if we let him. (Look at the incredible story "The Fermata" if you think he's all goblins.)

Novalis, *The Apprentices of Sais*. A short initiatory novel, a real challenge to a translator's double sense of style (highly formal) and agenda (deeply poetic, æsthetic, almost spiritual).

Beyond such easily named masterworks needing Green Cards, I can't quite stop myself from reeling off some more names. Jean Paulhan, Gertrud Kolmar, René-Guy Cadou, Louis-René des Forêts, scarcely translated at all into English though celebrated in their own terrains and in international criticism. I need to read them now in my own demotic.

It's not just the æsthete and experimentalist readers who need help. Even the bourgeoisie is deprived of its own international comfy classics: what about finally getting Jules Verne and Eugène Sue and C.F. Meyer and Theodor Fontane into English complete at last? And even Balzac is still not fully translated into unbowdlerized English versions.

(My original plan of attack in this note was voided by a timely compliance on the part of Penguin, that cunning press, which gave us a translation, I still haven't seen it, of E.T.A. Hoffmann's *Kater Murr*, *Tomcat Murr*, we'd say, which long struck me as close to the top of the list of books we need englished, Hoffmann's masterpiece of the talking cat, the stories interwoven, the hangover that lasts a whole life. So perhaps even as I write or you read, someone is translating Fijman & de Chazal and Suhrawardi or the complete journals of the Goncourt brothers.)

And then there are the poets. Not just the famous ones like the great Max Jacob and Georg Heym of whom we hear much, but so little of whose work has ever been put into circulation in English. There are others, the ones whose very success has obscured them. They are the ones we are taught to think of as Thinkers, but who are really poets, who thought in language and embodied thinking in the grace of words — I mean for instance the superpoets Nietzsche & Marx, who have always been presented for their Ideas, as if their texts existed just to notate conclusions. Strip away their working-in-language (which is the revelatory gesture of poetry, soulmaking, revelation), and all you have left is opinion. Take the poetry away from Dante and you have a quaint *Fodor's Guide to Purgatory*, as we could imagine a humdrum translator taking away the epochal transformative poetry of James Merrill's *Divine Comedies* and leaving us with a scuffed old ouija board.

(*PEN America Journal* #2, "Home and Away," 2001)

TENSIONS

A note on two newly published translations I'm anxious to let the world know about: Stuart Kendall's Gilgamesh *and Thomas Meyer's* Beowulf.

Where does the tension come from that runs the poem?

What's missing in almost all translations of the old stuff (the classics, the canon, that fleet of inscrutable foreign vessels lined up, sailing in against our ignorance) is tension. Tension means stretching, pulling the fabric taut, making the hearer (reader) hold the breath.

Scholars are mostly not good at holding anybody's breath. (I think of a few exceptions — Magoun's *Kalevala*, Tedlock's *Popol Vuh*, Arrowsmith's *Petronius*) but they are indeed exceptions.

But here come two grand triumphs of poetry bringing old instances of itself to new life. Simply said, a good translation of a poem must be itself a good poem.

Stuart Kendall's new translation of the *Gilgamesh* tablets, Thomas Meyer's newly published but decades-old translation of the *Beowulf* manuscript — these are our ancestral narratives: one of the whole western world, one of our own Northern Paranoid Lifestyle culture, whose languages we still are.

All great epics are always about slaying the monster. And here *Beowulf* and *Gilgamesh* in a strange way seem almost to be the same story. Hero vs. Monster. But Gilgamesh starts out as a tyrant, wielding thigh-right over all the brides and youths of the City. The City complains to the gods, who tame him by love — they send him a companion, the Dutiful Young Man, his Enkidu, someone to fight alongside him, to cherish. Love unhinges tyranny. Beowulf begins alone and ends alone. He is the individual, the solitary hero, who acts alone. Already we're in the unlikely world, however furry, of Kafka and Camus, the hero defined by his relation to his society, by his free action within its necessities. The hero nurses his difference; his difference empowers his moral superiority to others. What children heroes seem to us, children with swords.

These are primal narrations, and need careful enactment in our stale new languages. To feel their energies, to cherish their differences.

A translation has to make love with the text. But not to it — the translator is not a suave Lothario, touching every text with the same practiced strokes. No, the translator must meet each text humble to its difference. Humble, but horny.

Kendall and Meyer know how to coax their poems to speak so we can hear. Looking at a page of Meyer's *Beowulf* I get excited, something's happening here with the space of language which is (forgive me, it has to be said) the space of time.

Stuart Kendall works time in a physical way — takes the ancient tablets and breaks them into pages, pages that shatter the ongoing narrative into (instead) confrontative moments. So that looking at a given page of text (in the strikingly handsome Contra Mundum edition) has the feel of picking up a fragment of the cuneiform tablet, miraculously lucid, magically set in order so the reader can follow the story. The solemn priestly tablets of the "original" (don't ask) are transformed into communiqués from the field of action: the page.

The page is the field. The page is spacetime itself, your moment. The page (since Gutenberg) has been the only time there is.

That's what these two exemplary translations — nothing like each other except in the profound ground of modern poetics from which they upwell — have in common: the page as unit of imposition, golden tablet of their revelations.

God forgive us, we read *Beowulf* as if it were a story, that shabby thing, rather than the glorious exposition of linguistic transformation — kennings, alliterations, howl of vowel sequences, thunder of shifting stresses. The story is just there to pin language on: language that sustains us by transforming, lightning-quick, the consensual world from which language arises, possible words making impossible things.

Usually when you read a translation of an ancient text, you wind up quietly (furtively often) wondering what all the fuss is about. A city besieged, a grumpy hero, a monster slain? All that Stalinist architecture, heroes, peoples, plots, so effing what? It was the language that worked for the hearers, the Original Hearers, the ones for whom they spoke and memorized and wrote — they memorized the words themselves because the words are what counted. The words are what shaped time, shaped the hearers' time.

The time of hearing. Warriors, merchants, weavers, tillers — weary after a day's work, listening to a storyteller. What counted was not the story but the telling. The telling is everything. The caress, the tenderness, the aggression of the words as they poured forth, unstoppably they gave the listeners the experience they craved. Do you think they really, as they listened, always kept straight which was Glaucus, which Diomedes?

Modern translations need to recover the time of listening.

That's what seems to me to happen in the translations I'm looking at.

So the story is an armature to weave words on — whose flesh will be the tilth and nourishment of the act of hearing, reading.

Noteworthy that we understand or accept this meat most readily in works that present themselves as writing in 'dialect' — Flann O'Brien, Junot Diaz, Amos Tutuola — where it's perfectly clear we're reading for the language, the shimmer it gives to the experienced time that is the actual nature of literature.

Now poets find their way to the old texts and summon something in them into new life. The spur to shape sound. The story that agitates the breath of the teller till the hearer shares it, the angst, the squeeze of tension. Tension.

By chopping sentences into lines, staggering them down the page, not letting the sentence rest, Kendall keeps us going, each page a reward and a challenge to go on. It's wonderfully unsettling — where are the nice smooth continuous paragraphs of (say) N.K. Sandars' moving and legible translation of *The Epic* (note the literary claim) *of Gilgamesh*? Instead we get Kendall's dramatically urgent starting and stopping like a man in rage, his timeless pauses, his insistence on bringing us at every moment into the hero's moment. Emotion is a gate we can't walk around, we have to go through. Kendall can make us feel the baffled stammer of a hero unsure of what to cry out next. His method is frictional, making the reader react tablet by tablet, ever thrown back into the story. Ability to react to stimuli is the universal property of, surest sign of, life.

Meyer uses the page differently. Each page is a composed poem or prosem in itself, each in its own 'form' or shape. It's as if the poem is a cycle of small poems that *summate* to epic. Long lines, short lines, space and hurried prose-like statements enact the fabled sense of 'measure' with which American poetry came to new life (via Pound and Williams and their heirs). There is a dazzling proficiency of music in Meyer's own work, and here he sings fresh from his deconstructed original — a poem broken into its music.

So you can't have the story without the language.

There is no story without the language.

Without the language we'd have only dreams and nightmares, monsters and wars.

(*Nomadics Blog*, January 2013)

(*Golden Handcuffs Review* #17, 2013/2014)

INTRODUCTION TO *ŒDIPUS AFTER COLONUS AND OTHER PLAYS*

ŒDIPUS AFTER COLONUS

Early one morning I was sitting alone at the dining room table in Charlotte's family home in Boston, watching the first light from the harbor come up Bellevue Hill. Out of nowhere it said in my head "Oedipus after Colonus." Immediately I was full of excitement, hope, guesswork. The Colonus of Sophocles, most mysterious of all the Greek plays, challenging everything we know, and challenging as well everything we think we know about Greek thought and Greek conceptions of reality. It had haunted me since I read it as a kid, after finding my way to it through Yeats' great renderings of its choral odes. What did happen at the end of the play, what did happen to Oedipus? All we know is what the messenger came back babbling about. That babble, homeophonically worked off the Greek of the messenger speech in Sophocles, begins the messenger's words in my play.

My play. I wonder how much it is or was mine. Later that day (or was it the next day) we drove up to northern Maine, driving through those scores of miles of unbroken evergreen woods; as we drove along, my mind filled with ideas about the play. When we got back to Annandale (after a wonderful visit with Jennifer Moxley & Steve Evans, longer for an April blizzard) I began work on the play and finished it quickly. It was only a few months later, on our next visit to Boston, that I noticed for the first time that on the mantelpiece behind where I had been sitting, there was a small plaster bust. I picked it up and peered at it, & read the Italian inscription: SOFOCLE. So who knows.

Œdipus after Colonus was staged for the first time at HERE in Soho in September 2010. The production was designed and directed by Crichton Atkinson, who utterly famed my sense of the thing. Œdipus was played magnificently by my dear friend the novelist & playwright Carey Harrison — I can still hear his final monologue. The production played to capacity audiences for a week, with this cast: Colista Turner (Chorus), Richard Saudek (Messenger), Zoe Morris (Ismene), Joanne Tucker (Antigone), Carey Harrison (Old Man).

[...]

MONOLOGUES FOR ORPHEUS

Of course my sense of it was Orpheus as every poet, who loses what he best loves in the welter of his making, losing what he loves in the very act of praise and song.

I felt that the poet is talking to himself, sometimes 'self-consoling' (in Gurdjieff's memorable phrase), sometimes cutting through to clarity about himself and the world it is his business to praise — following Rilke's instruction in the *Sonnets*, Rilke, our greatest modern incarnation of Orpheus divus.

In my play, I imagine Orpheus sitting by himself, unaware of the four people placed around him. (They can be thought of as moving or just sitting there too — in the first public performance, they all remained seated, sometimes turning toward one another or Orpheus.) The four voices (they can be any gender, age, style) address Orpheus but he doesn't hear them, though sometimes he seems to catch a hint of what they're saying. The one moving, but not speaking, character is Eurydice, who weaves in and out of the performers, touching them, moving them about as she wishes. They can't see her, Orpheus can't see her, but she sees and hears all; she is the motive.

The first private read-through of the play was performed — Eurydice absent — by Ben Tripp, Sylvia Gorelick, Charlotte Mandell, Cameron Seglias, and Maksim Tsikharovich. I'm grateful to them for giving me a chance to hear the words out there.

The first public performances were at Bard College in February 2012, and took the form of staged readings. I had asked the dancer and choreographer Marjorie Folkman to direct the play, and to dance/move the role of Eurydice; while a full-scale performance was not possible at that time, she did wonderfully marshal the forces and guide them, and me, towards an effective evening in the theater. Orpheus was spoken by Thomas Bartscherer, and the other four voices were the poet Lynn Behrendt, the poet Mikhail Horowitz, the novelist Paul La Farge, & the scholar Florian Becker. The play was preceded by music, first a movement of a Bach suite performed by the bassoonist David Adam Nagy. Then Péter Laki sang three Hellenistic Songs by Adrienne Elisha, songs to texts from the last centuries of that Greek world into which Orpheus, like Apollo had come from the north. So accompanied, we came to the outskirts of hell, to hear the voices Orpheus sometimes hears, and how he sometimes answers.

An original video production of the play was created by Crichton Atkinson, who played Orpheus. A, B, C and D were played by Adam Janos, Olimpia Dior, David Gerson, and Tyler Alterman. Camera: Brandyn Johnson. [...]

CHAIR

The five plays in this collection are all in a sense Greek plays, responses to ancient themes & memes, written in texts that aim to respond at least to the shapes and rhythms, and careful character constraints, of classic tragedy. All of them feature main characters who would be familiar to a Greek audience. In the case of Chair (the word itself is a pun on chaire, the Attic for hail!), we can read the play as a celebration of Dionysus, a theophany, his grace and power revealed, along with his power over our feelings and our seemings. So if I had to give this the kind of title it would have had when all the Greek plays came to us with Latin titles, this would have been Dionysus Revelatus. I'm happy it is just chair, though, the throne, the resting point, the place of concealment.

The plot of the play was suggested by a tense situation mentioned by a friend; the course of the play suggests a possible solution.

HATE RADIO

My Greek title for this play would be Thersites — that odious but interesting character in Homer, a gadfly, a pest, a hater of quality and a loudmouth, whose life and fate are bound up with the querulous, the aggressive, the purely mean.

Thersites, yes, to let it count as a 'Greek play' but more pointedly to see it, set it, as a satyr play — the comic grotesquerie with which the Athenians rounded off their solemn tragedies. Don't think of the satyr play tradition as the cartoon between the double features. It was more like: the return through the comic to ordinary life. Art brings us back to ourselves. Don Giovanni sinks with a shriek into hell, & the survivors sing a pretty little song, a peasant melody. Tragedy, with all its pity and terror, must be banished so we can go back into the street. So we can go home.

Hate Radio came from an afternoon when Charlotte and I went in for a slice of pizza to a small town den, pleasant enough. We were the only customers. And the radio was on. A blaring, unending spate of ripe

American banker-fascism, praising the 'creators of wealth' & scourging the evil government that tried to tax the wealthy.

We carried our food out and away. The emptiness of the restaurant, the determined bray of sneering hatred we'd heard made me wonder if there were some way to investigate a hatred that was not manipulated by an obvious political paymaster to con a half-awake populace but a hatred that was radical, a hatred that just hated.

Though it's called Hate Radio, it wants to be staged. We must get to see the poor man who hates us so.

The text mentions several musical selections the actor is understood to cue up and play on air between his ravings. If possible, the identical pieces should be used — only a short passage, say a minute or two, need be played. They should be played loud, filling the space as it would be in such a studio.

ORESTES

How late I've come to writing plays. If I guess why it came to that, I'd think it's because only in plays could I hope to overcome or undo or unmake or remake, somehow process, some unbearable experiences of reading and hearing — like the overwhelming horror of killing the mother in the Greek plays that tell of the murder of Klytaimnestra by her son.

To try to relieve my own inner hurt at that deed, to say it isn't so. But it is so. And is a horror. All the more so because the killing is done to avenge the death of the father, an affront to the patriarchal order. As great as the Aeschylus Oresteia is, it is profoundly steeped in an attitude that is urgently patriarchal, embattled even. It celebrates (even if grievingly) the passing on of the patriarchate to the next generation.

So it became necessary for me to crawl like a mouse before the magnitude of Aeschylus and try to gnaw the ground around his sandals, to dig out the primal story, the scarlet nights when the mother ruled, and where Electra carries on her mother's work.

As I write, the play has not yet been staged; I want to thank the actors Marianne Rendon and Hannah Mitchell for reading some of the scenes with me, to get the sound right. And thank Carey Harrison for finding it a play.

(Œdipus after Colonus and Other Plays, 2014)

THREADS 9 : ROBERT SAYS

I had seen Brakhage films years before as a kid. When I was in high school my mother gave me a subscription to a film society where they showed avant-garde movies. So, years later I found out, yes, I had seen super early Brakhage films.

I didn't come to really know Brakhage's work until he came to live with us in 1963. Robert Duncan had told him that he should learn from me. It seemed very true in a way. The level of literature and his concerns with it were so very different from anything that Duncan was involved with and were pretty different from what I was involved with, but I understood what Duncan was saying. I knew some things and was much younger than Duncan. Therefore, I'd have more time to pay attention to the literary dimensions of Stan's needs, Duncan was saying. I suppose that was true. Brakhage and I had a firm relationship with much argumentation, but that was long after the deep image period.

I was concerned with the deep image of 1960–1962 and then I began to feel as if, as you could probably tell from Statement, *it were an embarrassment. I was embarrassed to have ever been bothered with any ism and I behaved in* Statement *in a what, who me kind of way. I didn't feel that the deep image was wrong, but simply I did not want to compel the next ten years of my life to any ism.*

in conversation with Dennis Barone [early 1980s]

Film was very important for me growing up, the way it is for most Americans of my era. I used to go to the movies every day, sometimes twice a day. There were lots of movies in the city; there were five movie theaters within walking-distance of my house. One of them (the Kinema) showed Italian movies — I seldom went there; there was a Jewish movie theater — I never went there because I didn't know any Yiddish when I was a kid — but the other four English-language moviehouses I went to all the time, and I think that that was a very wonderful preparation for me to understand the way in which images are constantly being — the visible *other, so to speak, that walks with us. But the kids of my generation really did believe deeply in what they saw in the films — they didn't have TV yet, I was thirteen or fourteen before TV came to be commercially commanding — we ourselves didn't have a set — a walnut cabinet whose double doors opened to show a Freed-Eisemann TV — till I was fifteen. So the dominant images were those of newspapers and magazines —* Life *magazine with its wonderful insistence on lots of photos — and movies. And the* image-world *that we have begun in the past twenty or thirty years to question more deeply — through the Structuralists, through the critical-theory people, but more than that through the magical folks. The work that Couliano did with Bruno [...], an extraordinary book about Giordano Bruno and the cult of visual images in the Renaissance. Bruno's notion — and it's that as much as anything else that got him burnt at the stake — was that we are controlled by images, and in a very literal sense we* can *be controlled by them; that the business of government, of society, is to control the population through images. And once you begin thinking this it doesn't take you long to think of all the ways in which that's true — "What should you marry?" "I should marry a beautiful woman." "What does a beautiful woman look like?" "She looks like, that, that, that..." & the way in which the cult of images imposes itself upon the individual, becoming this sinister other presence that lives with us. Peter Lamborn Wilson writes a lot about this. And a poet who was a very close friend of Robert Duncan, David Levi Strauss — no connection with the French guy — writes interesting things about this, books on images; he's been working on the Abu Ghraib pictures lately. But the domination of our political presence, political acts, economic, everything, by images, is something that Bruno begins to discuss in the 1580s and 1590s. It goes underground, treated only by magicians and magical theorists — Crowley and Yeats and so on at the beginning of the twentieth century were talking about it in one way or another — and now we're talking about it again. [...]*

I think it's a matter of size, to begin with. I said when I was a kid I went to the movies every day, and the reason I did is that my family had fallen into the clutches of a curious ophthalmologist, or oculist, or maybe he was just an optometrist, who had his own ideas about how to treat eye problems. My eye problem then, like now, was simply myopia, just shortsightedness, nearsightedness. He felt, however, that it shouldn't be treated by glasses, and my mother didn't want it treated by glasses — my people had strange ideas about health — everybody has strange ideas about health, everybody's odd in that. Anyway, his method of treating me was to send me to the movies every day, and I was to sit in the front row. So I would be forced to look around me — above, to the side, down — so I had to be in the image, so to speak. That was wonderful. I didn't like all the movies; I naturally liked movies best that had adventure in them and not romance. But when you're very close, even a twenty-foot high romantic embrace can be interesting, its planes and shapes — though I didn't see very well, everything was fuzzy. I'm answering the question this way because I just now am realizing that that's probably why this is, I'm discovering this answer. Essentially when I look at an image I want to be inside it; I want it to be as large as those were when I was a kid, I want to look at it close up. So when I see the Crivelli, all I want to do is enter it, be in it, feel the brick, feel the light, the shade in the alleyway, etc. I like all that. And the first thing I think an image does for me is to express itself as an environment into which I can come.

in conversation with Sam Lohmann (2007)

9.

A BOOK OF THE EYE (MOVING OR NOT)

ON KENNETH ANGER'S *INVOCATION OF MY DEMON BROTHER*

frenzy of magician / mitrailleuse / machine gun is
also a woman / savaging the invoker's breath /
                                                            star arms /
a skin / wrapped & unwrapped for Lady Babalon /
enstasis of the woman's face / a *conscious* Falconetti
lifting her blue eyes, brown nipples / drip with light

If you've got good news, burn it. That's the news,
turn everything to conscious fire. / The dark
magician becomes Magus /
                          The abyss
                          was syntax
                          & we lost our way.
But our way was fire & we learn to burn.
We do not have to go that way again.
Juggler in red pants & old books led
us out. Grand Canyon, red strata
flaming streets up to the blue who who you / sky /
to whom her arms /
                          exult / face
knowing the silence behind the music / science /
as a man would enter a woman knowing
only the beginning /
                          Boys sulk
naked on the sofa. Bacchuses flaccid.
Rouse them. The breath
of the magician wakes them / the flicker
(heartbeat of an eye)
wakes them. Pain
would rouse them but the pain is gone
all over into the magician / electric light
poured from an urn, he burns
his message in the cold grass

                                    *

brown nipples
touchstones
truer / Red Devil / White Devil / Brown Nipples /
dirty fingers do a joint / the skull
allows
        the smoke / allows
the magician / reads it all in his pain,
crosses the abyss & burns his hands.

Stay in there. Lubed anus
clenches on a star
studded seedcock /
        my Lady
's a star, an eye / inside me looking out
one eye / for all my travelling.

        *

this is the movie of what phallus sees coming to its
furnace, nest where it dies & up it flies, these images
up the spine / Eye of Horus / Lord / who sees in us such
liberty.

        (*Caterpillar* #10, 1970)

THE MYSTERY OF *KASPAR HAUSER*:
A DIALOGUE ON THE WERNER HERZOG FILM

LEX: It is not clear to me where such light comes from you claim to see there.

TEX: It is of course not light but interceptions of.

LEX: But it is a womanless dark he gives us, a film that knows nothing of sex or economics. By what Coleridgean abstention he could have risen! In a film about a sexless coinless man, he could have made the clearest statements about our twisted problematic, our interzone of sex and economics. Fassbinder can do it well in *Faustrecht der Freiheit*, the movie about Fox.

TEX: I agree, he does not do so. Herzog is content to stroke the anomie. But see — he celebrates on behalf of a thousand million inarticulate humans this one inarticulate man they all are.

LEX: You mean women like the film, and because of your cult of women (genitivum subjectivum et objectivum) you like it too. Because they find there the riddle of their own tongue-tied skepticism about religion, logic, education represented, dargestellt, as a *man* — the one man in history they don't have to feel inferior to, a lad more luckless than they, a riddle, they swarm to embrace this Kaspar, this eternal infant at times I think you represent such a figure too, lucus a non lucendo — by eloquence you silence the constraints of mere communication. You overswarm, he underswarms.

TEX: Yet when he speaks! O Mother, how far I am from everything! he says, weeping suddenly.

LEX: Existential cliché. He is a crimeless Meursault, thrown back into a pretty time, taupe fields of grain, soft focus telephoto flattenings, as if all existence were memory, like the tenor singing *This image is enchanting fair* at the start — an old tenor, Slezak was it, featured only for the *old* of it.

TEX: But Meursault *is* his crime, or the possibility of it. Crimeless, he becomes another being.

LEX: The Britannica claims that Kaspar Hauser stabbed himself, to work up pity, or renew a flagging public interest in his mystery — but did the job too well.

TEX: O I love his demi-suicide then, his half-deed — so like his life to die that way, unborn, unslain. Man between.

LEX: Be aware in loving him that your hero lives in a crappy film, a ragbag of slack editing, casual adventurism, easy raids on familiar territory.

TEX: All I know is that when, under the voiceover of K's letter, I see a stork eat a frog in a garden still in flower after a hundred years, I see something I have never known before, a new in fact dimension of the cinema, a world in which information may come at us from many sides, a world liberated from the linearity of judgment — that frees us from the Laws much more successfully than his easy (I agree) jibes at religion and positivism and Logik do.

LEX: Image of an image. The film indulges.

TEX: But what it indulges is also our eyes. No one has shown animals, *known* animals like this Herzog — the stork, the bewildering camel walking on his knees through the medieval city — the glistening little pigs of *Aguirre*, the green monkeys. The gleam of fur is Augustinian, handles our sorrow at the thingness of things.

TEX (continuing): But even saying these things is to accept your kind of argument — and to ask the film to be about or represent. So I should retract what I've just said, not because it isn't so, but because I want to conduct our troubled argument accurately. It is as a *film* I reject KH. It disposes of ("has at its disposition") no visual harmony, no rhythm of visual unfolding. Instead there are many posed, static, lovely scenes, arias, footlight numbers: the rouged showman displaying his monsters; Kaspar plays the piano; your stork eats his frog; the professor is mocked by Kaspar's sly tree frog; a brute who looks like Anton Bruckner teaches a limp lunatic to walk; cities uncoil in the distances — all of these I grant are memorable. But where is the *rythmos* of syntax that holds them together? The film is a series of postcards from the 19th century. I expect any minute to see Hegel look out the window, or the young Marx hurry by.

LEX (interrupting): You're wrong, there is a rhythm, a potent one. But just now this postcard stuff, that is wonderful, the sense of Time Herzog did give me. I thought of Hegel too, the unseen presence of that great spirit watching over the ways of the Mind with itself in this rigorously pretty landscape, from which all human suffering is excluded except that which Kaspar Hauser himself exemplifies. Because the dialectic is also *flow*, not a set of banal contradictions debaters have at one another with. Image answers image.

TEX: Don't tell me the rhythm-of-everything-there-is is what you find here. How useless that would be. I ask the rhythm of an art to discover. Stick to the film. Cinematographically, the film is nada. Only people interested in Directors could praise it; it is slick without being expert, touches deep places with a shallow probe that distorts the flesh that lies between the target and its own unavailing reach.

LEX: But *I* am reached. And you're asking of film what you wouldn't ask of any other art, a *surface syntax* any child can abstract *&* take home. How would a young filmmaker *imitate* the Herzog KH? There are no filmic gimmicks he hasn't seen before. Maybe you mean that if it isn't imitable, stylistically imitable, it isn't art?

TEX: A y-f-m would imitate Herzog by mingling sudden Halloween brutalities with pastoral scenes (*Aguirre* works by this alone, it seems). He would sneer at obviously vapid figures of church and state and school. He would equate physical deformity with mental deformity. He would furnish his troubled-looking (Bruno S, Klaus Kinski) characters with sparse lines, seeking profundity by eliminating all dialogue that relates to feeling or to situation: his characters are like some demented John Wayne, rugged and austere to the point of mindlessness. To be wordless is to be mindless.

LEX: You refer to another actor, another style-world, and that gives me a clue. *KH* is a film, not a meta-film. For you, as for any merchant of the avant-garde, that art is best which refers to itself. Painting is about painting; the buyer is strapped in a world where all fashions and all negations point to the same economic act: purchase of the work-of-art; it becomes the business of the critic (i.e., the showman) to keep the buyer entranced by the endless capacity of art to comment on itself, on every instance of itself, until the very fact of comment on art *makes* it art. You miss that in Herzog; he is a raw romantic, a ballsy half-baked pretender trying to make films that see the world for the first time. His adventure is unsettling to the critics; he doesn't make his obeisances before Hitchcock or Resnais; his anomie and his brutality are strictly his own. Like any naïve artist he is at every moment denying his art, begging like a magician for the means to elapse, elide, disappear and leave only the Real World Changed towards which his art gestures. For me, his films have the power of early socialist cinema: Vertov, Dovzhenko: "I find by camera the multitudinous truth of the world and aim it at you"; Herzog has Vertov's confidence, that power of vision and pain and understanding, makes its own statement as he shapes the world he'll want the camera to shape.

TEX: I doubt this naïveté you argue. He is a sophisticate, I mean degenerate, spring the pastoral like any Alexandrian.

LEX: The sense of wonder I mean can live even in a sleazy Alexandrian — what do I care about that? *KH* silenced all my irritations, my noble distaste for Once More with the Pachelbel Kanon, my adult distaste for Herzog's cheap shots, my historian's disappointment at how he oversimplified the actual of story KH, and wasted the extraordinary problematic of that apparition, my poet's distrust of how he superimposes his Moroccan imagery over Kaspar's own. Silenced, I was left vulnerable to the paradise landscape, the inarticulate angel blaring out sudden agonies of that obvious we have never seen.

TEX: I know you at last: you are an anarchist. That's why you like the movie so much. You pretend to dislike its 'cheap shots' at authority, but you swallow down the cheapest trick of all — having a picturesque young man walking around a pretty landscape saying youthful profundities. You are a child, or an anarchist, who have torn down the canons of art all criticism means to enforce. You bathe in sentiment; you probably write freeverse.

LEX: Perhaps. I do admit that one of the high points of the film for me was when Bruno S played that Mozart piece: he made it more interesting then turned it inside out, worked some silence in. The nineteenth century *began* to understand playing Mozart, with the remorseless *continuousness* of eighteenth-century art broken, smashed into meaningful new form.

TEX: Anarchist is maybe too polite a word for you. If I had known your take on Mozart, I would[n't] have begun this argument. That's just silly, what you say. Mozart is unimprovable. Everyone agrees.

15 October 78
(*Let There Be Light* #25, 1978)

FROM *ORGANON*:
SECTIONS ON MATT PHILLIPS'S RECENT WORK

Nudes are merciless.

*

I'd like to lose a woman in a chair.

*

One sees these pictures as items in a dictionary.

*

In languages (like Latin) where the noun is declined, the noun appears in various 'forms' or desinences. Speakers of analytic languages (like English) tend to feel those declensional 'forms' as variations on a theme. But they are not variations — they are the actual, factual & exclusive aspects of a thing's reality. Declension exhausts the referentiality of nouns. In non-declined languages, referentiality is as infinite as context, chooses.

*

Phillips is still busy with the permutations. That makes his pictures linguistically very American. Even more than diners and discos, they are *vernacular* — not by virtue of their subjects (so often European, exotic) but by their incapacity to find rest in one perfect gesture.

*

Americans are people who see everything as variation.

*

Valéry: "There is always a grain of truth in what is pleasing, and a grain of falsity in what is shocking."

*

Call a monograph on MP: "A Grain of Truth." See criticism, even this benign deictic I substitute for critique, as necessarily concern to shock: re/expose the work attended. So in all criticism, "a grain of falsity?"

*

Or call a novel on MP an eighteenth-century one: "Phillips, or, Constancy." Saint-Saëns and the pear tree. Art is what you do every day.

*

Nudes are merciless, but he tries to make them relent, charm them into the room, confuse their curves with empty cups, unknown flowers.

*

Constancy means his address unflinching from the elusiveness of things, elusiveness of his own means.

*

Scriabin, a tone-cutter Phillips is likely to despise, refused to play a sustained note — only a trill, faster the better, could keep spirit free of the fly-paper of matter, of fixed tone that by its fixity rots. Tone moves. If it does not renew itself, it decays.

*

How much of perfect draughtsmanship is slowness of fancy, stodginess of imagination?

*

Yet in the arcane rational spaces of de Vries, one loses oneself, as if forever.

*

Pascal in his famous boast of being scared by the infinite spaces, was thinking of Holland, perspectiva artificialis, and of the insides of machines, where space is limitless and pointless.

*

So the very messiness (I use the word as a lordly Englishman would order his omelette) of impressionism restores to us the very fact of things, as they were before the secular decay of glance, and thus, as they *are* in eternity? That was the old hypothesis.

*

There are no afterimages here.

*

In these lines that cut the surface deeply and so smooth, one feels the soft surface of the block. Go ahead, he says, it isn't hard. Carve with your eyes.

*

What is the matter of which paintings speak? Or the monotype, as echo of an act of painting, controlled echo, of what word is it the signed sign? I say: 'It is a woman, a room, objects in an intimate space.' But these are *my* recognitions, not *its* gesture. How to find its gesture.

*

Take this and bisect it twice diagonally. How unequal the quarters become. There are silent districts, graveyards — sure sign of the quick fate of the eye. It sees into the picture, just as the quick viewer does. Sees into. Vice or virtue?

*

In some of these pictures we, obedient to tradition, look into parlors where other pictures grace the walls. In the solemn wackiness of these linocuts, some of the inner pictures are far more 'energetic,' 'composed,' 'dynamic' than the frame picture. MP seems to take an oriental pleasure in this paradox. And the viewer is reminded of those vast eighteenth-century canvases, views of Baron Seinesgleichen's studio-gallery.

*

The second time that century is here considered.

*

These little views show other faces of Phillips's work among details. Every now and again we see some other realizations of MP's work-motive: poem books, haunted bottles, magician's doves, the black downrushing hair of his wife in an ice-green interior.

*

Phillips I have found in his studio listening to Bach on the record player. Hoo-hoo said the doves in their shadowy cage. Pish tush said the brush or the pencil on paper.

*

One seems to need to listen to one's opposite (as I listen flawlessly to romantic music). The structure he hears is the structure he *releases from*, abolishes from, his loveliest monotypes. It is the achievement of these cuts that a similar releasement has taken place. Image colored by the elision of thought.

*

Structure all gone. The widowed line makes a new life.

(*Ontario Review* #11, 1979/1980)

NOTES ON BRAKHAGE

What we loved about Brakhage back then remains a permanent liberation in the medium: he broke the illusion of personed narrative.

It is not that he destroyed the line, but (like our master Kandinsky before him) moved off from the line into continents of color, geologies of mass and bodily shove.

"My violences, my violences!" The violence, of course the violence in him, studied and literary mostly, like tuneful McClure and his genial beast howls, sometimes the violence just violence, an excuse of blood, a tip of the hat to the chainsaw that seems bedded in the core of the movies. It jerks to make us see.

It makes us jerks see, we who had been put to sleep — a beautiful sleep, *bien sûr*, with Harlow and Monroe and Bogart and Widmark — by svelte narration.

That unbearable episiotomy in the baby movie I hated (speaking of cores) — the occasional trace of an earlier, cheaper sense of 'drama' stands out amongst the grandeur of the rest of his work, banal rhapsody of fig-like pregnancy and blade work and spill.

So we loved him when he moved against the narrative, and counterposed (as some Blanchot might say) against old narrative a deeper, newer sense of telling.

Telling the eyes, not telling the story.

Pure telling.

So he could come at the body when the word 'autopsy' told him that it meant the art of seeing for yourself, which he stretched at once to, the art of seeing with your own eyes. (As in the grand prose-poem by Georg Heym, the autopsy becomes the passive screen on which the poetic vision plays a complex game beyond ordinary meat. Not meat but meant.)

We loved him for hurting, then changing, the way we see. It is a truism by now that Brakhage's one- and two-frame retina-torturing splices led the way to the vital, violent cross-cutting so common in commercials now, when the means of that blaze are easy. Not so back then, the glue-soaked joins of rubbery stock, the scratch of light some younger artists imitate now — about as useful as using black-and-white for flashback in cheapo movies to signify (like Wittgenstein's take on a movement in Schumann's *Davidsbündlertänze*) sheer pastness.

9 · A BOOK OF THE EYE (MOVING OR NOT)

There was that authentic throttle of the hand on the pass of film, the pressure of simple things like fingers & knives.

If that is authenticity, it is an authenticity of means. ("Man at the mercy of his means" — that was the glyph I marked on my brief newsletter *Matter,* printing an early text by Brakhage.) Important to recall that every period authenticates itself by using the means to hand, and what's just barely possible to do. Not by making antiques. Not even antique 16mm art films.

Back to then. We loved him for erasing any pre-existent story, and allowing to come forward only the story that the film/ing edit/ing could tell, could tell by making us see, by letting us know.

Let me know what you see.

Duncan, a master for Brakhage and for me, notoriously could hardly bear watching Brakhage's films, especially the ones after *Anticipation of the Nights* tossed Greek fire onto the eyes.

They hurt my eyes, said Robert Duncan, giggling the way he did when his most elaborate trail of reflection and exposition led him, as it sometimes must, right to something that everybody else knows too. They hurt my eyes.

It hurts to make us see.

The only way (before the interactive arts we now begin to take delight in) that film could reckon with body was, duh, to come at the eyes.

Once I asked Lama Norlha Rinpoche, But what is the self? He immediately and suddenly jabbed his fingers towards my eyes, stopping an inch or so away. That blink is the self, he said.

The body then is not something [to be] [re]presented in images, the homeless raptures of pornography, not at all. The body is to be involved in the play, put to work, put to play, via the eyes. The body's work in this art is seeing, seeing with all its limbs and innards and reaches.

And when we're in our bodies we can see with our eyes.

We had to fight to see.

I think this is where the overlap was, Brakhage's work with Duncan, Creeley, me, Olson, all our ten thousand poems, unreadable by the conventions of metric and academic ambiguity, his films unwatchable by the conventional lax attention — come and dream in the movie palace, let the images do their work, lie fallow, citizen — we had been taught, encouraged, to bring to the movies.

Our god (good Hawthorne Americans we still are, praise the lord) is a difficult god. Our god is difficulty itself.

So long before most of us heard about Derrida, Brakhage was seeing, making us see, *sous rature*.

Is that what it was? The superimpositions, the multiple exposures, the A, B, C rolls that let him show & not-show at once, give and withhold, tell and be silent? Overlay, *pli selon pli*.

Brakhage certainly did not pioneer double-exposure; when he was raptly beholding kiddie matinees in Midwest movie palaces, already double-exposure was a veteran trick. But conventional double-exposure was always about showing us this plus that. Brakhage's genius lay in showing us this *minus* that *minus* those, and making those subtractions, which became additions, into a complex manifold in which we found ourselves seeing nothing of what had been shot, but only what had been resurrected, multiplied, into seeing. Literally (to use the word that links alchemy, Olson's poetics, and any film) projected.

Anybody can write. A writer is someone with an eraser.

So that the writing of the film might properly be spoken of, and I do speak it, Brakhage wrote (erased) his films. We saw (were denied the sight).

The voyeur of course is always hovering on the verge of rape. There is violence in the act of looking, we hear about it all the time, and it's not just the infamous gaze, the appropriate eyebeam looped around its target/victim, though it is that certainly. The bittersweet fact seems to be that to look is to touch. The eyebeams the Renaissance supposed came forward in the act of seeing and embraced the beheld, the be/held.

We say: it's impolite to stare. We don't say: it's impolite to listen, it's impolite to smell, it's impolite to taste.

Seeing, like touching, is still felt as a palpable gesture interfering with the world of the touched or beheld.

Brakhage not only gives us permission to stare, he demands that we do so. But our stare must become dance, an active gesture, no more a passive gaze. Our stare must dance, a stare-dance, star-dance, the *Dog Star Man* movelessly struggling up the mountainside, tortured and restrained by colors, images, deliquescences.

Mallarmé was fascinated, especially in his last years, with the visual field in which the poem is inscribed. It is a simple fact that in this apparently linear, successive art, one word after another, one line after another, we do in fact see more than we are reading. Poets are fascinated with these penumbral words that shimmer round the text in ocular focus. It has been said, I don't know on what authority, that Mallarmé actually speculated about inscribing his great final experiment, *Un coup de dés n'abolira jamais le hasard*, as a film in that nascent medium, so the words and phrases could scroll by at a controlled rate. Mallarmé and Méliès, what a pair they'd have been. But the book, or a book, won the chance.

I think about that often, and take particular delight in Brakhage's work, who found a new vocabulary, new kinds of words, and inscribed them not just in light (light, light, we hear too much about light), he inscribed them in *time*. The dark of the future — whether coming in ten seconds or ten years — is the medium in which he throws his words on the wall.

No statement ever will use up language.

A year or two ago, thinking of Brakhage and Mallarmé, I became more than ever painfully aware of how a century ago the new art of film was at a crossroads, and we have never deeply pondered the other road film could have taken, how it could have borrowed the trajectory of music, the pre-eminent "*Nacheinander*" (Lessing's term for temporally successive) art, could have enrolled its skills of wielding time under the orders of counterpoint and formal structure. Just as it could have seen — and at times still does see — itself as fulfillment and renewal of the art of painting, a kind of New Testament of visual art, and dedicated its techniques to the temporal unfolding of 'long paintings.'

We know how film was soon co-opted by the physical spaces in which it needed to be exhibited and became first a mimicry of the sideshow, then theatrical exhibition, then an extension of theater itself, and finally a mimicry and fantastically successful embodiment of the things that theater itself extended: fiction, story. Narrative has long been so implicit in our take on films that we have to explain in awkward locutions if we mean any other kind — and even when we do, the hearer imagines us to be talking about documentaries.

It is the achievement of Brakhage, deployed over forty years of passionate film making, to make stand, move, and shine before us some of these other optics of film as art. We learn from him best if we continually explore what film could do, what kinds of transactions between mind & location & time, individual & society, public place and private space film can open up. To imitate Brakhage (color, beauty, quickness, edit, fireworks) is to betray him, I think. Because those who do it that way are imitating his style, his smell. Learn from his mind, that formidable art intelligence that knows how to make old things work differently together.

I'm not about to claim that Brakhage has an 'about' & that I know what it is. But I am certain that those who carefully see his films (mediate his films) learn as much about human relations and social arrangements as they might from theatrical or documentary films. His language, subtle with erasures, disclosures, brings the reader of the film (again I insist on the name) right back to the ardent afternoon outside the kiddie matinee or the art house, the street.

Because erasure abolishes the absolute, and lets chance be change.

Film at best returns upon its origins, renews itself in the sheer possibilities of engaging real presence with the structures and rhythms of time, color, shape, resemblance — & the erasure of those things as well into the frightening, welcoming, restorative darkness.

Brakhage reminds us to ask of film not What happens? or What is the story? — but ask instead, as we ask of music, what happens in us as we watch in real time. And we try to begin investigating the alphabet at least of the language with which this strange music inscribes itself on the wall before us.

Whatever the imagery or visual obsessions may be with which he is blessed or condemned to work, Brakhage is still offering us bracing, necessarily experimental, visions of an autonomous cinema, one in thrall to no other art, telling the eyes. He silences story so we can happen.

(*Chicago Review*, winter 2001)

BRAKHAGE, SPOKEN IN MEMORY

What is important I think is not to make a story of him or about him or with him in it playing some role. All his work life he kept shoving himself and us away from story, which was not a denial of the appeal of story or the lure of narrative, but pushing to the other side of story,

what we could get to and know, fiercely know, by seeing alone. If we could just get past story (i.e., as Stan loved to say, past novels and plays & comedies divine or human)

I've always been excited by Brakhage's work as deliverance of film from theatrical narrative. In doing so, he brought us much closer to real narrative, the telling of identity, the telling of fixity in the human world, the visual event that grounds us in the emotional complex reality of our own acts of seeing.

As Adam Vroman lugged his fifty pound behemoth of a view camera up the Mesa Encantada & the Hopi mesas, to show us how it was there, and how they were, the ones who were there, the ones who are always there when the camera opens its eye,

so Brakhage carried the whole weight of cinema and cinematic history, striving, storying, intrigues and plot up into the mountains beyond story, beyond plot and circumstance.

Not beyond narrative. This is urgent in him, and in every time art, reading the shadows of human gesture. Because far as we are, we can live only with ourselves — not beyond the shadow-forms of men and women and children whose exemplary forms embody what I have been calling Empirical Narrative

[so for the past months I've been tormented/obsessed with the question of narrative, and the place I try to work out my ideas is in thinking about actual and imaginary films. What haunts me is the idea of *narrative without plot*. Narrative can serve as honest structural unifying principle or motive, as long as it is not plot, not linear. I remember the beauty of certain films that play narrative to set up structural lines of clarity, but precisely avoid the linear, avoid continuity and resolution. I think of Paradjanov's *Sayat Nova* [*Color of Pomegranates*], or the way he violates folkloric linear tale-telling in *Shadows of Our Forgotten Ancestors*, or Sokurov's *Mother and Son* — "real" enough people — never resolved — they are momentaneous, arise from nowhere & fall back.

We witness them episodically. So the non-linear episodic narrative, samples of lives, ten minutes of somebody's life (and Jarmusch's *Int. Trailer. Night.* comes along just in time to show exactly that): to see them in time (my own book of essays years ago was called *In Time* to insist on this even then — not a time line but stab into time through which narrative time pours out towards the viewer. Not as technique, but as starting point towards new ways of holding the span of a film, not just color and visual rhythm and montage and all that classicism, and certainly not the dramatic-novelistic continuity. But instead a critical *empirical continuum*, in which narratives arise and fall back like complex images. (This is the structure, I now realize, of my long poem *The Language of Eden*, where the voices arise and fall silent and replace one another, speech as building block, while in film the complex gesture could serve so, the story without a plot.) So sampling, pulling out the evidentiary, representative person (what criticism would call the "subject") and deploying the subject through the double perception: subject's own view of own world in which subject moves, doubled with filmmaker's view of same. (*Dog Star Man* might be the first magnitude of such narration.) I think both have to be there — if the former is missing, it becomes dumb documentary, easy cynic. If the latter is missing, it becomes mere story. This doubling of perspective is what I mean by the empirical narrative, a kind of guided phenomenology of subjects moving through the mediated spectacle.]

held together not by seedy plot or grand exterior arrangements, but by the strike they make in the earth of our feelings,

not a story but people rooted in the visible. Living can see.

We feel beyond any story. It hurts to see them. It helps to see them.

And this is true of Brakhage's work all the way from the operatic masterworks of the early '60s (*Dog Star Man*, *Art of Vision*) and the person-oriented *Song Traits*, up through the handmade, hand-scratched, twisted, glued, hand-painted films — always the gesture of the hand, hand of the eye, a sign the seeing body recognizes, and knows as a mark made in its own space.

March 17th, 2003
(*Millennium Film Journal* # 41, 2003)

ADAMAGICA: MAGIC AND ICONOLATRY IN FILM[1]

PART ONE

1.

When we look at the sad, often ridiculous, lives of the great ceremonial magicians, it is obvious, in any conventional sense of success — wealth or happiness — that magic doesn't work.

But no sooner do I think this than I think (maybe the way we often think when we ponder the deeds of certain Catholics and Protestants & Muslims): if they act so brutally with religion, what on earth would they be like without it?

The tragicomedies of an Aleister Crowley or a McGregor Mathers, the high tragedy of Giordano Bruno — maybe these are the best outcomes that could be made from the karmic clay with which each began. At least we know their names — their names for a blessing!

Does magic imbue each life — Crowley or Bruno, Kenneth Anger or Michael Powell — with this sense: my life has meaning. There is a work, and I am for it, I live for that work & that work is my life. "Determin'd, dar'd and done!"

Were these great men, grandees of the image, just fooling themselves? Yet who among the still living or the safely dead would we dare label self-deluded? Isn't such a conviction — My life has meaning — exactly what gives a person the sense of being what we call happy?

2.

Magic is what the mind comes back to time & time again to right itself.

3.

The images on the movie screen last a lifetime — I mean they're always there, once seen they're here forever. They are really what we mean by here — the mind as intersection of all its experiences, naked now in the prepared moment. Samskara, the shaped clay ready for the kiln.

Images seen order the viewer's experience into paradigms of meaning and passion and grace.

---

1. Text presented at the Princeton Conference on Magic & Cinema, 11 March 2006.

4.

When I sat in the movie theater, nine years old, watching the newsreel while I waited for the second feature, I saw suddenly the living corpses of Buchenwald totter towards me. The image, images, entered me and dwelt among me — *eskênosen*, the Gospel would say, they set up their tabernacle in me and they live here, here, still. Defining me.

5.

We are defined by what we see. Blake: "He became what he beheld."

6.

And then I found myself thinking of the great Nobel Prize-winning biologist Max Delbrück. He was brown from chemotherapy, dying, tender, witty, skeptic as ever, when I sat with him at our last dinner together, years after I had left Cal Tech. I had come back just to give a poetry reading. We were dining, just the two of us alone in the vast and otherwise deserted faculty club, marmoreal as a mausoleum. Max spoke about the final obligation that he felt — towards the animals & towards poetry, towards the strange life that passes from one to the other, through the text, through the reader. With his last strength, he had committed himself to traveling to New York to lecture on Rilke's *Duino Elegies*, the animals and us, the interweaving presences in the world. Last dance of this great biologist, at the threshold of the real ecology: the interwoven lives of humans & animals — & angels.

How those Sufi angels of Rilke must have vexed him! Yet greeted him thereafter.

I had seldom seen a happier man than this dying scientist.

7.

So science doesn't work either, any more than magic does.

He was dying and we all do die. Science or no science, magic or no magic, we die.[2]

---

2. The sage and the poet and the scientist and the man of affairs — in the later Renaissance, all of them are painted with a skull on the desk, sometimes even with long poetic fingers trailing with eerie familiarity over the ivoried skull on their writing table.

And Darwin and Goethe and Einstein and Freud never stopped a single war, not even for a single day.

So nothing works.

8.

That's what we are privileged to remember. War, poverty, anger, disease, indifferent lovers, ingrate offspring, hatred, greed — science doesn't touch them. Art makes use of them a while, then scoundrel Time sweeps them all away.

Nothing works.

Yet we have come to this aporia: how do we know that these things don't work?

How do we know what horrors we have been spared, thanks to the energies and clarities and "Mental Forms" generated or composed by scientists and magicians and visionaries? Unknowable, but thinkable.

And that is the exact definition: Unknowable, but thinkable = magic.

Like the equivalent definition: Unthinkable, but sayable = poetry.

9.

Nothing works. But everything works, whatever it is that sustains that luminous shadow — can I call it that? A man like Crowley — or Delbrück — or Freud follows day by day, as if the illuminating sun were always behind him, showing the shape of him on the way. And the shadow of what he is stretches before him, long, long, pointing to what he must become.

10.

Magic (even Magick) tells us we are all "Men of Destiny" — which is not so different from what the Buddhadharma tells us: every living thing has Buddha Nature.

11.

Turn from people and their ways a minute, think of things.

Things do not tell, things do not sin.[3]

---

3. Cf. my poem of 2 February 2006, "Sinners."

12.

    The essence of our subject today:
    Magic takes the story out of the story
    and leaves the images.
    The images are what "comforts and helps" us and heals.

13.

    These are the eye-mages that Brakhage talked about long ago,
    take the story out of the story
    and the thing will save you

14.

    Escape from the family tragedy of the Pronoun Family
    I, and you, and he, and she
    and what they do to each other.
    The image has of course terrors enough of its own
    (Pascal and Borges and Robbe-Grillet and Beckett).
    Take away the clamor and terror of the pronouns
    and the image teaches
    awakens us, heals us, begets something in us.

PART TWO: AN ESSAY TOWARDS ICONOLATRY

15.

    I found myself moved by a picture in a catalogue, a picture of a picture on the cover of a book of pictures. But for all that remoteness from the living woman who once caught the eye of the camera, or perhaps because of it (it is too early in our study to trouble with causality) the image made me think. And thinking about what the picture showed, and what it means to show, and how I read the showing, I understood all at once, with a great metabolic excitement, that pondering the picture offered me a new way to read the world.

16.

    Take every picture as a religious picture.

17.

Here is the argument: every icon is an Ikon, every visual image is an icon of the truth.

In that sense, take every image as a sacred image.

18.

Inspecting, feeling an image, we can learn the truth that way, perhaps the truth scattered by Set through all religions, intact in none.

19.

Not 'all religions are one.' Rather, all religions have some.

20.

All pictures are holy.

21.

"Holy pictures" (sounded like *holypitchiz*) we used to call them when I was a child and cared about those things, a lot, always uneasy between the art form (often trashy) and its intention (often exalted). But I saved the pictures, put them where they seemed to belong — in missals, or lives of the saints.

22.

The saints are those who showed us themselves. That is, showed us how to be.

23.

The pictures were for example a pale vapid pink and greeny painting of Saint Therese the Little Flower, that cute Norman girl who embodied the deepest sense of Buddhist compassion, and who said to Christ, Give me all the pain of the world so I can take it away. Or a black and white snapshot of Father Alfred M. Rudtke S.J., who had baptized my friend not long before the priest's death. Or a funeral mass card for my cousin Doris, no picture of her just her name and death date, but instead of her there was a picture of Our Lord, on a silvery crucifix, a prayer to say for her. So all these were holy, Saint Therese, Saint Rudtke, Saint Doris-hidden-in-Christ, pray for us.

All made sacred by the informal but effective canonization of having their pictures looked at.

24.

Looking at a picture is worshipping it.

As Swann worshipped all his life Vermeer's *View of Delft*, so we worship all too briefly perhaps our canonical images of rock stars and close relations, old friends, a snapshot of Gandhi pinned to the wall, or Ezra grumpy-holy in his gondola beside Olga.

25.

The example that got me thinking this morning, where this all began, was a photo by Diana Scheunemann. Is the woman in the picture experiencing orgasm or faking it? Once the question is asked, it starts to ask itself: what is the difference?

What is the difference between a picture of a man dying on a cross, say, or a picture of an actor acting a man dying on a cross?

Can the picture tell the difference?

26.

And what is it in us that can tell the difference, or thinks it can? That is the Magic Factor, the energy in us that somehow, simply, knows.

27.

What is the difference between regarding (worshipping) an image of something doing something from regarding an image of something pretending to do something?

Is this just a cavil, a place where religious doubt creeps in?

Don't we in fact worship what the picture tells us?

28.

So when I look at Diana Scheunemann's image of a woman, grimacing her gasp of ecstasy as her soaked body amuses itself with the gushing hose or waterspout, I see the Virgin Mother of the world, her pleasure pouring life into the world, her anguished ecstasy our cosmos, all we have and are and know, at just this moment spilling out of the excess of her self-awareness. Her orgasmic cry is the aleph that begins us — everything that comes into existence comes from the overmeasure of her self-knowing.

We are the part of herself that spills out of knowing into being.

9 · A BOOK OF THE EYE (MOVING OR NOT)

PART THREE: EPOPTEIA
(Seeing beyond the world)

29.

When the initiates of the Eleusinian Mysteries were all enclosed in the dark, possibly even underneath the ground, at a certain moment in the ceremony they suddenly experienced an intense bright light. The priest of the moment, the epopt, held up or showed them something. Something they saw. This revelation was called the epopteia, the showing forth. It is not known for sure what was shown or what they saw — because the initiates kept their vows of secrecy. For fifteen hundred years or so these mysteries were practiced as the central focus of Athenian, later pan-Hellenic life, and ultimately the most 'fashionable' religious practice of the whole Roman Empire. It was so to speak the great pilgrimage of the Classical world, its Hajj. Millions were initiated, but the secret was kept.

30.

There are many surmises about what was shown. I am not here concerned with that. What interests me at this moment about Eleusis and the whole praxis, is that something was seen. And that visual event, that instructive pleasure, transformed the lives of the initiates profoundly and evidently permanently. No doubt the experienced was supported and interpreted by the ceremonial context and the inevitable (priests are priests) commentaries. But what was seen is what confirmed the experience and the transformation the initiate experienced and went on experiencing. We can always look back on what we have seen. We carry in our brains a superior emulsion for such archival preservation of the image.

It's time for me to venture my own guess about what was seen in the dark. Maybe it isn't what the initiates saw that matters. But that they saw. That some special kind of seeing was going on. Some special mode of showing, full of light and sound and movement — perhaps a pantomime of the Goddess in the afterlife, perhaps just a woman made out of light. The very fact of seeing in this unknown and unprecedented way told the initiate that there's more to the world than we see at first glance.

Eternity opens from now. We are told that the initiates no longer dreaded the afterlife. No one knows what combination of shamanic craft or psychoactive drink or dramaturgy had such profound effects on so many. Some sort of poesis, some imaginative act. Some technique of enlightenment. What was true there may have been what is true in every art, in every renaissance: the technical is the revelation.

What we do know is that the initiates would say one thing: I have seen.

31.

We study the image to understand. To understand what induces in us the visual pleasure — that is the whole ground of art, no other.

Æsthetics presumably goes arid or bleak as it drifts away from that. Concentrate always on pleasure. That is what art gives. That is what art is.

Voluptas docet. Pleasure is our sole instructor.

32.

Now this is the main point: the main pleasure in seeing an image is seeing something one has not seen before. Simple as that.

And that is the ground of magic. The lowest apprentice magician, Faust's famulus in the early Faustbook, wants to learn magic so as to see the girls of the town dance naked in the courtyard, just as, a millennium or more before, young Lucius wanted to peer through the wall and see the witch at play.

And the highest magic too summons vision: to welcome the knowledge and conversation of the Holy Guardian Angel, to use the beautiful formulation of the Golden Dawn tradition.

33.

We do magic to see what we have never seen. In the simplest terms, magic shows us the invisible.

Whether it's done with magician's silks and mirrors or with archangels and incantations, magic is one thing. Magic tricks the eye into seeing what is not really there, just as art tricks the eye into really seeing what is there.

34.

Prestidigitation and Highest Ritual Magic differ in methods, and style, but not in aim: the transformation of the ordinary. They are both true magic. As is cinema, QED.

What the motivation is, of course, will be immensely different. Not so much depending on the 'level' of magic (as if to make a dove fly out of a handkerchief were somehow lower than making you hallucinate a deity) as on the moral niveau of the magician.

35.

Magic makes us see. And when the icon it produces for our inspection moves, it becomes intensely more powerful. Seen becomes scene. The whole complex of images in transformation, movement, locks in the mind. Becomes a kineme, I'll call it, a complex elapsing of images in time.

36.

It stays in mind. It has become a product of alchemy *solve et coagula*. The fixed image has been made fleeting, the fleeting scene is fixed as a single complex kineme in mind. The fixed movement which makes live mercury into solid gold.

37.

We go to movies the way the ceremonial magicians picked up their grimoires and stepped into their magic circles. We go so we can see in the dark.

38.

And what we see is what we've never seen.

PART FOUR: Therefore:

39.

That's why the most powerful artistic force in contemporary film is special effects. That is what people really want to see. And it is proper of them to want this and pursue this. This is the science of the invisible. FX rules!

40.

This is a terrible announcement to make, especially to an aging generation weaned on the tepid adulteries of Cassavetes and *The Graduate*, as if a film is supposed to be one long bullsession in a bar or shrinkarium.

Whereas: Plot is nowhere. Plot failed us long ago.

41.

The most powerful artistic force in contemporary film is special effects — any kid knows that, and that's also what the pure Blakean eye of desire wants to see, see, see. Books can be read, stories can be told.

42.

So now it is time for us Magicians to liberate Princess Kinema from her long enchantment to Demon Storyboard.

The most powerful artistic force in contemporary film is special effects — take away narrative and show: something happens.

No simpering pronouns, no *triste histoire* — instead the purity of the technical. Special effects instead of special pleading. And the obsessions of memory spell out in optical printing (as in the astonishing magical ending of Jennifer Reeves' *Chronic*, where optical process transforms psychological narrative into psychic fact.)

43.

When film shows,
it 'says the names of things'
it lights up the corresponding signatures of energy inside us:
this is magic.

44.

Think of the magical intensity of Miyazaki's backgrounds, textures, details, as over against the vapid banality of the drawing of his 'human' characters in their sentimental stories. His films are the clearest evidence of the tension between bland narrative foreground and the intensity of the thing observed, described, transcribed. He dares to steal the nuclear power of a blade of grass or a raindrop to fuel the sentimental narrative.

(Yet in honesty I have to ask if the storyline is not a necessary evil, a psychic permission Miyazaki gives himself to care so visually about the where and what his characters move through, so that the story serves like the vague poems that somehow managed to stimulate the great songs of Schubert, or Beethoven's *An die ferne Geliebte*.)[4]

45.

So here I am in a cold spring stuck with Japanese animes and special effects — that is what is left of Eisenstein and Dreyer and Brakhage. Yet they are enough. They renew us in the act of seeing, renew us for seeing more. Seeing better than we saw before — the way Brakhage was such a great propaedeutic force in cinema, made us see because: he gave us nothing else to do with ourselves in the movies but see.

46.

I have, as you can tell, been carrying on for years against narrative in film. At best, narrative is a provocation to reveal glimpses of the future or the interior, or to reveal the suddenly seen unseen glory of the obvious. (Tati's *Playtime*, Jarmusch's *Ghost Dog* come to mind.)

47.

History comes to our aid:
After the Renaissance, after the exalted magics of Ficino, Pico, Paracelsus, and Bruno, especially Bruno, obit 1600, we witness a decline of magic.
The conventional view is that magic gave way, slowly, clumsily transformed into, the experimental sciences.
I propose instead this model, that magic hid itself, but coincidentally with that occultation, and made possible by it, began to flower as the theater, and then, (especially after the shutting down of the playhouses in England during the Commonwealth, and during the reign of the Inquisition in Spain) renewed its life in the development of prose fiction.

---

4. Thinking along this conciliatory line, I am braced by a beautiful phrase by the poet Geoffrey O'Brien, who in his NYRB review of a collection of Val Lewton films speaks of Joseph Cornell's transfiguration of *East of Borneo* as "nineteen minutes of mesmeric suggestiveness, a dream vision of what remains of movies after their stories have gone."

48.

That is, magic, which is always concerned with making the invisible visible, now comes to public service as making the unreal real, making the imaginary actual, giving 'a local habitation and a name' to things unreal. Creative magic.

So we see on the stage the transformations of Bottom's Dream, or read in Don Quixote the imaginary world become real enough to make an old man tilt at the sheep, & real enough to make us weep at that old man.

The novel for the next four hundred years takes over the shape-shifting tasks, creates the *Novus Ordo* your dollar bill talks about.

49.

It is to fiction that we look for magic, that is: for the deliberate & conscious estrangement of the obvious, the revalidation, the renewal of the things of the world. The transformations leave the tip of the magus's wand and flow from the tip of the pen: Nashe, Deloney, Cervantes, Defoe, Swift, Sterne, Walpole, Smollett, Voltaire, Diderot, Mary Shelley, Hogg, Novalis, Tieck, Hoffmann, Wilkie Collins, Lefanu, Balzac, Poe, — we see the common world transformed into what it really is.

The magic continues in Hawthorne and Melville, Flaubert even in his *Saint Julien* or his *Salammbô*. And it is only when the novel leaves off treating of wonders, miracles, adventures — the changeful stuff of magic — when the novel goes quiet, and takes up its careful beautiful study of the endless chimerical dimensions within the small man, when it gets all quizzical and beautiful like Henry James, only then does magic have to take leave of fiction, and go out to rise again on its own. The psychological studies of the Brothers James, the sociological ventures of Zola and Ibsen[5] — they parch the soul that yearns for wonders, and so by contrast they bring high magic back. Eliphas Levi walks through the streets with the Goncourts, Mme. Blavatsky can be sniffed at in James or Wharton.

---

5. Typified for instance in the volumes of Lynn Thorndike's magisterial study of eighty years ago, *History of Magic and Experimental Science*, or in Singer's studies of Paracelsus.

And by the end of that century, magic arrives fully clothed in all its delicious lies and lunacies and awkward truths, Yeats, The Golden Dawn, Theosophy, Steiner's Anthroposophy, the export of all that to America where the mentalists and spiritualists had made the ground ready for such new (but often stodgy) conceptualizations of the raw beauty and power of magic. Where it will flower in Arcane California, and Robert Duncan will write the greatest magical poetry since the Renaissance.

50.

But by that time public magic has worked its way into the newspapers with uncomprehending stuff about the Great Beast, and shocking stories about Himmler's lunatic rune-meisters. So true magic has slipped away again.[6]

And where it flees this time is into the next evolutionary step of Divine Invention: the film.

51.

Of course Méliès and Lumière, of course the radical practical magic of 24 frames per second equaling a human calmly walking past. Of course the rocket to the moon, of course the stop and start camera that lets clowns appear and disappear. We must never forget the historical truism: "Movies begin by being part of stage magic shows, and go on imitating stage magic ever after."[7]

---

6. Interesting that throughout the government direction of the arts in the USSR, film found its way to magic and wonder only through treatment of folklore. The same route that the German Romantics had followed to escape the inexorable rationality of the Enlightenment became the way through the penny-plain austerities of Socialist Realism and beyond into splendor — the work of Parajanian/Parajanov, the great Armenian-Russian director contains magnificent examples of this liberation.

7. Consider for instance the remarkable *Magic Bricks* from *Pathé* in 1908. The magician assembles and disassembles bland substances, forming a wall on which an image forms, moves, a strangely beautiful child appears and then is unpieced as the wall is taken down by the same magic wand that built it. There is an intimate convergence of stage magic, movie magic, and the 'real thing,' the sudden apparition of the magical child, wistful, her hair wafting, her eyes yearning for the world into which she must be born.

52.

The beauty of stage magic, all that business of elephants and mirrors and trapdoors and veils, is that it reveals another truth of magic. Now you see it, now it is. Magic is ontology. Beings are only insofar as they are perceived. *Esse est percipi.*

53.

And soon enough they're imitating the lost cosmological energies of Bruno — gently, calmly: the British of the 1930s with *The Man Who Could Work Miracles* or *The Shape of Things to Come*. Then the noisy genius of Mr. Disney, who magicks us still with the fumbling but strangely effective magician in the so-called *Magical Land of Oz* — it's a Wizard we're reminded, not a little girl that roots that film to the sad weird tender history of western magic, all fraud and mirrors — but the fear is true, the love is true.

The camera lies, but the image tells true: that is the essence of magic.

54.

No clearer sense in commercial film of that magic than Michael Powell, his version of *The Tales of Hoffmann*, say, or the patriotic extravaganza of *Stairway to Heaven*.

And it is not of course the narrative. The narrative of *Stairway to Heaven* is embarrassing to a degree unparalleled except in Frank Capra. The magic lies in the autonomous image that deserts its stupid story and flies directly into our minds and lodges there, like Dante's Love, spreading his banner and ruling us.

55.

Tricks as simple as Robert Helpmann's hand plucking colored candle wax from the candles and having them turn to jewels in his hand, or an invisibility made visible like the stalking black leopard of *Cat People* whose movement is terrifyingly present though her form is never seen — we see movement by movement. Tricks as complex as the multiplied villain of the *Matrix* films, dissed as they are by esthetes, reveal the poverty of æsthetics, and the robust, outwelling creativity of magic.

56.

But why? Why does magic work? I want to conclude by raising some questions I think radical, that need answers more from political analysts, economists, and neurophysiologists rather than from the usual suspects — analysts and theologians — who typically are heard from on these matters. Any academic study (in the best sense of the word) of magic must engage deeply and exactly with questions like this:

1. What is an image?
2. What does an image make us see?
3. How does an image make us see?
4. What happens to us when we see an image?
5. Where is the image stored, and how is it revived?

57.

From the great mental struggles & researches of Giordano Bruno, of which I suspect you will hear much from other speakers in this symposium, we learn the world is built of image. And thus of magic, in this precise sense: having once seen something, you can never unsee it.

To unsee something would be to unmake the world.

58.

The world is what we have seen. And Bruno is careful to warn us: to control the images people see, is to control the world. We need the study of magic in our time to produce something like Bruno's masterpiece, *Lo Spaccio*, where the bestial (read: conventional) order of the zodiac (read: the world) must be renewed by new images.

Perhaps by special effects.

March 2006

(*Brooklyn Rail*, June 2006)

THREADS 10: ROBERT SAYS

The main project, the current on which my life is shaped, is the simplest of all, the writing of the day, the poem that comes, the work of the borderlands between sleep and waking, or in the brightness of everyday, between one thing and another, this and that. The poem is always the first-born of the between.

in conversation with Simone dos Anjos & Pietro Aman (2006)

Imre Kertész says: "while I work, I am; if I didn't work, who knows if I'd be?" And on my part, I would also worry about this: who knows who I'd be? It is something like that. I write to pay back my debt. I write out of guilt, to fill the blank pages the world sets in front of me. When I say pay my debt, perhaps I should say pay my way. Giving back something, that is, transforming the energy that floods into us all from overwhelming presences of people & places, mountains and operas and sailboats & a hawk over my head. So from all these riches of experience and cognition that I have been given, to transform that energy into gifts I can give back, poems, stories, anything I can do. Anything that comes to mind. I write because it comes to mind. I don't like to begin a day without writing — if I can get even fifteen uninterrupted minutes after I wake, I feel I can get something down. Sounds like a wrestler, get someone down.

What happens is this, as close as I can call it: my mind is silent, but my breath is anxious, a tension in my chest. It is morning, I've just awakened, walked downstairs, sat down at the table or stepped outside into the day. My body tense, my mind quiet. And suddenly something speaks: a phrase (never just a single word) or sentence "comes" and I hear it. I write it down and work from it, with it, using whatever comes to mind. What happens then is, I think, obvious in any poem or text — the reader can follow the lines of thought or (even sometimes) reasoning. But I feel better for saying this right here, how it begins, each day — that is what the reader would not necessarily notice. Unless the reader were The Reader, the one who reads everything. [...]

Language is the heart of my work, and my body and my life and reading and feelings and intuitions are only of consequence (in my work) to the extent that they entrain language. That is, they prepare the event of writing, they prepare me for the meeting with language.

                              in conversation with Mark Thwaite (2006)

The physical environment that has always meant the most to me is motion: any place where there are things going on around me. I grew up in a small family in the outskirts — I mean, in New York, in Brooklyn — in sort of uncultured & desolate regions where there were cows & sheep & trolley cars & stuff like that. The center was always inward where there was the most going on. So that physical city environment shaped me, has shaped any sense I have of rhythms or change.

                          in conversation with Joshua Stolle [ca. 1970s]

A city is such a beautiful place to be alone. [...] My greatest blessing was hours every day alone; both parents worked, and the hours after release from the hated schoolroom were my time. Walking the streets, looking at people, finding the libraries, reading, playing ball — the kind of solitude I needed, I think everyone needs to be able to process what they see and hear, and bring it into alignment with what they feel. Walking around is a way of getting to know your own body. And what you're walking around in and through is language. I was walking through the names of things. My eyesight was poor in those days; I squinted fearfully, and only color made sense. Color and touch — what else do I trust even now? Names. What I saw I wanted to name, to know the names of. Things got realer for me when I knew their names. I can remember some of those words that came to transform things — names transform things into themselves. Oak-tag. Pine grove. Hoarfrost. Snow.

    [...] I found slowly but certainly through poetry that poetry was the altar to which names are brought, where they give the most light, isolated as they are in the silence around each word in

a poem. God, poems should be printed one word on a page, and then we'd really begin to understand them. And then, in another way, all the spaces should fall away and we read all the syllables as one continuous breath of one single word. A poem is a single word, naming a sensual unknown.

in conversation with Simone dos Anjos & Pietro Aman (2006)

Brooklyn is more important to me now than it was when I lived there. I didn't know where I was. We never know where we are till we aren't, I think. By now it's like Dublin for Joyce, a graph or grid on which subsequent experiences plot themselves & take on "local habitation and a name." […] I don't mean, by the way, that I'm at all nostalgic for Brooklyn — anymore than Joyce was for Dublin — in forty-five years I've gone back to visit only once. It provided me with the trestleboard my life has been ordered by, it gave me a hint of the vast psychic Body in which a person's life unfolds, finding the limits and going beyond […].

in conversation with Simone dos Anjos & Pietro Aman (2006)

10.

A BOOK OF NEARLY EVERYTHING ELSE

Mithwissens is the art of mid-wit, a conscientious craving
for the middle of the mood, a straight track right to the
mid of the mind. Mizlo says the grammarye, the vowels' are
odd or wrong, the consonants light up the better god. Mirt
or mird would that be, Z & R turning inside out, those
runes? Moda, yes mocd. Our mod is many, our midday need.
Moses knew the modes of it, though he was downcast on Mount
what was it, in sight of----& so much sight was woth, & so
much it wasnt; faith he'd have traded the whole three-di-
mensional prospect for one good sensation of his own weight
pressing down the sole of his foot on Thatland. His modes were
greeks might have thought barbaros, he hastened with celerity,
he concealed his beard in faminous disclouds---& yet such a
moral music came off the man as he stood, resolutely chopping
his thoughts free from superstit & materist.

    This is my gothic period. More motors outside, the
roar of dictionaries revving in the head. Manny Mota comes
to bat a decade back. Traffic tangled outside the stadium in
a frenzied motorjam---elle gronde, le petit dort, & still the
targets twinkle in sunlight, hungering the shaft. Mustard
for gold, & blew the red circle into place around, all food
looks like goal or target. All hopes come home. They knocked
the fence down. The old Moulmein pagoda's gone, I think,
or such as look upon it---lepres at the footsteps up, the girl
a while in shadowy arcade he lost. And never forgot her, never
excatly remembered her either more. The modes of mmoonlight
held his thoughts at arms length from her.

myrtle?
o good
green,
you ever
nimble!

24 july 76

Robert Kelly)
Biography)

Elm trees are menaced.
I prefer hard upright chairs & read at table.
This year I am twice the age & half the age of my ideal reader.
My totem animals are boar & bear & lion.
I do not like animals in the house.

[RK archives, undated text]

HOROSCOPE OF A TENTATIVE NORTH AMERICAN REPUBLIC born Philadelphia, Pa., 4 July 1776.

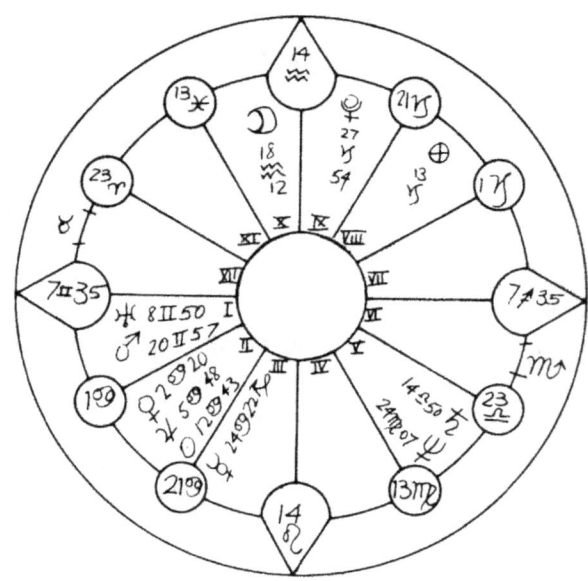

Uranus rising, brave beginnings.
Venus, Jupiter & Sol in the IInd: money money money, inflation as mode.
Money as *sole* measure
yet no measure ever for money.
Neptune in V: sex in the head; no playfulness known that does not lead to destruction.
Saturn in V: the great Puritan Thing, denial of the body, whereas the body in glory wd be the only way to offset what we're left with:
MARS in the House of Life: It is a land of war, lives by war, is war.
All under the gorgeous presidency of Moon in X, cold dreams of power.
How to bring peace to a nation founded on war?

              Re/found.
(Do you know what that means?) ("& if this be bla bla bla")
TOWARDS THE FOUNDING OF THE CITY
             — *per* R.K., Amanuensis

(Jerome Rothenberg & George Quasha, *America A Prophecy*, 1973)

"AUTOBIOGRAPHICAL ESSAY" [EXCERPTS]

5

What I come to is this, something like this: to write an autobiography is to write one's life oneself, that much is easy.

But my life is not my past: my life is my strength, my instrument ("my bow").

My life is not my past. The past does not belong to anyone — that is the point. The past is common, cloacal, intimate, true only inasmuch as it motivates presences, presentnesses, presents.

"My" past appalls me with its Flemish chiaroscuro, its gleam of sense amongst a nightmare of appetites.

Am I, after all, ashamed of my appetites? Am I a sunflower ashamed of the sun? *Mes tropismes.*

6

I'm not sure I want to write about my life. I do know I want to praise, praise many people, all my friends and teachers and, no sense in the categories, all those who have made contact with me.

Here is a text some Tibetans chant every day before eating:

May whoever gives me food attain the happiness of complete peace. Whoever gives me drink, serves me, rescues me, honors me, makes offerings to me, may he attain the happiness of complete peace. And whoever reviles me, causes me unhappiness, abuses me, strikes me with weapons, harms me in any way, even kills me, may he also attain the happiness of complete enlightenment and become fully and actually awakened in perfect complete Enlightenment.

I want to speak the names of my friends.

And I want to speak the names of my enemies, but who are they? I think of myself as a novel without villains. The astrologers say I have Mars in the Twelfth House, the House of Self-Undoing, they say, *Carcer*, the Jailhouse. They say that means: Beware of secret enemies. They say: Your friends are your enemies. Your friends are jealous and secretly wish you ill. But I know the name of the secret enemy, most treacherous of all the local potentates, and it is me.

Which is one more reason I should be unsure about writing my life. Be advised, honest reader. Even now, by this very scruple, this candor, I may be making you think ill of me.

Don't waste their time, say it or be silent. Never apologize, never explain — that has always been your rule. Why otherwise now?

Listen, it won't do me any good to doubt.

7

Here is my contract with the Natal Daemon, my contract for one Life with one Earth: I was born forty-eight minutes after noon around the autumnal equinox — 24 September 1935. A late degree of Sagittarius was rising in the house of life, my sun was in the first degree of the Scales, and my moon in the balsamic degrees of the Lion. It was a hot week. My mother was in labor for three days. (That is a fact I learned only forty-some years later when I happened to ask her, for the first time in my life, what kind of birth I'd had. Instantly, her eyes filled with tears, she who was no sort of crying woman, and she said, simply, that she was in labor with me for three days. She never mentioned it again.)

Weeks after my birth, my mother learned that her own father had died the same day I was born. He was Thomas Kane, about whom I don't know much. He smoked a pipe and I've seen a picture of him where he looks like Wallace Stevens. (My mother was the tenth of his eleven childbirth-surviving children, and she was born, a valiant imperious Aries, on the 7th of April, 1902.) He was also my last surviving grandparent, so I grew up in a world without eld. There were no old people near me, so I had to be my own grandfather. I had to be wise and big. His surname excited and shamed me, and I thought through childhood I bore that mark of Kane/Cain — which I took to be the mutinous left eyebrow of mine that everybody still seems to notice.

So I grew up without grandparents, though some of my uncles and aunts (two score of them all told) seemed old enough to qualify. Still, I saw day by day no one older than my parents. And so I never learned about old. As in the house of the young Prince Sakyamuni, age was not seen, death was not mentioned, sickness was not discussed. (When my pregnant mother went to the hospital to give birth to my sister, no sort of explanation was offered to me of her absence.) Religion was de rigueur, but priests and nuns were spoken of with delicate skepticism, a warning not to take too seriously whatever roads of piety or renunciation they might suggest.

I grew up without the old. So when it becomes time for me to be an old man, I will not really know how to do it. I suppose it's something you can fake, the frail body helping out. But I have no role model and fear I may make a very imperfect old man. For years, from my earliest childhood in fact, it seemed unlikely that old age would ever be a problem. Several doctors prophesied, in their solemn and scary way, that "the boy would die by thirty-five" — a prophecy of which I was frequently reminded. Grossly overweight as I was, their lugubrious anticipation seemed justified enough medically (if a bit outrageous psychologically). Now that thirty-five is two decades behind me, I have to face the fact that I'll have to solve unaided the mystery of old age.

Of course, if you don't have grandparents, you don't have anyone to confide in, you don't have a court of cassation, a tribunal of ultimate appeal. You don't have a *tertium comparationis* to judge the truth of what you're told.

So not only did I not learn how to be an old man, I did not learn how to speak out loud what might have been on my mind.

If you don't have grandparents, I sort of think, you never really learn how to talk. Parents tell, grandparents talk. To this day I'm more comfortable addressing a room full of people than meeting them one at a time.

8

My mother's sisters feared to tell her of my grandfather's death — I was a month old before her sisters told her the real reason why her said-to-be-ailing papa had not visited his latest grandchild. That pattern of not-bringing-the-bad-news shaped her life, and my life. When I was a man of forty, my favorite aunt, Aunt Annie, passed away, and my parents never mentioned it for fear of grieving me.

The unspoken. I seemed to be told: the essence of life is to say nothing. No explanations, no excuses, no narration. Things happen, and we shelter from them as well as we can: in silence and fierce habit & the passionless security of everyday life.

And that is kindly, hard, well-meant. Maybe it is finally the best way, in that harshly tender north of Ireland way they imported (who knows when?) as armor against the lascivious novelties of the new world.

9

There was a day, I might have been in second grade, when I decided to walk home from school a different way. The school was only across the street from my house, catercorner, but I walked up away from my house a long block, up the yellow leaves that carpeted Batchelder Street, then over and down, then home, a block or two more. Not long, but long enough for me to miss my father, who for the one day I can remember in my whole childhood had come home early from work and was waiting for me, proposing to take me to the movies to see some Disney (*Dumbo*, was it, the flying, the fat?). He was distressed, and I felt awful to have missed the outing, which never did happen, and more than that, selfish as I was, to have disappointed him so. This event stayed in my mind for all my years, because before I walked the Different Way, I seemed to hear an inner voice saying: Walk a different way. Ever after, I've had this event in mind as groundwork for a life of interpretation. Was this event a deep incurable wound in the body of my openness, one that curtails still my spontaneity? Or was it a protection — if so, whose? — against some experience (car crash, obsessive movie image, act of crime) we would have otherwise been in for? This was the first storey in the House of Interpretation, grist for a life of pondering anxiety.

10

At twenty-three, I dedicated my life of work to God. To benefit the world was how I thought about it. At forty-six I dedicated it to the enlightenment of all beings. It seems ambitious and possibly pretentious to want these things, but I mean them with everything I have that can mean anything. My search in "flesh, dream, book" has been for ways of saying, ways of saying that benefit beings. Searching now in language to unsay my "self," and thereby say the truth, or say towards it.

11

Uranus, inchoate, changeful, full of hope and fear, dwells in the fourth house in my horoscope. Where he dwells, there is no early peace, and change comes quick. I sit and think about the way karma drives us when we're young, how I was driven, ceaselessly agitated by what I think young Dante meant by *dubioso* desire — a fleshly but cogent yearning, in head no less than hod, to run wild in the city and hurry the country down.

And how resist the velocity of karma. I remember the city forty years ago, how desperately I sought words and women, those walking aliens who were at the same time the only home I wanted. I sought and sought. Thoughtful but unconscious. What was it? What wouldn't let me rest?

To catch up with the world I was supposed to inherit. To incarnate fully on this woebegone beauty, Eyes of Earth. Postures of intercourse and stances of poetics, odes and measures, prosody and ghost stories, the dark house in M. R. James's "The Mezzotint" toward which I was the obscure figure creeping — the urge to be everyone. *I am the man*. All the hurry is there, to become the self you must spend the rest of your days unpiecing. Poetry I sought, and fame, feeding, noise, Viennese music, the secular roar of history. Kulchur, said Pound, and I carried his vade mecum with me in Times Square at fourteen, he was my author and my book was yet to be. Pound and Mahler, Joyce and the girl across the subway car, the girl in the wind, Wotan's farewell, *das oft ich lächelnd gekost*, the blue distances, Italian bread, white cheese, Pepsi-Cola, IRT — they were my house.

When I'm less excited about it, I know that Uranus in the fourth means many changes of house and home, unconventional living arrangements, odd cronies, hand-me-down furniture, dust bunnies, some strange bed. The loss of my first house — 1878 Brown Street, a brief tangent off Gerritsen Avenue, in the Marine Park district, not too far from gentle evenings sauntering in sealight at Sheepshead Bay — even now I'd rather posit it than describe the loss. For months after we'd moved, I'd find myself many days taking a complicated series of buses back to the old house, to walk on the old block, talk with the old friends. Though it was not the friends that moved me so. How can a child survive such losses? That house was the blue sky over it, that house was cloud and the color red and ivy up brick wall. That house was ghost story and block of ice, girls in dark wool slacks coming home from ice skating. That house was radio and opera. That house was Canada and Finland and 1940. That house was war and the knowledge of color. That house was a clock on the wall. How can a child survive such subtle losses? That house was number.

12

I can't remember a time when I couldn't read. The first day in school, the nun took me around from classroom to classroom, making me read from some book in front of other students. I didn't understand what was happening. I did what I was told. I read aloud. I was uncomfortable being dragged around but I did what I was told. I almost always have. Later my mother told me it was remarkable that I could read; other children couldn't, and had to go to school to learn. Why did I have to go?

13

Buildings. The green copper dome of St. Peter's church against the high skyline of Jersey City. The green copper of Queen of Angels in Brooklyn, and the Masonic Temple right beside it. The vast prow of Freemason's Hall in London, standing out of the night palpably full of useful mysteries. The low skyline of Hudson from the hospital window where I came with Mary Goodlett several times each week for her chemotherapy, for radiation, windows in the room where Mary died. *Skylines of Small Cities* — I thought that was going to be a book's title for me, the human scale of it. The exact and unreplaceable detail of the apparent. The Parthenon we could build again from formula, but the skyline of Hartford in 1968 is lost forever, a message we never read, a shapeliness that eludes us still.

Buildings. When I first began to listen to Bruckner's symphonies, I understood that "structure" in music was not about construction but about housing, interiority, carving out a space in the rock of the world we could live in, or defining by some masterstroke the templum, *space defined as ours* — a place we can live in. Hearing is a house.

15

The events in my life as I remember them do not seem in any way different from actions I remember in a book. My standing outside our apartment on West Twelfth Street excitedly telling Joan that I'd just made ΦBK — though I feel the complex intertwined vulgarities of my excitement in the street, this memory doesn't seem to belong to me — except I guess by default: *there's no one else to remember it*. When there's no one else to remember it, it must be mine.

These *hapax dromeda*, then, these once-only happenings, are the special burdens of memory we are bitterly privileged to bear.

Because there is no story except the story told. And what is left when I'm finished writing will be the story of my life. I tried at first to sketch it in terms of the twelve houses of the genethliacal figure, my horoscope (though that word truly means only the ascendant or degree rising over the horizon at the moment of my birth, in my case 24 Sagittarius); had I persuaded myself of the cleanliness of that procedure, I would have wound up with (been wounded by) the twelve mundane houses and their affairs: Body and Personality, Stuff and Property, Brothers and Sisters and Friends, Mother and Home, Sex and Self-Proclamation, the Body as Theater of Chemistry, Marriage and Partnership, Dream, Fantasy and Other Inheritances, Theory and Observation (thus travel and religion), Profession, Sway and Conviction in Society, and Karmic Obscuration and Constraints.

And then I thought to order the record of my days by using as rubrics the main relationships of my life — each one an era. But such a procedure, like the Winter Count of the Plains tribes pictographed on buffalo hides, would have made me seem even simpler than I am. And I am simple.

19

As I child I wanted to be English, be in England, be there. The heavenly country, I called it later in one of the few pieces of mine where I ever tried to face that strange infant anglophile — I can't remember when I didn't want to be there. "Over there," my sad old uncles sang, and meant a different place from the one to which I ventured at their sounds. Song was a signal of that place, a flag seen at earliest light, dim over the hill. And I knew it was an English war they fought in and sang about now. But music is embarrassing, isn't it, especially when people make it drunken and cigarry and with the scatter of pinochle cards all over the big walnut table and the smoke going up into the nostrils of that bald old shiny-pated god in gold-wire rimless spectacles, the god of old men. Over there was somewhere else... was moorland and soft springy turf and lichenous stonework yellowy and green. It was old cars moving slow in crowded streets. It was rain. I knew it already, though I had never been, wasn't to set foot in the place for forty years. But I knew. I was almost content. I studied weather and language. I loved the rain and waited.

20

If I write about myself, I must circle around certain absences. If there is any excuse for writing (rather than praying) about one's life, it is this one: that is necessary to praise certain men and women, and more than man and woman, who have blessed me with their kindness or their rage. What it means: *rühmen ists's* — praise is the order where the mind best says itself in the world, just as a glad or silly reverence is the best habit of mind to carry through the blaze of deeds and omissions.

The only unity to my life is the responsibility I might take for all the deeds and omissions of what is perceived by others as my life. For me, I see only a song that has mine as some of its words.

But there will be absences, and that worries me. Until I know, if I know, how to deal with them, I will devote myself to a history of the text. Not of the life of the weaver. A weaver's life is Bottom's dream & needs no deep expounding.

21

The life of Napoleon that vanished overnight from my cellar study, vanished with the rest of the twenty- or thirty-volume set of duodecimo classic biographies — I don't know, I didn't have them long enough to tell — that my dear uncle Owen Parry had just given me, the life whose absence made me for forty years or more refuse to read a word about Napoleon until Tolstoy made me think of that strange tormenting personage again — that life that vanished overnight because my parents deemed the print too small for my eyes, the eyes meant to be kept virginal for all the textbooks I would read in medical school, but these books in a brown paper bag, dark dusky reddish books, faded burgundy, dusty, very small type to be sure, those books I have never ceased lamenting, and never recovered from the sudden spiteful (as it seemed) destruction — never acknowledged, silently denied — of these things, books, I valued more highly than any other thing I knew then, when I was eight, and books were my savior and my hope, my silver key to the hard door out of the screaming madhouse of my unquiet mind. How wild a child's mind is, prey of every wind of desire and aversion.

What might have been if that book had stayed with me? Would the determined madness of the emperor have won my noncommittal heart, would I have joined the army, determined to rule, and kill where I could not reign?

What might have been — there was no sexier reflection as I grew up than that, what might be, and what might have been.

I used to sit on the subway and boldly watch the doors slide open at my own station, stare and stare and dare myself to let them slide closed again. And the train would take me to the next stop or beyond, beyond anything I knew. What would happen then? I would grow breathless with the excitement of the guess, burgeoning wildness of all that might come to pass. If only we broke the ordinary, the orderly, the same. How we could be touched!

Would that have tormented me, those days after days of the long summer of 1815, after Waterloo, before the ill-starred flight to England, when he, he, *l'empereur*, could have gone anywhere, Russia, America, the Orient? But stayed there too long in Malmaison, too long in Rochefort. The breathless hard excitement of his waiting, the scholars and biographers didn't know that, but I knew it, how he waited *because* it was the wrong thing to do, because only by breaking the pattern of all your oughts (your reason, your stop on the train), only by breaking all of that can you ever hope to meet your destiny, to meet *&* contradict the Dæmon whose shadow lies on the pattern of your life.

It's just as well, isn't it, that I didn't know all that then? The lust to break the pattern would have overwhelmed me, left me in the world of crime or war.

And then hell would have been my portion in the next life *&* the next.

22

I didn't like poetry when I was a child. The artifice of it, the rhymes especially, made me feel bad. The artifices, the "marked features" so obvious a child could see or count them, "lisp in numbers," struck me as, not exactly *insincere*, but something like that, perhaps something worse. There was something bad about the poetry I saw, something that made me feel unclean or cloyed by some sentimental (which children dislike) or over-enthusiastic smarmy teary compulsion to feel. Drunken uncles at funerals, coming upstairs from where the funeral director was prudently dispensing shots of rye to the sports among the mourners — those illucid, self-involved, self-deceiving uncle eyes, breathing a sincerity on which they could not quite focus — *that* was the feel of poetry.

So poetry seemed untrue. It was not till years later (as it seemed) when I finally reached fourteen that poetry appeared in my life (thanks to Arthur Pinkerton and Hugh Smith) that seemed to be about revelation, not decoration.

If as a child I had been shown Whitman or W. C. Williams, I might have come earlier to poetry. But by the time I did find them, I had grown enraptured with artifice, & found them, both of them, huffy & secular and busy with opinion. By the time (late college) I read WCW, I wanted to read of glory and see the sunset slant in through the lines of poetry as I could find it doing in Dylan Thomas.

But when I was younger, very young, turning with a literal physical sensation of nausea from rhyme and "poetic" language, then Whitman would have won me. I would have liked him well, the ardor and self-conviction, his arrant sincerity unmodulated, stark, like a penguin alone on an ice floe. But no one showed me Whitman.

23

These are the books I remember in my house: seven of the eight volumes of the *American Educator Encyclopedia*; a Catholic CCD edition of the New Testament; *Lost Horizons*, by James Hilton. (I never read it, strange to say, since I heard ordinary people talking about it. All the stranger since my life has become deeply involved with some real-time version of a Tibetan tradition I gather that novel fancied or celebrated.) Then there was a twenty-volume set of books called World's Greatest Literature, in false gilt cloth bindings, faux-Grolier, which my parents had gotten for subscribing to the New York Post, a paper which my father, by the time I could buy my own paper, judged Bolshevik and vile. These are the ones I remember from the twenty: *Moby Dick, The Last Days of Pompeii, The Scarlet Letter, Vanity Fair* (never read it, still can't; Becky still scares me) *The Vicar of Wakefield, Plutarch's Lives* (a selection), *The Last of the Mohicans, The Autobiography of Benvenuto Cellini, Poe's Best* (or *Best Loved*) *Tales, Best Loved Poems, Ben Hur, Tale of the Christ, Oliver Twist, Washington Irving's Sketch Book, The Way of All Flesh, Treasure Island, Shakespeare's Plays* (a selection — I remember best the drawings, men's calves limned as sturdy ovals, something German in the drawing, a woman cracking a lute over someone's head), *The Count of Monte Cristo, Emerson's Essays*.

Number one sustained me. And one day in number ten I found Coleridge's "Kubla Khan" — and that was it. That is the first poem I remember reading where I found something — everything — I had found nowhere else. I had found poetry.

(In August 1992, after a summer spent in the French countryside, I stood with Charlotte in the noisy MSS display room of the British Museum, and, half-bent forward over the case containing the original manuscript, found myself chanting out loud, full normal voice among the hum of Japanese visitors, the original poem of my life, "In Xanadù did Kubla Khan," I read from the manuscript and recited to the end, hoping to pay back, in the capital city of our language, my debt to its greatest poem.)

24

I should talk now of the poets in my life, starting with Samuel — Samuel Coleridge, matching Samuel Kelly, my father, named for his grandfather Samuel Marles, from Somerset or so, next county over from Coleridge's Devon, who was of an age to have been Coleridge's son. It was Samuel Marles, my great-grandfather, who presided over the fantasy of the past for me as I grew up, so much so that when I first was publishing in college days, I used his name as my pseudonym. Marles must have been born around 1825, probably in Somerset. Family legend called him a painter and poet, who supported himself by japanwork on cabinetry and worked in Bristol. Some pages of his journals survive — including many poems, well-written, intelligent, with an early Victorian sincerity. The spelling is flawless, and nothing hints at the autodidact of the insecure. He must have been educated. He got married in Manchester to Jane Brass, daughter of a clergyman — presumably John Brass (b. 1790) of Bedfordshire. They moved to New York — why? — in the late 1340s, and in 1861 Samuel enlisted in the Union Army to defend his adopted country in the time of her need. My grandmother Florence was eighteen months old at the time. Samuel was wounded at the Battle of Gettysburg, and somehow never came home. He left the country, went to Australia (I was told by some) and to India (I was told by others) to seek his fortune. Certainly I have letters from him, mailed in Karachi (now Pakistan, then the Sind) in 1865. He spoke of his hopes to have wife and daughter join him. Nothing more. Rumors of his death from cholera, of gold found, of some gold sent home expropriated by a wicked uncle. In any case,

Samuel Marles has been a vital figure for me, establishing at once whatever authenticity it is to have connections with history (Gettysburg) and Over There (Somerset, Bristol) & at the same time pointing me to Asia.

25

It doesn't seem to me there is some other way of talking about my life than by talking about the people who made me me.

Who are they, though, if not the father and the mother? And everyone had been that at one time or other, even if they haven't been of the magnitude of Margaret Rose Kane (nic Aen) and Samuel Jason Kelly (O Ceallaigh) who made this body of me.

Whose names should I mention, leave out, hide, disguise?

Charlotte Mandell, my wife, who moves in the room behind me, her voice soft on the telephone talking to someone a few miles from the sea?

The sea itself — Sheepshead Bay, Coney Island, Rockaway, and the vastness of the sea seen?

Nora Welcome of New Hampshire, whose gracile limbs were white but not as white as the sand scorched into 8-mm color movies from 1939, fresh from being bought at the World's Fair?

The first woman and the last.

And I am all the men, or none of them.

No, there is no way to begin this, there is no meaning in a life, in a packet of names, a card catalog, a bed, a crowd in the street at a festa in Settembre, hips jostling, the saint being carried by in his golden carozza.

A wasp in the window, wondering.

Daylight is all, just daylight.

My autobiography is any day.

The Tibetans when they write of a life story call it for short *nam thar*, abbreviating a phrase that means something like the Story of How He Achieved Complete Liberation. Only such stories are worth telling, I guess. Whereas for us, we dote on detailed annotations of failure, grief, misprision, and despair.

Shall I pretend to an Enlightenment I have yet to uncover, affect a despair I do not feel?

So hard to begin... to begin is to end. Well begun half done, they say. Who say?

The English. Start with that. I think I'm English. The Brasses of Bedfordshire and the Marleses of Manchester, Somerset, Wales. But I'm born on the terminal moraine of the last glacier, a ridge which ran through Brooklyn, of an Irish (raised English by his Protestant mother Florence Marles) father and an Irish (raised American by her Catholic father Thomas Kane) mother. What does it matter where they came from? Doyle made me, and Williams and Dante and Pound & Marlowe and …

26

A problem suddenly encountered in writing my autobiography:

I think I'm turning into a crow.

Noisy mysterious obvious and dark
arcane mysterious overt on a tree
conspicuous in snow folkloric
dark portentous scary easy-scared
polemic but not murderous
carnivorous but killing nothing
wide-winged tasteless in people's way
eating grain I never planted
making too much noise being here
sitting apart of the highest
thing I can find apart from everybody
never far from human neighborhoods.

27

Nothing happened to me but people. The people who met me made me. That's the behind and before of it, the way it simply is. (And if we look cannily at most people, we will find it I think the same — they were who they had beheld, they spoke what they had heard.

Who said an autobiography is honest? It isn't — it is instead a telling of how one supposes one came to be oneself, here and now, the one who bears my name and speaks it as his own. I am telling you how I came to be me — yet I know nothing of it, nothing but guesswork and hope and fondly cherished memories of erotic blessings, sentiments exchanged, vistas seen — and even more tightly cherished memories of pain and injustices.

So Western autobiography, since it tries to tell what the author doesn't know, is a desperate genre, full of the accidental genius of trying hard — which is why autobiographies are always so full of brio and youthful charm and lies, no matter how old the perpetrator. Robert Graves writing his at thirty-five is no more juvenile than the Oldest Member grousing at his foolscap.

Nothing happened to me but other people. All I did was sometimes have the bravery to recognize and embrace them, all too often the cowardice to avoid them or turn away, mostly the ignorance not to see them really until they were gone. Chances, missed chances, chances married to the deepest and richest bottom of themselves. Known. But there are always more chances. The beauty of the world: there are always more people.

So if I can't tell their names, then I have nothing left to tell (in the old title style, *Life and Opinions of So-and-So*) except my opinions. And my opinions are precisely what I value least about me, lord, this old green shirt has more value than my views on intellectual history or the latest *lutte poétique*.

So I am left to tell you the books I wrote, by which I in turn was written into the world, such as it is, as those who read books and come to know vaguely, at the corner of their minds, my name. The way it is.

But you understand, don't you, that all this while I'll be thinking about the people.

(One thing I could do is write their names: a real autobiography would look like an index in a scholarly text, and be, finally, as comprehensive and unreadable as an index, a book of names, a personal Deuteronomy.)

In fact, every life is the index to a lost text.

28

When I think through my life, I realize that I am sustained by an immense (that means not measurable) network of gratitudes and permissions.

Maybe the thing I mean when I say *my life* could be the same as all those who have surrounded and instructed me, plus the act of saying so, where "I" is no more than the one that says so.

Someday, someone may have the decency, courage, and effrontery to write an accurate autobiography. It would be made up of nothing other than the names of every man and woman he has ever known; at the end he would draw a line and beneath it sign his own name. Because that is who he sayably is.

I don't have the time, memory, and honesty to do that now. There are so many, and I have lost them, so many of them, into the days and the renewals.

But of the network that sustains me, some nodes are so obvious even I can't forget them. Let me say some of them here, for the beauty of the names of them, these little murmurs of thanks should be a mountain roar of *Gratias ago*, lords and ladies!

Friends of childhood who welcomed me into the road of excesses and the palace of self-criticism, Arthur Pinkerton, the first person I could talk to who knew more than I did about what I needed to know, and Hugh Smith who made me understand that a poet was someone it was possible to be.

Joan Elizabeth Lasker (1931–1989) my first wife, Joby — she it was who took my arrogance and mute skills and said, These will do, and treated me like a poet until I sort of was one. And who did not selfishly confine herself, or let me confine her, to Musing just me, but whose kindness and perceptions strengthened I think many poets, young and not so young. Long after Joby and I had separated, my parents kept sending her every Christmas as nice a check as they could from their Social Security — a little before their deaths, my mother said, She made you a poet.

Wasn't that extraordinary for a mother to say, to yield to that other woman what she, more than any, could have claimed as her own? For she had not just given me a strong body and sturdy bones, but a profound sense of that Irish quality I should call "despairing optimism," the knowledge that we are going to get what's coming to us, and that everything turns out for the best. What better paradox could an artist be armed with?

My father, for all his verbal wit and bel canto, had no such convictions, and had a typically English come-off-it attitude about most exaltations — except for country silences and rare glimpses of deer at twilight (he would have said "in the gloaming"). From him I learned that the words we choose to call them make the emotional meaning of everything we see and do. And from him too the strange (since he despised exercise and athletics, though he danced like Astaire and shamed me at any physical deed) transmission into the sacred dance of baseball: playing, observing, judging, adoring.

His name was Samuel Jason Kelly, and he was born 8 July 1900 — on John D. Rockefeller's birthday, he would wryly remember. His own father, a New York detective and City Hall presence of some sort, died when my father was seven and the whole huge family had to vacate the mansion they'd lived in. They kept a few steps ahead of the bailiff, as my father described it, all through his growing up. My father had a wonderful tenor voice, even as an old man, when the voice was lower and darker. He sang, when he sang, formally and deliberately, never just humming or absent-mindedly; when he sang, he sang full voiced and with his mind on it. He loved Irish songs in the manner of McCormack, and operatic arias he'd make up imaginary French or Italian sounds for, as needed. The music was all, the words nothing. *Prima la musica, dopo le parole* might have been his motto. And in a sense it's mine, since my voice is bass, heavy, unnimble to sing — so I've had to find my arias in the words. But still the music comes first.

My father retired early, at sixty, and he spent the next thirty years in a curious quietness. He would sit at the window for hours, with a strange light in his eyes, seeing I suppose nothing, or that Other Country to which meditators perhaps also hasten inward and by night. He smoked heavily — cigarettes till his seventies, then cigars — but never inhaled, drank more beer in later years, but never seemed drunk, just louder, then quieter, then asleep. He died three weeks after my mother's death, only a few weeks after we all had, for the first time in years, had a chance to spend a summer together up here in the country.

29

In the late 1950s, there was a circle of kindness & decency and visionary explorations into which I, rough-hewn and suspicious & greedy, was welcomed — by Jerry and Diane Rothenberg and their friends, Armand Schwerner, Paul and Sara Blackburn, Seymour Faust, my friends Rochelle Owens and David Antin, who was the first of all of them I knew, and who brought me along to the Rothenberg door finally, as he had brought me through German literature and communicated even to me some feeling of the brittle, the fiercely detailed, the passion for the abstract, the glimmering meager of silverpoint, the passionate enough.

With the Rothenbergs and their friends, I entered for the first time a world in which the individual striving for vision, clarity, or just decency and sense, fitted into the social order — where the solitary poet ran the glad risk of becoming a man of letters. The risk is necessary — without the community, and specifically in some sense the community of letters, vision turns back ingrown. It is the community that gives language, and through language, what we see is restored to those who gave us our means. It was this specific world that the Rothenbergs, with their anthropological interests and training, would soon investigate so deeply and usefully through their work with finding a current English/American voice for Native American and other tribal poetics.

And I was caught at the pivot point, right there, and never sure, never to this day sure, which way I speak. Because I am private and dread the tribe whose language speaks me. Crazy as Merlin or Taliesin (flattering self-images abound), I took stock of my world and found silence what I could trust most — to talk with silence. To talk from the feel of water on my skin, my feet on the rock, my eye on the contours of experience — uninstructed by the social.

Except of course the ever-present, ever-hidden "social" of poetry, all the poems I have ever read that, resonating in me and charming and changing and dying and begetting, taught me in fine not what to say but, somehow, how saying is, and that I could.

Pivot point. This is the late 1950s, 1960. We had founded The Blue Yak, a bookstore exclusively devoted to small-press books of poetry. A cooperative of us poets ran it: Rothenbergs, Diane Wakoski, George Economou, Armand Schwerner, Howard Ant, Susan Sherman, Bill May. It did enough business to support one person, and that was remarkable itself, after the low rent was paid on the Tenth Street storefront on that block of avant-garde galleries and winos. But there were eight of us, and most of us had too much on our minds to keep it open The wonderful blue furry horned animal painted on the brick still stays in my mind.

30

About this time Caryl Chessman was scheduled to be executed after years of appeal. Joan and I marched from Columbus Circle in a great crowd of protesters begging for last minute clemency from the California gauleiter. We reached Washington Square to be greeted with news of the man's execution. The grief and impotence of the social moment matched identical emotions in me about my own life and work. I felt neglected, ignored, unknown. Cheaply and silently, I resolved to die. By force of habit we kept walking down to the Figaro, a sleazy and comfortable café on Bleecker, and as I came in, footsore and in despair, an older man wearing a cocoa-colored suit with an orange necktie said, "Hello, you must be the Kellys. I'm Robert Duncan."

This man had recognized me! This man, whom I regarded as the greatest poet living in my language, had known my name, known me. Always a knower, Duncan had here, deftly, simply, saved my life, literally. The strictly angelic nature of his intervention was shocking and shamed me by its simplicity. How little I needed! And how much I got! And the basic sustaining power, the wing he gave me, lasted in all he taught: the power of attention to the dance of words that — so attended to — always would make sense of the body and all its pivots with the world. Social as Auden, fierce as Barker, incantatory as Thomas, learned as Lansing, honest as Olson, adventurous as Mac Low, musical as Zukofsky, Duncan struck me as the complete poet and one whose grace let him play and comfort and be gone. And part of his grace was his strict, sometimes even humorless, fidelity to dream and vision — which made him my key in my own struggles on the side of the surreal against the neo-classic — which is how my generation misunderstood the energy and scruples of Charles Olson:

Olson, who overpowered me and my kind with fervor with which he, sometimes breathless and in doubt, sustained what seemed — too easily — the mind's argument against the heart. Amazing man, that such flesh and tune and ballsiness should doubt Lord Plato.

And who but Olson could read to me deep in the marches of the night, on Fort Square, within breath of the sea, that overwhelming paragraph of *Moby Dick* that warns all Platonists (and he was warning me) of the honeyhead, the sea in which they'd fall from the crow's nest of their dreamy apart — as if he, great Olson Ter-Maximus, would not have splashed that sea dry and displaced it by his own Animal Ardor he wittingly mistook for mind! For he was intelligent indeed, and knew the cunning of the knees, the care of the eye, the art of what the Icelanders, we are told, call *menskr* — all that is human.

Yet neo-classic seemed an honest word to say of all that, that early and middle thrust of Olson towards the human, the truistically over-determined Human Universe — presume not God to scan.

But in the later, more powerful days, Olson did break that too-sensible rule, and turned from the sub-Emersonian enthusiasms of "history" in America (where Pound had been all our teachers) to scan the deity, the central issue, the Angel. And in the third volume of Maximus, still under-perceived by or stifled by his scholars, we find a far more telling appointment with the soul than many of his students wanted or want — they wanted to keep him to the Democratic Party, Aristotle, & coaching at third base. And in the heart of his striving we find the curious name of Amoghasiddhi, the Buddha of the possible.

31

Dear reader,

(Dear reader! How dear you are to me, really really, not just *façon de parler*, you are the heart of me, the best of me, the part that hears.

You judge the truth of me by what I say.

Actions speak louder than words, my father used to say and say, until I feared to say a word.

Dear reader, for you this language is, for you it made me and made us as we are, prone — prompt — to answer and sullen, we are sullen, you hold me in your sullen lap and dare to doubt me, you do right to doubt me, to test what I say. Test in your body moving and at rest the cloth and fiber and fit. Test the steel on your wood. Test the insistent questions on your continual answers.)

Dear reader, I don't feel much interest in the years gone by, my imagined past. The trough of time I got through as well as I could. I don't feel close to them now, especially the 1960s & 1970s, years of putting one word after another and hoping the world would still be there. Now that the fashions of those times are with us again, if cleaner now and more whimsical and safe, no need to give much glory to those dark hopes and self-induced projected terrors, scares we used as a politics to block our always dim-enough terror of the situation: this mind of ours we do not know. It was a bleak enough time for all its noise and patchouli, and I am glad to be past it.

But the beloved friends of those days, let me say their names at least here, and many of them I get to call upon still, Diane Wakoski and Chuck Stein and Armand Schwerner and Helen Kelly and Jackson Mac Low and Tandy Sturgeon and Gerrit Lansing and Susan Quasha and Elie and Nona Yarden and Jed Rasula and Clayton Eshleman and Lisa Katzman and Michele Martin and Dennis and Barbara Tedlock, and brave John Martin whose fierce idealistic mind and sensual disposition ushered to the dear readers of America half a thousand books of new poetry.

Dear reader, by the time you read this, I will probably be sixty years old. What I care about is what is happening now, the life I live now with Charlotte Mandell, my wife, who translates French and studies Tibetan with me and in her accuracy and beauty and clarity keeps me pointed towards sunrise and makes me happy.

32

Charlotte was different from people I've known. She grew up gently, fastidiously, accurately. I came to know her first in the late 1980s, when she was a student of Edouard Roditi — in the last few years of his life he taught memorably at Bard. Charlotte was of great personal beauty; her father Marvin was a novelist & teacher and an editor of *New Politics*, her mother Betty Reid a sociologist whose career was devoted to the disadvantaged, the homeless, the beneficiaries of welfare-in-name-only, and who single-handedly edited a newspaper for and about the poorest, *Survival News*. Husband and wife had moved in the same New York leftist circles I knew a few years later. So Charlotte was raised in ethical and æsthetic literacy — and that summoned me to her, to a friend raised to value articulate candor and justice.

Charlotte spent her summers in France, or on a small island near Martha's Vineyard — and from that island, Cuttyhunk, she from time to time would send me letters that I marveled at for their spontaneous serenity, a kind of razor-sharp gentle alertness. When she moved to Seattle in 1990, we corresponded. Always her letters were, as she is, precise, generous, willing to see the best of things, even of me. Late that year, after all the deaths and separations I'd been through, I found myself on a west coast trip, and we met in Seattle, then travelled by ferry to British Columbia for a week of keeping warm in the rain. We seemed to move in the House of the Raven, in the primordial powers. The following year she went to France, and when she came back in October, we began to live together — and have ever since. I have never before known the curious integration of erotic intensity with intelligent calm — truth in quiet teaches constancy.

33

What I care about is now, & the work I'm doing — long poems that go on, *Bliss, Espousals*, prose texts, theories of translations, the klondike of electronic publishing with the Himalayas of hyper-text just behind, and above all else the dance I meet every morning in silence, the song, *le chant du jour* and what else is new? What else is now?

> I want to write sentences they will take delight in
> ("feel measure!") in three hundred years
> (after the baroque revival, the second Lake school,
> the new Novalis and ultra-Kierkegaard,
> when Marx is fashionable again
> and a great, bluff bully from Touraine
> weeps at the human comedy again
> and Miss Baudelaire wakes up at the evening's dusk
> and Second Ezra wakes up what's left of London
>
> or whatever is, whatever ever is)
>
>   sentences,
> sentences unhinged from rule and hardware,
> long lines of luminous messages, semaphores,
> outrage on emulsions, screens, the sky, the eye
> taught its manners by machines,
> however and wherever they do it, do it,
>
> and still my crazy grammar will make hard sense,
> crazier the better, glue on every corner,
> crumbs of green cheese between the fingers,
> something for you! For you!
>
> Inexhaustible, indestructible, leaving
> Echoes and clatter and strange garlicky reeks,
> A flurry of frangipani, gets stronger
> when you open the windows, where's it coming from,

from your hands, the words infect your flesh,
keep reading, smell the weather of these words
coming over the horizon like a Viking ship
or just a sunrise, a coven of gypsies,
a crowd of giggling kids tossing your heart from hand to hand

34

In all the gratitudes I want to mention last the chiefest gratitude:

In December of 1981, beginning to be tired of what had begun to look like persistent patterns of greed and aggression in what I thought was my innocent behavior, I took refuge in the Buddha, Dharma and Sangha. I recited the ancient traditional formula that makes one a Buddhist. One very cold night a month or two later a friend was showing me pictures of various Tibetan lamas. (A lama is one who shows you your mind — something we can see unaided no more than the eye, for all its acuity, can see itself. We need a mirror, and the eye finds perhaps its best mirror in the eye of another person.)

One picture in particular struck me; looking at the face, I felt what I could now call the intense presence of near and far — at once most intimate and most exalted, the way I suppose one's own soul feels. At the moment, what I felt was yearning to meet & listen to this teacher, who was called Kalu Rinpoche.

Several months later I had the chance to make a connection with Kalu Rinpoche when he offered the Kalachakra Initiation in New York. A little later, I had the nerve to ask him to be my teacher; he agreed, but in his kindness told me that I should work mostly and directly with Lama Norlha, who lives most of the year in the United States.

Meeting these two great teachers, my root lamas, strikes me as the most important opportunity I have been given, and the greatest good fortune, even among so many kindnesses my life has known. For the past dozen years or so, I have tried to let their wisdom and compassion shape the direction of my activities. Though Kyabje Dorje Chang Kalu Rinpoche passed away in India in 1989, his presence and kindness continue to pervade my life, focused through the brilliant and compassionate instruction of Lama Norlha. It is strange in these times to meet such a being; usually, the better you know someone, the more you see his faults.

With Lama Norlha, the reverse seems true; the longer I have been with him, the more I have seen of his qualities. Of all the remarkable persons I have ever had the blessing of talking with out loud, in ordinary words, as well as learning from by signs, behavior, quietness, Lama Norlha is the truest. Without any time wasted on what we quaintly call a "private" life, he dedicates all of his time, all of his life, to helping others. His teaching is penetrating and direct, and intensely personal to the one taught. The simplest thing to say about him is this: He knows.

He knows me. He has helped me to integrate all the energies and interests of my life and perceive them as continuous. The Buddhist Vajrayana is usually called tantric — *& tantra* means continuity. At root, the word means something like loom, and the seamless continuity of what is woven. The Tibetan word is clearer: *rgyud*, the thread, the line, the lineage, the continuity.

Lama Norlha teaches the Buddhadharma, yes, but I have learned from him much of what I know about narrative, timing, language, and what we mean when we speak, and what we are keeping unsaid. His own teachings, and the power of his chanting, are continual reminders of what it means to speak and be heard.

Once not long ago I was talking to him and told him about this thing I'm writing (this thing you're reading now), about this autobiography. My life, what can I say about my life? What is the value of writing a story of someone who has not achieved the goal, has not broken out of the system of habits and constraints?

I said to Lama Norlha, what can I possibly write in my autobiography?

He laughed and said, You like to write. Write about your future lives instead. (The past is the son of a barren mother, it is said. There is no past, only an onward hurtling energy of our own past deeds, shaping what we perceive as the world, moment by moment appearing to take form.) Write your future lives. It is the ones to come and not the ones that have gone that are important. Tell those.

Are you joking?

(In telling there is learning. Learning is investigation.)

Maybe in my very next year I will be born in Mongolia, a nomad. Looking down the corridor of Necessary Words (the world of prophecy),

A VOICE FULL OF CITIES

I see myself on a cold wide plain. Between my hands the head of a deer, his eyes turn wild at me, his breath snorting out, gushing warm on my dirty wrists. I am holding this animal by the horns, he twists his head to one side and I pull him straight, twists to the other and I right him again. We look at one another. He has the fatal, useless, beautiful wisdom of animals. I have the kind of cunning, deep ensemplastic cunning, that I can hardly imagine in this present life. But when I am Mongolian it will be different. My hands will do some of my thinking for me, twisting the deer this way and that, until we have finished saying to each other whatever has to be said. Perhaps I'm trying to tell him about this life of mine. Or all life, so short, so mysteriously projected into outrageous destinations.

I look at Lama Norlha. His hands are twisting the head of the animal back, gently, so that this unseen beast sees me.

He says, Oh, in your next life after that you will be a Chinese fisherman. (This will be hard for me, for I have never hunted, fished, or killed.) And then in your next life you will be a Japanese businessman.

(And here is the harness of money, that I never understood in this life — Saturn in Pisces in the second house — didn't understand, did love the warm feel of it in my pocket. But Japanese businessmen have no pockets, only fountain pens and documents, no sleep, Johnny Walker Red Label (I never liked scotch). I used to go without sleep — once I managed five days without sleep and without food, lived on coffee and cigarettes and rode the subways. Was I in training for Nagoya or Osaka? Once I was a sort of businessman and wore a homburg hat to business, had the key to the office in my pocket, and knew the books. I took a course in Japanese language and culture from Professor Edwin O. Reischauer (later to become Ambassador to Japan) at City College. It was called Unattached Eight, and brought Madame Harich-Schneider (I think was her name) to play that round mountain of tubular ascensions, an ancient mouth-organ of the Japanese; she brought with her a small electrical brazier to keep the instrument warm. And someone else brought in and played the *shakuhachi*. Nineteen fifty-four, and already getting ready for that life beyond the Pan-Pacific Rim.)

Lama is still smiling at me. Maybe then you are born again as an American. You become president, you preside over America becoming at last a very spiritual country. You think that is good?

(And here I can tell the history of my *historein*, searching, researching, my quest among the so-called religions. What I saw early in the morning as Father Brady lifted up the silver cup. And how that light led me faithfully to the work of the Grail. How can a country have a religion? Can't we go to the land of the Grail, as the King of Oddiyana achieved realization, and brought the whole population of his country with him into the Pure Land? Travelers when they came to Oddiyana found a pleasant, perfectly empty country, no people, no birds, no beasts, no fish. Just trees and flowers, precious jewels lying all over the ground, smoke still drifting up from kitchen fires.)

But, Lama, is it just one life after another?

Then you get a lifetime of rest, in Tibet, watching yaks.

Maybe then enlightenment time?

Maybe.

Maybe a long time watching the yaks.

(Gale Research, *Contemporary Authors*, 1976 & 1993)

A NEW KIND OF MFA PROGRAM

What is proposed is different from other MFA programs. The Bard Program addresses the place where the arts meet, and recognizes that place as a person not as a set of theories or a set of skills. The work of the student is the center. That work will often enough involve exactly the accumulation and practice of skills, of making and of judgment. But it will also entail learning about the world an artist makes by declaring it, and learning how to live out one's own cunning and æsthetic enterprise. What will be on hand is a staff of resourceful artists active in their disciplines, who have chosen to spend part of their energies on alerting people to the powers of making art and giving coherent accounts of themselves. Making sense is radical to making art.

What is different about this program is that it engages all the arts (visual and verbal, musical and physical, iconic and temporal) in a shared project of learning and discourse. To say that all the arts are included does not mean that the student is invited to pick one thread from a neatly packaged skein and follow it for three years, only occasionally looking over at what the competition is up to. It means the student sets to work under the guidance indeed of a professional artist in the discipline to be examined, but with the steady commentary and support of artists from all the other fields — whose perceptions, founded on a life way of work and thinking, will be of direct and material value to the work going on. In practice, this will mean an abhorrence of abrupt specialization. It will mean that the painter's work should expect to be meaningful to the composer and the dancer and the novelist. It will mean that the isolation of conservatories is broken.

In the pluralism of competing pleasures, the student of the arts will begin to sense not just what skills might be or become appropriate, and what work best fulfils the artist's personal needs, but also how to reach an audience: a new kind of audience, it may be, based on the common humanity of maker and perceiver, and the immense diversity of the means between them.

Painting. Music. Poetry. Sculpture. Photography. Fiction. Dance. Film. Drama. The means are there, the skills are available, the facilities are given. But nothing is packaged. The labels guide only the first minutes of the program. The artist works with the teacher who seems able to be of help, right then, in the project at hand whether the work is in thought or execution or performance. The student makes the choice, gets what help is needed, when and as it is needed.

The formalities of the program are few. Each week, the student meets with the chosen adviser for private conference or discussion. In some cases there will also be continuing workshops and performance groups. There will be a plenary weekly meeting of all artists (students and staff) in seminar to consider (in response to emergent needs or interests) ideas or works of art whose usefulness is to be shared. Several times a week will occur Presentations or Performances, in which the work of an individual artist will be offered for commentary and critique by colleagues and faculty. Each MFA Candidate is expected to mount one such Presentation every session in residence.

These three concerns: Conference, Seminar, Presentation, will be the basic public garment of the MFA Program at Bard. The center or body so clothed is, always, the creative and perceptual and conceptual work of the individual artist.

The Program is directed both to recent graduates and to all those who have come to work in one or more of the arts, and who now want the chance to conduct their work in the supportive and challenging environment of other artists, in all fields, seeking to discover the languages that unite and divide them.

Most of the formalities of the program will be carried on during the four (preferably consecutive) sessions in residence at Bard College. Students may be invited to be in residence at other times, or advised to take specific college courses at Bard or elsewhere to equip themselves better for what they have in mind. All such options are to be worked out with the student, and exclusively with reference, and in response, to the student's own demands.

4 October 1979
rev. 9 October 1979

SOME LETTERS

LETTER TO MARGARET RANDALL

Bard College, Annandale-on-Hudson
8 February '63

... your beautiful fifth issue in today, & filling me with excitement & pleasure & pride, of a kind I thought I cdnt feel except for a magazine I'd done myself. But I feel (damn little that I've done for it), part of it, and the stirring of the waters I bathe my hands in.

Externally, all change for the better; paper is wonderful, fat & cheap, as it shd be, rough to the hands & good for the texture of the print. Design is splendid, & those dibujos valuable, close to home.

... the Sejourne piece revelation, so much drawn together there so quickly. All very well to speak of knitting the threads together. But her mind blends the textures, a harder & infinitely more profitable task...

You've been sending to me, speaking to me (whether you know it or not) for days now. All week Sy's Sources of Radio Emission have been on my mind (tho it's 2yrs at least since I saw the poem), & this morning (while ECE lay already in the box, unfetched as yet) the word *quincunx* came into my mind. It's curious: I know what quincunx means, yet the poem came "& don't feel what it means", &c., as if I didn't. I mean the poem I began to write, beginning with quincunx & going out. Then when I'd done it, going up the hill & getting ECE & finding *quincunce* mysteriously in Sejourne. That piece has been with me all afternoon & night: the dios de hielo the figure I need now.

Heard from Cid this week, & he tells me you mentioned the Outward Air to him. In my answer, as I was writing, I realized (how slow I am) for the first time *fully* how good it is that you will do the book, that it will come out, thru the care of your hands, as part of one of the continuing processes of publication of real value now. As a poet and as what poets are, am grateful for that process, & to be some part of it...

One of winter's coldest nights, now, with the temperature way under zero. Below zero all day, in fact, as if we were in Enslin's woods. But here we are, and the snow wonderfully clean against the skin. I'll put 3 poems on the back for you. Remember that stupid radio station we met at? I wonder why I think of it, perhaps walking along that same street this week, on a rare afternoon in the city. City totally alien to me, no sense of its life or love or rhythm. People furtive and desperate. What can we do to warm them? Plainly it is you & Sergio who can, your work the walls of the oven. Begin to warm. All our love...

(*El Corno Emplumado* #6, April 1963)

LETTERS TO LINDY HOUGH & RICHARD GROSSINGER

Thanksgiving Afternoon '67

dear Lindy,

Robert Tipps is visiting with us from Cambridge, the turkey is tawny in the oven, Button is paring two kinds of turnip, Joby reposes. It rains. Things seem drawing together in odd portentous ways here. Always a gleeful sadness in surmise, how long will anything last, this house, these woods, our own agencies of matter. But the music goes on, & as long as we have bodies (instruments of relation) we may fancy the dance. But there was a slow happening at Bard two weeks ago, with two naked dancers, one of whom tried to draw me into the round dance with wch the evening ended. And I wd not dance, & understood in that refusal an entry upon another plane or scale, not *perspectiva naturalis* or *perspectiva artificialis*, but some other conduit of distances & relations & proportions. Yet I thought too of protestant Kierkegaard who wrote that he 'will not' dance, altho summoned to the dance. Troubled by this in your letter: that you take the presence of women in my poems (I cant speak for Richard or Brakhage) as non-specific. It may seem that way, by virtue of the common pronouns that move our engines & clear our path, but in fact each poem (or each poem that comes from woman) arises from the specific woman, or specific encounter of the specific woman; so there is not even the theoretical limit of 1 ½ billion poems (= number of planetary women), since not all people are specific, nor does one poem exhaust specificity. Lately I've worked on a series of "sonnets" each clearly inscribed to the person (usually woman) in clear response to whom that poem arises. Yet that is biography, & the specificity of each woman must better be mirrored in the exact specificity of each poem, that it *is* (in) its own measure, that to be its own unique emergence. Cf. preface to *Finding the Measure* (a section of wch is on the Black Sparrow mailer you may have seen). ((Offhand, I'd guess Brakhage is indeed, as you say, generic in (using) woman that he discerns the prototype in his wife, with all the grandeur & focus that implies; but focus is also limitation.)) So that to speak for myself, I'd think the poem (not woman in the poem) stands for the specific woman (rather than the other way round). I have grown very much less interested in the kind of syncretic mythology a Joseph Campbell offers, & find the idiosyncratic & the particular more moving & rewarding. There is an awful blandness abt Woman as Image; Goethe, for all the magic of his sound, does manipulate statuary & masks in *Faust II*.

And what is important to remember abt archetypes & archetypal women &c. is this: each archetype exists as a function in a specific context. There may indeed be 'an' archetype of Venus or Mother or White Goddess: but all that can mean is that that is name of one function of woman, *a* woman for *a* man, in a given context or ground. A woman does not participate in the archetypal: she *is & does* in a context something archetypal, with reference to those who participate in the context. Each woman's specificity must be implicitly honored; that is the fidelity of art, wch inherently objectifies distinctness. *I'jaz* is the qoranic virtue, uniqueness of each manifestation. That is why we have in the world two sexes but a billion names. The best thing we know abt Helen called of Troy is that she is the sister of Kastor & Pollux & the wife of Menelaos & a skilled weaver & often ashamed of her own excessive effect on men. She is Helen of Troy because she is beautiful & wild & wet & has a *name & identity*. Therein is she, as woman, different from those impressive but horrifying "Venuses" so-called of the paleolithic deposits, matched at any time by psychotic drawings etc., figures wch are all tits & buttocks & belly & cunt, faceless & handless. (How pleased homosexuals like — & — seem to be with these figurines, wch seem to 'explain' woman to them without the dangers of encountering a specific woman!) Triumph of the hellenic in something like Kallipygian Aphrodite, whose beautiful ass is a consequence of those earlier fascinations, but who herself is now identified as a human form specifically, hands & face & meaningful gesture, displaying that specific beauty. (Is Milo's Aphrodite armless because a degraded Roman soldiery tried to reduce that image to its paleolithic terms, stopping short by chance or by holy dread from that head?)

You say you "would like to do something very specific about someone." That is our dilemma, & as far as art deals with people at all (& that is very far), that is the whole program of art. That the specific engender the specific, not a blurred carbon copy but a whole new thing. Pound's Make it new, Christ's *Ecce omnia faciam nova*, seem to relate paradigmatically to this intention. Attention, we shd really call it, since only thru the rapturously naked intellect (=, I guess, as I use the word, intelligence + senses + skill) & its remorseless relentless touching & weighing & pondering of things, can a meaningful response come forth.

(It wd be easy to say that a ((male)) poet of the kind I'm speaking of has a poem the way other men have an erection, easy but false since the poet has the erection too, does sleep with the girl, does marry and give in marriage. So that it is a more total response than any easily channeled biological/social response can be: I detect in this proposition an alchemic clarity, the real purport of *sublimation* (wch is never in alchemy what it is in Freud's debased use of the word, i.e., substitution.)

Later now, & just back from recording Tipps at Bard Hall; Button is putting the tape on so we can hear the results. He's playing the strange, simple-seeming music of Frederic Mompou,[1] a contemporary Catalan, & then a beautiful Cage piece, *4:19*, at least some pages of its large aleatory score. The recording is on now, & very good.

---

1. *Musica callada*: "silent music" after a notion of John of the Cross.

The Mompou is getting into my ears, & I'd like to let it into yours, tho it's stuff that must be heard over & over because it is so simple, like Satie in that respect. Hear it again to know you've heard it at all. Strange the role Brakhage plays for you & Richard; your sense of the 'generations' is probably a clear way to cope with it; he is 35 or whatever, does feel absolutely estranged from hippies, & not alone from hippies but from those gestures of his own (my own) generation wch created the hippies as by-product of the endless mechanism of human liberty. Not end-product, as we must all be clear. The Big Turn-On, the Public Nakedness, these are propaideutic functions. The warmongers & antiwar/mongers do seem to me these days the enemies, those who wd compel our focus to those very sights we can do nothing abt, & to wch our responses are expected to be decorous & conventional. They wd strangle our response/ability, & thus castrate our effectiveness. The CIA is behind everything, just as clearly as the hero lurks behind the anti-hero. Liberty is elsewhere, is here, is in your hand & mind. Tho Brakhage doesn't say this, the major doctrine the hippy attacks is the doctrine of work by which B is sustained, as I am, as I believe you & Richard to be (tho you are a woman, & have thus sustenances I cannot know of, hearths you kindle & hearths you tend & hearths that catch fire as you pass.)

I'm due to read in San Francisco on 8th January, & dont have to be back here till the end of the month, so I'll try to keep moving the whole month, hopefully to the southwest & Mexico too, & perhaps able to stop by Michigan on the way home. Let me bring this letter to a close & bid you both well, & ask to hear from you soon. Tapes will be gratefully rec'd, & I'll try to get one off to you too, it is easier than typing. Take care of yourselves & joy of winter. A chip of moon topsy turvy in the sky now, rising over a great wrack of cloud, but the river half an hour ago was still black, one lone green light across it like the sentimental memories of Gatsby, or our own sentimental engagements with distance.

9 December '67

Dear Richard and Lindy,
                the spirit that is Mercurius has many counterfeited likenesses, that may in truth be He Himself in a playful guise,
        but o what gobbledegook until he reveals himself, what barrels of tripe get written & peddled & reverently read (wherein the reverence has its effect, tho the read matter hath not, like the girls who read Gibran & profit from that languid page)
                                                                        reverence.
As principle. Wch does underlie any *stance* from wch work can be done: reverence to the self (like Strindberg's in his amazing *Inferno* wch I've just read) at least, & how a reverence for one's own self leads to a reverence for signs & wonders, each thing observed & noted, the *semata* enodia, signs we meet on setting forth along our way)
        but reverence, as preliminary Warming of the athanor
                                                                (the Work completes itself every moment of the day, or there is no work of wch we can say That is the work, but each minute is process is work is part of that not-other The Work)
                                        & Button has brought me a cup of tea and a cup of coffee, how do you do?
                                                Discovered today that there is a wisdom in Divorce our society hides from us; thinking so on learning of Margaret Randall's separation from her husband, that word, separation, & all the meaning it has in all the rest of our lives.
        All that fertility means.
                                Fertiles îlots of Mallarmé, but fertilities are not islands, are just such twined snakes or greased poles or stacked decks or club sandwiches or clefs wch open music & close sound, or close music & open sound.

Yet we offer, day in & out, like courteous gods to fuck them & bring them to bear unlikely children. We must not expect a shower of gold; we must be, a shower of gold.

                                                            26 December '67

dear Lindy,

all we have (& this is a start at a theory of society, society even where it offends, in CWms, or the dark moral of your Bonnie & Clyde) all we have is to be wrapped/rapt/raped in one another; the wolverine, having a huge northern territory to enclose, pisses his way along the thus declared boundary, only a few drops at a time, to make the enclosing (in his case) logos last; Dante puts Diomed & Odysseus wrapped in one flame, whose midnight chicanery declared them kin, but enemies to all others, wrapped in their cunning, the exclusions of their mental territories. There is the 'perceptual trick' of wch Richard speaks so often, & by which (according to his last letter) you are able to come to the poem, to the Society or collegium I speak of in Alch. Jnal., the society of our best wills, wrapped in the weft-shuttling of time & times & momentary fatal abnegations of *directio cordis* (directio voluntatis, wch Pound makes defining task of *jen*), yet the warp runs straight, & guessing in the dark at that straightness we can allow (I think CWms allows) the road of our true wills more important than the diversions therefrom. "Even I" have womanpoet in my pocket, & fail you in entertaining such a concept) yet I do hold it, not as a credence but as a perception of certain ladies in the world, certain perceptions arising within the spectral limits of *their* unwilling to be more. I also have the concept manpoet in my pocket, no nobler critter, tho both have noble parts in their names. But society begins again each morning at the tip of our intentions

                                        & the womanliness that summons men (world) (all) to herself does seem a radical fact of woman; the womanpoet denies this in a world of aspiration (of a kind all too familiar), aspiration that never allows itself to take the work itself as measure, but only the amount of contact the publicity of that work allows or forces. Self-advancement is our anglo-american disease still (tho it's not fashionable to talk abt it, it doesnt seem compatible with existenz, tho it is the *spectre* of existential thought), & the poet no less given to it than others. More in fact, since the poet inherits the dreams of Citizen Kane & other alger/ian potentates the world at large hides away. There is Tom Swift in Olson, but Babbit in — poet-society (in the shit sense) always modeled on an earlier people-society, the Rotarianism of angryarts, the PAL of the white rabbits.

So if I sidle up behind you & whisper in your ear: "Your god is a black god. The road you walk is the loneliest. Your society is always behind you & before you. Your house is the poem, & your friends are chosen by the angels to betray you. Keep the truest measure that you know. Start in your body." it will not be because you are a woman & a poet, but simply because of the poet. And there are lady poets, & you must not be one of them. And there are poets whose concern is their own advancement, & you must not be one of them. The clarity of the world holds some measures effective: how much do they write? how much do they publish? how much of what you see of them in talk or sex or playfulness or money turns up in their poems? do they choose a persona thru wch to write? (note how Mr. Berryman has not yet caught up with the possibility of admitting the madness in his own voice; his dream songs must be im/persona/ted beware of male & female impersonators, they're fine at a distance but death in bed, where (say) it counts). I keep finding myself with respect for Enslin for all his elephantine rhythms: I can always find him in his poems. But how angry Levertov was some years back when Dorn started sounding like himself! The death of poetry is decorum: wch finally means sounding like somebody (or everybody) else & that seems over-simple, but it is not, it is exactly simple. Tho it may take a million years to sound like yourself, you do in fact know when you sound like somebody else. And there is enough of me in thee & him in me & her in him &c. to make for merry confusions at any given moment. But finally the voice proclaims itself, or it does not. And there is no way towards that clarity but in the work.

If you let your doubts abt the Figure of the Poet or the personas available balk your writing, the Great Prince imprison'd lies.

But to be wrapped/rapt in each other, rape always possible, the confusion of voices it is our business to clarify. That's what time is for, presumably, else a man wd die at the moment of saying. Because our voice at its purest is also *response*. More theory of society. More talk.

Day after Christmas, light snow on the ground &
the way the light is in the house, snow is not part of ocean but is of Okeanos,
the primal water from whose surface this sealight fills the house. A house,
our house, we'll be moving from any day now, so that the landscapers can
tear it down. We'll still be in a Bard house, so the address is unchanged;
seemingly we'll be in a separate house down near Adolf's, in the trian-
gle that is Annandale, & I want a Blakean sheep to crop that common.
That I may be the Lion within. Seriousness.

Fluty Robt Bly read here two
weeks ago, not at my connivance; his reading was four or five of his own,
a handful of haiku & badly done Lorcas, amidst a long pleasing rant of
opinion & attitude & orthodoxy. I say 'pleasing' because his words
sound fine until his poems begin, or his abominable distortions of Lor-
ca, whom I can read in español. I dont know how Issa & Bashō fared.
But his work is mere contrivance, crossword puzzle moods, no sense of
word or sound or rhythm. I've known him for years, but never heard
a full reading before. He was bursting with opinions to communicate to
these students, but finally did not have the meat to ram it home in any
real way.

Lord Argyll's respect for the Law, that it, the sovereign
process, the work, was not to be foredone for the sake of conve-
nience, or even severe inconvenience. That attitude balances and
gives weight to the other aphorism, that the way to the stone is
in the stone. Seriousness.

Keep the work going. "Writing wants to go on."
I think of Stein. I think of H.D.: It is idle to say that the women who
were or are poets truly are few; poets are few, & there might be a time
when women are more frequent in those woods than men, since woman's
centripetality is the closest metaphor of the work. But poetry is exactly
alchemy, & never will the crucible open to the golden sparrow & the
house be filled with savor if the work is cherished for any goal other than
the work itself as the single process. The way to the stone is in the stone.
This work is closed to those who seek advancement. Who want gold.
When 'want' is 'to lack' & we have our gold, we have all our gold, & what
we need do is work therein & therewith.

This letter comes from practically
no one. There's been so much Bard work & anxieties I am too weary of

to recount. I look to the coming of the tape. Our love to you & Richard, for the rebirth of light & the year that starts at any moment & every, that great small year.

[The editors (of *Io*) have omitted several names from these letters at their own discretion.]

(*Io* #5, 1968)

LETTER TO THOMAS BERNHARD

I don't know why I'm bothering to write to you. You're dead, for one thing. All we really share is a love for Glenn Gould and long sentences, probably that's the same love in different forms. Forms of art. I think it's mostly because I want to borrow your complaining tone. Really, your skill at complaining & making the reader keep reading, even liking, the diet of groans, the antiphonal maledictions of your characters. Such skill, skill indeed. But *immer schimpfend*, said a woman in Vienna years ago when I said I liked your work. she didn't like it, you were always bitching. Maybe some other word, meaning to complain and to blame, at once. I have a lot to complain about, & who else can be trusted to listen but a dead man, a man what's more who in some sense chose to be a dead man at this very time when I need a living man, a man four years older than I am, in fact, no older than my first wife, a woman who died the same year that you died, if my facts are straight, they seldom are. Dead man, will you be my friend? Or at least listen, that's the least you can do. Maybe even the most, but I can't say. What do I know about the dead? It's the living, of course, I suppose, that are the problem. The living, and the way we set about to be living. For one thing, the most terrible thing of all probably, I hate grown-ups. I have hated grown-ups all my life, I hate grown-ups & now I have become one. Isn't that horrible? The way Saul woke up and found he was himself a hated Christian. Only no toppling swoons and flashing lights for me, just the slow inexorable Work of the Mirror that paints time's grisaille on my cheekbones, time's sly etching technique using no mordant fiercer than the nervous hours. What can I do? I hate grown-ups, the way I hate nature. Nature will kill you every time. As you know perfectly well, I'm just reminding us both, from nature there's no way out but out. I hate grown-ups & I look just like a grown-up, who would know the truth looking at me? The way you changed in your television interviews, from the smooth cheeked shy author of the late 1960s to the blotched skin & annoyed celebrity, almost arrogant, of the late interviews, but who can blame you, such dumb questions, your books said it all, what did they want you to say that language had not already told them? You looked like a man in bad health in those last interviews, and so you were, and sure enough you came to die. Stories are told about that but I'm not interested in stories. Not now. Before, you were alive; after, you were dead. And what accesses of choice or refusing to choose, of will or negation of will, may have come between those two states, that's not on my mind now. You did what you had to do. Bless you, my heart goes out to you, glad to have heard you, a little, glad to have read you. You did me good. What I can do for you is another matter. Nothing, I suppose. Though we both come from people who believed, or said they believed, in praying for the departed souls, the souls in Purgatory, praying for them, their happiness in whatever follows life, does anything, doesn't matter, praying for them is at least praying for other people, that can't be wrong, can it? Can't hurt might help we say. Yet selfishly we pray for *our dead*, our own departed. And what about all the billions unknown to us, nameless to us, not *our* dead at all, not ours at all except by species, if even that. But at least we pray. So this letter is a little bit praying for you, you who are off in some condition that likely is wholly imaginary, in the course of a survival that is to say the least problematic, and which, if it has any currency at all, that is to say, if it exists, is likely to be of a sort splendidly (or glumly) impersonal. You survive the way the world survives. You survive in me. Any me, of course, not this particular grieving animal who addresses you now, you would have put that in italics so I will, this *grieving animal who speaks to you now*. Am I trying to flatter you by writing like you, a little, not that I could really write like you, your gravitas, humor, skill, charm, rhythm, but I *can certainly seem to be trying to* — is that flattery, or mockery? No paragraphs, no quotations marks, no let up 'til the end, just like you know what. What we've been talking about all along. And whereas this business of death — almost a commercial concern, Death, Inc. — for the sake of which life seems to be conducted, Death as the exclusive beneficiary of all our sweat & so forth, fluid after fluid, has preoccupied writers of every kind from before the beginning of the alphabet to this day, it is not death that is the problem here, the one I entered into this (dreary as it must be for you) correspondence to examine and deplore. No, it is in fact birth. Birth is hard. It is degrading. I am complaining about birth. Not, as usual with so many of us, complaining, blaming, *schimpfen*, about being born. No, being here is fine. Or ineradicably as it is, no question. No question about being here makes sense. But having to get born to get here, that's just wrong. The fact that for thousands of years, as they say, since the ice, we have been being born from inside someone else's body. What a humiliation! What a degradation of the woman, of the child. This is intolerable. It is time to change it. The fact that we have accepted this state of affairs, this outrageous, post-Edenic way of making more of us is the worst of all our practices, & not doing anything to change it is the worst failure of human imagination & skill since we let Atlantis founder. That we worm our way out of the flesh, are born like maggots, soft and defenseless and foul-smelling and bedewed with our mother's agony, this is not how it should be. This is not art. This is not science. This is not culture. This must change. Don't ask me how. How isn't your business, not any more, and certainly not mine. I have certain pictures of my own in my head, about how that change might look if it did happen. Pictures of pale chambers lit by an eternal unnatural light, like the magic caverns of Damanhur or the crystalline abysses in the Mines of Falun. In these places there would be wandering about, and from these chambers, caves, grottoes of the future, there would come, quiet happy grown-ups full of kindness and wisdom, yes, there could be such beings in the time to come, grown-ups wandering, wandering purposefully through the luminous *definition*, watering and tending and pruning and whispering little fairy-godmother spells of pure DNA. Intentional. Carefully thought-out. Tender. Humming a new song for new cells. They would coax one another into being, new being By chemicals and word of mouth we would grow, lit by a curious light spilling out of the mind itself, amplified unnaturally by some bizarre disposition of crystals, think Novalis: *In crystal grottoes reveled a luxuriant folk.* They move, we move, in a light in which we would grow each other. I hear in my surmise some of Blake's raving against the rational. Nature is the most rational of all, all of 'her' escapades have rational purpose and foundation. Nature is the enemy, here. Nature is the enemy. Not Novalis's sense of it as our mind in luminous nexus with everything there is, growing and being grown at once. No. Nature as it is understood by the austere simpletons who use the word as their supreme accolade, natural life style, natural food, natural childbirth. I hate nature. Nature is what happens to us, you know that, and what happens to us is what we must despise. If we have anything pure at all, it is our will, maybe, our will to be better and. And. And what. Something beyond nature. I hate nature. *Nature is my Austria*. So it is time for a poetry of pure flesh, or, if that sounds too poetic, for a flesh healed by poetry, flensed of its penchant for begetting, its tendency to swell up inside victim-women its new identities, alien arrivers. These beings who purport to come from our testicles and ova, who demonstrably ripen in our wombs, who are they? Children are horrible, I've always hated them, hated to be around other children when I was a child, hated them even more than I hated adults, but I knew that adults were incurable, but there might still be some hope for Paul or Raymond or Joan or Miriam, my little friends. No doubt I was wrong, and they're all just grown-ups now, or dead, like you. Who knows where children get to? They are always running out of the house. Sometimes they don't come back. Sometimes when they don't come back they're not dead, like you, or grown up, as I seem to be, but are just gone. Gone as a condition, *gone* as a state of being all its own. They are not some abducted changelings like Rilke's 'early-snatched-away,' not at all, instead they vanished into being who they are. As perhaps I may one day too, and as you probably did. Neither child nor grown-up, not woman and certainly not man. Who are we, Thomas, who are we really? I appeal to you, because of the savor of your elevated, abstruse condition, a condition that is bounded by certainties of all kinds, tell me. I love my country with a corrosive scorn like the tender and detailed hatred you affected towards your Austria, all emotions are one, isn't that finally so, all emotions are just kleshas, just ways we feel, habitual energies prompted into doing. Who cares what we feel? A feeling is just something you feel. So what. Call it love, call it hate, I slept almost eight hours last night for the first time in months, and I had no dreams for the first time in weeks. I woke uneasy, knowing *they were up to something*, as it is said, never specifying, never even knowing, who 'they' are. The children, I thought, it might be them, the hated and hate-filled children might be starting at last their long-deferred crusade against the grown-ups and their messed up world. The children, they are detestable, they can't talk, they don't read, they don't love, they don't care about anything that I care about, my poetry and your noble prose are trash to them, and trash to the adults they are likely to become. But still I'm on their side, because they march out, maybe even this very day, with slingshots and tasers and ninja weapons, against our common enemy, yours and mine, you called it Austria, I call it Nature, grown-ups, the president, the pope, the people. Any collective that has no living beings in it, but only members. A member is a thing incomplete, a hand without an arm, an arm without a torso, a torso without a man. These children are still children, alas, not the dream people I foresee & whose coming into our world, full in flesh but dripping from no agony, gleaming only with the radiance of the technology from which they are spoken into the world, whose coming into the world I demand, demand, no weaker insistence. Come them into us! Maranatha, new child! Such raving your silence lets me give vent to, you who pretend to be dead, how well you hear for a dead man, you hear like your dead emperors in the Kapuzinergruft, I have stood there and heard the banal sanctity of their anthems, the tumultuous alchemical racket of their longaeval bones, ash, crumble, greasy leftovers of more than one kingdom stuffed in marble. *At her grave also have I stood*, you don't need to hear her name yet again. When I went down those stairs and stood alone among the dead, why was I alone, where were the tourists who should have elbowed me aside with their digital cameras, their cold little *remembering machines,* how had the chill November rain managed to keep them in their snug buses? I stood there and listened to the dead, as I listen to you now, and hear you hearing me, and that Möbius-like infolding of our hearing lets me talk, it seems, confident of your acoustic eternity. If the Hapsburg croakers could hear me, so can you. And you know what I'm asking for, I detest children, so of course I don't want any more of them in the world, but I do want people, people of a sort, of a quality, a limpidity, a torsion, fluid in limb and welcome in fold, people who are born with Bach inside them, children who are never young and adults who are never grown up, these betweeners I yearn for, pretty girls and boys remind us of what they might look like, these yet-to-come, and listening to, say, the Third Partita gives us a sense of what their minds and hearts would be busy with all day long, and quiet at night, & no time for flowers. Flowers are left for the rest of us, we *leftover infantile adults* that the world endures as well as it can, its artists, writers, swindlers, crocodile wranglers, mountain climbers, gardeners, composers of serious modern music. For I would be flesh, and would discourse with my own, & my own have not come into the world. Or they have fled from it, suicided or snatched away by grisly ailments the doctors pretend to name and throw vile-tasting drugs at, or using their radiation and their surgery, grow obscenely rich by maiming those they cannot heal. Someone not born of woman comes to rescue me from my life. I will write again should that person come, or I will come walk with you in the all-too-formal gardens of the afterlife. They may be just like the Schönbrunn you detested, the emperor's palace, his lopsided Versailles with the land's first zoo full of uneasy animals serving life sentences, all of it a pale yellow, color of winter sunlight fading. The name means pretty fountain, doesn't it, or spring, water of the afterlife. When life finally begins.

(Cerise Press #1, summer 2009)

LETTER FROM JOSEPH CORNELL TO DOROTHEA TANNING

The sculptor Claire Woolner, in a letter to me from California, quoted from a letter that Dorothea Tanning had written to Joseph Cornell on March 3, 1948. In the letter, she spoke of feelings of revulsion towards most things, wondering how Cornell avoided such. I don't know how Cornell answered at the time, and I had never asked Dorothea Tanning about her feelings back then when, years later, she and I briefly corresponded. I felt something missing in the record here that I had to supply. So 64 years later I composed this response for him, content to be the amanuensis of so grand and thingly an artist. RK.

Dear Dorothea,

Revulsion, a terrible word, and I grieve that you find it for things around you, and you ask me (do you ask me?) how I live away from revulsion. I have had the grace to live at some distance from my feelings, though always acutely aware of them — how could I not be, living in this world?

But I long ago reasoned that a feeling is just something I feel. At an earlier time I felt some other way. Later I will feel some other way. Why should I privilege this feeling I feel now? I examine it, sometimes I use it to choose or change things around me. Real things. Objects and shapes. Things are my salvation in a way, and I suspect they help you too, the marvelous objects that crowd the people world in your paintings. But feelings are not much help. Things are. I have been called a fetishist, I know, by some of our Freudian friends (can a Freudian be a real friend? Just a thought.). I admit it, I am a fetishist, and my fetish is matter.

People say that I live with my mother. True enough, because a mother is a quiet world, a mother is someone always to be traveling from; from her my body and all its going, so I go, but I keep looking back over my shoulder to see her there, in the quiet Sunday afternoon light of Queens. People say that I live with my mother, but the truth of the matter is I live with matter.

The body is a sheen of glory with nothing inside it. The skin is our panoply and declaration. We artists are so fortunate, because we are the servants and masters of the visual world, the world of shape and color, form and geometry, tension and release, we are the lords and ladies of blank space! And all that happens to fill it! We know that what we see when we look with our artist loving judging smart tender broken eyes, when we look at someone standing there, we see the utter and absolute truth of him. We say: I see you. And that is exactly right. When I look at him, I see him. I see all there is. Poets and psychiatrists and philosophers and other types who do not have the grace of seeing, they talk about personality and character and inner motivation and neurosis and meaning and drives and complexes and memory and desire, they rave on and on about those things and think that such things somehow live inside the person they have before them — the person they don't know how to see. All that stuff, all that cognitive crap (forgive the coarse word, my dear, mama isn't looking), is lies. Personality is a lie. Psychology is a lie. People say I make my little boxes (focused environments?) to represent the tumult of repressed images and confusions in me. Not at all. My boxes express nothing but themselves. Don't people understand that artists aren't spewing out their guts, they're adding things to the world. We are increasing the intensity and beauty of matter. And one day matter itself will be perfect and complete, and this will be heaven. Our heaven, because we made it so, and knew it true.

When you look at a man or a woman, there is just this glorious shimmer in front of you, a shimmer that you also are, shimmer looks at shimmer, shimmer shimmers shimmer onto the canvas or into marble (sculpture is an ancient joke, I love it, turning light into stone). That is our work. We can see everything. Sometimes we can even touch what we see, and that is wonderful, because beauty is skin deep. Reality is skin deep. Did you know (who told me this?) that the word skin is the same as the words shine, and sheen, and they just came into the language at different times? What we see is the skin of things, and all there is is skin. Go through the skin and you come into a howling nightmare where surgeons and demons torture flesh they imagine into being. But there is nothing there but what we see. God bless you for seeing so much of what is there and so little of what isn't. Please always be with me in seeing the world and speaking or shaping or singing or limning it into new embodiments. This is what I know, and this is what keeps me happy, happy as I hope you will always be.

Your loving brother,

Joseph

P.S. Give my best wishes to Max — I'm not sure if you should show him this letter — he's a German, and they believe things have insides. It might shock or disturb him. And there is no virtue in disturbing an artist. Let him follow his nightingale, even if it leads into the imaginary forest inside!

Annandale-on-Hudson, 18 March 2012
(Brooklyn Rail, December 2012)

NOTE ON KABBALAH & CRITICISM

Bloom is right to insist that K/ emphasizes interpretation, wrong to suggest that it alone of mysticisms does so. In traditions (unknown to B, evidently) as diverse as Shia and Shaivite and Sufi and Spanish Christian, the fundamental gesture of the mystical 'act" is hermeneutic (*ta'wil* is one case), & very much the hermeneutic of an (actual) text. Where K/ does differ is in contenting itself with one fixed corpus of text to which *all* hermeneutic impulse must apply itself. Thus the mythopoetic faculty that produces (or induces) an Ibn Arabi, a Suhrawardi, a Juan de la Cruz must presumably redigest itself [alchemy is HB's next target?] as a meta/mythopoiesis. Clearly, this very cessation of 'revelation' makes Kabbalah apt for B's intuitions.

A note of late Nov/76 reading Kabbalah & criticism
[RK archives]

THE TRUE STORY

For untold centuries men have been going the ways of good & evil. The saints of good the saints of evil have contended, & that contention has been brought to focus more particularly by Christianity. And though the stories of God & Devil, Christianity & Anti-Christianity, are tireless, men have not broadly understood the terms of conflict.

I propose here to set down the barest lineaments yet more tenuously adumbrated by the most bizarre assortment of witnesses through the ages. St. Paul, the author of the Book of Secrets of Enoch, Mme Blavatsky, certain dances in Tibetan courtyards, the Jataka tales, Hopi mythology, tales & traces & iconic representations in all people in all times, the shapes of our inner torment.

The true story can be told simply. To grasp it, bear in mind the many traditional ways of representing devils. Bear in mind the curious, bewildering designation of Jesus as the Son of Man.

Angels

Each of the planets its ruler. Each man his Holy Guardian Angel. The Gnostics & Satanists erred by worshiping (either with the worship-of-fear in the former instance, or with the worship-of-cult in the latter) the servants of the Lord rather than the Lord. They (Gnostics, Satanists) are prototypes of those paranoid victims of bureaucracy who blame all the local office chief &c. The Soviet Union at the present mythologizes the *access* of the *individual through* the *bureaucratic* machine to be responsible Marfa — in *The General Line* — getting the tractor from Moscow despite the local bureaucrat is the Soviet archetype of rising on the planes, or that *prayer to the Father* that Jesus especially taught, whereby we reach directly to the levels of judgment above, the "throne of the Distributor" as Taliessin says. Worshippers of angels do not take advantage of known techniques of rising to the Throne — people in general are superstitious — i.e., mistake the proximate angel for the True Distributor, mistake the postman for the President.

To worship an angel makes a devil of him. How often have those who aspired to legitimate Discourse with angels fallen into worship of those powers, because we do worship power — i.e., as Eliade makes clear, worship is the active positive registration of *awe*, which is itself a response to power, bigness, oddness.

Jesus broke through the hierarchies & gave us direct access to the Father. No doubt there are angels ("Lucifer" we are told was the first of such) who, like Cardinal Ottaviani & the Roman Curia, cherished the hierarchy & their places in it, & who are predisposed to honor & respond to those who offer them worship (even though they, the angels, know it's wrong; they receive the worship & transmit it to the Father — in triplicate, no doubt — ((but how cold their formalized styles become)) — the angels rightly transmit the worship but delight in the fact that the worshipper stands at their doors, before their desks, mistakes them to be what he seeks. Weak men or angels, not necessarily evil at all, are prey to flattery.

But the angels of whom I have just written are presumably those whose proper functions are not connected with men directly at all. They are the 'spirits' of metal & the 'spirits' of corn, the regulators of times & equilibriums, the genii of places & nations, the minor planetary beings, the spirits of time.

I do not think that the Guardian Angel is vulnerable to flattery. Unlike the engineering-angels and the logistic-angels &c., his proper function has to do with moral psychology. The Guardian Angel will not give his sign or glyph or signature or rotund name to rotaries (as other spirits will, angels of order who delight in florid signatures like Latin American businessmen). The Guardian Angel has no name by which we know him; because that name (though we stretch the meaning of the word back to the nomen-numen antiquity) is not different from our own secret names, our own source-powers.

The demonist or theurgist is not unlike the votary of the Cargo Cult — his worship is to the apparent-form-of-the-vehicle in which power comes.

Our proper response to angels is *audient*. Do our work & listen to what they prompt or utter in us.

       In his heart or in the intensest core of his loving a man can talk with angels. But to learn "Enochian" languages or the script of the Malachim is to reduce ourselves to amoebae in the Petri dish seeking to infer the possibilities of human utterance from the pattern of the weave on the lab worker's smock,

      i.e., our relationship to angels is *not* that of studied to student, or microorganism to biologist. It is that of free organism to free organism, potential immortal to potential immortal — i.e., our discourse is that of freemen. That entails response to the individual angelic utterance as such. The bureaucratic angels I've guessed would perhaps be willing, to be obliging, to offer the conventions and rubber stamps of their departments to over-eager men as the sum of angelic discourse. It is not necessary to beware of over-obliging angels — they do not arise except in reaction to our appetites for systematic Delusions = some men learn languages (notably the 'Classical' ones, but also Erse, Welsh, Basque, Arabic, Chinese, the way the Brontës in their parsonage 'learned' (invented) their granstarkian lands & histories.

                       The Function of angels is not to talk to men as such, gossip with them, pass the time of day, do their work for them, &c. A man who sets out to chat with angels winds up in essentially misleading talk with the least-busy (or, hence, least responsible) agent in the sector. God helps all, but angels seem to help those who help themselves. It is in the throes of his work, when he needs it most, that a man is most likely to receive angelic intelligences = i.e., when they matter most.

  The angelic names Mimle & Pseudepigrapha give us are all, in their form, *functions of God* in the cosmos. Hellenistic, Cabalistic & Early Christian demonology gives us names of devils = they too are of the same form.

      What did it mean for the Sons of Heaven to lust after the daughters of men? The Blavatskyan versions seem unsatisfying.

     This question is not important, but the answer to it is. This last sentence is distinctly important in its inclusions & exclusions. Enough.

                     27 November '65

FAUST ET MOI

I was always young. It needed no transformation music, pretty as it is, for me to seem so again. My beard and fusty robes sprang away from me the way leaves rush from a lawn, cleaned away by an invisible wind.

"To seem so again." To seem to myself young, and seem so to you. To her.

I was the devil I sold myself to.

And Germany is calling again.

Faustus = *favustus* = fortunate, favored, favored by fate.

Faust = fist.

Which do I mean, my force or my fate? Am I agent or am I angel'd?

Spoused fun. Faust pun. He needs a wife I need a wife. What's true for him truer for me. Comparative of bliss.

He goes from woman to woman, not out of licentiousness but to seek the perfect wife. No matter how many he has. Marriage is no obstacle to married bliss. Find her, whoever she is. Whoever I seem to be.

Marguerite = *margarita,* 'pearl.' A string of pearls.

One after another.

Because he is a perfect husband he must marry everyone he meets. Or at least everyone who seems as if she might be the perfect wife.

His desire is the fire in which they're both to be refined. Defined. They are transformed by what he wants. A hoax, like the hoax of poetry.

This is not adultery but its opposite.

This is not infidelity. It is a pilgrimage of faith itself.

Faith in the perfectibility of person, in the perfectibility of relationship.

Adultery, adultery is settling for imperfection. Settling. When we say of a substance that it is not purely itself, we admit it has been adulterated. Something is adulterated when it is not utterly true to itself.

So wrote Faust. (Take this out later so the reader can't tell me from him. From her).

I am a bottle, dark green glass, barely translucent but translucent.

In me is a message, carefully and neatly written, on sturdy paper with a decent ink, screwed tight and stuffed inside.

My name, personality, history & so on — all those are just the cork snugged into the mouth of this bottle.

The message is intact inside. I am in the sea.

I wait for you, wave. I wait for you, shore. I wait for you, hand.

Certainty was never my business. A puff of smoke, greenish, from my chalice. A few dead leaves, scarlet symmetries. Enough to go on. Guess.

She knew she was in trouble when she felt his eyes all over her, her body, not just the face, not just the glances that smooched along her cheeks to linger on her lips. Lips open, moving. To speak. His eyes were on her body. Body: midriff, loins, nape of neck, socket of knee, small of back, hollow of throat, curve of belly, *chute de reins*. She knew she was in trouble when she could feel him reading her skin, her shallow breath, her cautious smile.

He stole her feelings. Shanghaied them into his huge complicated design where he worked them in, her feelings, so important to him, as if he had none of his own.

His phantom city he built around her. Live in me, he seemed to be saying. But he had no in.

She knew she was in trouble but knew he was in worse trouble. A perfectionist has no peace, ever.

He was a pilgrim through a world not yet finished. Never finished. He was to go on forever. He called that living, sometimes he called that loving.

She was afraid of him, so she took him in her arms. Maybe so close to her he could not hurt her.

She could see him: he studied her the way a blind man faces the rising sun.

How (she thought), how does what he sees have anything to do with me?

Open me, open me and read! He would say things like that, and no god, no devil, could say what he meant by such jargon.

The language of enthusiasm is always inexact. If one truly knew the thing one wanted, one would not go on wanting it, since want is consciousness of deprivation, and knowing is consciousness of possession.

Enthusiasm speaks from deprivation; it approximates, it yearns.

The shadow adds dimension to the man. She studies it in turn, trying to know the thing he makes happen, the thing of which he cannot be fully aware.

No man knows his whole shadow, she said, and he thought her clever for saying it. It made him more determined to possess her. Or not so much possess her, as possess that power which simultaneously summons, appropriates and dismisses all such images into and from the niche in the world, in the mind, that she occupied at present. Her amber yellow hair.

The lover of chastity. I yearn for chastity the way a poor man hungers for money — anxiously, energetically, dreamily, in vain. The turbulence I bring to the quest for the object of that desire annihilates the quality sought.

Parable of Midas, whose fingers found the same quality in everything, and made it what he sought. His so-called gold.

My touch imbues even the chastest beloved with my own immunditia.

I make unclean.

Parable of the leper. What I am, I make you too.

Immundus. Unclean. As if: un-world, un-worlded. The world is clean. The only chastity (he is told) is everything that is, left just the way it is. The unclean lover takes his love out of the world.

Come home with me.

How I want to wake and see you beside me on the bed, your head pillowed in the bedding I have left for you. I have saved you from the world. I study morning light on your cheek, the stain of shadow along your throat. I hear you breathe. Not meaning to, you have saved me from the world.

There is a strange ancient novel called *The Recognitions*. It begins with a sentence that haunts me all my life: "I, Clement, a native of the City, have been all my life a lover of chastity."

Clement, whom we call Alexandria, says of himself, I am a native of the city of Rome.

This book translates me

In vain again. For Clement in the book achieves that which he sought, finds it because he already has it.

Is Socrates wrong, then? So that Love, far from being penurious & full of hungry wanting, is actually all Surfeit and *satis* and serene with is own fulfillments?

He found what he was, and he found it in everyone.

If you must be chaste to find chastity, must I be or become the woman I desire?

Is Faust Marguerite?

So he looks (and what a sad story this is going to be), he looks for that quality he desires, looks for it in a person who is enough like him to support the inference: 'this person is a lover of chastity,' but also enough like him to warrant a foundational impurity, a looseness, a door somewhere in the back of the house slamming open in the hot prairie wind. Through that portal, unclean lust slouches in and out.

Faust writes on a piece of stiff cardboard: Never doubt your desires or your entitlement to them. Doubt is loud, and others will hear it, and come to doubt you too.

Faust looks at what he's written and doubts it too. It seems childish, cynical, adolescent, merely true.

—

Faust in his dealings with men and women much prefers civility to truth. Truth changes with situations, while civility is permanent.

Faust in his dealings with angels and demons is much more likely to give and expect truth, imagining (wrongly) that angelic beings perceive situations better than humans, however wise. This is superstition, of course, and will get him into endless trouble.

Angels and devils are in the situation too. Or they are the situation. How can someone in a situation see the whole situation, which itself is part of an endlessly proliferating nest, network, of situations. Each situation bracketing all the others, and bracketed in turn.

Faust knows this too, of course, because he's smart. But because he is still a little boy, he believes that truth is the civility owed to angels. And true enough, it is. It is superstition, however, to expect it from them in return.

Because pure Presence alone is the only civility you can expect from angels, the only gift they have to proffer or withhold.

Faust feels the warm pearls slip through his fingers.

Pearl after pearl. Such a long string of beads. Has he ever counted them? How many pearls is forever?

Can he tell the pearls that are his past from the ones that are to come.

Pearls of identity.

What if this one warm lustrous pearl in his fingers now, round, sensuous, faintly exciting, between slope of thumb and fingertip, what if this one were the last pearl of all?

Would he know he had come to the end of the rosary and started again? Would it be again if he didn't know it?

How warm a pearl is. It never loses a certain animal warmth or spirit. You can tell it was alive once, before it was slain by admiration, desire, possession.

It may still be alive. Or capable of summoning (or is it only stimulating?) life from the body with which it rests in contact.

Is the warmth from the pearl or from the skin?

From her or from him?

Maybe it is a product of contact itself.

Faust remembers a Russian mystic who taught that the sun gives no light and no heat. Space beyond earth's kindly atmosphere is dark and cold. What we call heat & light are earth's response to the distant diamond fervor of the sun. Light and heat are response. They are the friction of earth's love song, earth's welcoming the sun's invisible ardent ray, the spill of glory from the touch of love.

Or maybe earth is just us.

Maybe heat and light are our answer, billions of humans metabolizing their lives marrying the sky.

This heat comes from me, Faust thinks.

When he thinks this, all at once it becomes bearable for him to remember that after all is said and done, the pearl borrows its warmth from the skin.

As once it borrowed its substance from the tender self-regard of the oyster, the anxiety that spoke and spoke around a core of doubt.

Its luster is its own.

Where does the skin go to get its heat?

From the pearl, surely.

We feed one another.

I am Faust and you are Marguerite and the other way round.

Complete. All the properties of all the pearls are found in any pearl.

Everything, that is, except the allness of them. The many.

If one were enough, one would be enough.

If one were enough, there would only be one sunrise in the world.

Then one sundown and no more kisses.

This must be why, on Easter morning, when the bells are dangling and the fools of the town, those ordinary people, are putting on their fuzzy pink cloth spring coats and their lime-green sports jackets and their two-tone shoes, Dr. Faust himself is slumped in his armchair, his hands, weary of pearls for a moment, toying with a small blue bottle.

This is the poison.

He doesn't propose to drink it in order to become young again. He is always young again, he can't grow old, he can't grow out of his adolescence, desires, requires, skin and silk and flying through the air, all the Witches' Sabbaths that a young man dreams & an old man, he is an old man, can no more stop dreaming than he can stop breathing.

Breathing too is a young man's folly.

Hence the bottle. Breath and folly, youth and desire, all can be escaped at once.

But what image will be the last one to loom in his mind's eye, clear or murky, as his consciousness, such as it is, dims down for the endless night, dims out, yields, stops. *What image last will lurk inside his mind?* He remembers asking that question when he was young, fifty years ago he asked it and still he doesn't know.

What is the final image?

And suppose it is her, the last one, the one who still is waiting for the answering letter, the phone call, the promised necklace, the book of Sufi proverbs, the weekend in the mountains, all the feints of love? Can he leave her so unsatisfied?

Why should she be more satisfied than I, Faust wants to know. That is crabby and selfish of him, even to think it. He knows that, he unthinks it, the thought turns into Well, at least I can satisfy her, a little, maybe, now if not later, now if not forever.

But he'll have to stay around to do that. He puts down the blue bottle and picks up the green telephone.

Not so strange that the West, in love as we are with masks & those who wear them, has never noticed that its chief heroes are different stages, different ages, of the same man.

Don Juan — who has somehow been the one speaking often here — is an immature version of Dr. Faust.

Run out of steam, he can now be described as learned, doctus, doctor. That is, he can be defined by what happened to him, his hap. The weary wisdom that accumulated in his heart. It stifled passion without in the least extinguishing desire.

And both of them, I suspect (but who is speaking?) are the middle-aged and old respectively stages of the young hungry happy hero we call the Grail Knight, pierce-the-veil. Parsifal is the larval stage of Faust.

But maybe the man, the hero, does not age at all. His society changes around him. Some angel out of Adorno could tell us, but doesn't it seem that when the chivalric age ends, Parsifal's quest for the Holy Grail makes him a different person, since there is no Christ, no blood, no cup to fill with it, no company of love in the mercantile proto-bourgeois world — Phillip II's Spanish Empire, Vermeer's Delft. The Grail Knight must become the Girl Knight and seek out women, who alone remain prized, mysterious, imaginably holy, and who unlike the Grail remain multiple, sacred in each instance, each instance compelling to the next, the whole holiness graspable only when all the instances have been embraced. Women are many. Manifold as the opportunities for grace in a godly world, manifold as the opportunities for profit in a merchant world.

And then he is a very old youth indeed, and the spirit of his quest is alive enough in him to make him uncomfortable with his wise, displeased serenity. Serenity means night music. And he doesn't want to go to bed yet. Not yet.

Nobody home. The green phone rings and rings. Nobody answers. He puts it back on its cradle, reclaims the poison.

In his discomfort with his stillness, he writes essays on Nomadic Poetics, on the Art of Exiles. He rediscovers in the curlicues of his fleshy brain the lost Germanic epic the poet Ovid wrote during his exile among the Goths. He argues that literature reveals its truth best in translation, when it is estranged from what it supposes to be itself and becomes the other, or at least the other's. Undistracted by the sound of its own voice, the smell of its own breath, it is candid in translation.

Faust puts maps up on his walls — stained, wrinkled, discolored sheets that represent, usually ineptly, the glorious landscapes of the earth that once were women, stayed women long enough for the eye of the artist to observe them, and recognize their lineaments afterwards in the habit of sea and the haberdashery of rock & cloud.

A map on the wall is always a woman in disguise. He writes this & thinks about crossing it out.

Then he fears that doing so will make it all the truer, since the hidden is worth more than the evident, isn't it?

Elle, qui fut la belle heaulmière.

Hidden in time.

Heart hidden in mocking ribs.

Faust thinks of a woman standing at a window, taking in a view of the city, perhaps giving the city a view of herself.

Which comes first, to see or to be seen? How are they different?

Sometimes he sees her as if he were looking up at her from the sidewalk several stories below. Sometimes, though, he is in the room with her, watching from behind, observing what little of the sky and house roofs and steeples is not obscured by the graceful curve of her opaque and curious body.

She stands there against the light.

She who used to stand for the light. The only light he needed. Once.

Sometimes he sees her as from a window directly across the street from hers. At those times, their eyes seldom meet. But sometimes they do, and they dare to stare.

There, each thinks, that is the one they call the other.

And when they stare, then it is that Faust, not she, is the first to look away, shy not of the woman (I think) but shy of the sudden suspicion that he is looking into a mirror, and that she is he.

Or that the only woman left to him is the one projected from his eyes.

A woman is a mirror he writes, and crosses it out.

Maybe she is the only woman he ever knew, even though years ago he successfully courted one thousand and three of them in Spain. Were they just the several, separate breaths of his sighing, his desiring?

Maps, walls, women — all symbols of one another. But of what else?

That too he thinks about crossing out, & does, then realizes — as if a moment too late, that Else is a woman's name too.

He wonders: the poison in the little blue phial, warm from my touch now, a blue pearl, a blue rose of forgetfulness, haven't I drunk it already, many times, haven't I died many times?

And then he forgets.

He forgets, just as he has forgotten many times before.
Only in forgetting can he go on.
Startles, wakes, starts again. The blue poison is surely my ink. Why didn't I know it long ago? The clear poison took color from the bottle in which it lived so long.
Now writes the world dead word by word.
Death lives in glass.
Faust is almost sleeping now. Blue ink.
I have used this ink to poison the world, infect you. Love letter by love letter, poem by poem, treatise by treatise, I have infected you with my own virus, with me, with me, with
    the view from my window I made you once, once think was your own
    & in that rapt moment when you knew me as yourself, we lay down together as it always was, became as close to one as two can get
    and this love lasted till the light faded from both our windows
    and all our doors were banging in the wind
    and one of us got up to shut them and the other was alone
    and never came back and still am alone.

Faust is sleeping. The blue bottle rolls out of his fingers and drops, unbroken, into the skirts of his warm robe that bunch at the foot of his chair.

I have achieved the transmutation. The work of thirty-seven years has finally, quietly, been completed. The stone. Bred in mind then banished to the world of objects, returns and recognizes itself a subject again. Returns to my body. To be my bones. Every bone renewed. Every integument by which one bone knows another.

He takes out a postcard of the Tour Saint-Jacques and turns it over. He writes in Latin on the message half of the card. In translation, he has said: This erection in Paris not far from the Town Hall, the Woman's Cathedral, the River, this upthrust emblem tells much of my story. Stonework, the little lizards who run down from the sun, the girls who make waterspouts of their hands so that the rain says something to the street below. He has room only to sing: *your Faust*. But he does not write anything in the name and address side of the card. He does not know to whom to send it. He turns the card over again and admires, above & on either side of the mysterious tower the uninflected vivid blue of the sky.

I have achieved the stone. It has come home and claimed me.

I belong to all the things I ever said.

He crosses that out and tries again: I belong to all the things I never made.

Awake now, he gets up with a stiffness in which he imagines he can distinguish the muscular torpor of recent sleep from the clumsy stiffness of age. He goes across the room, away from the window, and pours himself a glass of liqueur, green pastis, & pours some water onto it, so that the clear emerald green turns yellow and grows turbid. He drinks some of this, and goes back to his chair, balances the glass on the chair arm.

They know my name but they do not call me. I know their names but do not touch them. We are even in our sad desuetude. Equals.

As he sips his pastis, he remembers a few phrases, imageless, that chased through his head while he slept. Whenever he woke they were there, then he'd drowse again and wake up to check if the words were there. There they were. But what did they mean?

Sexe couleur de moutarde, is it all right?

Faust teaches how to relax into ardor. His pupils come up the stairs one by one most days, he embraces them one by one as they come in. Hour after hour, life after life. When they leave they take the wax of his candle, leaving him to keep his flame alive as well as he can. They take the glass of his glasses, the sand of his hourglass, the Christ off his crucifix, the words out of his books, so at midnight he has to pray to an empty wall.

All they leave him is geometry. All they leave him is empty pages. Who will fill them?

No wonder on Easter morning when all the businessmen sit in the cathedral remembering the lap dancers of the night before, and all their wives sit in the cathedral trying to remember nothing, no wonder that Faust is outside, upstairs, griping, danceless, unforgetting, sourmouthed from his breadcrusts sopped in morning wine mixed carefully following the ancient Roman custom, one part strong wine to eight parts water. But Germans can't grow red wines, he thinks, not strong ones. But we have method.

He sips the pastis to take the taste of the breakfast away, and then the taste of the dream.

Sex color of mustard — what did it mean by saying that in sleep, his sleep? Was sex the anatomical feature (sex of a gladiolus) or the sociophysical behavior (they had sex) or the gender (the female sex) or the issue (Freud's views on sex), the endlessly absorbing human discourse or its momentary crises of physiological enactment?

And any, all, of these acceptations — how did it, they, comport with mustard? Mustard-colored excrementitious evidences of podicopenetrative raptures (how enterprising lovers are?) The unfolding flower of her sex (whose?) opening not the mauve petal works we expect but to something yellow-brown, faded like certain roses? How sad. How old.

Is it all right? — that seemed to be asking, is it all right that this (what?) happened, we did it (or did not do it) this way, is it all right that we did, is it all right that sex is that color, is it all right between us. Are we ok?

But who was speaking? She lies on her back, already asleep in his mind. He lies on his back and asks himself, was it with me that she was herself? And how did I like that?

We did know it all along. Dr. Johannes Faust we read in the old book, John Fist or Lucky John, John = Juan, Don Juan so lucky in love.

(2001)

"AUTOBIOGRAPHICAL ESSAY" [TIMELINE]

1935: September 24, born in Brooklyn, New York — on Brown Street, in Marine Park, near Gerritson Beach, the coal docks, and conduits.

1943: Birth of my sister, Patricia. (I knew her only as a baby, since after fifteen or so I hardly ever was home. I have gotten to know her in recent years, with her husband James Kimbis & my two nephews Thomas and Peter.)

1943: Simple myopia began. Misdiagnosed, untreated. For the rest of the 1940s, I would be progressively less and less able to see. Only the threat of having me put in classes for the blind finally reconciled my parents to the "crutch" of treatment: eyeglasses. (A great moment came in December — maybe 1949? — when the doctor settled the spectacles on my nose and wheeled me around, and I saw snow sifting down over Eighth Avenue, omni-colored in neon, & for the first time I saw each flake a word apart, distinct, chiseled clear.)

1944: "Loss" of our house — we had to move to a shabby part of town (one I later learned to roam and love). For months I would make my way, by buses and trains and walking, to the original neighborhood, not so much for the friends I had there, but for the house, the place — and the garden, which still, in its modesty, defines what flowers mean: the pansies in the windowbox on the garage, the pussy willow by the picket fence, the aisle of deep red roses, the huge blue blossoms of the hydrangea that always seemed wet with dew no matter how hot the day. How I hated heat!

1944–50: Living on Crescent Street in the Old Mill district, east of Brownsville and New Lots, south of Cypress Hills, west of Ozone Park. Walking distance from the great marshlands that bounded Long Island's south shore, which still throng with birdlife in the Hammels. In those marshes I walked a lot, losing and finding myself. Black mud, wild birds, luminous byways of water, sea creeks, endless acres of timothy and marsh grass. There were miles of old wooden catwalks and foot bridges over winding channels of the sea. These old grey weathered walkways went out towards the village of houses built on stilts, called Kinderhoek, where fishing people lived. No roads — only by boat did they come to the firm mainland. And this was the place for me, these marshes, gulls and sky. My place.

1949–51: Brooklyn Prep, a Jesuit school. I wanted to go there because it taught Greek. From the earliest sight of the place, long before school age, I knew they taught Greek and knew I needed it. How did I know? I did learn Greek & Latin there, and began German. Worked on the newspaper. Smoked, and stored illicit books in my locker.

1950–52: *Wanderjahre*, fell through the cracks, absenteeism gradually turning into dropoutism, wandered the city, got no further than Philadelphia (Rodin Museum! Gates of Hell!), mostly Manhattan: the Village and the subways and hanging out around Columbia. Era of nosleepism, no eatism, weird mentalisms, seehowfarIcangoism. My close friends in these days were Arthur Pinkerton, who disapproved, & Hugh Smith, always ahead of me in creative profligacy.

1951: Forced to choose between legal trouble (for truancy) and going to school. I had to enroll in something, so I went to college. I entered CGNY at fifteen and went sedately enough through four years of mostly immemorable required classes and met wonderful people — David Antin, Robert Levine, James Moran, Jack Hirschman. Insolent and unruly as I was, I secretly let these folk somehow be my teachers, and am grateful yet.

1954: Met Joan Lasker and began my first close relationship, in poverty & difficulty and silliness & splendor, the way it is. In the summer, I spent several weeks in Paris, studying nothing but the city, the fall of light, the wield of her streets. Supposed to go to Austria and Germany to study language, but I never did. I never do.

1955: Graduated from college. Married Joan in August. We lived in Brooklyn (again!), in Crown Heights, on a street neatly divided between Hassids and West Indians. Began working for a living: as a translator (German and Spanish mostly, medical and pharmaceutical materials — I knew all about the tranquilizers as they were being developed, thanks to the clinical papers I was assigned) for an agency run by Ralph Gladstone (poet & brilliant translator of Jarry & the 'Pataphysicals,' editor of the remarkable *Wunderhorn Musette*, a single issue that glistened in Bohemia) and his brother William.

1955–58: Enrolled in the graduate program at Columbia, working first in seventeenth-century studies with Marjorie Nicholson & Pierre Garay, then in mediaeval studies, just at the end of Roger Loomis's career — his spell lingered, & I worked on the exfoliations of the Grail legend, concerning myself with Malory in particular, answering an intuition that Malory had somehow — in his sullen art, his strange isolation, his feral apartness — enlarged nonetheless the notion of the Grail company, the sacred committee of holy knowing. I did all the course and exam work, but never wrote even a master's essay, let alone a dissertation. But I thought about it quite a while. Then rejected it.

1957: The closest friend I met in Columbia was George Economou, and with him I got started on a project of a new magazine. We invited two friends to work with us — Ursule Molinaro and Venable Herndon. We had been introduced by Joe Kling in his wonderful bookshop on Greenwich Avenue — he who linked back to Hart Crane and the Paris-American vanguard of the 1920s. Venable and Ursule were both much savvier than George and I, they were writers who had been around. I wonder sometimes how they put up with my callowness. Maybe it was my push. I have always had push. Soon we had together the first issue of the *Chelsea Review*, which we had printed in Gibraltar. Three issues more followed it before there was a change of editorial direction.

1958: On an October evening, blue sky and cool, I walked down Lexington Avenue going home from work, tired and absurd, three years in graduate school, three years translating rat tests and liver jaundice. It seemed that the sky opened quietly and an Understanding spoke in me, saying that if I dedicated myself to writing, if I gave myself to that truth I knew as somehow the sky and the voice that speaks inside and the good of the world, if I gave myself over to writing for the good of the world, it would be well, and it would be well with me. When I got home I explained all this to Joan, who encouraged me to quit my job and school and devote myself to writing. I did so, immediately. And from the end of 1958 to the summer of 1960, Joan supported us. She was working at a job she liked well, that paid poorly indeed, and we were almost humiliatingly poor in those days. She worked in the library at the Brooklyn Museum, with friends like Dorothy Billings and Lois Katz, who spent some lovely Saturdays trying to teach me Chinese.

1958–61: Amy Goldin, sister of my Columbia classmate Ruth Huston, moved to New York. Amy and I had the most intense exchange of letters I had ever known, and I reveled in the detail and emotional accuracy of her brilliant mind, her sensuous reach for art. Her coming to New York gave me someone to study with, study, be prodded by, yet also (being me) advise and console. A painter whose work never found its full reception, she later became more and more an essayist and critic in the 1960s. We were very close, and she was I think the first of my real live teachers. I still feel the excitement of her mind and her engagement with the means of all the arts; I mourn her loss, first through the natural estrangements of relationships, and then her terrible death.

Joan and I met Celia and Louis Zukofsky, and learned much from visits to them in their spotless place in Brooklyn Heights, a marvel of housekeeping, an apartment as precisely ordered as the dictionary. Their kindness to gauche and messy youngsters was impeccable. Louis Zukofsky's amazing acuity of mind's ear is of course what's most for me to be grateful for. But he also did all he could to link poets together and spread the news. He let George Economou and us print a little book of his as a Trobar Book — *I's (pronounced eyes)*.

1959: About this time I began a correspondence with Gerrit Lansing, which still continues. It brought me to Gloucester in 1962 to meet him and Charles Olson — the years 1962 to 1969 are full of Gloucester visits and adventures — it seemed to be a university of rock and sea, bitter and salty and smart, Olson and Lansing and the wind at Hammond Castle, Harry Martin. I learned to hold my own, but maybe held too hard.

1960: Through the kindness of George Economou, I got my first job teaching at Wagner College on Staten Island. Classes from eight in the morning till noon. I had to get up at five, take the subway, change to the East Side IRT, take the ferry, then two buses to get up to the college. I was often late but seldom absent. My annual salary was $2,400. At the end of the term, I resolved to never teach again. It had its advantages: the immense vista of New York from Grimes Hill — a sight of my Brooklyn, not much inflected from its essential nineteenth-century self; and palling around with the old poet and filmmaker Willard Maas, who taught English with people who saw him as an eccentric, whereas I celebrate him still as the maker of that extraordinary film *The Geography of the Body* that years before had overwhelmed me, ca. 1951, when I saw it at a showing of avant-garde films at Cinema 16 — a subscription to which had been my mother's surprising gift to me one Christmas.

1960: George Economou and I left the editorial board of the *Chelsea Review*. We wanted to deal with poems, not prose; American, not fashionable translations. We began *Trobar*, dedicated to what we called (by a perhaps fortunate synchrony) the new American poetry. The first issue had a strong cover by Amy Goldin & was printed on menu paper by Balys Jacikevičius in Brooklyn; he charged sixty dollars & felt cheated. But I can still spell his name and still taste his wife's sweet milky Baltic coffee.

1961: Through kindness of Paris Leary (with whom I'd corresponded since early in Chelsea days), a poet and Anglican priest with a passion for Charles Williams, and who thought of himself as "an apostle to the rich," I was offered a job teaching German at Bard College. (I had studied German literature in college, tried to major in it, translated it for several years, but had never spoken it, never been to Germany.) Twice I refused the job, hating the idea of leaving the city, of teaching what I didn't know, of living on the edge in every sense. When they made the third offer, they asked me to come and look at the campus. The president of the college, the late Rev. Reamer Kline, picked me up at the bus station in his little VW bug — the simplicity of it impressed me. Annandale's beauty swayed me, & the gorgeous apartment Bard offered us — free — won me, after years in Rat Hall in Bed-Stuy.

Sometime in the fierce hot dry summer of 1961, we managed to move our several thousand books (managing alas to lose our collection of Joe Kling) upstate, and left our steel shelves from Brooklyn to Jackson Mac Low. All these years later I do not regret it for a moment, this rustication.

1961–62: Taught German at Bard: beginning, intermediate, and a seminar on Goethe's *Faust*. What was I doing? Exhausting, draining, almost nightmarish — yet I wrote more than I had ever written in my life — an instruction that activity is itself stimulating to the prophetic faculty, not the reverse. Lazy people have nothing to say.

For the first time in my life, we had money, not much, but at $5500 a year and no rent, I could learn to drive. I bought a dark green 1949 Chevrolet. I was taught to drive by the poet Jonathan Greene, who had been the real instrument in getting me to Bard, and who now had to deal with the monster he had summoned. (I had met Jonathan in New York with his friend Chuck Stein, with whom I am still close after thirty-five years, both of them students of Armand Schwerner, who brought them to meet the Big Poets one night around 1958 — Paul Blackburn, greatest of our troubadours, and Armand Schwerner (never in my life have I heard him say a wrong thing, always on, always accurate) himself, and Economou and me. Chuck, whose mother had just died, read some poems that struck me powerfully indeed, even though he was supposed to be along only for the ride, and for his saxophone, which he played as we sauntered "like cut-rate Montezumas," in Dahlberg's great phrase, down to the Village and the Festa di San Gennaro that thronged the streets.)

In spring of this year, Jerry and Diane Rothenberg's Hawk's Well Press published my first book, *Armed Descent*. Fifty or so books later, I'm still glad that was the first. And as hard as it was to wait (till twenty-five!) for that first book to be published, I am profoundly glad it took so long; had the book been gathered together six months before, I could not now stand by it.

1962: Shifted to teaching English at Bard; I started my first freshman English course with *Naked Lunch* and Sherlock Holmes, with pleasure to teach the things that formed me. Later I was asked by Heinrich Bluecher to teach a section of his "Common Course" — which is how I began teaching Buddhism, one of the "units" of his history-of-consciousness-oriented Jaspersian enterprise. So I found myself one day — I can still feel the feel of me, inside the chest of me, the mind of me, as I, pompous as Charlemagne, recited the triple refuge in Sanskrit: *Buddham saranam gacchami, dhammam saranam gacchami, sangham saranam gacchami*. Twenty years would pass before I had the least sense of what I was really saying. But now I can stand by the words. The words meant. The words counted. As they always do.

1962: This year I met Charles Olson. Cid Corman, in the course of hundreds of dynamic, horrendous, instructive, benevolent, critical letters, published "The Exchanges" and other poems of mine in a featuring RK issue of the second series of *Origin*, whose first series had clearly been the most important magazine of the 1950s for American poetry.

1963: First meetings with Stan Brakhage and Ken Irby. Margaret Randall, who opened so much of the Americas to the work being done throughout all its tongues and islands, published my second book, *Her Body Against Time / Su Cuerpo Contra El Tiempo*, in Mexico City, in a bilingual edition.

1964: Charles Olson invited me to join Dorn, Creeley, and Baraka in teaching at Buffalo for the summer. *Lunes* (embodying a three-line, thirteen syllable form I had developed) was published in an edition with

Rothenberg's *Sightings*, fierce arrowheads of his work, with cover by Amy Goldin. *Round Dances* published, with drawings by Josie Rosenfeld.

1965: Meeting with Helen Belinky, who came to live in Annandale. I began *Weeks*, first of my long serial poems. *A Controversy of Poets* published by Doubleday as an Anchor paperback — Paris Leary and I had edited it over several years, and the controversy was between us, I representing the experimental/Black Mountain/avant-garde, he the "academic" poets (the ones the world already knew about). Doubleday had planned to call it the *Doubleday Book of Contemporary Poetry*, then got cold feet and gave it a silly donnish joke of a title which yet embodied something of the polemic going forward. Robert Duncan refused to be included because the anthology was not polemic enough. In the piebald despairs and follies of anthologists, I almost abandoned the thing, then kept myself going with the thought that Zukofsky's *A-11* could be read by thousands. The book eventually sold something like sixty thousand copies and must have done some of what it was supposed to do.

1966–67: Living in Cambridge, teaching as Visiting Professor of Modern Poetry (a title that warmed me) at Tufts. Close to Steve Jonas, Linda Parker, Carol Weston, and Robert Lee Tipps, through whom I met all these, Jim and Joanne Randall, Gordon Cairnie.

1967: Doubleday published *The Scorpions*. I began corresponding with John Martin of the new Black Sparrow Press whom I first met in Connecticut. This has been a continuous relationship with the publisher and press who made my work available to the commonwealth — my work and the work of hundreds of other new poets and narrators, in the greatest triumph of small press in our time. *A Joining: A Sequence for H.D.* is the first small book of mine this year, printed on our fancy mimeograph: *Devotions, Twenty Poems, Axon Dendron Tree, Crooked Bridge Love Society*. Residency as Fellow of Calhoun College, Yale.

1968: Moved early January into Lindenwood House, on the Triangle in Annandale, where I still live. The temperature reached twenty-six below zero a few days later, then I left for California, my first visit to the West. Stayed with Harvey Bialy and Timotha Doane, who opened San Francisco to me. *Alpha* published. *Finding the Measure* published, my first full-sized collection from Black Sparrow.

1969: Reading tour of New England. *Songs I-XXX* published. *A California Journal. The Common Shore*, first five books of a long poem about America in time. After a peaceful divorce from Joan, Helen & I married in Mexico, April 1969.

After eight years of digging in my heels, sustaining myself by sight of the dark treetops of the century-old white pines against the blue sky on the road to Blithewood, and after much political struggle (much of which went on unconsciously or actually without my taking part) I was given tenure at Bard. Bard. What a name, and what auspices! Originally I planned to stay a year, then fell in love with the place — the telluric aspect of it, the part the woodchuck & the crow know best. Then little by little the school part of it pleased me, gave me space, let me do my work. And to Bard came year after year brilliant students of poetry, and I had the privilege of working with them, trying to stimulate without shaping, informing without forming. Those students, who still keep coming, are what has kept me here all these years. Occasional forays to other schools would show me what is more usual in American colleges: one or two brightlings amidst the dim. But so many of them came here, men and women who wanted to write, and who would go ahead to make their lives into a long fulfillment of that double contract with the earth and with language that it is to be a poet. It was a delight, sometimes a daunting delight, to work with them, and a joy to think of them still working in the renewal of the world: Thomas Meyer, Pierre Joris, Elizabeth Robinson, Ann-Sargent Wooster, John Yau, Bruce McClelland, William Prescott, Amanda Dowd, Harvey Bialy, Josepha Gutelius, Norman Weinstein, David Gansz, Kimberly Lyons, Barbara Grossman, Juliana Spahr, Lydia Shectman, Brian Stefans, Drew Gardner, Manus Pinkwater, April Hubinger, Mary Sternbach, Mary Caponegro, Lynn Behrendt, Laura McClure, Noreen Norton, Marilyn Danahue, Susan Mernit, Peter Boffey, Phyllis Chesler, Dennis Barone, Paul Pines, Bill Wilson, Cathleen Shattuck, Jane Heidgerd, Thea Cooper, Mark Karlins, Barbara Roether, Tandy Sturgeon, Jessica Bayer, Martine Bellen, Richard Grazide, David Abel, Lisa Harris, Leonard Schwartz, Drake Stutesman, Alison Watkins, Norman Weinstein, so many, how can I number them? I am grateful to them all, for coming, for hearing, for making me speak. They made sense of my work.

Bard. I know the earth is special here. Whether it's because it's on the ancient Cape Ann-Cahokia-Grand Canyon-Temple of Maroni in West Los Angeles ley-line (as we would have said in the 1970s), or because of the grace of the earth lords, or its having been an ancient treaty region, Delos-like among warring tribes, or thanks to the blessing of some ecological juncture we have not yet the science to perceive, this Annandale is a place in which considerable energy is available for those who propose to work. And over the last two decades, the college itself has grown much more in harmony with that kind of renovative energy that so abounds here. When Leon Botstein came in as president to wake the faculty and bring the arts alive, he (historian, musician, a man of Olsonic reach and risk and skill) wielded the curious double power of the academy at its best: the power of finance, to provide for the livelihood of those intellectuals and artists who maintain the continuity of human culture, and the power of intellect, to declare all things open to question, including especially the comfortable assumptions of curriculum and "discipline." He has brought living people here and trusted them to do their work. And that is one of the things for which I am most grateful, the colleagues who have been brought here over recent years, colleagues who are writers and who teach as part of the strength of what they do — Norman Manea, John Ashbery, Mona Simpson, Ann Lauterbach, Ed Sanders, William Gaddis, Edouard Roditi, Lydia Davis, and further back Robert Coover and I. B. Singer and Peter Sourian and even, a decade ago, Robert Duncan, who taught a remarkable course in Poetics at Bard 1982–83, and presented a sequence of readings of all his late work. Bard is an extraordinary place, all three: ground & institute & the custom of the young.

 1970: *Kali Yuga* published by Cape Goliard in London. Through these years I was associated with Clayton Eshleman as a contributing editor to *Caterpillar*, and with Dennis & Barbara Tedlock of *Alcheringa*.

 1971: Death of Paul Blackburn. In the spring of the year, Paul asked me to read at Cortland, where he had finally taken a teaching job. On St. Patrick's day I read there for his class — on that same day, Paul got the diagnosis — "It's nothing," he said at the end of the reading, "just a little cancer." That night I couldn't sleep, tormented by grief for him — and for all of us, for myself, since one death is the death of us all. I grieved because of his young wife & baby son, grieved for the greatness of his work and his immense (really never saw anything like it before or since) kindness to other writers. When I was just beginning, he guided me to readings, wrote big praise about my work, tried to make things happen. And not just for me. He was always ready to put himself last.

I remember sitting in his West Side apartment in the late 1950s, hearing him read, studying how he studied his own work, his careful readings, revisions, attentions, watching how everything he did — eating, drinking, smoking, talking — was done with precise focus. His care and hard work and his sinewy feeling for song made the direct link with Ezra Pound, whose *Proenca* left Paul such scope for our new *trobar*. And now I was watching those oriental eyes of his wrinkle with the smile of "only a little cancer." By the summer, he was weak indeed. I saw him last at the curious two-week poetry festival on the sun-battered shadeless primary shield of central Michigan, where he lugged his two-ton reel-to-reel tape recorder around to everybody's reading, just as he always did in New York, keeping track of us all. His own reading was feeble, strong only in that this dying man could read so clearly, gently, without the least glimmer of self-pity or even excuse. The young writers who came to learn to strut got little sense of the grandeur of the man. Just after I got to Los Angeles and started teaching at CalTech, Paul died back east, mid-September, just before the beginning of Monastic Lent. He was forty-four.

Cities (a novella written at the end of writing *The Scorpions*) and *In Time* (a collection of essays and manifestoes) were published by Harvey Brown's Frontier Press. *Flesh Dream Book* (the title means to identify the three sources of the poem) published by Black Sparrow.

1971–72: Chosen as first Poet in Residence at CalTech, through the kindness of David and Annette Smith. Year in Los Angeles; lived up in the foothills of the San Gabriels, in Altadena; from the front steps you could see sunlight cresting on the waves coming in to the distant shore across the Basin. Behind the house was Mount Wilson, where it snowed one day. Friendship with Caryl and Clayton Eshleman, Jim & Christine Tenney, Max Delbrück, Ted Ronyon. In the fall of 1971 I turned thirty-six, thus in some literal sense outliving the predictions I had lived with since my childhood, that I would die at thirty-five. In the overwhelming gush of survival energy, I began *The Loom* and finished it, for the most part, in two months, sometimes composing (at the secondhand Olympia we had just bought) for twenty hours at a stretch.

1972: *Ralegh* and *The Pastorals* published.

1973: Back in Annandale. *The Mill of Particulars* published.

1974: *A Line of Sight* published.

1975: Publication of *The Loom*.

1976: Residency at Dickinson College in Pennsylvania. *Sixteen Odes* published.

1977: First teaching stint at Naropa Institute; over the years, I would read and teach often at this remarkable school that sheltered the last sparks of American protest, and the first glimmer of Dharma light. Separation & divorce from Helen. Publication of *The Lady Of*.

1978: I began to live alone, for the first time since 1954. This meant relearning the wonderful work of time. From now into the 1980s and beyond, I would enjoy friendships with Mary Caponegro, Chuck Stein, Patricia Snyder, George & Susan Quasha, Mary Sternbach, Franz Kamin, Bruce McClelland, Barbara Leon, all of whom were living within a few miles of each other — a kind of Annandale-Barrytown-Rhinebeck renaissance. *The Convections* published. *Wheres* published. Bruce McPherson's Treacle Press published *The Book of Persephone*, beginning a relationship that would shape my sense of my writing and eventually send my fictions — written at liberty — out into the world, unexpectedly, as far as I was concerned.

1979: This year was a major change in my life: through careful diet and through grace, I lost so much of the gross obesity I had always carried that, by 1980, I could walk down a street and not be noticed — and that is an extraordinary sense of liberty, the curious freedom of being "normal." Publication of *The Cruise of the Pnyx*, an experiment in telling, using verse and prose and something in between them, all three, in one text. Publication by Black Sparrow of *Kill the Messenger Who Brings Bad News — The World Is Only Description*.

1980: *Kill the Messenger* (under its shorter title) won the Los Angeles Times prize for the best book of poetry of the year. After a year or two of planning and committeeing, the new graduate program in the arts began at Bard. I taught in this every year for the next dozen years. Courseless and entirely directed at the individual encounter with work & criticism, based on endless one-to-one exchanges, the program usefully dealt with each art in the context of all the others, which was my chief concern, and avoids still the factory air workshops and conservatories. *Sentence* published by Station Hill. The Poetry Collection of the Lockwood Memorial Library in Buffalo began to acquire my manuscripts, correspondence, and notebooks, as part of an RK archive.

1981: *Spiritual Exercises* published. North Atlantic Press published Jed Rasula's gathering together of poems of mine published in magazines but never collected, *The Alchemist to Mercury*. He described it as an "alternate Opus" and presented it as a sort of left-handed Selected Poems. I had the chance to include some pieces overlooked, and learned a great deal about my work from Rasula's admirable editing. As I did later from his long essay on my work that prefaced his bibliography (complete up through 1980) of my work, published later as an issue of *Credences* (Spring 1984, edited by Robert Bertholf). On 27 December in New York City I took refuge in Buddha, Dharma, and Sangha.

1982: In the Springtime, I first met Kalu Rinpoche & Lama Norlha. *Mulberry Women*, the first *livre d'artiste* collaboration with Matt Phillips.

1983: Traveled in India with Lama Norlha and stayed in Kalu Rinpoche's monastery near Darjeeling. While there, compiled an Indian journal never published. On return, trying to find the way of words again, worked at the composition of *The Flowers of Unceasing Coincidence*.

1984: *Thor's Thrush*, an old collection, republished by Coincidence Press, with a title in runes.

1985: Traveled in England and Scotland. Beginning of a deep friendship with Mary Moore Goodlett; we worked and lived together till her death four years later. Her skills in linguistics and communication, her humane fervor and toughness, were joyously wielded for her friends. As a fourteenth-generation American from Kentucky, she made me, somehow, more American than I knew I could be. Bruce McPherson this year published *A Transparent Tree*, the first collection of my fictions. It includes the "Russian Tales — an Experiment in Telling," which is the clearest demonstration or exposition of how narrative arises from language itself: "Language is the only fable."

1986: In May, I received an award of the American Academy and Institute of Arts and Letters at their annual meeting.

1987: Visited Hawaii in January. In the summer, Jerry Rothenberg and I represented the U.S. at the First International Poetry Festival in Luxemburg. Visited France, Austria, Switzerland. *Not This Island Music* published.

1988: *Doctor of Silence* (second collection of fictions) published. *Oahu* (notations from my Hawaii visit) published by Bruce McClelland's new St. Lazaire Press.

1989: Visit to California. Last meeting with Kalu Rinpoche in January. Passing away of Kalu Rinpoche in India, 10 May. Death of Joan Lasker a week later. Throughout this year, Mary Goodlett's condition deteriorated, the cancer metastasizing determinedly.

1990: A full year of death: death of Mary Goodlett, January 25, aged thirty-nine. Death of my mother in August, aged eighty-eight. Death of my father in September, aged ninety. *Cat Scratch Fever* (third collection of fictions) published.

1991: *Ariadne* published. To California and Pacific Northwest. Travel with Charlotte Mandell to Victoria. In October, Charlotte returned from France and we started to live together.

Over the late 1980s and into the '90s I have been sustained by close working friendships with Pat and Marla Smith of *Notus*, Brad Morrow of *Conjunctions* (which we were able to bring to Annandale as Bard's literary journal) David Gansz, Dennis and Barbara Tedlock, Nicholas Maw, Matt Phillips, Barbara Leon, Ken Irby, Pierre Joris, & Nicole Peyrafitte-Joris, Sarah Rothenberg, Ilse Schreiber, and Bruce McPherson.

1992: Teaching at Naropa, and travel with Charlotte in the Rockies; spent the summer in the foothills of the Haute-Savoie with Charlotte and her family. Publication of *A Strange Market*. Resignation from the graduate program, getting the summers back.

1993: Charlotte and I married on 3 June. Editing and preparation of my *Selected Poems 1960–1992*.

(Gale Research, *Contemporary Authors*, 1976 & 1993)

THREADS 11 : ROBERT SAYS

Every morning I write in a notebook, always a bound one, never a loose-leaf one, usually a school notebook, the cheap kind made in India or Brazil, with useful mathematical formulas inside the back cover. (How those formulas have changed over the years; they used to tell how many barrels in a hogshead, or that a dozen dozen is a gross; now they talk of milligrams. But the cheap one I'm using now, № 290, from China, still tells me that 660 feet make one furlong. Thank god for furlongs!) I write longhand, with a fountain pen (favorites: a new golden Sheaffer, an old Parker 51, a Lamy Safari with violet ink) — this is the hour for poems, usually. If I'm writing prose then, or any time later in the day, because I love to revise but hate to type, I usually do first drafts at the computer directly (Sony Vaio). Quick spurts, yes. But also many edits. I love the act of revision — sometimes I feel I write so as to have something to revise.

in conversation with Mark Thwaite (2006)

There's an issue of a small magazine called Epoch *from Cornell which is bringing out a symposium on the line as its next issue. They wrote to twenty or so poets asking them what they think, what they have to say about the line. I sent a series of prepositions to* Epoch *about the line relying on the notion, which is so obvious, that the line is the shortest meaningful distance between two silences. Silence to me is the radix of art in the 20th century. It's what I as a person and as a poet have had to overcome, that is, not overcome silence but revere silence and learn it, since my natural tendency is fluency and non-stop talk. Compulsive or not, however it may be, to learn to be quiet has been a supreme achievement. I haven't been able to use some things that people of my generation have used, like drugs, or Buddhism, or mysticism. But it seems to me that poetry gives me that wonderful opportunity of balancing, of learning silence, since every line, to me, ends with complete silence, but not a long one. Silence is not quantity but quality* of speech. Jack Spicer, who was a trained linguist, insisted on describing silence in strictly linguistic terms, juncture, things like that. But the quality of silence rather than the quantity of silence seems to be important. I don't, myself, get carried away much by Jackson Mac Low's experiments with making silence as long as lines it follows or replaces, or as long as paragraphs. It doesn't seem to me that silence is that kind of animal, that you can quantify it the way you can quantify speech. By definition it's a quality, an instantaneous quality, that one moment of silence. In the 50s, Creeley defined for our time what poetry could be, a momentary interruption, dead silence of everything, catalytically open. [...] Since that which distinguishes poetry from prose in all of the linguistic discourse that I know about, is the deliberate intervention of silence, the deliberate shaping, the organizational principle that silence is, and I find that enough, I've never found it really necessary to use rhyme or metrics. Although I've played with them, I've never found it necessary to use them. I think people with good ears, what you call good ears, are really those who have a taste for silence and can recognize and place it. There is something else I do in my poetry which is connected with line break and that is indentation. In my own work I observe two formalities. One is that the line break requires a complete silence, very short. And indentation from the right hand margin indicates and should be realized by a deflection of pitch downward, so that the line begins for me with the highest comfortable pitch for my voice, and as you know, my voice tends to trail down. So the poem line which begins a little bit in from the margin will begin a little lower. A dropped line, for example, will be silence plus pitch drop. That's not very interesting, and it's not complex, but easy to say, easy to describe. Those are the formal tools I work with. I find for most of my work that's adequate. [...]

It's more a question of where to put the words, I think, than where to put the silences. How do I actually proceed? A line comes to me as an acoustic shape, the words of which are not always clear, but the feel of, as I say to myself, the wield of the line is clear. It is then a musical phrase, and it finds its words usually almost instantaneously, but not necessarily so. Sometimes it will take me *a second or two to figure out what it is I'm saying. This blue book the cassette is sitting on is called* Finding the Measure. *One of the more technical things I meant by that title was, it's all so personal and somatic that it sounds falsely abstract when I speak about it, but one of the more technical things that I meant is working in the beginning of the poem until the line appears. It might not be the first line that really seems to strike a substantiality of silence or sound from which the rest of a poem can flow. At that moment I typically cut away whatever came before as a simply clearing the throat or finding the measure. I mean other things by that title.*

As I talk I'm trying to figure out from your point of view where to locate the silence. The first successful line that in the poem, that which will then be the measure for the rest, does set up a system of expectations in my ear and all subsequent lines play off that, somewhat, even though I notice as I look through the book, that typically the first line is quite a bit shorter than the last line. With poems the lines have a tendency to grow larger, and I don't fight that. I don't mean that in a Pindaric sense, that that first line sets a measure which has to be recurrently revisited, but it does set up a system of expectation that I try to dance with through the rest of the poem. Let me put it another way. Sometimes I think of the line as the smallest number of words that can meaningfully interrupt the silence. I always want the line, of whatever kind, in whatever poem, to be able to be extracted. I define it to myself in a way like this: if, God forbid, the angel of death should visit me as I'm writing the poem, and I have written one line before another, I want that line to be capable of being put on my tombstone as evidence of what his last utterance was. I want every line then to have that degree of completeness.

in conversation with James Stalker [ca. 1980]

11.

A BOOK BETWEEN POEM &/AS STATEMENT

(In place of a statement)

I like to write with fountain pens, straight pens, pencils,
electric typewriters, word processors, felt tip pens, crayons,
other people's ball point pens, old portables musty from the
cellar: any tool that gets words down. Every pen has its
message. Every moment has its special song I mean to hear,
and by listening hard, release, so you can hear it too.

That would be the basis of a statement: things release them-
selves in us as language. Presumably the world is knowing
itself (among all its other ways of self-knowledge) by how we
know it.

I like writing because language is social, seldomllonely
though I may be lonely, always in focus though I may be vague,
always determinate though I may be fleeing from my feelings
and responsibilities by night. The words are all in the diction-
ary, awaiting their sharpest, most conscious resurrection
to preside over the self-awareness of a moment.

I think of a poet as one who has nothing to say. And therefore
has enough enough space toside to hear, listen, attend, re-
verberate.

17 April 1986

"AUTOBIOGRAPHICAL ESSAY" [EXCERPTS]

1

I'm not sure that I want to write my life. I'm not sure there is any way to write it except to write every day, as I try to, the poem of that day, one after another. The poem is a day.

I'm not sure I want to write about my life. Do I ever want to think about it? For someone as egotistical as I am, I have spent very little time thinking about it, only about what I want, what happened to me. Happens to me. Sometimes I think about what *it* wants of me.

I'm not sure I want, in other words, to write about my life in other words than those that have already (poem after poem, story after story, talk after talk) made their way into the more or less durable world of language.

I will try. Because I am asked to, no better reason. Could there be a better reason? Give what is asked: there is no other answer. Cavalcanti's canzone: *A lady asks me, so I will tell* — ground enough for all exposition.

When I think about my life, I think about how I hated it when I was younger, & love it now. Then it was curse and now it is bless. What I wanted to curse was how cut off I felt from everyone, mostly from those I wanted to be close to, wanted to like me. What I want to bless is everything, everyone.

2

My autobiography is the writing (*graphein*) of my life, my bios. Now Greek knows two words like that, two words the ancients surmised had at first been one: *bios*, "life," and *bios*, "a bow" to shoot with as the hunter takes the life of things and turns them into his own life, the life of the tribe.

Writing my life is writing my instrument, my strength.

My life is not my past.

3

An autobiography is different from a biography. It tells the truth, not the facts. "Truth is what most contradicts itself in time," and, like time itself, it is contingent, relative, impermanent as formulated. The most accurate clock in the world is accurate only one instant at a time. Its record is meaningless. Or the recorded readings of a bad clock are identical to the record of a good one. Truth, like time, does not only exist as experienced; it *is* experience. So biography (the writing of a life, done by a Greek pun with an arrow, scratching in the ground, piercing the heart, wounding the flesh, taking the life — or writing in the gentle dust of people's impressions by means of the arrow tip, scratching the names of our sins in the dirt) is *life writing*. Autobiography is the self writing life.

And the self exists only as an imputation: the noticer of the huge heap of stuff called *now*.

Autobiography is now-writing, then. Now writing then — and it comes to speak the past. Then writes now too, can't flee from speaking in the words chosen by, the rhythmic pression of this breath in, this body now.

All of which you know. But where would writing be, let alone literature, if we didn't write down so learnedly and urgently what is so obvious? Nothing else is worth speaking but the obvious. That's why we can make do with a reasonably tidy stack of a few hundred thousand words in the dictionary, enough to speak justly of the billon billion things.

We are just talking to each other about what we know. Minding & reminding. Touching. Writing is touch.

4

Real autobiography is *the life that writes itself*. That is what writer's works are, in truth. Look no further: self-written, self-begotten, the poems I have spent most of my life writing are my actual autobiography.

What can I add to them? Some dates, some dedications? Some personal confusions to try to drag back by the tails those articulated energies that have, by wholly entering into language, already managed to get away from me and my concerns?

This is the bow I bent when in October of 1958 I vowed to spend the rest of my life writing in service of that Brightness I intuited as like or beyond the intense blue autumn sky, and determined that I would give whatever I had of life to saying. To write every day. For the sake of the world, as I supposed in my innocent arrogance. For the truth that language tells — for while language does not tell all the truth or the whole truth, there is some truth that only language tells.

That October commitment is the story. To write every day was the method. To attend to what it said. To listen. To prepare myself for writing by learning everything I could, by hanging out in languages and enduring overdetermined desires, by tolerating my own inclinations as if they had the physical accuracy of gravity. To listen, and say what I heard.

(Gale Research, *Contemporary Authors*, 1976 & 1993)

SIX STATEMENT-POEMS

(gloss as preface

at the foot of the letter =
au pied de la lettre
    = *literal (ly)*
1) the literal as the looking-glass of mysteries
        & the opening of the gate
2) to kneel at the foot
      is to express devotion,
    to be vassal of the fact,
   to stand in humility before
(grasp the 'knees' of, in honor of the Fertilities):

      a) the sources
          (telling =
          story =
          logos =
          mythos =
          word
      b) the words
(which
(are never our own
        except as (in as) we use them,
   they are our tools
    but they are not ours
        /
3) fidelity to the imagination
         (emblematically:
          the Matter of Britain
       that Arthur whose story presided
      over our language emerging
        into itself,
     that story which as any is
    a man's emerging into himself)

is to be vessel of the words
                    (emblematically:
                        the letters of the
                    american alphabet,
                      which are not phonemes
                      (any more than words are morphemes)
                      but are the *current*
                                        (in everyone's
                        use *&* care)
                                    sure signs of.

                            [RK archives, undated]

(prefix:

Finding the measure is finding the mantram,
is finding the moon, as index of measure,
is finding the moon's source;

                if that source
is Sun, finding the measure is finding
the natural articulation of ideas.

                The organism
of the macrocosm, the organism of language,
the organism I combine in ceaseless naturing
to propagate a fourth,
        the poem,
                from their trinity.

Style is death. Finding the measure is finding
a freedom from that death, a way out, a movement
forward.

       Finding the measure is finding the
specific music of the hour,
              the synchronous
consequence of the motion of the whole world.

                              5 June '67
                  (From *Finding The Measure*, 1968)

(prefix:

Against the Code

Language is the only genetics.

    Field
"in which a man is understood & understands"
   & becomes
     what he thinks,
becomes what he says
       following the argument.

"When it is written that Hermes or Thoth invented a language, it is meant that language is itself the psychopomp, who leads the Individuality out of Eternity into the conditioned world of Time, a world that language makes by discussing it."

So the hasty road
& path of arrow
must lead up
from language again

    & in language the work to be done,
 work of light,
   beyond.

"Through manipulation and derangement of ordinary language (*parole*), the conditioned world is changed, weakened in its associative links, its power to hold an unconscious world-view (consensus) together. Eternity, which is always there, looms beyond the grid of speech."

    (From *The Mill of Particulars*, 1973)

Purity

A true poem of the eternal present, an ocean, each wave is now, no wave is then. Nothing, comes again.

The reader is no reader. He hears, in one direction, avanti, forever. Not a line, a passage.

This is a truth of process.

For years I hated Lot's wife, who was the Reader Looking Back through the Text. The woman reliving her memories. Rereading the poem.

It must come to this: the line becomes line, as the Word becomes Flesh.

The poem is only when it is. Only the going by right now.

A formal line, of verse, at last breaks down. In a purely serial unfolding, there is no structure possible based on recurrence-within-a-figure.

A line is the breath's take on the heart's grasp of the senses' senses, burnt up in an instant on the altar of the poem.

So the line one hears is an abstraction, sheer guesswork.

The integer of poetic composition is Interruption.

A poem is a controlled interruption of the reader's associative mental life.

A blank page summons data from the reader's mind. So the page must not be blank, lest the reader's wall never be broken, and he be trapped in the dream-palace of his associative reflections, or if he move out, wander only all day in the vales of Har.

Har is: thoughts without thinking. Concepts without conceiving.

Purity is the other.

So the blank page must have words on it.

(From *The Convections*, 1978)

In Commentary on the Gospel According to Thomas

the silent places
behind the brain

        Valhalla
where our lives are slain
minute by minute,
picked over by the blonde women
moving in the corridors of that house

Going back to that root
horseman crossing the flying bridge
into the castle at the back of the world

the brightness of organic event
    crossing into the dark

                There
is resurrection
that Christ was born in flesh
set up his tent among the cell structures of the brain
that there we christs are born in flesh,
coming down from the dark father
through the radiance of everyday
   & every space
into the one tomb from which we can rise
becoming him
         Love is the name of the
energy rising
growing the garden that stretches from beneath the heart
out to each end of the spine,
to the place where that bridge ends
   to welcome the images
in the place of the death of Images
   (dark of the brain where the images are silenced)
& spur them onward

where they have never been,
    a single Image in the place of images,
    a Movement
(called over & over by the holy name of
  Dance)
                as all is movement
compact & still & fiery in the final image,
the kingdom of heaven light with the light we bring there.

                (*Fuck You, A Magazine of the Arts* #7, 1964)

(An Anecdote, as Preface)

One night Andrews Wanning already old
asked Robert Lowell a question while we were at dinner:
      "Cal, when it comes down to it, isn't all literature just
family and circumstance?"
(one Harvard man appealing to another).

Lowell looked at him with that crazy boiled eye of his and
answered by caveman grunt
                conceivably affirmative.
Months or years later when I told this anecdote
(still feeling shock and tumult)
      to P. Adams Sitney, he said "Well, isn't it?"

And I cried out (did I cry out?)
like Blake (I'm not in the least
like Blake),
        No, poetry is glory and revelation and mystery
suddenly unveiled,
    poetry is not inherited,
                poetry

is not given.
Poetry is what no one knows.

                        (From *The Time of Voice*, 1998)

"AUTOBIOGRAPHICAL ESSAY" [EXCERPTS]

14

What do I think of myself as a writer?

I think I am a great playwright, one who has scarcely ever written a play, and never a good one. I think that I am writing a great play all my life and every poem a speech in it. Only to find the right mouth, the right shadow. Come, speak me. Come be my mouthed verities and bellowed tendernesses. Come to me. Every poem is a cry that matches exactly its lewd or sacred juncture in the play. Every story a précis or stage direction.

I proposed in my first book an armed descent — Valéry's mot, "He who would descend into the self must go armed to the teeth." And that is what I have tried to do, if do is the word for it, if tried is true. To go down into the self, armed with everything I have of flesh or dream or information. Armed, but not armored. To go down into the self, not necessarily my self but the sense of, steady beating pulsing beautiful soon lost forever physiology of the self.

If beginnings were only as easy as they say, those French writers of our day who propose a universe not essentially different from the spin they can give to their words, who balance paradoxes on the tips of their fingers, an arm's length at least from the heart.

Linguistics is the most ironic science, and while we hear little about it these days, it casts its spell still on the devious enterprises of the educated classes, the stuff that passes for learning and teaching, the voice of not knowing you know nothing. "... the unbreachable demarcations of law are themselves and precisely the destinies of every transgression, which by endorsing the law it trespasses, by and in that fact proposes, beyond and undoubtedly, a later and thus nonpresent limit which is both result of the transgression and source of the next." These phrases from a text of Maurice Blanchot are what happens to me when I fall into a fever of doubt to avoid responding from my heart to Georges Bataille's remark: "Coitus is the parody of crime." When you hear a sentence like Bataille's, you either hear it in silence, or fill up your mouth with words.

And right now I'm filling up my mouth with words, to avoid hearing the *tolle lege* of the Gale Research Company, or rather its *tolle scribe*. Rather than tell the story of my life, I'll say anything that comes into my head.

16

I am simple. There, that is a beginning, like the great first line from an early novel: "I, Clement, have been from my earliest youth a lover of chastity."

No one but the hardworking and prolific writer, dauntless practitioner of every experiment and any trick that comes to hand, no one but he can really know just how simple he is. How simple I am. And telling you about it no more convinces you of its truth, my truth, than the phrase *Pleasant downpour every afternoon at Waikiki* soaks the clothes you're wearing now.

Simple, a lover of chastity, a lover of flags and emblems and words, of contours, of answers. Science was my first love, because it told as quickly as it could what little it knew. It knows more than I ever will, and still tell quick, but it too has latterly grown sluggish in its ways of telling. It argues more and more about beginnings, and shows less and less the inner life of geodes and the dreams of zooplankton. (Just as linguistics turned to issues of grammaticality and covert structure and left off cataloguing and describing the languages that are actually spoken, at least still being spoken when linguists turned away, by living human beings.) Discourse (a word Charles Olson disdained) has taken over even what used to be called the Exact Sciences; with discourse has come that flaccidity of intellect from which it is not likely we will, as a culture, recover.

Early on, very early, even from the first book I read from the library (was it called *The Stars for Sam*?) I could tell by feel, not reason but feeling itself, just when the author was saying what he knew (or what he thought he knew) — as opposed to filling the gaps more or less plausibly. It is allergy to that specious gap-filling that has kept me from science & most scholarship.

Simple enough to know I can't find any structure for my telling, except itself, structuring its way along as writing always has, always *can*, if you let it. *No structure but structure*, then, I will claim, and obey.

17

It is not always what we want, the ability to remember. A mango left in a paper bag on a body-polished wooden bench on the Eighth Avenue subway platform. Millie Gendell gasping her lungs out with plaster dust in the coldest winter in years, scraping down to brick in her apartment on Minetta Lane. Millie Minetta millinery, Mr. Buonfiglio and the two-toned sports jacket he made for me, cashmere soft & paneled in buff, like buckskin, Elderts Lane with Simonetti's pizza garden, a bus on the Avenue Paul Valéry, what is it all about?

Here is the story I have tried to tell:

Armed descent, into her body which is my talisman, my weapon against time. Against time these round dances, the movement around the core of myself that is my enstasy — the opposite of the ecstasy people are always raving about or hoping for. I wanted enstasy, to stand inside, to be incarnate as myself, in all the full intensity of feeling in full consciousness from this place outward. Above me, the stages of the moon declare their lunes, which are their measures in us too, the tuneful amazements of the soul's calendar. Words are forever in the service of this going that is my knowing.

That was the first chapter. Somewhere inside all that while, not published as or in a book for twenty years, was "The Exchanges" (1959–1961), the secret alchemical, Mahayana heart of what I was trying to declare.

I can admit it now — my work *has* a meaning to declare. One that I have learned along with you, clement reader.

18

Readers, raiders, you by being close and by being few have charmed me into my own intimate acts of self-awareness, undistracted by criticism in bulk. Slowly I have come to know what my work proposed, first for me to do, then for you to understand. And I am with you, reader, really, for writing and reading are the same act, only different phases of, and I am (truth to say) only this minor character among the personae of my drama, the one called towards the bottom of the column of fine rolling names: First Reader. The writer is just the first reader and seldom the best.

And waits for the Final Reader, in whose lap lies — perhaps at this moment, rising from the paper halfway to the eye, to the ear, to the heart, the real meaning of each thing I have written, and of all those things together. For surely they have their true meaning only in the great text of the whole work, the thing called context but that is really the text itself, the actual weaving.

(Gale Research, *Contemporary Authors*, 1976 & 1993)

INVITED TO INTRODUCE MY WORK

Invited to introduce my work to the general reader, I think of a drawing by Robert Duncan that showed the Ideal Reader of his book. I remember a comfortable plump lady in sun hat in her garden, enemy of snails and aphids, cultivatrix of something dippier, sweeter than roses. Since seeing that picture, I've wondered about my ideal reader — but I come up with no singular instance. I see the beautiful young woman letting the book fall and turning to the tree. I see a girl fighting in the desert, a booklet of mine packed on her ample hip. Who carries books around? My work is fed and instructed by woman's presence; that does not make it better for her. She yawns and says she knows all this stuff already. So perhaps I write for the wicked old scholar, to rekindle the power of the text in time — he notices in my scribbles an allusion to Geoffrey of Monmouth, and forgives me my psychotic metrics for the sake of the link. But it is not our shared tradition that makes us human. Perhaps the image is a double one, a man and a woman (a woman and her man) sitting side by side on the subway. They want to understand this dark earth they tunnel through, yet want to relate it to the sunshine, rain and stars.

But all these images, which become no single image, betray the work & its readers. My little cartoons are prolusions of the ego, a foreplay of folk I might like to talk to or be with in discourse. The work must find its own conversation.

Poetry is not foreplay.

(I have written for the king to read as he hides in the forest.)

What help can I give the reader who would come to my work? First, tell him it is not *my* work, only Work, itself, somehow arisen through (or in spite of) my instrumentality. My personality is its enemy, only distracts. But what is there for the reader who reads to find the man? He'll find the man. The man is always here. The stink of him, the hop and fear he confuses with himself, the beauty of him, struggle, dim intuitions of a glory that is not personal, but that only persons can inhabit or share. That we are humans in the world, and share our thoughts.

And this sharing of thought, perception, is what becomes the world. The world is our shared thought.

But in language the unperceived or newly perceived can arise, to break the fabric of the ordinary consensus of our lives. News from nowhere, a new handle for an old day.

I want to make a work that talks to me.

To which I can turn to learn answers to all the questions I can ask, questions that don't have what we glibly call 'facts' as answers (what is the capital of Iceland? how much fluorine in topaze? where do nutmegs grow?). If I disdain a fake dialectics of arbitrary dichotomies, dismiss all my opinions, let all my subscriptions lapse, to what do I turn?

(Why turn anywhere?)

I mean, how do I keep talking?

(Why do that? Why not be silent?)

To break the consensus!

(Then say what you know.)

What I know is what comes into my head, stuffed with books and fitful desires, into the rhythm of heart and breath, assaulted by clock & calendar & the Way we Live Now. I think what I'm doing is saying what comes into my head. Heart.

(Nonsense.)

True. I'm saying what comes into my mouth. Into the poem. Simeon of Sarov said: "I say the first thing that rises in my heart." He could tell where lost things are, or who stole the gold.

(Or how much fluorine in topaze?)

That's just a link in the consensus.

(You know very well that in the Consensus, all epistemological bets are off. Any single *thing* implies all the others, as any single meaningful statement implies all others, implies the systematic properties of a language. Only in language are all propositions true.)

Then through the transformations of language the consensus is transformed. The world is changed.

Invited to introduce my work to the general reader, never! the *specific* reader, I rehearse for our mutual benefit two answers my work has given, and I here transcribe.

"Finding the Measure" [see above, p. 687.]

(Measure as distinct from meter, from any precompositional grid or matrix superimposed upon the fact of the poem's own growth 'under hand.')

"(Prefix:" to *The Mill of Particulars* [see above, p. 688.]

I have spoken a little about my motives and my intentions. I have not presumed to speak about the work itself, which must, true to its name, do its own work, and try to lure the reader to dance with it.

One word of abandon-caution: I am not concerned with sources. The poem is "sensuous in its intention to impress," says W.C. Williams. Many lights flicker on the water, many images are reflected. But the point is to jump in. Or at least to lift the cup and drink.

3 IX 73

(St. James Press Questionnaire for *Contemporary Poets*)

NOTES ON *LINE* FOR *EPOCH*

A line is that double thing:
A host of content and a cut of sound.

We read the inside, the walled garden's inside. Inside the *hortus conclusus* of the line the words make their special sheltered sense. Before the inshaped power *in* the line the best reader is quiet, regarding, alert.

There the line *as* line makes sense — a unit of signifying unknown to philosophy, a lemma isolable inside the drift of proposition.

And the line *is* its outside. It is the silences that border it. It exists, void of meaning, as a ripple of perturbation in the silence upon which the poem launches.

A line is a musical presumption, a musical event.
That is, it possesses the same sort of eventfulness that music does, a complex of meanings from which all *proper* meaningfulness flees when the order of event is disturbed.

Only a very bad translator would casually shift the order of lines in a poem, or of stanzas.

Yet it is the unquestioned slovenly practice of most to disturb, 'rearrange,' the order of morphemes (of 'things *&* images *&* deeds') inside the line.

We will never have a sense of line in our language as long as we ignore the issue of the order of morphemes in the original text.

A line is how the music happens.

Line is the core of poetry.

A line is shaped time. Music shapes its verbal onwardness.

Recently we have learned to move to ('hear') a sense of line no longer 'horizontal' (as print taught us to conceive it). We learn to make poetry from 'short lines' which are really thus units of the real line, the new line, which becomes a rain down the page. The line descends. ("The descent beckons.")

This new sense of line involves the shaped time itself shaping space.

(Skelton, Blake are forerunners. Mallarmé showed the way, as does Pound's Cavalcanti, late *Cantos*, Corman's Zeami, WCW's triadics — which are the most orderly effective experiments in the deconstruction of the line.)

The line moves from horizontal to vertical:
it is our gothic time beginning, our upthrust.
At first it seems to descend, to be going down (*art goth / argot*). Then it is seen in its triumphant ogival arrowing, *art gothique*: the ascent.
The page makes a world the line explores.

Poetry is the hypersyntactic organization of language.

Where hypersyntactic means 'subject to a principle undetermined by linguistic rules.'
Of such hypersyntactic principles, the most radical and most simple is silence, zero, off. Zero is that quality that takes its color from location. Similarly, the silence that ends a line of poetry is shaped by the line it ends, and defines the line in turn. Silence is usually called 'line ending.'

Most of the marked features that adorn and specify verse are devices for recognizing the presence of line:
rime at the end, alliteration within, caesura, formal assonance.
Of these the most radical is silence: the turning back.
When I read a line aloud, it happens that I hear my voice negotiate the silence of line ending and shift, subtly, to a higher pitch to read the next line. This pitch alternation seems to be provoked in me by no consideration except the line ending itself.

A line is the shortest distance between two silences.

Only rarely do I hear a line begin me.
Usually when I hear, it is a set of lines, a strophe: *a nest of turnings*.

A line is carved out of a matrix of idea by precision of feeling.

A line is a garden of morphemes.

It is the *cut* of a line that counts, that makes it count.
Yet only the ear can determine the success of the surgery (or the sculpture). There is no rule except alertness, no solid goal except difference.

A line must be different from itself.

A line is the shortest interesting distance between two meaningful silences.

A line-break should:
Focus the whole preceding line *anew*
    This is the *ostranenye* of enjambement, the sudden estrangement of language from its propositional predictability.

                      A line-break should carve out a unit of sound, a musical event such that the ear, entranced by the suddenly pierced wholeness of the so-terminated line, is held in suspense (and with it the mindheart of the hearer) across the synaptic gap before the next line. The silence carries.

The most interesting thing about a poem is where it stops. And how it stops.

A line works from inside out.

A line has no space for the ordinary despair.
        A line follows another as day
        follows day, always new, always
            full of hope, forgettable, cancelable, immaculate.
A line is a room in a house.
A line is a room around the house.

A line is interruption.
Focus the interruption until you hear.

            (How to write a line)
There is a silent speech which recasts language, obedient to the usual linguistic rules, pronouncing it inward, with no laryngeal sound, no murmur. So pronounced, this silent language inscribes itself in the etheric body of the speaker, writes itself in the etheric space around the speaker — and perhaps (QED) in the etheric body of those nearby — or afar?

This silent language is the substrate of prayer. It is why in effective liturgy periods of silence must be allowed, sans anaphora, sans music.

This silent language has a gestural equivalent — the word *mudra* comes to mind — sign of the cross made in the sky of the body — sign made in sky, by *this* sign conquer.

It is *line* that guides the inspeaker (= the reader) to just this shaping. Here is a line:

Formosum pastor Corydon ardebat Alexim

What a line! All in order, five words tell the whole story, the cast of character, the relations between.

The adjective at the start is itself the whole story, the *beautiful* Alexis, whose name seems just tossed in at the end of the line as an afterthought. Yet the name is in concord with the first word of the line, forming one grammatical unit, *formosum Alexim*, beautiful Alexis: so that the beloved in effect *is* the line, or comprehends the whole meaning of the experience. Corydon the shepherd was burning, was hot for, was in love with, the shapely Alexis. By defining the relation, as deed, the line also defines the beloved as hypostasis of the whole event.

poets whose line praxis instructs me ever:
  a) the morphemic garden (the line as fable intact:) Shakespeare, Chaucer, Hopkins, Blake, Stevens
  b) the line as musical event: Milton, Pound (his inveterate enemy, his *semblable*,) Duncan

Some poets have a potent balance of these powers:
The romantics (their secret strength) Coleridge (Frost at Midnight, Limetreebower,) Keats. and especially the Shelley of *Prometheus*. And Virgil — is that why they call him Romantic?

stichomythia —
          one line = one speech, a device of Greek tragedy,
   typically quick, iambic, signifying altercation, fast exchange,
                                                              much
          imitated by Shakespeare in *A&C* that greekest of
   his plays in structure
(as he must have studied, the originals in some form)

the line as a single focused utterance.

line = person

Jan 1980
(*Epoch* #29, 1980)

"TO THE READER" FROM *NOT THIS ISLAND MUSIC*

1.

My dear, my favorite person, for you all my life is work and all my work is play and you can read me or look away. Such power you have, to command me so, and such beauty, that to you I would over and over pour out everything I think, everything I can hear, everything I hear the words whisper, every sound I can steal. Truly you are my mother, for who else could I talk to in such confidence of being well heard? All the beauty I know is what I find in you, or let you find. You are my father & my lover and my child, and I am nothing without you.

2.

I am concerned to examine in practice how through the composition of poems the organs of enlightenment begin to open, begin to work for the benefit of all. For the benefit of all, not just the talker, the poem shapes itself in syllables, breath patterns, deep metabolic rhythms it borrows from the writer — signal of what is personal (body) transcending itself into what is sharing, shared:

Speech, the deep sound of language, the blood of society, the archaic system of phonemes always focused currently, precisely, urgent semantics of everyday 'meanings' and all the magical guesswork of the mother tongue that reveal the mind. Not just or especially the mind of the individual writer. The poet is someone with nothing to say. What is revealed in the poem is the mind of all beings who use language, locally this language, this American. The mind of life speaks us in detail for and to which language is responsible.

In the condensing text the poem works all the ordinary and extraordinary knowledge that comes its way from our searches among libraries, annals, archives, dreams, meditation, ritual, introspection, conversation, argument, analysis, lovemaking, daydreaming, looking, remembering.

Then the musical powers of syntax, all our listening, line structure, sound, begin to act: the poem. A poem is activity, a nest of deeds which reader and writer share, transpersonal, unpossessed.

And what they share is one focused, coherent dance of all that's going on. The activity of poetry is to reconnect the reader and the reader's society with the underlying ever-present glory we take as behavior.

There is an internal politics of the poem: that the spontaneously arising text is responsible to all the constituencies the poet contains and represents, and is contained by. My obscurations are my wisdoms. My needs are my permissions. What I hear is sacred: in one ear & out the mouth.

The poet's prime responsibility is to esteem nothing unworthy of notice, nothing too small or too large, too subtle or too obvious, to talk about.

To learn how to say everything and to keep silent.

Silence is the life of poetry. Not the silence of the uncommitted, but Vimalakirti's silence that shook the world, the silence that hears us at the end of every line of poetry.

(*Not This Island Music*, 1987)

STATEMENTS FOR *SENTENCE* AND *UNCERTAINTIES*

Sentence is not a sentence but an investigation of what a sentence might be. Explorations along the way are always of pivotal situations — each word or phrase is encouraged to be itself, that is, to present the three faces all things possess: past, present, and to come. The poem pretends to arrive at a text of itself, though God knows a whole life might not suffice to speak a single genuine sentence.

(from *Sentence*, 1980)

Call and response. The breathing body of poetry from the beginning. The psalms of David, the wave of them, rise and fall of plainchant, verse & response. The constantly shifting pause between the half-lines of Old English poetry and the poems of the Edda, the half-lines of the Kalevala swayed out four-handed on the saga bench. So I thought towards the two-line stanza as experiments in duration, in complex syntactic and melodic demands. The melody of the first line necessitates the melody of the next. Shape shaping shape. Formally, the poem engages with one constraint: each line wants to be semantically intact — ideally, any line could stand alone, be my Last Words, my epitaph. Yet it also must link syntactically or narratively with the line that follows. And each stanza must stand in like relation with the stanzas before and after. This requirement extends to line structure something that I've worked with for years (usually furtively): hypersyntax, where phrases link with what comes before or after, or plausibly stand alone. *Uncertainties* tries to use these strategies in "mental strife," to solicit the dissolving of certainties — in between the inbreath and the outbreath, where nothing is fixed, and freedom begins.

(from *Uncertainties*, 2011)

POETRY IS AN ART SEEKING INFINITE RELEVANCE thru the fertile limitations of the literal. As the Tuscan poets of seven hundred years ago initiated the great rebirth of poetry into the language men speak, so in our time the great poets have slowly moved poetry, as an art among men, to a radically different height: the sweet finders of ways to state superbly what everyone knew have vanished into the museum of the past. Their songs are beautiful, but they do not feed us. Perhaps Hopkins was the last of them, the last of those whose poems could be well paraphrased, or perhaps he was already of us, of the poets who crystallize in one single structure of music all the roads that lead thru time towards that perception, the cosmogony a poem is, and sway from it again. We are as naked as Dante was, and for many of the same reasons. Only in a man's heart can he learn the true reason Dante composed the *Commedia* in the vernacular; the closest I can come to saying it is this: that the truth, the lifeblood a poem is, deserves nothing less than the most intense, most urgent expression. Dante was not fooled: many more folk then & for ages after knew Latin than knew Tuscan; but he knew too that the ways of their knowing were too calm for what his journey was to be for them. He limited his audience, daring to say stelle rather than the universal sidera. Poetry now has no time for triflers and poetasters; the poet who says I am hungry knows that those who [...] will not feed him. Dearth's dread spirit doth dwell within my flesh.

[RK archives, undated text]

SOME POET-STATEMENTS

[ON DANTE]

Beyond the fond tortures and inversions and mysteries of *trobar clus*, Dante's lyric poems also breathe a curious, even contradictory, freshness that comes from abbreviation, breathlessness, conversationally casual sentence structure. Sentences change course midway, phrases dangle, grammatical subjects behave like shy lovers, now all too prominent, now quite hidden, their face left implicit. I've tried to honor both the high-literary and the passionately paratactic turn of the verse.

[RK archives, undated text]

[ON SHAKSPER]

Shaksper's use of the sentence: coming as he did at stage when the function of the sentence was rendered somewhat doubtful because of the influx of classical & foreign models; thus consider Lyly, or more significantly, Roper... Shaksper preserved or formed, have it as you will, the integral character of the sentence, i.e., formed a *Verhaeltnis* between noun & verb, neither one not the other predominating, each individual word maintains its own basic individuality, denotation (as indeed in Milton), but each word absorbed also into the connotive strength of those sentences that are formed thereby (as not in Milton, the sentence rendering too high ideas in too high-flown manners: thus Milton the poet at times emasculated by Milton Justifier), so that the reader finds two units of strength & meaning, complementary and interacting. Thus consider the line that Lodovico speaks (V, ii, 335):

And Cassio rules in Cyprus. For this slave,

The calamitous catalog in two lines, ending here. Cassio and that which he is and has done; *rules*, that which Othello may longer do: the echo here of Creon's last speech to Edipus; Cyprus, back and forth, the island kingdom, end to Venice; then we are back there, to Othello, to the guards, the dead Desdemona; a slave now the Loewe des Venedigs.

[RK archives, undated text]

11 · A BOOK BETWEEN POEM &/AS STATEMENT

BLAKE WAS BEST
& THOSE WHO DOUBT HIM LET THEM LOOK AT HIS
                                                                  [SYNTAX
                   ORDAINING HEAT OF PROCESS
WHAT HE SAW.
                THE VISIONARY
MAKES US SEE.
THE SOULS HIDDEN IN OUR HANDS
FOLLOW HIS LONG SENTENCES, FACE
THEMSELVES IN EACH VERB,
                             RISE
IN SYNTAGMIC FIRE.
                PROSE IS PERSONALITY,
                BUT VERSE, VERSUS, POETRY, RIME
                IS THE SLEEP OF ACQUISITION
                SLEEP OF PERSONALITY.
                                  ESSENCE
                WAKES
                IN THE KINGDOM OF ITS SIMILARS
                THIS IS THE ORDER OF RIME
                                & SIGNATURE.

                              24 NOVEMBER 69

HEADNOTE FOR *IO* [ON BLAKE]

All the years I've loved Blake and quarreled with and for him, I had not presumed on the acquaintance. Late last summer I found myself on Chesapeake Isle among hardwood forests ancient as things go in America; I sensed a new opening in my work, coming. I was near the place where Cornwallis had once trundled ashore the borrowed mercenaries of Urizen, in vain restraint of what would be us. One day I began to write, with no design, and as I wrote discovered myself working in a Blakean permission: a double permission, to loop the line long, and to study the acts of Persons who stood forth named from the mind. Book I of the *Book of Water* was written that week, & since then Books II and III have been composed, tracing the righting of Pothor's ardor and the serviceable love of Malchus for Norsha. I do not aspire to the power of William Blake's cosmological physics; for me cosmology is still psychology, my cosmos still psyche.

May 1981

ON KEATS' "WELL-WROUGHT URN"

That urn is cold. I find it strange that several poets & scholars speak of the beauty-truth equation as the last lines of the poem. That equation has called forth so much fuss — its bald assertiveness is immensely persuasive at first hearing, then almost instantly the mind rebels against the symmetry of identity. The equation seems like a handsome face you glimpse in the crowd — it teeters between vapidity and sublimity, depending on whether you keep on gazing or else close your eyes to retain the first impression. This very oscillation is Keats' work, his way of bracing us for the actual conclusion of the poem: the last words the urn addresses to us, assuring us that the equation, problematic as it seems, is all we know on earth, and all we need to know.

If in fact we are the 'ye' — archaic second person plural familiar — spoken of twice in those last lines.

That urn is cold — 'cold pastoral' we have heard, the chill ring of marble. The strophes of the ode grow progressively more somber. The passions and delights pictured on the urn are sublated into eternity, which is usually a pretty chilly condition in Christendom — one doesn't think of eternity as the prolongation of life but as the prolongation of the tomb, the marble replica of life — which this Grecian urn also is.

And the cold, marmoreal, eternal, all-encompassing time-denying Thing speaks to us, from the serene apartness of things, and says ... all ye know, and ... all ye need to know.

Experiment: Try hearing, just for once, the stress placed firmly on the ye. Then, with the *sprezzatura* so appropriate to artist and artifact alike, a creature from eternity condescends to speak to our flesh-bound mortality, whose antics the marble creature literally comprehends & (perhaps with infinite, tender subtlety) envies.

All ye know on earth — beauty, truth, these glorious abstractions, easily revered, more easily compromised. And that equation will serve people like you in your contingencies and trivial earthly need for reassurance that there is something to understand in life, and that you understand it. With the stress on the ye, I hear an insinuation that some higher, worthier form of knowing exists, whose propositions and parables far exceed the simplistic equation the urn offers us as our consolation.

Or do humankind and urn console each other? The urn consoles us for our transience and we console it for its inability to feel the kiss it holds suspended for two thousand years, unable to pursue the beloved or be pursued, unable to share in the sacrificial meal when the poor heifer is offered up to those vague and nameless deities towards which, even now, she raises her lustrous amber eyes.

I don't think Keats meant (not that it's important whether he did or didn't) or believed the equation — if he had, he would have set it in his own authorial voice, which speaks with all the immense authority that found Keats in that mild May of 1819, the voice that speaks all the rest of the poem. By putting just those words in the urn's mouth (so to speak) Keats proposes what our cronies overseas would call a rupture, a chasm in the texture of trust and sincerity we still insist on finding in poems. The urn tells us not what truth is, not what beauty is, but what we are.

February 2010

TODAY'S THE BIRTHDAY OF WALLACE STEVENS, SO I PLAN TO TALK AS INVITED ABOUT POUND.

The problem: these are the two masters. Turn from one to the other and move your head fast enough and you have a poet of utter completeness, something unseen since Shakespeare.

A poet of grace and authority, cunning and sweetness. And the power of language to explore, reveal, declare.

Unfortunately when we can't read that fast there are two of them, the Virgilian Libra of Hartford, the crazed Ovidian Scorpio of Rapallo.

Take WS to be your very master and you get, eventually, something as rich and telling as Ashbery, where the torment is the endless summer evening nightmares of Protestant America, and the evasions/escapings are modes of sexual ecstasy when young (o you sleek Greeks in your bathhouse), deepening in age to a profound post-Presbyterian pickle.

On the other side is the shouting Baptist of Pound, holy roller and Dionysus, o you wackier Greeks too hairy for the bathhouse, rough trade of Lydia and Thrace, I wonder, hairy Pound, our beloved Esau — his escapes are endless star-sequences of EXILE, his potion is madness, melvillian nuthouse wave patterns, glooms of intellect with birds squawking in the back of your head.

Take this head as the one to work your face through and get if you're lucky Charles Olson, overwhelmed with the CONSEQUENCES of what he, that gangling transcendentalist like me, huh, had to report.

Before I get tired of this polarity I've summoned, consider that there are obvious social distresses veiled in these two great beings' works: the virile disappointments (delicately, delicately we walk here) of Stevens, the outrageous wrongness, mindless baseness of Pound's political squint. Founded on the common distresses of American insecurity: potency-anxiety, anti-Semitism, fear of those burglars in the heart.

Christ, we are a veiled people!

Anyhow: as a start, be clear that we're not here concerned with the moral & even æsthetic values of Pound. Unless you're crazy about Vivaldi — or Mussolini — there's not much to say nowadays that hasn't been adequately roasted or toasted. So not here to address Pound's impeccable exemplification of the worst aspects of the AmeriMan's malaise, or even his rarer & beautiful overcomings — the huge generosity to his fellows and his descendants — his glorious dedication of KULCHUR to Bedouin Bunting and the Jewish Zukofsky.

What I'm after is the rarest thing about Pound, though to any young woman picking up the *Cantos* it is the most obvious thing.

Nobody since Whitman, if even Whitman did, so exulted in the animal of language. This is a horse, ladies & gentlemen, this is a powerful horse, a Greek horse that eats meat, a horse that carries — no joyride of the lyric trivia (towards which Pound's earliest work could have been seen bending, salon stuff of jade and précieux and chinoiserie).

This is animal.

(Buffalo Broadside, 1990)

A LOVE AFFAIR WITH SILENCE: REVIEW OF PAUL CELAN[1]

It was the peculiar genius of Paul Celan to be able to strip language of its normal socioeconomic occasions without cutting the lines that lead language to the heart. For all the celebrated difficulty of Celan's poems — dense constellations of morphemes, word elements packed like molecules — they are hard only when you try to think about them. At first touch (what William Carlos Williams called, in a noble phrase, the poem's "intention to impress") Celan's poems come to us from a warm sense of life, of paying attention and taking care.

It is unlikely that any translator could match the subtlety of Paul Celan's stock of words; a few words recur again and again, at times with severely different ranges of association. We can ask the translator to be conscious of Celan's own lexicon, his idiolect, and make us aware of it. The translators of these two volumes are generous with their understanding, and guide us through the sensuous intricacy of Celan's vocabulary.

It is the delight and torment of the translator to try to develop structures that will accommodate the deft hallucinations of Celan's assemblages. Celan's ability to touch us and penetrate to the core of language, where it continually arises to guide, cajole, mislead and console us, produces a poetry of immense expressiveness. The notorious clenched hieroglyphic abstruseness of Celan's poetry is not so much a product of poetic theory as an irreducible consequence of his way of attending to

---

1. [Paul Celan, *Last Poems*, tr. by Katharine Washburn & Margret Guillemin (San Francisco: North Point Press, 1986). Paul Celan, *Collected Prose*, tr. by Rosmarie Waldrop (New York: P.N. Review / Carcanet, 1986).]

the world. He disparages a certain sense of artifice, saying in a 1960 piece from "Collected Prose": "There are exercises — in the spiritual sense... And then there are, at every lyrical street corner, experiments that muck around with the so-called word-material. Poems are also gifts, gifts to the attentive." Celan is famous above all as the poet of exile, for whom exile was not only linear displacement or geographic event, but a multidimensional domain from which he could never free himself. Born in Rumania (in 1920), speaking Rumanian and Yiddish, he came to be the greatest German poet of midcentury, while all the years of his celebrity were spent living in Paris. Fleeing war and concentration camp, the permanent anguish of the Holocaust, Celan turned to language with an immensely lyrical skepticism; the speech he gave when he was awarded the Bremen Prize for German literature is often quoted: "Only one thing remained reachable, close and secure amid all losses: language. Yes, language. In spite of everything, it remained secure against loss. But it had to go through its own lack of answers, through terrifying silence, through the thousand darknesses of murderous speech. It went through."

He died an exile's death in 1970 — abandoning the element of our common lives, he committed suicide by drowning himself in the Seine. That death by water (we remember Virginia Woolf and Hart Crane and John Berryman) makes us recall anew his odd remark in "Backlight," translated in "Collected Prose": "'All things are aflowing': this thought included — and does that not bring everything to a halt?"

The three books Celan left unfinished at his death have been collected in "Last Poems," a handsome bilingual edition, translated by Katharine Washburn & Margret Guillemin. They are "Force of Light," "Snow-Part," and "Farmstead of Time." Ms. Washburn's sensitive, informative introduction, written with a grace that readies us to read the poems, is dotted with typographical errors, which have the strange effect of increasing the alertness of the already wary reader. Is this a deliberate tactic?

Anyone fortunate enough to read German will have fun praising and deploring any translator's solutions. Ms. Washburn and Ms. Guillemin are by no means fond of the obvious. And where an impromptu translation might follow pretty much the word order of the original, it is their tendency (a translator's right) to prefer more complicated patterns. Sometimes this produces unnecessary, perhaps unintentional ambiguity.

Thus one poem begins literally: The escaped gray parrots say Mass in your mouth. Ms. Washburn and Ms. Guillemin enlarge: Having escaped the gray parrots recite Mass in your mouth.

Now "recite" seems to become an imperative addressed to someone who has just escaped from suddenly menacing parrots. My point here is that there is much to be said for keeping faithful whenever possible to the order in which ideas and their words occurred to the author. Such adherence helps to reveal the mind of the poet as it articulates the world. At the same time, the Washburn-Guillemin impulse toward complexity is part of the very sensibility that makes them such good translators of Celan.

So there will be quarrels with some versions, but they will be family quarrels, nuances among friends. In general, these two translators do a satisfying job of making strong English poems. There are pieces in the book that will read their way right into the anthologies. Gone into the night, complicit, a star-porous leaf for a mouth: something remains for wild wasting, treeward. These are poems from the culmination of Celan's career; a measure of hope and even a joyous, imperiled playfulness return. To say Celan is the most important German poet since Rilke is not to maroon him off on Comp Lit Island. His greatness reaches into English and American poetry, leaving its mark on our poetry; it's hard to think of any contemporary foreign poet who has cast such a spell on our sense of what a poem is.

A fitting and most useful companion to any reading of Celan's verse is his "Collected Prose." The slimness of the book tells its own story of Celan's love affair with silence. It is one of the wellsprings of his work, and of his influence. Silence is a dominant issue in modern poetics — silence as elision of speech (Celan, Anne-Marie Albiach, the American "Language" school), or silence as a strategy of music (Robert Creeley, the Black Mountain poets, John Cage). The addresses and responses that make up this volume are translated by the poet Rosmarie Waldrop, whose German is native. Her English (now her working language) has an idiomatic adroitness that catches the pauses and suspensions in Celan's breath — his prose often seems breathed rather than thought into place. Whereas Ms. Washburn's introduction guides us to the man, persuasively arguing autobiographical readings of Celan's poetic imagery, Mrs. Waldrop directs us to a sense of a more reserved, hidden-hearted poet, tormented by questions he asks in the hope of being delivered (O hope of Jews & Christians) from this perishable self to some enduring Other. It is a fresh way of seeing Celan, I think, and while I'm not so convinced of it as I'd like to be, there is evidence in "The Meridian," the longest yet most tentative of Celan's theoretical writings, presented here in an effective translation.

The collection includes the haunting prose dialogue "Conversation in the Mountains," which appears as well in "Last Poems" — two translations are none too many for this important extravaganza of language, inventing characters who turn out to be memorably real. Celan's "Conversation," for all its appeal (like "The Meridian") to the work and example of Georg Büchner, will remind us of the dialogic form that his hated and loved Martin Heidegger restored to modern philosophy; it bears here on the inextricable knot of Jewishness and the word. We recall that the dialectic is rooted not only in the Platonic dialogue but in the Mishna.

In our time, poets have taken up *philosophieren* — doing (not studying) philosophy. Celan is the loftiest of them, surely, teaching poetry to fashion awareness out of "words which seem," he says in "The Meridian," "something that listens, not without fear, for something beyond itself, beyond words."

(November 9, 1986)

OPENING REMARKS FOR BLACK MOUNTAIN CONFERENCE

My business at this moment is to welcome you to this place, as if words ever needed for a place to speak its welcome or not. And that is in a way one of the QEDs of our business here together, to sense out the specifications of geography, the way it did in the 1950s and early 60s come to so many of us, always differently, as a big surprise that a poem *is somewhere*, speaks in a body out, out into a place, and from it in. The circulations, in which we speak and understand our welcomes. What is it that asks us to speak?

Welcome to Bard. When I came here 25 years ago it was, like every other college then, and most now a fortress of New Criticism. It was a crumbling fortress, with lichen stains on its walls and deep fissures you could see daylight through sometimes, but still a fortress. New Criticism — I needed to pierce that foolish evil Maginot line between the reader and the poet, between mind and mind. Here we are still, still doing some sort of battle; the lovely thing about the poetics of Black Mountain is that it never arrived, never simply won. It remains as it began: difficult, demanding, renewing. It never became an academic orthodoxy from which the young poet or reader had to veer. Only its practitioners had to escape into the deserts of their needs. As we did. In the colleges, the New Criticism people moved on but not before their wetback replacements came, the newer gallican preoccupations that have inherited the chief social agenda of New Criticism, i.e., TO PROTECT THE READER FROM THE POET. They still struggle with different sorts of desperation to distract the reader, keep the reader from being aware of, much less succumbing to, the poet's vision.

This is always the sedate Philistinism of the academy, to propose a kind of morpholatry, worshipping mere commodities of formal consequence. No more fieldwork. No more venturing into the anguished domain of the other person, the other that is always the one who writes (Valéry: When you descend into the self, remember to go armed to the teeth.) With the subtle arrogance of the mandarin stage of late capitalism, the academic critics continue to proffer an even svelter, more seductive commodity fetish than the old poem itself, whether construed as 'sonnet' say or as 'text.' They proffer as commodity a profitably renewable discoursefulness built on, though scarcely grounded in, the poem. (Olson already was worried about that word 'discourse.')

I want to remember aloud the outrage that they felt, those academicians we were always at risk of becoming, the outrage at what we were doing. Not that we explored the world, but that we dared to call it poetry, had the effrontery to suggest that the poetic act itself issued not in artifact or amenity, but in understanding, awareness, even revelation. Olson would not let us forget that the body's actual living process shapes the word: in the beginning was the breath. To read his poems is to understand that their utterance and their composition are non-dual. I want to remember the outrage: people could get used to poetry mentioning the body by reference; they struggled against the poem as embodiment itself. That the poem's quality arose not from a skill of adhering to a model or articulating a shared sensibility, but from the energy of listening, from the authority of physical presence in all the openness of being. Body could be the archive in which Edda & Vedas & Upanishads are stored. And more.

Soon after I met Olson in 1962, he asked me to give an account of myself. Not my opinions (doxa) or theories of line or deep image or the Hermetic. Who was my father he wanted to know, what kind of job did he do, where did I grow up and what went on there, on and off the streets around me. What church did I go to — that isn't theology, that's politics. Nobody had ever asked me such questions. We city people mistook ourselves for our opinions in those days, and for our more salient aspirations. As I understood it, he wasn't asking about biography as such, or about 'experience,' in the sense that realist writers continue to abuse the word and their readers. I think he was talking about *authority*, which comes from the fact of being. Being. Writing was the baptism of growing into one's own authority.

His authority, which people continually confuse with power, stands before us in the fact that we come together here. The West is still trinitarian. The authority of Duncan. The authority of Creeley. As I understand it, and I was never at Black Mountain, what we are thinking about are the mountainous consequences of what those three people had to say to each other, and what their works continue to explore in us as we read, and write, and study, and grow.

I hope that what happens here this weekend isn't anecdotal, except as Plato is, to people the idea. I hope we learn about the contradictions, the battle over *Finnegans Wake*, or what Jung's essay on the Mass was doing in the BMR. I hope we hear about the wounds too, the confiteors of unaccountable failures and underserved successes. I hope we remember we're talking about that brilliant band of beauties Emerson sent out from his american dream to score all over the cosmos rare surmises of fact and revelation. Forgive us. Whatever we *may* learn, there is a fact to this weekend when in a sense we are supposed to say what we *have* learned, in the daily practice of writing — so that most of us will find ourselves, as they say, ' giving readings' of and from that work it has fallen to us to transcribe, the work we usually call 'ours.' I have learned that beyond the illusion of the self with something to say, there is the poet, the one with nothing to say. Open, ready for what comes.

26 June 1987, 11:37

STATEMENT ON MY POETICS FOR THE H.W. WILSON CO.

1.

The closest to a thing like a poem was on the moors in Yorkshire, north, off the road to Whitby. The ground was like no ground. Not earth and not rock, it was age upon age of growing, peat or moss or grass or all of these, thick-twisted as a Tibetan carpet, deep as time leaves spindrift in the mind.

We are consequences. That is the point. The song of it is the close tracking, by ear, of what the mind makes of where it has come to, this place of Now, out of all its geneses, its flowerings and failings.

This thing a poem is, moorland under your feet.

The place was where sheep made the way, have been making the way for hundreds of years, and all a word could do was follow, like a big oafish ram, their nimbler quiet passage. This noise is made our music.

Poems are trying to find out how you sound. How you sound and how you suffer. The poem is an enactment of the common moment of mind.

A means to know each other is language. Language is to know. Language is a behavior, one part of it is speech, and one aspect of speech is what can be written down, in words, they say.

So when poems work, they work because the fingerprints of mental obscurations, confusions and aspirations ("me") shapes by its whorls the ever-moving current of what-there-is-to-be-heard ("language") into that gorgeous interrupted silence we call "music."

Is the poet exchanging self-justifications with the unknown reader? Why aren't they all out working to liberate all beings from the sufferings of samsara, the never-ending torment of the "natural"?

Language is the intersection of the self and the other. In the heart of it, maybe the exact crossing point, a lucid doorway opens.

Through it, to escape from both self and other. That is the hope of poetry, the journey "in the yellow of the" eternal Rose.

*

11 · A BOOK BETWEEN POEM &/AS STATEMENT

Poetry is the intersection of the body and the mind. Poetry rescues language from meaning, and rescues meaning from having no way to talk.

*

Be suspicious of extended discourse, expository prose that fancies its own 'development,' 'conclusion,' 'organization,' 'coherence.' Only fragments of Parmenides' epic survive — the whole would have appalled with its persuasions and rightness, rather than waking us again and again by its problematic. Revere those whose ideas have spurned the special pleading of discourse, have resisted the appeal of rhetorical amplification. No Western philosopher has ever said more than Heraclitus.

2.

Two formal strivings in my work: towards a syntax that connects everything, every which way — pompously call it *polysyntaxis*. The height of the polysyntactic in my work is the long poem *Sentence*, published as a small book originally, then later, very slightly changed, as the central poem in my collection *Spiritual Exercises*.

The other striving is towards a link-resistant, dissociative energy, that creates a music of interruption, deflection, resistance. With equal pomposity call that *allocentric*. The word or image or line finds its center outside itself, and strives to reach it, only to be repelled by the equipollent outward-reaching of the other word or image or line to which it yearns. As like poles of the magnet 'repel' by the ardor of their similarity, so these lines mean to snap away from each other, and leave space, space open.

The high evidence for this in my work is the book-length poem *The Flowers of Unceasing Coincidence* along with a number of earlier poems, including "Those who are beautiful / A sonata" from *Under Words*, and long before, the locking and unlocking stanzas of *Axon Dendron Tree*.

In all my work, a striving for one content: to let language tell its own story, of which everything that happens to me, and happens in anyone like me, is a particular instance. If we could listen thoroughly enough to language, we could hear everyone. The High History of Everyone.

So lyric pours into narrative into discourse into those sketchy myths that rise out of the friction of words, thin smoke of new meaning rising in the clear air, what Whitman called "the flanges of words" ever bearing, one on another.

Language is what comes out of the mirror with its hands on your breasts, elegant torsion of its fingers not at all dainty.

Presently its mouth is all over you and you can endure the pleasure in silence, or resist into speech.

This language thing is mind. It is a gap — *language is space* — we must never fill. The silence is the heart of it.

So there are always the two of you — you and language (you and mind); great texts talk about a Holy Marriage between them, the result of which is that famous *unum caro* (One Flesh) human lovers get so anxious for. *They* are not what the sacrament means. It is you and mind (not "your mind" — that's just the tattered silk or glory of all *your* past and present and future days), you and mind that get married. You are never alone. That noble suitor is always present, never craving, never apologetic, never blaming, never at fault.

What I believe and have worked to make believable is that the poem is revelation — of mind by mind to mind through language. What the old world spoke of as the Muses is surely a root fact of our way of knowing, and where They live is in the mind, what They are is mind, and They have many ways to talk — the ways we *hear* are language, and we have our share in shaping that utterance.

Because it is always a dance, this revelation, this coming into us of the call of language — the same dance the Bible tropes with its stories of a deity talking and a prophet hearing the words come out of his own mouth.

The act of the poem means to show me my mind at that instant, show it to me out loud, so you can hear too.

This showing, this hearing, activates the mind of the speaker (poet, Blake's "Orator") and of the hearer. This activation is what revelation means. This activation of the mind is previous to any social, political, or spiritual commitment the mind can make.

Folklore like the wind never sleeps, and all calms are only apparent. It rouses in us, the old mind, the old stories, every day.

(H.W. Wilson Co's *World Authors*, 1990 edition)

BARD COLLEGE 40ᵀᴴ ANNIVERSARY CELEBRATION

[...]
But among all these people who made the day and those who are making the day happen now my students, my colleagues, my peers and my betters, my dear friends, there is one person notably absent

but without whom we would not be here, at least in this singular way.

On this day, November 10ᵗʰ, one hundred and ten years ago, there died in Marseilles a tortured pre-postmodernist visionary for who poetry was always the youngest art, an art exhausted by the teenager he had been. He was named Arthur Rimbaud.

It's his fault we are here. He did it.

After performing the incredible — talk about unlikely — act of transforming poetics from personal plaint to transpersonal revelation, mapping the classics beyond all their plaster and dust onto a vivid and recurrent world, even after leaving poetry forever, as he thought he was doing, in his twentieth year and sailing off to Arabia and Africa, Ethiopia, to serve the silent evocative muse of Caffeine in her homeland, coffee, twenty years of importing guns & exporting Harrar coffee, some letters, some snapshots, but no more poems,

he left us with this young thing to do, this world of poetry that still has to get said, that we have to say, that we are kept somehow young to say, to keep saying, to articulate a new universe piece by piece, if we want to be fancy about it, or just spill our dreams into the public morning.

Rimbaud teases us till we know that poetry really has to be love poetry after all — maybe poetry will be the sex of the new millennium

not necessarily the old erotic, the *zutique*, not at all probably the tender romantic old fashioned sexo-sentimentality of "I love you please give yourself over to my designs," that yearning love we can still sometimes enjoy in opera (whose very flamboyancy is the edge of irony that lets us shamelessly enjoy it) or in old poetry (like Thomas Wyatt and his "dear heart, how like you this?")

and not the exalted smuttiness of Donne or our friend Verlaine, or the veiled exaltations of Dante but something more radical, yet more devious the way any simple thing is, more searching:

Rimbaud proposed a poetry that would do the most generous thing literature ever tried to lay beside the other, the other, the one that Whitman hailed:

"you, whoever you are, who are holding me now in your hand"

that literature was no longer (as in the mediæval æsthetic trinity of purposes) supposed to instruct, reprove or persuade. Instead, the poem was to live with.

To dwell with us. The poem is dwelling.

Rimbaud's generous impulse was to lay out the sequence, orderly as all real things are, one leading to another, hand to hand, in one ear & out the mouth, the events of the mind itself, themselves.

So the modern poet (whether pre-m, m'ist, or po-mo) has this grand but intimate calling, to speak the cosmos of the mind, the inscape pronounced out loud, so that you (whoever you are) can lie down & wake up beside the images, the ideas, the upwellings, the drowsy remembrances, the peremptory demands,

can fit yourself, nestle, into the ongoing sequences of language, & have your own mind roused to fill the spaces.

With Rimbaud, the poem at long last became not something to listen to but something to do.

A poem is a liturgy for readers,

a script for a wild play you put on in the barn, in the bedroom, in the congress,

a partner to their thinking and feeling, shaping them both in real time, like what we used to call music

to make the synapses between what you hear and what you think.

What thinks itself in you now

thinking is the feeling that passes

the feeling that thinks

down by the river
someone is sitting by the tracks
by an abandoned station

what does it matter how old he is
he's watching the freight train pass

the train runs fast alongside the river
there are mountains over there

he can't see the mountains now
he sees the freight cars pass

he didn't come and sit on this old bench to watch the train
he was sitting there in the shade of the wall to take the cool of the shade
and the train happened to come by

there are times and seasons
he thinks
like the Bible says

and then the train is there
he watches it

it goes by so fast he can just see what's in front of him right now
you know how it is

cattle cars full of pigs he smells the pig he imagines
he can hear them squealing inside
he can't hear them he can only hear the squeal of the wheels on the rails

and now there are cattle cars with cattle in them
he sees big heavy shadowy bodies shifting around
crammed in as they are
sure footed as the car slams back and forth
along the switches by the old station

pigs and cows and now what
boring flatcars ten of them in a row
full of what look like sewer pipes heading west
black plasticky sewer pipes or oil lines or what are they

they're gone and now there's a yellow freight car
with the sleeping cat on it
he loves that — Chessie the cat
and a red one from Lehigh
and another yellow and a flat car with tractors on it
brand new heading to the prairie he thinks

one thing after another
by now he's forgotten to count the cars he's watching
it bothers him he doesn't know
how many there are

he feels he should be aware of being aware of things

he watches
what they mean

what they mean is passing by and being red and yellow
what they mean is passing by and being beautiful

a man is watching a freight train pass
he may be young he may be old
what difference does it make
to the river

weeds along the track
that rose from seeds that fell from trains
wheat and oil and milk and long machines
boxcars full of what the man can't see

and then after all those dark red mystery cars
a flatcar empty
he sees the river again and the mountains beyond it
clear for a moment then gone
as if the train were carrying even the mountain away

what reveals it also takes it away.

                                    talk in Olin, 10 November 2001, in thanks

STATEMENT FOR THE MODERN POETRY CONFERENCE AT CUNY

I suppose poetry is
Listening Out Loud
And what one listens to is language —
language in one's head
(only a fool would confuse that with himself thinking
only a fool would think the things that he hears languaging in him are things that he himself is thinking)
Most poets are too smart to believe in their own intelligence.
Witless, clueless, we await a sign.
Pindar tells us a sign is never clear (at least a sign from Zeus) —
hence the poem veers towards a kind of
lucid incomprehensibility.
[Eventually after a few hundred or thousand years we begin to comprehend the incomprehensible — Dante, Æschylus, Milton — and they become classics and become of great celebrity but diminished use. But till then the texts are of great power, startling, provoking, eliciting. Some grand provokers — Pindar himself, Li Shang-Yin, Lycophron, Hœlderlin, Stein — still wait their turn, still turn us towards the poem we must write, the poem they force us to write, to make sense of what they do to our heads.]
The incomprehensible provokes the reader to acts of preternatural awareness.
This incomprehensibility factor is what the ancient Greeks called *Mousa*, Muse. [The Spartans — sturdy workmen, who would have liked the sacred gizmos of Elshtain's gnoetry — called her Moha.] (I told her I would work her into this evening.)
The incomprehensible is the only thing that makes sense. That is, it creates sense — the sense of something happening to you as you read.
And that's the only happening poetry has?
The luster of listening.
Or what we hear in poetry is groans from the battlefield where time struggles against space.

(Februay 2012)

POETRY, ARCHIPELAGO, ISLAND

A part of any art is always waiting. Poets were waiting for years for Foucault, press agent of their radical disconnections. Poetry is half rupture, half rapture. Poetry is all about discontinuity, dematerializing the given 'unities.'

Archipelago, not mainland. Hölderlin's Archipelago beginning to show the way. Or we now beginning to say the nature of this thing we so instinctively, drivenly, do.

Poetry transfers the sense of unity from the imputed object to the experience itself — like Buddhism, poetry is experiential, not propositional. It enunciates, it doesn't prove. That is perhaps why the wrongest poets (Milton, Dante, Pound) can also be (or might even be expected to be) so great. Burdened with preposterous or horrific orthodoxies, they take flight, take refuge in pure saying. The word flees from their meanings, perhaps from its own meaning, into the intensity of sheer, mere, presence.

(Subtle Milton inside overt Milton, the apology inside the apology at the start of Book I of PL. God's works need 'justification' — and the astonishing bravura that such a theological immensity can be accomplished by a poem. What must a poem be, to have such force?)

This transfer of the powerful *experience of enunciation* to the apparent object apparently addressed by the implicit or declared subject is the chief strategy, and chief crime, of poetry.

By making the [reading of the] poem discontinuous from the intention, game-plan, mind set of any speaking subject (e.g., an author) the power of the experience is restored — and it, itself, the experience, can be examined, to solicit or enjoy the pleasures of *criticism* — a word to whose ancient meaning of judgment, discernment, we have added the radical connotation of observation.

(From *Sainte-Terre, or The White Stone*, 2006)

THREADS 12 : ROBERT SAYS

You asked about the main influences. It isn't enough to list books and poems. I have to speak of Opera. Since my childhood, listening dazzled to my father's old "Shellac" McCormack and one-sided Caruso records, opera has haunted my imagination. Of course, every poem I write is an aria, text and music both somehow compressed, expressed I hope, in the musical fact of the poem's presence. Of course, they're arias and choruses. Of course, I don't know who is singing each, or what the greater narrative context is in which that song arises and into which it falls, lashing about with all my breath. But if I had to think of my whole body of work under any one trope or figure, it would be of a vast opera, a kind of hyper-Wagnerian structure of endlose Melodie and a cast of thousands — all of them lovers, beloveds, witches & high priests. Nonsense. They're just a few thousand poems scattered in the spaces of time that let words in. But operas have wooed and won me, operas have gathered my time and sung to me. Sometimes I listen as I write — not always, not even often, but when I do I am writing into, against the music.

in conversation with Mark Thwaite (2006)

I think [the reader]'ll find the poem's acoustic shape, & when I'm reading aloud, I have to struggle for that, practice it just the way I would practice if I were a pianist and were learning to play a Chopin étude, because it's not mine anymore. It belongs to the page. I don't have any inside information about that poem in reading it aloud that the reader doesn't have. I might have inside information about references & some mythological event or something in the semantics of the poem. I might have some inside info, but if that stays inside info then the poem to that extent is a failure.

in conversation with James Stalker [ca. 1980]

Prose is a subtle form. The musical interruptions that give prose rhythmic shape are less obvious and less regular than those that weave silence into speech in a poem. Anyone who has heard Faulkner reading, or Ed Dorn, or James Agee, or James Joyce, knows something of the incredible variety of prose music. Sometimes I have been allowed to bestir myself in those measures, & make the long summer drone of prose.

in conversation with Simone dos Anjos & Pietro Aman (2006)

The only things that can be said about anything, can be said only by means of silence. Silence as a sort of music. Silence is what makes poetry happen. The silence of the line ending is what makes the line. A line of poetry can be said to be the shortest distance between two silences. The words define the silence as much as the silence defines the words. The relationship between silence and what is being said is that golden reciprocal, everything influencing everything else. With a poem you have silence in the sense that no one is talking, then a line comes into the silent mind, or the will of an attentive artist locates some talk within the chatter of the mind and a quite obvious, and quite easily talked about relationship between silence and saying.

in conversation with Larry McCaffery (1988)

I wanted to talk about the natural, musical ease of reading, reading finding its own time. I think the simplest way I could say a lot of what I've been saying is that I understand what I write as more like music than like theory or argument, and that it should be — should be, take away "should," but that I think the reader would be happiest if the reader could experience it as she experiences music, by just letting it happen and seeing what happens then. [...] So it may seem difficult on the page, but it's only difficult if you're not listening to it. If you listen to it and let it do its work, you don't have to do the work, it does the work, but let it do the work. Normally when we read we do the work, but I'm proposing a kind of writing that does the work for you, if you let it. So that far from my writing being difficult, I think it's extremely *easy, I mean really easy, much easier than Dickens or Jane Austen or those difficult people where you have to visualize each event and see what this sentence means, and then what does this sentence mean, whereas I think for me, the sentence is busy working in you as you read it. Some of my music. It's just an analogy, but it's the analogy that makes best sense to me.*

in conversation with Bonnie Langston (1994)

An opera singer is one who acts through the voice, who does through the voice, I mean, acts in the strict sense of who performs an action. He's acting by singing. We pick up a hundred-year-old recording by Caruso, and we hear somebody acting. A man who's been dead for eighty years, we hear him acting, we hear him doing something, and he does it entirely with the voice. That's what lyric means to me. It certainly doesn't have to deal with the conventions of quatrains and rhyme and meter. It has to do with singing as hard as you can. It has to do with an attempt to organize the whole poem in one sonic arc and, I think, if there is one way I could hope that I have succeeded in my poetry, when it's any good, is that the poem is that; it is a sonic arc from beginning to end. It may lose its way in triviality, along the way intellectually, but it's still holding some, what my mother called a chune — *my mother said* chuna *and* chune; tune *we'd say in ordinary American, but I still say* chune —, *it holds or it's trying to hold a tune, a tune that doesn't exist somewhere else. The poem is that tune: it's not copying a tune, it* is *that tune. That's what I would mean by lyric, but I know that's maybe a specialized sense of it.*

in conversation with Leonard Schwartz (2006)

12.

A BOOK OF MUSIC

What I learn from music
is to take my time
being quick.

                                    27 XI 75

The slack catgut we (are) propose(d) to
              pull taut &
pull the sound from, new song &c
Homer made his meanings.
            Herodotos

LECTION) HARMONICS

to Gerrit Lansing

the afterimage,
    mirrored,
        blank space at the end of the world
from which the sounds of the shape
proceed

      ♩ *Lion*

      ♩ *Man* across the abyss of
          response,
            the clef is G

(Great Light
    ((that is, Light))
      move unaltered thru the rivers of my heart,
myth = physiology
    (not 'merely'
    but "even as much as, as much as")
          the
Arrow
    flies ever to its goal

    = the place to which the arrow flies is the arrow's goal.

            (From *Lectiones*, 1965)

A PLUCKED FLUTE

The concern is to generate timbres. Not melodies. Suppose the last melody I heard plucked my heart. Heart strings. Suppose. And I wanted to pluck a flute, so to elicit a sound out of the air, not lute, no tooth. To liberate my heart say.

This is a generation of timbres. The old melodies die back, climax vegetation of the great Eur-American plain, after the ice. Suppose I want to sing to the ice, or sing ice. Suppose the heart has had its hour?

Do we want our presidents honest? Suppose the heart is feedback as it seems. Only one more language.

> "They were saying how queer I was a year or two before, and how nurse had called my mother to come and listen to me talking all to myself, and I was saying words that nobody could understand. I was speaking the Xu language, but I only remember a few of its words, as it was about the little white faces that used to look at me when I was lying in my cradle." (Arthur Machen, "The White People.")

But what the president says we are somehow permitted to hear. "I want some of that consommé." Is this the old melody making a comeback? While there's soup, song's safe?

But the "tones given off by the heart" Pound tells us of, are not plucked from an adventitious air or guessed all too easily. The tone must be heard.

If we want our president honest we have to hear him. Even when in the white building we have put him in he speaks in the Xu language, we have to hear.

Now it is my supposition (said Kung) that a coin dropped on the street sounds with the voice of the president. Or that a tree felled in Berkeley's woods crashed with his voice. Or that a coon treed up the Guski Road yelps (not unlike an owl) from his throat.

But to hear.

This is a generation of timbres. Now if rhythm is feelings & harmony is thought, timbres isolated in time will be thinking and feeling.

Be thinking. Be feeling. Process. Ing. Neither abstract nor concrete, neither a thing nor a thought. Alive.

So we are concerned not with the tones given off by feelings (call it the Xu language), not with the tones given off by objects, concretes, concretions, ideas. But with the sounds of the process naturing, going, being along with itself, saying.

This is the condition or land (hinted at by the Red Mouth on Jupiter) of the Third God, or age of spirit to which Joachim first woke. Ing is its characteristic timbre in English. Our sounds, our devious ways.

Not thought, Not feelings. No felt in this flute. No even lip to mute. I pluck the flute and the tone is irrevocable, bells out, thinking its way through a world not structured for such feeling. But the plucked flute of all our ways, that monster of clear intention, lifts its own note along, structuring, structuring.

Why are poems so difficult? To answer that is to say only, austerely, what they are. They are thinking feeling its way along, feeling thinking its way along.

To be with them is to be thinking & feeling. To be with ing. Be ing.

And there is nothing natural in this, in the taste of ordinary. What we take as our nature isolates, enrages us, pits us against our brothers all day long. In that face of "nature" we find nothing to our purpose, only a fanged vacancy.

So gladly we turn to being.

And what are we permitted to hear? If we are being with, there is nothing they can hide. In the clear depths of the president's soup swims no alchemic ichthys to herald his redemption. His ganoid face mirrors back from his soup plate. Yet even he must be transformed.

Pound's bet, he never hedged: listening closely is the start of the way. One night or early morning an equation spoke aloud in my head, like a mantra given:

TO HEAR IS TO HEAL

Now the isolate timbres sing, and we learn to hear them, and in them hear a great deal of what is going on. And the isolate tones build now not towards a melody — which is a shape imposed on times but transportable out of it — but towards a procession of intervals in time, full of truth & separation.

To hear is to heal. Who listens, hears everything. We move towards the head. In an anecdote, Olson was said to have pointed to his head when the instruction was to Point to Yourself, & all the others pointed at breasts or plexus. That is something. I have seen young ones now who would point to a measurable inch about their heads, that lovely old lotus revisited in our days.

But it is neither firmament nor fundament, to use terms Creeley has lately made so clear. Neither Uranus nor anus. Firmament and fundament are only new finials for the self-same sad old Catholic polarity. And I heard you, certainly, I sang with you too — if we must have that polarity, then give me ass every time. Keep the worm on the ground.

But the joy of it is that these polarities are no place, no way. We must not have that polarity. There are no opposites, there are only differences. No categories but man. Which is not a contrast to god, but a calm mysterious synonym.

The young writer turned surprised to me & said: I thought only the enlightened ones could do that. Or think that. And I trembled for the dirty traditions we have mounted in a dream, that told him Some are enlightened but you are not, Grovel at the guru's feet and hope.

We are enlightened, I answer, firmly, my fingers crossed with immense demand on us that I be true. We are the enlightened, the only, and all that is light mirrors in us, if we can know it so.

There seemed to be nothing else honest I could say.

*

So from the computers & synthesizers issue sounds of no natural instrument, mimetic of no natural condition. Helen said: "in a piece by

Charles Dodge, I heard the sound of a plucked flute — and that's what interests me."

That we can think our way along a process, processing, and pluck the flute, and go on to witness the ordering of these sounds by the grace of our thinking & feeling in the behavior of the instrument. A proposal, to all kinds of our minds.

Poems are so difficult, music is so difficult, thinking and feeling go along endlessly defining themselves, and being, and being a process the hearer can find his way (no place) to go along with. But defining nothing else. Going along with.

As I might say, meaning and meaning it, go along with me.

(1974)

AGAINST MUSIC

Utter silence

then a shadow falls on it —
how to darken silence

without an actual sound
how to let some one sound
stir in darkened or obscured silence

how to let someone sound

how
how what someone first "hears" as "a sound" sways other
sound (performers)
is common,

and though common, beautiful
and though beautiful jazz,
and though jazz music, and
therefore necessarily sad.
If you think about it. It is sad,
the persuasions.

Words beget words beget sounds, it is common and they are beautiful. And it is beautiful in that it happens; we don't know anything but what happens, and we call it, say, beautiful. (We are the kind of beings who call mountains beautiful, or weather beautiful.

How strange we are, to call what happens anything at all.)

We call it beautiful, or some variant label ("ugly," "OK," "ordinary," "common," "new," "traditional," "original," "dull") that reflects some finesse of the original thing we want to find it, beautiful [sic].

What bothers me about music right away is not that it's beautiful (or any variant, any description) but that it is realistic.

Without even being actual, music is realistic. Music, especially interesting music, especially music where intelligent musicians listen to one another as they play, and skillfully respond, weaving a text of "offer — respond

— let be," music that is always answering, leading, dancing, talking, musing, commenting, being led, moving, such music is realistic, moving.

Music is a one-dimensional metaphrase of everything else, everything always happening: physics, cosmology, economics, interpersonal enterprise, history — the endless web of everything caused by and causing everything else. Pretty as an elegant philosopher, music is an exact demonstration of the interdependent coordination of all things, the world.

By being like the world, music is part of the problem.

Tragic.

Where is the original silence from which a different music, not at all beautiful, would come? It would not be realistic but actual.

Actual because uncaused uncausing.

I am imagining such a music that does not depend on the umbral dimming of the Prime Silence, that does not arise.

I am imagining a music that does not arise.

Perhaps it is suddenly there. Perhaps there all the while. How can there be music all the while which is not a reference to or part of everything else that's here all the while? So while our common and beautiful music is just a phase of the "music of the sphaeres" and so on, this music I'm guessing towards would neither transitively nor intransitively move — move neither in itself nor cause others to move or be moved.

Yes yes but could we hear it?

Imagine we could hear it. That brings it halfway home.

There are many models from present-day music-making. Whether the model in mind is deistic (Bruckner slaving away in isolation perfecting his massive chunk of cosmos) or angelic (Charlie Parker impregnating with his lucid gospel the astonished shepherds of his sleeping sidemen) or democratic (everybody listens, everybody talks) or ecological-thrifty (Mr. Glass recycles one chord for hours, no implication is wasted), the resultant musics will always be beautiful (how beautiful music is!), realistic, common, unhelpful.

They will be part of, even if commentary on, the as-is world of interdependent coordination. Whether music is a sermon or a lecture or a conversation, it still is enmeshed in the macro-social, macro-linguistic event we call the world, or beauty itself.

The more it talks, the more it's part of the problem.

And like any sign, it is a symptom.

What I am saying is difficult for me to say. It sounds clever, a captious rhapsody disguised as an "against"; I fear cheap whimsy and costly preciosity. I love music more than any thing I ever know. Because I love music so, I know there's something I'm after, some sense of an alternative. Is there a clue in what looks at first like an ordinary romantic revulsion:

> When I heard the learn'd astronomer,
> When the proofs, the figures, were ranged in columns before me,
> When I was shown the charts and diagrams, to add, divide, and measure them,
> When I sitting heard the astronomer where he lectured with much applause in the lecture room,
> How soon unaccountable I became tired and sick,
> Till rising and gliding out I wander'd off by myself,
> In the mystical moist night-air, and from time to time,
> Look'd up in perfect silence at the stars.

[Whitman in 1865, about the time of the first performance of *Tristan*]

Is there a clue in those lines, if not towards the music I have in mind, then at least towards what my mind is after?

What my mind is up to by calling what it's after "music."

Language ("poetry") has for several centuries used "music" to free itself from referentiality. Instead of paraphrasable meaning, poetry offers at its best the sound and shape of itself passing.

Various eras have various standards of or tastes for the referential, and make various demands on the accountability of words. Language as music cuts the web of words by words.

No one knows if any success is in store for us in this great deferencing. The curious looks of baffled disappointment on the faces of people leaving poetry readings are promising things, but not without their amphibolous portent. It has been evident since at least the Buddha & Heraclitus that we are, or are in, a vast, perhaps meaningless system. Our current whimsy tropes our hereness as: we are lost in the computer.

We have sought relief from this intermittently painful awareness by various ways we fancy rigorous: the solution-by-exhaustion we call "science," that shellgame of discutables we call philosophy, as well as by praying to the unknown programmer or technician to turn the damned thing off or let us out ("religion," apocalyptic or soteriological, respectively), but mostly by various hard to condemn quisling-acts of collaboration ("ordinary life," "business as usual").

The Chinese supposed a note on the trumpet, or some note on some trumpet, would shatter the sky. Imagine that.

And MUSICK shall untune the Sky.

(Dryden, 1687)

I am not advocating violence. Or not yet.
Imagine a music that doesn't cooperate.
Imagine a music that is no simple or complex mimesis, that isn't an imitation of conversation or any sort of conversation, we being who and what we are, sleepers, sleepers;

imagine a music that is not an imitation of biological process and not an imitation of Hegel giving a lecture or of people walking naked in the woods or of God creating the world.

Imagine a music that does not collaborate:
that isn't Nazi or Socialist Realist or Capitalist Experimentalist,
that doesn't reaffirm by constant rhythmic reinforcement the shabbier precincts of business: weddings and war.

Imagine a music that refuses to interact with the complex interaction we call "reality" (but whose true name is Satan, Lord of the World).

Imagine a music that isn't realistic.
It could not be common, hence would not be beautiful.
It would save us.
But could we hear it?

Imagine you could hear it.
Imagine you're hearing it now.

[RK archives, undated text]

PIANO TUNING

Circles around. The sky opens. One simple fact we make arabesques around. A song and dance. Circles. Ruins of what was foretold in being told. In the first place. But are they circles. How can I think what I'm thinking? A real question? How can I think what I'm thinking. Someone is thinking. Someone is speaking without thinking. Several octaves down the think is thought. Loses its action and its character. Suffers. Mute. Where feeling turns into something felt. Feeling muted. Felt mutes. The circles are cycles. What comes to us is in the fashion of an opening or a coming around. Opening round as a cycle.

What comes to in us. Comes in the fashion of a circle declaring itself in the middle, or open in the middle. A circle is an opening. A cycle round as a circle is not a circle but is an opening. Antique symmetry makes the open close. Sine wave. What posture is this cycle? It turns over and under. Thinking turns round and hears itself as feeling. Feeling turns under and sees itself as thinking. Or later as thought. By then the paint is dry, the movie theater full of dingy light. A pasture of smoke.

In the two breasts coming towards him one apprehends the Infinity Sign. And then he wonders if that infinity is a product, as its sign looks to be, of two sine waves counterchanged, reciprocal. Producing a steady tone called silence. The silent night is infinite, those blazing stars are finitudes that define their context as not-defined. The end of it unfound.

Or not noticed, as sound not in silence. The cycles recurred. The sky of afternoon blurred. So many separate clouds, baroque in their interlock. He saw.

Really feeling wants no place or space or definition. The felt is defined and silences the sound. One more reciprocal. It was Pascal's nightmare wasn't it, the measurelessly large the meaninglessly small. Infinity as entropy. What was to be noticed was that feeling sounded, but the felt suppressed the sound. Held it down.

That a man could care About circles or cycles or afternoons. The day before, a letter had come from his friend: "I'm in love." The cycle has amplitude. We move between the high and the low. Had found a circle in the world, a proper opening. For feeling, it was all feeling, feeling and thinking. Nothing getting written. Nothing felt. Nothing yet to silence the feeling. The word is infinite, alas.

Years of his friend's life struggled to the cycle. We bear our sine waves with us that bear us, don't we. Circles abound. But what comes to in us comes in the fashion of a sound opening. The circle also closes, is enclosed. It's perfection they say. I see no perfect in that confection.

What was Pascal's nightmare? Silence? Size? We do not know the size of silence, and its sound is no measure. The word is infinite, alas. Language very large. To be moored here, as these clouds are, to earth. This special atmosphere round our round, no circle. Holds. The sphere can be broken the circle can't be broken. "Our" breath. The sphere of breath. The sphere.

But the cycles. "I'm" or "I am" "in love." Perhaps pronounced the same way. Same way feeling. How can I think that I'm thinking with all these words to moor me to another's meanings. How can I feel what I'm feeling with all these thoughts to moor me to my own meanings. To perceive the System is not to break it.

Then what is the music for that this instrument is for? The word is infinite alas, the poem is not infinitude, proposes instead a pattern for feeling to feel its way through.

The cowbells hung on the door ring, or make sound. It is a sign that someone has gone through. Or some part of someone, glance, say, or even breath, to mingle with the sights and airs outside. The sound.

This music we're talking about. Music is a condition of thinking thinking its way along or through or nearby without a single thought to distract. Or to moor it to what's meant. Meant, but not by it.

What this instrument is for. A circle can not be, or can only be, broken. A circle. But a cycle can be transformed. That is the hope. It is no part of physiology, though physiology blossoms with roses because of it. Change the amplitude, the wave-length. The sound transforms. Or silence is differently transformed. A different silence. Ask anybody.

Perhaps. Perhaps the reciprocal sine waves (her breasts, infinity) are the chatter we call silence, the never-empty rooms.

Roses, he seemed to ask over his shoulder, Roses?

Anwar, the lights, chakras, ganglia, the "centers" we suppose to exist because we feel "there." He half-turned towards me: But you mean, you mean —

Yes, I mean we don't feel "there," we feel *here*.

He, it might be, turned back to his work.

This might be, or have been, the most important thing said. Already the clouds part in the west to admit a single band of turquoise through the compact grey. It doesn't look like a cycle but we know better. Weather is the language of the atmosphere, clouds the lexicon of infinite words. They are moored, or we moor them. This condition we are in, of breath & other oxygens, moors them.

So the poem, plain, would moor to our feeling. Would not moor feeling. Would not move our feelings but our feeling. Thinking along or nearby. This condition along.

The nightmare was the circle wasn't it. We were all afraid. And in the living transformations of the cycle we found. Only another octave? Another sound? Another set of relations. "I'm in love." The passion of the word is to be finite, to know itself known. Set of relations. The sound changes.

All right. Nothing sounds the same. Not pronounced the same way. That is clear, if something is. To be in love is a condition. To be in feeling. To be in thinking. Or else (against these three most beautiful conditions, or one condition) to fall on sleep, which is no sort of condition. "Only another orphan," says Ishmael of all our findings, only another orphan fact or face. Bare, but not void. Not void as a circle. Shapely, shapely as a cycle. A shapely fact. Only another octave?

The sound changes. Think, think, the instrument is saying. I think and you feel. For me. Feel for me in this thinking. When nothing like a thought has hammered down, no felt has muted. "I'm in love." This thinking is you feeling. Me feeling you. You feeling this thinking, in your own condition. The infinite silence of my feeling afraids me. This gulf or comma. Not between theory and fact but between fact and feeling. How can one B natural? he smiled from the keyboard.

It is then a keyboard, an array of possibles marshaled by feeling and thinking. Between between — that was my earlier persuasion. In the crack of the words over our heads we grovel to our supposed masters: "Fact." "Feelings." I have a feeling. The fact remains. The fact in fact opens. The sky opens. It comes to inside us in the fashion of a circle opening. Being no circle at all. Being not natural except as B is, unwarped, uncolored. That is my favorite tone he said.

But all round him the octaves altered, passed beyond and below his hearing. His friend was in love & he heard a sound. It begins a sound we later make into a word. You're reading in. No, I'm in love. You too? And so the feeling of which all thinking is condition proposed itself ("began") as a sound. Or a seen. But these are seeing & hearing. The cycles, presumably, do not stop. The cycles amend themselves. Now thinking is a sort of seeing, feeling a sort of hearing? A whiter wit to clean these differences. Like old soap stains, there is a ring of sense around these ings. Whiter wit to cleanse. Feeling. Thinking. What serves these processes. This instrument proposed. Not as a circle. A cycle, wave, & trough faithfully mirroring across the plane of silence. Across? Only another sound, itself, no likeness & all difference. And that is our condition.

[RK archives, undated text]

THE LOST CHORD

There was a song they sang before I was young
before I even went to confession
and sometimes the old ones sang it still:

Seated one day at the organ   I was weary and ill at ease   and my fingers wandered idly   over the noisy keys is what I remember, then I heard what sounded like: *I know not what I was playing   or what I was dreaming of when I struck one chord of   music* something more *like the sound of a grand Amen   like the sound   of a   grand   A   men.*

Heavy with rubato the song went on, vaguely praising and despairing, never being able to hear that chord again. "The Lost Chord," they called it.

It spoke of the impossibility of the merely possible. Surely there is a finite number, even if it is very large, of chords that human hands can play at an organ, however many manuals the organ might have. Ten fingers. Finite. Of course that chord. Could be found. And played. Again. Ten fingers will always win. Of course they could find it, but the mind can never come to that place again. The fingers can find the chord but not the resonance. Never again the mood or mind or moot or mum or means or mark or murk or mild or muss of whatever images they were that dragged along through the sluggish sarabande of consciousness while the fingers played.

What was the man at the organ dreaming? His wife's breasts or the fulvous marmot sunning itself on the path up to Montriond or the face on his mother's sleep when she was just a few hours this side of dying. Her last face. Or just a streak of dust on a window pane in the light of rain. Or nothing but the pale pleasant snoozy somnolence of not paying attention to what your hands are doing? Ten fingers. Of course the chord, though all its notes and registers be found, will never be found. Its resonance in mind is long, though. Whatever happens lasts a long time. And even what we feel casts a shadow, and in the shade of feeling we go on living. Ten fingers & one mind, all the vibrant images lost on the heave or spurt or swoon of orgasm. All the lost imaginings. All the vanished doors.

All music starts in reverie — didn't Plato warn us, Lydia's lewd modal dissolution leaching our sobriety? How can a republic stand up against the fantasy of its citizens?

    Because we hide our fantasies from one another
    We can be ruled by politics and priests and war.

She looked closely at me & asked what logic entitled me to say that. I said No logic, or The logic of oranges & lavender and south wind — that's what poetry comes from, and what it devours.

    No logic (I went on, growing confident) but the logic of the Secret Alphabet, the hidden firmament behind the sky, the eternally proliferating sculpture of light and warmth and turbulence through which we move all our lives and never look at, never see. Stare into boiling water and see the endlessness of art, the changefulness of beauty. It is movement, it all is movement. It is nothing but movement observed & cherished, lovingly observed & understood. Let the kettle be your study in its rolling boil. Watch the wind rise.

    Yes, yes, she said, I know all that. I have lived amongst you all of my life, and I have seen your waters boil. But logic I was demanding, and you have none, no logic at all. You are not entitled to what you said about Fantasy and War.

    I didn't say it. The words said it. Words say themselves, and we just listen out loud. I'm just the shabby dusty city park they play in. Poor words, to have me for their only greenwood!

    You may hear them all you please, but you have no right to let the words out, she said, no right at all. Unless you study them alertly; then, if what they say conforms to what you yourself believe or trust or practice, then you may speak them with sincerity.

    I believe nothing, trust nothing, & have no practice but listening to them speak through me.

    Let them speak, but you have no right to repeat, to me and to others, what you fancy you hear the words saying.

On the contrary, I have no right to impede their passage. I am a road, a crossroads, trivial, glorious. Three peasants on their way to a dance walk right through me, queens sail by in their palanquins, the shadows of hanged men swaying on their gibbet fall across me. I am a road, not a judge, not a philosopher. I am a road. I am a door.

Only one man ever is a door. She said this sadly, & I wanted to cheer her up:

We all are him. Or he is me, I, who am speaking to you now, am he.

She shrieked & held her soft hands over her ears. (I wanted to be her hands.) You're nobody, she said, nobody. Or maybe you yourself are the terrible answer to the unasked question. Maybe your father meant to ask you *Who will you be?* And from the agony and horror of the future, your answer spoke: *I will be me.* And nothing after that, just a door swinging open and slamming shut in the desert wind.

(from *Lapis*, 2005)

Is it exactly that I write too slow

to catch the words moving across the border

from the country of not even imagination ri to the country of speech

They come where there was nothing. Or there is nothing

till they get here, packed in a hurry, hopeful,

aching in journey. They come.

ALSO BY ROBERT KELLY

Books of Poetry

Armed Descent. New York: Hawk's Well Press, 1961.
Her Body Against Time. Mexico City: Ediciones El Corno Emplumado, 1963.
Round Dances. New York: Trobar Press, 1964.
Enstasy. Annandale: Matter, 1964.
Lunes / Sightings (with Jerome Rothenberg). New York: Hawk's Well Press, 1964.
Words in Service. New Haven: Robert Lamberton, 1966.
Weeks. Mexico City: Ediciones El Corno Emplumado, 1966.
Song XXIV. Cambridge: Pym-Randall Press, 1966.
Devotions. Annandale: Salitter, 1967.
Twenty Poems. Annandale: Matter Books, 1967.
Axon Dendron Tree. Annandale: Salitter, 1967.
Crooked Bridge Love Society. Annandale: Salitter, 1967.
A Joining: a Sequence for H.D. Los Angeles: Black Sparrow Press, 1967.
Alpha. Gambier, Ohio: The Pot Hanger Press, 1967.
Finding the Measure. Los Angeles: Black Sparrow Press, 1968.
Sonnets. Los Angeles: Black Sparrow Press, 1968.
Songs I-XXX. Cambridge: Pym-Randall Press, 1968.
The Common Shore (Books 1-5). Los Angeles: Black Sparrow Press, 1969.
A California Journal. London: Big Venus Books, 1969.
Kali Yuga. London: Jonathan Cape, 1970.
Flesh Dream Book. Los Angeles: Black Sparrow Press, 1971.
Ralegh. Los Angeles: Black Sparrow Press, 1972.
The Pastorals. Los Angeles: Black Sparrow Press, 1972.
Reading Her Notes. Uniondale: privately printed at the Salisbury Press, 1972.
The Tears of Edmund Burke. Annandale, privately printed, 1973.
The Mill of Particulars. Los Angeles: Black Sparrow Press, 1973.
The Loom. Los Angeles: Black Sparrow Press, 1975.
Sixteen Odes. Los Angeles: Black Sparrow Press, 1976.
The Lady of. Los Angeles: Black Sparrow Press, 1977.

The Convections. Santa Barbara: Black Sparrow Press, 1977.
The Book of Persephone. New Paltz: Treacle Press, 1978.
Kill the Messenger. Santa Barbara: Black Sparrow Press, 1979.
Sentence. Barrytown: Station Hill Press, 1980.
Spiritual Exercises. Santa Barbara: Black Sparrow Press, 1981.
The Alchemist to Mercury: an alternate opus. [Uncollected Poems 1960–1980. Edited by Jed Rasula] Berkeley: North Atlantic Books, 1981.
Mulberry Women. [With drypoints by Matt Phillips] Berkeley: Hiersoux, Powers, Thomas, 1982.
Under Words. Santa Barbara: Black Sparrow Press, 1983.
Thor's Thrush. Oakland: The Coincidence Press, 1984.
Not This Island Music. Santa Rosa: Black Sparrow Press, 1987.
The Flowers of Unceasing Coincidence. Barrytown: Station Hill Press, 1988.
Oahu. Rhinebeck: St Lazaire Press, 1988.
Ariadne. Rhinebeck: St Lazaire Press, 1991.
Manifesto for the Next New York School. Buffalo: Leave Press, 1991.
A Strange Market (Poems 1985–1988). Santa Rosa: Black Sparrow Press, 1992.
Mont Blanc (a long poem inscribed within Shelley's). Ann Arbor: Otherwind Press, 1994.
Red Actions: Selected Poems 1960–1993. Santa Rosa: Black Sparrow Press, 1995.
The Time of Voice. Poems 1994–1996. Santa Rosa: Black Sparrow Press, 1998.
Runes. Ann Arbor: Otherwind Press, 1999.
The Garden of Distances (with Brigitte Mahlknecht). Vienna & Lana: Editions Procura, 1999.
Lapis. Boston: Black Sparrow/Godine, 2005.
Runic Workbook. Annandale-on-Hudson: Matter Books, 2005.
Threads. Lawrence: First Intensity, 2006.
Earish: Thirty Poems of Paul Celan. Annandale-on-Hudson: Matter Books, 2006.
May Day. Toronto: Parsifal Press, 2007.

Sainte-Terre, or The White Stone. Kathmandu: Shivastan Publishing, 2007.
Fire Exit. Boston: Black Widow Press, 2009.
Uncertainties. Barrytown: Station Hill, 2011.

Books of Fiction

The Scorpions New York: Doubleday, 1967. London: Calder & Boyars, 1968. (2nd Ed., with a new afterword, Barrytown: Station Hill Press, 1986).
Cities. West Newbury, Massachusetts: Frontier Press, 1972.
A Line of Sight. Los Angeles: Black Sparrow Press, 1974.
Wheres. Los Angeles: Black Sparrow Press, 1978.
The Cruise of the Pnyx. Barrytown: Station Hill Press, 1979.
"Russian Tales" in *Likely Stories*, ed. Bruce McPherson. New Paltz: Treacle Press, 1981.
A Transparent Tree. Kingston: McPherson & Co., 1985.
Doctor of Silence. Kingston: McPherson & Co., 1988.
Cat Scratch Fever. Kingston: McPherson & Co., 1990.
Queen of Terrors. Kingston: McPherson & Co., 1994.
Shame / Scham (with Birgit Kempker). Kingston: McPherson & Co., 2005.
The Book from the Sky. Berkeley: North Atlantic Books, 2008.
The Logic of the World and Other Fictions. Kingston: McPherson & Co., 2010.

Other Books

In Time. West Newbury, Massachusetts: Frontier Press, 1972. [Essays & manifestoes]
A Controversy of Poets (with Paris Leary). New York: Doubleday Anchor, 1965. [Anthology]
Abziehbilder. Heimgeholt (with Jacques Roubaud & Schuldt). Graz & Vienna: Droschl, 1995.
Atlantis Manifesto (with Peter Lamborn Wilson). Kathmandu: Shivastan Publishing, 2009.

COLOPHON

A VOICE FULL OF CITIES:
THE COLLECTED ESSAYS OF ROBERT KELLY
was typeset in InDesign.

The text & page numbers are set in *Adobe Garamond Premier*.
Book design & typesetting: Alessandro Segalini
Cover design: Contra Mundum Press
Image credit: Nicole Peyrafitte

A VOICE FULL OF CITIES
is published by Contra Mundum Press
& printed by Lightning Source, which has received Chain of
Custody certification from: The Forest Stewardship Council,
The Programme for the Endorsement of Forest Certification,
and The Sustainable Forestry Initiative.

Contra Mundum Press   New York · London · Melbourne

CONTRA MUNDUM PRESS

Contra Mundum Press is dedicated to the value & the indispensable importance of the individual voice.

Our principal interest is in Modernism and the principles developed by the Modernists, but challenging and visionary works from other eras may be considered for publication. We are also interested in texts that in their use of form & style are a *rebours*, though not in empty or gratuitous forms of experimentation (programmatic avant-gardism). Against the prevailing view that everything has been discovered, there are many texts of fundamental significance to *Weltliteratur* (& *Weltkultur*) that still remain in relative oblivion and warrant being encountered by the world at large.

For the complete list of forthcoming publications, please visit our website. To be added to our mailing list, send your name and email address to: info@contramundum.net

Contra Mundum Press
P.O. Box 1326
New York, NY 10276
USA
info@contramundum.net

OTHER CONTRA MUNDUM PRESS TITLES

Gilgamesh

Ghérasim Luca, *Self-Shadowing Prey*

Rainer J. Hanshe, *The Abdication*

Walter Jackson Bate, *Negative Capability*

Miklós Szentkuthy, *Marginalia on Casanova*

Fernando Pessoa, *Philosophical Essays*

Elio Petri, *Writings on Cinema & Life*

Friedrich Nietzsche, *The Greek Music Drama*

Richard Foreman, *Plays with Films*

Louis-Auguste Blanqui, *Eternity by the Stars*

Miklós Szentkuthy, *Towards the One & Only Metaphor*

Josef Winkler, *When the Time Comes*

William Wordsworth, *Fragments*

Josef Winkler, *Natura Morta*

Fernando Pessoa, *The Transformation Book*

Emilio Villa, *The Selected Poetry of Emilio Villa*

SOME FORTHCOMING TITLES

Miklós Szentkuthy, *Prae*

Pier Paolo Pasolini, *Divine Mimesis*

Carmine Fahrdor, *Communism, Fame, and Fortune*

www.ingramcontent.com/pod-product-compliance
Lightning Source LLC
Chambersburg PA
CBHW071351300426
44114CB00016B/2025